# Compton's
## by Britannica

VOLUME 10
# H

ENCYCLOPÆDIA
Britannica®

# 2007 Compton's by Britannica

Library of Congress Catalog Card Number: 2006927678
International Standard Book Number: 978-1-59339-298-7
International Standard Book Number: 1-59339-298-2

Printed in the U.S.A.

Britannica may be accessed at http://www.britannica.com on the Internet.

"To inspire ambition, to stimulate the imagination,
to provide the inquiring mind with accurate
information told in an interesting style,
and thus lead into broader fields of knowledge—
such is the purpose of this work."

www.britannica.com

# HERE AND THERE IN VOLUME 10

*From the A-1 satellite to the zygote cell, thousands of subjects are gathered together in Compton's Encyclopedia and Fact-Index. Organized alphabetically, they are drawn from every field of knowledge. Readers who want to explore their favorite fields in this volume can use this subject-area outline. While it may serve as a study guide, a specialized learning experience, or simply a key for browsing, it is not a complete table of contents.*

*The wigs of 18th-century French aristocrats were fashioned with false hair, padding, extravagant decorations, and special powders. What did poor people use for powder? Page 10.*

*Which bird, called "kiss-flower" by the Portuguese, is the only one that can fly backward? Page 346.*

# EXPLORING VOLUME 10

*This statue of the Indian hero of 'The Song of Hiawatha' is a landmark in Ironwood, Mich. Who was the real Hiawatha? Page 150.*

*Why was Halley's comet named for the 18th-century English astronomer? Page 15.*

Does the human heart ever rest? Page 100.

Why was the national hero of Bohemia burned at the stake? Page 358.

Name the Midwestern university that abandoned intercollegiate football despite its great football tradition established over decades. Page 360.

Name the painter who was a Quaker minister. Page 153.

What American patriot said, "I only regret that I have but one life to lose for my country"? Page 14.

Who was the first president of the United States to die in office? Page 50.

Where is the Peace Palace, seat of the International Court of Justice? Page 5 illustration.

What is the second oldest republic in the Western Hemisphere, after the United States? Page 11.

Who discovered an inexpensive method of separating aluminum from its oxide? Page 15.

Who is called the father of history? Page 145.

Name some animals that hibernate. Pages 150–1.

"Back to normalcy" was the campaign slogan of which United States president? Page 40.

What is finnan haddie? Page 4.

What animal can regrow whole parts of its body? Page 362.

Which blues song was originally written as an election campaign song for a Tennessee mayor? Page 31.

*(Right) Name the United States writer who received both the Pulitzer and the Nobel prizes. Page 128.*

*(Top left) Winslow Homer's 'Shore and Surf, Nassau' is typical of his famous sea paintings. What was his first big assignment as an illustrator? Page 224.*

*(Bottom left) What is the name of Germany's largest seaport? Page 21 illustration.*

Why do some horses wear blinders? Page 255.

What was the original meaning of the term "coat of arms"? Page 139.

Which of the Founding Fathers of the United States was killed in a duel with Aaron Burr? Page 22.

What was the name of Gen. Robert E. Lee's favorite horse? Page 254.

What is the world's busiest seaport? Page 39 illustration.

Why did Leonardo da Vinci use mirror writing? Page 30.

Which character in 'The Thin Man' was based upon an internationally famous playwright? Page 23–4.

Which city was named for two people—a British prime minister and then an African chief? Page 35.

Why have Cuban Americans been more economically successful than other Hispanics? Page 172.

Where did the horses used by the Spanish explorers come from? Page 275.

Where did handball originate 1,000 years ago? Page 28.

What white horse is dark at birth? Page 267.

How does the thyroid gland affect a person's disposition? Page 247.

What is the highest mountain range on Earth? Page 156.

Russ Kinne—Photo Researchers                                                    Pamela J. Harper

*The red and green of holly are worldwide symbols of Christmas. What Chinese holiday also uses holly for decoration? Page 208.*

*Who were the first people to use special indoor growing areas to speed up plant growth? Page 294.*

What gas was identified in the sun before it was found on the Earth? Page 126.

How large is the human heart? Page 100.

What common herb grows its male and female flowers on separate plants? Page 130.

What are some commercial uses of animal hair? Page 8.

How soon after birth can a foal walk? Page 255.

What American poet was also a surgeon? Page 208.

While working for the Geological Survey, which president of the United States tried to prove that a mule could scratch its head with its hind foot? Page 236.

What poem saved a historic ship from destruction? Page 208.

What was the Hanseatic League? Page 33.

Who was the "man without a country"? Page 14.

What classics are supposed to have been created by a blind wandering minstrel? Pages 224–5.

What city is often called Insurance City? Page 53.

What famous early explorer was set adrift by his men to perish in the Arctic? Page 322.

What is the origin of the celebration of Halloween? Page 17.

What Greek god had wings on his shoes? Page 144.

Why is helium the best gas for inflating lighter-than-air craft? Page 126.

What is the average number of strokes per second for a hummingbird's wings? Page 346.

Which newspaper publisher took credit for starting the Spanish-American War? Page 99.

Why did cartoonists like to picture President Benjamin Harrison in a "grandfather's hat"? Page 47.

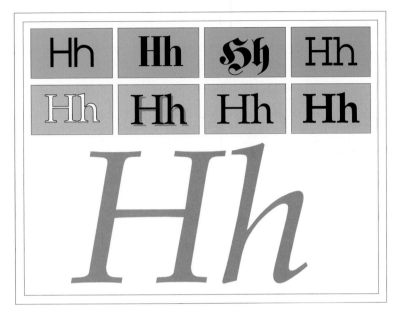

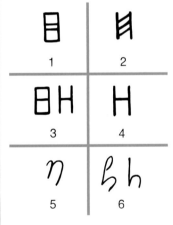

**The letter H** may have started as a picture sign of a fence, as in very early Semitic writing used in about 1500 BC on the Sinai Peninsula (1).

In about 1000 BC, in Byblos and other Phoenician and Canaanite centers, the sign was given a linear form (2), the source of all later forms. The sign was called *heth* in the Semitic languages, which may have meant "fence." The sound expressed by the *heth* sign stood for a pharyngeal sound which is not found in the English language.

The Greeks renamed the sign *eta* and used it in two functions—first for the consonant h and then for the long vowel e (3). The Romans took over the form H (4), with the sound value of the English h. From Latin the capital letter came into English unchanged.

A small Greek *eta* with curves (5) was developed from the capital letter. By the 9th century the corresponding Latin letter acquired a shape (6) much like the English handwritten and printed small h.

*The ancient history of letter forms is illustrated at the far left. The letter forms shown above are some styles used in modern printing.*

*A collection of letters and other characters of one design is called a typeface, or face. A typeface of one size is called a font. A font usually consists of numbers, punctuation marks, capital letters called uppercase letters, and small letters called lowercase letters. Some fonts also have other characters.*

*The small extensions at the ends of letter strokes are serifs. A typeface without serifs is called a sans-serif face. Letters drawn with only one line width are called monoline.*

***Top row:*** *examples of typefaces with very different features. Left to right: Avant Garde is a late 20th-century sans-serif monoline typeface. Bauer Bodoni Bold Condensed has serifs, very wide vertical strokes, and very narrow letters. Fette Fraktur is a type style that developed in Germany in the late 15th and early 16th centuries. Lubalin Graph is a modern monoline design with slab serifs.*

***Middle row:*** *various styles of a single face called Palatino. Left to right: open-face, shadow, lightface, and boldface. The open-face and shadow designs are examples of display type. (Display type is used primarily in advertising and for titles and headlines in some magazines and books.) The wide vertical strokes of boldfaced type make it darker than lightfaced type.*

***Bottom row:*** *Palatino lightfaced italic. Italic typefaces mimic handwriting. (Nonitalic typefaces are known as roman.) The articles in Compton's Encyclopedia are set mainly in various styles of the elegant Palatino typeface.*

**HAAKON, Kings of Norway.** Seven kings of Norway were named Haakon. From Haakon I to Haakon V they were all descendants of Harald the Fairhair, the first king of Norway (*see* Norway).

**Haakon I, the Good** (born 920?, ruled 946–61?), was the youngest son of Harald the Fairhair. He defeated his half brother Erik Bloodax, who had seized the throne. In about 961 he was killed by Erik's sons, who had taken refuge in Denmark.

**Haakon II, the Broadshouldered** (born 1147, ruled 1157–62), was the illegitimate son of Sigurd Munn. He was killed in battle at the age of 15.

**Haakon III Sverrsson** (ruled 1202–04) may have been poisoned by someone acting for his stepmother, Queen Margaret of Sweden.

**Haakon IV Haakonsson, the Old** (born 1204, ruled 1217–63), was the illegitimate son of Haakon III. He is remembered for having brought Iceland and Greenland under the control of Norway.

**Haakon V Magnusson** (born 1270, ruled 1299–1319) was the last male in the line of Harald the Fairhair. At his death the throne went to his nephew Magnus VII, who was also king of Sweden.

**Haakon VI Magnusson** (born 1339, ruled 1355–80), the son of Magnus VII, married Margaret, daughter of Valdemar IV of Denmark. As a result, Norway, Sweden, and Denmark were eventually united (*see* Denmark; Sweden).

**Haakon VII** (born 1872, ruled 1906–57) was the name assumed by Prince Charles of Denmark when he became the king of Norway in 1906, after Norway had regained its independence.

**HABEAS CORPUS.** An essential safeguard of personal liberty is the writ of habeas corpus. The term comes from the first two words of an old Latin legal form, which said "thou shalt have the person" of the accused in court at a given time. When a person is held prisoner, a judge may upon reasonable demand issue an order compelling the jailer or other custodian to bring the prisoner to court and explain why he is held captive. If no lawful reason is found, the prisoner must be released.

The origins of the writ are uncertain. The Magna Carta (1215) laid the foundations of the present form in English-speaking nations (*see* Magna Carta). King John was forced to promise that "no free man shall be taken or imprisoned except by the lawful judgment of his peers and by the law of the land." In the Habeas Corpus Act of 1679, the British Parliament strengthened the law by imposing severe penalties upon judges and officers who refused to grant the writ of habeas corpus.

The United States Constitution (Article I, Section 9) says: "The Privilege of the Writ of Habeas Corpus shall not be suspended, unless when in Cases of Rebellion or Invasion the Public Safety may require it." The privilege was suspended by President Abraham Lincoln at the outbreak of the Civil War. The Supreme Court later ruled that the power of suspension must be authorized by Congress.

The habeas corpus remedy is generally not found in civil-law countries, though some countries in Europe, Africa, and South America have adopted procedures similar to habeas corpus. During times of social or political strife, however, the writ is known to have been revoked. (*See also* Citizenship.)

**HABIT AND ADDICTION.** Often the origin of a word can reveal a great deal about its true meaning. This is certainly true of the words habit and addiction, which entered the English language many centuries ago. "Addict" is a term that originated in Roman law, when it referred to a person who was "formally made over or bound [to another] or attached by restraint or obligation." "Habit," on the other hand, originally referred to the way in which a person held or exhibited himself, as in his manner of dress. The original meaning of "habit" has been retained in the expressions nun's habit and riding habit. This difference in etymology reflects the essential difference between the actual phenomena of habit and addiction. The principal characteristic of addiction is a loss of control and freedom, while a habit is something that is donned or assumed, perhaps often, but that can nevertheless be removed if desired.

When after ingesting even a small amount of a narcotic drug a person feels compelled to continue taking larger doses, the person experiences a gradual failure of self-control as the body becomes "bound to another": the drug. This is the beginning of addiction.

Addiction is always considered harmful. On the other hand, while there are harmful habits as well as helpful ones, the process of habit formation can actually be beneficial. Many habits make it possible to carry out a host of necessary tasks swiftly and automatically. Learning to drive an automobile, for example, involves mastering a series of automatic behaviors, or habits, which help drivers react with the swiftness and decisiveness that driving demands.

In everyday speech, the words habit and addiction are often—and improperly—used interchangeably. Persons refer to "drug habits" and to "addictions" to food, gambling, work, and even to such activities as running and skiing. In order to clarify the distinction between the two terms, particularly when they refer to substance abuse, the World Health Organization (WHO) has supplied its own definitions. Addictive drugs are defined as those that produce in the great majority of users an irresistible need for the drug, an increased tolerance to its effect, and a physical dependence as indicated by severe and painful symptoms when the drug is withdrawn.

A habit-forming drug, on the other hand, is defined as one that can cause an emotional or psychological, rather than a physical, dependence in the user and one that can be withdrawn without causing physical harm or pain. Thus the principal difference between habit and addiction, according to WHO, involves the type of dependence. If the dependence is purely psychological, it can be considered a habit. If it is physical, it is an addiction.

## Habituation

Forming a new habit involves a process called conditioning, the basic principles of which were first discovered by the Russian physiologist Ivan Pavlov (*see* Pavlov). In his work with dogs, Pavlov found that after he repeatedly linked feeding with the sound of a bell, he was able to induce salivation in the dogs merely by sounding the bell. Hunger is a basic drive, and salivating is a normal response to the presence or anticipation of food. Salivating at the sound of a bell, however, is a conditioned response in which the sound serves as a stimulus that becomes reinforced or rewarded by the food. All learning, including the learning of habits, follows this pattern. The stimulus can be external, such as the red traffic signal that triggers the habit of stepping on the brake, or it can be internal, as when a person anticipates the satisfaction to be gained from playing a musical instrument or from displaying good manners. (*See also* Learning.)

In one famous and controversial experiment, the psychologist John B. Watson conditioned an infant to fear all furry animals. Watson would sound a loud noise, for example, as the infant was petting a rabbit. This began a process of negative reinforcement—the child became conditioned to link the frightening noise with anything furry. After the experiment, the infant would recoil in fear from anything with fur including animals, fur coats, muffs, and even Santa's beard.

In a similar way it is possible to break a habit by following the undesirable behavior with a negative reinforcement, or punishment. In test animals, habitual behavior can be changed or eliminated by applying an electric shock or other painful stimulus after the behavior. In humans, undesirable habits can be changed by punishment or other forms of negative reinforcement, such as our own dissatisfaction with our behavior or the disapproval of others.

Conversely, some habits can be broken by substituting a positive reinforcement for a negative

one. This was the method used by Watson to remove the infant's fear of fur. In this case, Watson brought furry objects to the baby under soothing circumstances, such as during the child's mealtime. As a result, the child overcame its fear because it no longer associated fur with unpleasant occurrences.

Whether habits are ever completely destroyed is unclear. Some scientists believe that habits establish specific, persistent patterns in the brain so that long-unused habits may reappear, particularly when a person is under stress. One example is the driver who, in an emergency, tries to step on the nonexistent clutch of an automatic-transmission car.

### Addiction and Withdrawal

Because addiction involves physical dependence, trying to change it with negative reinforcement would be futile. Addiction is an entirely different—and far more powerful—phenomenon than is habit. Test animals that have become physically dependent on drugs will consistently choose the drug over food and water and will continue to do so until they die. Studies indicate that this type of physical dependence begins at the most basic biological level, the cell. Cells in the central nervous system that have become accustomed to working in the presence of high levels of narcotic drugs soon are unable to operate normally when the drug is absent.

Scientists have learned that the brain makes its own pleasure-producing chemicals, called endorphins and enkephalins. These chemicals lie at the surface of certain specialized nerve cells, or neurons, in the brain and fit into the neurons like keys into keyholes. Narcotics, such as morphine and its relatives, contain chemicals that also fit into these keyholes, which is why these drugs produce feelings of pleasure. As a result of relying on increasing doses of narcotics, however, the brain stops the production of its own endorphins and enkephalins. Thus a narcotic actually changes the body chemistry in such a way that normal

*The effects on children of parents addicted to alcohol is poignantly illustrated by a child's drawing shown in a national art exhibit.*
Courtesy of the Children of Alcoholics Foundation, NYC

functioning becomes impossible unless the drug is present. (*See also* Brain; Narcotic and Sedative.)

While the process of breaking a habit may be very difficult, it is far different from the process of withdrawal from an addictive drug. Withdrawal produces many symptoms, ranging from yawning, crying, profuse sweating, and runny nose to more painful and frightening symptoms such as shaking and shivering, vomiting, and increases in blood pressure, temperature, and rate of breathing. In severe cases convulsions, respiratory failure, and even death may result. (*See also* Drugs, "Drug Abuse .")   Timothy Larkin

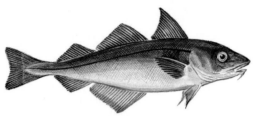

**Haddock (Melanogrammus aeglefinus)**

**HADDOCK.** A member of the cod family, Gadidae, the haddock (*Melanogrammus aeglefinus*) is a bottom-dwelling, carnivorous fish. It differs from the cod by having a smaller mouth, a black lateral line in place of the cod's white line, and a distinctive dark spot on each shoulder. Its average size is about 1 ½ to 2 feet (45 to 60 centimeters) and 5 pounds (2.3 kilograms), though haddocks as large as 3.3 feet (1 meter) and 36 pounds (16 kilograms) have been recorded.

The haddock is found on both sides of the North Atlantic. It lives deeper than the cod and feeds on invertebrate organisms and small fishes. Spawning occurs from January to June on the offshore banks. The female lays a large number of eggs, which float on the surface and hatch after two to three weeks. Then the young seek the bottom and, unlike other codfishes, spend their first years in the open sea.

Haddock are caught in the same areas and in the same ways as are cod (*see* Cod; Fisheries). The catch is often sold fresh, dried, or as packaged fillets. Smoked haddock is known as finnan haddie. The process of smoking the fish originated in the 18th century at Findon, a fishing village in Scotland. Originally the product was known as "Findon haddocks."

**HADES** *see* **HELL AND HADES.**

**HADRIAN** (76–138). Publius Aelius Hadrianus, called Hadrian, was Roman emperor from AD 117 until 138. He regarded his 20-year reign as a golden age of peace and prosperity, comparable to that of his great predecessor Augustus more than 100 years earlier ( *see* Augustus). Monuments to Hadrian's reign are the Tivoli villa near Rome; Castel Sant'Angelo, adjacent to Vatican City, built as a mausoleum for himself; the Pantheon, a temple to the gods, in Rome; and Hadrian's Wall in the north of England.

Hadrian was born in Italica, Spain (near modern Seville), on Jan. 24, 76, to a Roman family. He was a relative of the emperor Trajan, who ruled from 98 to 117. Hadrian was probably educated in Rome. Through the emperor's good will he was rapidly promoted in military and political posts. While on a military campaign with Trajan in the Middle East, the emperor adopted him—a sure sign Hadrian was destined to succeed him. Two days later, on Aug. 11, 117, it was learned that Trajan had died. The army immediately proclaimed Hadrian emperor.

His reign began under a cloud with the execution of four senators suspected of conspiracy, and it ended in similar fashion 20 years later. Yet he was a man of culture, sensitivity, and religious devotion. His artistic temperament manifested itself in his poetry, his architectural designs, his very style of life. The most notable feature of his reign was his traveling around the empire. For 12 of his 20 years he was absent from Rome, mostly in the eastern provinces and in North Africa. He especially loved Athens and its culture. He visited it three times, revised its constitution, and brought to completion the vast temple of Olympian Zeus, which was begun 500 years earlier.

During the last years of Hadrian's reign there was a serious Jewish rebellion in Palestine, led by Bar-Kokhba. Palestine was left ruined and largely depopulated. Hadrian adopted the future Antoninus Pius to succeed him, and Antoninus in turn adopted the boy who would become Marcus Aurelius. Hadrian died in Baiae, a seaside resort, on July 10, 138.

**HAFNIUM** *see* Fact-Index.

**HAGUE, THE, The Netherlands.** The seat of government of The Netherlands and its third largest city, The Hague lies in the province of South Holland about 2 miles (3.2 kilometers) from the North Sea. The legislature convenes at The Hague, but Amsterdam is considered the capital because the constitution requires the sovereign to be crowned there. The original Dutch name of the city, 's-Gravenhage ("the count's private dominion"), was shortened to Den Haag. The counts of Holland had a hunting preserve here in the 13th century.

The heart of the city is the quadrangle of government buildings known as the Binnenhof, or Inner Court. In the courtyard is the Ridderzaal, or Hall of Knights, built about 1280. Every September the sovereign is driven in a golden carriage to the Hall of Knights to open a new session of the States-General, or parliament. Behind it is the Counts' Palace.

Immediately to the north of the Binnenhof is a lake, the Hof Vijver. West of the Binnenhof is the Buitenhof, or Outer Court. The original entrance was the medieval prisoners' tower and gate, now a museum. Northeast of the Binnenhof is the Mauritshuis, a palace

*Construction of the Peace Palace was inspired by peace conferences held in The Hague between 1899 and 1907.*

Academy of Fine and Applied Arts are located in the city.

The luxurious seaside resort of Scheveningen adjoins The Hague. Renovation and reconstruction here were completed in 1983 following legislation to allow gambling. In a wooded park in the area is the miniature town of Madurodam. Built to a scale of $\frac{1}{25}$ the actual size, it shows the evolution of Dutch architecture.

Heavy industry is not a major part of The Hague's economy and does not employ many workers. Services and trade play more significant roles. Light industries include printing and publishing and the manufacture of pottery and glass, chocolate and other food products, metal and electrical products, and chemicals. The international headquarters of several petroleum companies are located in The Hague.

The Hague grew up around the castle built by Count William II in 1248. It was a center of diplomatic negotiations in the 17th century. It declined in power and influence during French rule, but after liberation in the early 1800s it became the capital of the Kingdom of The Netherlands. Revenues from the Dutch East Indies also increased the city's fortunes after 1850.

During World War II the Germans destroyed whole sections of the city to build fortifications. Afterward, much work was done to restore and expand The Hague. Population (1999 estimate), 440,743.

begun in 1633. It houses the royal art gallery with masterpieces by Dutch and Flemish artists, including Rembrandt, Jan Steen, and Jan Vermeer. It was restored and reopened in 1987.

Other buildings of interest in the old part of the city are the Great Church of St. Jacob (15th to 16th century), the Cloister Church (14th century), and the Old Town Hall (1564). In addition to the Mauritshuis there are many other cultural institutions. The Mesdag, Bredius, Royal Coin Collection, and The Hague Municipal museums are especially notable. The Meermanno-Westreenianum Museum, which is a branch of the Rijksmuseum in Amsterdam, exhibits rare books and antiquities.

The 17th-century palace formerly occupied by the royal family is the seat of the International Institute for Social Studies. The royal family, when in The Hague, lives in the Huis ten Bosch (House in the Wood), built in 1645.

Northwest of the Binnenhof is the Peace Palace, completed in 1913 with funds provided by Andrew Carnegie. The Peace Palace is the seat of the International Court of Justice, the supreme court of the United Nations (*see* Hague Peace Conferences; United Nations). More than 100 international conferences are held each year in The Hague.

The garden in Westbroek Park has thousands of rosebushes. Lange Voorhout Park has a weekly flea market from May through September. Nightlife ranges from jazz and movies to The Hague Philharmonic Orchestra and the Royal Theater. The Royal Conservatory of Music and Dance and the Royal

**HAGUE PEACE CONFERENCES.** Before World War I the most promising movements for world peace were two conferences held at The Hague, The Netherlands, in 1899 and 1907. They were called by the czar of Russia. Twenty-six countries, including the United States, were represented at the first meeting; 44 sent delegates to the second. A third conference, planned for 1915, was not held because of the outbreak of World War I.

The chief goals of the conferences were to secure an agreement for reducing or limiting national armaments and to formulate a plan for settling international disputes by arbitration. The first objective was not attained mainly because Germany refused to limit its armaments.

Both conferences proposed agreements, or conventions, that concerned international disputes. Included were regulations that defined the rights of neutral nations and outlawed such military tactics as the naval bombardment of undefended towns and the use of poison gases and aerial bombs. Because none of these agreements was ratified by all the participating countries, they were not considered binding. Most of the provisions of the Hague conventions were disregarded in both world wars.

A plan for optional arbitration, drafted during the conferences, led to the Permanent Court of Arbitration, known as the Hague Court. This court consisted of a panel of judges from the member states. When two nations quarreled—for example, over a boundary line—they could request a judge to arbitrate the dispute (*see* Arbitration). When the League of Nations established the Permanent Court of International

Justice, known as the World Court, in 1920, the older Hague Court nominated candidates to the World Court bench. Under the United Nations charter, the two older courts were virtually merged into the new International Court of Justice. (*See also* United Nations.)

**HAHN, Otto** (1879–1968). The German chemist Otto Hahn is credited, along with radiochemist Fritz Strassmann, with discovering nuclear fission. This development led directly to the creation of atomic weapons during World War II and to the modern nuclear power industry (*see* Nuclear Energy). Hahn was awarded the Nobel prize for chemistry in 1944 and shared the Enrico Fermi award in 1966 with Strassmann and Austrian physicist Lise Meitner.

Hahn was born on March 8, 1879, in Frankfurt am Main, Germany. He attended the universities of Marburg and Munich and received his doctorate from Marburg in 1901. After a year of military service and two years teaching at Marburg, he studied radioactivity in London and Montreal. He returned to Germany to work in the chemistry laboratory of the University of Berlin. From 1912 until 1944 he was at the Kaiser Wilhelm Institute for Chemistry (later the Max Planck Society for the Advancement of Science).

During World War I Hahn was a chemical-warfare expert. After the war he and Meitner announced the discovery of the radioactive element protactinium. Inspired by Enrico Fermi's work on bombarding uranium with subatomic particles, Hahn and his associates obtained results indicating that atoms were split in the process. To this action they gave the name nuclear fission. The implications of this discovery were immediately apparent to scientists (*see* Nuclear Weapons). After time in England after World War II, Hahn returned to Germany. He died at Göttingen on July 28, 1968.

**HAHNIUM** *see* Fact-Index.

**HAIFA, Israel.** Israel's major port and third largest city, Haifa has been compared to San Francisco for its mountainous seaside beauty. Located in the northern part of the country on the shore of the Mediterranean Sea, Haifa has majestic views from Mount Carmel, looking northward over Haifa Bay.

Haifa is an industrial, commercial, and educational center. Its principal industries include steel manufacturing, food processing, shipbuilding, and the production of chemicals, textiles, and cement. Haifa has an electric power plant and petroleum refineries, and its Dagon silo can hold 100,000 tons of grain.

Haifa University and the Technion, or Israel Institute of Technology, draw Israeli students as well as many students from other countries. The world headquarters of the Baha'i faith is in Haifa, and its neoclassical temple made of white marble with a gold dome is

*The gold-domed Baha'i temple on Mount Carmel overlooks the lower city of Haifa and its harbor.*

surrounded by majestic Persian gardens. The Haifa Museum and several smaller museums attract many visitors. These include the National Maritime Museum, located near the port; the Tikotin Museum of Japanese Art and the Mane Katz Museum on Mount Carmel; and a music museum devoted to folk-music instruments of Asia, Africa, Europe, and South America. Also frequently visited are Elijah's cave and the Carmelite monastery of Stella Maris. The city also has a professional orchestra, a youth orchestra, and a theater company.

Haifa is laid out in four major sections. The lower city near the port is both a residential and commercial area. The bay area is heavily industrial. Hadar Hacarmel, at the foot of Mount Carmel, houses the shopping district, movie theaters, and many restaurants. This and the other lower areas are connected with Mount Carmel by Israel's only subway, called the Carmelit. Mount Carmel is mostly a residential area, with some of the houses and apartments atop the mountain facing the bay.

Haifa was first mentioned in the Talmud and has since been claimed by many people. In 1100 the Crusaders conquered the city, slaughtering Arabs and Jews. The city was destroyed by the Mamluks in 1291, captured by the Turks in 1517, and fortified by the Bedouin Sheikh Dahir el 'Amr in 1750. Jewish settlers from North Africa and Germany came to Haifa in the 19th century. In 1933 the modern port opened with plans that had been started by the British during their occupation, which began in 1918. During the War of Independence in 1948 the Arabs of Haifa surrendered the city to Jewish fighters of the Haganah, or underground defense organization. Population (2001 estimate), 270,500.

**HAILE SELASSIE** (1892–1975). When Haile Selassie came to the throne of Ethiopia, he was a progressive ruler and the hope of young moderates hoping to modernize their country. By the end of his reign he had become a virtual dictator, overthrowing the old constitution and taking all power into his own hands.

Haile Selassie was born Tafari Makonnen on July 23, 1892, near Harar, Ethiopia. Because his father was right-hand man to Emperor Menelik II, he was quickly given the responsibilities of a young nobleman. By 1910 he was governor of his native province. When the emperor's daughter Zauditu became empress in 1916, Tafari was named regent and heir to the throne. In 1923 he brought Ethiopia into the League of Nations, and in 1924 he visited Europe—the first ruler of Ethiopia to travel abroad.

He assumed the title of king in 1928, and upon Zauditu's death in 1930 he had himself proclaimed emperor as Haile Selassie. The name means "Might of the Trinity." Ethiopia was a Christian nation, and the emperor was supposedly descended from ancient Israel's King Solomon. Another of his numerous titles was Lion of Judah. In 1931 a new constitution greatly limited the powers of the parliament and within a few years it had become defunct.

His rule was interrupted in 1935 by Italy's invasion of Ethiopia, which forced him into exile. He returned in 1941 when British and Ethiopian troops recaptured the capital. Although restored as emperor, he had to re-create the authority he had once held. In 1955 he issued a new constitution, giving himself all governing authority. Except for an army revolt in December 1960, Haile Selassie ruled with little opposition until 1974, when he was deposed by a provisional military government. He died under uncertain circumstances, a captive in his own palace, on Aug. 27, 1975. ( *See also* Ethiopia.)

**HAIR.** A slender, flexible structure found on the surface of mammals, as well as on some insects and plants, is hair. One of the characteristics by which mammals are distinguished from other members of the animal kingdom is the presence of hair. Plant hairs called trichomes occur on roots, stems, and leaves.

In mammals a coat of hair is called a pelage. A fine, soft, and dense coat is usually referred to as fur. The woolly coat of sheep is called fleece. In hogs the hairs are stiff bristles; in the porcupine and hedgehog they are enlarged and toughened to form a protective coat of quills. Sensory hairs on the antennae, palps, and legs of insects inform the insects of their surroundings and their body position.

Most mammals have three distinct kinds of hairs. Guard hairs protect the rest of the pelage from abrasion and frequently from moisture and usually lend a distinctive color pattern. The thicker underfur is primarily insulative and may differ in color from the guard hairs. The third common hair type is the vibrissa, a stiff, typically elongate hair that functions in tactile sensation. All mammals except humans have vibrissae, usually found around the lips, nostrils, eyes, and cheeks. The cat's whiskers are examples of these tactile hairs. Vibrissae grow from specialized follicles with a rich supply of sensory nerves. Hairs may be further modified to form rigid quills. The "horn" of the rhinoceros is composed of keratin, a protein also found in horns, hooves, nails, claws, and baleen.

The amount of hair and where it grows vary with different mammals. The entire body of the dog, the sheep, the cow, and the horse is covered with a hairy coat. The whale and the hippopotamus have only a few hairs. In humans, hair is not found on palms of the hands or the soles of the feet.

The coloration and pattern of coats in animals serve both as a camouflage for protection against enemies and as an allurement to mates. The color of hair is caused by the presence of melanin, a pigment made by special cells called melanocytes. All humans have the same number of melanocytes, but the activity of the cells varies among individuals and races. When groups of cells responsible for melanin production cease to function, the result is the uncolored white or gray hair characteristic of aging.

Human hair consists of a root, embedded in the skin, and a shaft, projecting from the skin surface. The root ends in a soft, whitish enlargement, the hair bulb. The bulb is lodged in an elongated pit in the skin, called the follicle. If the hair is long, the follicle extends into the subcutaneous fatty tissue beneath the skin. At the base of each follicle is a conical swelling, the papilla, supplied with nerves and blood vessels. Hair growth takes place at the junction of the follicle and the papilla. As the cells are pushed up the follicle, they harden and become the horny shaft. (*See also* Skin.)

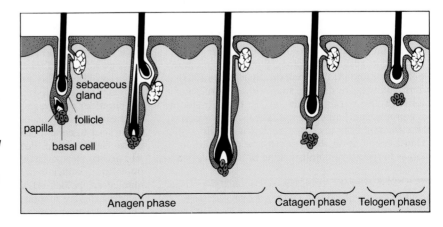

*All types of fur, including human hair, are subject to a cycle that can be divided into three phases: the anagen, or growth, phase; the catagen, or intermediate, phase; and the telogen, or resting, phase. In the anagen phase the papilla induces basal cells to begin development of a new hair. The new hair, growing both upward and downward, moves alongside the old hair and eventually pushes it out of the hair follicle. Hair growth stops in the catagen phase. Basal cells and the follicle migrate upward in the telogen phase.*

sebaceous gland

follicle

papilla

basal cell

Anagen phase

Catagen phase   Telogen phase

A small erector muscle is attached to each hair follicle. If the muscles are contracted, the hairs become more erect and the follicles are dragged upward, producing small bumps on the surface of the skin, called gooseflesh. Sebaceous (fat) glands attached to each hair release a substance, sebum, that lubricates the hair. Straight hairs are cylindrical, wavy hairs are oval, and curly hairs are flattened in cross section.

Hair growth is not a continuous process but progresses for a variable period and then stops. The 150,000 hairs of the scalp are able to grow for years without interruption. Most animals have shedding (molting) periods. Baldness, or alopecia, occurs because of a natural tendency of the follicles of the scalp to become very small as humans age. Common baldness is hereditary and occurs more frequently in men than in women. In 1988 the United States Food and Drug Administration approved the use of minoxidil as a treatment for some types of baldness. The drug was originally formulated for treatment of high blood pressure. Some types of baldness show a rather sudden loss of hair, in patches or over the whole head. These types sometimes result from high fevers, medical treatments, or glandular or emotional disturbances. The hair usually regrows once health is restored. Dandruff is a skin condition in which loose scales of dead cells and dried oil secreted by glands are found in the hair.

Cloth is made from the hair of sheep, goats, camels, and other animals. Felt for hats is made from hare and rabbit hair. Carpet padding and gymnasium mats use cow hair. Horsehair from tails and manes is sometimes used for upholstery and for stiffening garments. Hair from squirrels, camels, badgers, and sables is used to make artists' brushes. Hog hair is used for brushes and in upholstery. Human hair is used for wigs and for hairnets. Artificial fibers such as nylon have replaced animal hair in many products.

**HAIRDRESSING.** The processes of cutting, cleaning, coloring, styling, and arranging hair are known collectively as hairdressing. When the practice of hairdressing relates specifically to men and includes the grooming of beards and mustaches, it is known as barbering. These grooming practices are not limited to humans; animals such as apes, baboons, and cats clean and smooth each other's fur with their paws and tongues. Humans use a wide variety of tools, however, and attach much importance to hairdressing.

As a science, called trichology, there has been much late 20th-century study of hair and its components: carbon, nitrogen, hydrogen, sulfur, phosphorus, and chlorine. Sulfur bonds are involved in the permanent wave process, and other elements are significant in understanding how to change the color of hair.

Hairdressing as an art form uses the principles of color, as in the art of painting. One of the features that

. . . . . . . . . . . . . . . . . . . . . . . . . . . . . . . . . . . . . . . . .

*This article was contributed by Esther R. Teller, formerly a hairstylist and makeup artist for Broadway theaters in New York City.*

sets it apart from painting is that the product has an opinion about the work of art. Some of the mediums used to color hair are temporary color rinses, sprays, and lotions that can be brushed or washed out of the hair immediately; semipermanent color in various forms that deposit on the cuticle, or outer layer of hair, and that require several washings to rid the hair of the effect; permanent tints that add color to darken hair or disguise gray hair; and bleaches that remove color or lighten hair.

The tools used in the sculpture or shaping of hair include brushes, combs, scissors, razors, hairpins, clips, such curling implements as hair rollers or curling irons, hairdryers, setting lotions, sprays, and mousses. Perhaps the single most important element in the art of hairdressing is communication between the hairdresser and client and that between the client and the world at large.

### History

Boxwood combs from the Stone Age, about 10,000 BC, indicate early examples of hairdressing. Cave paintings show mud, feathers, and animal skins used as hair adornment as much as for protection. The Bible mentions the barber's trade at the time of the prophet Ezekiel, and the Book of Judges refers to the long, flowing, unbound hairstyle of warriors dedicated to liberation. Female barbers have gained and lost popularity since Delilah cut Samson's hair and thus took his strength.

**Ancient Egypt.** It is evident that hairdressing was an aspect of life in Egypt, as hairdressers are depicted prominently on frescoes, urns, and ceremonial coffins. Elaborately decorated cases were used to carry combs, hairpins, scissors, razors, tweezers, and bottles of lotions used to restore and strengthen hair. The Egyptian court of gods had a barber god, and wealthy people had personal barbers who came to their homes daily or were their personal attendants. A traveling barber set a stool under a tree to perform his services for poorer people.

Shaven heads and smooth, hairfree bodies were signs of nobility in Egypt from about 3000 BC, but fashion required men and women to wear wigs of real hair or sheep's wool. False beards, braided and curled, were popular with men. Indigo dyes were used to achieve the favored black color for wigs and beards; and henna, a powder made from the leaves of a shrub, gave hair, nails, and toes a red-orange cast. After 1150 BC wigs were dyed more fanciful colors such as red, green, and blue. The most popular styles were bluntly cut hair, which varied in length from the chin to below the shoulder and was usually worn with bangs on the forehead.

**Ancient Greece.** Barber shops first came into vogue in the Greek period. Political, sports, and social news and gossip were exchanged by philosophers, writers, poets, and politicians while they were shaved, curled, manicured, pedicured, and massaged. Rituals of hairdressing are mentioned in the writings of Homer ('Iliad'), Aristophanes, and others. Some barbers were skilled artists and respected community members. Others were household slaves who were punished if they allowed a hair out of place. Hair was mainly thick and dark and worn long and curled naturally or artificially in definite patterns. Fillets, headbands made of ribbon or metal, were popular. It is in the frescoes of Crete that ponytails worn by women first appear. Cosmetic preparations, oils, pomades, waxes, and lotions were used to give the hair shine and a pleasant scent. Blond hair was rare and admired by the Greeks, and both sexes tried bleaching their hair with potash water and infusions of yellow flowers. In the 5th century BC Athenian men began to wear shorter hair, cutting it in ritual offering to Hercules. Beards, real and fake, remained popular until the reign in the 4th century BC of Alexander the Great, whose soldiers had to shave their beards to avoid having them seized in hand-to-hand combat.

**Ancient Rome.** Many Greek grooming traditions were followed in ancient Rome. Barbershops remained familiar social institutions, and barbers were in plentiful supply in the marketplace and in public baths. Prosperous citizens offered guests the services of their household barbers. Hair and beards were curled with oven-heated curling irons or tongs. Wealthy Romans sprinkled gold dust on their hair to obtain the popular fair-haired look, and some dyed their hair with caustic soap to achieve a red color. Potions made of such ingredients as ashes, earthworms, and boiled walnut shells were made to prevent hair from falling out or turning white.

The writer Ovid describes the many hairstyles worn by Romans, but the most popular for men were short, brushed forward, and with arranged curls. Beardless faces remained fashionable. Women's hairstyles were most often parted in the center, waved or curled over the ears, and left hanging in long curls or put up in chignons or buns.

**Middle Ages.** In the Middle Ages barbers also performed as surgeons, a practice previously attended to by monks, priests, and other clergymen. From 1163 until 1745 barbers were called doctors of the short robe and practiced tooth pulling, bloodletting, and the treatment of abscesses. It was during this period that hairdressers first became associated with a variety of technical instruments and chemical compounds that were later developed as methods of tinting and dyeing hair. Early medieval styles showed a return in popularity of the beard and longer hair for men, and braids were very fashionable for women. The bowl haircut and the pageboy, which curled under the chin, emerged as the popular men's hairstyles of the period, though both men and women wore a variety of hats or ornate and unusually shaped headdresses that covered the head. Blond hair continued to be admired, and the favored medieval bleaching formulas included henna, gorse flowers, saffron, eggs, and calf kidneys. Hair and scalp conditioner was a lizard boiled in olive oil, and egg whites gave hair body and stiffness. Curl papers, crimpers, and ribbons were tools used to produce desired styles.

*The portrait of Battista Sforza (left) by Piero della Francesca depicts a hairstyle worn by some women during the Renaissance. The "punk" hairstyle (right) of the 1980s became popular in tandem with the emergence of punk-rock music.*

**Renaissance.** In the Renaissance there was more freedom in the spirit of dress, and headdresses again allowed more hair to show. In England a variety of beards, mustaches, and hairstyles for men became popular during the reign of Henry VIII. The popularity of Queen Elizabeth I inspired her subjects to imitate her by wearing red wigs or by dyeing their hair red and shaving their hairlines to give the appearance of a high forehead. The high collars and starched ruffs of this period led to upswept styles that were sometimes dressed over a wire frame to achieve a heart shape. In the last years of the 16th century, the Italian artist Titian popularized a red-blond hair color in his paintings. Venetian women who wanted to achieve the color applied mixtures of alum, sulfur, soda, and rhubarb to their hair and sat in the sun to let it dry. In Renaissance France the new custom was to pulverize flowers in a powder and then apply the mixture to the hair with a gluey substance.

**17th century.** In general, men's hair got longer and beards got smaller in the mid-1600s. Wigs (especially for men) gained in popularity again, getting progressively fuller, curlier, and more exaggerated. The upswept feminine style of the Elizabethan period became flatter on top, with soft curls worn over the ears and forehead and the back of the hair pulled into a bun and decorated with ribbons, pearls, nets, feathers, and flowers. In England King Charles I introduced the lovelock, a long ringlet usually separated from the rest of the hair, brought forward on the shoulder, and tied with a ribbon or rosette. A stricter mood influenced hairstyles as the poorer population and the Puritans wore shorter, uncurled haircuts under caps. In the New World in 1634 the students at Harvard (they were all men) were forbidden to engage in the fashion extremes of hairdressing, including long hair, lovelocks, and hair powdering. The very formal Spanish mode of women's dress tried to find balance in hairstyles through the use of wire frames to emphasize width. Popular hair colors were blond, brown, and black, but perfumed powders were gaining use on hair and wigs.

**18th century.** Wigs for men throughout Europe and the American colonies continued to be popular and were worn throughout the century. Fashion shifted from bulky, exaggerated, and full-bottomed wigs to wigs of a smaller proportion—most frequently worn with a ponytail at the back, which was tied with a ribbon or tucked into a bag. These wigs were called cadogans, or tie-wigs, and could be worn in natural hair colors but were made with white hair, or powdered, for formal occasions. Women's hairstyles became very fanciful in the middle of the century. False hair and padding were used to build them to great heights, and extravagant decorations—from jewels and flower and feather adornments to models of ships, bird cages, and entire flower gardens—were worked into them. The messy practice of dressing and powdering the hair took several hours, and wealthy people set aside a special powder room in their homes for this purpose. White powder made of flour, starch, or plaster of Paris was used for most hair and wigs, but pastel-colored powders were also favored. Poorer people who desired to maintain fashionable hairstyles wore plainer wigs, called scratch wigs, and powdered them with sawdust. Wigs worn in the 20th century by British judges, barristers, and royal coachmen are based on some of the 18th-century styles.

**19th century.** The French Revolution at the end of the 18th century had a great deal to do with bringing hair fashion back down to Earth. There was a return to the classical Greek hairstyles, with hair dressed closer to the head and fillets or bands of ribbon worn by women. Hairpins, clips, and tortoiseshell combs became popular hair ornaments. Wigs were rarely worn in the 19th century, and men once again wore facial hair in a wide range of styles—from mutton-chop sideburns to the walrus-style mustache. Treatments and cures for baldness were concocted of substances as varied as bear's grease, beef marrow, onion juice, butter, and flower water. They were sometimes such toxic substances as sulfur or mercury. The most widely used hair preparations of the century were Macassar oil and brilliantine, whose functions were to give hair shine. In general, hair fashions changed faster as news traveled faster from one country, and even continent, to another. The simplicity of the smooth, center-parted styles worn by women in the Victorian era lasted until the 1870s, when the Parisian hairdresser Marcel Grateau created a new, natural-looking wave by turning a curling iron upside down. The Marcel wave remained popular for almost half a century and helped usher in a new era of women's waved and curled hairpieces, which were mixed with the natural hair. Another major innovation at the end of the 19th century was the invention in 1895 of the safety razor by an American, William Gillette. Barbers now concentrated on cutting hair and trimming beards and mustaches, and a new age of at-home grooming practices began.

**20th century.** Women's hairdressing salons appeared, and women not only went to have their hair "done" but to socialize, gossip, and be pampered in much the same way that men went to barber shops from ancient times. Scientific research on the hair and scalp began as personal hygiene became the way to prevent lice and dirt that were masked by the wigs, powders, perfumes, and potions of preceding centuries.

The advent of electricity sparked a major change in the concept of hairdressing, when in London in 1906 hairdresser Charles Nestlé invented the permanent-wave machine. The bulky machine took up to ten hours to complete the process of waving the hair to withstand washing, weather, and time, but it saved women countless hours with the curling iron and forever united fashion with 20th-century technology. The next year a Parisian chemistry student, Eugène Schueller, founded the company L'Oréal by creating a dye to cover gray hair with natural-looking colors in a permanent process.

At the end of World War I a short haircut for women, called the bob, was considered scandalous but gained popularity because of its practicality for women working outside the home. The advent of motion pictures in the 1920s set new standards in fashion for both clothing and hairstyles. Women all over the world quickly adopted the styles and colors of Hollywood actresses. In the 1930s Jean Harlow and Mae West started the trend for platinum blond waves, and little girls were having their hair curled or permanently waved to look like Shirley Temple. The 1940s were more encouraging for brunets like Katharine Hepburn and Hedy Lamarr, and red hair became popular once again in the 1950s with Lucille Ball.

Fashions in men's hair did not change quite as radically or as rapidly in the first half of the 20th century, and a clean-cut look prevailed from the military influence of the two world wars. The rock-and-roll singer Elvis Presley helped change this with his long sideburns and shiny pompadour. But it was the singing group The Beatles that repopularized longer hair for the first time in many decades with their bowl haircuts.

Changes in women's hair appeared in the 1960s as well, with the return of straight hair and the asymmetrical haircuts created by English hairdresser Vidal Sassoon. From the 1970s there was a wider acceptance of variety in hairstyles for both men and women—from the straight and free-swinging through the naturally curly, to spiked-up "punk" hairdos.

**FURTHER RESOURCES FOR HAIRDRESSING**

**Charles, Ann, and De Anfrasio, Roger.** The History of Hair (Mediterranean Press, 1970).
**Contini, Mila.** Fashion: From Ancient Egypt to the Present Day (Odyssey, 1965).
**Cooper, Wendy.** Hair: Sex, Society, Symbolism (Stein & Day, 1971).
**Corson, Richard.** Fashions in Hair: The First 5,000 Years (Peter Owen, 1965).
**Masters, T.W.** Hairdressing in Theory and Practice (Oxford Technical Press, 1966).
**Schroeder, David.** Engagement in the Mirror: Hairdressers and Their Work (R & E Research Assoc., 1978).
**Zviak, Charles.** The Science of Hair Care (Dekker, 1986).

**HAITI.** Located in the Caribbean Sea, Haiti covers an area of 10,695 square miles (27,700 square kilometers) and occupies the western third of Hispaniola, the second largest island of the Antilles. Haiti shares the island with the Dominican Republic, but the two neighbors have little in common. Haiti's population has French and African cultural roots, while the Dominican Republic is more closely associated with Latin America. Haiti is the second oldest republic in the Western Hemisphere, after the United States.

## Land and Climate

Haiti possesses some of the most rugged terrain of the Caribbean islands. Its mountain systems and the parallel ribbons of lowland that separate them are oriented in an east-west trend. To the north there is the Massif du Nord, which belongs to the main mountain backbone of Hispaniola (called the Cordillera Central in the Dominican Republic). To the south there is a long and relatively narrow mountainous peninsula formed by the Massif de la Hotte and Massif de la Selle. The latter contains the country's highest peak, Mount Selle, 8,773 feet (2,674 meters) above sea level. Between the mountain regions, central Haiti is characterized by alternating uplands (Chaine des Mateux and Montagnes Noires) and lowlands (the Cul de Sac, the valley of the river Artibonite, and the Plaine Centrale). The nation's capital, Port-au-Prince, is located in the Cul de Sac depression. In the northeast around Cap-Haïtien there is a patch of lowland called the Plaine du Nord.

The complexity of terrain is matched by a wide variety of climatic conditions. Tropical conditions resulting from the low latitude of between 17° and 20° N. are modified by the trade winds, the surrounding ocean, and high elevations. In most areas, however, temperatures are moderately high and vary little from season to season. Rainfall is normally higher on mountain slopes that receive the northeasterly trade winds and decreases on leeward slopes and in the major valleys, especially in the Cul de Sac and the Artibonite Valley. The lowlands of central Haiti are so dry that fields must be irrigated for crops. Prolonged droughts in 1965, 1975, 1977, and 1980 affected coffee and sugar exports and led to a severe food shortage. Hurricanes also had a devastating effect on Haitian agriculture in 1979, 1980, and 1998. Earthquakes are another hazard. Port-au-Prince was destroyed twice in the 18th century, and Cap-Haïtien had a similar fate in 1842.

## Plant and Animal Life

Haiti was once almost entirely covered with pine, hardwood, and mixed pine-hardwood forests, but fire, uncontrolled cutting, and the conversion of woodland

## Facts About Haiti

**Official Name.** Republic of Haiti.

**Capital.** Port-au-Prince.

**Area.** 10,695 square miles (27,700 square kilometers).

**Population** (2002 estimate). 7,064,000; 660.5 persons per square mile (255.0 persons per square kilometer); 36.3 percent urban, 63.7 percent rural (2001 estimate).

**Major Languages.** French and Haitian Creole (both official).

**Major Religions.** Roman Catholicism and Voodoo.

**Literacy.** 45 percent.

**Highest Peak.** Mount Selle.

**Major River.** Artibonite.

**Form of Government.** Republic.

**Heads of State and Government.** President and prime minister.

**Legislature.** National Assembly, composed of Senate and Chamber of Deputies.

**Voting Qualification.** Age 18.

**Political Divisions.** 9 departments.

**Major Cities** (1997 estimate). Port-au-Prince (917,112), Carrefour (306,074), Delmas (257,247).

**Chief Manufactured Products.** Cement, essential oils, cigarettes, malt liquor, beer, garments, travel goods and handbags, sports equipment and toys.

**Chief Agricultural Products.** *Crops*—sugarcane, cassava, plantains, bananas, mangoes, corn (maize), yams, sweet potatoes, rice, sorghum, avocadoes, coffee, cacao. *Livestock*—goats, cattle, pigs, horses.

**Flag.** *Colors*—red and black. The state flag also has the national coat of arms at the center (*see* Flags of the World).

**Monetary Unit.** 1 gourde = 100 centimes.

to agriculture destroyed most of the trees. Firewood is still the principal source of energy. Some pines, mahogany, cedar, and rosewood still exist in the humid upper mountain ranges. There are also wild varieties of coffee, cacao, and coconut trees with many native tropical fruits, including avocado, orange, lime, and mango. The vegetation of subhumid areas such as the Artibonite Valley is generally savanna with scattered palms. The Cul de Sac and other arid zones are characterized by cactus and thorn scrub. Many species of insects are found, but there are no large mammals or poisonous snakes. Ducks, guinea hens, flamingos, and wild pigeons are common.

## People

Haiti is one of the most densely populated nations in the world. Opportunities for employment are scarce, and roughly three fifths of the population still lives in the countryside. Like the capital cities of most developing countries, however, Port-au-Prince has grown rapidly and now has more than 1.5 million inhabitants, many in shantytowns surrounding the city. Other major towns are Cap-Haïtien, Carrefour, Delmas, and Pétionville.

The inhabitants of Haiti are descendants of African slaves brought by French colonists to grow sugar in the 17th and 18th centuries. Ten percent still speak French, and most are nominally Roman Catholics, but the

culture retains African roots. Ninety percent speak a
Creole patois that is basically a mixture of French,
Spanish, and English. Most Haitians practice voodoo,
a combination of African and Roman Catholic beliefs
that involves rituals of dance, music, magic, and cults
of the dead (*see* Voodoo).

The staple elements of the diet are corn, cassava,
millet, rice, and fruits. The average annual income of
most urban Haitians is roughly 300 dollars; thus
protein sources such as meat, fish, or eggs are rarely
consumed. More than 80 percent of the rural population lives below the poverty line, and malnutrition is
high. Malaria, tuberculosis, and hepatitis are endemic,
as is infection with HIV. On average, there is one
physician for every 10,000 people; in rural areas, the
ratio is much greater. Literacy is low among Haitian
adults; less than half are able to read and write, and
more than half have received no formal schooling.

## Economy

Haiti is the poorest country in the Western
Hemisphere. The economy is heavily dependent on
farming, which employs much of the labor force. Only
a third of the land is considered suitable for
cultivation. Ever since the French sugar plantations
were destroyed in the struggle for independence,
Haitian agriculture has been carried out mainly on
small peasant farms that became increasingly
fragmented through inheritance. Cultivation is
principally by hand, using such simple tools as hoes or
machetes. Few farmers can afford fertilizers or
insecticides. The low productivity does not keep up
with the large population growth rate, and thus a
large portion of the country's food is imported. The
entire population of pigs was destroyed in 1983 by
African swine fever.

The principal cash crops are coffee, sugar, sisal, and
essential oils. Mangoes are an important export, as is
coffee. Sugar production has fallen dramatically
because of growing local consumption and the
production of rum.

The industrial sector is small and concentrated in
Port-au-Prince. There are a few medium-sized
factories, which produce cement, malt beverages, oils,
and refined sugar. The most significant development
from the 1960s has been the rapid growth of light
industry, which produces at least 25 percent of Haiti's
export revenues. Many foreign companies have been
attracted to Haiti by the low cost of labor, the absence
of employment legislation, and exemption from taxes.
Most light industries specialize in the labor-intensive
assembly of components shipped from the United
States to produce sports goods, clothing, toys, and
electrical goods. Haiti's industry now employs almost
6 percent of the labor force. Additional revenue once
came from bauxite mines, but resources are exhausted,
and the aluminum company closed its Haitian plant in
1983. Another major source of income, the tourist
industry, has had severe difficulties since 1980.

The nation's road system consists of approximately
2,500 miles (4,000 kilometers) of main roads, of which

Bob Krist—Black Star

*The citadel on the summit of Bishop's Bonnet Mountain in Haiti was
built as a gesture of defiance to the French.*

almost a quarter are paved. Most unpaved roads are
impassable in the rainy season, and produce for local
markets is largely transported by burro or by humans.

## History

Christopher Columbus made his first landing in 1492
on an island in The Bahamas, but the first part of
America to be settled by the Spaniards was Hispaniola.
At that time there were more than a million native
inhabitants on the island. Within 50 years most had
died from overwork in the gold mines, lack of food,
and epidemics of such European diseases as measles
and smallpox. This is why there is no significant
indigenous population in present-day Haiti and the
Dominican Republic. The gold that could be obtained
using 16th-century placer-mining techniques was
exhausted by 1530, and Spain lost interest in
Hispaniola with the discoveries of Mexico and Peru.
The Spaniards who remained on the island turned to
cultivating sugarcane, using black slaves brought
from Africa.

In 1697 Spain ceded the western third of Hispaniola
to France. By the end of the 18th century, the new
French possession, known as St-Domingue, was one of
the world's richest colonies, producing vast quantities
of sugar and cotton. Of its 524,000 inhabitants, 88
percent were African slaves. France eventually gained
control of the whole island in 1795.

After many futile revolts, the black population
united in 1798 under Henri de Toussaint-Louverture, a
freed slave (*see* Toussaint-Louverture). Captured by
trickery, Toussaint died in a French prison, but his
successor, Jean-Jacques Dessalines, "The Tiger," drove
out the French in 1803. In 1804 Dessalines proclaimed

the colony's independence and massacred almost all the remaining white inhabitants.

In 1806 Dessalines was assassinated and was succeeded by his general in chief, Henry Christophe. Declaring himself emperor, Christophe attempted to reconstruct the ravaged country. After Christophe's suicide, a succession of military despots seized power. (*See also* Christophe, Henry.)

By 1915, revolutions and banditry had reduced Haiti to misery. Under the Monroe Doctrine, the United States Marines intervened, remaining until 1934. In 1957 François Duvalier was elected president (*see* Duvalier, François). He became a dictator, enforcing a reign of terror with his secret police, the Tontons Macoutes, until his death in April 1971. During his dictatorship, Haiti's already weak economy deteriorated, and the resultant extreme poverty caused increasing civil unrest.

In 1971 the Haitians voted to approve Duvalier's 19-year-old son, Jean-Claude, as his successor. The Tontons Macoutes continued to terrorize the population, and corruption was rampant among public officials. In July 1985 Duvalier held a fraudulent election that showed him with 99 percent of the popular vote. Anti-Duvalier riots broke out in several towns, and he and his family fled Haiti in February 1986.

For the next four years Haiti was ruled by its generals, except for the six-month presidency of Leslie Manigat in 1988. He was deposed in June 1988 by Gen. Henri Namphy, who was ousted in September by Gen. Prosper Avril. The latter held power until forced to resign in March 1990 because of antigovernment protests. Supreme Court Justice Ertha Pascal-Trouillot was appointed acting president, becoming the first woman to lead Haiti.

In December 1990 Jean-Bertrand Aristide became Haiti's first democratically elected president. Aristide was a leftist former Roman Catholic priest who had gained an ardent following among the Haitian people. Nine months after taking office, however, he was removed by a military-led coup. General Raoul Cédras became head of state. Aristide set up a government-in-exile in the United States and persuaded the administrations of George Bush and Bill Clinton to help him regain power. Violence between the president's supporters and factions within the army led to many deaths. The United States imposed trade sanctions, which destroyed Haiti's industrial base. Thousands of Haitians fled the country. In 1994 Clinton's threat of military invasion and forceful diplomatic pressure led General Cédras and his associates to agree to relinquish power. More than 20,000 United States soldiers landed on the island to police the handover of power to Aristide, who returned to Haiti in October 1994. René Préval succeeded Aristide as president in February 1996. In 2000, Aristide was again elected president. Opposition to his rule increased, however, and he fled the country in February 2004 amid antigovernment protests that had turned into a full-scale rebellion. Population (2002 estimate), 7,064,000.           Gustavo Antonini, Sarah Cameron, Ben Box

*Silver hake* (**Merluccius bilinearis**)

**HAKE.** Fish of the hake family, Merlucciidae, are found in many parts of the world. Hakes and their relatives have two dorsal fins and a long ventral fin. On the top of the head is a V-shaped ridge. Most hakes are slate gray above and white or silver below and on the sides of the head.

The white hake (*Urophycis tenuis*) is actually a member of the cod family, Gadidae. It is a major food fish in the New England states. It grows to a length of about 50 inches (127 centimeters) and may weigh as much as 40 pounds (18 kilograms). The smaller red, or squirrel, hake (*U. chuss*) is closely related. True hakes include the silver hake, also called whiting, of the Atlantic coast, and the Pacific hake (*Merluccius productus*) of the West coast.

**HAKLUYT, Richard** (1552?–1616). When England first won glory at sea, Richard Hakluyt recorded his country's achievements. He spent much of his lifetime gathering accounts of the voyages of the time. His work represents a valuable source of information about the many accomplishments of this age of discovery.

Richard Hakluyt was born in London in about 1552. His father died when Richard was 5 years old, leaving his family to the care of a cousin—a lawyer with many prominent friends. Richard attended school in Westminster. After a cousin introduced him to "bookes of Cosmographie, with an universall Mappe," young Hakluyt decided to become a student of geography. In 1570 he entered Oxford University. There he began collecting books and manuscripts that dealt with explorations and voyages to distant places. After his graduation he stayed on at Oxford for several years as a lecturer on geography.

Some time before 1580 Hakluyt, like many university graduates of his day, became a clergyman. His first book, 'Divers Voyages Touching the Discoverie of America' (published in 1582), brought him to the attention of the queen's court. He was introduced to sea captains, merchants, and mariners who gave him firsthand accounts of English voyages.

In 1583 he became the chaplain to the English ambassador to Paris. During the next five years he collected information about Spanish, Portuguese, and French explorations. In 1584 he wrote 'The Discourse on the Western Planting', in which he appealed to Englishmen to establish colonies in America.

Hakluyt returned to England in 1588 and completed his chief work, 'The Principall Navigations, Voiages and Discoveries of the English Nation' (1589). Hakluyt was a promoter of the Virginia Company of London. He died on Nov. 23, 1616, in England.

## HALE, Edward Everett

**HALE, Edward Everett** (1822–1909). A clergyman and author, Edward Everett Hale wrote the famous story "The Man Without a Country." Published in the *Atlantic Monthly* in 1863, it tells of a man, Philip Nolan, who is sentenced never to see his homeland again and who learns too late what it meant to him.

Edward Everett Hale was born on April 3, 1822, in Boston, Mass. As a student at Harvard College he reported meetings of the Massachusetts legislature for his father's paper, the *Boston Daily Advertiser.* He graduated in 1839 and taught while studying for the Unitarian ministry. He was ordained in 1846 and spent ten years as minister of the Church of Unity in Worcester, Mass. He then went to the South Congregational Church in Boston, where he stayed for 43 years. In addition to novels, Hale wrote several volumes of reminiscences. He considered 'In His Name', published in 1873, his best book, but 'A New England Boyhood' (1893) was very popular. His other works include 'James Russell Lowell and His Friends' (1899) and 'Memories of a Hundred Years' (1902). From 1903 until his death on June 10, 1909, in Boston, he was chaplain of the United States Senate.

## HALE, Nathan

**HALE, Nathan** (1755–76). Captured by the British and condemned to hang as a spy, Revolutionary War hero Nathan Hale said, "I only regret that I have but one life to lose for my country." Hale's words still stand as a lasting testimony to patriotism and courage.

Nathan Hale was born in Coventry, Conn., on June 6, 1755, the son of a prosperous farmer. He studied under a village minister and then entered Yale College in 1769. There he played sports, joined a literary fraternity, and talked about politics. One of the plays he probably read at Yale was Joseph Addison's 'Cato'. Hale's last words paraphrased a speech made by a character in that tragedy. Hale graduated in 1773 and taught school in East Haddam, Conn., and then, a year later, in New London, Conn. People admired his learning and athletic prowess and the way he maintained discipline without severity.

When news of the British-American clash in Lexington, Mass., arrived at New London, Hale enlisted in the patriots' army. Commissioned a first lieutenant on July 1, 1775, he fought in Boston, Mass., and was promoted to captain on Jan. 1, 1776. In March the British evacuated Boston, and George Washington moved his army to New York City. Washington was defeated in the battle of Long Island in August. He needed to know the British plans, and Hale undertook the dangerous spy mission. Dressed as a civilian, he crossed to Long Island from Norwalk, Conn., where he secured the information.

On the night of September 21 Hale was captured by the British as he tried to return to the American lines. Taken before Gen. William Howe and faced with the notes and maps that had been found concealed on his person, he admitted his rank and purpose. Howe ordered his execution. At 11:00 AM on Sept. 22, 1776, Hale mounted the gallows, uttered his famous words, and was hanged.

## HALFWAY HOUSE

**HALFWAY HOUSE.** Residences for individuals who have been released from institutions—prisons, drug rehabilitation centers, clinics for alcoholics, or mental hospitals—are called halfway houses. These are places of transition, homes in which people may live as they prepare to reenter society and the world of work and family. Similar homes have been set up for victims of child- and wife-abuse. Some halfway houses are privately funded and operated, while others are state supported.

Since the mid-1970s the overcrowding of prisons and the high costs of prison systems have led to the suggested use of halfway houses for prisoners who have committed minor offenses. California has about 290 such homes, but most states have been reluctant to establish them. This approach is similar to the released-time prison facility: prisoners are allowed to leave the institution for work or school, but they must return each evening and on weekends. The released-time prisons, however, are far more expensive to operate than halfway houses.

Halfway houses are similar to private homes or apartment buildings in their appearance. They normally have only a few residents at a time, and the atmosphere is more like being in a home than in an institution. The residents are people who need support and—in the case of alcoholics and drug addicts—care and protection but not medical care. The houses are staffed by nonprofessionals. Halfway houses for recovering alcoholics, of which there are about 400 in North America, are normally associated with Alcoholics Anonymous (*see* Alcoholism).

Although the term halfway house came into general usage only in the mid-1960s, the concept is much older. As early as 1788 the Philanthropic Society of London, England, opened cottages for children who had been arrested for stealing or other minor crimes. There are today more than 40 halfway houses in Great Britain. They are privately operated, but they receive some funding from government sources.

From about 1900 until the Great Depression of the 1930s, there were a few privately operated halfway houses in the United States. The first of these, called Hope Halls, were started with aid from the Volunteers of America. When the states began using parole as a means of releasing convicts from prison, officials declared that halfway houses were no longer needed. The economic crisis of the 1930s forced their closing. It was not until after World War II that state prison officials expressed interest in halfway houses to ease the transition from prison to society.

Support for halfway houses grew after 1970 because of the advantages they offered. New facilities did not have to be constructed. Existing buildings—including small hotels, apartment buildings, and homes—were used. A drawback, however, was the unwillingness of many communities to accept halfway houses, because they felt that these institutions and their residents would pose a threat to property values.

**HALIBUT** *see* **FLATFISH.**

**HALIFAX, N.S.** Nova Scotia's capital and largest municipality is Halifax. It is situated on the southeastern coast of the province and has as its primary geographical feature one of the world's largest natural harbors. In 1996 the city of Halifax merged with several neighboring communities to become the Halifax Regional Municipality. Halifax has long been the province's center of education and culture. One of its several institutions of higher learning is Dalhousie University. The Nova Scotia Museum of Natural History and the Maritime Museum of the Atlantic are local cultural sites. Province House, the Capitol, is noted for its Georgian architecture. Halifax Citadel, a massive 19th-century fortress built by the British, looms above the harbor.

Eighty-five percent of the area's employment occurs in the service sector. Some leading service areas are trade, health care, government, and education. The harbor is part of the regional economy as well. The year-round harbor handles everything from container ships filled with trade goods to cruise vessels carrying tourists. It is also the site of the Canadian navy's Atlantic headquarters.

Native Americans known as the Micmac lived in the Halifax area before the first Europeans arrived. Permanent British settlement began in 1749 as a counterbalance to a French stronghold in Cape Breton. Halifax continually served as an imperial army and navy base until its facilities were taken over by the Canadian government in 1906. In 1917 a munitions ship exploded in the harbor, killing about 2,000 people and razing much of the city's north side. During World Wars I and II Halifax was Canada's major naval base. In 1996 Halifax merged with Dartmouth, Bedford, and the rest of Halifax County. Population (2001 census), regional municipality, 359,111.

*The Old Town Clock, built in 1803, overlooks the harbor of Halifax from its site on Citadel Hill.*
© Gary Crallé—The Image Bank

**HALL, Charles Martin** (1863–1914). On Feb. 23, 1886, a young man of 22 stood anxiously over a complicated mass of electric wires, crucibles, and heating apparatus in a woodshed in Oberlin, Ohio. For two hours Charles Martin Hall watched as the contents of one of the crucibles grew hotter and hotter. Finally, he turned off the powerful current and poured out the molten mass. Little silver-colored drops had separated and hardened into shining buttons of aluminum metal. Hall's discovery of the electrolytic method of aluminum production brought the metal into wide commercial use and became the foundation of aluminum production as we know it today. The problem was to find a mineral that melts at a low temperature and, when melted, dissolves aluminum oxide. Hall found the answer in cryolite. (*See also* Aluminum.)

Hall was born in Thompson, Ohio, on Dec. 6, 1863. Eight months after graduating from Oberlin College, he made his discovery. In April of the same year a Frenchman, Paul-Louis-Toussaint Héroult, who had made the same discovery at almost the same time as Hall, was granted a French patent for the same process. Hall applied to the United States Patent Office in July 1886 for a patent for his discovery, but it was not granted until 1889.

At first Hall could not get financial backing. When production was under way, he was sued for stealing the Héroult process. Hall won the suit in 1893. He died on Dec. 27, 1914, in Daytona Beach, Fla.

**HALLEY, Edmond** (1656–1742). The English astronomer and mathematician Edmond Halley was the first to calculate the orbit of a comet later named after him. He also encouraged Sir Isaac Newton to write his 'Philosophiae Naturalis Principia Mathematica', which Halley published in 1687 at his own expense. (*See also* Comet; Newton, Isaac.)

Halley was born in Haggerston, Shoreditch, near London, on Nov. 8, 1656. He began his education at St. Paul's School, London, and in 1673 entered Queen's College at Oxford University. There he learned of John Flamsteed's project at the Royal Greenwich Observatory using the telescope to compile an accurate catalog of stars visible in the Northern Hemisphere. Halley proposed to do the same thing for the Southern Hemisphere. Leaving Oxford without his degree, he sailed for the island of St. Helena in the South Atlantic in 1676. His results were published in a star catalog in 1678, establishing the youth as a prominent astronomer. Halley, who sometimes spelled his first name Edmund, published the first meteorological chart in 1686 and the first magnetic charts of the Atlantic and Pacific areas, which were used in navigation for many years after his death. Continuing his work in observational astronomy, he published in 1705 'A Synopsis of the Astronomy of Comets', in which he described 24 comets.

He accurately predicted the return in 1758 of a comet—now known as Halley's comet—previously observed in 1531, 1607, and 1682. Halley died in Greenwich, on Jan. 14, 1742.

**HALL OF FAME.** On the campus of Bronx Community College, which is part of the City University of New York, stands the Hall of Fame for Great Americans. Located in University Heights in the west Bronx, the site was originally part of the uptown campus of New York University. The hall of fame, designed by architect Stanford White, is a granite colonnade 630 feet (192 meters) long. Along the colonnade are panels fitted with bronze tablets. Each tablet is inscribed with the name of an honored American, that person's birth and death dates, and a selected quotation. Above each panel stands a specially commissioned bronze bust of the person honored.

According to conditions made in 1900 by Helen Gould Shepard, who provided the original funding for the memorial, only persons dead ten years or more were to be eligible. In 1922 that time period was extended to 25 years. Although 50 names were to be inscribed in 1900, only 29 were elected from more than 1,000 nominations. New names were to be added every fifth year thereafter until all the panels were filled. After 1970, selections were made every third year until 1976 when the project lapsed because of a lack of funds. All names in the hall of fame are listed in the accompanying table.

Various classes of citizens were recommended for consideration, including statesmen, authors, artists, scientists, educators, physicians, businessmen, inventors, explorers, and philanthropists. Foreign-born Americans were eligible after 1914. In 1914 a colonnade site was set apart as a Hall of Fame for Women, but in 1922, after the names of seven women had been chosen, the decision was made to use the existing colonnade to honor notable Americans of both sexes.

The idea of honoring special achievements by election to a hall of fame has become an increasingly popular one since 1901, when the Hall of Fame for Great Americans was dedicated. A number of different sports have organized halls of fame. In addition to honoring and commemorating outstanding players of the various sports, these institutions also serve as museums where sports fans may look at collections of pictures, equipment, and memorabilia that provide an overview of the history of a favorite sport.

One of the first of these, and a very popular attraction for baseball fans, is the National Baseball Hall of Fame and Museum in Cooperstown, N.Y. The Baseball Hall of Fame was established in 1935, when it was organized to celebrate baseball's centennial. The Cooperstown location was chosen because of its association with the origins of the game (see Baseball).

Other sports halls of fame are the Naismith Memorial Basketball Hall of Fame, located in Springfield, Mass., established in 1963; the Pro Football Hall of Fame in Canton, Ohio, which opened in 1963; and the International Tennis Hall of Fame in Newport, R.I., established in 1953. There is a Hockey Hall of Fame, honoring ice hockey, in Toronto, Ont. There is also a United States Hockey Hall of Fame in Eveleth, Minn. The Indianapolis Motor Speedway Hall of Fame is in Indianapolis, Ind. Some halls of fame honor animals as well as people. For example, the National Horse Racing Hall of Fame in Saratoga Springs, N.Y., honors jockeys, trainers, and horses.

Most sports have more than one hall of fame. Some of these honor professional athletes; others are limited to amateur players. Some deal with a single state, province, or county or cover a specific region, such as New England. Others may list women who are outstanding athletes in a given sport. Altogether there are more than 200 sports halls of fame.

---

### Members of the Hall of Fame (with year elected)

| | |
|---|---|
| John Adams (1900) | Sidney Lanier (1945) |
| John Quincy Adams (1905) | Robert E. Lee (1900) |
| Jane Addams (1965) | Abraham Lincoln (1900) |
| Louis Agassiz (1915) | Henry Wadsworth |
| Susan B. Anthony (1950) | Longfellow (1900) |
| John James Audubon (1900) | James Russell Lowell (1905) |
| George Bancroft (1910) | Mary Lyon (1905) |
| Clara Barton (1976) | Edward A. MacDowell (1960) |
| Henry Ward Beecher (1900) | James Madison (1905) |
| Alexander Graham Bell (1950) | Horace Mann (1900) |
| Daniel Boone (1915) | John Marshall (1900) |
| Edwin Booth (1925) | Matthew Fontaine Maury (1930) |
| Louis Dembitz Brandeis (1973) | Albert Abraham |
| Phillips Brooks (1910) | Michelson (1970) |
| William Cullen Bryant (1910) | Maria Mitchell (1905) |
| Luther Burbank (1976) | James Monroe (1930) |
| Andrew Carnegie (1976) | Samuel F.B. Morse (1900) |
| George Washington | William Thomas |
| Carver (1973) | Green Morton (1920) |
| William Ellery Channing (1900) | John Lothrop Motley (1910) |
| Rufus Choate (1915) | Simon Newcomb (1935) |
| Henry Clay (1900) | Thomas Paine (1945) |
| Samuel Langhorne | Alice F. Palmer (1920) |
| Clemens (1920) | Francis Parkman (1915) |
| Grover Cleveland (1935) | George Peabody (1900) |
| James Fenimore Cooper (1910) | William Penn (1935) |
| Peter Cooper (1900) | Edgar Allan Poe (1910) |
| Charlotte S. Cushman (1915) | Walter Reed (1945) |
| James Buchanan Eads (1920) | Franklin Delano |
| Thomas Alva Edison (1960) | Roosevelt (1973) |
| Jonathan Edwards (1900) | Theodore Roosevelt (1950) |
| Ralph Waldo Emerson (1900) | Augustus Saint-Gaudens (1920) |
| David G. Farragut (1900) | William Tecumseh |
| Stephen C. Foster (1940) | Sherman (1905) |
| Benjamin Franklin (1900) | John Philip Sousa (1973) |
| Robert Fulton (1900) | Joseph Story (1900) |
| Josiah Willard Gibbs (1950) | Harriet Beecher Stowe (1910) |
| William Crawford Gorgas (1950) | Gilbert Charles Stuart (1900) |
| Ulysses S. Grant (1900) | Sylvanus Thayer (1965) |
| Asa Gray (1900) | Henry David Thoreau (1960) |
| Alexander Hamilton (1915) | Lillian D. Wald (1970) |
| Nathaniel Hawthorne (1900) | Booker T. Washington (1945) |
| Joseph Henry (1915) | George Washington (1900) |
| Patrick Henry (1920) | Daniel Webster (1900) |
| Oliver Wendell Holmes (1910) | George Westinghouse (1955) |
| Oliver Wendell | James Abbott |
| Holmes, Jr. (1965) | McNeill Whistler (1930) |
| Mark Hopkins (1915) | Walt Whitman (1930) |
| Elias Howe (1915) | Eli Whitney (1900) |
| Washington Irving (1900) | John Greenleaf Whittier (1905) |
| Andrew Jackson (1910) | Emma Willard (1905) |
| Thomas Jonathan | Frances E. Willard (1910) |
| (Stonewall) Jackson (1955) | Roger Williams (1920) |
| Thomas Jefferson (1900) | Woodrow Wilson (1950) |
| John Paul Jones (1925) | Orville Wright* (1965) |
| James Kent (1900) | Wilbur Wright (1955) |

*The rule that a person nominated must have been dead at least 25 years was waived in this case.

*The Hall of Fame for Great Americans, designed by architect Stanford White, stands on the campus of Bronx Community College in New York City.*
Courtesy of The Hall of Fame for Great Americans, Bronx Community College, New York

Many other activities and professions regularly honor outstanding people who work in specific fields. Some of these, like the Rock and Roll Hall of Fame in Cleveland, Ohio, or the National Cowboy Hall of Fame and Western Heritage Center in Oklahoma City, Okla., are rather specialized (*see* Rock and Roll Hall of Fame in Fact-Index). Others, such as the United States Business Hall of Fame, make their selections from a larger segment of the population. Behind this diversity, however, there is a single objective that inspires each of these institutions. Each hall of fame that has been organized is an indication of the desire of a group of people to pay homage to those who in one way or another have made a special contribution in their chosen field.

**HALLOWEEN.** Customs and superstitions gathered through the ages go into the celebration of Halloween, or All Hallows Eve, on October 31, the eve of the Christian festival of All Saints. It has its origins, however, in the autumn festivals of earlier times.

The ancient Druids had a three-day celebration at the beginning of November. They believed that on the last night of October spirits of the dead roamed abroad, and they lighted bonfires to drive them away. In ancient Rome the festival of Pomona, goddess of fruits and gardens, occurred at about this time of year. It was an occasion of rejoicing associated with the harvest; and nuts and apples, as symbols of the winter store of fruit, were roasted before huge bonfires. But these agricultural and pastoral celebrations also had a sinister aspect, with ghosts and witches thought to be on the prowl.

Even after November 1 became a Christian feast day honoring all saints, many people clung to the old pagan beliefs and customs that had grown up about Halloween. Some tried to foretell the future on that night by performing such rites as jumping over lighted candles. In the British Isles great bonfires blazed for the Celtic festival of Samhain. Laughing bands of guisers (young people disguised in grotesque masks)

carved lanterns from turnips and carried them through the villages.

In the United States children carved faces on hollowed-out pumpkins and put lighted candles inside to make jack-o'-lanterns. Halloween celebrations today reflect many of these early customs. Stores and homes display orange and black figures of witches, bats, black cats, and pumpkins. People dressed in fanciful outfits go to costume parties, where old-fashioned games like bobbing for apples in tubs of water may be a part of the festivities. Children put on costumes and masks and go from house to house demanding "trick or treat." The treat, usually candy, is generally given and the trick rarely played. Some parents feel this custom is dangerous. There have been numerous instances in which sharp objects or poisons have been found in candy bars and apples. To provide an alternative to begging for candy from strangers, many communities schedule special, supervised parties and events at Halloween. The United Nations has used the Halloween observance to collect money for its children's fund.

*The jack-o'-lantern, carved from a pumpkin and lit with a candle, is a popular symbol of Halloween.*

F. Rivera—Four By Five/SUPERSTOCK

**HALLUCINOGEN.** While many drugs speed up or depress the central nervous system, there is a class of drugs that distorts how we feel, hear, see, smell, taste, and think. Called hallucinogens because users often hallucinate, or experience nonexistent sensations, these drugs are also known as psychedelic, or mind-bending, drugs. Some hallucinogens come from natural sources; others are made in laboratories. Examples of natural hallucinogens are mescaline, psilocybin, DMT, and marijuana.

Mescaline, which has been used by American Indians in religious ceremonies, comes from the peyote cactus. Psilocybin, also used by the Indians and believed to have supernatural powers, is found in about 20 varieties of mushrooms. Once ingested, psilocybin is converted to psilocin, which is responsible for the drug's hallucinogenic sensations. DMT (dimethyl-trypta-mine) is a short-acting hallucinogen found in the seeds of certain West Indian and South American plants. In the form of snuff, called cohoba, it has been used in religious ceremonies in Haiti. Marijuana is a plant belonging to the hemp family (see Hemp). The active principle responsible for the drug's effects is tetrahydrocannabinol (THC), obtained from the amber-colored resin of the flowering tops and leaves of the plant. Hashish is also made from this resin.

Of all drugs, synthetic and natural, the most powerful is LSD, or lysergic acid diethylamide. Twenty micrograms, an almost infinitesimal amount, is sufficient to produce a hallucinogenic effect; just 3 pounds (1.4 kilograms) could induce a reaction in all the inhabitants of New York City and London. This extraordinary potency makes LSD especially dangerous since it is usually impossible to determine how much is contained in doses offered by drug dealers.

LSD is chemically derived from ergot, a parasitic fungus that grows on rye and other grains. An odorless, colorless, and tasteless substance, LSD is sold on the street in tablets, capsules, and sometimes liquid form. It is usually taken by mouth but can be injected. Often LSD is placed on a blotter or other absorbent paper and marked into small squares, each representing one dose.

Synthetic hallucinogens with effects resembling those of LSD include DET (diethyltryptamine), a synthetic compound similar to DMT, and DOM (2,5-dimethoxy-4- methylamphetamine), a compound that combines some of the properties of mescaline and amphetamines, as do the drugs MDA (3,4-methylenedioxyampheta-mine) and MMDA (3-methoxy-3,4-methylenedioxy-amphetamine).

The effects of hallucinogens on the body are unpredictable. They depend on the amount taken and the user's personality, mood, expectations, and surroundings. Although hallucinogens do not produce a physical addiction, users do develop a tolerance, so that increasing amounts must be taken to achieve the same effect. Psychological dependence on hallucinogens is well documented.

It appears that each drug carries its own risks. For example, unlike hallucinogens such as LSD and synthetics such as DOM that consist of a single chemical, marijuana has been found to contain more than 400 separate substances. These substances are in turn broken down in the body into a great many more chemicals, and the effects of these chemicals on the user are poorly understood. It has been found, however, that the most potent of these chemicals are attracted to and accumulate in fatty tissues, including the brain and reproductive organs.

Studies indicate that frequent marijuana users may experience impaired short-term memory and learning ability and reproductive problems. Other studies suggest that frequent or chronic marijuana use may contribute to damage of the immune system, increased strain on the heart, delayed puberty, and chromosome damage.

The most pronounced psychological effects induced by hallucinogens are a heightened awareness of colors and patterns together with a slowed perception of time and a distorted body image. Sensations may seem to "cross over," giving the user a sense of "hearing" colors and "seeing" sounds. Users may also slip into a dream- like state, indifferent to the world around them and forgetful of time and place to such an extent that they may believe it possible to step out of a window or stand in front of a speeding car without harm. Users may feel several different emotions at once or swing wildly from one emotion to another. It is impossible to predict what kind of experience a hallucinogen may produce. Frightening or even panic-producing psycho-logical reactions to LSD and similar drugs are common. Sometimes taking a hallucinogen will leave the user with serious mental or emotional problems, though it is unclear whether the drug simply unmasked a previously undetected disorder or actually produced it.

Among the short-term physical effects of hallucinogens are dilated pupils, raised body temperature, increased heart rate and blood pressure, sweating, loss of appetite, sleeplessness, dry mouth, and tremors. The long-term effects are less certain. LSD users may experience involuntary flashbacks during which the drug's effects reappear without warning. Such flashbacks can occur days, months, or even years after the drug was last used. Some LSD users develop organic brain damage, manifested by impaired memory and attention span, mental confusion, and difficulty with abstract thinking. It is still unclear whether such damage can be reversed when LSD use is halted.

Although hallucinogens can pose a threat to health when used indiscriminately, they may also have therapeutic uses in medicine when administered under controlled circumstances. A synthetic form of THC, the active principle in marijuana, has been approved for prescription use by persons who suffer from the severe nausea that often accompanies cancer chemotherapy and for whom other antinausea drugs are unsuitable or ineffective. LSD was once used to treat persons with certain mental disorders, but such use was abandoned because of the drug's harmful effects. (See also Drugs; Narcotic and Sedative.)

Timothy Larkin

**HALOGENS.** The five nonmetallic chemical elements that make up the halogen family are fluorine (the symbol for which is F), chlorine (Cl), bromine (Br), iodine (I), and astatine (At). The halogens are in Group VIIa of the periodic table (*see* Periodic Table).

Most of the halogens are found in relatively small amounts in the Earth's crust. The single exception is astatine, which does not occur naturally because it consists exclusively of short-lived radioactive isotopes. The only practical source of this element is its synthesis by nuclear reactions. The halogens, particularly fluorine, are highly reactive, so that they never occur uncombined in nature. They readily react with most metals and many nonmetals to form a rich variety of compounds. (*See also* Nuclear Energy; Radioactivity.)

The members of the halogen family closely resemble each other in general chemical behavior and in the properties of their compounds (*see* Chemical Elements). Each halogen atom carries seven electrons in its outermost orbitals. Potentially, each halogen atom can hold one additional electron; in acquiring such an electron the atom acts as an oxidizing agent and in the process assumes a negative electrical charge and becomes a negative ion. Halogen elements exist in their salts as halide ions, which are very stable. (*See also* Chemistry; Chlorine; Fluorine; Iodine.)

**HALOPHYTE.** Plants adapted for living in an environment that is high in salt content are called halophytes. They have evolved structural and functional mechanisms to cope with high-salinity environments such as coastal salt marshes and salt deserts.

Some agricultural crops, asparagus and beets for example, are resistant to relatively high salt concentrations in the soil. The most salt-tolerant plants are those that already exist in habitats where salt concentrations are always high. Salt-marsh grass (*Spartina alterniflora*) is the most abundant and widespread halophyte in the tidal marshes of North America. Its roots and stems are constantly washed by ocean waters. Saltwort (*Batis*) and glasswort (*Salicornia*) are found in coastal regions. Mangroves are woody plants that thrive in coastal regions throughout the world (*see* Mangrove). Some species can live in aquatic habitats with salinity levels approaching that of seawater.

A common feature of many halophytes is the presence of salt glands, which consist of special groups of cells that collect salt from the body of the plant and then excrete it onto the plant's leaves or stems. Some halophytes excrete salt by means of tiny bladders on the outer layer of leaf cells. These plants adjust the rate of excretion in response to the level of salt in the environment. Many halophytes also tolerate high internal concentrations of salts.

Halophytes respond to arid or drought conditions by dropping their leaves to reduce water loss through them. They also sometimes develop extensive root systems to increase potential water uptake from the soil. In addition, halophytes have a variety of other physiological mechanisms to reduce dehydration. (*See also* Plant; Water Plants.)

J. Whitfield Gibbons

The Metropolitan Museum of Art, Gift of Henry G. Marquand, 1890. Marquand Collection, 91.26.9

*'Portrait of a Man'*, an oil painting by Frans Hals, measures 43½ inches by 34 inches.

**HALS, Frans** (1580?–1666). Now recognized as one of the greatest portrait painters of all time, the Dutch painter Frans Hals was generally ignored for two centuries. Then, in the 1800s, Édouard Manet, Vincent van Gogh, and others rediscovered his work and were influenced by his freedom of style, use of color, and technique that approached 18th-century impressionism. Critics today rate Hals next to Rembrandt at the head of the Dutch School, and some consider him the greatest of all painters for truth of character (*see* Painting).

Born in Antwerp, Belgium, in about 1580, Frans Hals moved to Haarlem, Holland, when he was a young man. Public records, which provide most of what is known about Hals, indicate that he was married twice and had ten children.

Plagued by debt most of his life, Hals was pensioned by the city in 1662. The warmth and enthusiasm he showed in portraying merrymakers and tavern goers have caused speculation that Hals's financial problems might have resulted from too much high living, but the level of his work and the commissions he received make this seem unlikely.

Hals's group portraits of local guilds and military societies, the first of which dates from 1616, frequently show his subjects in relaxed, natural poses, talking, eating, and enjoying each other's company. Eight of these great canvases, portraying a total of 84 men and women, hang in the Frans Hals Museum in Haarlem. The last of the series was painted in 1661. There on the walls may be traced the artist's development. The picture painted in 1633 shows him in his most vigorous period when his brilliant color and jovial spirit were at their height. The later groups are painted in somber colors—blacks, whites, and grays—but the brush technique has become even freer and more deft.

**HAMAD IBN KHALIFA AL-THANI, Sheik** (born 1950). Sheik Hamad ibn Khalifa al-Thani overthrew his father, Sheik Khalifa ibn Hamad al-Thani, the emir of Qatar, in a bloodless coup on June 27, 1995. The elder sheik, who himself had seized power from a cousin in 1972, was vacationing in Switzerland when his eldest son took the reins of government.

Hamad was born in December 1950. He attended Britain's Royal Military Academy at Sandhurst, where he was an excellent athlete. Upon his return, he organized and subsidized athletic programs in Qatar. Sheik Hamad was commander in chief of the armed forces from 1972 and minister of defense from 1977.

Prior to becoming emir, Sheik Hamad managed the day-to-day government administration and military affairs of Qatar. He had major responsibility for petroleum, trade, and foreign policy. The 1995 coup followed two years of political rivalry between father and son. Soon after the coup, Sheik Hamad gave permission for Qatar's first official stock exchange to be located in Doha, the nation's capital. He also appointed a new cabinet, published the rules of government and royal succession, and named himself premier. He retained his posts as minister of defense and commander in chief of the armed forces. He named his brother as deputy premier. Regarded as a liberal Arab leader, Sheik Hamad moved toward normalizing relations with Israel and permitted the United States to build military facilities within Qatar.

**HAMAS (or Islamic Resistance Movement).** The militant Palestinian group Hamas is dedicated to the creation of an Islamic state in historic Palestine and has used terrorism against both Palestinians and Israelis to achieve its goal. The group was founded by Sheikh Ahmad Ismail Yasin, a Muslim religious leader.

Hamas was established in 1987 by members of the Muslim Brotherhood, a religio-political organization dedicated to restoring Islamic values and rejecting westernization, and by religious members of the Palestine Liberation Organization (PLO). Hamas viewed Palestine as an Islamic homeland that must never be surrendered to non-Muslims and stressed jihad, or holy war, against Israel. By maintaining social service organizations in the Gaza Strip and the West Bank with which to spread their ideas, enlist members, and raise money, Hamas quickly grew to include thousands of supporters throughout the Arab world. In the early 1990s Hamas began a violent *intifadah*, or uprising, against Israel. Israel responded with increased security and military force.

In 1994 Israel signed an agreement with the Palestinian Authority (PA), a newly established body charged with governing the occupied territories. Israeli forces withdrew from Gaza and parts of the West Bank, and Palestinian self-rule was established in Gaza and the West Bank city of Jericho. Hamas, not recognizing

Israel as a legitimate country, rejected the accords and expanded the *intifadah,* ordering suicide bomb attacks against Israelis. Periodic peace talks failed, and the violence continued. In 2004 an Israeli missile strike killed Yasin in Gaza; his successor was killed a month later. Despite the setbacks, Hamas went on to win more than half the seats in the 2006 election for the Palestinian Legislative Council. ( *See also* 'Arafat, Yasir; Palestine; Palestine Liberation Organization.)

**HAMBURG, Germany.** Located on the Elbe River, 75 miles (120 kilometers) inland from the North Sea, Hamburg has long been Germany's greatest harbor city. Hamburg is the second largest city in Germany and is also one of the country's 16 *Länder,* or states, with an area of 292 square miles (756 square kilometers).

The Altstadt (Old Town), a former medieval settlement, forms the center of Hamburg. Its boundaries include the harbor and several roads that follow the outline of the old fortifications. The layout of the Altstadt can be seen in the canals that connect the Alster River with the Elbe's docks. Two major fires—in 1842 and 1906—and bombing during World War II destroyed many of the older structures.

The canals carry traffic from the main stream to the warehouses. The Alster was dammed during the 18th century and forms a lake at its southern end. Two bridges, the Lombardsbrücke and the Kennedybrücke, divide the lake into the Binnenalster (Inner Alster) and the Aussenalster (Outer Alster).

**Culture and Education**

The Deichstrasse is a historic street of merchants' buildings that date from the 17th century. Reminders of the city's 1,000-year history are five rebuilt churches: the Katharinen, Jacobi, Michaelis, Petri, and Nickolai. South of the Binnenalster is the Rathaus, or city hall, which was built in the late 1800s. Between 1890 and 1910, many large, elegant homes were built around the Aussenalster. Many now house consulates of various countries. The 1920s and 1930s were also an architectural boom time, known for the revival of traditional north German red brick. Modern style is represented by the Congress Centrum Hamburg, a vast exhibition and conference center.

Hamburg is known for its excellent museums—especially the Kunsthalle, an art gallery featuring works from the late Middle Ages to the present. Since its founding in 1839 the Museum of Hamburg History has grown from covering only Hamburg's history to providing information on all German emigrants who left the country through the harbor from 1850 to 1914.

The composers Felix Mendelssohn and Johannes Brahms were born in Hamburg, and the city has long

*Tugboats line the Elbe River waterfront near the Old Town of Hamburg, Germany's largest seaport.*
Victor Englebert—Photo Researchers

maintained a musical tradition. The State Opera dates from 1678 and is the site for classical and modern opera and ballet. There are three fine orchestras as well as smaller groups specializing in a variety of musical styles. The neobaroque Musikhalle was built in 1904–08 and is a center of the city's musical offerings. Several theaters, including the German Theater, offer plays and dramatic presentations.

Hagenbeck Zoo, founded in 1907, was the first zoo in the world to house animals in open-air pens. Planten un Blomen is a large park famous for its many rare trees and shrubs. Alsterpark offers a fine view of the skyline of Hamburg. The Hirschpark and the Jenischpark are both on the Elbe. The Stadtpark, north of the Alster, includes a planetarium and many miles of footpaths.

The University of Hamburg was founded in 1919 and is one of the largest in Germany. In 1982 the Technical University of Hamburg-Harburg opened to provide higher education in technological subjects. Several state schools specialize in the arts and music. More than 200 research centers in fields from oceanography to economics are located in the city.

### Economy

Among Hamburg's many industries are the production of machinery, electrical equipment, vegetable and mineral oils, cigarettes, and chemicals. Most of the country's copper resources are treated here, and the Norddeutsche Affinerie is Europe's second largest copper plant. Steel making and shipbuilding employ many workers, but the latter has declined because of Japanese and Korean competition.

Major exports from the city-state are machinery, electrotechnical products, processed petroleum and lubricants, copper, and pharmaceuticals. Since 1960 it has been the site for large trade fairs. The Übersee-Zentrum is the world's largest roofed warehouse. After Berlin it is Germany's top newspaper and periodical publishing center, an industry based in the city since the 17th century. Daily newspapers include the *Hamburger Abendblatt,* the *Hamburger Morgenpost,* and the *Bild-Zeitung*.

More than 15,000 ships from all over the world sail through its harbor. The German rail network as well as international lines pass through the main train station. Buses and subways provide local public transportation. A tunnel that is part of the Stockholm–Lisbon highway was opened in 1977 to route long-distance travel away from the central city. It has been a major air-traffic center since before World War II.

### History

Hamburg was founded by Charlemagne, who built a fortress here in 808 for protection against the Slavs. In 811 he founded a church on the Elbe. This was the beginning of the Christianization of Northern Europe. In spite of repeated looting and burning by Danes and Slavs, the early Christians rebuilt the town many times. An archbishop was installed in 834.

Hamburg's commercial growth began in the 12th century. Frederick I granted franchises to the city, including fishing rights on the Elbe. Early in the 13th century Lübeck and Hamburg formed the Hanseatic League. Other towns soon joined the federation. The league became powerful enough to protect its land and sea trade from pirates and other marauders (*see* Hanseatic League). In 1510 Maximilian I proclaimed Hamburg a free imperial city of the Holy Roman Empire. Local and coastal commerce flourished.

When Napoleon won the battle of Lübeck in 1810, Hamburg was occupied by French troops. There were looting and heavy taxation, and the population shrank from 100,000 to about 55,000. After occupation, the city gradually returned to its former prosperity. In 1842 fire destroyed much of the business district.

Because Hamburg's harbor is ice-free all year and because it had the finest equipment, the port grew. Its exports and imports were vast in variety and quantity. The harbor teemed with activity.

In World War II mass bombings destroyed three fourths of Hamburg. The population fell to less than half. After the war Hamburg recovered swiftly. In the 1960s a large business district, City-Nord, was built and became a symbol of Hamburg's commercial rebirth. The population peaked in 1965 at 1,850,000 but has been slowly decreasing since then.

The constitution of 1952 places legislative authority in the Bürgerschaft (State Parliament), which is composed of 120 members elected to four-year terms. The Bürgerschaft elects the Senat, which represents the Free and Hanseatic City of Hamburg in its dealings with the other German states. Population (1999 estimate), 1,701,800.

**HAMILTON, Alexander** (1755?–1804). One of the youngest and brightest of the founders of the United States, Alexander Hamilton favored strong central govern- ment. As the nation's first secretary of the treasury he established responsible financial policies that helped the country prosper.

Hamilton was born on the island of Nevis, in the British West Indies, of Scottish and French descent. He was born on Jan. 11, probably in 1755. For years his birth year was given as 1757, but research now indicates he was probably born two years earlier. When he was about 15 he was sent to school in New York City and was studying at King's College (now Columbia University) when the American Revolution began. He enlisted in a New York artillery company and soon became a captain. He was introduced to George Washington. The American commander in chief liked the young officer, and from 1777 to 1781 Hamilton served on Washington's staff with the rank of lieutenant colonel.

During the war Hamilton decided that the new nation would need a strong central government. In the critical period after the war, he advocated writing a new constitution to replace the weak Articles of Confederation (*see* Articles of Confederation). He persuaded New York to send delegates to the Philadelphia Convention and was one of the three chosen. The other two were bitter anti-Federalists who, until they withdrew from the convention, constantly outvoted him. Hamilton signed the Constitution for New York.

Hamilton believed a limited monarchy like that of Britain to be the best form of government. Failing that, he would have preferred a strong aristocratic republic, with members of the government elected for life. Nevertheless, he exerted his great influence in support of the new Constitution. With James Madison and John Jay he wrote a series of essays in its defense. They were signed "The Federalist." These essays not only helped win New York's ratification but also had a tremendous influence throughout the country. Written to serve a particular purpose in Hamilton's time, they continue to be of great value to students of law and political science. They are regarded today as classic commentaries on the Constitution. (*See also* Federalist Papers.)

Washington chose Hamilton to be the first secretary of the treasury. It was in this office that he did most to shape the struggling young government. Hamilton's interpretations of the direct and implied powers of the Constitution later influenced the thinking of John Marshall, the fourth chief justice of the United States (*see* Marshall, John).

Hamilton's financial measures assured payment of the foreign and domestic debts of the United States. Under his leadership the federal government also took over the debts contracted by the separate states as a result of the Revolution. Hamilton gained congressional support for this provision by agreeing to locate the federal capital in the South on the Potomac River. Hamilton restored the credit of the United States—his greatest achievement. He also established a national bank.

Thomas Jefferson, Washington's secretary of state, opposed Hamilton's efforts to strengthen the federal government. Jefferson was a firm believer in states' rights. In foreign affairs Hamilton was pro-British. Jefferson favored revolutionary France. These two men became the leaders of the first organized political parties in the United States: the Federalists and the Democratic Republicans. (*See also* Jefferson; Political Parties; States' Rights.)

Jefferson resigned from Washington's cabinet in 1793, and Hamilton left in 1795, but their political feud continued. John Adams was elected president in 1796, and in the election of 1800 Jefferson and Aaron Burr ran for president against him. Jefferson and Burr received equal numbers of electoral votes, and Congress had to decide which of the two should become president. Hamilton distrusted Burr. He also knew that the voters wanted Jefferson to be president. Therefore, he temporarily abandoned his feud with Jefferson and swung the Federalist majority in Jefferson's favor (*see* Burr). Then, in 1804, Hamilton further alienated Burr by using his influence to prevent Burr from being elected governor of New York.

Burr, infuriated, challenged Hamilton to a duel. Hamilton reluctantly accepted. Early in the morning of July 11, 1804, Hamilton and Burr faced each other at Weehawken on the New Jersey shore of the Hudson River, opposite New York City. The first shot mortally wounded Hamilton, and he died the next day.

**HAMILTON, William Rowan** (1805–65). The Irish mathematician and astronomer Sir William Rowan Hamilton made several distinctive and original contributions to the fields of mathematics and physics. The development of modern abstract algebra was aided by his theory of quaternions, a complex form of calculus useful in performing geometric operations in three-dimensional space. His unification of optics and dynamics has had a lasting influence on mathematical physics, though the full significance of his work was not appreciated until the appearance of quantum mechanics in the 20th century. He also discovered the phenomenon of conical refraction, regarded in his lifetime as his most brilliant achievement.

Hamilton was born in Dublin, Ireland, on Aug. 4, 1805. While a very young child he was recognized as a prodigy. At age 5 he could read Latin, Greek, and Hebrew. At 11 he was proficient in Syriac, and at 14 he could write Persian. His interest in mathematics and astronomy began at 15 when he read the works of Isaac Newton. He entered Trinity College in Dublin at 18, graduating with the highest honors. At 22 he was made a professor of astronomy and Royal Astronomer of Ireland. In October 1827 he took up residence at Dunsink Observatory, where he lived for the rest of his life working on his research. His first major work, 'Theory of Systems of Rays' was presented to the Irish Academy in 1827. It transformed optics into a new mathematical science. 'On a General Method in Dynamics' was published in 1835, 'Lectures on Quaternions' in 1853, and 'Elements of Quaternions' in 1866, after his death. Hamilton was knighted in 1835 and two years later became president of the Royal Irish Academy. He died in Dublin on Sept. 2, 1865.

Bill Brooks—Masterfile

*The Rock Garden is one section of the Royal Botanical Gardens in Hamilton, Ont., which opened in 1941.*

**HAMILTON, Ont.** Located on the western shore of Lake Ontario, Hamilton forms part of the Hamilton-Wentworth Municipality. It is the seat of Wentworth County and one of Canada's leading industrial cities.

The Royal Botanical Gardens and two 17th-century mansions are tourist attractions. Dundurn Castle hosts a summer light-and-sound spectacle. There is a symphony orchestra, and Hamilton Place opened in 1973 as a performing arts center. A park and monument mark Stony Creek, the site of a decisive battle in the War of 1812. McMaster University, noted for nuclear research, was founded in Toronto and moved to Hamilton in 1930. The Canadian Football Hall of Fame is located here.

Hamilton has produced steel since 1893 and is now Canada's largest steel-producing city—more than half the national output. Other manufactures include electrical products, tires, farm implements, and chemicals. Industry benefits from nearby Niagara Falls as an inexpensive source of electricity and both rail and port facilities. The city is also a financial hub and a marketing center for the rich Ontario fruit district. It is the home of Canada's largest open-air market.

French explorers first visited the site in the early 1600s. The numerous streams from the Niagara escarpment and its location on Lake Ontario established the area as a milling and transportation center. The city was founded in 1778 by United Empire Loyalists, former citizens of the American Colonies who remained loyal to the British in the American Revolution. It was named for George Hamilton, who laid out the original town in 1813 at the foot of what is now called Mount Hamilton. The city prospered as a rail and port center following the construction of a railroad in the early 1850s and the opening of the Burlington Canal in 1830, which linked Hamilton Harbor to Lake Ontario. The harbor is protected from the lake by a 4-mile (6-kilometer) sandbar. Population (1996 census), 322,352.

**HAMMETT, Dashiell** (1894–1961). One of Humphrey Bogart's most memorable roles was as private detective Sam Spade in the film version of 'The Maltese Falcon'. The movie was based on the novel by mystery writer Dashiell Hammett. Although all of his published works were written within a ten-year period, Hammett probably had more influence on the detective story than any other American author after Edgar Allan Poe. His books were the first and best attempt to render realistically the world of American crime. He created the hard-boiled school of detective fiction, a tradition that was later taken up by Mickey Spillane, Ross Macdonald, and others.

Samuel Dashiell Hammett was born on May 27, 1894, in St. Mary's County, Md. At 14 he left school to work at odd jobs for eight years before joining the Pinkerton Detective Agency. He served in World War I, where he contracted tuberculosis, and spent several years afterward in Army hospitals. He began to publish short stories in about 1923 in pulp magazines. His first novels were 'Red Harvest' and 'The Dain Curse', both published in 1929. 'The Maltese Falcon' came out in 1930 and 'The Glass Key' in 1931. In 'The Thin Man' (1932), his last book, he created the characters Nick and Nora Charles, a detective couple about whom several movies and a television series were made. Nora was based on his friend, playwright Lillian Hellman (*see* Hellman, Lillian). Hammett served in World War II as an enlisted man. He died in New York City on Jan. 10, l961. (*See also* Detective Story.)

**HAMMURABI** (ruled 1792?–1750? BC). In a small room in the Louvre museum in Paris, France, stands a black diorite stela, or column. On it is inscribed in Akkadian, a Semitic language, the Code of Hammurabi. (For picture, *see* Law.) This collection of laws has been ascribed to the reign of Hammurabi, the sixth and best-known king of Babylon's First dynasty.

**Life.** The dates of Hammurabi's life and reign are uncertain. It is believed that he succeeded his father, Sinmuballit, in 1792 BC, when Babylon was but the center of a small city-state about 50 miles (80 kilometers) in radius (*see* Babylonia and Assyria ). Knowledge of the events of his life is derived from historical and building inscriptions, the prologue to his laws, his correspondence, and other materials. The length of his reign is established by what are called date formulas—the naming of years for significant accomplishments or acts of the king.

The area over which Hammurabi ruled is Iraq today. Formerly it was Mesopotamia, the land between the Tigris and Euphrates rivers. He is credited with uniting most of this area under one extensive empire for the first time since Sargon of Akkad did so in about 2300 BC. To do this, Hammurabi waged several military campaigns. The purpose of most of his operations was to gain control of the Tigris and Euphrates waters, on which agricultural productivity depended. Some campaigns were over control of trade routes or access to mines in Iran.

The king began his military campaigns in 1787 by conquering the cities of Uruk and Isin to the south. He then turned his attention to the northwest and east. The power of Assyria prevented him from achieving any significant results, and for 20 years no major warlike activity was reported. He used the time to fortify cities on his northern borders.

The last 14 years of Hammurabi's reign were overshadowed by war. In 1763 he fought against a coalition east of the Tigris that threatened to block access to metal-producing areas in Iran. The same year he conquered the city of Larsa, which enabled him to take over the older Sumerian cities in the south. He followed this victory with the conquest of Mari, 250 miles (400 kilometers) upstream on the Euphrates. During his last two years the king concentrated on building defense fortifications. By this time he was a sick man, and the government was in the hands of his son, Samsuiluna.

Hammurabi effected great changes in all spheres of life, mostly from the transformation of a small city-state into a large empire. Most of his rule was given to the establishment of law and order, religious buildings, irrigation projects, and defense works. He personally oversaw the administration of government.

In doing so he failed to create a permanent bureaucratic system. This failure was a primary reason for the rapid deterioration of his empire after his death. Hammurabi's accomplishments are believed by historians to be exaggerated. This is partly because of the fame he gained when his law code was discovered. His lasting achievement was to shift the main theater of Mesopotamian history northward, where it remained for 1,000 years.

**The laws.** The Code of Hammurabi is the most complete remnant of Babylonian law. The background to the code is the body of Sumerian law under which city-states had lived for centuries. The code itself was advanced far beyond ancient tribal customs. The stela on which the code is inscribed originally stood in Babylon's temple of Marduk, the national god. It was discovered at the site of ancient Susa in 1901 by the French archaeologist Jean-Vincent Scheil. He presented it to the Louvre.

The code consists of 282 case laws, or judicial decisions, collected toward the end of Hammurabi's reign. The decisions deal with such matters as family, marriage, and divorce; tariffs; trade and commerce; prices; and criminal and civil law. From the code it is evident that there were distinct social classes, each of which had its rights and obligations. The right of private property was recognized, though most of the land was in the hands of the royal house. Ownership of land brought with it the duty to provide men for the army and public works.

Families were dominated by fathers. Marriages were arranged by parents, and control of the children by the father was unlimited until marriage. Adoption was common, either to ensure continuance of a family line or to perpetuate a business.

In criminal law the ruling principle for punishment was the ancient *lex talionis,* or law of retaliation. Penalties were calculated according to the nature of the offense. Capital punishment was common, and the various means of execution were prescribed, depending on the nature of the crime. Neither imprisonment nor forced labor is mentioned in the code. Unintended manslaughter was punished by a fine. Willful murder was not mentioned. Carelessness and neglect in the performance of work was severely punished. In general, the penalties prescribed were an improvement over the brutality of previous Assyrian law.

**HAMPDEN, John** (1594–1643). A Puritan statesman who opposed the autocratic government of Charles I, John Hampden figured prominently in the controversies that led to the English Civil War. He was a man of wealth and position, a cousin to Oliver Cromwell, and one of that leader's ablest advisers.

John Hampden was born in London and attended Oxford University. In 1635 he refused to pay the ship-money tax levied by King Charles to outfit the navy. His example broadened resistance to the tax and made him a popular hero. In the early days of the Long Parliament (1640–60), Hampden was the principal lieutenant of the Puritan leader John Pym. He also was one of five members of Parliament whose arrest King Charles ordered on Jan. 4, 1642. This act led rapidly to war.

When hostilities began, Hampden joined the parliamentary army. Wounded at Chalgrove Field on June 18, 1643, he died on June 24 near Thame, Oxfordshire. His abilities as both statesman and soldier prompted the historian Thomas Macaulay to say that if Hampden had lived he would have been the George Washington of England.

**HAMPTON, Va.** Located on the southeastern tip of the Virginia peninsula on Chesapeake Bay, Hampton is the oldest continuously settled English community in the United States. As an Indian village called Kecoughtan, it had been visited by the first English colonists before they sailed up the James River to settle in Jamestown.

The first free public schools in the United States were founded in Hampton by Benjamin Syms and Thomas Eaton and are commemorated in the Syms-Eaton Museum. Hampton is the site of Hampton Institute (now University), established in 1868 to educate freed slaves, and Thomas Nelson Community College. St. John's Episcopal parish was founded in 1610, making it the oldest in the country.

Military installations, tourism, and fishing form the basis of Hampton's economy. Fort Monroe, the only active moat-encircled fort in the country, dates from 1819. For a long period during the American Civil War the fort was the only Union outpost in the Confederacy. The famous battle between the first ironclad battleships, the *Monitor* and the *Merrimack*, was fought just offshore. Today Fort Monroe serves as headquarters for the United States Continental Army Command. Langley Air Force Base and the Langley Research Center for the National Aeronautics and Space Administration (NASA) are also in Hampton.

The actual settlement of Hampton began in 1610, when settlers built two forts for protection against Indian raids. The town was organized in 1705 and named for the third earl of Southampton. Attacked during the American Revolution and again during the War of 1812, Hampton was burned in 1861 by the Confederates to prevent its capture by Union forces.

Hampton is governed by a council-manager form of government. Population (1990 census), 133,793.

**HAMSTER.** A close relative of the rat and mouse, the hamster is valued both as a pet and as a laboratory animal. Several species of these small rodents occur naturally in Europe, Asia, and northern Africa.

Hamsters are popular as pets because of their good nature, attractive appearance, and normally excellent health. In addition, they are easy to feed and will reproduce readily in captivity. These same traits have made hamsters a common laboratory animal. Because they are susceptible to many of the same diseases as humans, they are often used in medical experiments designed to find cures for human diseases.

The most common species, and the most popular as a pet, is the golden, or Syrian, hamster. All golden

**Golden hamster** (Mesocricetus auratus)

hamsters in captivity are apparently derived from a single litter captured in Syria in 1930. Adults are 5 to 6 inches (12.5 to 15 centimeters) long and weigh about 4 ounces (110 grams). Their fur is soft and silky and is yellowish brown to red. The belly and underside of the legs are creamy white. Hamsters have large ears and a tiny tail. Their large cheek pouches resemble those of a chipmunk and are used to carry food.

In the wild, adult hamsters eat various grain seeds and plant materials, although some species also eat insects and other small animals. In captivity, they thrive on food mixtures containing seeds and grains and will also eat many kinds of vegetables and fresh fruit. They require a ready supply of fresh water, which is normally dispensed from a glass bottle attached to the side of the cage.

Most hamsters live in arid regions, retreating to their burrows for hibernation during cold weather. They are generally nocturnal. The golden hamster is a native of the steppe country of Asia Minor and the Balkans. The common, or black-bellied, hamster is a solitary animal, not as well suited to captivity as the golden hamster, and inhabits the steppes and cultivated lands of Europe and parts of Western Asia. It digs an elaborate burrow system with separate chambers for nesting and for storing food, which it gathers in great quantities.

A female hamster is able to bear young when she is 6 weeks to 2 months old. The gestation period is about 16 days. Although an average litter size is from five to ten, hamsters commonly have as few as three or as many as a dozen offspring at a time. Mothers will sometimes eat their own young, particularly when the number of offspring is large. Females may produce litters at monthly intervals up to an age of about 15 months. The blind, hairless young begin to grow fur in two to three days. Their eyes open after about two weeks. After ten days they begin eating solid food, though the mother will continue to nurse them for about two more weeks. In captivity, a typical hamster may live for two to three years.

Hamsters belong to the order Rodentia and the family Muridae. The scientific name of the golden hamster is *Mesocricetus auratus;* the common hamster is *Cricetus cricetus.* (*See also* Pets; Rodents.)   J. Whitfield Gibbons

**HAMSUN, Knut** (1859–1952). The Norwegian novelist, dramatist, and poet Knut Hamsun represents a return to Romantic fiction at the end of the 19th century. His desire was to rescue literature from the excessive realism and naturalism that had preoccupied writers from the 1850s (*see* Novel, "Romanticism" ). He was impatient with books about social problems. Instead he concentrated on a psychological analysis of an individual's attempts to cope with simple realities. Hamsun was awarded the Nobel prize for literature in 1920.

Hamsun was the pen name of Knut Pedersen, who was born in Lom, Norway, on Aug. 4, 1859. He spent most of his childhood in the Lofoten Islands and had almost no formal schooling. He started writing at age 19 while working as a shoemaker's apprentice in Bodø. For the next ten years he worked at various jobs, and during this period he twice visited the United States. For a time he was a streetcar conductor in Chicago and a farmhand in North Dakota.

Hamsun's first novel, 'Hunger', published in 1890, was published after his return to Norway. His other works include 'Pan' (1894), 'Children of the Age' (1913), 'Growth of the Soil' (1917), 'The Women at the Pump' (1920), and 'Vagabonds' (1927). His contempt for Western culture led him to support the Nazi occupation of Norway during World War II. After the war he was imprisoned for treason but was soon released because of his age. He died near Grimstad on Feb. 19, 1952.

**HANCOCK, John** (1737–93). The man whose name heads the list of signers of the Declaration of Independence, John Hancock was a Boston patriot and a leader of the American Revolution. His prominent signature is familiar to anyone who has seen a picture of that document.

John Hancock was born on Jan. 12, 1737, in Braintree, Mass. His father died when John was a child, and he was adopted by his uncle, a rich Boston merchant. Hancock inherited his uncle's wealth when he was 28 years old. In 1768 his sloop, *Liberty,* was seized by British authorities for nonpayment of duty. Its cargo of wine had been smuggled ashore. The seizure precipitated a riot on shore. The British used the ship as a coast guard vessel until it was burned by a patriot mob in Newport, R.I.

The episode was a prelude to the Revolution. Hancock's opposition to British rule was no doubt inspired by business interest, but, whatever his motives, he was valuable to the cause. In 1770, after the Boston Massacre, he was one of the committee that went to the governor to demand the removal of British troops from the city. At the funeral of the victims he delivered an address that led to an order for his arrest. He presided at the revolutionary Provincial Congress that met in Concord and later in Cambridge, and his arrest was one of the objects of the British expedition to Concord.

This expedition led to the battle of Lexington and Concord.

Elected president of the Second Continental Congress in 1775, Hancock held that office for two years. In 1780 he became the first elected governor of Massachusetts and, except for two years (1785–87), held that office until his death. The support he was persuaded to give to the Federal Constitution in 1788 was the decisive factor in the struggle for ratification in Massachusetts.

Hancock was a man of strong common sense and sound patriotism. His wealth, social position, and education were of great help to the colonial cause. He died on Oct. 8, 1793, in Quincy, Mass.

**HANCOCK, Winfield Scott** (1824–86). One of the best Union officers of the Civil War, Hancock was a fearless and capable leader. Ulysses S. Grant said of him, "Hancock stands the most conspicuous figure of all who did not exercise a separate command."

Winfield Scott Hancock was born on Feb. 14, 1824, in Montgomery County, Pa. He graduated from West Point in 1844 and fought in the Mexican War. A captain when the Civil War broke out, Hancock was soon commissioned brigadier general. He helped organize the Army of the Potomac, and in 1862 served in the battles of South Mountain and Antietam. At Fredericksburg, that December, he led a desperate attack on Maryes' Height through a deadly fire. At Gettysburg in 1863, his appearance on Cemetery Ridge on the first day of the battle was equal to reinforcement by an army corps. Men who were fleeing stopped and the troops were restored to order.

Hancock commanded the Second Corps, and it was his forces that, on the last day of the battle, stopped the charge of Pickett's men, depriving the South of all hope of victory. Hancock was wounded, but he stayed on the field until victory was won. He recovered and in 1864 took part in the hard-fought battles of the Wilderness, Spotsylvania, and Cold Harbor. At Spotsylvania his troops broke through the Confederate defenses, capturing 3,000 prisoners. He was promoted to the rank of major general in 1866.

In 1880 the Democratic party nominated him for the presidency. He lost the election to James A. Garfield, who, in addition to his military career, had also served in Congress. Hancock remained in the Army, serving his country for more than 40 years. He died on Feb. 9, 1886, on Governors Island, N.Y.

**HAND.** Human beings, alone in the animal kingdom, are tool makers and tool users. The ability to make and use tools depends in great part upon the use of the hands guided by the intelligence of the brain. It is believed that in the evolution of humanity the development of the brain and dexterity in the hands were mutually dependent processes.

All vertebrates have hands or something like them. In some animals they are called paws; in the case of birds and some reptiles they are claws. Horses and cattle have hooves. The hand may be defined as the

**Structure of Some Animal Hands**

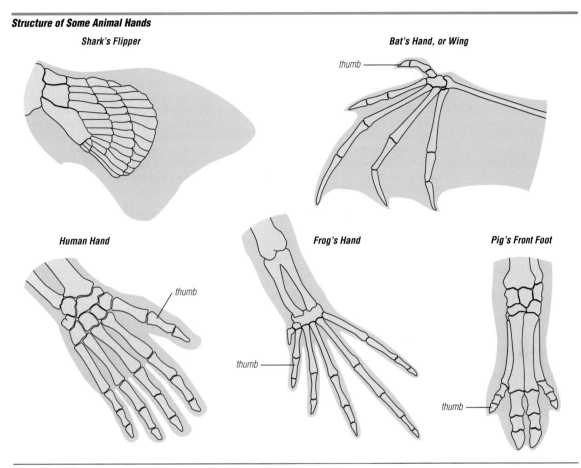

**Shark's Flipper**

**Bat's Hand, or Wing**

thumb

**Human Hand**

**Frog's Hand**

**Pig's Front Foot**

thumb

thumb

thumb

*While the human hand (bottom left) is particularly versatile, other creatures also have hands adapted to various purposes. The bat's fingers (top right) have evolved to support its wings, with the thumb remaining free to be used as a clinging hook. The shark's flipper (top left) is broad and short, and almost all of its fingers have been lost or fused. In the frog's hand (bottom center), the fingers are plainly represented even though they are longer than the fingers on the human hand. The fingers in the pig's hand (bottom right) have been modified to allow for the pig's use of its limbs for digging and rooting.*

grasping end of the forelimb. In many animals it exhibits a great amount of mobility and flexibility in its use. The hand is most highly developed in the primates, an order of mammals that includes lemurs, apes, monkeys, and humans.

The human hand is located at the end of the arm, with the ball-and-socket joint at the shoulder, the hinge joint at the elbow, and a peculiar joint at the wrist. The eight bones of the wrist are called carpal bones, the five of the palm are the metacarpals, and the 14 in the fingers are the phalanges. These phalanges are so called because they are arranged side by side, as were the Greek soldiers in the military formation known as the phalanx. All these bones are bound by tough flexible ligaments.

The muscles that move the hand are mostly upon the forearm and have long tendons by which the pull of the muscles is communicated to the different joints. An individual can feel and see some of these tendons in the wrist when bending the fingers. There are more

than 30 pairs of muscles involved in producing hand motions.

In humans the thumb is set at an angle from the other fingers. In apes and humans it rotates on what is called the carpometacarpal joint and is therefore opposable to the other fingers. It is this feature that makes it possible to pick up and hold objects. Among some apes and New World monkeys the four fingers are elongated to make it possible to swing on vines and tree branches.

In primates the tips of the fingers are covered by fingernails. The palms and undersides of the fingers are marked by creases and covered by ridges called palm prints and fingerprints. These serve to increase sensitivity and gripping power. Human fingerprints, because they are distinctive for each individual, are also used for identification.

The sensitivity of the hand is more highly developed than in many other parts of the body. There are numerous little elevations or papillae on the skin of the palm, and fine nerve fibers extend from these to the brain. Thus the skin is made very sensitive to touch, heat, and cold.

While the human hand is the most completely developed in the animal kingdom for all-around purposes of protection, strength, blows, grasping, delicate movements, and sensitiveness, it is interesting to note that the forelimb of all mammals is formed on the same general plan. The horse's front hoof is just a modified fingernail; all the fingers but one have disappeared or are represented only by the remnants called splints. In these animals the modifications are for purposes of speed in running. In the bat, very long fingers are developed to support the web that, instead of feathers, constitutes the wing.

**HANDBALL.** A fast-paced, energetic game in which competitors hit a ball with the hand against the walls of a court, handball originated in Ireland about 1,000 years ago. For hundreds of years the game's popularity was limited primarily to Ireland. Then in the 1880s the Irish brought it to the United States.

Handball is most frequently played on either a four-wall court or a one-wall court. The four-wall game is most like the one that originated in Ireland. The one-wall variation was developed in New York City around 1900. The standard four-wall court is basically a rectangular box. The front wall is a 20-foot (6-meter) square, and the side walls are 40 feet (12 meters) long and 20 feet high. The short line crosses the middle of the floor, dividing it into two 20-foot squares. The service line also crosses the floor, 5 feet (1.5 meters) in front of the short line. The area between these two lines is called the service zone. The back wall is usually 12 feet (3.7 meters) high, with a gallery above where the referee and the scorer are stationed. Spectators may watch the game from the gallery. Some courts also have a glass back wall that gives spectators a better view of the action.

The ball used is made of black rubber, 1 ⅞ inches (4.8 centimeters) in diameter and 2.3 ounces (65 grams) in weight. Although soft, it can sting the bare hands on its lively rebound from the walls. Players wear special gloves for protection. The gloves also keep moisture from affecting the ball during play. Players may strike the ball with either hand, but they may not use their feet or other parts of their bodies.

Two, three, or four persons may play. When two play, one is the server and the other is the receiver. In doubles, with four players, the server and his partner form the serving side and their opponents form the receiving side. The three-person game is called cut-throat handball. In it, a single server plays against two receivers, continuing to serve until put out. When that happens the left-most receiver takes over the serve and plays against the other two. The serve rotates in this way until one player wins by scoring 21 points.

To serve, the server stands in the service zone. The server drops the ball to the floor of the service zone and strikes it on the bounce so that it hits the front wall first and, on the rebound, lands on the floor behind the short line. A served ball landing in front of this line is a short. Two shorts in a row score an out against the server, who then becomes the receiver, and his opponent becomes the server. In doubles, the server's partner must stand in the service box with his back to the wall until the ball passes the service line.

The receiver must stand behind the short line while the ball is being served. He must play the served ball either on the fly or on the first bounce so that the ball returns to the front wall without hitting the floor. The server then hits the ball on its rebound from the wall, and play continues with the opponents alternately hitting the ball until one of them fails to return it legally to the front wall.

If the server fails to make the return, an out is scored against him, and he then becomes the receiver. If the receiver fails to make the return, a point is awarded to the server, who continues to serve until he is out. Thus only the server or the serving side scores points. A game is 21 points; a match goes to the first player or team to win two out of three games.

The rules permit a served ball, after hitting the front wall, to strike one side wall before landing behind the short line. A returned ball is permitted to strike the side walls and ceiling before hitting the front wall. From there the ball may bound to the back of the court and may be played from the back wall.

One-wall handball is played on a court having a wall 20 feet wide and 16 feet (4.9 meters) high. The court is 20 feet wide and 34 feet (10.4 meters) long. The same ball and the same system of scoring are used as for four-wall handball. The basic difference is that because there is no ceiling or side and back walls, the ball must always be played off the front wall. The court is open on three sides, and considerable skill is required to keep the ball within bounds during a fast game. The one-wall court permits the game to be watched by more spectators than the four-wall court, and it costs less to build. The wall is often built long enough so that several courts can be laid out on both sides of it. This makes the one-wall game popular at playgrounds as well as in gymnasiums.

Another variation of the game uses a three-wall court. Three-wall courts may have two full side walls in addition to the front wall, or the front wall may be flanked by two triangular wings. The four-wall game, which allows play off all four walls plus the ceiling, is probably the most demanding form of the game. All of the versions of the game require both stamina and agility, however, and the fact that handball requires only two players and can be played indoors makes it an ideal way to keep in shape when darkness or bad weather makes some outdoor sports difficult.

**HANDEL, George Frideric** (1685–1759). A musical giant of the late baroque period, George Frideric Handel was born in Germany but spent most of his adult life in England. He successfully combined German, French, Italian, and English musical styles in about 40 operas, 20 oratorios, and numerous other vocal pieces, instrumental works, and church music.

**George Frideric Handel**

Handel was born on Feb. 23, 1685, in Halle, Brandenburg (in what is now Germany). In addition to musical studies, he was trained in the law at Halle University. Although appointed organist of the Halle Cathedral in 1702, he moved to Hamburg the next year, where he obtained a position as violinist, and later harpsichordist, in the opera orchestra. His 'St. John Passion' was performed in 1704 and his first opera, 'Almira', in 1705.

Handel then went to Italy, which was the musical center of Europe, where his work was already known. He met the leading musicians of the day and composed the operas 'Rodrigo' and 'Agrippina', many Italian solo cantatas, Latin church music, and the oratorio 'La Resurrezione'.

In 1710 Handel became the director of music for the elector of Hanover. A few months later he traveled to London. His opera 'Rinaldo' was received enthusiastically there in 1711, and he made several more trips as his popularity increased. Handel's 'Ode for the Queen's Birthday' and 'Utrecht Te Deum' and 'Jubilate' in celebration of the Treaty of Utrecht in 1713 won him a royal pension. Except for a few visits to the European continent, Handel spent the rest of his life in England.

In 1718 he became director of music to the duke of Chandos, for whom he composed the 12 'Chandos Anthems' and 'Haman and Mordecai'. The latter was later reworked as 'Esther', which introduced the musical form of the English oratorio (see Oratorio). This was the first of many oratorios that Handel wrote, including the famous 'Messiah', which was written for a performance in Dublin, Ireland, in 1742.

Handel began to have trouble with his eyes in 1751. Two years later he was nearly blind. He died on April 14, 1759, and was buried in London in Westminster Abbey.

**HANDICAP** *see* **DISABILITY.**

**HANDICRAFTS.** Strictly speaking, handicrafts are occupations that involve making usable or decorative products by hand. Before the Industrial Revolution all such products were handmade, often in the home. The age of the machine nearly did away with the traditional crafts by fostering mass production.

During the mid-19th century, however, a reaction against the machine took place in Great Britain. Called the Arts and Crafts Movement, it urged a new appreciation for decorative, handmade products. The movement did a great deal to bring about today's interest in handicrafts, often as a hobby, for limited production of quality goods.

Whether as a hobby or a vocation, handicrafts encompass activities that require a variety of skills. They also usually require some equipment and, because they do, the term handicraft may seem misleading. Knitting, for example, requires the use of needles.

Among the common handicrafts are model building, needlework, lace making, pottery, woodworking, scrimshaw (whale- and walrus-bone carving), ornamental metalworking, glassblowing, and the making of stained glass, jewelry, and mosaics. Handicrafts as a hobby have become a major industry. There are packaged kits for models of ships, automobiles, airplanes, rockets, military vehicles, human anatomy, birds, and animals; painting; mosaics; needlepoint; embroidery; and crafts that use plastics, wood, leather, textiles, metal, cork, wool, yard goods, and laces. The sciences are represented by kits for chemistry, biology, physics, astronomy, and the earth sciences.

Some hobbyists reject the use of kits as too commercial. They use their own materials, often discarded goods, for their craft. A quilt, for instance, can be made from squares of colorful cloth sewed together. Rugs can be made on a hand loom from old rags. Newspapers, paste, and powdered glue are the basis of papier-mâché for masks, puppets, float displays, and other artifacts.

---

### FACT FINDER FOR HANDICRAFTS

The subject of handicrafts is a broad one. Readers will obtain additional information in the related articles listed here. (See also related references in the Fact-Index.)

| | |
|---|---|
| Basketry | Lace |
| Batik | Mask |
| Bead and Beadwork | Metalworking |
| Book and Bookmaking | Models and Model Building |
| Calligraphy | Mosaic |
| Candle | Needlework |
| Embossing | Pottery and Porcelain |
| Enamel | Puppet |
| Finger Painting | Quilt |
| Folk Art | Rug and Carpet |
| Hobby | Spinning and Weaving |
| Jewelry and Gems | Stained Glass |
| Knitting | Taxidermy |

---

**HANDWRITING.** John Hancock signed the American colonies' Declaration of Independence in a large bold script so that, he said, King George III of England would have no trouble reading it. The handwriting of adults is not as individualized as their fingerprints, but it is distinctive enough that it is highly unlikely that any two persons write exactly the same.

Handwriting, as distinguished from printing, has come to refer to the form of writing peculiar to each person. Individuality in handwriting occurs among members of the same family as well as among classmates who are taught the same system of writing by the same teacher. This individualization apparently begins very early in life, when a preschool child is still scribbling and drawing.

An unusual feature of some childhood efforts is called mirror writing. This is script that reads from right to left and can be read as normal left-to-right writing only when held up to a mirror. The great artist Leonardo da Vinci used mirror, or reverse, writing in his books, presumably to keep his scientific thoughts secret. Left-handed children often write in reverse because it is easier for them to move their hands from right to left across a page. As they write, the words become visible because the hand uncovers them. When they write from left to right, the words are covered by the hand as they write. Right-handed persons, by contrast, can easily move their hands from left to right, and the words are uncovered as the hand moves across the page. Left-handed children after a while tend to conform to the left-to-right standard taught in schools.

The teaching of writing normally proceeds in stages. First, children are taught what is called manuscript writing. This is more like printing. Both capital letters and small letters are formed individually and are not run together. The characters are written vertically rather than slantwise. Many letters are made of several individual strokes of the pen.

After manuscript writing has been mastered, pupils are taught cursive writing. This term is what many people mean when they use the term handwriting and script. In cursive the letters of a word are written in a continuous motion without lifting the pen from the paper. Thus all the letters of a word are joined. Such writing ordinarily slants to the right, and several of the letters, such as *f* and *s*, look very little like the printed or manuscript forms. Generally speaking, manuscript writing is easier to learn and to read, while cursive has the advantage of greater speed in composition.

A compromise between manuscript and cursive called joined manuscript is sometimes taught. The letter forms are those of ordinary unjoined manuscript, but many of them (such as *m* and *t*) are given "tails" that connect them with the following letters. Joined manuscript may be used to make the transition between manuscript and cursive, or it may be taught as a regular form of handwriting. There is also a very artistic, stylized kind of writing called calligraphy, which is used for decorative manuscripts (*see* Calligraphy).

### Handwriting Identification

Although not as distinctive as a person's fingerprints or voice, the identification of handwriting is often a vital procedure in law, when the authenticity of a signature is in question. There are also times when the signature itself is not doubted, but there is concern about the conditions under which it was written. This is particularly true in determining the validity of wills and other legal documents. It sometimes can be demonstrated that the writer's hand was forced or guided, or that the writer was not in a proper mental condition to sign his or her name.

If a signature or other handwriting is questionable, it is necessary to obtain some of the person's known handwriting for comparison. The writing characteristics that experts use in determining authenticity presuppose that each individual's writing has certain permanent features. These can be identified and compared to other samples of the person's handwriting. Although no two signatures of an individual are exactly the same, the overall characteristics are always present. The signature of a forger, moreover, usually represents a combination of his own writing habits and his imitation of someone else's.

Several methods have been devised to detect forgery in documents. The age of the paper can be compared with the supposed date of the writing. It can be determined whether writing at creases in the paper preceded or followed the creasing. Chemical analysis of paper and ink are used to determine the date of manufacture of each. It is difficult, for instance, to create a convincing forgery of a pre-20th century document because the chemical composition of paper and ink have changed markedly since 1900. (*See also* Counterfeiting and Forgery.)

### Graphology

It has long been believed that character and personality traits can be inferred from a person's handwriting. The name for this study is graphology. Derived from the Greek, it means simply "knowledge of handwriting." The theory holds that a systematic analysis of the way words and letters are formed can reveal the inner nature of the individual. Factors such as the size and slant of letters, spacing between letters, degree of connectedness, and other measurable aspects of writing have been studied. There are also indicators of the speed and pressure of writing.

One of the problems besetting graphologists is finding a scale by which to rate all the separate handwriting elements in order to assign them specific meanings. It has been stated, for example, that unusually large handwriting indicates an ambitious and imaginative person. Those who regard graphology as a false science counter by saying that large handwriting, rather than indicating a personality trait, may be no more than evidence of poor eyesight. The chief problem graphologists have faced is the development of valid scientific methods and experiments under controlled conditions.

**HANDY, W.C.** (1873–1958). The title of W.C. Handy's autobiography, 'Father of the Blues', is an accurate assessment of his contribution to American music. The man who composed the immortal 'St. Louis Blues', written in 1914, and other classics—such as 'Beale Street Blues', 'Memphis Blues', 'Careless Love', and 'Yellow Dog Blues'—forever changed the course of American music by integrating a blues idiom with ragtime.

William Christopher Handy was born on Nov. 16, 1873, in Florence, Ala., the son of former slaves. As a 15-year-old he left home to work in a traveling minstrel show, but he soon returned when his money ran out. He attended Teachers Agricultural and Mechanical College in Huntsville, Ala., and worked as a schoolteacher and bandmaster. In 1893, during an economic depression, he formed a quartet to perform at the World's Columbian Exposition in Chicago. For several years afterward he drifted around the country working at different jobs. Eventually he settled in Memphis, Tenn.

Handy wrote music during the period of transition from ragtime to jazz. The music he had absorbed during his youth consisted of spirituals, work songs, and folk ballads. His own work consisted of elements of all of these in addition to the popular ragtime and the blues notes that he inserted. His work developed the conception of blues as a harmonic framework within which it was possible to improvise. His own chosen instrument was the cornet. Although he lost his eyesight at age 30, he conducted his own orchestra from 1903 until 1921. His sight partially returned, but he became completely blind after a fall from a subway platform in 1943.

Composing the blues began in 1909 when Handy wrote an election campaign song for the mayor of Memphis, Edward H. "Boss" Crump. With some changes, the song was published in 1911 as 'Memphis Blues'. In all he wrote some 60 compositions. Handy spent his last years in New York City, where he died on March 28, 1958.

**HANGZHOU,** or **HANGCHOW, China.** The capital of Zhejiang Province, Hangzhou is situated at the head of Hangzhou Bay in eastern China. It is renowned for its scenic hills and the buildings and gardens around West Lake. The city is linked by water, rail, and highway to the interior of Zhejiang and is the southern terminus of the Grand Canal.

Hangzhou has long been an intellectual and cultural center and is now the seat of Hangzhou, Zhejiang, and Zhejiang Agricultural universities. Tourists visit the city's two monasteries, the stone bridges and pagodas around West Lake, and the many gardens, two of which are modeled after gardens of the Southern Sung Dynasty (see China). The city has an ancient look that it has tried to maintain. In the early 1980s pollution of West Lake led officials to move the factories and to enforce strict rules regarding sewage disposal.

In addition to tourism Hangzhou's economic ventures include silk and cotton industries, chemicals and machine tools, tea processing, and grain milling. An electric generating plant and a tractor plant brought many jobs to the city.

Hangzhou is one of the six ancient Chinese capitals and has a reputation for paradiselike beauty. Its site was first developed during the Ch'in Dynasty. It became a wealthy port when the extension of the Grand Canal reached the city in 609. It was a state capital during five dynasties and was China's cultural center as the capital of the Southern Sung Dynasty from 1126 to 1279. In the 13th century the Venetian explorer Marco Polo visited Hangzhou and was reportedly overwhelmed by its beauty. The city was damaged during the 1861 Taiping Rebellion. The Japanese controlled the city from 1937 to 1945. Rail and highway development in the 1950s made Hangzhou the focus of traffic from the province to Shanghai. Population (1999 estimate), 1,346,148.

**HANKS, Tom** (born 1956). Oscar-winning actor Tom Hanks got his break in the television series Bosom Buddies, which ran from 1980 to 1982. In many of his films, including 'He Knows You're Alone' (1980), 'Splash' (1984), 'The Money Pit' (1986), 'Nothing in Common' (1986), 'Big' (1988), 'A League of Their Own' (1992), 'Sleepless in Seattle' (1993), and 'Saving Private Ryan' (1998), he played an ordinary, decent man caught up in extraordinary circumstances. In 1994 he was awarded the Academy award for best actor for his role in 'Philadelphia' (1993), in which he played a homosexual attorney fired from a law firm when it becomes known he has AIDS. He followed that performance with the critically acclaimed box-office blockbuster and winner of the Academy award for best picture, 'Forrest Gump' (1994). Hanks again won the best actor Academy award for his work in the title role, becoming the first person in fifty years to win back-to-back Academy awards for best actor. He was nominated for an Oscar in 'Apollo 13' (1995). He was nominated again for 'Saving Private Ryan' (1998). In 1999 he starred in 'The Green Mile', a film which was nominated for best picture. In 2000 he starred in 'Cast Away'.

**HANNA, Mark** (1837–1904). Few men in United States history have exemplified the close ties between business and politics better than Mark Hanna. He was an industrialist who became convinced that the welfare of industry, and therefore the nation, was bound with the fortunes of the Republican party. To further his goals he waged the most expensive political campaign the nation had ever seen to get William McKinley elected president in 1896.

Marcus Alonzo Hanna was born in New Lisbon (now Lisbon), Ohio, on Sept. 24, 1837. The family moved to Cleveland in 1852, where he attended

Western Reserve College for a few months before entering his father's wholesale grocery business. After brief service in the Union Army during the Civil War, he went to work in his father-in-law's iron and coal business. He became very successful and expanded his interests to include banking, publishing, and transportation. In 1885 the iron and coal company was reorganized as M.A. Hanna and Company.

In 1890 he was impressed by Ohio congressman William McKinley's support for a tariff bill. This support cost McKinley the 1890 election, but in 1891 he was elected governor of Ohio. Hanna managed McKinley's campaign for reelection two years later and retired from business to give full time to promoting McKinley for the 1896 presidential campaign. Hanna raised an unprecedented 3.5 million dollars from industrialists and corporations to defeat William Jennings Bryan, the Democrat-Populist candidate. After McKinley's victory, Hanna became his closest and most influential adviser. President McKinley appointed Senator John Sherman of Ohio secretary of state, and Hanna was appointed to fill Sherman's unexpired Senate term. Hanna remained in the Senate until his death on Feb. 15, 1904.

**HANNIBAL** (247?–183? BC). "I swear that so soon as age will permit . . . I will use fire and steel to arrest the destiny of Rome." The boy Hannibal said this as he stood at the altar beside his father, the great Carthaginian general Hamilcar Barca. The father and son were leaving for Spain, where Hamilcar hoped to make up for the losses that Carthage had suffered in the First Punic War.

Hannibal learned quickly. After his father's death he took command of the army in Spain. Then in 218 BC he launched the mission to which he had been sworn. As the Roman Senate made plans to invade Carthage, Hannibal started one of history's most daring marches. He led his forces along eastern Spain, over the Pyrenees Mountains, and across the Rhône River. His 90,000 infantry, 12,000 cavalry, and nearly 40 elephants traveled all autumn. When they reached the Alps, the cold was intense. Some of Hannibal's soldiers died of exposure. Others fell to their death.

Only about half of them reached northern Italy, but Hannibal's skilled cavalry tactics crushed the Roman forces at the Trebia River and at Lake Trasimene. Alarmed, the Romans appointed a dictator, the wise statesman Quintus Fabius Maximus, and gave him extraordinary power. Choosing not to risk an engagement at once, Fabius instead followed the Carthaginians, delaying and harassing them. At last, in 216 BC, the Roman army met Hannibal's band at Cannae in southeastern Italy. Hannibal outwitted and annihilated them, slaying an estimated 60,000.

Hannibal's triumph was brief, however. Neither his own countrymen nor the Italians he had subdued during his 15 years in Italy supported him. His brother Hasdrubal, bringing reinforcements from Spain, was defeated by the Romans and killed. Hannibal finally returned home when a Roman army

under Scipio Africanus invaded Carthage. There at Zama he suffered a crushing and final defeat.

Hannibal now showed that he could be a statesman as well as soldier. He reformed the government of Carthage and paid the heavy tribute exacted by Rome. The Romans, alarmed by this prosperity and fearing that Hannibal might renew the war against them, demanded his surrender, but he fled to Asia. Several years later the Romans hunted him down. Hannibal took poison, ending the life of one of the greatest military leaders of ancient times. (*See also* Carthage.)

**HANOI, Vietnam.** Since 1976 Hanoi has been the capital of Vietnam. Located on the western bank of the Red River approximately 85 miles (137 kilometers) inland from the South China Sea, Hanoi has an almost tropical climate. The rich soils of the Red River have made the city an agricultural center.

Co Loa, a citadel dating from the 3rd century BC, the Temple of Literature, and the Temple of the Trung Sisters are among the historical sites. The Temple of the Trung Sisters is dedicated to two women for their leadership during the first Vietnamese movement. They led the rebellion against the Chinese Han Dynasty. A scenic feature is Lake Hoan Kiem. The city itself reflects its French heritage in its architecture. Cultural centers are the University of Hanoi, the Army Museum, the Revolutionary Museum, and the National Museum.

The city is a major center for communications, industry, and agriculture. Machine tools, electric generators and motors, textiles, and matches are among the products manufactured. Many small rivers make it easy for small boats to reach Hanoi. Roads and railways connect the city to its outport, Haiphong, to Kunming, China, and south to Ho Chi Minh City. Hanoi has two airports.

Hanoi has been the scene of many political changes. Ly Thai To, the first ruler of the Ly Dynasty (1009–1225), chose Hanoi as his capital in 1010. Hanoi's status remained unchanged until 1802, when the capital was moved to Hue. Restored as the capital in 1902 by the French, Hanoi survived French rule, Japanese occupation from 1940 to 1945, and extensive damage in 1965, 1968, and 1972 from bombing by the United States during the Vietnam War. Population (1992 estimate), 1,073,760.

**HANOVER, Germany.** The capital of Lower Saxony is the historic city of Hanover. It has an irregularly built old town with many quaint stucco-front houses and a highly industrialized modern city. There are many beautiful parks, gardens, museums, and picture galleries to house a rich collection of art. For years the city has attracted foreign students eager to study Hanover's reputedly pure form of the German language. The city is a major traffic junction of northern Germany. It is a financial and commercial center. Its many manufactured products include motor vehicles and machinery.

Dave Bartruff

*Hanover's train station, seen at the end of Bahnhofstrasse from Kröpcke Square, was first built in 1833–34 at the edge of the city. It is now in Hanover's city center.*

In the war between Prussia and Austria in 1866, Hanover was allied with Austria, and the victorious Prussia then annexed Hanover as a province. After World War II it was made part of the new state of Lower Saxony.

As a center of industry and transportation, it was heavily bombed in World War II, and many historic buildings were destroyed. Reconstruction came after the war. The city's German name is Hannover. Population (1999 estimate), 515,200.

**HANSEATIC LEAGUE.** A fleet of tall-masted ships gathered near the Denmark coast in 1368. The ships came from north German cities belonging to the Hanseatic League, which was at war with the king of Denmark. For two years the ships harassed the Danish coasts and waters, sacked Danish cities, and carried off their treasures. At the end of that time the king of Denmark made peace, but the terms were humiliating. The cities of the league demanded a share in the Danish revenues for 15 years, the possession of Danish strongholds, and the final voice in the selection of the Danish kings.

This episode in the history of the loose confederation of north German cities known as the Hanseatic League gives an idea of the power it then possessed. The league had developed gradually. More than a hundred years before the action against Denmark, a few cities had formed hansas, or alliances to protect their traders from plundering barons along land routes and from marauding pirates upon the

seas. These alliances proved so useful that gradually more towns joined the strongest league, of which Lübeck was the center, and this union became known as the Hanseatic League.

Just how many towns were in the league no one knows. Even its ambassadors in London, when asked for the number of towns, replied that they could not be expected to know all the places, large and small, in whose name they spoke. At the height of its power in the 14th century it probably included nearly 100 cities, extending from Belgium to Poland.

In these foreign trading posts the league's representatives lived almost like monks. They were forbidden to marry as long as they remained abroad. They could not leave the post at night. Iron doors, watchdogs, and guards enforced this rule. The representatives were allowed to associate with the people of the country only for business purposes, and they were required to be rigidly honest in their dealings, for the dishonesty of one league member would bring the wrath of the townsmen upon all.

But the advantages more than made up for these inconveniences. Merchants of the league were exempt from the taxes and tolls paid by others. In some places they had a monopoly of a certain trade, such as the herring fisheries off the coast of Sweden. At the height of its power the league not only protected its merchants but also maintained its fleet and even engaged in war to safeguard its interests. It played an important part in suppressing lawlessness, in carrying comforts and conveniences into remote lands, and in promoting the exchange of ideas throughout Northern Europe.

Quarrels among the towns gradually weakened the influence of the league, for it was only a loose union whose assembly met every year or two and had no authority to enforce its decisions. The rise of strong political states such as Denmark created rivals and enemies for the league, and the commercial importance of its cities diminished after the discovery of the Americas and the route around Africa. The deathblow came when the herring suddenly deserted their haunts off the shores of Sweden for the coast of Holland. The exclusive control of the herring trade had been the most highly prized league privilege, and with that gone the members lost interest. By 1630 most of the towns had deserted the alliance. The free cities of Hamburg, Lübeck, and Bremen, however, continued to be known as Hansa towns until the latter part of the 19th century (*see* Bremen; Hamburg).

**HANTAVIRUS.** The hantavirus is a rodent-borne virus that causes a severe, sometimes fatal, respiratory infection called hantavirus pulmonary syndrome (HPS). The infection occurs when the person comes in contact with infected rodents, their droppings, or their urine. It was first isolated on a Navajo reservation in the Four Corners area of New Mexico, Arizona, Utah, and Colorado. There were more than 50 cases of the infection reported in the United States in 1993.

**HANUKKAH.** Also spelled Chanukah, Hanukkah is a Jewish festival, that celebrates the triumph of the few over the many, the weak over the strong, and the faith in one miracle-making god.

Jerusalem was ruled as part of the Seleucid Dynasty beginning in about 198 BC. One member of the dynasty in particular, Antiochus Epiphanes IV, who ruled from 175 to 163 BC, brought Greek culture to the land of Israel and insisted that the Jews living there worship the pagan gods idolized by the Seleucid Greeks. Mattathias, a high priest from the village of Modi'in, led a revolt against the rule of Antiochus. When Antiochus ordered the Jews to make animal sacrifices and pay homage to Greek gods and pagan idols, Mattathias refused. Antiochus threatened those refusing to abandon their Judaism with the death penalty, and his armies desecrated the Temple in Jerusalem. The small army of Jews was led first by Mattathias and subsequently by his son Judas Maccabeus, or Judah Maccabee. The name Maccabee came from the Hebrew word for hammer. The Maccabees regained access to the Temple in Jerusalem after seven years of fighting. In 165 BC the Maccabees purified and rededicated the Temple. The festival of Hanukkah took its name from the Hebrew word for dedication.

A later story found in the Jewish oral law compiled in the Talmud told of a small vial of oil found by the Maccabees when they came into the Temple. There was enough oil to last for only one night, but the oil miraculously lasted for eight nights, during which time Judah Maccabee was able to obtain fine fresh oil for the temple lamps. Some scholars believe that this story was added to move the focus of the story from the military victory to the sacred realm of God and miracles. Hanukkah became known as both the Festival of Lights and the Festival of Dedication.

The holiday, which is not a holy day requiring fasting or praying, has been celebrated continuously for thousands of years by Jews all over the world. It begins on the 25th of the Jewish month of Kislev, which usually falls sometime in the civil month of December, and is celebrated for eight nights to commemorate the eight days during which the oil lasted. The holiday involves worship that is centered more in the home than in the synagogue. People light candles on a menorah, or hanukkiah, adding a new candle for each night. The menorah is an eight-branched candelabra with a ninth holder for a helper candle called shamash. Since the menorah could not be used as the only source of light, and since no candle was to light another, the shamash was used to light each nightly candle. Two blessings are said each night; one is a blessing over the candles, and the other is in remembrance of the miracle of the oil. An extra blessing of thanksgiving is added on the first night. The menorah is displayed prominently in a family's window. Many of the customs and rituals surrounding the holiday relate to oil. The foods prepared for Hanukkah include latkes, or potato pancakes fried in oil, and round donuts, called *sufganiyot,* that are filled with jelly and fried in oil. The

*During the Hanukkah celebration a young boy lights the menorah.*
C. Orrico—SUPERSTOCK

tradition of giving gelt, or Hanukkah coins, to children began in Europe in the Middle Ages.

Occasionally the gelt is used to create a pot for a game of dreidel. The dreidel is a spinning top with a different letter on each of its four sides. The letters are the first initials of the words in the phrase *nes gadol haya sham,* meaning "a great miracle happened there." Children and parents play the game until someone wins all of the gelt. In modern Israel the letters of the dreidel were changed to reflect the translation "a great miracle happened here." The dreidel is called *sevivon* in Hebrew.

In contemporary Israel Hanukkah is a national holiday, and students present plays, sing holiday songs, and have parties. Schools are closed, and menorahs are displayed atop such prominent buildings as the Israeli parliament, or Knesset. The highlight of the eight-day festival is an annual relay race from Modi'in to Jerusalem. Runners carry burning torches through the streets beginning in Modi'in. The runners continue until the final torchbearer arrives at the Western Wall, which is the last remnant of the Temple. The torchbearer hands the torch to the chief rabbi, who uses it to light the first candle of a giant menorah.

In countries where Christmas rituals are widespread, some echoes of those rituals appear in Hanukkah celebrations. Some families, for example, exchange gifts or decorate their homes. The word Hanukkah in Hebrew also means "education," and rabbis and Jewish educators try to instill in their congregants and students the notion that the holiday celebrates Jewish continuity. They teach that Mattathias and his sons had stood up to their oppressors and that modern Jews must also insist on Jewish continuity.

### FURTHER RESOURCES FOR HANUKKAH

**Corwin, J.H.** Hanukkah Crafts (Watts, 1996).

**Goodman, Philip, comp.** The Hanukkah Anthology (Jewish Publication Society, 1992).

**Kimmel, Eric.** A Hanukkah Treasury (Holt, 1997).

**Koralek, Jenny.** Hanukkah, The Festival of Lights (Lothrup, 1990).

**O'Hare, Jeff.** Hanukkah, Happy Hanukkah: Crafts, Recipes, Games, Puzzles, Songs, and More for a Joyous Celebration of the Festival of Lights (Boyds Mills, 1994).

**Simon, Norma.** The Story of Hanukkah (HarperCollins, 1997).

**HAPSBURG, HOUSE OF.** Atop the 1,682-foot- (513-meter-) high Wülpelsberg, a mountain near Aarau in northern Switzerland, stands the ruins of the Habichtsburg, or Hawk's Castle. This castle, built in 1020, was the original seat of the famous Hapsburg (or Habsburg) family. Members of this family ruled Austria from 1278 to the end of World War I.

With only one exception, Charles VII, who ruled from 1742 to 1745, all the rulers of the Holy Roman Empire from 1438 until the abolition of the empire in 1806 were members of the House of Hapsburg. One of these rulers, Emperor Charles V (1519–56), a Hapsburg by descent on his father's side, was also king of Spain as Charles I (*see* Charles V; Holy Roman Empire).

Before his death, Charles V divided his dominions between his brother and his son, creating two Hapsburg houses. One of these houses ruled Spain until the extinction of that line in 1700; the other house continued to rule Austria.

A full lower lip and a long pointed chin—the famous "Hapsburg chin"—were family features inherited from a Bohemian princess who married into the House of Hapsburg in the 15th century. (*See also* Austria-Hungary; Vienna, Austria.)

**HARARE, Zimbabwe.** Formerly known as Salisbury, Rhodesia, Harare is the capital and largest city of Zimbabwe in southeastern Africa. At an altitude of 4,865 feet (1,483 meters), Harare has a pleasant climate with annual average temperatures of 64° F (18° C) and 30 inches (76 centimeters) of rainfall. It is located in the northeastern part of the country and is a modern, well-planned city with high-rise buildings, wide tree-lined avenues, and many parks.

Harare is Zimbabwe's commercial, financial, industrial, and transportation center. Its major

**The Stanley Street Travel Centre is one of the newer government buildings in Harare, Zimbabwe. The city's name was changed from Salisbury in 1982.**
Dennis Cox—Tony Stone Worldwide

industries include food processing, metal products, textiles, automobile assembly, chemicals, paper, fertilizers, and Virginia tobacco products. Harare is the center of the country's tobacco industry with one of the largest single tobacco markets in the world. Corn, tobacco, cotton, dairy products, and fruits are produced in the surrounding farmlands. There also are a few gold mines in the vicinity. Harare is linked by railways with the ports of Beira and Maputo in Mozambique.

Almost three fourths of the population are of African origin, but there are large white and small Asian communities. Harare's major points of interest include the Queen Victoria Memorial Library and Museum, the National Archives, the University of Zimbabwe, and the Rhodes National Gallery.

Founded in 1890, the city was originally named for the then British prime minister, Robert Cecil, the third marquis of Salisbury. Created a municipality in 1897, it was chartered as a city in 1935. Salisbury was the capital of the self-governing colony of Southern Rhodesia from 1923, the Federation of Rhodesia and Nyasaland (1953–63), and Rhodesia (1965–79). The independent country of Zimbabwe retained it as its capital and in 1982 renamed it Harare after the local African chief Neharawe. Population (1999 estimate), 1,686,000.

**HARBIN, China.** The largest city and capital of Heilongjiang Province in the northeastern part of China known in the West as Manchuria, Harbin is situated on the south bank of the Songhua River. It has a subtemperate continental climate with mean annual temperatures of 38° F (3.3° C) and annual rainfall of 21 inches (53 centimeters).

Harbin is one of the leading transportation and industrial centers of northeastern China. Its modern industries include electrical machinery, electronic instruments, chemicals, paper, machine tools, agricultural and mining equipment, and boilers. Its traditional food-processing industries are soybean and flour mills and sugar refineries. Wheat, soybeans, sugar beets, corn, and flax are grown in surrounding areas. Harbin is linked by air with Beijing, Shenyang, and Shanghai. It also has good road, waterway, and rail connections. It is the seat of Harbin Shipbuilding Engineering College and Harbin University of Science and Technology. There are several theaters, hospitals, and libraries in the city.

Recorded history of Harbin dates back to 1097. A small fishing village before 1896, it grew with the construction of the Chinese Eastern Railway by the Russians. After the Russo-Japanese War in 1904–05, Harbin was jointly administered by China and Japan. It was a haven for Russian refugees after the Revolution of 1917 and became for a time the largest Russian city outside the Soviet Union. During the time Japan dominated Manchuria, calling it Manchukuo from 1932 to 1945, Harbin was known as Pinkiang. Soviet troops occupied the city in 1945, and the following year Chinese Communist forces gained control. Population (1999 estimate), 2,586,978.

*A man-made coastal breakwater shelters the small harbor at Nice, France, from stormy seas.*
Ric Ergenbright

**HARBORS AND PORTS.** The chief doorways of the world of international commerce are its harbors and ports. Through them pass cargoes and travelers from one part of the globe to another. A harbor is any sheltered body of water where boats or ships may moor or anchor. A port is an installation that has been built around a harbor with facilities for loading and unloading such vessels.

Ordinarily a harbor, either natural or man-made, must exist before a port facility can be set up. Some large harbors—San Francisco Bay on the California coast, for example—are used by several ports. Some ports, such as Chicago, Ill., on Lake Michigan, are served by several small harbors.

The major requirements of a good harbor are direct access to the open water and sufficient depth for vessels to enter and exit safely. Ocean harbors are commonly 40 feet deep or more. The harbor should be well protected against storms and large waves. The bottom of the harbor should provide good holding ground for anchors—it must not be too rocky, too sandy, or too muddy. The harbor should also be spacious enough for ships to ride at anchor and to maneuver. Currents and tides must not be excessive.

### Types of Harbors

Harbors are classified according to their location and structure. A natural coastal harbor is formed by a bay (New York City, for example) or by an offshore barrier such as an island (Hong Kong, China). A coastal breakwater harbor (Casablanca, Morocco) is sheltered by one or more man-made breakwaters. A tide gate harbor has locks that enclose areas of the harbor at high tide. As water leaves the harbor with low tide, the water level in the locked-off areas remains constant. At the port of Liverpool, England, tide gates

are a necessity, for the tidal range of its harbor is approximately 21 feet.

A natural river harbor (New Orleans, La.) is sheltered from storms by virtue of the narrowness of the river. A river basin harbor (Rotterdam, The Netherlands) has slips dug into the riverbanks to accommodate vessels. A lake harbor or canal harbor (Brugge, Belgium) is on a small lake or an artificial canal that is connected with the open water by means of a navigable waterway. An open roadstead harbor offers little protection from storms, though it may serve as a port. Many harbors of this type are found along the coasts of Africa.

### The Parts and Structures of a Harbor

Breakwaters are massive, wall-like structures that partially enclose a harbor, protecting it from waves and currents. They may provide a harbor's total shelter or supplement protection present in the natural state. Breakwaters are made of stone, concrete, or rubble. Jetties, less substantial than breakwaters, are found within a harbor and are used to contain currents or to control the deposit of sediment. They are often made of timber, steel sheeting, or concrete.

Harbor channels are marked with buoys. These are floating objects moored to the bottom. The anchorage is that part of a harbor in which ships lie at anchor. Many narrow harbors, particularly those on rivers, have turning basins in which ships are turned around.

### Types of Ports

Ports are classified according to the types of traffic which they handle. An industrial port specializes in bulk cargo—grain, sugar, ore, oil, chemicals, and similar materials. A commercial port is one which handles general cargo—packaged products and

*Container loaders along the huge port at Elizabeth, N.J., load and unload the container ships speedily so the cargo can be on its way.*
Bob Krist—Black Star

manufactured goods, for instance—as well as passenger traffic. Comprehensive ports handle bulk and general cargo in large volume. Most of the world's great ports are classified as comprehensive.

### Where Ports Develop

The development of a harbor into an economically thriving port depends upon several basic conditions. The contiguous land areas should be suitable for piers, wharves, loading and unloading facilities, and warehouses. The surrounding region should be geographically favorable to the development of a population center and supporting industries, such as railroads and ship repair. There should be an accessible interior which furnishes products for export and provides a market for imports.

River dredging and canal construction have made inland cities into seaports. Manchester, England, is connected with the sea by the Mersey River and by a 35-mile canal, so steamers may unload cargoes directly into the city's mills. Hamburg, Germany, 75 miles from the North Sea, is a major port because continuous dredging has deepened the Elbe River channel. Houston, Tex., is linked with the Gulf of Mexico by means of a ship canal.

Chicago, whose port is used mainly for Great Lakes shipping, also handles cargo via a dredged tributary to the Mississippi River. The completion of the St. Lawrence Seaway in 1959 made every port on the Great Lakes available to oceangoing vessels. This was made possible by dredging shallow sections of the waterway to a minimum depth of 27 feet. (*See also* Great Lakes; Saint Lawrence River.)

### Cargo Handling; Repair Facilities

When a ship reaches port, it may be assigned a berth, which is a mooring space along a wharf or a pier. A wharf—sometimes called a quay (pronounced *kē*)—lies parallel to the shore. A pier projects lengthwise into the harbor.

Solid bulk cargoes, such as coal and limestone, are generally loaded from shoreside stockpiles to ships by means of conveyor belts. Iron ore is usually loaded from ore docks. These are elevated railways with chutes which drop the ore into the holds of waiting ships. Grain is loaded through chutes from dockside or from floating elevators. The unloading of solid bulk cargoes is often done with mechanized shovels or by conveyor systems. Large "vacuum cleaners" are frequently used to unload grain, copra, and similar bulk cargoes. Liquid bulk cargoes are pumped through hose between shoreside storage tanks and ships.

Transit sheds on a pier or wharf provide storage for general cargo. The men who do the work of loading or unloading general cargo are called longshoremen or stevedores. General cargo is usually handled by means of winches on the ship's deck. Items of cargo that weigh hundreds of tons, however, are customarily handled by means of a dockside crane or by a crane floated on a barge next to the ship. Dockside gantry cranes transfer semitrailer-size cargo containers to and from container ships.

Ports situated on open roadstead harbors are often too shallow to permit oceangoing ships to reach shoreside installations. The transfer of cargo and passengers to and from such ships must be done by means of shallow-draft lighters, which shuttle back and forth to shore. Some ports have been constructed on artificial islands supported on stilts.

All large ports have dry docks and other facilities for repairing ships. Dry docks are of two types—graving docks and floating dry docks. A graving dock is a concrete basin that can be closed

with watertight gates after a ship has entered. The water is pumped out or allowed to run out with the tide, the ship being held upright by timbers. This facilitates the repair of parts of the vessel that are normally underwater. A floating dry dock is mobile. It can be submerged or raised by increasing or decreasing the amount of water within its hollow side walls, and it can be taken wherever it is needed—across oceans if necessary.

### Planning, Maintenance, and Operation

The planning of harbors and ports, whether for transportation, reclamation, or conservancy, has recently included the use of model studies. Once regarded as scientific toys, scale models of harbors, ports, and the surrounding areas are in many instances essential to any large-scale redevelopment of a coastal area and are useful even for minor modifications or additions. These models are made so that water can be caused to flow in such a way as to reproduce the various tidal and wave effects of the existing coastal system.

In the United States, harbor maintenance and the operation of port facilities are the responsibilities of several federal and local government agencies. The port authority assigns berthing and anchorage space to ships. It also operates cargo and passenger terminals. Some large harbors that include the port facilities of several municipalities are under the jurisdiction of a single port authority. The Port Authority of New York and New Jersey is an example.

### The World's Greatest Ports

Rotterdam is the world's busiest port. The city's center was devastated by German and Allied bombing during World War II. Its development was favored by its commercially strategic location on the Rhine River delta—some 15 miles from the North Sea.

Today most cargo entering Rotterdam from the sea—by way of a ship canal—passes on to Europe's interior. Much of the city's industry centers upon petroleum, which constitutes about half of Rotterdam's imports. Other major imports are iron ore, coal, and wheat. Exports include manufactured goods and chemical products.

In the 1950s a complex of port installations and related industrial facilities—known collectively as the Botlek—was set up to handle the growing needs of the European Economic Community as well as of The Netherlands itself. Today a much larger complex, called Europoort, consists of industrial sites and harbor basins. It handles chiefly vessels too large to reach Rotterdam, including oil tankers and iron ore bulk carriers. (*See also* Rotterdam.)

Once the busiest port in the world, the Port of New York remains one of the major ports of the Western Hemisphere. It is located at the mouth of the Hudson River in New York City and is the largest port in the United States, handling about one tenth of all of the country's imports. It is also one of the best natural harbors in the world. It is deep and well sheltered, and the rise and fall of the tide is relatively small. In addition, it can accommodate an almost unlimited amount of traffic.

The Port of New York encompasses all waterways and port facilities within a 25-mile radius of the Statue of Liberty. The port's total frontage along navigable waters is 751 miles. There are more than 250 berths for deep-draft general cargo vessels. In one year nearly 100 million tons of coastal and foreign cargo are handled. Foreign-trade cargo predominates.

Courtesy of Europoort, Rotterdam and Netherlands Consulate General

*Rotterdam in The Netherlands is the world's largest and busiest seaport, as well as a transshipment port for Europe.*

The Port Authority of New York has jurisdiction over marine cargo terminals, marine passenger terminals, heliports, and four airports: John F. Kennedy International Airport and LaGuardia Airport in New York and Newark Airport and Teterboro Airport in New Jersey. (*See also* New York, N.Y.)

On the East coast of the United States other major ports are Hampton Roads, Va.; Baltimore, Md.; and Philadelphia, Pa. The significant ports on the Gulf coast are New Orleans, La., and Houston, Tex. The two chief ports on the Pacific coast are Oakland and Los Angeles, Calif. The busiest ports on the Great Lakes are Chicago; Detroit, Mich.; Toledo, Ohio; and Duluth, Minn.-Superior, Wis.

Canada's chief Pacific seaport in terms of traffic and cargo turnover is Vancouver, B.C. Its most significant ports on the Atlantic coast are Montreal, Que., and Halifax, N.S. On the Great Lakes, Toronto and Thunder Bay, Ont., handle large amounts of tonnage annually.

London, England, which for years had been Europe's leading seaport, continues to rank as one of the world's foremost shipping centers. Milford-Haven and Southampton are also among the world's leading seaports. Hamburg and Bremen, Germany, are not far behind Rotterdam as European centers of waterborne commerce.

The two leading ports of South America, in terms of cargo turnover, are located in Argentina—Santos and Buenos Aires. Asia's major ports include Hong Kong; Singapore; and Chiba and Yokohama, Japan. Africa's port with high-tonnage turnover is Casablanca, Morocco. (*See also* Ship and Shipping.)

U.S. Army Engineer Waterways Experiment Station

*A working scale model of New York Harbor has been constructed by the United States Army Corps of Engineers. It is used by the staff of the Waterways Experiment Station. Tidal currents, water salinity, and silting are mechanically reproduced to study the long-term effects on the harbor.*

Bettmann Archive

*29th President of the United States
(1865–1923; president 1921–23)*

# WARREN G. HARDING

"Back to normalcy" was the campaign slogan of Warren G. Harding, 29th president of the United States. War-weary American voters of 1920 liked the idea so much that they elected this Ohio newspaper publisher by a plurality of 7 million votes. Harding died Aug. 2, 1923, before his term ended, but his conservative policies were followed by other Republican presidents during the prosperous 1920s.

## Growing Up in Ohio

Born in the village of Corsica, later Blooming Grove, Ohio, Nov. 2, 1865, Warren G. Harding was the eldest of eight children of George Tryon and Phoebe Dickerson Harding. The growing family had a hard time making ends meet in the trying days following the Civil War. The father worked as a farmer, a country doctor, and a general "trader."

Warren grew into a strapping, big-boned, handsome youth. He learned the chores of the pioneer farm—felling trees, splitting rails, chopping wood, planting and harvesting crops. When his father traded for an interest in a village newspaper, the lad taught himself typesetting.

## Schooling and Early Career

He started school in a little red schoolhouse in Caledonia, Ohio. When he was 14 he went to an academy in Iberia, called Ohio Central College. Though he had to drop out to earn money, he was graduated in 1882. A popular student, he edited the yearbook, played an alto horn, and entered speaking contests.

Warren also played his alto horn in the town band in Caledonia and later in Marion, Ohio, where his family moved. He became manager of the Marion Citizens' Cornet Band. The story goes that he was so eager to lead the band in contests at county fairs that he plunged it into debt to buy uniforms. The investment proved a good one, for the Marion band won third prize in a state band festival in competition with units from Ohio's large cities. The $200 award paid off the debt. Warren also played substitute first base on the town baseball team and joined in the other sports and amusements of a small town.

Like many another 19th-century statesman, he began his career by teaching school for a term. He later called it the hardest job he ever had. In Marion he tried his hand at reading law and selling insurance. He was only 19 when he found his life's calling—newspaper work. Politics lost him his first job as a reporter on the *Mirror,* a Democrat weekly paper. Warren was already a strong Republican. As a supporter of the "plumed knight," James G. Blaine, in the 1884 campaign, he dared to wear a Blaine campaign hat to work.

## Harding Buys the 'Marion Star'

Within a few weeks, however, young Harding had become a publisher. A bankrupt daily paper, the *Marion Star,* was available to anyone who could pay the sheriff $300 and take over the mortgage. Warren persuaded two young friends to invest in the project and borrowed his own share from his recent employer, the publisher of the *Mirror.*

The survival of the daily, with its broken equipment, scanty advertising, and 10-cents-a-week subscription price, has been called a "minor miracle." Warren at times did every task around the office from washing the inky rollers to writing editorials and selling printing and advertising. He pioneered in selling advertising as a business builder. His political activities helped increase revenues from official printing and advertising. As Marion grew, the fortunes of the *Star* improved. Harding was an enthusiastic Marion booster—active in all moves to bring in new industries that would increase population.

## Marriage to Florence Kling De Wolfe

On July 8, 1891, Warren married Florence Kling De Wolfe, divorced daughter of a Marion banker. Mrs. Harding's business ability and ambition proved

## Time Line of Presidents, Events, and Periods

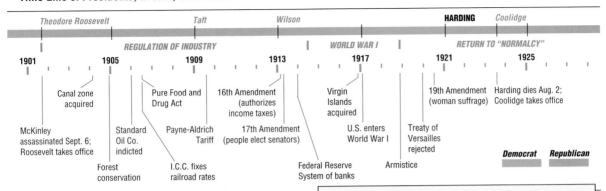

Theodore Roosevelt | Taft | Wilson | **HARDING** | Coolidge

REGULATION OF INDUSTRY | WORLD WAR I | RETURN TO "NORMALCY"

1901 | 1905 | 1909 | 1913 | 1917 | 1921 | 1925

Canal zone acquired

Pure Food and Drug Act

16th Amendment (authorizes income taxes)

Virgin Islands acquired

19th Amendment (woman suffrage)

Harding dies Aug. 2; Coolidge takes office

McKinley assassinated Sept. 6; Roosevelt takes office

Standard Oil Co. indicted

Payne-Aldrich Tariff

17th Amendment (people elect senators)

U.S. enters World War I

Treaty of Versailles rejected

**Democrat** | **Republican**

Forest conservation

I.C.C. fixes railroad rates

Federal Reserve System of banks

Armistice

Ohio Historical Society

*Harding stands in the composing room of the* **Marion Star.** *He enjoyed every phase of newspaper work. As president, he still carried his printer's rule as a lucky piece.*

### HARDING'S ADMINISTRATION 1921–23

Budget Bureau established.
Bill restricting immigration passed.
Peace with Germany and Austria declared (July 2, 1921).
Washington Conference on Limitation of Naval Armaments.
Fordney-McCumber Tariff Act restores high protection (1922).
Republicans lose 14 seats in the Senate and 150 in House.
President Harding dies (1923).

important factors in her husband's success. She went to his office to help while he was ill. She stayed to take charge of the circulation department and other aspects of business management. The *Star* prospered and her husband had time for politics.

Young Harding enjoyed practicing his oratory at county political meetings. (He later coined the word "bloviate" for the rousing, "flag-waving" public speaking common in his youth.) At one of these rallies, when Harding was only 35, he met Harry M. Daugherty, a Columbus lawyer and political leader. Daugherty's enthusiastic support later was to take Harding to the White House.

In 1898 Harding was elected to the state senate. His party loyalty and his ability to get party agreement on

programs gained him popularity. He became lieutenant governor in 1904 but met defeat when he ran for governor in 1910. In 1914 he was elected United States senator from Ohio.

### A Popular Senator

In Congress he quickly gained popularity. He was placed on important committees. He voted for the two constitutional amendments of the period—the 18th, or Prohibition, Amendment, and the 19th, giving women the right to vote. On domestic issues he usually voted according to Republican policy. After America entered World War I he voted to give special war powers to the Democratic president, Woodrow Wilson.

After the war, President Wilson asked for ratification of the Treaty of Versailles. Harding allied himself with the "strict reservationist" group of the Republican senatorial majority. The treaty included the Covenant of the League of Nations, which these senators held would limit national sovereignty. They proposed reservation after reservation and finally defeated the treaty on Nov. 19, 1919 (*see* Wilson, Woodrow; World War I, "The Peace and Its Results").

### Nomination and Election as President

In 1920 Americans were upset by the restrictions, sacrifices, idealism, and disappointments of the war years. Business, though enjoying high profits, wanted relief from war regulations and high taxes. Labor held that its wartime gains had been wiped out by the mounting cost of living.

A business decline came in the spring of 1920. It brought unemployment and the collapse of farm prosperity. The people blamed their troubles on Wilson and the Democrats.

## Major World Events During Harding's Administration

**Soviet Union.** *Constitution adopted, 1923*

**England, United States, Japan.** *5–5–3 naval ratio treaty adopted at Washington conference, 1921*

**The Hague.** *Permanent Court of International Justice established, 1922*

**Colombia-Panama.** *Treaty ratified giving Colombia $25,000,000, 1921*

**Austria, Germany, United States.** *Peace treaties ratified, 1921*

**Italy.** *Mussolini granted dictatorial powers, 1922*

Brown Brothers

**Harding speaks to a crowd from his front porch in Marion, Ohio, during his presidential campaign in 1920.**

Republican senators felt that Wilson had extended the power of the presidency at the expense of the legislative branch. They wanted one of their own men in office. Although Harding had never gained much voter support, he felt his plea for a "return to normalcy" for the country would make him a favorable candidate. Harding announced his candidacy for president, with Harry Daugherty as his campaign manager. At the Republican nominating convention in Chicago, neither of the chief candidates, Gen. Leonard Wood or Governor Frank O. Lowden of Illinois, could gain a majority. Leaders met and selected Harding as their compromise candidate. He was nominated on the next ballot. Governor Calvin Coolidge of Massachusetts was selected as the vice-presidential candidate. The Democrats nominated Governor James M. Cox of Ohio for president and Franklin D. Roosevelt of New York for vice-president. On Nov. 2, 1920, Harding was elected president.

In Washington the Hardings opened the gates of the White House, locked since before the war. They welcomed their friends and well-wishers. Harding followed as many of his hobbies and interests as he could. He was an enthusiastic golfer and he also enjoyed boxing, motoring, fishing, baseball, and card playing. The Hardings had no children.

### Legislative Program and Cabinet

After his inauguration, the new president called a special session of Congress and recommended a conservative program. It included strict government economy, the creation of a federal budget system, higher tariffs, tax reduction, restriction of immigration, and aid to veterans and farmers. A cooperative Congress quickly passed a joint resolution declaring World War I officially ended. Other legislation included the budget and accounting bill and a temporary tariff bill. The Fordney-McCumber Act of 1922, with the highest tariffs in history, and an immigration restriction bill, setting a quota for aliens from each country, were also passed (*see* Migration of People).

Harding's administration was also responsible for the Washington Conference of 1922, at which treaties limiting and reducing naval strengths among world powers were negotiated. Congress adopted a liberal program of care for disabled veterans, but when it passed a soldier's bonus bill, Harding vetoed it on economic grounds. His chief service to labor occurred when he personally induced "big steel" to drop the 12-hour day.

Harding's Cabinet was a mixture of distinguished men and personal or political friends. He had great and unquestioning confidence in them all. The chief accomplishments of his term reflected the leadership of Charles E. Hughes, secretary of state; Andrew Mellon, secretary of the treasury; and Herbert Hoover, secretary of commerce.

### Foreign and Economic Affairs

Hughes presided at the Washington Conference on Limitation of Naval Armaments, which Harding called for Nov. 12, 1921. The principal naval powers invited were Great Britain, France, Italy, and Japan. Invitations

**Warren Harding was an ardent golfer, and he was on the course as often as possible in the typical golfing attire of the 1920s.**

also went to China, Belgium, Portugal, and The Netherlands. Hughes boldly proposed that there should be a naval building holiday for ten years. He also proposed that several United States, British, and Japanese ships should be scrapped and that the ratio in capital ships power between these nations should be 5-5-3 respectively. The Hughes program was largely adopted. Other treaties provided for the maintenance of China's territorial integrity and sovereignty and the principle of the "open door." Japan agreed to withdraw from Shantung.

Under Secretary Mellon both the national debt and federal tax rates were reduced. Congress, however, refused to cut taxes on high incomes as much as Mellon requested.

**Oil Leases and Other Scandals**

Harding's faith in certain appointees proved misplaced. He named Albert B. Fall, a former senatorial associate, secretary of the interior. Fall induced Edwin Denby, secretary of the Navy, to transfer naval oil reserves to the control of the interior department. Harding signed the executive order making the transfer. Fall then leased drilling rights in the Elk Hills, Calif., and Teapot Dome, Wyo., reserves to friends who were oil promoters. When a senatorial committee investigated the transaction it appeared that he had received large "loans" and blocks of Liberty Bonds from the lessors. In the meantime Fall had resigned from the Cabinet. He was later prosecuted and, after long delay, convicted for his part in the affair. He served nine months in prison. The leases were canceled in 1927.

Other scandals arose regarding graft by the Alien Property custodian and the director of the Veterans' Bureau. Harding's friend Attorney General Daugherty resigned and was tried on charges of corruption.

President Harding was spared the pain of most of these revelations. Early in 1923 he had a severe attack of influenza, followed by other disorders. His wife's health was also poor. Harding was concerned over the Republican loss of seats in both houses of Congress in the 1922 election. He decided that a speaking tour would be helpful alike to his health and to his popularity. Accompanied by his wife and a party of 65, he set out on a transcontinental trip that included a visit to Alaska. Instead of helping him relax, the trip exhausted him. He became ill in Seattle and was taken to San Francisco, where he died on August 2 under somewhat mysterious circumstances. Calvin Coolidge became president (*see* Coolidge). Mrs. Harding immediately returned to Washington and burned all of Harding's papers.

Harding had been a popular president, and he was deeply mourned. He was buried in a memorial tomb erected in Marion by public gifts. (For Harding's Cabinet and Supreme Court appointments *see* Fact-Index.)

**FURTHER RESOURCES FOR WARREN G. HARDING**

**Kane, J.N.** Facts About the Presidents: A Compilation of Biographical and Historical Information, 5th ed. (Wilson, 1990).
**Mee, C.L., Jr.** The Ohio Gang: The World of Warren G. Harding (M. Evans, 1981).
**Russell, Francis.** The Shadow of Blooming Grove: Warren G. Harding in his Time (Easton, 1988).
**Wade, L.R.** Warren G. Harding: 29th President of the United States (Childrens, 1989).

**HARDY, Thomas** (1840–1928). Essentially a tragic novelist, Thomas Hardy wrote books that strike many readers as overly gloomy and pessimistic. A great novelist of the Victorian era, Hardy was also an accomplished poet (*see* English Literature).

Hardy was born on June 2, 1840, in Upper Bockhampton, near Dorchester in Dorsetshire, England. He passed most of his long life in this region of woodland, heath, and moor. It forms the setting of most of his writings, under its old name of Wessex. He attended local schools until he was 16, when he became an apprentice in an architect's office in Dorchester. In 1862, Hardy went to London to work as assistant to an architect. He had already begun to write verse and essays.

Hardy returned to Dorchester in 1867 because of ill health and soon began writing prose fiction for a living. His first really successful novel, published serially in 1874, was 'Far from the Madding Crowd'. Others are 'Under the Greenwood Tree' (1872); 'The Return of the Native' (1878); 'Tess of the D'Urbervilles' (1891); and 'Jude the Obscure' (1895). His poetry includes 'Wessex Poems' (1898) and 'Time's Laughing-stocks' (1909). 'The Dynasts' (1903–08) is an epic drama in three parts.

Hardy viewed nature as a real power affecting the lives of his characters. His novels are realistic, but they resemble Greek tragedies in the way they show their characters as helpless victims of an unfeeling fate. Hardy's sympathy for his characters, even when they had done wrong, caused some of his works to be condemned as immoral.

In 1874 Hardy married Emma Lavinia Gifford, who died in 1912. In 1914 he married his secretary, Florence Emily Dugdale. He died in Dorchester on Jan. 11, 1928. His ashes were placed in Westminster Abbey, but his heart, at his request, was buried in Stinsford, near his birthplace.

**HARE** *see* **RABBIT AND HARE.**

**HARE KRISHNA.** In Hinduism Krishna is one of the most widely revered and popular gods (*see* Hinduism). He became the focus of a large number of devotional cults. One of these was inspired by a mystic from Bengal, Caitanya (1485–1533), who worshiped Krishna with ecstatic song and dance. In time Caitanya came to be regarded as an incarnation of Krishna.

In 1965 another Hindu mystic, the swami Prabhupada (A.C. Bhaktivedanta, 1896–1977), arrived in the United States and founded the movement originally called the International Society for Krishna Consciousness. More commonly known as Hare Krishna from the chant its members use, it claims a direct descent from the beliefs and rites of Caitanya. By the time swami Prabhupada died he had published more than 50 books and founded about 100 centers throughout the world.

The general public in North America and Europe became aware of the Hare Krishna movement from seeing its devotees dressed in saffron robes and singing, dancing, or chanting on street corners and in public buildings. They were especially visible in railroad stations and in airports soliciting funds for their organization. Most members are young, and many are alienated youth who came out of the hippie culture of the 1960s. They associated themselves with a highly authoritarian cult that emphasizes enthusiastic religious devotion. Devotees accept a four-caste system, whose positions are determined by ability rather than birth as in the Indian caste system (*see* India, "Caste").

Hare Krishna believes that human beings are souls composed of Krishna's energy and bodies made of the lowest matter. To achieve peace and happiness believers try to return to an original relationship, called Krishna Consciousness, with the god. This is done through a type of yoga called bhakti yoga, which involves recognizing Krishna as a god and doing his work with no thought of reward. All possessions are surrendered to the organization.

Members live in communes in which unmarried men and women live separately in celibacy, while married members have their own quarters. There are prohibitions against gambling, the use of alcohol, and eating meat. Each commune, or temple, has its own officers, and each supports itself by selling the organization's publications.

Culver Pictures

*The spinning jenny invented by Hargreaves could spin eight threads at the same time; it greatly improved the textile industry.*

**HARGREAVES, James** (1730?–78). The obscurity of James Hargreaves's life contrasts sharply with the worldwide influence of his invention, a yarn-spinning machine called the spinning jenny. Almost nothing is known of his life. He was probably born in Blackburn in Lancashire, England. While still a boy, he became a carpenter and spinner in Standhill, a village nearby. At that time Lancashire was the center of England's manufacture of cotton goods. The industry was still confined to workers' homes, however, and the cards, spinning wheels, and looms were operated by hand.

It is said that an accident gave Hargreaves the idea for his spinning jenny. In his crowded cottage, which served him both as home and workshop, he was experimenting with spinning two threads at one time. His experiments were unsuccessful, however, because the horizontal spindles allowed the threads to fly apart and become tangled. After his daughter Jenny overturned the experimental machine and its wheel continued to revolve with the spindles in a vertical position, it occurred to Hargreaves that a machine with spindles in this position might be successful. He proceeded to build a spinning machine, probably in 1764, that would spin eight threads at the same time. He called his new invention a spinning jenny.

The amount of cotton yarn he and his children began to produce alarmed other spinners, who feared that the machine would put them out of work; so they broke into his home and destroyed his machine. In 1768 he moved to the town of Nottingham, where he set up a fairly profitable yarn mill to supply hosiers. In 1770 he patented the spinning jenny. Since he had sold several of his machines, the patent was declared invalid when challenged in court. This left others free to use the invention without paying him royalties.

Before Hargreaves's death on April 22, 1778, in Nottinghamshire, mechanical spinning was fully developed by Richard Arkwright and Samuel Crompton. Later Edmund Cartwright invented the mechanical loom. (*See also* Arkwright; Cartwright; Crompton.)

**HARNESS RACING** *see* **HORSE RACING.**

**HAROLD, Kings of England.** Only two kings of England were named Harold. Both of them reigned before the Norman Conquest, which took place in 1066.

**Harold I** (ruled 1035–1040), called Harefoot, was a son of the Danish king Canute, who ruled Denmark and Norway as well as England (*see* Canute the Great). When Canute died, his rightful heir, Harold's half-brother, Hardecanute, was in Denmark. In his absence Harold was made regent. His brother's delay in returning to England led Harold to claim the English crown in 1037. He died at Oxford on March 17, 1040. On Harold's death, Hardecanute succeeded to the English throne.

**Harold II** (born 1022?, ruled 1066), the last king of the Anglo-Saxon period, reigned for only nine months. He was the son of the powerful Earl Godwine and was himself earl of East Anglia and of Wessex before he was chosen king. Most of the time from 1055 until 1066 was spent in conflict with other claimants to the throne. He first defeated the house of Leofric of Mercia and its allies.

Harold paid at least two visits to the Continent, probably in 1056 and 1062. He fought for William of Normandy against Conan of Brittany. It was at this time he may have taken an oath to support William's claim to the throne of England.

When Edward the Confessor, the king, was dying, he named Harold as his successor. Hardly had Harold come to the throne, in January 1066, before he was compelled to take his army north to face an invading Norwegian force that included his brother. After defeating the Norwegians he soon had to hasten southward to face another invading army under William, duke of Normandy. Harold met William at Hastings and fell on the field of battle. (*See also* William, Kings of England.)

William based his claim to the English throne on the promise he declared he obtained from Harold while Harold was in Normandy in the days of Edward the Confessor. The famous Bayeux tapestry shows Harold taking the oath to support William. One cannot be sure of this incident because the tapestry, which was made by Norman artisans, doubtless presents William's claim in a strong way. (*See also* England, "Norman Conquest (1066)"; Hastings, Battle of.)

**HARP** *see* **STRINGED INSTRUMENTS.**

**HARPERS FERRY, W. Va.** Harpers Ferry is located in the Blue Ridge Mountains on a strip of land at the junction of the Shenandoah and Potomac rivers where West Virginia, Virginia, and Maryland meet. It is famous as the site of John Brown's ill-fated raid on a United States armory, an incident that preceded the outbreak of the American Civil War (*see* Brown, John).

*Harpers Ferry lies at the confluence of the Potomac and Shenandoah rivers in the Blue Ridge Mountains. It is now a quiet residential town.*

Harpers Ferry is now a residential and resort area. The old town has been restored to its 19th-century appearance. The site of the famous raid is now Harpers Ferry National Historical Park. On the former Storer College campus, a college established for freed slaves after the war, is the reconstructed engine house of the armory from which Brown and his men fired their last shots. A visitors' center and museum are in the paymaster's headquarters of the old armory. The National Park Service maintains a training center in Harpers Ferry.

Harpers Ferry was settled in 1734 by Robert Harper, who ran a ferry service across the Potomac. President George Washington chose the site in 1796 for a federal armory because of the area's abundant waterpower.

On the night of Oct. 16, 1859, a small group of armed abolitionists, led by zealot John Brown, seized the armory as part of a plan to form an "army of emancipation" to free slaves. Brown was a militant abolitionist who had witnessed the proslavery attack on Lawrence, Kan., in May 1856. He planned to establish a stronghold for escaped slaves in the Virginia and Maryland mountains. State and federal troops, led by Col. Robert E. Lee, stormed the armory and forced its surrender. Seventeen men, including two of Brown's sons, died in the fighting. Brown survived the battle but was convicted of treason and hanged. Brown became a martyr to the cause of emancipation, and the raid did much to increase tensions.

Harpers Ferry was a strategic location during the American Civil War because of its proximity to a natural pass through the Blue Ridge Mountains. It also served as a key link in the defense of Washington, D.C. Harpers Ferry was repeatedly attacked by both Union and Confederate forces. Confederates under Gen. Stonewall Jackson captured the town in 1862. Railroad tracks were destroyed and reconstructed nine times. The armory never reopened. (*See also* Civil War, American.) The town has a mayor-council form of government. Population (2000 census), 307.

*Brer Rabbit captures Brer Wolf, who is in the chest. The drawing by A.B. Frost is from 'The Awful Fate of Mister Wolf'.*

**HARRIS, Joel Chandler** (1848–1908). Creator of Brer Rabbit, Uncle Remus, and a score of other characters drawn from the experiences of his childhood, Joel Chandler Harris was one of the most popular writers of his time. Based on the folklore of the South before the American Civil War, his stories were eagerly awaited by his readers.

Harris was born on Dec. 9, 1848, in Eatonton, Ga. He lived with his mother, a poor widow, and was able to go to school only because a neighbor paid his way. Harris loved to read and spent hours at the post office and general store reading newspapers. In one paper he read an advertisement from someone looking for a boy to learn the printing business. Harris replied and went to work for Joseph Turner, a publisher and owner of a nearby plantation.

After the war, Harris worked for newspapers in the South. In 1876 he joined the staff of the *Atlanta Constitution,* which published his first Uncle Remus story, "The Wonderful Tar Baby Story," in 1879. Harris's stories were published in several books, including 'Uncle Remus: His Songs and His Sayings' (1880); 'Nights with Uncle Remus' (1883); 'Uncle Remus and His Friends' (1892); and 'Uncle Remus and Brer Rabbit' (1907). Other writings included 'Little Mr. Thimblefinger and His Queer Country' (1894) and the autobiographical 'On the Plantation' (1892). Harris's books owed their great popularity to their humor, their humanity, and the accuracy with which he was able to reproduce the speech, the ideas, and the atmosphere of a special place and time. Harris died in Atlanta on July 3, 1908. His home, near Atlanta, is maintained as a memorial to him.

**HARRISBURG, Pa.** The capital of Pennsylvania, Harrisburg developed from an Indian trading post into a modern transportation and manufacturing center. Harrisburg, stands on the east bank of the Susquehanna River and is the seat of Dauphin County.

The state Capitol, located in a 68-acre (28-hectare) downtown park, has a 272-foot (83-meter) dome modeled after St. Peter's Basilica in Rome. It was built after the first Capitol was destroyed by fire in 1897. The William Penn Memorial Museum and Fort Hunter Museum, the site of an outpost to protect settlers from French and Indian raids, preserve some of the city's early history. Educational facilities include the Capitol campus of Pennsylvania State University, the Pennsylvania State University Center, and Harrisburg Area Community College. Harrisburg is also home to the Milton S. Hershey Medical Center, endowed by the chocolate company founder. The largest chocolate factory in the world is located in nearby Hershey.

Transportation and manufacturing are a large part of Harrisburg's economy. The Pennsylvania and Reading railroads, five national highways, and the Pennsylvania Turnpike run through the city. Harrisburg is also served by domestic and international airports and by trucking terminal facilities. Manufacturers produce steel, clothing, shoes, electronic equipment, and precision and road machinery. The New Cumberland Army Depot, the United States Navy Supply Depot, the United States Army War College, and Fort Indiantown Gap Military Reservation are nearby.

Harrisburg is named for John Harris, an Englishman who settled here in 1718 to trade with the Indians and to run a ferry service for pioneers traveling through the Lebanon and Cumberland valleys. The settlement was first known as Harris's Ferry. His son, John Harris, Jr., had the area laid out in 1785 and named it Louisbourg in honor of Louis XVI. He set aside land for the use of the legislature in the hope that it would become the state's capital. It was later named Harrisburg.

The city prospered as a busy river port when the Pennsylvania Canal opened in 1834. An American Civil War skirmish was fought at Camp Hill, 3 miles (5 kilometers) southwest of Harrisburg, in June 1863. Harrisburg began producing steel soon after the war.

Harrisburg was chosen as the third capital of the Commonwealth of Pennsylvania in 1812 but was not chartered until 1860. (The first and second capitals were Philadelphia and Lancaster.) Harrisburg has a mayor-council form of government. Population (2000 census), 48,950.

Brown Brothers

**23rd President of the United States
(1833–1901); president 1889–93**

# BENJAMIN HARRISON

Nearly half a million people stood in the rain to watch the inauguration of Benjamin Harrison in 1889. This was the nation's centennial inauguration. Just 100 years earlier George Washington had become the first president of the United States.

Some old people in the crowd remembered the inauguration of Benjamin Harrison's grandfather (*see* Harrison, William Henry). "Grandfather's hat fits Ben" was a Republican campaign song. Cartoonists, however, liked to picture the new president in a "grandfather's hat" much too large for him. He was a little man, barely five feet six inches tall.

President Harrison's single term fell between the two terms of Grover Cleveland, a Democrat. Cleveland was popular with the people but unpopular with political leaders. Harrison was popular with neither. There was indeed something of a mystery in his being elected at all. He was serious and dignified, not a hand-shaking politician and not a leader of men.

Benjamin Harrison was born Aug. 20, 1833, in his grandfather's beautiful home at North Bend, Ohio. He was the second son of John Scott Harrison and Elizabeth Irwin Harrison. He was named Benjamin after his great-grandfather, who signed the Declaration of Independence as "Benj. Harrison."

William Henry Harrison had a large estate. He gave 600 acres to John Scott, and soon after Ben's birth the family moved into their own home. Their farm lay between the Ohio and the Miami rivers and was called The Point because it tapered to a point where the two rivers join. The house stood on a bluff facing the Ohio. From the porch Ben could watch flatboats floating downstream carrying pioneer families with their household goods and farm animals.

Ben's father had nine children of his own and adopted two. He hired a governess to teach the young children and a tutor for the older children. Ben cut wood and carried water for the black cook so that the cook would have time to go with him to fish or hunt. In his later years, however, he never cared for sports.

### He Goes to College

When Ben was 14 he went to Farmers' College, near Cincinnati. One of his professors, Dr. John W. Scott, had an attractive young daughter, Caroline (Carrie) Lavinia. When Dr. Scott moved to Oxford, Ohio, Ben decided that Miami College, at Oxford, would be a fine place to continue his education.

At Miami Ben showed skill in debating. Words came easily to him, and his shrill voice and earnest manner commanded attention. He entered Miami as a junior and was graduated the next year (1852), ranking fourth in a class of 16. Before leaving he became secretly engaged to Carrie. Then he went to Cincinnati to read law in the office of a well-known attorney.

### He Marries and Becomes a Lawyer

Ben married Carrie when he was 20. The next year they moved to Indianapolis, Ind. Clients were few for a lawyer who looked like a boy, and Ben earned his first money as a court crier at $2.50 a day. The young couple lived in a boardinghouse until their first child, Russell, was born, in 1854. Then they moved to a three-room cottage. Their second child, Mary, was born in 1858.

At this time the struggle over slavery was dividing the nation. Harrison joined the new Republican party. In 1860 he was elected reporter of the Indiana Supreme Court. When the Civil War broke out, he was working day and night to pay for a new house.

### He Answers the Call to Arms

On July 1, 1862, Lincoln called for more troops. Harrison went to the governor, who asked him to recruit a regiment. On his way back to his office, he bought a military cap and hired a fifer and a drummer. Then he put a flag out of his office window and began recruiting. When the regiment was complete, the governor commissioned him a colonel, and Harrison set off with his troops. By day he drilled his men; at night he studied tactics. Always he looked after his soldiers' needs. They called him Little Ben.

## Time Line of Presidents, Events, and Periods

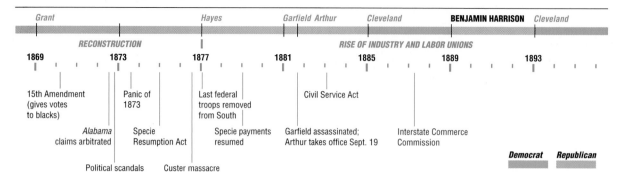

Grant     Hayes     Garfield Arthur     Cleveland     **BENJAMIN HARRISON**   Cleveland

RECONSTRUCTION     RISE OF INDUSTRY AND LABOR UNIONS

1869    1873    1877    1881    1885    1889    1893

15th Amendment (gives votes to blacks)

*Alabama* claims arbitrated

Panic of 1873

Specie Resumption Act

Last federal troops removed from South

Specie payments resumed

Civil Service Act

Garfield assassinated; Arthur takes office Sept. 19

Interstate Commerce Commission

Political scandals    Custer massacre

Democrat    Republican

In the summer of 1864 Harrison was marching into Georgia with General Sherman (*see* Sherman). He fought gallantly in many battles and took part in the siege of Atlanta. Before he was discharged he was breveted a brigadier general of volunteers. Thereafter he was called General Harrison.

### Back to Law and Politics

General Harrison went back to his work at the Supreme Court and his law practice. He also took over again his large Bible class in the Presbyterian church, where his wife taught Sunday school.

In 1876 Harrison ran for governor of Indiana. The Democrats called him "cold as an iceberg" and nicknamed him Kid-Glove Harrison. (Harrison thought it was necessary to wear gloves to guard against infection.) The Democratic candidate, nicknamed Blue Jeans, won the election.

Four years later the Indiana legislature elected Harrison to the United States Senate. He served from 1881 to 1887 and won the good will of veterans by supporting the many private pension bills that came to him.

### He Is Elected President

Great was the confusion in the Republican nominating convention of 1888. Senator James G. Blaine, the leader of the party, had been defeated by Cleveland in 1884 and refused to run against him again. The field was therefore open. Harrison was finally nominated with Blaine's support. Levi P. Morton, a New York banker, was named for vice-president.

Manufacturers gave money to the Republican campaign because they feared Cleveland, who demanded a lower tariff. Cleveland polled about 90,000 more votes than Harrison but lost the election because the Electoral College gave him 168 votes to Harrison's 233 (*see* Electoral College). Harrison appointed Blaine his secretary of state.

### The Harrisons in the White House

Mrs. Harrison, beautiful and gracious, did what she could to make friends for her husband, but congressmen preferred to visit the Blaines. The White

> **BENJAMIN HARRISON'S ADMINISTRATION 1889–93**
>
> McKinley Tariff Act (1890).
> Sherman Anti-Trust Act (1890).
> Sherman Silver Purchase Act (1890).
> Dependent Pension Act (1890).
> North Dakota, South Dakota, Montana, Washington, Wyoming, and Idaho admitted as states (1889–90).
> Territory of Oklahoma opened to settlement (1889).
> First Pan American Conference (1889–90).
> Bering Sea controversy with Great Britain settled (1893).

House was crowded, however, with the Harrisons' own family—Mrs. Harrison's aged father; her niece, Mrs. Mary Scott Lord Dimmick, a young widow; and the Harrisons' daughter Mary (Mrs. McKee), with her husband and two young children. The Harrisons' son Russell made frequent visits.

Congress appropriated $35,000 to have the White House renovated, and Mrs. Harrison spent the money carefully. When the White House was wired for electricity, the Harrisons asked one of the electricians to stay on because they were afraid to turn the lights on and off. The man they selected was Ike Hoover, who remained on the White House staff for 42 years. (*See also* White House.)

### The Billion-Dollar Congress

Harrison kept aloof from Congress and left lawmaking to its leaders. Thomas B. Reed, speaker of the house, won the title of Czar Reed because he pushed through new parliamentary rules to speed up lawmaking. First on his list was the Dependent Pension Act. This provided money for Civil War veterans who had a disability, no matter where or when they got it. Extravagant appropriations were made also for the Navy and for rivers and harbors. The 51st Congress was the first to spend a billion dollars in peacetime. It easily disposed of the large treasury surplus that had troubled earlier administrations.

Six states were admitted to the Union. Four were Western mining states. Congressmen from these Western states wanted more silver dollars coined to raise the price of silver. Congressmen from the East wanted higher tariffs. The two groups agreed to

## Major World Events During Benjamin Harrison's Administration

**Greenland** *proved to be an island by Peary, 1892*

**France and Russia** *form Dual Alliance, 1891*

**Japan.** *Great earthquake, 1891*

**Brazil** *dethrones Dom Pedro, 1889, and proclaims a republic; first constitution, 1891*

Bettmann Archive

**President Harrison, seated, is listening to his secretary of state, James G. Blaine, who shaped many administration policies.**

### Harrison Loses to Cleveland

The Republicans renominated Harrison in 1892. The Democrats nominated Cleveland again. The new People's party, or Populists, put up James B. Weaver of Iowa, who had run and lost as the Greenback party candidate in 1880. The Populists represented farmers in the West. The farmers were suffering from low prices and "tight" money. They wanted cheap money—silver or greenbacks—to raise the prices of their products.

Already there were warnings of the approaching Panic of 1893. Because of the Sherman Silver Purchase Act the government was buying all the silver produced in the United States. Still, the price of silver did not rise because of the large world production. Precious gold was being drained away from the treasury, and cheap silver piled up. People and banks began to hoard gold coins. Foreign investors sent their American bonds back to be sold for gold while the precious metal was still to be had.

Cleveland was elected by a large majority (*see* Cleveland, Grover). Harrison's wife died on October 25, near the end of the campaign. After Cleveland's inauguration Harrison returned to his Indianapolis home to resume his law practice and to write. His excellent book on federal government, 'This Country of Ours' (1897), was widely read.

In 1896 Harrison married Mary Scott Lord Dimmick, who had nursed Carrie through her last illness. By her he had a child, Elizabeth. Harrison died on March 31, 1901, and was buried in Indianapolis, beside the wife of his youth. (For Harrison's Cabinet and Supreme Court appointments *see* Fact-Index.)

support each other. The McKinley Tariff Act raised duties on almost every article that competed with American products, thus making permanent the duties enacted during the Civil War. The Sherman Silver Purchase Act forced the treasury to buy 4½ million ounces of silver each month.

The 51st Congress also passed the Sherman Anti-Trust Act to curb monopolies ( *see* Monopoly and Cartel). No serious attempt was made to enforce this law until the administration of Theodore Roosevelt.

### FURTHER RESOURCES FOR BENJAMIN HARRISON

**Clinton, Susan.** Benjamin Harrison: 23rd President of the United States (Childrens, 1989).

**Kane, J.N.** Facts About the Presidents: A Compilation of Biographical and Historical Information, 5th ed. (Wilson, 1990).

**Sievers, H.J.** Benjamin Harrison (Easton, 1989).

**Socolofsky, H.E., and Spetter, A.B.** The Presidency of Benjamin Harrison (Univ. Press of Kansas, 1987).

**Stevens, Rita.** Benjamin Harrison: 23rd President of the United States (Garrett, 1989).

Gramstorff Brothers

**9th President of the United States**
**(1773–1841; president March 4–April 4, 1841)**

*W. H. Harrison*

# WILLIAM HENRY HARRISON

On March 4, 1841, General William Henry Harrison rode briskly down Pennsylvania Avenue in Washington, D.C., to be inaugurated ninth president of the United States. Slender and slightly stooped, the victor of the battle of Tippecanoe was 68 years old—the oldest man to be elected president in the 19th century. Just one month later, on April 4, he died in the White House—the first president to die in office.

This tragedy, so soon after triumph, was typical of the ups and downs of Harrison's life. Born of a wealthy family, he left home when only 18 years old to make his own way. After a long career in the Army, he suffered political attacks on his skill as a military leader. As a farmer and businessman, he slipped from prosperity to heavy debt. When he was elected president of the United States he was glad to be earning a small salary as county clerk. Yet, through all adversity, he was always a gentleman—kindly, mannerly, and strong with steady courage.

William Henry Harrison was born on Feb. 9, 1773, at Berkeley, the family plantation on the James River in Charles City County, about 20 miles southeast of Richmond, Va. He was the third son of Benjamin Harrison and Elizabeth Bassett Harrison. Benjamin Harrison, a landed aristocrat and governor of Virginia, was usually called "the Signer," because he signed the Declaration of Independence. Young William was educated at home until he attended Hampden-Sydney College in Virginia (1787–90). He then went to Philadelphia to study medicine.

The death of his father in 1791 changed his plans. Under the old Virginia law, most of the handsome Berkeley estate went to his older brothers. Young Harrison decided on an army career. President George Washington appointed him an ensign in the Army, which at that time numbered only one infantry regiment and one artillery battalion.

In Philadelphia the 18-year-old ensign recruited a motley force of 80 men. He marched them afoot through the mountains to the Ohio River, then by flatboats to Fort Washington at Cincinnati—a little settlement of some 30 log cabins. This was Harrison's first post in the vast Northwest Territory—the pioneer land he was to serve for the rest of his life.

### Service on the Frontier

Thrust into the brawling, drinking life of a frontier post, young Harrison had to win the respect of his men. Tall, slim, and gentle-mannered, he seemed younger than his 18 years. He was determined to succeed in the Army, making himself three promises—to be temperate, never be provoked into a duel, and to learn all he could about military science. He was so successful that in just two years he became aide to "Mad Anthony" Wayne (*see* Wayne). In Wayne's campaign against the Indians, Harrison served with distinction at the battle of Fallen Timbers, 1794, thus ending 20 years of border warfare. As a lieutenant, Harrison then commanded Fort Washington.

### Marriage and New Career

While at Fort Washington, he eloped in 1795 with Anna Symmes, 20-year-old daughter of Judge John Cleves Symmes, wealthy landowner at North Bend, near Cincinnati. When the angry judge heard of the marriage, he demanded of Harrison, "How, sir, do you intend to support her?" The young lieutenant answered, "My sword is my means of support, sir!"

The marriage was long and happy despite many periods of debts and scrimping. The Harrisons had ten children—six sons and four daughters. In 1797 Harrison was promoted to captain but resigned in 1798 and settled on a farm at North Bend.

The growing family lived in a four-room log cabin, which Harrison gradually enlarged to 16 rooms covered with clapboard. Through the years the large family was visited almost daily by friends, travelers, territorial officials, and politicians. Harrison's hospitality was so extensive that his table took most of his farm produce, including a ham a day. The expense often drained his income, but he managed to give his sons a college education.

## Time Line of Presidents, Events, and Periods

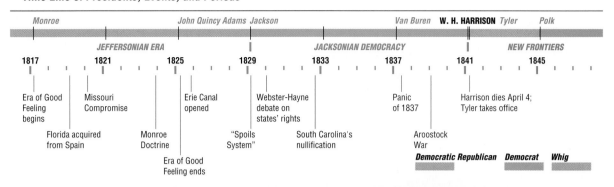

| | | | | | | | |
|---|---|---|---|---|---|---|---|
| Monroe | | John Quincy Adams | Jackson | | Van Buren | W. H. HARRISON | Tyler | Polk |

JEFFERSONIAN ERA      JACKSONIAN DEMOCRACY      NEW FRONTIERS

| 1817 | 1821 | 1825 | 1829 | 1833 | 1837 | 1841 | 1845 |
|---|---|---|---|---|---|---|---|

Era of Good Feeling begins

Missouri Compromise

Florida acquired from Spain

Monroe Doctrine

Erie Canal opened

Era of Good Feeling ends

"Spoils System"

Webster-Hayne debate on states' rights

South Carolina's nullification

Panic of 1837

Aroostock War

Harrison dies April 4; Tyler takes office

**Democratic Republican**    **Democrat**    **Whig**

**This handsome plantation home, the birthplace of William Henry Harrison, was built about 1726. It is a Virginia showplace.**
Charles Phelps Cushing

### Enters Government Work

In June 1798 President John Adams appointed Harrison secretary of the Northwest Territory. In 1799 he was its first delegate to Congress. To aid the people, young Harrison pushed through a bill changing the government's land policy. Formerly the land was sold in huge tracts, which only the wealthy could buy. Harrison's bill put smaller tracts, on easier terms, within reach of settlers with less money.

In 1800, when the Territory was divided into Ohio and Indiana territories, Harrison became governor of Indiana Territory. He also served as superintendent of Indian affairs, with headquarters in Vincennes.

At scores of council fires Harrison made treaties with Indian tribes. He gained millions of acres for settlement in Indiana and Illinois. He sympathized with the Indians, but his duty was to the government. Tecumseh, a chief of the Shawnee Indians, claimed that the land cessions were not valid until all the tribes agreed (see Tecumseh). The result was an Indian war, in which Harrison defeated the Indians at Tippecanoe River, near Lafayette, Ind., in 1811. This victory

brought national acclaim to Harrison and the admiring nickname Old Tippecanoe.

In the War of 1812 Harrison, appointed a brigadier general, commanded all forces in the Northwest. After Commodore Perry's victory on Lake Erie, Harrison took the offensive. Relieving British-held Detroit, he led his army into Canada. In the battle of the Thames, Oct. 5, 1813, he defeated the British, ending the war in Upper Canada. (See also War of 1812.)

### Congress and the Presidency

In 1814 Harrison resigned his commission as general. He farmed in North Bend but also undertook several disastrous business ventures. He was, however, enormously popular in Ohio and was elected successively to Congress, the state Senate, and United States Senate. In 1828–29 he was minister to Colombia.

In 1836 the Whigs nominated him for the presidency, but he lost to Van Buren (see Van Buren). The Whigs again nominated him in 1840; John Tyler of Virginia was named the vice-presidential candidate.

The campaign, based on the slogan "Tippecanoe and Tyler too," was like a giant carnival. The Whigs

*Harrison, mounted on a dark horse (top), turns to call up more of his troops in an assault on the Shawnee Indians, led by Tecumseh and his brother, the "Prophet" (in white buckskin), who shouts defiance. The Whigs in 1840 (bottom) used hard cider and log cabins as symbols to contrast with Van Buren's wealth.*

promised "better days for everyone" in the wake of the severe recession of 1837, and Harrison won 234 electoral votes to Van Buren's 60.

The strain of the campaign, however, and the pressure of office seekers were too great for the aging Harrison. He died of pneumonia on April 4, 1841. (For Harrison's Cabinet and Supreme Court appointments *see* Fact-Index.)

---

### FURTHER RESOURCES FOR WILLIAM HENRY HARRISON

**Fitz-Gerald, C.M.** William Henry Harrison: 9th President of the United States (Childrens, 1987).

**Kane, J.N.** Facts About the Presidents: A Compilation of Biographical and Historical Information, 5th ed. (Wilson, 1990).

**Peterson, N.L.** The Presidencies of William Henry Harrison and John Tyler (Univ. Press of Kansas, 1989).

*Bret Harte*

**HARTE, Bret** (1836–1902). Originator of the American local-color story, Bret Harte wrote of the lawless, burly life of early California mining camps. Known for his stories of the American West, he grew up in the East and spent his last years in England.

Francis Brett Harte was born in Albany, N.Y., on Aug. 25, 1836. In 1854 he went to California, where he worked at various jobs, teaching, mining, and setting type. In 1860 he took a job with a San Francisco newspaper and published the first of his sketches. As editor of the *Overland Monthly,* he wrote his most famous stories, "The Luck of Roaring Camp," published in 1868, and "The Outcasts of Poker Flat," a year later. Other stories include "The Twins of Table Mountain" (1879) and "Ingénue of the Sierras" (1893). A comic poem, 'Plain Language from Truthful James' (1870) is also known as 'The Heathen Chinee'.

Bret Harte returned to the East in 1871 a famous man. *The Atlantic Monthly* paid him a large sum of money to write for them for a year, but Harte soon ran out of fresh ideas. He lectured for a time on California life and then served as consul, first in Crefeld, Germany, and later in Glasgow, Scotland. After 1885 he lived in England. He died in London on May 5, 1902.

**HARTFORD, Conn.** One of the chief cities of New England, Hartford is the capital and the second largest city of Connecticut. Many insurance firms have their headquarters here, and Hartford is often called Insurance City.

Standing at the head of navigation on the Connecticut River, Hartford developed into a trade center and shipping port in colonial days. Its bankers wrote marine insurance. The first Hartford fire-insurance policy was issued in 1794. During the War of 1812, which hampered shipping, companies were established to handle other types of insurance. Today the many factories in the Hartford area manufacture a wide range of products, including aircraft and electrical equipment and tools. In the 19th century several Hartford men, notably the firearms inventor Samuel Colt, experimented with interchangeable-parts manufacture and mass-production methods. Their efforts helped make the city a center for precision articles.

Opposite the marble and granite Capitol is the Museum of Connecticut History, which houses many items of historical interest. The Wadsworth Atheneum, opened in 1844, is the oldest public art museum in the United States. Constitution Plaza, the city's nationally known urban renewal project, was completed in 1964.

The city is the seat of Hartford Seminary Foundation, Trinity College, and Hartford College for Women. The University of Hartford is in West Hartford.

Four years after Hartford's founding in 1635, delegates from the river towns met here and adopted a constitution known as the Fundamental Orders of Connecticut. In 1662 considerable autonomy was given to the colony through a charter granted by England's King Charles II. When Governor Edmund Andros in 1687 demanded that the charter be given up, it was hidden in an oak tree. A Charter Oak Avenue monument marks the historic tree's site. Hartford became the capital of Connecticut Colony in 1665. It was the joint capital with New Haven beginning in 1701. In 1875 Hartford became the sole state capital. Hartford has a council-manager form of government. Population (2000 census), 121,578.

**HARUN AR-RASHID** (766?–809). The fifth caliph of Baghdad's 'Abbasid Dynasty has been forever memorialized in one of the world's literary masterpieces, 'The Thousand and One Nights' (*see* 'Arabian Nights'). Harun ar-Rashid (also spelled al-Raschid) was neither a great nor a good ruler. His fame rests on the opulent luxury of his court and his lavish patronage of the arts.

Harun was born in about 766 in Rayy, Iran. His father, al-Mahdi, was the third 'Abbasid caliph and his mother, al-Khayzuran, was a former slave. His tutor was Yahya the Barmakid. His mother and tutor exerted a powerful influence on Harun and on the empire throughout most of his life. As early as age 14, Harun was given military commands against the Byzantine Empire, though military decisions were usually made by older men. After a successful expedition in 782 he was given the title ar-Rashid, meaning "the rightly guided one." He was named second in succession to the throne and was made governor of Tunisia, Egypt, Syria, Armenia, and Azerbaijan. His father died in 785 and his elder brother in 786. Harun became caliph of an empire stretching from modern Morocco in the west to India in the east.

There were occasional revolts, but his reign was mostly a time of increasing prosperity, development of industry, and expansion of trade. Administration was overseen by his former tutor and the tutor's two sons until 803. Once they were gone, Harun divided the empire between his two sons, setting up a struggle that lasted for 50 years. Harun fell ill on his way to quell a revolt in Iran in 808, and he died on March 24, 809. (*See also* Caliphate.)

**HARVEY, William** (1578–1657). From dissecting many creatures, including humans, English physician William Harvey discovered the nature of blood circulation and the function of the heart as a pump. Before his discoveries blood was thought to ebb and flow through the body by the contraction of arteries. Harvey's work also laid down the foundations of physiology, the study of body functions.

William Harvey was born on April 1, 1578, in Folkestone, Kent, England. He was the oldest of the seven sons of Thomas Harvey. At age 10 he was sent to the King's School in Canterbury, and at 16 he entered Gonville and Caius College, Cambridge, where he received a bachelor's degree in 1597.

Harvey then studied medicine at the University of Padua in Italy, the finest medical school of its time. One of his teachers was Hieronymus Fabricius, a noted surgeon and anatomist who had already discovered the one-way valves in veins, but was not sure of their purpose. Harvey later proved that they prevent blood from flowing backward. He returned to London after receiving his medical degree in 1602.

*Marble bust of William Harvey by Edward Marshall*
Courtesy of the Hempstead Parish Church, Essex; photo, the Royal Academy of Arts, London

Shortly after his return to England Harvey married Elizabeth Browne, daughter of a physician to Queen Elizabeth I. In 1607 he received a fellowship at the Royal College of Physicians, and in 1609 he became assistant physician. He was then a physician at St. Bartholomew's Hospital until 1643.

In 1618 Harvey was appointed one of the physicians to King James I. When King Charles I ascended to the throne Harvey became his personal physician. King Charles took a personal interest in Harvey's research in circulation and growth, and he provided Harvey with animals for experimentation.

From 1615 to 1656 Harvey was appointed to a college lectureship. The manuscript of the notes on which the lectures were based is entitled 'Lectures on the Whole of Anatomy'. His famous book 'On the Motion of the Heart and Blood in Animals', published in 1628, gave a unique and accurate account of the circulatory system (*see* Circulatory System; Heart). The book made Harvey famous throughout Europe despite initial attacks on it.

Harvey explained that blood does not contain bubbles of air. He proved that blood does not pass through the heart's septum, and he explained the function of the valves in the heart and larger veins. Harvey died in London on June 3, 1657.

**HASTINGS, Warren** (1732–1818). India's first governor-general, Warren Hastings consolidated and organized British power in India, building on foundations laid a few years earlier by Robert Clive. Hastings's administrative skill enabled the British to counter threats both from internal interests and from the French at a time when the British were involved in the American Revolution. Hastings also established sound procedures for administering justice and collecting revenues during a difficult time of transition.

Hastings was born on Dec. 17, 1732, in Churchill, Oxfordshire. He was left at an early age in the care of an uncle, and attended Westminster School in London. Hastings became a clerk with the East India Company and, at the age of 18, arrived in Calcutta. Clive recognized the young man's abilities. Before he left India he made Hastings agent for the East India Company in the court of an Indian prince, the nawab of Bengal. Later Hastings served the company in Madras. In 1772 the company recalled him to Calcutta as governor of Bengal. Hastings, finding the administration in confusion and the company in debt, instituted reforms.

The East India Company was originally a mere trading corporation that governed only its own trading posts. Clive had extended the rule of the company from Calcutta over all Bengal, a vast continental area (*see* Clive). The British government saw the need to exercise stricter supervision over a corporation that collected taxes, maintained armies, and, in return for giving them protection, exacted large sums of money from Indian princes. In 1773 Parliament appointed Hastings governor-general of all the company's possessions in India.

During the American Revolution France joined the American Colonies in their war with Britain. In India the French hoped to take this opportunity to expel the British. French officials plotted with Indian rulers, and French officers drilled Indian troops. Hastings took decisive action.

An army was dispatched across the peninsula to Madras to put down Hyder Ali, the sultan of Mysore. Hastings's action saved India for the British, but the wars cost money. To pay for them, Hastings exacted increased tribute from the raja of Benares and the nawab of Oudh.

Hastings also had to uphold his authority against a faction in his own governing council, a faction led by his personal enemy, Sir Philip Francis, whom Hastings had wounded in a duel. When Hastings returned to England in 1785, Francis, then a member of Parliament, denounced him for corruption and cruelty. The orator Edmund Burke and the playwright Richard Sheridan took the lead in demanding Hastings's impeachment. The trial opened in the House of Lords in 1788 and dragged on a full seven years. Hastings was finally acquitted in 1795. He retired to the country and lived there quietly until his death on Aug. 22, 1818, in Daylesford.

**HASTINGS, BATTLE OF.** The Norman Conquest, which brought tremendous changes to England, began with the decisive battle of Hastings on Oct. 14, 1066. Harold II, the last of the Saxon kings of England, was killed in this battle. On Christmas Day William, duke of Normandy, was crowned king. He became known as William the Conqueror (*see* William, Kings of England).

After long preparations William set sail from Normandy. On September 28 he landed his army of 4,000 to 7,000 cavalry and infantry at Pevensey on the English Channel and moved eastward along the coast to Hastings. Harold hurried from the north of England with his army of about 7,000 men, many of whom were half-armed, untrained peasants. On October 13 Harold took a strong position on a hill between the port of Hastings and the present-day village of Battle. At dawn the next day William roused his troops and set out on an 8-mile (13-kilometer) march to join battle before Harold's troops were rested.

All day the battle raged. Norman horsemen pressed up the hill. Standing close together and protected by great shields, the English wielded their long-handled battle-axes with terrible effect. Throughout the day William alternated cavalry charges with flights of arrows from his archers. Pretending retreat, he drew the English from their entrenched position and annihilated them. Harold was killed when an arrow pierced his eye. His brothers had already been slain. The English fought on until dusk. Then they fled, leaving the field to William. After the battle William and his army moved northward to isolate London. (*See also* England, "The Norman Conquest.")

Hastings, which gave its name to the battle, is now a thriving Sussex town and seaside resort. Population (1982 estimate), 76,500.

*The painting 'Portrait of Giovanni Arnolfini' by Jan van Eyck shows a man wearing a chaperon, a type of hood common in the Middle Ages. The painting is at the Berlin Gemaldegalerie.*

*The painting 'Portrait of a Lady' by Francesco Bacchiacca shows a young woman wearing a turban. Of oriental origin, the turban consists of a long scarf wrapped around the head.*

# HATS AND CAPS

Like other things we wear, hats and caps have two purposes—protection and ornament. They have also been worn since very early times to show the rank or importance of the wearer. This type of headwear is seen today in the hats and caps worn by soldiers and sailors, in the bishop's mitre, the cardinal's scarlet hat, the priest's biretta, and the scholar's mortarboard.

The ancestor of all hats was probably the fillet. This was a band tied around the head to keep the hair in place. It was worn in ancient Egypt, Babylonia, and Greece. Turbans and crowns developed from it, and today it survives as the band on our hats.

Probably the first real hat was the broad-brimmed petasos of the ancient Greeks. It was worn only for traveling, as a protection against the weather. A chin strap held it on or allowed it to hang down the back when not needed. It was so practical that people all over Europe wore it throughout the Middle Ages.

In ancient Rome slaves were not allowed to cover their heads. When a slave was freed, he at once put on the small cone-shaped Phrygian cap as a sign of his freedom. French revolutionists revived this "liberty cap" as the bonnet rouge (red cap).

The common people of Rome wore a cloak with an attached hood. Some kind of hood continued to be worn outdoors by both men and women throughout the early Middle Ages. If it was separate from the cloak or cape it was called a chaperon. If it was attached, it was a cowl, or capuchon. The earliest hoods looked somewhat like the Phrygian cap. By the 13th century the tail, or tippet, had lengthened until it almost touched the ground and was called a liripipe. Later the liripipe was wound round the head, making a turban shape called the roundlet.

**Men's Hats Since the Renaissance**

During the Renaissance men of wealth began to wear hats of various shapes, richly decorated to match their splendid costumes. The beret originated in Italy at this time. It was made of a circular piece of cloth gathered onto a band decorated with jewels or embroidery. Inside the band was a string, which could be tightened to fit any head. The tiny bow on the inside of men's hats today is a survival of that string.

Louis XIV of France, who reigned 1643 to 1715, was proud of his fine head of hair. He wore it in long curls. His courtiers, to look like him, wore wigs of natural hair. Later, powdered horsehair wigs came into style. When furs from America became plentiful, men of fashion began to wear the wide-brimmed beaver hat, trimmed with drooping ostrich plumes. To show off their curls, they turned up the brim—first on one side and later on two sides. This was called "cocking the hat." Finally they turned up the back also, forming the tricorne. The tricorne lasted more than a century.

During the French Revolution, men's clothes became much plainer, and the tall-crowned pot hat came into style. This gradually developed into the high silk hat, or "topper" (from which we get the expression high-hat, meaning "snobbish"). By 1900 the hard round bowler (called a derby in America) had replaced the topper for street wear. By this time also the hard straw boater, or sailor, the soft straw panama, and many kinds of cloth caps for sports had appeared. In about

*In the portrait 'Sir Richard Southwell' (left) by Hans Holbein the Younger, the subject is wearing a beret, a kind of headgear that appeared in the 16th century. Philip IV of Spain (center), in a portrait by Peter Paul Rubens, is wearing a cavalier, originally associated with knights. A painting by Jean-Baptiste Chardin (right) shows a boy wearing a tricorne.*

*In the process of making a custom-made hat, a conformateur (top) establishes the size of the hat on a paper mask. In one of the final steps in manufacturing a hat (bottom), a trimmer hems the brim, sews in the lining and sweat leather, and puts the band on the outside of the hat.*

1908 the soft felt fedora began to replace the derby. The silk topper continued to be worn for inaugurations until President Eisenhower broke with tradition in 1952 by wearing the semiformal Homburg—a stiff-brimmed felt with a soft crown.

Practically all men's hat styles worn today originated in England. America contributed only the Stetson, or "ten-gallon hat," of the Western ranchers and cowboys. This hat could be punched into any shape and used as a roof, umbrella, sunshade, or water carrier. It was modeled on the Mexican sombrero.

## Women's Headwear Since the Middle Ages

During the Middle Ages religious practices concerning dress were based on a few New Testament injunctions that required women to cover their hair completely, both indoors and out. The earliest and simplest head covering was a piece of linen that hung to the shoulders or below. It was called a wimple.

The wimple survives today as the bridal veil and in the lovely lace mantillas worn by Spanish women. In the 13th century chin bands and forehead bands were pinned on under the wimple to make a frame for the face, somewhat like the headdress that is worn by some nuns today.

In the later Middle Ages women draped the wimple over a large wire frame. The shapes were fantastic—a pair of great horns, a heart, a butterfly, or a "steeple," 1 to 3 feet high. The headdresses tilted backward. If a woman's hair grew low on her forehead, she shaved it so that no hair would show.

In about 1500, women began to wear hoods, highly jeweled and embroidered. Some form of hood or lace cap continued to be worn until the late 1700s, when milliners' shops began to take hatmaking out of the home. The milliners made hats to order in all shapes and sizes. They made them of straw, felt, or fabric, and trimmed them elaborately to go with the piled-up masses of powdered hair. Great favorites were the plumed Gainsborough and the wide leghorn, trimmed with a circle of flowers.

Bonnets, tied under the chin, came into vogue during the French Revolution. They were made of fur, velvet, satin, or felt for winter and gauze or straw for summer and were trimmed with plumes, ribbons, flowers, and lace. They took such shapes as the coal scuttle, the poke bonnet, and the calash, so huge it was named for the hood of a carriage (calèche).

Hatpins began to replace bonnet strings in about 1860. On top of their elaborate hairdress women now pinned small porkpies, covered with trimming. About 1900 they began to wear large hats, heavily trimmed.

*Empress Eugénie hats (left), named for the wife of Napoleon III, are pictured in the painting 'Frozen Out' by George Dunlop Leslie. In 'The Bow' (center) by Talbot Hughes, a woman wears a Gainsborough hat, named for the English artist. A woman of the late 20th century (right) wears a tailored version of a man's hat. Such hats can be made of felt or straw.*

During World War I many women bobbed their hair and pulled tight-fitting cloches down over their ears. After World War II, many women wore no hats at all, except for rather formal occasions.

### Hatmaking—A Mass-Production Industry

The best felt hats are made from the soft underfurs of animals. Cheaper felts are made of wool. The chief fur used is coney (rabbit). For finer qualities fur from the hare, beaver, or muskrat is added.

Real panamas come from Ecuador and Colombia. They were named "panamas" in the gold-rush days by prospectors who bought them in Panama when returning from California. Panamas are made by hand from split, bleached leaves of the palmlike toquilla.

Factory production of women's hats began after World War I, when block and diemakers began to produce highly styled wood head blocks and metal dies in all sizes. Every season manufacturers and designers visit the showrooms of the hat-block makers in New York City to select basic styles. New York City is also the wholesale center for straw braids and straw hat bodies from Italy, Switzerland, and the Orient, and for felt hat bodies, buckram shapes, fabrics, veilings, linings, and trimmings. (*See also* Dress.)

**HAUPTMANN, Gerhart** (1862–1946). The most prominent German dramatist of his time, Gerhart Hauptmann won the Nobel prize for literature in 1912. He established his reputation in 1889 as an exponent of naturalism, an artistic technique that deals realistically with human emotions and motives. Much of his writing was of the neoclassical type of romanticism.

Gerhart Hauptmann was born on Nov. 15, 1862, in Obersalzbrunn, Silesia (now Poland), where his father owned a hotel. After he left school, at the age of 15, he tried various pursuits, from farming to sculpture. In 1884 he took acting lessons in Berlin and decided to make his career as a poet and dramatist.

'Before Dawn' brought overnight success. Greatly encouraged, he wrote in rapid succession a number of other plays on such naturalistic themes as heredity, the plight of the poor, and the clash of natural science and religion. The most gripping, but the most objectionable to the political authorities, was 'The Weavers' (1892), a compassionate drama about the Silesian weavers' revolt of 1844. He also became an ingenious director of his plays as well as those of others. Beginning in the 1880s, he published prose, poetry, and essays that demonstrated his range.

Although honored as a national figurehead in public appearances, Hauptmann was isolated from the literary and intellectual life of the time. Indecisive about Nazism, he remained in Germany, where he died in Agnetendorf on June 6, 1946.

**HAVANA, Cuba.** Cuba's capital and largest city, Havana, is a commercial and industrial center and the focus of Cuba's economic, cultural, social, and political life. It lies on the northwestern coast of Cuba in the Gulf of Mexico. Its landlocked harbor is less than 100 miles (160 kilometers) south of Key West, Fla. Its location in the tropical zone gives it a balmy climate. The people are mainly whites of Spanish descent, blacks descended from slaves brought to sugar plantations in colonial times, and mestizos (of mixed ancestry).

Before the Revolution of 1959 led by Fidel Castro, Havana was world-famous as a tourist center. The *Habaneros* (people of Havana) provided tourists with

Ewing Galloway

*The Academy of Sciences, built as the capitol in 1929, was modeled after the United States Capitol in Washington, D.C.*

abundant entertainment. Bathing beaches and yacht and golf clubs offered recreation in the sun. When the flashing neon signs lit the streets at night, the guests turned to the restaurants, cafés, night clubs, and gambling casinos. Jai alai, baseball, soccer, and racing were favorite sports and are still popular today.

Tourism declined swiftly with the Revolution of 1959 and its anti-United States policy. American assets and all foreign and domestic property were nationalized with the establishment of a socialist system of government.

The city's appearance reflects its long history. Founded in the early 16th century, Havana quickly became an important port in Spain's rich trade with the New World. The historic walled town, Old Havana, lies near the docks. Here are found narrow awning-shaded streets and quaint Spanish colonial houses and churches. The city hall on the ancient Plaza de Armas was built in 1790 as a combined governor's palace, council hall, and prison. The cathedral on a nearby plaza held the bones of Christopher Columbus, now lying in Santo Domingo, for 100 years (*see* Columbus, Christopher).

Attacks and plunders by pirate ships and by fleets of Spain's enemies led to the erection of strong fortresses on both sides of the channel leading from the Gulf of Mexico into the harbor. Still standing are the Castillo de la Fuerza, Castillo de la Punta, Fortaleza de La Cabaña, and Castillo del Morro.

The growing city spread beyond the old walls and developed into a handsome Latin capital. It has broad tree-lined avenues, flower-decked plazas, and elaborate Spanish baroque public buildings. The capitol, finished in 1929, is now the Academy of Sciences, standing at the end of a promenade, the Paseo de José Martí,

formerly called the Prado. A seaside boulevard, the Malecón, follows the shore for several miles. It leads to the beaches and residential sections of Vedado and Marianao, where skyscraper hotels and business houses spread during the decades of the 1940s and 1950s.

In the 1950s a five-tube vehicular tunnel was built beneath the harbor of the city to give quick access to Habana del Este (East Havana). The National Library founded in 1901, today is located in the Plaza de la Revolución.

Railways and roads fan out from Havana to all parts of the island. Its port was formerly the busiest in the West Indies. Today, however, trade is chiefly with Russia, Canada, China, and Spain. Sea and air traffic to and from the United States has been restricted. Industries include sugar refining, cigar and cigarette making, textile mills, brewing and distilling, and packing and canning. Other manufactured products are cement, furniture, shoes, fertilizers, and agricultural machinery.

Havana was founded in 1515. It remained the chief city of the Spanish in the West Indies until the end of the 19th century, when the island sought its independence from Spain. In February 1898 the United States battleship *Maine,* sent to guard United States citizens and property, was mysteriously blown up in its harbor. During the Spanish-American War that followed, the city was blockaded by the United States fleet (*see* Spanish-American War). When Cuba was freed from Spanish rule in 1898, Havana became the capital of the republic.

Havana underwent changes after Castro came to power. Its luxury hotels and apartments housed technicians from the Soviet Union and other Communist countries. La Cabaña became a prison and a place of execution for Castro's enemies. The Plaza de República was renamed Plaza de la Revolución. There was a shortage of many supplies. (*See also* Castro; Cuba.) Population (1999 estimate), 2,198,716.

**HAVEL, Vaclav** (born 1936). Czech playwright and political leader Vaclav Havel was born in Prague. His first essays were published when he was 19. His first plays were performed in the 1960s. He was imprisoned for a total of more than five years for speaking out against government abuses. He was the leader of the peaceful "velvet revolution" that ended Soviet-style Communism in Czechoslovakia. In December of 1989 Havel became the first non-Communist president of Czechoslovakia since 1948. In 1990 he discussed Czechoslovak membership in the European Communities with leaders of other European nations. He resigned the presidency in 1992 when Slovakia's regional parliament declared sovereignty, the Slovaks in the federal parliament blocked his reelection, and Slovakia and the Czech Republic agreed to break up the federation. He was elected president of the new Czech Republic in January 1993 and was reelected in 1998. He served until 2003. His literary works include 'The Memorandum', 'The Conspirators', 'Audience', 'Largo Desolato', and 'Letters of Olga'.

© 1994 Douglas Peebles

*Lava from Kilauea Crater on the Big Island of Hawaii flows into the Pacific Ocean. The state has the world's largest active and inactive volcanoes.*

# HAWAII

Millions of years ago fiery basalt rock erupted through a crack in the floor of the Pacific Ocean. Gradually the lava cooled and formed great undersea mountains whose summits protruded from the ocean. Over the centuries the action of wind, water, fire, and ice on the chain of volcanic peaks created the islands that became the state of Hawaii—a land of exotic flowers, shining beaches, and majestic mountains.

The first inhabitants of Hawaii were Polynesian seafarers who came to the islands in sturdy outrigger canoes more than 1,500 years ago. When the British sea captain James Cook discovered the islands in 1778, he found a preliterate but thriving people who bred fish for a better catch and irrigated their taro fields. (Taro is an edible plant that grows underground tubers.) Today Hawaii has a population more varied than that of any other state: its inhabitants include descendants of the original Polynesian population, of 19th-century sailors and traders, of the New England missionaries who brought Western ways to the native people, and of the Asians and Portuguese who came as field hands to work on the islands' sugar and pineapple plantations—mixed with the service personnel from the United States mainland who arm the great Hawaii-based naval and air fleets.

. . . . . . . . . . . . . . . . . . . . . . . . . . . . . . . . . . . . . . . . . . . . . . .

*This article was critically reviewed and updated by Roger A. Ulveling and the staff of the State of Hawaii Department of Business, Economic Development, and Tourism.*

Military expenditures are one of the island state's most important sources of income. The production of sugarcane and pineapples, long the mainstay of its agriculture, has become highly mechanized. Since the islands' annexation by the United States, Hawaiian agriculture has been diversified by a variety of tropical crops. World War II, which brought greater unity and widespread unionization, spurred Hawaii's industrialization. The more fast-paced economy has not detracted from the charm of the Aloha State. Its mushrooming tourist business—since 1961, the state's largest industry—is a challenge to Hawaiian ingenuity, and the general harmony of its multiracial culture sets a positive pattern for the world.

In many ways the 50th and last state in the Union is the most unusual one. It lies almost entirely in the tropics. It has the world's largest active and inactive volcanoes. Separated from the United States mainland by the world's biggest ocean, the Pacific, it is the only state that does not fall within the continent of North America. It is the only state that was once an independent kingdom and the only one with a royal palace. It is the only state that is composed entirely of islands. And it is the only state not dominated by Americans of European ancestry.

The nickname of the Aloha State comes from a late 19th-century Hawaiian word for love that is used as a greeting and to say farewell. Another nickname is the Paradise of the Pacific. Mark Twain characterized

## State Symbols

**FLAG.** The islands of Hawaii, constituting a united kingdom by 1810, flew a British Union Jack received from a British explorer as their unofficial flag until 1816. In that year the first Hawaiian ship to travel abroad visited China and flew its own flag. The flag had the Union Jack in the upper left corner on a field of red, white, and blue horizontal stripes. King Kamehameha I was one of the designers. In 1845 the number of stripes was set at eight, one to represent each major island.

**SEAL.** The basic design of Hawaii's state seal has been in use since 1845. In 1894 the republic was established. The legend now reads "State of Hawaii" rather than "Republic of Hawaii." The Hawaiian coat of arms is supported by Kamehameha I and the goddess of liberty, with a rising sun behind. The motto "Ua Mau ke Ea o ka Aina i ka Pono" (The Life of the Land Is Perpetuated in Righteousness) is along the bottom edge. Below the shield are various symbols: a phoenix rising from flames, taro leaves, banana foliage, and maidenhair ferns.

**MARINE MAMMAL.** Humpback Whale.

**TREE:** Kukui (Candlenut)

**FLOWER:** Yellow Hibiscus

**BIRD:** Nene (Hawaiian Goose)

## Facts About Hawaii

**Nickname.** Aloha State.

**Motto.** Ua Mau ke Ea o ka Aina i ka Pono (The Life of the Land is Perpetuated in Righteousness).

**Song.** 'Hawaii Ponoi' (Hawaii's Own).

**Entered the Union.** Aug. 21, 1959, as the 50th state.

**Capital.** Honolulu.

**Population** (2000 census). 1,211,537—rank, 42nd state. Persons per square mile, 188.6 (persons per square kilometer, 72.8)—rank, 13th state. (Islands—Oahu, 872,478; Hawaii, 143,135; Maui, 105,336; Kauai, 50,947; Molokai, 6,838; Lanai, 2,989; Niihau, 230; Kahoolawe, none.)

**Extent.** Area, 6,459 square miles (16,729 square kilometers), including 36 square miles (93 square kilometers) of water surface (47th state in size).

**Elevation.** Highest, Mauna Kea, Hawaii, 13,796 feet (4,205 meters); lowest, sea level; average, 1,990 feet (607 meters).

**Geographic Center.** 20°15' N., 156°20' W., off Maui Island.

**Temperature.** Extremes—lowest, 12° F (–11° C), Mauna Kea summit, Hawaii, January 20, 1970; highest, 100° F (38° C), Pahala, Hawaii, April 27, 1931. Averages at Hilo, Hawaii—January, 71.4° F (21.8° C); July, 75.7° F (24.3° C); annual, 73.6° F (23.1° C). Averages at Honolulu, Oahu—January, 72.6° F (22.6° C); July, 81° F (27.2° C); annual, 77° F (25° C).

**Precipitation.** At Hilo—annual average, 128 inches (3,251 millimeters). At Honolulu—annual average, 21 inches (533 millimeters).

**Land Use.** Crops, 7%; pasture, 23%; forest, 29%; other, 41%.

*(See also HAWAII FACT SUMMARY.)*

***The State Capitol in Honolulu rises from a reflecting pool (not visible in this photograph) that symbolizes Hawaii's ocean setting. The structure was completed in 1968. Iolani Palace was the former State Capitol.***

James P. Rowan—Tony Stone Worldwide

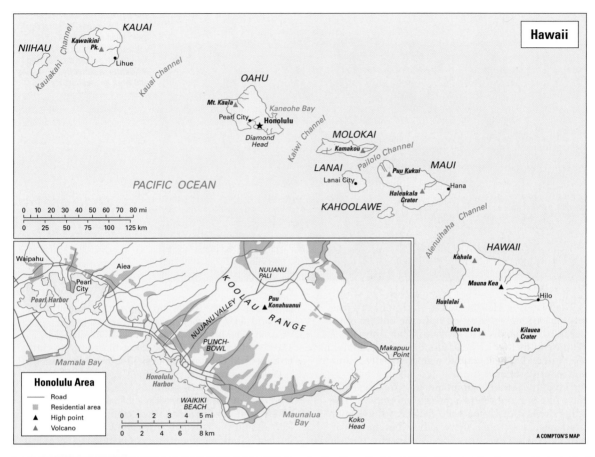

KAUAI

NIIHAU

Kawaikini Pk.▲

Kaulakahi Channel

Lihue

Kauai Channel

OAHU

Mt. Kaala ▲

Kaneohe Bay

Pearl City ●  ★ Honolulu

Diamond Head

Kaiwi Channel

MOLOKAI

Kamakou ▲

Pailolo Channel

LANAI

Lanai City ●

Puu Kukui ▲

MAUI

Haleakala Crater ▲  ● Hana

PACIFIC OCEAN

KAHOOLAWE

| 0 10 20 30 40 50 60 70 80 mi |
| 0 25 50 75 100 125 km |

Alenuihaha Channel

HAWAII

Kohala ▲

Mauna Kea ▲

Hualalai ▲  ● Hilo

Mauna Loa ▲  Kilauea Crater ▲

**Hawaii**

Waipahu

Aiea

NUUANU PALI

KOOLAU RANGE

Pearl City

Pearl Harbor

NUUANU VALLEY

Puu Konahuanui ▲

PUNCH-BOWL

Makapuu Point

Mamala Bay

Honolulu Harbor

WAIKIKI BEACH

Maunalua Bay

Koko Head

**Honolulu Area**

— Road
■ Residential area
▲ High point
▲ Volcano

| 0 1 2 3 4 5 mi |
| 0 2 4 6 8 km |

A COMPTON'S MAP

***Iao Needle on the Island of Maui is an erosional remnant in an ancient volcano caldera. It is in Iao Valley State Monument near Wailuku and rises about 2,200 feet.***
Robert Frerck—Odyssey Productions

Hawaii as the "loveliest fleet of islands that lies anchored in any ocean." The name of the state may have derived from Hawaiki, the former name of one of the Society Islands, home of some Polynesians. According to an island legend, Hawaii Loa was the name of the man who discovered the paradise.

### Survey of the Aloha State

The state of Hawaii is a chain of rugged islands, coral reefs, and rocky shoals located in the North Pacific Ocean. It occupies all except for the 2 square miles (5 square kilometers) of the Midway Islands. The Hawaiian Archipelago is crossed near its northwestern end by the Tropic of Cancer. It is some 2,400 miles (3,860 kilometers) away from the West coast of the United States mainland.

There are about 132 named islands and islets in the chain, which curves 1,523 miles (2,451 kilometers) southeast to northwest. Hawaii's land area of 6,459 square miles (16,729 square kilometers) is less than that of any other state except Connecticut, Delaware, and Rhode Island.

*The petrified hot lava bed at Hawaii Volcanoes National Park gives vivid evidence of past volcanic activity on the island. Next to the park is the Volcano Art Center, a collection of folk art and work by local artists.*
Catherine Sternbergh—Stock South

The islands of Hawaii are the worn tops of great volcanoes. They were raised from the bottom of the ocean by tremendous upheavals millions of years ago. Because of their volcanic origin, the islands do not have the variety of physiographic regions usually found in the other 49 states.

Typically, Hawaii is mountainous. The larger islands have one or more central spines of mountains. This spine drops to a slanted plain that then slopes more gradually down to the shore. Where beaches occur along the shore they are either white with coral sand or black with pulverized lava. In the interior are a few valleys and gulches.

Some parts of the islands rise from the sea in a sheer cliff called a pali. The cliffs are thousands of feet high in some places. Some of the smaller islets in the Hawaiian Archipelago are barely above sea level when the ocean tides run high.

### Eight Main Islands

The state of Hawaii is composed mainly of eight principal islands. In order of size they are Hawaii, Maui, Oahu, Kauai, Molokai, Lanai, Niihau, and Kahoolawe.

**Hawaii** is also called the Big Island, with a land area of 4,028 square miles (10,433 square kilometers). It is composed of five volcanic masses, with Mauna Kea at 13,796 feet (4,205 meters), Mauna Loa at 13,679 feet (4,169 meters), and Hualalai at 8,271 feet (2,521 meters) the highest peaks. Kilauea, whose slopes merge with those of Mauna Loa on the north and west, is the world's largest active volcano. As a result of a series of eruptions that began in early 1983, the glacier-type flow from the volcano moved across the island and destroyed many homes, causing millions of dollars in damage in 1990. The island of Hawaii has a generally rugged coastline, lava deserts, valleys, and gulches.

**Maui** is known as the Valley Island and has 729 square miles (1,888 square kilometers) in land area. It is composed of two mountain masses that constitute east and west Maui. They are connected by an isthmus. The highest peak is Haleakala—10,023 feet (3,055 meters). It has the largest extinct volcano crater in the world (20 square miles; 52 square kilometers).

**Oahu** is sometimes called the Capital Island because the city of Honolulu is located there. It has a land area of 594 square miles (1,538 square kilometers). It is formed of two mountain ranges, the Koolau and the Waianae. The island has no active volcanoes but many extinct craters, notably Diamond Head, Koko Head, and Punchbowl.

**Kauai** is popularly called the Garden Island and occupies a land area of 549 square miles (1,422 square kilometers). It has one central mountain mass. Its highest peak is Kawaikini—5,243 feet (1,598 meters). Waimea Canyon is nearly 3,000 feet (914 meters) deep. Kauai has fertile valleys, deep fissures, many caves, pinnacles, and waterfalls.

**Molokai** is famous as the Friendly Island because its inhabitants extend such a warm welcome to visitors. It is 261 square miles (676 square kilometers) in land area. The island is composed of three volcanic masses. In the east is Kamakou, at 4,961 feet (1,512 meters) Molokai's highest peak.

On the northern side of Molokai is a precipice rising from 500 to 3,250 feet (152 to 991 meters). Its highest part is indented by deep gorges and valleys. At the northern base of this cliff, cut off from the rest of the island, is the Kalaupapa peninsula, which is the site of the state's Hansen's Disease (leprosy) Treatment Center.

**Lanai** is known as the Pineapple Island because it is mostly owned by a pineapple company, which employs most of the residents. With a land area of 140 square miles (363 square kilometers), Lanai consists of a single mountain mass. At 3,370 feet (1,027 meters) Lanaihale is its highest point. Cliffs line its southerly coasts.

**Niihau** occupies a land area of 70 square miles (181 square kilometers). Its east-central third is a tableland 1,300 feet (396 meters) high with cliffs on the ocean side. The balance of the island is arid lowland of coral origin. All of Niihau's inhabitants are at least partly of ethnic Hawaiian ancestry, and tourism is prohibited.

**Kahoolawe** is sometimes called the Target Island because United States military forces once used it as a target. The smallest of the main islands, it is 45 square miles (116 square kilometers) in area and is uninhabited. It is a single mountain mass; its highest point, Puu Moaulanui, is 1,477 feet (450 meters). Native Hawaiians regard it as a sacred island, and many remnants of prehistoric Polynesian life remain on the island.

Uninhabited rocky islets and coral reefs in the Hawaiian chain include Kaula, Nihoa, Necker, Gardner Pinnacles, Lisianski, and Pearl and Hermes Atoll. Four of the Northwestern Hawaiian Islands were inhabited in 1980: French Frigate Shoals (in which lies La Perouse Pinnacle), Laysan Island, Kure Atoll, and the Midway Islands (not part of the state). (*See also* Oceania.)

### Climate

The mild, uniform climate of Hawaii is famous all over the world. Wide temperature changes are unknown in the state. Despite Hawaii's location in a tropical zone, cooling ocean currents keep the climate moderate. Although Hurricane Iwa caused extensive damage in 1982 and there were devastating tsunamis, or great sea waves, in 1946 and 1960, violent weather conditions are comparatively rare. The average annual temperature is about 75° F (24° C) throughout the lowlands.

The mild temperature of the islands is matched by dependable patterns of sunshine and rainfall. These patterns vary according to location and altitude and are governed by the northeast trade winds. On the western, or leeward, side of Hawaii's mountains a tropical savanna climate prevails. Puako, on the Big Island, has about 10 inches (25 centimeters) of rainfall during an average year. It is the driest area in the Hawaiian chain.

On the northeastern, or windward, slopes the climate is tropical wet (rain forest). There, mountain heights and deep valleys receive more rain than coastal areas. Waialeale, on the island of Kauai, is one of the wettest spots on Earth. It receives about 444 inches (1,128 centimeters) of rain in an average year.

### Natural Resources

One of Hawaii's most valuable resources is its soil. Only 7 percent of the land is used for crops, yet agriculture is one of Hawaii's major sources of wealth. Hawaii's fertile soil is composed of lava ash and soft, sandy stone. In places it has yielded up to 11 tons of sugar per acre, the largest yield on Earth. Because of the mild climate and fertile soil, the crop year never ends.

The value of mineral production reached its peak (in current dollars) in 1992. Stone, cement, sand and

*A greenhouse worker examines a crop of anthuriums. Some of the world's most exotic flowers are grown commercially in Hawaii. The state's orchids are in great demand around the world.*

gravel, and lime are the most abundant minerals. Lava ash and rock are used as building materials. Unusual minerals found in Hawaii are red and blue cinders, which are used in landscaping, and black coral, which is used in jewelry.

Hawaii's water-resources problem is basically one of geographic distribution. Groundwater serves approximately 46.2 percent of the state's total water supply. Surface water, drawn through miles of aqueducts and tunnels, is used mainly for irrigation. Groundwater for domestic use is brought to the surface by huge pumping stations.

**Plant and animal life.** Hawaii's landscape is a perpetual flower show. Hedges of hibiscus bloom everywhere. Shower trees shed their blossoms along the streets. Bougainvillea vines, night-blooming cereus, and ginger plants make the islands a paradise of bloom. There are more than 1,700 species of flowering plants and trees in Hawaii—many found only in this state. Some species have been imported from Asia, Africa, Australia, Mexico, and Brazil. A great many originated in the East Indies.

Wild animals are found on six of the islands—Hawaii, Maui, Oahu, Kauai, Molokai, and Lanai. They include deer, wild goats, and wild pigs. No snakes (except for one very small species) are found on the islands. The only land reptiles are small skinks and geckos, commonly called lizards, and toads. More than

*Waikiki Beach, in Honolulu, is world-famous and attracts thousands of tourists. Huge hotels rise along its warm, sandy shores. Beyond it rises Diamond Head, a well-known landmark.*

60 percent of the nearly 90 native bird species and more than half of about 24 native land and marine mammals, reptiles, and amphibians are threatened, endangered, or extinct.

### People of Hawaii

Located in the mid-Pacific, Hawaii is a natural meeting place of East and West. A mixture of many cultures, its citizens trace their lineage back to nearly every area and major cultural region in the world. The original inhabitants were probably Polynesians who sailed from the Marquesas Islands, perhaps as early as AD 400. Of the present population about one out of every three citizens is a member of the Caucasian race, with fully a third of mixed ancestry. They include Japanese, Hawaiian, Chinese, Spanish, German, Korean, Puerto Rican, Filipino, Portuguese, Indian, Samoan, Vietnamese, and Anglo-Saxon.

The population of Hawaii in the 2000 census was 1,211,537. This was an increase of 103,308, or 9.3 percent, since 1990. The two largest racial groups are Caucasian and Asian, followed by Native Hawaiian and other Pacific Islander.

**Hawaiian language.** The English language is the one most used in Hawaii. Many ancestral languages are still spoken on the islands, however, and many Hawaiian words are heard in everyday speech. The Hawaiian alphabet has only 12 letters: the vowels *a, e, i, o,* and *u,* and the consonants *h, k, l, m, n, p,* and *w* (sometimes pronounced like *v*). Each vowel is pronounced separately. A pidgin English, which differs from standard English in both word use and inflection, is also spoken.

In giving directions, a place is said to be *makai,* "toward the sea," or *mauka,* "toward the mountains." Nearly all cities and towns and most of the streets bear Hawaiian names.

### Cities and Manufacturing

Honolulu, the capital and largest city, is the state's industrial and tourist hub, with high-rise hotels, shopping centers, and the crowded sands of famed Waikiki Beach (*see* Honolulu, Hawaii). The second largest is Hilo. Pearl City is about one tenth as large as Honolulu. Both Honolulu and Pearl City are part of a single municipality, the city and county of Honolulu. The port of Lahaina on the west coast of Maui was an early whaling center.

Hawaii's more than 921 manufacturing plants are located chiefly on Oahu. Many of the Oahu factories have been built in industrial parks and special areas on the southern part of the island. The industrial region forms a 20-mile (32-kilometer) arc around Pearl Harbor between Barbers Point and central Honolulu. There are also a number of plants in Hilo and Kahului. Food processing is Hawaii's leading manufacturing industry. Printing and publishing and textile production are also valuable industries.

## AGRICULTURE, INDUSTRY, AND RESOURCES

HONOLULU
Food Processing,
Printing & Publishing,
Clothing

Commercial fishing

Sugarcane

Fruit

Commercial fishing

Commercial fishing

Commercial fishing

Sugarcane

Pineapple

Honolulu

Commercial fishing

Pineapple

Commercial fishing

Pineapple
Sugarcane

Pineapple

**DOMINANT LAND USE**

Diversified Tropical Cash Crops

Livestock Grazing

Forests

Urban areas

Nonagricultural land

Major industrial areas

Commercial fishing

Commercial fishing

Commercial fishing

Cattle   Sugarcane

Fruit

Coffee

Sugarcane

Commercial fishing

Cattle

A COMPTON'S MAP

## Agriculture

The Hawaiian agricultural economy is based largely on sugar and pineapples. The state produces less than 3 million tons of sugarcane for sugar annually. The value of the crop is more than 85 million dollars. The first Hawaiians probably brought sugarcane from the South Pacific. The industry got its real start on Kauai in 1835 when three New Englanders grew a crop on land rented from King Kamehameha III. By 1874 more than 13,000 tons a year were being exported. Today Hawaii raises more cane sugar than any other state, except Florida. Raw sugar is sent to the United States mainland for refining, most of it to California.

In the early days many extra laborers were needed on the islands' sugar plantations. Immigration was encouraged, and field hands were brought from China, Japan, Portugal, and the Philippines. Many stayed on in Hawaii. Today the industry is highly mechanized and requires fewer workers. Mechanization has enabled Hawaiian sugar growers to compete successfully with low-cost labor areas. In the mid-1980s the illegal crop of marijuana far surpassed the value of the sugar crop.

The largest legal crop grown in Hawaii is pineapples. The plants are set out to mature in rotation, so picking never stops. The heaviest harvest months are June, July, and August. More than 300,000 tons of pineapples are harvested annually. The fruit is grown on Kauai, Oahu, Lanai, and Maui. Most of the crop is exported as fresh fruit. Pineapple is canned only on Maui.

Dennis Cox—Tony Stone Worldwide
*Sugarcane is grown commercially on Maui. Hawaii has the most advanced sugar technology of any area in the world.*

Cattle raising is a major source of income, especially on the island of Hawaii. That island produces more than 65 percent, by volume, of the state's livestock. One of the largest privately owned cattle ranches in the United States, the Parker Ranch, is located there.

Scattered throughout the islands are cattle ranches, as well as sheep and horse ranches and pig and poultry

*In addition to pineapple and sugar cane, macadamia nuts have become a significant export crop. This macadamia tree orchard is on the island of Hawaii.*

*Hookipa Bay (top) on the island of Maui claims the title of windsurfing capital of the world. The bay became popular with windsurfers in the late 1970s because of its favorable wind conditions. Tourists who want to see authentic hula dancers visit the Kodak Hula Show (bottom) in Kapiolani Park, Waikiki. Before the arrival of tourists, the hula was considered a religious dance.*

farms. Almost 24 percent of the land in Hawaii is used for grazing. The annual value of livestock production in the islands, including dairy products, is well over 70 million dollars.

Exports of macadamia nuts, papayas, and other Hawaiian specialties have expanded rapidly. Vegetables, melons, and taro are also grown on the islands. Taro is used to make poi, a pasty but digestible starchy food. Hawaii is the only state that raises coffee. It has the largest orchid-growing business in the world. Tourists spend more than 10 billion dollars annually, making tourism the state's most valuable industry. By the end of the 1990s Hawaii was among the states most visited by foreigners (more than 2 million). Federal defense expenditures are another large source of income.

**Transportation and Communication**

Hawaii is the center of a vast transportation system that extends to all areas of the Pacific and around the world. Air and sea transportation is available to almost every major port and airport ringing the ocean.

Interisland freight shipping is conducted primarily by air and by barge. Honolulu Harbor is the center for intrastate and overseas shipping. Travelers within the island chain use the interisland commercial air system almost exclusively. Good highways link the intra-island towns with scenic regions and plantations. Railway mileage is small, as trucks have totally replaced the plantation railroads.

Since 1957 a transpacific submarine telephone cable has formed a link between Hawaii and the United States mainland. In 1964 a second cable linked Hawaii with Japan, completing the first transpacific service between the United States and Japan. Hawaii is the site of ground relay stations for satellite communications systems that link people throughout the world.

**Recreation**

Hawaii's year-round summer encourages residents and visitors to enjoy life in the open air. Many houses have verandas, called lanais. People throng the beaches, such as Waikiki—one of the world's most famous playgrounds. Hawaii has its own special sports and pastimes. The most popular is surfboarding, the sport of the Hawaiian kings and chiefs. Surf riding in an outrigger canoe is also enjoyed. Skin diving, windsurfing, running, spear fishing, and some spectator sports attract many. Honolulu is the site of American football's annual pro bowl game.

Outdoor Hawaiian feasts, called luaus, are popular. They feature whole roast pigs cooked by means of hot rocks in a pit. A native dish called poi is usually served also. Entertainment often includes native songs

*Iolani Palace in Honolulu once served as the capital building. Since Hawaiian monarchs once lived in the structure it is the only royal palace in the United States. The stone structure was built in 1882 in Italian Renaissance style.*
David R. Frazier Photolibrary

James P. Rowan—Gartman Agency
*The magnificent Akaka Falls are an attraction in a state park on the Hamakua coast of the Big Island. Hawaii's lush foliage can be enjoyed by the tourist throughout the year.*

and dances, especially the graceful hula—an art form of words, rhythm, and gestures. It was originally an expression of religious belief dating from the days when the Polynesian settlers believed in pagan gods.

Sparkling beaches, public parks, playgrounds, and other recreational facilities dot the main islands. On Oahu more than 260 recreational areas are maintained by the city. Major places of interest for tourists are Hawaii Volcanoes National Park on the island of Hawaii, which has two active volcanoes, and the USS *Arizona* National Memorial on Oahu, which marks the spot where the USS *Arizona* was sunk in Pearl Harbor on Dec. 7, 1941. In all, the state has seven national sites, including national parks and historical parks, 77 state parks, and 569 county parks. (*See also* National Parks.)

A favorite attraction among visitors is the Iolani Palace, with its throne room, royal portraits, replicas of original thrones, and *kahilis* (feather standards). The palace was built in 1882 by King Kalakaua, who lived there until his death in 1891. In 1893, when Queen Liliuokalani was dethroned and a provisional government took over, the building was used for executive purposes. Legislative sessions were held there from 1895 until the completion of the new State Capitol in 1968.

The original frame buildings erected by the first American missionaries also attract many visitors. Educational lectures are given at the Honolulu Academy of Arts, which has 30 galleries of artworks. The Bishop Museum, founded in 1889, is a treasure house of Polynesian folklore. The Foster Botanical Garden displays unusual tropical trees and plants from the Pacific area.

### Education

American missionaries set up Hawaii's first schools in the early 19th century. In the 1840s the government of Hawaii took over the school system. Today Hawaii's public schools are administered by the State Board of Education.

The University of Hawaii was founded in 1907. The main campus is at Honolulu, and there are four-year branch campuses at Hilo and West Oahu, as well as seven affiliated two-year colleges throughout the state. The university excels in such subjects as marine sciences, astronomy, and tropical and cultural studies. The East-West Center, located on the Honolulu campus, is a federally financed institution. The center encourages the exchange of cultural and technical information between students from Asia and the United States. Other schools include Chaminade University of Honolulu, Hawaii Pacific University at Honolulu, and Brigham Young University–Hawaii Campus at Laie.

*The University of Hawaii is located in the Manoa district of Honolulu. The school was founded in 1907 as the College of Agriculture and Mechanical Arts.*

## Government and Politics

In 1900 Hawaii officially became the Territory of Hawaii. As a territory, it had only one representative in the United States Congress—a nonvoting delegate. The governor and secretary of Hawaii and the territorial court judges were appointed by the president of the United States. The islands had no electoral vote, and the citizens could not vote in presidential elections.

To prepare for statehood, delegates from all the islands convened in Hawaii in 1950 to draft a constitution. It was ratified by Hawaii's citizens in a general election on Nov. 7, 1950. The National Municipal League praised the document for setting a new standard in modern state constitutions.

Hawaii's constitution is patterned after the Constitution of the United States. It provides for an elected governor and a two-chamber legislature. A governor is limited to two consecutive terms. Hawaii sends two senators and two representatives to the United States Congress. It is the only state that has but two levels of government—state and county. There are no municipalities or other smaller government jurisdictions in the state.

Honolulu remained the capital when Hawaii was admitted to the Union in 1959. Iolani Palace served as the meeting place of the state legislature until construction of the new Capitol was completed in 1968.

Until the mid-1950s Republicans dominated the legislative elections. Hawaii was among the few states that supported the losing Democratic candidates in the presidential elections of 1968, 1980, and 1988. In 1974 Hawaii's George R. Ariyoshi became the first state governor of Oriental ancestry. He was succeeded by John Waihee, the first elected governor of Hawaiian ancestry. The first Democratic representative from Hawaii (1959–63) was Daniel K. Inouye, who was the first Japanese American Congressman; he was elected to the Senate in 1962.

## HISTORY

Hawaii was settled more than 1,500 years ago by the Polynesians—a race of seafarers who probably originated in Southeast Asia. Little is known of their arrival except through old Hawaiian legends.

The island chain first became known to the Western world and recorded history in January 1778. Captain James Cook, a British explorer, came upon the islands during one of his voyages (*see* Cook, James). He named them the Sandwich Islands, after the earl of Sandwich. The islands then consisted of individual kingdoms ruled by local chiefs. By 1810 one ruler had conquered the others. Kamehameha I and his descendants then ruled the islands for almost a hundred years (*see* Kamehameha, Kings of Hawaii).

In 1820 the first companies of American missionaries arrived from New England on the *Thaddeus.* Other missionaries followed, from Europe as well as America. They became advisers to the Hawaiian rulers and were influential in liberalizing the government and in advancing education, including a written language. Christianity, both Protestant and Roman Catholic, became the national religion.

As early as 1826 a United States Navy captain negotiated one of the first commercial treaties with Hawaii. Whaling ships from New England and fur-trading ships from Russian America (Alaska) used Hawaii as a supply point. In the next decades trade increased tremendously.

### Annexation by the United States

In 1858 the Kingdom of Hawaii applied for annexation to the United States but was refused. In 1893 Queen Liliuokalani tried to replace the so-called "bayonet" constitution forced on her predecessor in 1887 (*see* Liliuokalani). This led to a revolution. A group of residents, mostly Americans who had become prominent in the Hawaiian economy, engineered the overthrow of the monarchy.

The new government applied for annexation to the United States. When this request was again refused, the rulers established a republic in 1894, with Sanford Ballard Dole as president (*see* Dole, Sanford Ballard). Finally, in 1898, a treaty of annexation was concluded. In 1900 the Territory of Hawaii was established. The Organic Act gave the people greater political power than they had possessed under their kings. American institutions and influences spread throughout the islands, and the economy made rapid progress.

### Pearl Harbor and World War II

By a treaty in 1887 Oahu's Pearl Harbor had been turned over to the United States to be used as a ship coaling and repair station. In 1908, as the Navy was being upgraded, the building of a great naval base began there; the War Department, meanwhile, ordered the construction of Schofield Barracks. United States Army and Navy installations were expanded.

On Dec. 7, 1941, the Japanese attacked Pearl Harbor (*see* World War II). Honolulu proved to be the only

David R. Frazier Photolibrary

James P. Rowan—Gartman Agency

*The colorful mural interior of St. Benedict's, commonly called the Painted Church, near Kona was done by the parish priest between 1898 and 1902. He used oil-based paints.*

*A statue of King Kamehameha I stands in a public square in Honolulu. It was under his reign, from 1782 to 1819, that the islands were unified for the first time.*

American city under attack during the war. Fearing an invasion attempt, the Army proclaimed martial law (later found to be unconstitutional by the Supreme Court). Civil government was not restored until October 1944. Anxiety arose at the presence of more than 150,000 people of Japanese birth or extraction on the islands. Suspected leaders were interned, but the vast majority worked peaceably on the plantations and on construction projects (*see* Asian Americans ). Hawaiian-born Japanese American troops achieved a notable combat record in Italy during the war.

**Statehood**

After the war the people renewed their plea for statehood. A bill for Hawaiian statehood was passed by the House of Representatives in 1947 but did not meet Senate approval. Finally, on March 12, 1959, Congress voted to admit Hawaii as the 50th state. On June 27 Hawaii's voters approved immediate statehood. President Dwight D. Eisenhower signed the proclamation making Hawaii a state effective August 21.

After attaining statehood Hawaii's economic development was rapid, particularly in industrial diversification and tourism. To deal with the fast pace of construction, in 1961 it became the first state to adopt a statewide land-use program. It was also the first state to institute the office of ombudsman, in 1967, to handle citizens' complaints against the government.

During the late 1960s, in an effort to keep pace with tourist needs, the Hawaii Visitors Bureau set up special planning committees to maintain a balance between construction, personnel needs, transportation, and recreation. When Ferdinand Marcos, former president of the Philippines, fled that country in 1986, he found exile in Hawaii.

In the mid-1980s a geothermal plant began producing electricity on the island of Hawaii. New telescopes for the Mauna Kea Observatory have helped Hawaii become a major world center of astronomy. (*See also* United States, "Hawaii" ; individual entries in the Fact-Index on Hawaii persons, places, products, and events.)

**FURTHER RESOURCES FOR HAWAII**

**Carpenter, Allan.** Hawaii, rev. ed. (Childrens, 1979).
**Daws, Gavan.** Shoal of Time: A History of the Hawaiian Islands (Univ. of Hawaii Press, 1974).
**Feeney, Stephanie.** Hawaii Is a Rainbow (Univ. of Hawaii Press, 1985).
**Fradin, Dennis.** Hawaii: In Words and Pictures (Childrens, 1980).
**Lye, Keith.** Take a Trip to Hawaii (Watts, 1988).
**McNair, Sylvia.** America the Beautiful: Hawaii (Childrens, 1990).
**Morgan, J.R.** Hawaii: A Geography (Westview, 1983).
**Nordyke, E.C.** The Peopling of Hawaii, 2nd ed. (Univ. of Hawaii Press, 1989).
**Rublowsky, John.** Born in Fire: A Geological History of Hawaii (Harper, 1981).
**Tabrah, Ruth.** Hawaii: A History (Norton, 1984).

## Notable Events in Hawaii History

**Between 300 and 600.** Islands settled by Polynesians believed to have arrived from Tahiti.

**1778.** Capt. James Cook, English explorer, visits the islands; names them Sandwich Islands for sponsor, earl of Sandwich; killed by Hawaiians in 1779.

**1792–94.** Captain George Vancouver makes three visits to the islands; introduces cattle and sheep.

**1795.** Chief Kamehameha wins battle of Nuuanu Valley; conquers most of the islands; proclaims kingdom, which lasts until 1893.

**1819.** First American whaler calls at Honolulu, Oahu; whaling reaches peak in 1858. Ancient religious system of taboo ended.

**1820.** First New England missionaries arrive; organize schools.

**1835.** Three New Englanders, as Ladd & Company, establish first successful commercial sugar plantation, on Kauai.

**1840.** King Kamehameha III proclaims constitution.

**1848.** Feudal landholding system broken up by the Great Mahele, or division of land.

**1849.** Hawaii concludes its first treaty with the United States.

**1875.** Reciprocity treaty signed with the United States for free exchange of goods; stimulates sugar industry.

**1886.** Captain John Kidwell founds pineapple industry; starts a pineapple cannery in 1892.

**1887.** United States granted exclusive right to Pearl Harbor for coaling and repair station; naval base authorized by Congress in 1908.

**1893.** Revolutionists dethrone Queen Liliuokalani, install provisional government in anticipation of union with United States, elect Sanford B. Dole president.

**1894.** Republic of Hawaii created.

**1898.** President William McKinley signs resolution annexing Hawaiian Islands to United States on July 7.

**1900.** Organic Act creates Territory of Hawaii; capital, Honolulu; Capitol, Iolani Palace; governor, Sanford B. Dole.

**1901.** First successful commercial pineapple cannery organized.

**1903.** Territorial legislature petitions Congress for statehood for first time. Telegraph cable links Hawaii and United States.

**1906.** Fort Ruger established; Forts Shafter and Armstrong, in 1907; Schofield Barracks and Forts Kamehameha and DeRussy, in 1909.

**1907.** University of Hawaii founded at Honolulu.

**1916.** Hawaii National Park established; section on Hawaii named Hawaii

Volcanoes National Park and section on Maui, Haleakala National Park, in 1961.

**1927.** First nonstop flight made from United States mainland.

**1929.** Air service begun among the islands.

**1931.** First interisland and transpacific radio-telephone service.

**1935.** China Clipper makes first commercial flight across Pacific from San Francisco, Calif., to Honolulu.

**1941.** Japanese attack Pearl Harbor.

**1947.** First statehood bill for Hawaii fails in Senate.

**1950.** Constitutional Convention draws up a constitution for the "State of Hawaii"; effective in 1959.

**1959.** Hawaii becomes 50th state.

**1961.** City of Refuge National Historical Park created.

**1968.** New State Capitol completed.

**1972.** Hawaii's first full medical school approved; first law school established in 1973.

**1974.** George Ariyoshi becomes first Japanese American to be elected governor of a state.

**1986.** Molten lava from Kilauea volcano destroys dozens of buildings and forces evacuation of 400 persons.

**1994.** United States Navy returns control of Kahoolawe Island to the state of Hawaii. A 1941 agreement had given the island to the Navy for use as a target site for gunners.

*An oil painting entitled 'The Death of Cook' depicts the killing of explorer Capt. James Cook in 1779, on the beach at Kealakekua. He was about to set out for a discovery voyage in the North Pacific.*

Bishop Museum

## Some Notable People of Hawaii

*The people listed below are associated with Hawaii, though some of them may not have been born there. Some prominent people are not included below because they are covered in other articles in Compton's Encyclopedia (see Fact-Index).*

**Bingham, Hiram** (1789–1869). Missionary and translator. Born on Oct. 30, 1789, in Bennington, Vt. He worked for the American Board of Boston in the Hawaiian Islands from 1820 to 1840. While in Honolulu, he helped reduce the Hawaiian language to writing and devised a 12-letter alphabet. The missionaries taught the native people to read, and between 1825 and 1839 he and several associates translated the New Testament of the Bible into Hawaiian. His publications include, 'Elementary Lessons in Hawaiian' (1822) and 'First Book for Children' (1831).

**Bishop, Bernice P.** (1831–84). Princess and philanthropist. Born in 1831 in Honolulu, Hawaii. She was the last direct descendant of King Kamehameha I and was raised with her adoptive sister, who later became Queen Liliuokalani. She attended the Royal School and married Charles Bishop, an American banker and philanthropist in 1850. With money she provided in her will, the Kamehameha Schools for Hawaiian children were established.

**Damien, Father** (1840–89). Belgian priest. Born on Jan. 3, 1840, in Tremelo, Belgium. He was ordained as a priest in Honolulu in 1864. In 1873 a settlement of lepers was founded on Molokai Island and Father Damien volunteered to take charge. While there he improved water and food supplies and housing, and founded two orphanages. He contracted leprosy in 1884 but refused a cure because it would mean leaving the island. He was nominated for a place of honor for Hawaii in the National Statuary Hall in 1965.

**Dole, James D.** (1877–1958). Founder of Hawaiian pineapple industry. Born on Sept. 27, 1877, in Jamaica Plain, Mass.

After graduating from Harvard University in 1899, he moved to Hawaii. In 1901 he established the Hawaiian Pineapple Company (now Dole Company) and began producing and marketing mass quantities of canned pineapple. In the 1930s the company was reorganized and Dole was given the honorary title of chairman of the board. He was responsible for such innovations in pineapple growing as paper mulching, motor trucks, and sulfate spray. In 1948 he resigned as chairman of the board.

**Fong, Hiram L.** (born 1907). United States senator. Born on Oct. 1, 1907, in Honolulu, Hawaii. He was the deputy attorney for the city and county of Honolulu and served in the Hawaii House of Representatives. In 1959 he became the first United States senator of Asian ancestry. He retired from the Senate in 1977.

**Inouye, Daniel K.** (born 1924). United States senator. Born on Sept. 7, 1924, in Honolulu, Hawaii. After earning his law degree, he became involved in politics and in 1959 became the new state of Hawaii's first United States Representative. He was the first Japanese American to serve in Congress. In 1962 he became a senator. In 1972 he was appointed to the Senate Watergate Committee to investigate the Nixon Administration. In 1986 he was picked to be chairman of the Senate Select Committee to investigate the Iran-*contra* scandal.

**Kahanamoku, Duke** (1890–1968). Swimming champion. Born on Aug. 26, 1890, near Waikiki, Oahu, Hawaii. He won the 100-meter freestyle event in the Olympic Games of 1912 and 1920 and was a member of the United States team that won the 800-meter relay race in the 1920 games. He developed the flutter kick and was considered the greatest swimmer of his time. He was the sheriff of the city and county of Honolulu from 1932 to 1961.

**Midler, Bette** (born 1945). Entertainer. Born on Dec. 1, 1945, in Honolulu, Hawaii. In 1966 she was cast in the chorus of 'Fiddler on the Roof'. After she left the show in 1969, she performed at a cabaret in New York City, where she did comedy song and dance. It was there she was first called The Divine Miss M. This recognition led her to a serious film role in 'The Rose' (1979), for which she was nominated for an Academy award. After a five-year slump, Midler made a comeback, appearing in four successful comedies within two years. She then took on a more serious role in the movie 'Beaches' in 1988. She won a Grammy for best song of the year ('Wind Beneath My Wings') from the 'Beaches' soundtrack in 1990. Other movies include, 'Down and Out in Beverly Hills' (1986), 'Ruthless People' (1986), 'Outrageous Fortune' (1987), 'Stella' (1990), and 'For the Boys' (1991).

**Duke Kahanamoku**　　AP/Wide World

**Bette Midler**　　AP/Wide World

**Bernice P. Bishop**　　Bishop Museum

**Father Damien**　　Courtesy of the Damien Museum

**Hiram L. Fong**　　AP/Wide World

# Hawaii Fact Summary

## POPULATION TRENDS

| Year | Population | Rank Among States |
|------|-----------|-------------------|
| 1890 | 89,990 | |
| 1900 | 154,001 | |
| 1920 | 255,881 | |
| 1930 | 368,300 | |
| 1940 | 422,770 | |
| 1950 | 499,794 | |
| 1960 | 632,772 | 43 |
| 1970 | 769,913 | 40 |
| 1980 | 964,961 | 39 |
| 1990 | 1,108,229 | 40 |
| 2000 | 1,211,537 | 42 |

## THE LAND

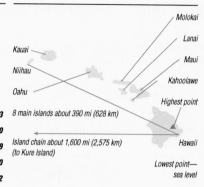

Kauai
Niihau
Oahu
Molokai
Lanai
Maui
Kahoolawe
Highest point
Hawaii
Lowest point— sea level

8 main islands about 390 mi (628 km)

Island chain about 1,600 mi (2,575 km) (to Kure Island)

## LARGEST CITIES AND OTHER PLACES (2000 census)

**Honolulu** (371,657). Capital and chief port of state on Oahu; commercial and industrial center; hub for transpacific shipping and air routes; pineapple canneries, sugar refineries, clothing, steel, aluminum, petroleum, cement, dairies; Iolani Palace; University of Hawaii (*see* Honolulu).

**Hilo** (40,759). Chief city and port on island of Hawaii; sugarcane, orchids, macadamia nuts; gateway to Hawaii Volcanoes National Park; Lyman Mission House and Museum; Rainbow Falls nearby; University of Hawaii at Hilo.

**Kailua** (36,513). Residential city on Kailua Bay of Oahu; twin community with Lanikai; excellent white beaches; temple ruins in vicinity.

**Kaneohe** (34,970). Residential town near Kaneohe Bay on Oahu; coral gardens; Waikalua, home of legendary Tahitian prince who introduced the hula to Hawaiians.

**Waipahu** (33,108). Residential city on Oahu.

**Pearl City** (30,976). Industrial and residential city on Oahu.

**Mililani Town** (28,608). City on Oahu; near Wheeler Air Force Base.

**Wahiawa** (16,151). In central Oahu; pineapple-growing area; adjoins Schofield Barracks.

**Schofield Barracks** (14,428). On Oahu; Tropic Lightning Historical Center; assortment of weapons from World War II.

## VITAL STATISTICS 1998 (per 1,000 population)

**Birthrate.** 14.4 (1999)
**Death Rate.** 6.8
**Marriage Rate.** 17.5
**Divorce Rate.** 4.0

## GOVERNMENT

**Capital.** Honolulu (since 1850).
**Statehood.** Became 50th state in the Union on Aug. 21, 1959.
**Constitution.** Adopted 1950; amendment may be passed by two-thirds vote of each legislative house at one session or by majority vote of each house at two sessions; ratified by majority voting on it in an election.
**Representation in U.S. Congress.** Senate—2. House of Representatives—2. Electoral votes—4.
**Legislature.** Senators—25; term, 4 years. Representatives—51; term, 2 years.
**Executive Officers.** Governor—term, 4 years; may succeed self once. Other officials—lieutenant governor; elected; term, 4 years.
**Judiciary.** Supreme Court—5 justices; term, 10 years. Intermediate Court of Appeals—4 judges; term, 10 years. Circuit courts—28 judges; term, 10 years.
**County.** 5 counties.

## MAJOR PRODUCTS

**Agricultural.** Pineapples, sugarcane, flowers, macadamia nuts, coffee, papayas, cattle, pigs, chickens, milk, fish, shellfish.
**Manufactured.** Food products, canned pineapple, preserved fruits and vegetables, apparel and textile products, printing and publishing, processed sugar.
**Mined.** Cement, gem stones, construction sand and gravel, crushed stone.

## EDUCATION AND CULTURE

**Universities and Colleges.** Brigham Young University/Hawaii Campus, Laie; Chaminade University of Honolulu, University of Hawaii at Manoa, Hawaii Pacific University, Honolulu and Kanouke Campuses; University of Hawaii at Manoa and Hilo Campuses.
**Libraries.** Bernice P. Bishop Museum Library, Hawaii State Library System, Library for the Blind and Physically Handicapped, University of Hawaii Libraries, all in Honolulu; Hawaii Volcanoes National Park Library, Hawaii Volcanoes National Park.
**Notable Museums.** Bishop Museum, Honolulu Academy of Arts, Mission Houses Museum, Conteporary Museum, all in Honolulu; Grove Farm Homestead, Lihue; Hale Hoikeike, Bailey House Museum, Wailuku; Lyman House Memorial Museum, Hilo; Pacific Botanical Garden, Lawai.

## EMPLOYMENT Percentage by Industry

**Total Number of Persons Employed: 745,000.**

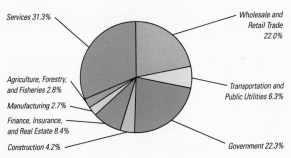

Services 31.3%

Wholesale and Retail Trade 22.0%

Agriculture, Forestry, and Fisheries 2.8%

Manufacturing 2.7%

Finance, Insurance, and Real Estate 8.4%

Construction 4.2%

Transportation and Public Utilities 6.3%

Government 22.3%

## GROSS STATE PRODUCT Percentage by Industry*

**Total GSP: $40,914,000,000. Per Capita Income: $28,221.**

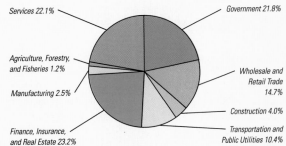

Services 22.1%

Government 21.8%

Agriculture, Forestry, and Fisheries 1.2%

Manufacturing 2.5%

Wholesale and Retail Trade 14.7%

Construction 4.0%

Finance, Insurance, and Real Estate 23.2%

Transportation and Public Utilities 10.4%

## PLACES OF INTEREST

**Ala Moana Park.** In Honolulu; 118-acre (48-hectare) beach; picnicking.

**Bishop Museum.** In Honolulu; exhibits of Polynesian and early Hawaiian culture; natural history exhibits.

**Black Sand Beach.** In Kalapana; jet black sand.

**Captain Cook Monument.** At Kealakekua Bay; marks spot where Hawaiians killed explorer.

**City of Refuge National Historical Park.** Near Keokea; ruins of ancient sanctuary; prehistoric home sites; royal fishponds; spectacular shore scenery.

**Diamond Head.** Crater overlooks Waikiki.

**East-West Center.** In Honolulu; federally financed institution for Asian and United States students.

**Foster Gardens.** In Honolulu; flowering orchids; collection of tropical plants and trees.

**Halawa Valley.** Near Halawa on Molaki; picturesque valley.

**Haleakala National Park.** Near Koali; dormant volcano 10,023 feet (3,055 meters) high; one of largest craters known; birdlife.

**Hana.** Waterfalls, cliffs, beach.

**Hanalei Valley.** Near Hanalei; scenic valley.

**Hawaii Volcanoes National Park.** Near city of Volcano; two active volcanoes; rare plants and animals.

**Hickam Field.** Near Honolulu; Air Force base.

**Honolulu Academy of Arts.** In Honolulu; art exhibits.

**Honolulu Aquarium.** In Honolulu; tropical marine life.

**Iao Valley State Monument.** Near Wailuku; 2,250-foot- (670-meter-) high monolith called the Needle.

**Iolani Palace.** In Honolulu; former territorial and State Capitol; former residence of Hawaiian royalty.

**Kalaupapa Peninsula.** In north-central Molokai; state's Hansen's Disease Treatment Center.

**Kapiolani Park.** In Honolulu; bandstand, zoo.

**Keaiwa Heiau State Recreation Area.** Near Aiea; old healing temple; collection of medicinal plants; picnicking; trails.

**Kona Coast.** West coast of Hawaii; coffee farms; deep-sea fishing.

**Lava Tree State Monument.** Near Pahoa; volcanic formations.

**McKenzie State Recreation Area.** Near Kalapana; ironwood grove; picnicking, camping.

**Manuka State Wayside.** Near Naatehu; botanical collection.

**Mauna Kea State Recreation Area.** Near Huumula; one of Hawaii's highest mountains; hunting, hiking.

**Menehune Fish Pond.** Near Lihue; built by first inhabitants, the legendary Menehunes.

**Mormon Temple.** In Laie; large religious edifice.

**National Memorial Cemetery of the Pacific.** In Punchbowl Crater, Honolulu.

**Nuuanu Pali.** Mountain pass near Honolulu.

**Old Russian Fort.** Near Waimea; built in 1817.

**Parker Ranch.** Near Kamuela; huge cattle ranch.

**Pearl Harbor.** United States naval base near Honolulu.

**Puu Ualakaa State Wayside.** Near Honolulu; scenic views.

**Queen Emma Summer Palace.** In Honolulu; summer home of former queen.

**Royal Mausoleum.** In Honolulu; burial ground of Hawaiian kings.

**Schofield Barracks.** Army post near Wahiawa.

**Spouting Horn of Koloa.** Near Eleele; water geyser.

**University of Hawaii.** In Honolulu, Manoa, and Hilo.

**Waikiki Beach.** Near Honolulu; famous beach; surfing.

**Wailoa River State Recreation Area.** Near Hilo; landscaped park; picnicking, fishing, boating.

**Wailua River State Park.** Near Kapaa; former royal coconut grove; camping, water sports; Fern Grotto; Opaekaa Falls overlook.

**Waimea Canyon State Park.** Near Kekaha; deep gorge cut by Waimea River; trails; picnicking; hunting, fishing.

**Wet and Dry Caves of Haena.** In Haena; great caverns.

*All Fact Summary data are based on current government reports. Details may not total 100% due to rounding.

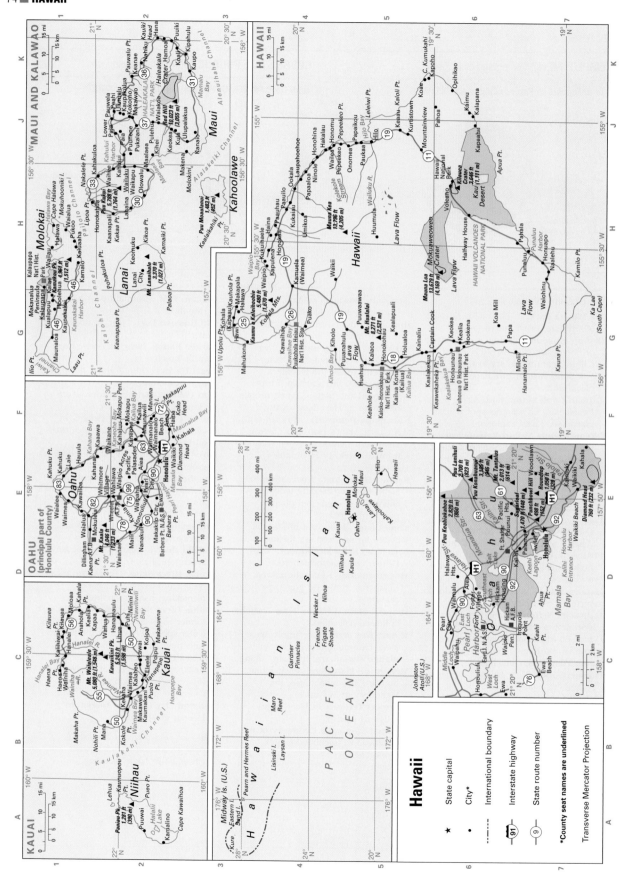

# Hawaii

2000 census information is unavailable for cities listed without population figures.

**HAWK** *see* **BIRDS OF PREY.**

**HAWKE, Bob** (born 1929). When the Australian Labour party (ALP) defeated the Liberal-National coalition in 1983, Bob Hawke achieved his lifetime ambition to be Australia's prime minister. The flamboyant labor leader was reelected in the early election he called in 1984 and then won an unprecedented third term in 1987. For a time he seemed cool and invincible, but in 1990 his party barely managed a parliamentary majority in the closest election ever held in Australia to that time. Hawke won a fourth term as prime minister even though his economic reform program had failed after his first six years in power.

Robert James Lee Hawke was born in Bordertown, South Australia, on Dec. 9, 1929. Hawke earned a law degree at the University of Western Australia in 1950 and spent two years (1953–55) at Oxford University in England as a Rhodes scholar. Back in Australia, he became a research scholar at the Australian National University in Canberra.

After joining the Australian Council of Trade Unions (ACTU) in 1958, Hawke quickly earned a reputation as an effective negotiator of wage settlements. From 1970 until 1980 he served as president of the ACTU. A member of the ALP since his student days, Hawke served as the party's national president from 1973 to 1978. In 1980 he was elected to Parliament. In 1983, after Prime Minister Malcolm Fraser had called for new elections, Hawke was the surprising choice for ALP leader to run against him. Hawke led the Labour party to a landslide victory over the Liberals.

During the 1990 election campaign, Hawke dropped his previous emphasis on economic issues. He lost support during his fourth term because of a deep recession and was ousted in December 1991 by Paul Keating, Hawke's former treasurer and deputy prime minister. Hawke was the first Australian prime minister to be ousted by his own party.

**HAWKING, Stephen** (born 1942). One of the most admired and brilliant theoretical physicists of the 20th century, Stephen Hawking became a widely known celebrity as well after his book 'A Brief History of Time: From the Big Bang to Black Holes' unexpectedly became a best-seller in 1988 (a motion picture based on the book followed). He specialized in the study of black holes, the elusive remains of collapsed giant stars (*see* Black Hole). He also worked in the areas of general relativity, thermodynamics, and quantum mechanics in seeking to understand how the universe began. His achievements have proved all the more amazing because he suffered since the early 1960s from the severely debilitating amyotrophic lateral sclerosis—Lou Gehrig's disease—which gradually destroys the nerve and muscle systems.

Stephen William Hawking was born on Jan. 8, 1942, in Oxford, England, and grew up in London. He attended St. Albans School and entered Oxford University in 1959. Upon graduating in 1962 he moved to Cambridge University to study theoretical astronomy and cosmology. It was at this time he was diagnosed with amyotrophic lateral sclerosis. As the disease worsened, Hawking was confined to a motorized wheelchair. In time, he was unable to write and barely able to speak. He, however, proceeded to work on his doctorate and in 1965 married a fellow student, Jane Wilde. (The marriage lasted until 1990.)

After receiving his doctorate in 1966, he remained at Cambridge as a member of the department of applied mathematics. He was appointed professor of gravitational physics in 1977 and Lucasian professor of mathematics (a chair previously held by Sir Isaac Newton) in April 1980. His earliest work, in collaboration with Roger Penrose, dealt with Einstein's general theory of relativity, black holes, and gravity. The great success of 'A Brief History of Time' surprised him. He followed it with a series of essays, 'Black Holes and Baby Universes and Other Essays' in 1993, and with 'The Universe in a Nutshell' in 2001.

**HAWTHORNE, Nathaniel** (1804–64). Although his friends included a number of noted transcendentalists—such as Ralph Waldo Emerson, Henry David Thoreau, and Bronson Alcott—Nathaniel Hawthorne's works show little of the optimism and self-confidence that marked transcendentalism. Instead, he preferred themes drawn more from a Puritan preoccupation with guilt and the natural depravity of humans.

Hawthorne was born on July 4, 1804, in Salem, Mass. His family, early Puritan settlers in America, had lived in Salem since the 1600s. One of his ancestors may have been a judge in the Salem witchcraft trials. Hawthorne's father, a ship's captain, died when Nathaniel was only 4, and his mother became a virtual recluse. Hawthorne attended Bowdoin College in Brunswick, Me., where he befriended Franklin Pierce, who later became a president of the United States.

Hawthorne decided to become a writer, but until the 1840s he wrote little except for an amateurish novel, 'Fanshawe', published anonymously at his own expense in 1828. Some stories he sold to magazines were published as 'Twice Told Tales' in 1837. The publication cost of the collection was underwritten by another of his college friends, Horatio Bridge. He worked in the Boston Customhouse from 1839 to 1840, after which he spent a few months at Brook Farm, a cooperative agricultural community in West Roxbury, Mass. The Brook Farm experience was later described in his novel 'The Blithedale Romance' (1852).

In 1842 Hawthorne married Sophia Peabody. The young couple spent the next three years in the Old Manse in Concord, where he wrote a second series of 'Twice Told Tales'. 'Mosses from an Old Manse', published in 1846, describes their happy life in Concord. In 1845 Hawthorne returned to Salem and again worked in a customhouse. Relieved of that job in 1849, he found time to write. His best-known work, 'The Scarlet Letter', was published in 1850. Moving from Salem to Lenox, Mass., Hawthorne wrote 'The House of the Seven Gables', which came out the following year. At Lenox he made the acquaintance of

*Nathaniel Hawthorne, in a photograph by Mathew Brady*
The Granger Collection, New York

Herman Melville, a fellow writer whose novels show Hawthorne's influence. After a short stay in West Newton, Mass., the Hawthornes returned to Concord, where they purchased a house that had belonged to Bronson Alcott, renaming it Wayside.

In 1853 Franklin Pierce became president. He offered Hawthorne a consulship in Liverpool, England, a post that Hawthorne held until 1857. After resigning his position as consul, Hawthorne traveled in Europe, mostly in Italy. In 1860 the Hawthornes returned to their home in Concord. After 'The Marble Faun', published that year, Hawthorne wrote little. He aged rapidly and found it increasingly difficult to write. On May 19, 1864, while traveling with his friend Pierce, Hawthorne died in Plymouth, N.H.

Hawthorne wrote relatively little, but if he had written only 'The Scarlet Letter' his position as a major American writer would have been assured. The symbolism, psychological insight, and clarity of expression found in his writing have provided a model for generations of American writers.

**HAY.** One of the most useful farm products is hay, the principal winter fodder of cattle and horses. Hay is not a single crop. It is cut from legumes such as clover, alfalfa, and soybeans and from grasses such as timothy, upland grasses, and midland grasses. Even cereals such as rye, oats, and barley may be cut and cured as hay. Some hayfields, such as alfalfa and red clover, produce two or more crops a year.

To retain the sugar and other nutrients in the stalk and leaves, hay must be cut while in flower and before the seed matures. If left standing too long the stems and leaves become too dry for feed.

After it is cut the hay is left in the field for several days to cure in the sun. To keep it from drying too rapidly farmers rake it into long rows, called windrows, or into small piles, called cocks. Curing develops the flavor and keeps the hay from spoiling when stored; properly cured hay, with a moisture content of 20 percent or less, may be stored for months without danger of spoilage.

When the hay is dry enough, farmers either bale, stack, or chop it. Baling machines compress the hay into tightly packed rectangular or cylindrical bales weighing from about 50 to 100 pounds (23 to 45 kilograms) and tied with wire or twine. The bales can then be transported and stored either in barns or outdoors. A hay stacking machine may also be used to pile hay into large mounds.

The farmer may chop the hay using a forage harvester, which cuts the hay into short pieces. The hay is then stored in the barn in a pile called a haymow.

When farmers leave their hay drying in the field, they run the risk that heavy rains may ruin their entire crop. To avoid such a loss, many farmers now cure the hay artificially in ventilated haymows, where large fans blow air through the hay. If ventilation is inadequate, the hay may generate enough heat to catch fire.

Sometimes farmers choose an alternative method of treating hay. They cut and chop the hay while it is still green and, after one day of drying, put it into silos where fermentation changes it into silage (*see* Silo).

**HAYDN, Joseph** (1732–1809). Called the father of both the symphony and the string quartet, Joseph Haydn founded what is known as the Viennese classical school—consisting of Haydn, his friend Mozart, and his pupil Beethoven. He lived from the end of the baroque period to the beginning of the romantic and presided over the musical transition between them. His distinct style combined elements of the baroque, the gallant style from Italy and France, and the emotional *empfindsamer Stil,* or "sensitive style," of the north Germans. (*See also* Music, Classical.)

Franz Joseph Haydn was born on March 31, 1732, in Rohrau, Austria. When he was 7 he entered the choir school of St. Stephen's Cathedral in Vienna. He composed avidly but had no formal training until his late teens, when he worked with the Italian Niccolò Porpora. In 1761 Haydn was engaged by the Esterházy family, and until the death in 1790 of Prince Miklós József Esterházy, Haydn directed an orchestra, choir, and opera company. At their castle Esterháza Haydn composed a continuous stream of works for performance. His fame spread throughout Europe, and his works were published, but he tired of the confinement. Prince Miklós's successor, however, cared nothing for music, and Haydn was suddenly free.

The impresario Johann Peter Salomon offered Haydn a contract for 12 new pieces to be performed in London. Haydn was lionized in London, and he stayed for 18 months, returning again in 1794. His two sets of symphonies known as the 'Salomon', or 'London' (Nos. 93–104), and the six 'Apponyi Quartets' are among his greatest works.

He returned to Vienna in 1795, and his late oratorios—'The Creation', first performed in 1798, and 'The Seasons' (1801)—were finally successful with the Viennese public. Haydn died in Vienna on May 31, 1809. His enormous output includes 107 symphonies, about 50 divertimenti, 84 string quartets, about 58 piano sonatas, and 13 masses, among numerous other works.

Hayes Memorial Library

*19th President of the United States
(1822–93; president 1877–81)*

# RUTHERFORD B. HAYES

The presidential election of 1876 between Rutherford B. Hayes and Samuel Tilden was the most bitterly contested in United States history. Both the Democrats and the Republicans accused each other of fraud. Not until March 2, two days before President Grant's term expired, was the issue at last settled. The electoral commission decided in favor of the Republican candidate, Hayes.

### Birth and Boyhood

Rutherford B. Hayes was born in Delaware, Ohio, Oct. 4, 1822. Five years earlier his father, Rutherford Hayes, had moved to Ohio from Vermont with his wife, Sophia Birchard Hayes, and Mrs. Hayes's brother, Sardis Birchard. Mr. Hayes invested his money in good farmland, which he rented, and built for his family the first brick house in Delaware. He died 10 weeks before Rutherford, who was known as Ruddy, was born. Her brother took over the guardianship of her three children, Lorenzo, Fanny, and Ruddy, and acted as a father to them.

Before Ruddy was two years old his brother, Lorenzo, then nine years old, was drowned while skating. Mrs. Hayes determined to protect little Ruddy, who was delicate, from all perils. She would not allow him to play with the boys in the neighborhood or go to school; and she herself taught him reading and spelling. The boy's sole companion was his sister Fanny, a bright, active girl two years older than himself. The two children read together and played together. Fanny loved poetry; she was also a tomboy and could always think of something exciting to do.

At 14, Rutherford was sent to a school in Norwalk, Ohio. The next year he attended an academy in Middletown, Conn. At 16 he entered Kenyon College, in Gambier, Ohio. The next year Fanny married William Platt, who had a jewelry store in Columbus. Mrs. Hayes gave up the old home to live with the Platts in Columbus.

Rutherford was a serious student, and his diary (which he kept all his life) shows that he tried constantly to improve his character as well as his mind. At 19 he wrote: "I am determined to acquire a character distinguished for energy, firmness, and perseverance." He resolved also to "preserve a reputation for honesty and benevolence." He even decided to stop laughing "entirely in future, if I can" because "the tendency to carry it to extremes is so great." His chief interest in school was debating, in which he excelled. His recreations were fishing, playing chess, and reading novels (though he called novels "trash").

### He Becomes a Lawyer and Marries

After graduating from Kenyon, Hayes spent a year in Fanny's home reading law and studying German and French. Then his Uncle Sardis furnished money for him to study at the Harvard Law School. Hayes was almost 21 when he arrived in Cambridge, Mass. Dressed in a modish manner, he looked like a proper Bostonian. He studied until he was weary and tried hard to be still more serious. "Trifling remarks, boyish conduct, are my crying sins. Mend! Mend!" In January 1845 he received the bachelor of laws degree.

Instead of returning to Columbus, Hayes went into a law office in Lower Sandusky (later called Fremont), where his Uncle Sardis lived. He spent nearly five years in the small village waiting for clients. Then he became restless and despondent and had spells of weeping. After a vacation in the East, he decided to move to Cincinnati, then a growing, thriving city.

In Cincinnati, Hayes and another young man rented an office and partitioned off one corner for a bedroom. Hayes joined the Literary Club, where he made influential friends, and the Sons of Temperance, for whom he made his first public speech. He also entered local politics in the new Republican party. Within a few years he had made a name for himself as a criminal lawyer and began to think of marriage.

Hayes's mother chose a girl for him. She was Lucy Ware Webb, whom Hayes had first met at his home in Delaware when she was 15. They became engaged after she was graduated from Wesleyan Female College in Cincinnati and were married in December 1852. Hayes was then 30. Lucy, nine years younger, was warmhearted, popular, and very religious. "A better wife I never hoped to have," Hayes confided to his diary. Their first son, Birchard Austin, was born in 1853.

### He Serves in the Civil War

When the Civil War broke out, in 1861, Hayes at once volunteered and was given the rank of major. Camping in the beautiful mountains of western Virginia (later West Virginia) he "enjoyed" the war, he said, "as if it were a pleasure tour." In 1862 he suffered a wound in an arm and Lucy went to the camp to nurse him. In 1864 he was in the thick of the fighting in the Shenandoah Valley with Sheridan. Grant commended him for conspicuous gallantry, and he left the army a brevetted major general of volunteers.

### As Congressman and Governor

Hayes was nominated and elected to Congress while still in the army, but he refused to leave his command until the war was over. He took his seat in the House in December 1865 and was reelected in 1866. He made few speeches and took no part in the bitter debates over reconstruction but voted consistently with his party.

In 1867 and again in 1869 Hayes was elected governor of Ohio. He proved a capable and economical administrator. He took great interest in prison reform and in hospitals for the mentally ill. His beloved sister Fanny had been hospitalized more than once for mental illness.

In 1873 Hayes declared he was finished with politics and moved his family to his uncle's house at Fremont, called Spiegel Grove. His uncle died the next year and left the bulk of his large estate (chiefly land) to Hayes. The Hayeses now had five children (three had died in childhood). The oldest boys, Birchard, Webb, and Rutherford, were at college. At home were Fanny, seven; and Scott Russell, four. Hayes was the leading citizen of Fremont and was listed in the directory as a "capitalist."

Hayes's retirement was brief. After one year he was persuaded to run for Congress; but the Democrats swept the country in 1874 and he was defeated. Ohio itself had elected a Democratic governor in 1873. The Republicans, knowing Hayes to be a good vote getter, nominated him for governor again in 1875. Hayes's success in a hard-fought campaign made him a presidential possibility in 1876.

### The Disputed Presidential Election

The Republican nominating convention met in Cincinnati. Grant's decision not to seek a third term left the field open. The leading candidate was Senator James G. Blaine, the so-called "plumed knight." Blaine had been accused of graft, and reformers controlled the convention. Hayes suited the reformers as well as the practical politicians; moreover, he would bring in

Hayes Memorial Library

*Hayes, blue-eyed and auburn-haired, was an earnest young man. Lucy was earnest too; she detested slavery and intemperance. Large black eyes gave her face its particular beauty.*

the needed Ohio vote. Gradually the drift to Hayes gathered strength, and Ohio's "favorite son" won out over the brilliant senator. Congressman William A. Wheeler of New York was nominated vice-president.

The Democratic party also nominated a reform candidate—Samuel J. Tilden, who had helped to overthrow the Tammany Hall Tweed Ring in New York City. The new National Independent party, commonly called the Greenback party, nominated Peter Cooper, a New York philanthropist. The campaign was bitterly fought, although the platforms of the two major parties differed little. Both were for "hard money," civil service reform, and an end to corruption in government. The Greenback party wanted to raise farm prices by inflating the currency with paper money. The Republicans had many handicaps—the scandals of Grant's administrations; the abuses of reconstruction in the South; and the hard times that still persisted following the panic of 1873.

On election night Hayes went to bed convinced that he had lost the election. The next day, however, the Republican campaign manager, Zachary Chandler, boldly proclaimed Hayes the victor.

Three Southern states—South Carolina, Florida, and Louisiana—had sent in double returns. In these states the election boards were dominated by Republicans (some of them "carpetbaggers" from the North). They refused to accept the apparent Democratic majorities and certified that the states had gone Republican. The Democrats, however, sent in their own returns. On both sides there was undoubtedly fraud.

Week after week congress debated the election. The Senate, which was Republican, declared for Hayes. The House, which was Democratic, said Tilden had won. The year ended with no decision reached. Finally

## Time Line of Presidents, Events, and Periods

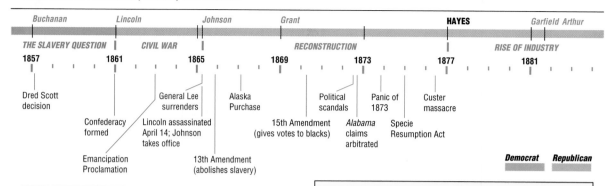

Buchanan | Lincoln | Johnson | Grant | **HAYES** | Garfield Arthur

*THE SLAVERY QUESTION* | *CIVIL WAR* | *RECONSTRUCTION* | *RISE OF INDUSTRY*

1857     1861     1865     1869     1873     1877     1881

Dred Scott
decision

Confederacy
formed

Emancipation
Proclamation

General Lee
surrenders

Lincoln assassinated
April 14; Johnson
takes office

13th Amendment
(abolishes slavery)

Alaska
Purchase

15th Amendment
(gives votes to blacks)

Political
scandals

*Alabama*
claims
arbitrated

Panic of
1873

Specie
Resumption Act

Custer
massacre

**Democrat**    **Republican**

The Bettmann Archive

*Carl Schurz, secretary of the interior, is at the piano during a Sunday evening's entertainment at the White House, while Margarethe stands leaning on the piano. William M. Evarts, secretary of state, stands beside President Hayes. Behind Schurz sits Mrs. Hayes with young Scott next to her.*

### HAYES'S ADMINISTRATION 1877–81

Civil Service reform begun.
Federal troops removed from the South and Reconstruction ended (1877).
Halifax award in fisheries dispute with Great Britain (1877).
Miners' strikes ("Molly McGuire" outrages) and railroad strikes (1876–77).
Right of states to regulate railroad rates upheld (1877).
Greenback party at height of its power (1878).
Bland-Allison Act passed over the president's veto (1878).
Specie payments resumed (1879).

### The Hayes Family in the White House

A new order began in the White House when the Hayeses moved in. Like Queen Victoria in England, they determined to set an example in their home life for the nation to follow. They had no dances or card parties, and wine never appeared on the table, even at state dinners.

In informal gatherings they continued the customs of their Ohio home. The family consisted of the youngest children, Fanny and Scott, and Webb. Webb, a Cornell graduate, was his father's confidential secretary. Birchard was at Harvard Law School, and Rutherford was at Cornell.

Every morning at breakfast a chapter of the Bible was read, each person in turn reading one verse. Then all joined in the Lord's Prayer. Each evening there were hymns as well as prayers. On Sunday mornings President and Mrs. Hayes walked to the small Foundry Methodist church near the White House.

Mrs. Hayes was hospitable and liked to fill the house with young people. At times, Webb said, there were cots in the hall and couches in the reception room, and he considered himself fortunate to sleep on the billiard table (which had been relegated to the attic). Sometimes his father "had to lock himself in the bathroom to prepare some important state paper."

The most unusual social event was the Hayes's silver wedding anniversary, in 1877. Mrs. Hayes wore her original wedding dress, and the couple repeated their vows before the same minister who had married them 25 years before. Then the Hayes's two youngest children were baptized and christened.

Congress appointed an electoral commission to re-count the entire vote. The commission consisted of eight Republicans and seven Democrats. The vote on every count was eight to seven.

When it became clear that the commission would decide for Hayes, the Southern Democrats agreed to accept him if the Republicans would enter into a "bargain." More than the election of Tilden—a Northerner—they wanted Federal troops withdrawn from the South and the return of self-government to the states. The Republicans agreed; and on March 2 the commission announced that Hayes had 185 electoral votes and Tilden 184. Tilden would have been elected if only one of the 20 disputed electoral votes had gone to him. His popular vote was 4,284,020; Hayes's was 4,036,572.

Hayes had to set off for Washington before he knew with certainty what the commission's decision would be. Although he felt some doubt, he sincerely believed he was entitled to the election.

## Major World Events During Hayes's Administration

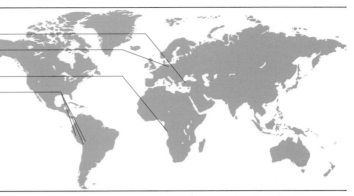

**Russo–Turkish War,** *1877–78*

**Congress of Berlin,** *1878, reduces Russia's gains*

**Africa.** *Stanley reaches mouth of Congo, 1877, after crossing Africa*

**Chile, Peru, Bolivia.** *War of the Pacific begins, 1879*

**Spiegel Grove, the residence of the Hayes family in Fremont, Ohio, has been preserved with its original furnishings. At the main entrance to the 25-acre wooded estate stands the Hayes Memorial Library and Museum.**
Hayes Memorial Library

### A Strong and Conscientious Administration

The presidency was weak and Congress strong when Hayes moved into the White House. Powerful senators had impeached President Johnson and overawed Grant.

They expected to control Hayes also and were by no means pleased with the tone of his inaugural address. The people of the country, however, applauded his much-quoted statement, "He serves his party best who serves his country best."

Hayes incurred the enmity of many Republican leaders by carrying out the "bargain." The "carpetbag" governments to which Hayes owed his election at once collapsed, and the South thereafter became solidly Democratic.

In April 1877 the last Federal troops were withdrawn from the South, and the long bitter period of reconstruction that followed the Civil War was at last ended (*see* Reconstruction Period).

Hayes next attacked the corrupt "spoils system"— the giving of government jobs to party workers as a reward for securing votes. In this he had the help of his secretary of the interior, Carl Schurz. Congress refused to pass civil service legislation or to appropriate money for examinations; but Hayes did succeed in awakening public interest, and civil service reform clubs sprang up in many states.

The worst abuses of the spoils system were in the customhouse of New York City. Hayes incurred the bitter enmity of Senator Roscoe Conkling of New York by dismissing Conkling's political friends from the top posts. One of the officials he dismissed was Chester A. Arthur, collector of the port of New York, who was later to become the twenty-first President of the United States. The other official he dismissed, Alonzo B. Cornell, became governor of New York in 1879.

### The Money Question

Hayes was anxious to return the country to the gold standard by carrying out the provisions of the Specie Resumption Act passed in Grant's administration. This act called for making United States paper money redeemable in coin by Jan. 1, 1879. Hayes's secretary of the treasury, John Sherman of Ohio, sold bonds to build up a gold reserve to be used on the day of resumption of specie payments.

In Congress there were inflationist groups in both the major parties that wanted plentiful, cheap money. There was also the small Greenback party, which demanded a larger circulation of paper money. These groups passed, over the president's veto, the Bland-Allison Act of 1878, which required the secretary of the treasury to purchase not less than 2 million dollars of silver bullion each month and coin it into dollars. Silver dollars had not been coined since 1806. Because of their weight and bulk they proved unpopular, and most did not circulate but remained in the treasury.

Resumption of specie payments began quietly on Jan. 1, 1879. Knowledge that every paper dollar was worth a gold dollar gave confidence to the businessmen, and the run on the treasury that had been expected did not take place. Foreign trade revived, and the depression began to lift. When Hayes left the White House the country was again prosperous.

**Return to Spiegel Grove**

Hayes had said before his election that he would not be a candidate for a second term. No one pressed him to change his mind. He stayed away from the nominating convention of 1880 and took no part in the campaign, though he approved of the candidate chosen—James A. Garfield. After leaving office Hayes was a man without a party, but he had won the affection and admiration of many people.

Back in Spiegel Grove, the Hayeses lived in ease and comfort and were never long without guests. Hayes worked for prison reform and crime prevention and became president of the Peabody Education Fund, which aimed to promote education in the South. He worked for improved education and training for black people. Rutherford B. Hayes died on Jan. 17, 1893. His wife, Lucy, had died four years before. Both of them were buried in Spiegel Grove. (For Hayes's Cabinet and Supreme Court appointments *see* Fact-Index.)

**FURTHER RESOURCES FOR RUTHERFORD B. HAYES**

**Davison, K.E.** The Presidency of Rutherford B. Hayes (Greenwood, 1988).

**Hoogenboom, A.A.** The Presidency of Rutherford B. Hayes (Univ. Press of Kansas, 1988).

**Kane, J.N.** Facts About the Presidents: A Compilation of Biographical and Historical Information, 5th ed. (Wilson, 1990).

**Kent, Zachary.** Rutherford B. Hayes: 19th President of the United States (Childrens, 1989).

**Robbins, N.E.** Rutherford B. Hayes: 19th President of the United States (Garrett, 1989).

**HAZEL.** The hazel—also called filbert—is a nutbearing plant that grows as a shrub or tree. There are about 15 species native to the North temperate zone. Various species are termed filbert, hazelnut, or cobnut, depending on the relative length of the nut to its husk (*see* Nuts). The large cobnut is a variety of the European species. The hazels form the genus *Corylus* and are members of the birch family Betulaceae.

*The hazel* (Corylus avellane)

The hazel is a deciduous plant with hairy leaves. The term hazel comes from the medium-brown shade of the acornlike nuts that lie in leafy cups at the end of the short branches. The plants range from 10 to 120 feet (3 to 36 meters) in height. In late winter yellow male catkins and smaller, red-centered clusters of female flowers appear on the same tree.

The oil pressed from European hazelnuts is used in food products and in perfumes and soaps. The branches, which are very tough and flexible, are used to make tool handles and walking sticks. California, Chinese, Japanese, Manchurian, Tibetan, and Turkish filberts are valuable hedgerow and ornamental trees.

**HAZLITT, William** (1778–1830). A vigorous writer with an easy, straightforward style, William Hazlitt wrote essays that have the flavor of conversation. His descriptions of his contemporaries, as in 'The Spirit of the Age', published in 1825, provide valuable insight into the life of the time.

William Hazlitt was born in Maidstone, Kent, England, on April 10, 1778. The son of a Unitarian minister, he spent his childhood in Ireland and America. When Hazlitt was 9, the family settled in Shropshire, where he read widely, forming the basis for his later writings. At this time he said, "I did nothing but think . . . or dip into some abstruse author, or look at the sky, or wander by the pebbled seaside."

Hazlitt studied painting for three years before turning to writing. He first struck his characteristic style in a series of familiar essays called 'Table Talk', published in 1821. After that he wrote essays and criticism and gave lectures, which were also published. Characteristic works include 'Lectures on the English Poets' and 'Lectures on the English Comic Writers', published in 1818 and 1819, respectively. In addition to 'The Spirit of the Age', his 'The Plain Speaker' (1826) is considered particularly effective.

**HEADACHE.** Pain involving the head is one of humanity's oldest and most common complaints. While headaches affect nearly all people at some time in their lives, it is estimated that one out of every ten people suffers chronic headache symptoms that may appear as seldom as once a month or as frequently as several times a day. For children the ratio is even higher—approximately one in every four will experience significant headaches by age 15. Among sufferers of all ages, the severity of headache pain can vary widely from a slight ache in the forehead or at the base of the skull to more intense pain involving one or both sides of the head.

The onset of symptoms may be gradual, as in the case of most tension headaches, or sudden, as with headaches caused either by an injury or by some physical disorder. Headaches may be accompanied by visual disturbances, dizziness, sweating, chills, nausea or vomiting, muscle weakness, confusion, or emotional reactions. These symptoms offer important clues for proper diagnosis and treatment of the headache and of any underlying, more serious problems.

Headache pain does not involve the brain tissue or bones of the skull, which are insensitive to pain. Headache pain is associated with nerves and blood vessels around the brain; certain nerves of the face, mouth, and throat; and the muscles in the head and neck. When the nerves in these structures become overstimulated, inflamed, or damaged, pain signals flash along neural pathways to the brain, and the person experiences a headache. (For information on transmission of nerve impulses *see* Nervous System.)

Psychological factors account for almost 90 percent of all headaches. Anxiety, depression, repressed anger or fear, stress reactions, and other strong emotions can cause chemical changes in the body and overstimulate pain-sensitive nerves in the neck and head. The remaining 10 percent of headaches can be traced to physical causes such as a misaligned jaw or bite (known as temporomandibular joint dysfunction, or TMJ); an injury to the head or neck; a brain tumor; or diseases such as meningitis, encephalitis, glaucoma, and diabetes. In some individuals headache pain may be triggered by allergic reactions to certain foods, drugs, or other substances, or by withdrawal from caffeine or sugar.

Although some headaches are intracranial, involving tissues inside the head, most are extracranial, or in the tissues surrounding or covering the skull. Intracranial headaches are caused by swelling of the arterial blood vessels at the base of the brain, by inflammation or bleeding around these arteries, or by a tumor or other mass pressing on certain veins or tissues inside the head. Extracranial headaches result from swollen extracranial arteries or from sustained contraction of face and neck muscles. The best known of these headaches are migraine, cluster, and tension headaches.

Approximately 12 million persons in the United States suffer migraine attacks. These are characterized by some of the following symptoms: severe pain on one or both sides of the head; loss of appetite, nausea and vomiting; and heightened sensitivity to light and sound. An attack may last from three or four hours to three or four days. Before migraine headache pain begins, some sufferers experience warning symptoms (collectively called an aura) such as a blank spot in their vision, a visual sensation of flashing or zigzag lines, weakness or tingling in arms or legs, or mental confusion. Women are more susceptible to migraines than men, and sufferers often have a family history of migraines. Although the exact cause is unknown, attacks are associated with reduced blood flow in the head and may be linked in some women to menstrual periods, birth control pills, or menopause. They can also be triggered by low blood sugar, high blood pressure, fatigue, stress, alcohol, glaring or flickering lights, tryamine (a chemical contained in some foods), and strong odors.

Cluster headaches, named for their occurrence in groups or clusters, begin with a sudden, intense throbbing pain around one eye, in the forehead, or on one side of the head. The nose and eyes generally water. The pain usually does not persist more than two hours for each episode, but there may be several attacks daily, weekly, or monthly. Some patients may then go for months or years between bouts. Cluster headaches affect men more often than women and usually start between the ages of 20 and 40. Their cause is unknown.

Tension headaches are familiar to people of all ages and in all lines of work. They usually develop in response to such emotional triggers as stress, depression, or anxiety and result from muscle contractions in the neck, face, and scalp. In some cases, physical factors such as degenerative arthritis or poor posture are the cause.

Medical science uses drugs, biofeedback, and dietary changes to relieve most types of headache pain. Analgesic drugs, or pain relievers, help reduce inflammation, relax muscles, and constrict or dilate blood vessels, but they often have unwelcome side effects. While aspirin produces fewer adverse reactions, it offers little relief in cases of severe or chronic headache. Drug therapy is often combined with biofeedback, which teaches patients to relieve or avoid headaches by relaxing the mind and body (*see* Biofeedback). Some headache sufferers can cure or reduce their symptoms by changing their diets to avoid certain foods, such as dairy products, chocolate, nuts, and alcohol, that can cause headaches in sensitive individuals.

Continued research into the nature, cause, and treatment of headaches offers hope to many sufferers. Scientists are learning more about the variety of headache symptoms. They are studying the complex interaction of vascular problems, hormone imbalance, hereditary factors, and environmental influences that may underlie both temporary and chronic headache pain. This growing body of knowledge, in turn, has enabled researchers to develop safer and more effective treatments to prevent or relieve this common, often debilitating ailment. (*See also* Health.)

*Children under 15 years of age are the group most prone to contracting a variety of communicable diseases. Immunization, required by many school districts, can protect against many childhood diseases.*
© Jim Olive—Peter Arnold, Inc.

**HEALTH.** The ancient Greeks believed that illness was a punishment sent upon them when the god Apollo was angry. The only way for sick people to get well was by praying to this god and assorted others. Apollo's son,

Aesculapius, was the god of medicine. The words panacea, a nonexistent remedy for illness, and hygiene, conditions and practices conducive to health, come from Aesculapius' two daughters, Panacea and Hygieia. (*See also* Aesculapius; Apollo.)

Beliefs that gods and goddesses could influence health were discarded when the ancient Greek physician Hippocrates separated myth and superstition from the study of medicine (*see* Hippocrates). The modern concept of health is defined as the general physical, mental, and emotional ability to function effectively and in harmony with one's environment.

Health is a dynamic condition that represents a range of physical and emotional states. Good health is more than the absence of disease. A person afflicted with a temporary illness, such as seasickness, for example, does not necessarily have bad health as a result of such a mishap. Moreover, physical condition and health are not synonymous terms. A basketball player in excellent physical condition can still have poor health.

**Private Health and Public Health**

Private health and public health are two areas that overlap to a considerable degree. Private, or individual, health concerns one's physical, mental, and emotional well-being. Good individual health, like many other human traits, depends partly on heredity. Some people are not born with strong minds and bodies, but even those born with good health cannot completely control its maintenance.

Public health deals with the maintenance and improvement of the health of a community or of the public as a whole. Many public-health activities are planned, directed, and carried out by various governmental and private agencies. Examples of public-health activities are water fluoridation, seat-belt laws, and restrictions on smoking in public places.

---

### FACT FINDER FOR HEALTH

The subject of health is a broad one. Readers will obtain additional information in the related articles listed here. (*See also* related references in the Fact-Index.)

| | |
|---|---|
| Adolescence | Health Maintenance |
| Aging | Organization |
| AIDS | Heredity |
| Alcoholism | Hormones |
| Allergy | Hospital |
| Analgesic | Immune System |
| Anatomy, Human | Lymphatic System |
| Anorexia Nervosa | Medicine |
| Birth Control | Menstruation |
| Child Development | Muscles |
| Circulatory System | Nervous System |
| Death | Nursing |
| Digestive System | Pain |
| Disease, Human | Personality |
| Drugs | Public Health |
| Emotion | Reproductive System |
| Exercise | Respiratory System |
| Fatigue | Sexuality |
| First Aid | Skeleton |
| Food and Nutrition | Skin |
| Gland | Sleep |
| Habit and Addiction | Stress |
| Health Agencies | Therapy |
| Health Education and | Vitamins |
| Physical Education | Weight Control |

(*See also* fact finders for BIOLOGY; DISEASE, HUMAN; GENETICS; MEDICINE; PHYSIOLOGY.)

Since the early 1900s public health has made major advances, particularly in the welfare of mothers and children and in the health of schoolchildren. In the United States, public-health policies require that students be vaccinated for some diseases before they may be enrolled in school. Some youth camps also require health records and proof of vaccination. Applicants for marriage licenses are required by law to have their blood tested for syphilis. Public-health nurses and other personnel engaged in educating and caring for the general public often visit schools to examine students, administer shots, and give talks on personal health and methods of disease prevention.

## What Determines Health

The habits and behaviors established within a family group can have a great effect on an individual's health. Good health habits are usually begun in the family. A child who is brought up in a family that practices healthful behaviors is more likely to continue the regimen as an adult.

Health is continually subjected to such internal and external challenges as varying external temperatures, bacteria, viruses, and stress. The various systems within the body must constantly adjust to these changing conditions.

Some health-influencing factors can be controlled, such as eating habits and environment. Others are not controllable, such as age and heredity. Among the many factors that can affect the health status of the individual are physical activity, nutrition, safety, smoking behavior, stress adaptation, and personal health practices. Many healthy people remain healthy by practicing behaviors that maintain or improve their health status.

There are a number of ways to determine health. Certain aspects of health can be measured. For example, a person having normal body temperature, pulse and breathing rates, blood pressure, height, weight, vision, hearing, and other normal measurable characteristics might be called healthy. Other factors that play a part in the individual's overall well-being, such as personal values, life-style choices, and beliefs, are more difficult to measure. However, they still play a vital role in a person's overall health status.

## Food and Nutrition

Nutrition is the study of how the body ingests food and uses it. It provides information about the type of food a person must eat to promote and maintain good health. Such knowledge helps the person develop and apply proper nutritional habits to maintain healthful living.

A diet, or the food regularly eaten, must contain all the essential nutritional elements: proteins, carbohydrates, fats, vitamins, minerals, and water. If a person's diet is consistently deficient in any of these nutrients, health is impaired and disease may result. Lack of the mineral iron, for example, is typical of the disease anemia; scurvy is a disease caused by a deficiency of vitamin C.

A healthy body is able to perform two basic physiological functions. It has both the capacity to grow and to convert certain substances into energy. Growth means an increase in size, not only of the entire body but also of every body part. It also involves replacement of worn-out tissues and the healing of wounds caused by injury or disease. The body requires a steady supply of building materials and fuel to produce the energy that powers all the body's vital processes. Since the body does not maintain an unlimited supply of building materials or fuels, these must be obtained from an outside source—food.

Food cannot be used in its original form as tissue-building substances or as fuels. Meat, for example, cannot be used directly to build new tissues. Similarly, a candy bar cannot be instantly converted into body energy or a glass of milk into bones or teeth. All food must first be changed into chemical compounds that the body is able to use. The most essential of these compounds are amino acids, the body's building blocks, from which new tissues are made; calcium, the mineral used to build and maintain bones and teeth; and glucose, a simple sugar that serves as a fuel. (*See also* Calcium.)

Pure amino acids themselves are not eaten to provide the body with its quota of usable substances. A food high in protein is eaten instead. The digestive system is

*Junk foods, those high in fat content, may promote such illnesses as cancer, diabetes, and high blood pressure.*

de Casseres—Photo Researchers

able to convert natural proteins into the necessary amino acids. All tissue-building substances or fuels are obtained from food by the process of digestion. (*See also* Protein.)

**Eating habits.** For many years the three-meals-a-day routine was considered essential, and eating between meals or before bedtime was thought to be a poor habit. In recent years nutritionists have found that while three meals a day are adequate for some people, others are unable to digest sufficient amounts of food at one time. They must instead eat smaller, more frequent meals. The objection to between-meal snacks is based on concern for overweight, especially when nonnutritious snacks are eaten in addition to three full-size meals.

The growing trend in the United States toward skipping breakfast does not lend itself to a healthful life-style. A glass of orange juice is not an adequate breakfast meal. The interval between the evening meal and noon lunch the following day is too long for the body to go without food. A long time without food often causes the level of glucose (sugar) in the blood to fall. The body is thus deprived of a vital fuel, and its energy is drained. This condition may result in inefficiency, irritability, weakness, and dizziness. It can also lead to accidents.

The process of digestion begins in the mouth. Here, as it is chewed, the food is mixed with saliva. Saliva contains an enzyme called amylase, which breaks down starch (*see* Enzymes; Starch). Since complete mixing of the food and saliva is necessary to break down starch and smaller particles are easier to dissolve in the stomach, thorough chewing is essential to good health.

Liquids taken with meals cannot replace the essential process of chewing. Water, however, is one of the critical elements necessary for normal body functioning. Milk is another liquid often taken with meals. When fluid milk reaches the stomach it combines with digestive juices to form a solid mass. Small swallows produce small milk solids in the stomach that are easier to digest. (*See also* Milk.)

**Eliminating waste.** What cannot be absorbed into the blood through the digestive system must be eliminated from the body. A healthy body accumulates waste residues as by-products of digestion. These must be eliminated regularly as the body signals its demand for their expulsion.

When the empty stomach receives food, it starts a movement in the digestive system. This movement contracts the colon, which is the signal that the bowels can be moved. Failure to have a daily bowel movement is not considered abnormal. The condition of having difficult bowel movements is called constipation. Many people take drugs called laxatives to relieve constipation; however, many of these drugs are habit forming. Other waste products that gather in the body are eliminated by the lungs and the kidneys.

**Weight control.** Many physicians believe that obesity is one of the greatest threats to good health. Overweight people often have shorter lives and are

Will McIntyre—Photo Researchers

*School lunches, consisting of a balanced diet while limiting the amount of sugar, offer children a variety of foods.*

also more apt to contract such diseases as diabetes, hypertension (high blood pressure), heart disease, arthritis, and various disorders of the digestive system.

In the late 1980s scientists discovered strong evidence that there is a genetic basis for obesity—that is, that children of obese parents will probably become obese themselves. Nevertheless, it is still true that a person's weight is directly related to the amount of food eaten and to the level of energy expended. All foods are fattening if eaten to excess. Butter, lard, oils, oleomargarine, and meats contain more calories than do the same weight of vegetables or fruits.

In reducing, the maximum safe body weight loss is about two pounds per week. The sensible way to lose weight is to decrease caloric intake and increase activity levels. An adequate supply of proteins must be maintained in any weight-reducing diet in order to rebuild worn-out tissues.

Two eating disorders that have gained notoriety in recent years are anorexia nervosa and bulimia. Both have physical and psychological consequences (*see* Anorexia Nervosa).

## Physical Fitness and Exercise

There are two basic types of physical fitness: health-related physical fitness and motor-related physical fitness. Despite some overlap between these classifications, major differences exist between them. Health-related physical fitness is primarily influenced by an individual's exercise habits. Thus it is a dynamic state subject to change. Characteristics that determine health-related physical fitness are strength and endurance of skeletal muscles, joint flexibility, body composition, and cardiorespiratory endurance.

Motor-performance physical fitness is the ability of the neuromuscular system to carry out specific tasks. Tests can be used to assess this type of fitness. The major health-related characteristics measured by these tests are the strength and endurance of the skeletal muscles and the speed or power of the legs.

Exercise contributes to overall body fitness. An adequate exercise program is necessary to maintain physical and emotional fitness and to deal effectively with everyday stress situations. The body's ability to adjust to stress is linked to physical fitness.

The muscles of an inactive person become soft and flabby (*see* Muscles). Hollow organs, which function through the action of muscles, lose their efficiency. Such a loss of fitness affects one's general health.

Proper exercise does not mean violent exertion. It should be looked upon as a pleasure, not as a task. For most people personal sports offer the best opportunity for keeping fit. Examples of suitable personal sports are dancing, active games, bicycle or horseback riding, hiking, and swimming. People who cannot find time to engage in personal sports may keep fit by means of simple exercises.

Among the goals of an exercise program is the enhancement of cardiovascular efficiency. Activities with an aerobic component, such as jogging, swimming, cycling, walking, and dance, are examples of such activities.

### Sleep and Rest

Sleep is essential to good health. Without the proper amount a person becomes nervous, irritable, and physically fatigued. Such fatigue makes the body particularly susceptible to attacks of various diseases.

Little is known about the nature of sleep. It appears that the amount required to maintain health varies among different individuals. Some need more, others less. The following daily schedule may be used as a guide: from 1 to 4 years of age, 12 hours of sleep; from 4 to 12 years of age, 10 hours; from 12 to 16 years, 8 to 10 hours.

The best conditions for natural sleep are a good bed (neither too hard nor too soft), a quiet room, and darkness. Covers should be warm but not heavy. Electric blankets or heating pads may be used to avoid creating more heat than is necessary to prevent chilling.

Excitement or active play just before going to bed may interfere with proper sleep. Heavy eating at bedtime is not advisable. Sleeping pills should be taken only on the advice of a physician.

### Aging

Aging is a natural phenomenon occurring in all species. From a physiological perspective, aging is a gradual decline in the body's ability to continue self-maintenance. Certain changes are normal, such as a decrease in metabolism, loss of skin tone, and thinning of hair.

Despite some of the physical degenerative aspects of aging, individuals have the capacity to maintain a vital health status throughout their lifetimes. Recognition of the positive aspects of aging can help older people to lead fulfilling years as active members of society. Improved life-style behaviors of the past several decades are beginning to yield a healthier, happier, more productive aged population.

© Estate of Sybil Shelton—Peter Arnold, Inc.

*An active life is one means of preventing osteoporosis, a bone-deforming disease that often occurs in older women.*

The spectacular advances made by medical science—especially during the 20th century—led to the avoidance of many diseases. In 1900, for example, the average life expectancy at birth in the United States was only 47 years. By 1985 it had risen to 74.7 years. The 1915 infant mortality rate for those under 1 year of age was 99.9 per 1,000 live births. In 1985 this rate had been reduced to 10.6 per 1,000 live births.

### Mental Health

Health implies more than physical fitness. It also implies mental and emotional well-being. An angry, frustrated, emotionally unstable person in good physical condition is not necessarily healthy. Mental health, therefore, has much to do with how a person copes with the world as he or she exists. Some physicians say that a person who is able to function reasonably well is mentally healthy. Others hold that a person is healthy mentally if his behavior is like that of the majority of people. Still others make comparisons with an ideal. According to these physicians, mental healthfulness may be approached but not attained. Another concept stresses the changes in a person's behavior that take place with the passage of time as criteria of the individual's mental health. Many of the factors that influence physical health also affect mental and emotional well-being.

Having a good self-image means that people have positive mental pictures and good, positive feelings about themselves, about what they are capable of

*The Amish, whose religious beliefs dictate certain restrictions in diet and style of life, are less prone to cancer than the general population of the United States.*
Jeff Greenberg—Peter Arnold, Inc.

doing, and about the roles they play. People with good self-images like themselves, and they are better able to like others. Having a good self-image is based on a realistic assessment of one's own worth and value and capabilities.

Stress is an unavoidable, necessary, and potentially healthful reality of our society. People of all ages encounter stress. Children begin to experience stress during prenatal development and during childbirth. Examples of stress-inducing events in the life of a young person are death of a pet, pressure to achieve academically, the divorce of parents, or joining a new youth group. The different ways in which individuals respond to stress may bring healthful or unhealthy results. One person experiencing a great deal of stress may function exceptionally well while another may be unable to function at all. If stressful situations are continually encountered, the individual's physical, social, and mental health are eventually affected.

Satisfying social relations are vital to sound mental and emotional health. It is believed that in order to initiate, develop, and maintain effective and fulfilling social relationships people must possess the ability to know and trust each other, understand each other, influence, and help each other. They must also be capable of resolving conflicts in a constructive way.

The mental and emotional health of a person is often judged by the ability to develop and maintain meaningful social relationships with a variety of people of both sexes.

### Health Hazards

Potential threats and hazards to human health have changed significantly over the past 100 years. Changes in the leading causes of death and disease show a shift from infectious diseases (such as pneumonia, influenza,

and tuberculosis) to chronic degenerative diseases (such as heart disease, cancer, and stroke). These chronic diseases are greatly influenced by personal life-style.

Today life-style is considered more of a health determinant than it was in 1900, when the leading cause of death was pneumonia and influenza. Through the development and widespread use of antibiotics and vaccines, communicable diseases have been effectively controlled in the United States, where the leading cause of death is heart disease. It is estimated that health-life-style factors contribute to 54 percent of all deaths due to heart disease. Health-life-style risk factors for heart disease include smoking, hypertension, lack of exercise, obesity, and stress. Most of these risk factors can be controlled by the individual. Although health status is often determined by environment, heredity, and the available health-care-delivery systems, personal health life-style is a major factor. Major risks include alcohol and drug abuse, high blood pressure, exposure to occupational health hazards, poor safety habits, and nutritional deficiencies.

Smoking is considered the leading preventable cause of death and disability in the United States. It is closely linked to heart disease, cancer, stroke, influenza, and pneumonia. Efforts to inform the public of the hazards of smoking have increased the number of former smokers, but it is still a major health problem (*see* Tobacco).

Alcohol and drug use and abuse have been common practices for centuries. Studies have shown alcohol and drug abuse to be linked to violent crime, suicide, motor vehicle accidents, and cirrhosis of the liver.

High blood pressure has been called the silent killer. Because there are no physical symptoms, people are often unaware that they have the condition. High blood pressure has been linked to heart disease and stroke.

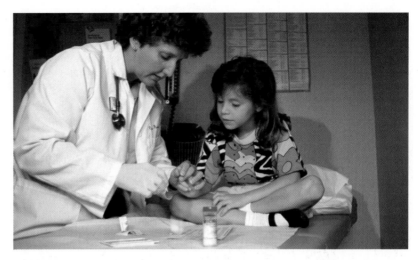

*Periodic checkups by a physician are necessary for young children as well as adults.*
© William Campbell—Peter Arnold, Inc.

With proper care and treatment, either through medication, diet modification, exercise, or stress management, high blood pressure can be effectively controlled.

Exposure to environmental and occupational hazards such as radiation and toxic substances is a significant risk factor. Many of the cancers that affect humans can be linked to such hazards. Most communities and companies take extra precautions to ensure safety against hazardous environments.

Many accidental deaths and disabilities can be avoided with proper safety procedures. It is estimated that accidents and injuries from automobile accidents in the United States could be reduced by 50 percent if seat belts were always used.

### Health Maintenance

Among the obvious challenges to health are bacteria, viruses, and other microbiological agents. A healthy body is able to protect itself and adjust to challenges through various internal mechanisms. Homeostasis is an internal mechanism by which the body maintains internal biological systems under variable environmental stresses. Other mechanisms defend against microbiological agents, repair and regenerate damaged tissue or cells, or clot blood to prevent excessive bleeding.

There are many ways to preserve and maintain good health. They include individual preventive-care measures such as regular physical examinations and the proper care of the body. Other preventive-care activities include immunization and social control over abusive practices. Most individual preventive-care measures focus on appropriate life-style behaviors and safety activities, such as cleanliness, wearing seat belts, eating well, and exercising.

**Health examinations.** One of the best ways to maintain good health is to make sure that the body and mind are functioning properly. This is possible through routine—usually annual—health examinations.

A health examination is likely to include a series of tests. Some of these tests are more descriptive than quantitative and can indicate the presence of disease in a seemingly healthy person. An electrocardiogram test, for example, detects some forms of heart disease. Electromyograms help to determine primary muscle disorders. An electroencephalogram monitors the activity of the brain. There are liver- and gallbladder-function tests and many types of X-ray techniques for determining disease or malfunction of internal organs. The efficiency of the respiratory, circulatory, excretory, nervous, and digestive systems are also determined in a health examination. The doctor inspects the eyes, ears, nose, throat, mouth, skin, and scalp. The person's weight, height, and posture are examined and daily activities discussed. If the physician discovers any handicaps or deficiencies, the proper measures to correct them are recommended.

In addition to the annual physical checkup, health specialists recommend dental examinations at least twice a year. Young people's teeth require particular attention since immediate correction of a dental defect helps prevent later complications that might seriously affect a person's general health.

**Eye care.** About 80 percent of everything people learn about their surroundings is gathered through sight. Thus, an eye defect that interferes with proper vision can be a handicap to work, pleasure, and health. Most vision disorders can be corrected by the use of glasses. A health-care professional educated, trained, and licensed to diagnose and prescribe treatment for vision problems, eye diseases, or other abnormalities is called an optometrist (*see* Optometry).

Good vision also depends upon adequate lighting. Daylight provides the best illumination for such activities as reading, writing, and sewing. Modern artificial lighting, however, is now almost as good as daylight, so long as glare is avoided.

Television viewing does not injure the eyes, but focusing on the same distance and area for long periods may tire them. The individual should sit far enough from the set so that the scanning lines on the

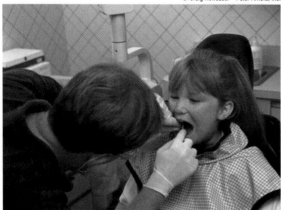

© Craig Newbauer—Peter Arnold, Inc.

*Proper oral hygiene and regular preventive dental care can keep an individual's teeth and gums healthy for a lifetime.*

picture are not visible. The room should be dimly lighted. (*See also* Lighting.)

**Ear care.** Like the eyes, the ears are complex and delicate organs. Indistinct hearing may be a temporary condition that can be easily corrected. It may also be a sign of impending deafness. In either case, only a physician can determine the exact reason for the hearing failure and prescribe corrective measures where possible. Buzzing or ringing in the ears may be a symptom of a serious condition. On the other hand, these sounds may only indicate that there is an overaccumulation of wax in the ear canal.

A person should never attempt to remove excess earwax with hairpins, toothpicks, matchsticks, or similar objects. There is an obvious danger that the eardrum may be punctured or scraped. Even if the object does not touch the eardrum, it may push the wax so far back into the canal that it presses against the eardrum. The advice often heard from many physicians is: "Never put anything smaller than the elbow into the ear."

**Skin and hair care.** The skin is the largest organ of the body. Its condition influences a person's general health. Preparations for the care of the skin form a major portion of cosmetics. They include cleansing

*Hearing tests, especially for persons regularly subjected to loud noise, should be taken frequently.*

© Werner H. Muller—Peter Arnold, Inc.

creams, lotions, and cleansing milks. Emollients are heavier cold creams that help prevent water loss from the skin. Hand creams counteract dryness from exposure to wind, sun, and detergents.

The daily bath is a common practice in many parts of the world. Some skins, however, cannot endure daily bathing, especially in winter. An oily skin requires frequent washing. A dry one should be bathed only often enough to keep it clean.

At one time some cosmetics contained poisonous substances. Certain hair dyes and face powders, for example, contained lead and pigments from poisonous chemicals such as mercury or cadmium. In the United States the Food and Drug Administration now determines the substances that may be used in cosmetics, and all cosmetics, except fragrances, must have labels listing ingredients.

Hair preparations are also part of health care. They include shampoos, which are actually scented detergents. Unlike soap, shampoo does not leave a film on the hair. Some shampoos control dandruff, the flaking of the scalp, but do not cure diseases. Scalp diseases require a physician's attention. (*See also* Cosmetics; Hair; Soap and Detergent.)

**Immunization.** The process of producing increased resistance to infection is called immunization. Immunization can provide a significant preventive guard against most major infectious diseases. Immunity may be naturally acquired or artificially induced by vaccination. There are now vaccines for a great many of the once fatal diseases, including polio, diphtheria, tetanus, German measles (rubella), measles (rubeola), whooping cough (pertussis), and mumps. Some immunizations are recommended only when needed, such as flu shots for the elderly and chronically ill. Other immunizations, such as those for tropical disease, are recommended or required for those planning trips to some foreign countries.

James M. Eddy

**FURTHER RESOURCES FOR HEALTH**

**Books for Children**

**Jones, L.H., and Tsumura, T.K.** Health and Safety for You, 7th ed. (McGraw, 1986).
**Neff, Fred.** Keeping Fit: A Handbook for Physical Conditioning and Better Health (Lerner, 1977).
**Simon, Nissa.** Don't Worry, You're Normal (Harper, 1982).
**Stiller, Richard.** Your Body Is Trying to Tell You Something: How to Understand its Signals and Respond to its Needs (Harcourt, 1979).
**Ward, Brian.** Smoking and Health (Watts, 1986).

**Books for Young Adults**

**American Association of School Administrators.** Raising Your Wellness Grade (American Assn. of School Administrators, 1986).
**Astrand, P.O.** Health and Fitness (Barron's, 1977).
**Brody, Jane.** Jane Brody's The New York Times Guide to Personal Health (Times Books, 1982).
**Combs, Barbara and others.** An Invitation to Health: Your Personal Responsibility, 2nd ed. (Addison, 1983).
**Read, Donald A.** The Concept of Health, 3rd ed. (Allyn, 1983).

(*See also* bibliographies for Disease, Human; Food and Nutrition; Health Education and Physical Education; Medicine.)

The headquarters of the American Red Cross is in Washington, D.C. The American Red Cross is part of the International Red Cross, which has affiliates in nearly every country. Its activities include disaster relief, accident prevention, and the maintenance of child welfare centers and medical clinics.
Doris DeWitt—Tony Stone WorldWide

**HEALTH AGENCIES.** Individual health problems are handled by visits to a physician's office or a stay in the hospital. Communities of people have wider health needs that must be overseen by governmental or voluntary agencies. The great variety of services performed by health agencies fall into at least four categories: epidemic disease control, public sanitation, preventive medicine, and social medicine.

### Community Efforts

A high incidence of disease in a limited geographic area is called an epidemic. If an outbreak of a communicable disease occurs, an agency of the local government can enforce a quarantine of those who have the disease in order to control its spread. Measures are also taken to trace the source of the outbreak, whether it be from carriers of the disease, poor sanitation, an unknown virus, lack of immunization, or some other cause. These measures involve the cooperation of a variety of health professionals, including physicians, nurses, and laboratory technicians.

Public sanitation services are vital to every community's well-being. Garbage collection is not usually looked upon as a health measure unless the collectors go on strike, but it is one of the most basic services provided to maintain personal health. Other agencies monitor the water supplies, keep the streets clean, inspect restaurants and food supplies, and test for atmospheric pollution or radiation hazards.

When natural disasters such as floods or earthquakes occur, it is necessary to warn people to take precautions against contaminated drinking water, to clear away debris, and to look after the needs of those who have been injured or displaced from their homes. Unusual disasters, such as the leak of poisonous gas that killed thousands in Bhopal, India, in 1985, require massive assistance from national agencies and volunteer organizations such as the Red Cross.

Preventive medicine is normally undertaken at the local level. One of its most common features is immunization of school-age children to prevent such ordinary, but sometimes life-threatening, diseases as measles, scarlet fever, chicken pox, and polio (*see* Immune System). Local health agencies also provide information to the public on nutrition and dangers to health, take surveys of communal health problems, and undertake health-education programs (*see* Health Education and Physical Education).

Social medicine encompasses a variety of tasks, some of which are performed by local hospitals. There are rehabilitation programs for accident victims, unwed mothers, problem families, and alcohol and drug abusers. Community nurses visit schools to record and update immunization records, perform hearing and vision tests, and offer other services. They also screen the general population for diabetes, heart disease, and high blood pressure and visit homes to care for the aged and the handicapped. (*See also* Nursing.)

Cities and towns often have transportation services to assist the aged or victims of sudden illness. Ambulances are able to reach homes and scenes of accidents quickly and provide some preliminary care on the way to the hospital (*see* Ambulance). Senior-citizen centers sometimes provide transportation for older people who need to visit a doctor's office. Many of these services are supported by taxes.

### National and International Agencies

The United States is less involved in the direct delivery of health-care services to individuals than many other nations—except through its Veterans Administration and military hospitals. In the United Kingdom, Germany, and other countries that have national health plans, the government is much more closely tied to the work of physicians and hospitals. In China all health care is managed by the state.

In the United States there is no national health plan, but those over 65 are eligible for Medicare. This program pays a portion of hospital and physicians' expenses, though the federal government sets guidelines for allowable costs. The Medicaid program provides grants to the states for health services for the needy.

The chief health agency of the United States federal government is the Public Health Service (PHS), which is part of the Department of Health and Human Services. The PHS was established by an act of Congress on July 16, 1798, to provide hospital care for American merchant seamen. Since then its scope of activities has broadened considerably. The PHS is directed by an assistant secretary for health and the surgeon general of the United States.

The major branches of the PHS are the Substance Abuse and Mental Health Services Administration, or SAMHSA; the Centers for Disease Control and Prevention; the Agency for Toxic Substances and Disease Registry; the Food and Drug Administration; the Health Resources and Services Administration; the Indian Health Service; the Agency for Healthcare Research and Quality; and the National Institutes of Health.

SAMHSA was established in 1992 to improve the quality and availability of substance abuse prevention programs, addiction treatment, and mental health services. Its major components are the Center for Mental Health Services, the Center for Substance Abuse Prevention, and the Center for Substance Abuse Treatment.

The Centers for Disease Control are based in Atlanta, Ga. This branch of the PHS has 12 subdivisions: the Epidemiology Program Office; the Center on Birth Defects and Developmental Disabilities; the Center for Chronic Disease Prevention and Health Promotion; the Center for Environmental Health; the Center for Health Statistics; the Center for HIV, STD, and TB Prevention; the Center for Injury Prevention and Control; the National Immunization Program; the National Institute for Occupational Safety and Health; the Public Health Practice Program Office; the Center for Infectious Diseases; and the Office of the Director.

The Agency for Toxic Substances and Disease Registry is also based in Atlanta. It devises and helps implement programs to protect both the public and the work force from exposure to the adverse effects of hazardous substances in storage sites or released in fires, explosions, or transportation accidents.

The Food and Drug Administration (FDA) is dedicated to protecting the health of the nation against unsafe foods and drugs. It also conducts research on the development, manufacture, and testing of both new and old products. Its subdivisions are the Center for Drug Evaluation and Research, the Office of Regulatory Affairs, the Center for Biologics Evaluation and Research, the Center for Food Safety and Applied Nutrition, the Center for Veterinary Medicine, the Center for Devices and Radiological Health, and the National Center for Toxicological Research.

The Health Resources and Services Administration is directly involved in programs to improve health services and provide adequate health-care delivery systems in all the states. Its subdivisions are the Bureau of Primary Health Care, the Bureau of Health Professions, the Maternal and Child Health Bureau, and the HIV/AIDS Bureau.

The Indian Health Service provides health services to Native Americans and to indigenous peoples in Alaska. Members of more than 550 tribes receive medical and dental services through the agency.

The National Institutes of Health conduct and support research into the causes of disease and support training research. Some of its subdivisions are the National Cancer Institute, the National Institute of Diabetes and Digestive and Kidney Diseases, and the National Institute of Allergy and Infectious Diseases. The Agency for Healthcare Research and Quality conducts research to determine how health care can be improved.

Other departments of the government also have agencies to deal with specific health problems. The Department of Labor, for example, has the Occupational Safety and Health Administration and the Mine Safety and Health Administration.

Great Britain's National Health Services was established on July 5, 1948, as a comprehensive program to assure adequate health-care delivery to all citizens of the United Kingdom. The NHS underwent considerable reform in the early 21st century and is now divided into a Department of Health and a Modernisation Agency. The Department of Health oversees the Strategic Health Authorities, each of which administers health services for a given region. Health care services are divided among a group of trusts. These include the Primary Care Trusts, which oversee medical and dental services; the Care Trusts, which administer social services; and the Mental Health Trusts, which supervise mental health services. There are also trusts that manage hospitals and ambulance services. The Modernisation Agency implements reforms. There is also a Public Health Laboratory Service, which is similar to the U.S. Centers for Disease Control.

In the Western Hemisphere the Pan American Health Organization, with headquarters in Washington, D.C., is an international agency for coordinating efforts among nations to combat disease. The organization was founded in 1902 as the International Sanitary Bureau. It was given its present name in 1958.

The World Health Organization (WHO), with headquarters in Geneva, Switzerland, is the largest international health agency. It was founded by the International Health Conference, convened by the United Nations in New York City in 1946. The WHO began operations on April 7, 1948. It functions in three broad areas. It is first a central clearinghouse of information and research. The occurrence of pestilential disease anywhere in the world is broadcast over an international radio network to national health authorities, seaports, airports, and ships at sea. The WHO also keeps member nations informed about new developments in medicine and vaccines, control of drug addiction, and hazards of nuclear radiation. Second, it assists with measures for controlling epidemics by mass campaigns against communicable diseases. Third, it seeks to strengthen and expand the health services of member nations, especially in developing countries.

*Youth organizations sponsor Special Olympics for children who have physical or mental handicaps.*
Mel Digiacomo—Image Bank

**HEALTH EDUCATION AND PHYSICAL EDUCATION.** An individual's physical and mental well-being is the concern of two similar areas of education: health education and physical education. Both deal with habits of exercise, sleep, rest, and recreation. Since physical well-being is only one aspect of a person's overall health, physical education is often thought of as a part of health education.

Health education is an activity aimed at the improvement of health-related knowledge, attitudes, and behavior. It is used in schools to help students make intelligent decisions about health-related issues. There are many ways to teach health in schools. Usually instructors create and facilitate learning experiences that develop the student's decision-making skills. Above all, teachers provide health information

and a concern for factors that influence the quality of life.

Health behavior plays a major part in a person's overall well-being. Since health-related behaviors are both learned and amenable to change, formal health education usually begins when a child is most flexible—in primary school. This is also when a child is more apt to accept positive health behaviors. It is in these early years that the negative effects of a lifetime of health abuse can be prevented. Many health problems are known to be linked to smoking, poor nutrition, obesity, lack of exercise, stress, and abuse of drugs and alcohol (*see* Alcohol; Drugs; Exercise; Habit and Addiction; Stress; Weight Control).

Basic to health education is the principle of preventive care. Health educators attempt to teach

*Nurses give lessons in dental care to grade school classes.*
Larry Brooks—Nawrocki Stock Photo

*Soccer is one sport played (top) in physical education classes to foster fitness. An emphasis in a high-school classroom (below) is learning about such health hazards as the deadly disease AIDS.*
(Top) Cathlyn Melloan—EB Inc.; (below) Steve Woit—Picture Group

people to be responsible for their own health and health care. They also discuss the benefits of medical technology and research. They often promote behavioral changes and modifications to improve health. (*See also* Holistic Medicine.)

Health education and physical education programs exist throughout the world. In the United States, most health education and physical education programs are managed by governments (federal, state, and local), communities, schools, and organizations.

### Government Programs

Many federally sponsored health and health-related programs are offered by the United States Department of Health and Human Services. The Health Resources and Services Administration, primarily through its Division of Maternal and Child Health, also has particular interests in the health of school-age children. This governmental body develops elementary school programs on human genetics and on accident and injury prevention.

The President's Council on Physical Fitness and Sports, based in Washington, D.C., promotes physical fitness and sports throughout the United States. The group recommends the Youth Fitness Test, developed by the American Alliance for Health, Physical Education, Recreation, and Dance (AAHPERD), as the most effective physical fitness battery for use in public schools.

This test consists of six items: pull-ups (for boys) or flexed-arm hang (for girls), standing long jump, 50-yard dash, shuttle run, sit-ups, and a long endurance run. Based on the results of the test, children 10 to 17 years of age can earn the Presidential Physical Fitness Award.

The Youth Fitness Test received some criticism that despite its usefulness in measuring athletic performance, it was not a valid indicator of health-related fitness. As a result of this concern, AAHPERD developed the Health-Related Physical Fitness Test in 1980. It measures cardiovascular function, body composition, flexibility, and abdominal strength.

The Office on Smoking and Health, originally in the Bureau of Health Education, is now part of the Office of the Assistant for Health. It maintains an inventory of information that is used by schools and often provides them with technical assistance.

The National Highway Traffic Safety Administration within the Department of Transportation provides schools with educational materials related to the use of alcohol, traffic safety, pedestrian and bicycle safety,

*Convincing arguments against drug use are made by a classmate telling of his own problems with substance abuse.*

Ellis Herwig—Gartman Agency

and housing-occupancy protection. Its curriculum materials are directed to people of all ages. (*See also* Health Agencies.)

### School Programs

There has been some controversy about the differences between physical education and health education in schools in the United States. Some states and local school districts treat these two phases of education as being identical. In recent years, many schools have begun to treat health education and physical education as separate disciplines.

In order to facilitate school health and physical education programs, health education professionals combine and categorize generally accepted health education concepts into easily accessible forms. These forms include pamphlets, books, films, audio tapes, video tapes, and curriculum guides.

**Primary and elementary school.** Health and physical education usually begins in primary school. Activities are carefully selected according to the child's age, needs, sex, and physical condition. Children are encouraged to participate in running, climbing, jumping, swinging, and throwing. Such play activities help children to grow and develop.

Health education curricula are often tailored to the age, intellect, and interest of the students. They may include the following health-related concerns: mental health, body systems and the senses, nutrition, family life, alcohol, drugs and tobacco, safety and first aid, personal health, consumer health, diseases (chronic and communicable), environmental health, aging, and death. Each of these concerns is composed of dozens of topics. For example, personal health encompasses dental care, personal care, exercise, rest, physical fitness, and other topics. The general attitudes within a

*School health fairs bring together a great variety of information in colorful exhibits that appeal to young children.*

Larry Brooks—Nawrocki Stock Photo

*Junior high school students do sit-ups as part of the program outlined by the President's Council on Physical Fitness. Many communities have mobile units where health professionals offer blood pressure checks and other services (below).*

Courtesy of the President's Council on Physical Fitness; (below) William Means—CLICK/Chicago

program for all students; (2) an instructional program in which games or sports have been adapted for special needs; (3) an intramural program; and (4) an interscholastic program. Intramural, or "within the walls," games involve competitions between teams of the same school. When different schools compete, the contests are called interscholastic (high school) or intercollegiate (college).

Complex team sports, such as football and basketball, are also introduced. The variety of sports activities is increased so that all students are given an equal opportunity for sports participation. Rather than having a program with monotonous exercises aimed at strength or discipline, modern physical education programs are designed to provide students with the opportunity to learn those natural activities that contribute to their personal development. Health and physical education curricula in many secondary schools and colleges reflect the recent concerns about problems associated with alcohol, drug, and tobacco abuse. They also include sex education. Different schools have varying means of providing information about these matters. By the time students enter high school, they have acquired some health knowledge as well as certain health attitudes and practices.

### Organizational Programs

Numerous private and public health organizations and community groups have an interest in promoting health. Some may focus on particular diseases, disabilities, or an assortment of health problems. Others take on specific health projects to serve their community. Many of these organizations provide informational material and allocate funds for both health instruction and services. Nonprofit organizations also serve the community by providing health-related information to the general public (*see* Health Agencies).

community may affect the elementary school curriculum. In some communities, for instance, sex education is considered a vital part of health education; in others it is felt that the subject should not be a part of the curriculum (*see* Sexuality).

**Secondary school and college.** At the junior high school level, activities are selected in terms of individual and group needs. Other determining factors are the age, sex, and physical condition of the student. Competitive sports are introduced at this level, usually for both boys and girls. General health practices are reinforced in junior high school, and new practices, particularly those associated with group responsibility, are begun.

Physical education programs in high schools and colleges often have four parts: (1) an instructional

Programs with health and physical education activities are also found in community centers, fitness clubs, churches, and many other recreational and social organizations. Youth organizations, such as the YMCA, YWCA, and scouting groups, play a particularly vital role in health education in local communities. Many promote Olympic development programs, Special Olympics programs, aerobics, and exercise (see Youth Organizations).

During the past decade, many large companies have provided health and fitness programs for their employees. These corporate programs have been found to reduce health-care costs and absenteeism. They also improve morale, job-satisfaction ratings, and the general health and attitude of employees. The corporate setting represents a logical link between the work site and the health and fitness of the employee. In the 1980s there were more than 50,000 such programs in the United States, and corporations spent about 2 billion dollars annually on fitness programs. Many companies have in-house health and fitness facilities, education seminars, and workshops.

### History

The physician has always tried to formulate rules of health based on knowledge and experience. These rules were probably the first attempt at health education. Two such regimens are attributed to the ancient physicians Hippocrates and Galen (see Galen; Hippocrates). Another was produced by the medieval medical school at Salerno, Italy. The health information provided by these programs was based on experience rather than on scientific evidence. In modern times, however, health and physical education is a more exact science and many of its teachings are based not only on scientific fact but also on the knowledge of the motivations behind human actions.

**Health education.** In the United States sporadic attempts at teaching hygiene in the schools were made in the middle of the 19th century. The activities were more crisis oriented than preventive since epidemic diseases were the primary concern. By the turn of the century the need for health education was recognized, but improvements came slowly. In 1924 only four states had certification requirements for health education teachers in the secondary schools. Formal health education took the form of instruction in anatomy and physiology. Health was taught purely as a science, and emphasis was placed on cognitive information. As health education evolved, health teachers became more concerned with the attitudinal and behavioral aspects of students' health as well.

Finally, by the 1930s, the idea of health education was thought of as a distinct, independent science. The first program of graduate training for health was established at the Massachusetts Institute of Technology in 1921. By the 1960s many institutes had embarked on the professional preparation of teachers of health education. The crisis-oriented approach to health education was eventually replaced with the modern preventive health education. In the mid-1980s at least 43 states offered preparation programs for teachers of health education.

The beginning of health education in Great Britain is attributed to Sir Allen Daley, a medical officer of health. Daley saw the usefulness of public talks on health topics and pioneered the field of preventive medicine. He was instrumental in setting up the Central Council for Health Education in England.

**Physical education.** The revival of gymnastics in the 18th and 19th centuries marked the beginning of large-scale physical instruction. In 1826 Harvard College established the first college gymnasium in the United States. In 1893 it became the first college to confer an academic degree in physical education. Many colleges issued entrance requirements and selective admission for entering students. The main emphasis was on sports participation. Remedial physical education and aquatics were also offered.

By 1925 city supervisors of physical education were employed to organize programs and assist classroom teachers in many elementary schools. The city could dictate the required number of classroom hours for physical education, usually 150 minutes per week for grades one through six.

By 1930 laws requiring physical education in the public schools had been enacted in 36 states. During World War II, physical education classes often lasted 30 minutes daily and included such activities as games, folk dance, story plays, tumbling, and health instruction. General physical education programs were developed at the college and university level for the general student, and professional programs were designed for students seeking a bachelor's degree in physical education. Professional physical education at all levels in the educational spectrum has recently undergone major modifications.

In the 1950s there was much concern over the physical fitness of students in the United States, partly because of the results of a comparison between the physical fitness of students in the United States and those in Europe. Students from schools in the eastern United States were given a test, called the Kraus-Weber minimum muscular fitness test, in 1952. About 57 percent of the students failed one or more parts of the test. In Europe only about 8 percent of the students failed. The implications of the test led to the establishment, in 1956, of the President's Council on Youth Fitness, shortly followed by the creation of the Youth Fitness Test Battery, designed by the American Association for Health, Physical Education, and Recreation.

James M. Eddy

**FURTHER RESOURCES FOR HEALTH EDUCATION AND PHYSICAL EDUCATION**

**Anspaugh, D.J., and others.** Teaching Today's Health (Bell and Howell, 1983).

**Cornacchia, Harold J. and others.** Health Education in Elementary Schools, 6th ed. (Mosby, 1983).

**Creswell, W.H. and Anderson, C.L.** School Health Practice, 8th ed. (Mosby, 1984).

**Greene, W.H. and Simons-Morton, B.G.** Introduction to Health Education (Macmillan, 1984).

**HEALTH INSURANCE.** All insurance is a form of risk management (*see* Insurance). To deal with the unforeseeable risks to health through accident or illness, various types of health insurance programs have been devised. Health insurance is offered to individuals in two forms: individual plans and group plans. The insurers may be private companies or governments. Since the early 1970s another type of health-care coverage has become prominent: the health maintenance organization, or HMO (*see* Health Maintenance Organization).

In some countries no insurance companies offer health care because governments have taken over the entire responsibility. China is a primary example. The United States has a combination of private and government-sponsored insurance. Some government programs are limited to specific groups within the population, such as veterans, members of the armed forces, and government employees. Others, specifically Medicare and Medicaid, are open to most of the population. (For government programs *see* Social Security; Welfare State.)

The purpose of health insurance is to provide protection against loss of income and to cover the expenses of hospitalization and some of its associated costs. Some policies also carry disability provisions, which will pay insured individuals should they be unable to work because of extended illness or permanent physical disability. (Temporary disability is usually covered by workmen's compensation.) Accident insurance covers sudden and unexpected injuries, while sickness insurance applies to illness or disease. There are policies that cover accidents only, while normal health insurance covers accidents as well as illness. Some policies are designed only to provide extra income during hospitalization. Many of these are known as mail-order policies, because they are sold to individuals who answer mailed solicitations or reply to ads in newspapers and magazines or on television.

Health insurance covers a variety of costs. Some policies cover a stay in the hospital and services offered by the hospital. Surgical expense coverage provides benefits for surgery resulting from illness or accident. Beyond this, a policy may cover what are called regular medical expenses, including doctor's fees, home nursing, diagnostic tests, and ambulance service. Some policies also cover prescription drugs.

Major medical, or catastrophic coverage, was introduced in 1949. It entails an added cost, or premium. This coverage pays only for large medical expenses, such as open-heart surgery or organ transplants. Because of enormous increases in medical costs since the 1950s, major medical coverage has grown rapidly in popularity.

Health insurance policies frequently carry a deductible clause. This means that the policyholder is required to pay the first part of his or her expenses, usually a nominal amount, before the insurer makes any payments. Deductibles are included in automobile and property insurance as well, to relieve the insurer from having to pay frequent, small claims.

Health insurance policies are offered in two basic forms: cancelable and noncancelable. Some policies can be canceled at any time by the insurer, presumably because of having to pay large benefits. Some are noncancelable during the time the policy is in force—normally one year—but may be renewed only if the insurer is willing.

Health insurance policies are issued by a variety of companies. Some are independent profit-making insurers; others are fraternal nonprofit societies. One of the best-known plans in the United States was developed by the Blue Cross–Blue Shield companies. These are nonprofit associations, usually sponsored by physicians through their medical societies. Whereas most health insurance policies pay benefits directly to the policyholder, Blue Cross makes direct payment to hospitals and Blue Shield to physicians.

One of the most valuable employee benefits offered to working people is group health coverage. Group health insurance is a 20th-century innovation that has expanded rapidly since 1950. The United States has developed a broader system of privately insured health coverage than any other nation.

The major advantage of group plans is lower cost to the individual. In most of these plans the individual employee pays part of the cost of premiums from payroll deductions. Premiums are lower because rates are based on a group, which is often very large, instead of on the individual with his or her known health history. Another advantage of group policies is coverage for dependents of employees. Some group plans include eye- and dental-care policies. Eye-care policies were introduced in 1957. The first comprehensive dental plan was started in 1959.

In a group policy, master contracts are issued by the insurer to the employer for the persons to be covered. People who work for government bodies, unions, churches, schools, and other associations are also covered by group policies. The employer is, in effect, the policyholder, though the individuals are given policies detailing the extent of their coverage. Retired persons are normally able to continue their policies as a supplement to Medicare coverage.

Types of coverage are much the same as with individual policies: protection against income loss, hospital and physician expense coverage, major medical, and disability. Disability income plans are designed to supplement workmen's compensation insurance.

A new type of health insurance developed in the 1980s offered coverage for most nursing home costs (*see* Nursing Home). This long-term coverage was designed for the over-65 age group, an increasingly larger segment of the population. Without such policies many people would have to liquidate their savings. Neither government assistance nor other plans are meant to defray more than a fraction of such expenses. In response to public concerns regarding rising private health-care costs, a governmental task force was appointed in 1992 to address the possibility of enacting federally funded, universal health-care insurance coverage for all people in the United States.

### Temperature and Specific Heat

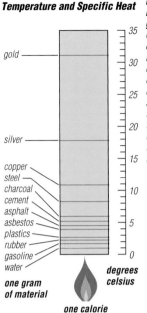

one gram
of material

one calorie

*By definition a calorie of heat raises the temperature of one gram of water by one degree Celsius. Thus the specific heat of water is one calorie per gram. From the chart we see that one calorie raises the temperature of one gram of silver by 17.8 degrees. To calculate the specific heat of silver, divide the specific heat of water (1) by the temperature rise in one gram of silver when it absorbs one calorie of heat: $^1/_{17.8} = 0.056$ calorie per gram.*

### Increase in Length with Temperature Rise

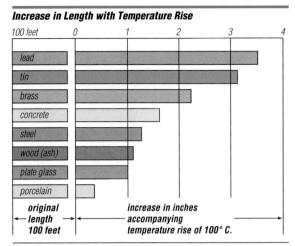

*Solid materials expand, by different amounts, with increase in temperature. The expansion cannot be readily noticed for short pieces. However, if the original length is 100 feet, the increase in length can be easily seen.*

body to rest. The kinetic energy of the moving body is changed into energy of motion within the molecules of both bodies. This kind of work is called friction. The increase in molecular motion results in an increase in the amount of heat contained in these bodies, and their temperatures rise.

The exact relationship which exists between heat and work has been determined. It is called the mechanical equivalent of heat. One calorie of heat energy equals 4.1840 joules of mechanical energy.

### Other Properties of Heat

The specific heat, or heat capacity, of a substance is the amount of heat that is required to raise the temperature of a unit weight of the substance by one degree. The value for specific heat varies widely for different substances. In the metric system the unit of specific heat is the calorie. It is defined as the amount of heat that is required to raise the temperature of one gram of water by one degree Celsius. The specific heat of water is set at 1.000 calorie per gram. All other values are based on this unit. The relationship between temperature and specific heat is shown in the chart above.

In the English system of measurements the British thermal unit (B.T.U.) is the unit of specific heat. One British thermal unit (252 calories) is the amount of heat required to raise the temperature of one pound of water by one degree Fahrenheit. In measuring the heat content of fuels the British thermal unit is the unit of specific heat used. The heat of reaction is the quantity of heat that is absorbed or lost by the surroundings when a chemical reaction takes place. Q is the symbol for the heat of reaction. If heat is lost, Q is a positive number and the reaction is called exothermic. If heat is absorbed, Q is a negative number and the reaction is called endothermic.

A measurement of the heat of reaction can be made with an instrument called a calorimeter, a vessel placed in a larger vessel filled with water. This reaction vessel is provided with a sensitive thermometer, and the larger vessel is insulated from the surroundings. A weighed amount of the substance under test is completely burned in the reaction vessel. The rise in temperature of the wat⸱⸱ is measured. Since the amount of water and t̶ ̶ ̶ ̶ ̶ ̶rature are known, the amount of as the heat of reaction or ⸱⸱⸱

The latent heat of vaporization is the amo⸱⸱ absorbed on vaporization at boiling temperature. For water this value is 539.6 calories per gram. The latent heat of fusion is the amount of heat required to change a crystal into a liquid at the melting point. For water this value is 79.7 calories per gram.

### Expansion and Contraction with Heat

All matter increases in volume when there is an increase in temperature. In the case of gases the increase is a large one. If the pressure and the weight of gas remain the same, the increase in volume will be in direct proportion to the increase in temperature. The application of heat to a solid causes it to expand also but to a much smaller degree than a gas. In a metal rod every unit length of the rod becomes longer when it expands. The increase in length for each unit of length per degree rise in temperature is called the coefficient of linear expansion. Liquids in general behave like solids and expand slightly when the temperature is raised. (*See also* Water.)

### The Transfer of Heat

Heat transfer helps to shape the world in which we live. Great loss is suffered by man when heat transfer

### Three Methods of Heat Transfer

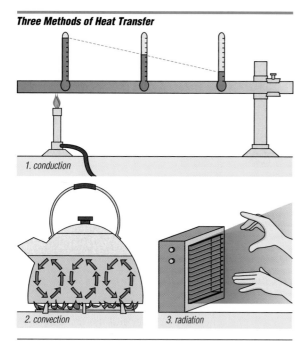

1. conduction

2. convection

3. radiation

*(Top) heat flows from the hot end to the cool end of the rod. As the distance from the burner flame increases, the temperature of the rod falls by a proportional amount. In a tea kettle (bottom left), hot water rises and cold water descends until all the water is at the same temperature. A home heating lamp (bottom right) produces its heating effect by direct transfer of radiant energy.*

is impossible. If a way could be found to transfer heat to the polar regions they could support large populations just as the temperate countries do. Fortunately man has been more successful in making use of the natural methods of heat transfer on a smaller scale. A quantity of heat is useless if it is where it is not needed. It may be useful if it can be moved to another place.

Heat, by its very nature, helps to make this possible. Heat always travels, or flows, from a high temperature to a low temperature. It can do this by three different methods. These are called conduction, convection, and radiation.

#### Conduction

Conduction is a point-by-point process of heat transfer. If one part of a body is heated by direct contact with a source of heat, the neighboring parts become heated successively. Thus, as shown in the diagram, if a metal rod is placed in a burner, heat travels along the rod by conduction. This may be explained by the kinetic theory of matter. The molecules of the rod increase their energy of motion. This violent motion is passed along the rod from molecule to molecule.

In considering the flow of heat by conduction, it is sometimes helpful to compare the flow of heat to the flow of electricity. The temperature difference can be thought of as the pressure, or voltage, in an electrical circuit. The ability of a substance to transfer heat (its

thermal conductivity) can be compared to electrical conductivity. When the temperature difference (or voltage) between two points is great, the driving force to move heat (or current) is high. The quantity of heat (or current) transferred will depend upon the temperature diffence (or voltage difference) and the resistance to the flow of heat (or current) offered by the conductor.

#### Convection

The method of heat transfer called convection depends upon the movement of the material which is heated. It applies to free-moving substances; that is, liquids and gases. The motion is a result of changes of density that accompany the heating process. Water in a tea kettle is heated by convection (*see* diagram). A stove heats the air in a room by convection.

When a liquid or gas is heated, its density (mass per unit volume) decreases; that is, it becomes lighter in weight. A warmer volume of gas will rise while a colder, and thus heavier, volume of gas will descend. This process is described as natural convection. A familiar example of natural convection is the circulation of air from a hot-air furnace. When a liquid or gas is moved from one place to another by some mechanical force, the process is known as forced convection. The circulation of air by an electric fan is an example of forced convection.

#### Radiation

The third method of transferring heat energy from one place to another is called radiation. This process begins when the internal energy of a system is converted into radiant energy at a source such as a heater. This energy is transmitted by waves through space, just as the sun radiates heat outwards through the solar system. Finally the radiant energy strikes a body where it is absorbed and converted to internal energy. It then appears as heat. An electric heater produces radiant energy in this way (*see* diagram). It may be absorbed, reflected, or transmitted by a body in its path. When the radiant energy is absorbed, the internal energy of the body increases and its temperature rises.

All bodies, whether hot or cold, radiate energy. The hotter a body is, the more energy it radiates. Furthermore all bodies receive radiation from other bodies. The exchange of radiant energy goes on continuously. Thus a body at constant temperature has not stopped radiating. It is receiving energy at the same rate that it is radiating energy. There is no change in internal energy or temperature.

Heat transfer by radiation is not proportional to the difference in temperature between the hot and cold objects as it is in the case of heat transfer by conduction and convection. It is proportional to the difference between the fourth powers of the absolute temperatures of the two objects. Thus heat transfer by radiation is enormously more effective at high temperatures than at low temperatures. Radiation transfer depends also upon the shape of the radiating object. (*See also* Radiation.)

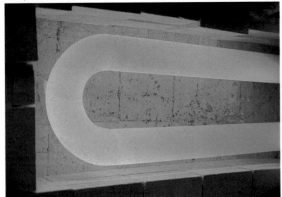

Courtesy of the Gas Research Institute

*A radiant heat exchanger is used in industrial furnaces to heat working materials, such as nuts and bolts. This experimental model is made of a ceramic tube surrounded by ceramic insulation blocks.*

## Thermodynamics and the Theory of Heat

The nature of heat has been a major subject for study since the beginnings of modern science. Early investigators, including Galileo, Boyle, and Newton, explained heat as the motion of tiny particles of which bodies are made. In the 18th century scientists advanced understanding by concentrating on the flow of heat. It was thought of as a fluid, and experiments were made on the heat conductivity of metals.

Antoine Lavoisier attempted to develop a quantitative theory of heat. He showed that the heat produced in chemical reactions could be studied quantitatively. He developed a system of thermodynamics that helped to explain the relations between heat and chemical reactions. Lavoisier's theories were still based on the idea that heat was a fluid.

## Kinetic Theory

In 1798 the physicist Benjamin Thompson (Count Rumford) revived the kinetic theory of heat. He became interested in the subject by observing the vast quantities of heat produced by friction during the boring of a cannon. Thompson decided that heat was not a material fluid but the result of a conversion of energy. Forty years later, the British physicist James P. Joule also proved that heat was a form of energy. Joule also proved the equivalence of mechanical energy and heat. He concluded that the amount of work required to bring about any given energy exchange was independent of the kind of work done, the rate of work, or the method of doing it. Therefore, in an isolated system, work can be converted into heat at a ratio of one to one. This discovery later became known as the First Law of Thermodynamics.

Nicolas L.S. Carnot did research on heat that explained the mechanics of the flow of heat from a hot region to a cooler region. Lord Kelvin used Carnot's concepts to develop his absolute thermodynamic temperature scale. By applying mathematics, Willard Gibbs and Ludwig Boltzmann refined thermodynamics into an exact science.

**HEATH, Sir Edward** (1916–2005). The major achievement of Prime Minister Edward Heath was gaining French acceptance for British membership in the European Economic Community, or Common Market. Heath served only from 1970 to 1974. After a Labour party victory in 1974 he was replaced by his predecessor, Harold Wilson (*see* Wilson, Harold).

Heath was born on July 9, 1916, at Broadstairs in Kent, England. He attended Oxford University, where he became a member of the University Conservative Association and thus involved with the Conservative party. As chairman of the Federation of University Conservative Associations he opposed the government's policy of appeasing Adolf Hitler during the late 1930s. After service in the army during World War II, he worked for the Ministry of Aviation in 1946–47. He edited the *Church Times* for nearly two years before going into a banking firm.

Heath was elected to Parliament as a Conservative in February 1950. He served in a succession of posts under prime ministers Anthony Eden, Harold Macmillan, and Alec Douglas-Home. Upon Douglas-Home's resignation as party leader, Heath was elected to replace him in July 1965. His party suffered a decisive defeat in March 1966, but it won the June 1970 election. His term was disturbed by violence in Northern Ireland and economic troubles. After Conservative losses in the election of Feb. 28, 1974, he was replaced as prime minister by Labour party leader Harold Wilson. Margaret Thatcher replaced him as head of the Conservative party in 1975 (*see* Thatcher). Heath was knighted in 1992. He died on July 17, 2005, in Salisbury, Wiltshire, England.

**HEATHER.** The songs and stories of Scotland are filled with praises of the "bonnie blooming heather." It covers the rugged Highlands with a cloak of purple and mingles its delicate fragrance with the upland air.

Heather—or ling, as it is sometimes called—is a small evergreen shrub, sometimes rising only a few inches above the ground, but often growing to a height of 3 feet (0.9 meter) or more. On its purplish-brown stems are close-leaved green shoots and feathery spikes of tiny bell-shaped flowers. The flowers are usually rose lilac in color, but range from deep purple to pure white. White heather, which is somewhat rare, is the most prized of all—in Scottish superstition it is thought to bring good luck.

The hardy heather plant serves many useful purposes. The tops afford winter forage for Highland sheep and cattle. The flower is a favorite of the bee, and heather honey has a delicious flavor. The larger stems are made into brooms, the smaller into brushes. Because of the scarcity of wood in earlier times, the Highlanders built cabins of heather stems cemented with mud. The same plant served to thatch the roofs. The ripe seeds of the heather are eaten by a great many birds.

The common heather (*Calluna vulgaris*) belongs to the heath family (Ericaceae). It is widespread in Europe, North America, and Asia.

Libby Owens—Ford Glass Company

**Noon Sun, December 21**

**Noon Sun, June 21**

*A contemporary solar house is warmed by the low angle of the rays of the sun on winter days (top right). The broad eaves protect it from the more nearly vertical rays of the sun in summer.*

**HEATING AND VENTILATING.** Heating of living quarters dates from earliest times, when people who lived in cold climates used open fires for warmth. Open fires were later replaced by stoves or fireplaces that heated only single rooms.

Central air heating, which distributes heat evenly throughout a building, was used in Roman times. Today central heating is the most economical form of heating for year-round homes and is a necessity for large buildings.

### Central Heating Systems

Central heating systems obtain their heat from burning fuel in a furnace. The furnace may heat water, it may turn water into steam (in which case it is called a boiler), or it may heat recirculated room air. These fluids are then the medium used to distribute the heat through the various rooms of the building. If central air

. . . . . . . . . . . . . . . . . . . . . . . . . . . . . . . . . . . . . . . . . . . . . .

*This article was contributed by Fred Landis, Professor of Mechanical Engineering, University of Wisconsin—Milwaukee.*

conditioning is also desired, hot-air systems are generally most effective because the same system can provide heat in the winter and cool air in the summer. (*See also* Air Conditioning.)

**Hot-water and steam systems.** In hot-water or steam systems, the hot fluid is generally distributed from the furnace through insulated pipes to radiators placed in strategic areas of a building. The cooled water or condensed steam is then returned to the furnace for recycling.

Most hot-water systems have two pipes attached to each radiator, one for the hot supply water, the other for the cold return. In systems that are fed by gravity, the hot water rises as the cool water runs down to a boiler in the basement. Since water expands on heating, an expansion tank must be supplied at the highest point of a gravity system. The expansion tank consists of a closed vessel partly filled with air; the air is compressed as the water is heated. Larger buildings invariably use a water pump for circulation. Such systems can work under higher pressures and with smaller water pipes.

### HOW A PULSED-COMBUSTION GAS FURNACE WORKS

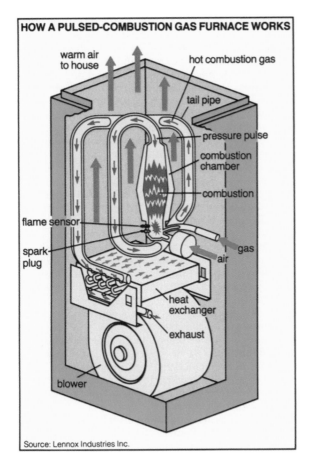

warm air to house
hot combustion gas
tail pipe
pressure pulse
combustion chamber
combustion
flame sensor
spark plug
gas
air
heat exchanger
exhaust
blower

Source: Lennox Industries Inc.

In each room, the actual heat transfer takes place by a combination of radiation, conduction, and convection (*see* Heat). Thus cold air in contact with the hot radiator rises by convection and circulates through the room. Because hot air rises, radiators are generally located near the floor of a room, away from any obstructions. At the same time, the radiator transmits heat to colder walls and furniture by radiation.

In older hot-water and steam heating systems, cast-iron radiators are frequently used. Newer hot-water systems generally use convectors, which consist of one or more water tubes covered with a large number of thin metal sheets or fins attached at right angles to the tubes. Convectors are normally placed near the floor along room walls. They are often partially enclosed in a rectangular sheet-metal casing, open near the bottom and top. The casing acts as a chimney, drawing in cold air from the floor, passing it up over the fins, and then discharging it back into the room. Both radiators and convectors have valves to control the amount of heating. In buildings with concrete floors, hot-water pipes may also be embedded in the concrete to heat the floor directly by conduction and the rest of the room by radiation.

Steam systems require smaller pipes than hot-water systems and are used primarily in large buildings. In some large metropolitan areas, inexpensive low-pressure steam is available as a by-product of electric power generation. In a system known as district heating, this steam is piped to nearby buildings for use in their heating systems.

**Hot-air systems.** Hot-water residential heating systems have remained popular in Europe. However, for private homes in the United States and Canada, hot-air systems are less expensive to construct and, because they can be combined with central air conditioning systems, they have become widely accepted for use in large buildings as well. In hot-air systems a circulating blower and air filters are encased in the same housing as the furnace. The hot air is distributed to the various rooms through ducts; the air flow through the ducts is regulated with adjustable dampers. In each room, the air is discharged through outlet registers, located near the floor, from which the hot air rises and circulates. Registers have louvers that can be opened or closed to control the amount of hot air entering the room. The air is drawn back through return ducts, located near the floor at a distance from the inlet registers, and is fed back to the furnace. If the same circulation system is also used for air conditioning, additional ducting outlets and return inlets are required.

**Furnaces and boilers.** A furnace consists of two basic components: a combustion chamber where the fuel is burned, and a heat exchanger where the hot combustion gases transfer heat to the distribution medium (water, steam, or air). In water or steam heating systems the heat exchanger may line the combustion chamber; in hot-air heating systems the hot gases come into contact with the heat exchanger after they leave the combustion chamber. The hot combustion gases are then vented to the outside through a stack or chimney.

Although coal was a common fuel for furnaces through the 1940s, it has been largely replaced in North America by fuel oil and natural gas. Before oil can be burned efficiently, it may have to be preheated and it must be atomized, or broken into tiny droplets. This atomization may be achieved by using an air jet, by forcing the oil under high pressure through small nozzles in a gun-type burner, or by using a centrifugal device that spins the oil off a rotating disk or cup. A separate blower usually supplies the air required for combustion, which is then initiated by an electric arc. Fuels for domestic furnaces are similar to diesel oil; for large commercial units they may be heavier oils.

Gas furnaces require a stream of gas and air for combustion, which can be started by a pilot flame or, more economically, by an electric sparkplug. In remote locations where natural gas is not available, compressed gaseous fuels, such as propane, may supply a gas furnace. However, their relatively high cost makes them an economical alternative only in temperate regions or in houses used only part of the year.

All types of furnaces have temperature overload protections. If the heat exchanger surface gets too hot, combustion is shut off until the temperature drops to an acceptable level.

Conventional gas furnaces have efficiencies of from 70 to 80 percent—that is, 70 to 80 percent of the heating energy in the fuel finds its way into the home. In oil furnaces, the efficiency may drop to as low as 60 percent unless the furnace is tuned up and cleaned frequently. Most of the remaining energy is lost as hot exhaust. If the exhaust temperature can be reduced, the overall performance of the system is substantially improved. This improved performance is the aim of modern gas-fired high-efficiency furnaces, which have efficiencies of from 93 to 97 percent. High-efficiency furnaces significantly increase the surface area of the heat exchanger, where hot combustion gases on one side transmit heat to house air on the other side. To further increase their efficiency, these furnaces take in only outside air for combustion rather than warm inside air, and they use a sparkplug to initiate combustion instead of using a pilot flame.

One such furnace uses a type of pulsed combustion. Air and gas are fed into a combustion chamber with a long tail pipe and are initially fired by a sparkplug. A pressure pulse closes the air and gas inlet valves while the hot combustion gas empties through the exhaust pipe into the heat exchanger sections. A low-pressure wave reflected from the end of the tail pipe admits a fresh air/gas mixture and another combustion pulse begins. This pulsing takes place about 60 to 70 times per second. (*See also* Furnace and Boiler.)

**Heating control.** Most home furnaces are controlled by a thermostat. The heart of the thermostat is a primary, or sensitive, element, which has physical properties affected by temperature changes. Generally it is an element that expands or contracts with increases or decreases in room temperature. Changes in the primary element usually activate an electric switch, which is called the secondary element. Usually, when the temperature falls by about a half degree below a preset amount, the switch is tripped, closing an electric circuit and starting the burner. Then, when the temperature has risen above the setting, the switch is opened again and the burner stops.

Some thermostats use tilting mercury contact switches. These contain a spiral strip made of two metals, one of which expands and contracts in response to temperature change more rapidly than the other one. This uneven response causes a bending in the strip. Thus as the room temperature drops below the desired level and the spiral cools, it contracts, allowing a tiny capsule half filled with mercury to tilt to one side. There are two wires at one end of the capsule; when the mercury fills that end, it completes a circuit that turns on the burner. Other thermostats use entirely electronic switching. In large buildings the heating system is usually subdivided into zones that can be individually controlled by separate thermostats.

### Other Heating Systems

Furnace-operated heating systems are not the only ones in use. For some regions other heating systems may be more practical. Such systems include solar heating, electric radiant heating, and heat pumps.

**Solar heating.** A simple form of solar heating is used in greenhouses. Glass and certain plastics are transparent to short-wavelength solar radiation. When these materials are used in roofs and walls, the solar radiation readily passes through them and into the space within. The plants in the greenhouse reemit radiation, but because they are at a relatively low temperature, the radiation is at longer wavelengths and cannot pass through the glass. Thus much of the solar heat is trapped within the greenhouse, which becomes warmer than the outside air.

Solar radiation can also be used to heat homes and other buildings. Solar heating systems used in buildings typically include a solar collector, a water or air distribution system, and a storage system. Most often a flat-plate solar collector is mounted on the roof, facing south and preferably positioned at a steep angle. In water systems, the collector typically consists of an outer glass plate, a small airspace, and a bottom heat-absorption plate through which water is pumped in closely spaced tubes. To provide heat when the sun is not shining, a large hot-water storage tank is used. As room heating is required, the hot water is pumped, either directly from the collector or from the storage tank, through one side of a heat exchanger. On the other side the building air is forced through with a fan. About 20 to 30 percent of the incident solar energy can actually be utilized in such a system. A backup heating system using a conventional furnace is also required.

Hot-air solar systems use more complex collectors that heat air directly. Because air cannot store much thermal energy, however, supplementary storage systems must be added. They consist of rock beds or assemblies of large pebbles that are heated by the air flowing through the collector. Room air then passes over the storage bed and absorbs heat from the rocks.

Solar systems can be active, whereby the circulating water or air is pumped through the system, or passive. If passive, circulation relies solely on the rising of warm fluids and falling of cooler ones. Solar heating systems, particularly passive systems, designed into a building before its construction, can be quite economical in moderate climates and sunny areas. At present, active solar systems and solar heating in less ideal climates are generally less economical.

**Electric radiant heating.** In some heating systems electric resistance heaters are buried in concrete floor slabs. These heaters warm first the floor by conduction and then the rest of the house by radiation and convection. Although this type of heating is very comfortable, its high cost makes it impractical except in areas where electric power is inexpensive and the seasonal heating requirements are low.

**Heat pumps.** A home refrigerator takes warm air out of a cold region, raises it to a higher temperature, then discharges it into the room (*see* Refrigeration). This requires mechanical energy. For many home refrigerators the amount of heat extracted is equal to about six times the mechanical energy required to extract the heat, and the heat discharged is about

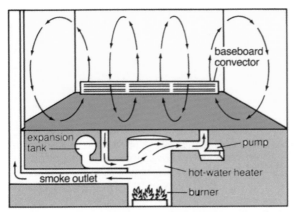

Hot-water systems run hot water from a furnace to convectors. Heat circulates, and the cold water returns to the furnace.

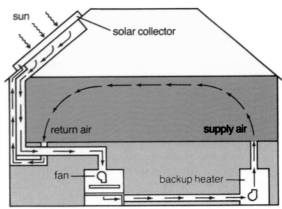

In solar air systems, air is circulated past the solar collector, over the storage system, and into the rooms.

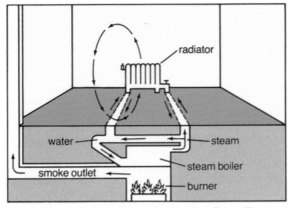

Steam systems boil water and pass the steam to radiators. The steam gives off heat, condenses, and flows back to the boiler.

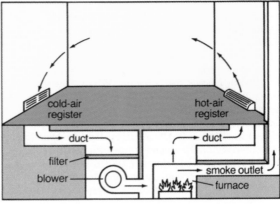

Hot-air systems have a blower that circulates warm air from the furnace through ducts to room registers.

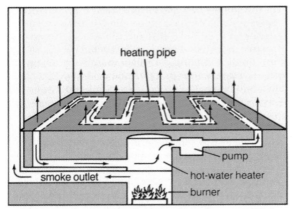

Radiant hot-water resembles other hot-water systems except that a continuous hot-water pipe is embedded in the floor.

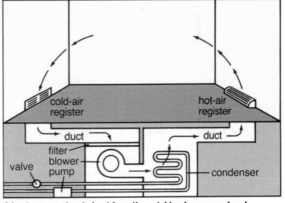

A heat pump extracts heat from the outside air or ground and releases it at a higher temperature into the building.

seven times the mechanical energy. These values decrease when the difference between the high and low temperatures is increased.

A heat pump works like a refrigerator. It extracts heat from the atmosphere or from the ground and releases it at a higher temperature into the building. For moderately cool outdoor temperatures, the heat

discharged is many times the mechanical and electrical energy supplied to the system. Thus a heat pump can be a practical heating system in climates where the air temperature does not drop much below 50° F (10° C). At lower air temperatures, heat may be drawn from the ground or from groundwater, though this can be costly. Heat pumps may eventually become more common in moderate climates. Today, however, the high initial cost has restricted the use of such systems.

**Stoves and fireplaces.** In the United States, the use of domestic wood stoves rose sharply after the energy crisis of the early 1970s. In northern parts of the country where firewood was cheap, they provided a simple and economical means of heating the home. Their use has been limited, however, because of the dangers of accidental fire and carbon monoxide poisoning, as well as the rising cost of firewood.

Fireplaces have long been a favorite means of heating areas of the home. However, though a fireplace will warm its immediate environment, it may actually cool the rest of the house because it draws in large amounts of surrounding air. This heat loss can be reduced by narrowing the damper opening after the fire has settled to a slow burn. Nevertheless, a fireplace is only effective for space heating if it is flanked by separate ducts, or heatolators. These allow room air to enter at the bottom of the fireplace, draw heat from the fireplace walls, and then reenter the room from the top of the fireplace.

**Space heaters.** Supplementary heat for a single room or for an area that is used only occasionally can be supplied by electric space heaters. When electric current passes through the heater's resistance elements, the elements become red hot. A reflective surface at the back of the unit may serve to concentrate the heat toward the front of the heater. Heat transfer takes place principally by radiation and conduction, which may be aided by a fan that directs air past the elements and reflective surface. For safety, many space heaters have a shut-off device that is activated if the heater is tipped over. Because the cost of electric heating is usually much higher than that of gas or oil heating, space heaters are generally used only for supplementary, short-term heating.

### Seasonal Heating Needs

In the winter human comfort requires not only a certain temperature range, but also a certain humidity level. The relative humidity—the percentage of moisture in the air compared to the maximum amount of moisture that the air can hold at a given temperature—should range from 30 to 70 percent. Due to increased evaporation from the skin, persons in a room at 75° F (24° C) feel colder if the relative humidity is too low than they do in a room at 70° F (21° C) with moderate relative humidity. Thus, because cold air can hold less humidity than warm air, the relative humidity of outside winter air, once heated, will be too low for comfort. This can be remedied in central hot-air heating systems by adding a humidifier in the furnace. For steam and water systems, separate room humidifiers may be required.

In general, heating is required if the daily average outside temperature falls below 65° F (18° C). A system of "degree days," based on degrees Fahrenheit, is sometimes used to estimate the annual fuel requirement for a given region. For each degree Fahrenheit that the average temperature falls below 65° F, one degree day

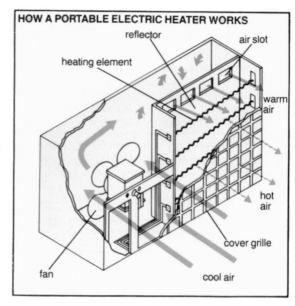

**HOW A PORTABLE ELECTRIC HEATER WORKS**

reflector
air slot
heating element
warm air
hot air
cover grille
fan
cool air

accrues. Thus if the daily average temperature is 20° F, 45 degree days will accumulate. The total number of degree days in a year is a measure of the annual fuel requirement, though the actual amount of fuel required depends both on the exact number of degree days and on the temperature at which the home is maintained. The higher the average inside temperature, the greater the fuel consumption.

Heating requirements also increase with strong winds, which hasten the heat loss from a building. In all cases, heating costs can be greatly reduced by lowering the thermostat setting during the night, when room temperatures between 60° F and 65° F (16° C and 18° C) are comfortable for most persons.

### Building Insulation and Air Exchange

To a large extent the heating requirements of a building depend on the amount of insulation in the building. Modern frame houses in temperate parts of the United States typically have 2 to 3 inches (5 to 8 centimeters) of insulation in the walls and 6 inches (15 centimeters) or more in the attic floor.

This insulation may be in the form of matts or battens (insulation packaged in paper covers). Or, for wall insulation, it may be blown into the spaces between the studs.

Much of the heat loss from a building does not take place through the walls, however. Instead it takes place through glass windows and cracks in the walls, often near window frames.

Thus a building's heat loss can be reduced by installing double- or triple-pane windows, in which the panes of glass are separated by a small airspace that acts as an insulator. Heavy curtains over windows can also lower heat loss. Radiation loss from buildings can be reduced by applying special coatings to the inside window pane that reflect radiation back into the room. (*See also* Insulation.)

Heat loss through cracks in building walls can be minimized by careful caulking of all joints with a sealing compound. However, no house should be completely airtight—a continuous exchange between inside and outside air must be allowed. Normally it is recommended that between 15 and 25 cubic feet (0.4 to 0.7 cubic meter) per minute of fresh air per occupant be allowed to enter a building. This does not present a problem in most residences, where even a well constructed building will normally have half of its air exchanged every hour. For particularly drafty houses this number may even approach two complete air exchanges per hour. However, insufficient air exchange can pose a problem for large buildings. In such cases ventilation should be provided.

**Ventilation**

Large buildings require ventilation to distribute fresh air to all parts of the structure, particularly if windows cannot be opened. The degree of ventilation required depends on the building's use, the height of the ceilings, the number of door openings, and the number of occupants. A ventilating system may be required to supply an amount of fresh air ranging from 7.5 to 40 cubic feet (0.2 to 1.1 cubic meters) per minute for each occupant.

Ventilation systems draw fresh air from outdoors, filter it, and then distribute it through a system of ducts by means of blowers. Part of the room air is returned through separate ducts and is often mixed with the incoming air, particularly if the system also includes air conditioning. Filters for industrial and commercial building ventilation are made of many materials. Replaceable fabric or glass fiber filters, also used in home air heating systems, remove particles from the air. They must be replaced when they become clogged. Electrostatic filters charge particles in the air and deposit them on oil-coated plates, which must be washed periodically. Activated charcoal filters are effective in removing odors and tobacco smoke and are often used when a high percentage of the air is recirculated.

Buildings containing laboratories or manufacturing areas that produce objectionable gases or fumes used to have special ventilating hoods that drew off the bad air and discharged it directly outdoors. To pollute the air in this manner is no longer feasible. Environmental laws require filtering the air before it leaves the building.

In the home, special ventilation may be required if an occupant is allergic to materials normally found in the air, such as pollen. In this case the incoming air may be filtered before distribution. For general circulation, exhaust fans may be used to discharge stale air from the building while drawing in fresh air through windows and doors. Attic fans may be used to ventilate closed spaces under a roof. Closed ventilating systems, which do not bring outside air into the home, can assist circulation and, to a smaller extent, heating in the home. Because hot air rises, the upper floors of an open house are likely to be much warmer than the lower ones. The heat can be more evenly distributed through the home by using a recirculating blower system. Similarly, ceiling fans can redistribute warm air by pushing down the hot air that accumulates near ceilings and providing air movement. (*See also* Fan, Electric.)

Ventilation plays a critical role in many industrial sites, such as in chemical processing plants and paint shops, where poisonous or combustible fumes and vapors can accumulate. A continuous supply of fresh air is also necessary in underground mines and in long vehicular tunnels.

Today heating and ventilating, along with air conditioning and noise and vibration suppression, are considered part of the larger field of environmental engineering. Engineers in this field recognize that human comfort and efficiency, as well as the proper operation of mechanical and electronic equipment, are affected by the immediate environment. Thus they attempt to take environmental factors into account in the original design of a building.

**HEBEI, or HOPEI.** Located in northeastern China, Hebei is one of the country's most advanced provinces. It is bordered by the Bo Hai, a gulf of the Yellow Sea, on the east; the provinces of Liaoning on the northeast, Shandong on the southeast, and Shanxi on the west; and the Inner Mongolian Autonomous Region on the northwest. Carved out of the center are the special-status municipalities of Beijing and Tianjin. The provincial capital is Shijiazhuang.

The Hebei Plain is bound by the Yen Mountains. Along this range is the Great Wall of China. The climate is continental with hot, wet summers and cold, dry winters. The heaviest rainfall is in the months of June, July, and August. The rains and the rich, fertile soils of Hebei produce cotton, wheat, millet, corn (maize), peanuts, sorghum, soy beans, and sesame. Fruits grown are pears, grapes, peaches, persimmons, dates, and apples.

A reflection of the major coal-mine and railway development, Hebei's heavy industry is centered on steel, cement, and railway repair. Other manufactures are textiles, paper, ceramics, leather goods, and woolens. Serviced by seven major railroads and by sea transport, Hebei is a dominant force in Chinese trade.

An early hominid called Peking man roamed the Hebei Plain approximately 400,000 years ago. The Ch'ing Dynasty ruled Hebei province from 1644 to 1911. Until the Japanese occupation in 1937 it was ruled by the Nationalist government. In 1945 the Japanese surrendered to the Chinese Nationalists, and in 1949 the Chinese Communist forces took control of the province. Population (2000 estimate), 67,440,000.

# HEBREW LITERATURE

**HEBREW LITERATURE.** The language of ancient Israel was Hebrew, one of the Semitic languages of the Middle East. It is the language in which most of the Hebrew Bible—what Christians call the Old Testament—was originally written (*see* Bible). Literature in Hebrew has been produced continuously since at least the 12th century BC. Until about AD 200 Hebrew was a spoken and written language, though it had been supplanted by other Semitic dialects in some places. From AD 200 until about 1880 Hebrew was a literary language only. Jews used other languages for speaking and for most of their writing.

From the time of the Roman Empire to the present, many Jews have written in the languages of the countries in which they lived. During the 19th century Yiddish—another distinctively Jewish language—became prominent, especially in Eastern Europe (*see* Yiddish Literature).

## Background

Jews, ancient and modern, share a powerful two-fold heritage: the Hebrew Bible and an attachment to the land of Israel. They lost political control of the land by the 1st century BC, and it was not restored until the founding of the modern state of Israel in 1948. The Biblical tradition remained, however, and it formed the main basis of Jewish literature for hundreds of years (*see* Judaism; Talmud; Torah).

The influence of the Bible, especially the Torah, was so overwhelming that it virtually stifled any attempts to formulate a literature not based upon it. A modern literature in Hebrew—novels, short stories, poetry, and drama—did not appear until about 1880. It owes much of its inspiration to the philosopher Moses Mendelssohn, who lived a century earlier. He urged that Jews adopt Hebrew as their distinctive language in order to promote unity in the face of intolerance (*see* Mendelssohn, Moses).

The critical factor in the emergence of Hebrew as both a written and spoken language in the 20th century was the Zionist movement and the founding of the state of Israel. Zionism and the resurgence of Hebrew literature were parallel developments. Much of modern Hebrew literature, in fact, deals with the resettlement of Israel and the problems occasioned by it (*see* Zionism). Hebrew is the first so-called dead language that has been revived for popular use.

## Themes of Modern Hebrew Literature

Whereas traditional Hebrew literature was religious, the modern literature is primarily secular. Yet it has never entirely disengaged itself from its ancient roots in Biblical history. Problems posed about human nature and society in the Hebrew Bible are woven into today's literature.

This is, in fact, one source of the conflict evident in the literature: how to relate the modern Jewish experience—especially the violent European persecutions and the horrors of the Holocaust—to a past that embraced the belief in being God's chosen people (*see* Genocide; Holocaust).

Jewish identity itself has been a source of difficulty. During the Enlightenment many Jews turned away from their traditions to become involved in the new waves of thought and scientific discovery (*see* Enlightenment). To some, being distinctively Jewish no longer mattered. They were content with being citizens of the nations in which they lived. This tension between modernism and tradition has persisted.

Since the start of the Zionist movement, attitudes toward it have proved a source of conflict. Many yearned for a return to Palestine as a promised land. Others rejected the notion out of attachment to lands of their birth. As resettlement in Palestine began around 1900, high hopes and expectations were often disappointed by the reality of the land itself as well as by the hostility of the Arabs.

The nature of the new state of Israel also proved a source of division. Some Jews desired to form a Semitic state in cooperation with the Arabs. Others insisted on a Jewish state. Even among those who favored a Jewish state there was disagreement. Would it be a state based on traditional religious law, or would it be a secular state? Another theme that prompted comment is: "What is Israel?" Some view it only in its present geographic terms. Others speak of the "true Israel," or the "greater Israel," the longing for a nation as large as that of the ancient period.

Since resettlement began in about 1900, thousands of Israelis have been born there. Between them and those who have moved there since, there has arisen tension. Those who were born in Israel had no special relationship with the Jews dispersed throughout the world. Israelis spoke and wrote Hebrew, while the others used different languages. For the Israelis, Palestine was home, but for the newcomers it was a strange place to which they had to grow accustomed. The native Israelis could view the Holocaust with horror, but they did not share in it.

These conflicts and disagreements provided some of the themes for modern Hebrew literature as it developed in Eastern Europe after 1880 and matured in Israel. The conflicts have been so prominent because they are still playing themselves out in the social and political life of Israel.

## The Literature

The first modern writers of Hebrew were of European origin, native to such areas as Austria-Hungary, Russia, Poland, and Lithuania. They were among the first people to join the resettlement in Palestine. More recent writers are a mixture of immigrants and native-born Israelis.

**Novelists.** The early generation of novelists includes Moshe Smilanski (1874–1950), Joseph Chaim Brenner (1881–1921), Abraham Kabak (1883–1944), Shmuel Yosef Agnon (1888–1970), Asher Baras h (1889–1952), and Hayyim Hazaz (1898–1922). Smilanski went to Israel from Ukraine in 1890. His stories deal with the early settlers but also show a great fondness for the Arabs. His 'Palestine Caravan' was translated into English in 1935. Brenner arrived in Israel in 1908 and was killed during Arab rioting in 1921. In contrast to the optimism of Smilanski, he expresses a keen awareness of how difficult it is to create a Jewish homeland surrounded by hostile Arab societies in 'Between the Waters' (1920) and 'Breakdown and Bereavement' (1922).

Russian-born Kabak's early writings concern the difficulties Jews had living in Eastern Europe. The novel 'Alone' (1905) examines the conflict between Zionist hopes and the communist ideology to which many European Jews were attracted. His major work is the trilogy 'Solomon Molcho' (1928–30), a story of the Middle Ages.

Agnon was one of the 20th century's most prominent writers and a joint winner of the Nobel prize for literature in 1966. Most of his writing deals with the Jews of Europe. Only after living in Israel for many years did he begin writing about his adopted country. 'Bridal Canopy' (1930), his best-known novel, is about a father who travels around his native province seeking dowries for his three marriageable daughters. 'Just Yesterday' (1947) tells of immigrants living in Israel prior to World War I. His stories were collected in 'And the Crooked Shall Be Made Straight' (1916), 'Twenty-one Stories' (1951), and 'Tehilla' (translated in 1956).

Barash's early novels are about the Jews of Eastern Europe: 'Pictures from the Brewery' (1928) and 'Strange Love' (1938). Of his later works about Israel, the short story "He and His Life Were Ruined" is among the best.

Hazaz's novel 'The People of the Forest' (1942) portrays refugees from Ukraine living in Israel. His major works—'Those Who Live in the Gardens' (1944) and the four-volume 'Yaish' (1947–52)—are minor epics about the Yemenite Jews.

Among the best-known writers of the later 20th century were Binyamin Tammuz (1919–89), Aharon Megged (born 1920), Moshe Shamir (born 1921), Nathan Shaham (born 1925), Abraham B. Yehoshua (born 1937), Amos Oz (born 1939), Aharon Appelfeld (born 1932), and David Schütz (born 1941). Most of these writers lived through the years of struggle leading to the founding of Israel.

Tammuz tackles the issue of Jewish identity in 'At the Edge of the West' (1966) and 'The Orchard' (1971). Megged, mainly a satirical novelist, explores the contrast between the early idealism of the Israeli kibbutz, or commune, and the later materialistic, pleasure-loving city dwellers in 'Hevda and I' (1954), 'Fortunes of a Fool' (1960), 'The Living and the Dead' (1965), and 'The Short Life' (1972).

Primarily a political novelist, Shamir tells of his life on a kibbutz in 'He Walked in the Fields' (1948). In 'The Border' (1966) he deals with the differences between the native-born Israeli whom he idealizes and the immigrant from Europe whom he holds in contempt. Shaham presents a far more optimistic picture of the modern Israeli in 'There and Back' (1972).

Yehoshua's goal was to depict the conflicts in modern Jewish identity. His novels include 'Early in the Summer of 1970' (1971), 'The Lover' (1977), and 'A Late Divorce' (1982). His shorter works were collected in 'Facing the Forests' (1968).

Oz was the most popular writer of his generation. His symbolic and poetic novels reflect the divisions and strains in modern Israel. He saw clearly the splits between rural and urban populations, between Asian and European Jews, and between the secular and the religious demands. Some of his books are 'Elsewhere Perhaps' (1966), 'My Michael' (1968), 'Unto Death' (1971), 'Touch the Water, Touch the Wind' (1973), and 'In the Land of Israel' (1982).

The novels of Appelfeld relate the modern Israel to its ancient past and traditions, often in a pessimistic way. The need to come to terms with the past was impressed upon him by living in Europe during World War II. His best novel is 'The Age of Wonders' (1982). Earlier works are 'Skin and Clothes' (1971) and 'Badenheim 1939' (1975).

Schütz was one of the last of his generation of novelists. As did others of his colleagues, he viewed his nation within a larger historical context dating from early Zionism. He shows an awareness of the European past and the first decades of resettlement in his successful novel, 'The Grass and the Sand' (1978).

**Poets.** The most significant of the early poets was Hayyim Nahman Bialik (1873–1934), considered by many critics to be the major poet of 20th-century Hebrew literature. He contributed greatly to making Hebrew a flexible medium of poetic expression. Some of his early poetry, such as 'The City of Slaughter', deals with the persecution of Jews in Russia. This theme runs though the collection 'Songs of Wrath'. 'Orphanhood' was written in Israel shortly before his death. Other poets of his generation were Saul Tschernikowski (1875–1943), Zalman Shneour (1887–1959), Deborah Baron (1887–1956), Uri Zvi Greenberg (1896–1981), Yitzhak Lamdan (1900–54), Avraham Shlonsky (1900–73), and Nathan Alterman (1910–70).

The most significant later 20th century poets were Leah Goldberg (1911–70), Hayyim Guri (born 1921), Yehuda Amichai (1924–2000), Nathan Zach (born 1930), David Avidan (1934–95), and Daliah Ravikovitz (born 1936). In addition to treating standard Israeli themes, the female poets also devoted themselves to women's issues in what is basically a male-dominated society.

**HECTOR.** In Homer's epic poem the 'Iliad', Hector is the son of the Trojan King Priam and the greatest of the Trojan heroes. When the Greeks besieged Troy, Hector's wife, Andromache, begged him not to fight, but Hector embraced their child and left to join the battle. Hector killed Patroclus, a friend of the Greek hero Achilles, and in revenge Achilles killed Hector. Achilles then drove his chariot around the walls of Troy, dragging Hector's body behind him. Priam finally begged his son's body from Achilles. The Trojans, mourning, burned Hector's body, and buried his ashes. When the fighting resumed, Troy fell to the Greeks. (*See also* Achilles; Homeric Legend.)

© Manfred Danegger—Peter Arnold, Inc.

*The hedgehog lives in hedges and thickets. When frightened it can roll into a tight ball.*

**HEDGEHOG.** When the spiny hedgehog is frightened or attacked, it rolls itself into a ball to protect its vulnerable face and underparts, exposing only its sharp prickly spines. Hedgehogs belong to the family Erinaceidae and are divided into two types: the spiny hedgehogs and their spineless, soft-furred relatives, the hairy hedgehogs. Both kinds are found in many parts of Europe and Asia. The hedgehog sleeps by day, and at night it pokes and burrows in the ground, feeding on such food as insects, frogs, and occasionally small mammals. About the size of a large rat, it spends the winter in hibernation.

**HEDGES.** Fences formed by living shrubs or trees are known as hedges. Some are planted as windbreaks not only for flower gardens but also for crop-planted fields. Others are used as enclosures to provide privacy, and some serve exclusively as ornamentals.

Hedges of myrtle, laurel, and boxwood were cultivated in the gardens of ancient Rome. The French introduced hedges made of tall trees such as elm, linden, hornbeam, and beech. The geometrically designed gardens of Elizabethan England were enclosed by magnificent yews that are still tended today.

Hedges vary in size and may be extremely formal and regular in outline or entirely natural. They can be grown from almost any plant with thick foliage that grows close to the ground and that has a fine, even texture, including deciduous as well as evergreen trees and shrubs, and even herbs and vines.

The American arborvitae (*Thuja occidentalis*) has been used ever since the early settlers first domesticated it, and the Osage orange (*Maclura pomifera*) has long been grown as a spiny hedge tree. The Canada hemlock (*Tsuga canadensis*), the hardiest of the hemlocks, is also frequently used. The California privet (*Ligustrum ovalifolium*) and the Japanese barberry (*Berberis thunbergii*) are ornamental hedges. Many European formal gardens are hedged with the dwarf boxwood (*Buxus sempervirens suffruticosa*).

**HEDIN, Sven Anders** (1865–1952). The Swedish explorer Sven Anders Hedin spent a great part of his life leading expeditions through Central Asia, where he made valuable geographical and archaeological discoveries. For these efforts he received the highest awards of the geographical societies of Europe, was made a Swedish nobleman, and was named honorary knight commander of the Indian Empire.

Hedin was born in Stockholm on Feb. 19, 1865. He attended Uppsala University in Sweden and the universities of Berlin and Halle in Germany. He traveled through Persia (Iran), the Caucasus, and Mesopotamia (Iraq) at age 20. In 1890 he was appointed translator for a Norwegian-Swedish mission to the shah of Iran. This marked the beginning of his explorations. In 1891 he visited Khorassan and Russian Turkestan. Between 1893 and 1898 he crossed Asia to reach Peking by way of the Ural and Pamir mountains and Lop Nor. He explored the Gobi Desert from 1899 to 1902. He was the first European to visit the Trans-Himalaya range of Tibet and make a detailed map of the country (1905–08).

His pro-German sympathies during World War I cost Hedin much support, but he resumed his explorations in an expedition of 1927–33, which located 327 archaeological sites in China. Among his books are 'Through Asia', published in 1898, 'My Life as an Explorer' (1926), and 'The Silk Road' (1938). He died in Stockholm on Nov. 26, 1952.

**HEGEL, Georg Wilhelm Friedrich** (1770–1831). One of the most influential of the 19th-century German philosophers, Georg Wilhelm Friedrich Hegel also wrote on psychology, law, history, art, and religion. Karl Marx based his philosophy of history on Hegel's law of thought, called the dialectic. In this dialectic an idea, or thesis, contains within itself an opposing idea, called antithesis. Out of the inevitable conflict between these opposing concepts is born a third, totally new thought, the synthesis. Applied to history by the Marxists, Hegel's concepts were used to formulate the notion of the class struggle. From the strife over the ownership of the means of production would arise a new classless society—the synthesis. Søren Kierkegaard's rejection of Hegelianism influenced the development of existentialism. (*See also* Existentialism; Kierkegaard; Marx.)

Georg Wilhelm Friedrich Hegel was born in Stuttgart, Germany, on Aug. 27, 1770. His father was a government official. Hegel went to Tübingen in 1788, where he studied philosophy and theology. After graduating he supported himself by tutoring until 1801, when he began to lecture at the University of Jena. Forced to leave because of the Napoleonic wars, he became principal of a gymnasium (high school) in Nuremberg. There he married Marie von Tucher. The older of Hegel's two sons, Karl, became an eminent historian.

At Nuremberg Hegel worked on his 'Science of Logic', which was published between 1812 and 1816. The success of this work brought him three offers of professorships. He taught at Heidelberg for a time and then in 1818 went to the University of Berlin. Students came from all parts of Europe to study with him. He became rector of the university in 1830. He died of cholera in Berlin on Nov. 14, 1831.

The significance of Hegel's ideas stems in part from the fact that they can be applied not only to abstract thought but also to psychology, religion, and history. An essential element of his system was his belief that reality can only be grasped when examined as a whole and that any attempt to discover truth by scrutinizing a single facet of reality is doomed to failure.

**HEIDEGGER, Martin** (1889–1976). The philosophy of Martin Heidegger is, for a variety of reasons, extraordinarily difficult to comprehend. His major book, 'Being and Time', published in 1927, is so complex as to be almost unreadable. He was mainly an asker of questions, not an answerer. His chief question, "What is it to be?" placed him in the tradition of 19th-century existentialism. He placed himself within the school of phenomenology. Yet it is not known whether his questions were philosophical, or perhaps entirely religious, influenced by his early training.

Heidegger was born in Messkirch, Germany, on Sept. 26, 1889. After finishing high school he joined the Jesuits as a novice. He studied philosophy and theology at the University of Freiburg and started teaching there in 1915.

He remained there until 1945 except for a five-year period at the University of Marburg (1923–28). When the Nazis came to power in 1933, he briefly supported Adolf Hitler. The Allies investigated him after the war but did not find his offense serious. He continued lecturing until 1958 and retired in 1959. He died in Messkirch on May 26, 1976.

**HEIFETZ, Jascha** (1901–87). Recognized as one of the greatest violin virtuosos of all time, Jascha Heifetz played with unmatched technical brilliance. He was born on Feb. 2, 1901, in Vilnius, Lithuania, and began studying the violin with his father at the age of 3. At 4, Heifetz was admitted to the Royal School of Music, and two years later he was performing major concerti in public. At the age of 9 he became a pupil of Leopold Auer at the St. Petersburg Conservatory. Following concerts in Russia, he made a successful European tour in 1914.

After the family fled the Bolsheviks in Russia, young Heifetz made his Carnegie Hall debut in New York City in October 1917. He became a United States citizen in 1925 and began a career of world tours that drew capacity crowds.

From 1962 Heifetz taught at the University of Southern California in Los Angeles, where the Heifetz Chair in Music was established in 1975. He retired from the concert stage in 1972. His recordings are classics, and he commissioned many works by modern composers. He also is known for his arrangements of both classical and modern works for the violin. He died in Los Angeles on Dec. 10, 1987.

**HEILONGJIANG,** or **HEILUNGKIANG.** The northernmost of China's 22 provinces, Heilongjiang is one of the three provinces that make up what is known in the West as Manchuria. Heilongjiang is bounded on the north and east by Russia along the Amur and Wusuli rivers, on the west by the Inner Mongolian Autonomous Region, and on the south by Jilin Province. It covers an area of 179,000 square miles (463,600 square kilometers), and its capital and largest city is Harbin (*see* Harbin).

Heilongjiang's Songhua-Nen River plain is surrounded by mountains. The Amur River is the international boundary for 1,180 miles (1,899 kilometers). Its main tributary, the Songhua River, is the province's major waterway. Heilongjiang has severe winters, and its short summers can be rainy.

Agricultural products include wheat, soybeans, and half of China's sugar beets. Lumber, petroleum, and coal are plentiful. The major industries include iron, steel, and machinery manufacturing; papermaking; and food and sugar processing.

In 1650 Russians built a fort on the Amur River, and border clashes, which still continue, began. Japan invaded Manchuria in 1931. During its occupation, industrial and transportation systems, including a railroad network, were established. (*See also* Manchuria.) Population (2000 estimate), 36,890,000.

**HEINE, Heinrich** (1797–1856). Along with Johann von Goethe and Friedrich Schiller, Heinrich Heine is one of the three greatest names in German literature. He is best known as a poet. He also wrote prose, much of it satiric criticism of German politics and society.

Many of Heine's poems were set to music by composers such as Felix Mendelssohn, Franz Schubert, and Robert Schumann. 'Die Lorelei' (The Lorelei) and 'Du bist wie eine Blume' (Thou art like a flower) are two of the best known.

Harry Heine was born in Düsseldorf, Germany, on Dec. 13, 1797. A wealthy uncle financed his education in law at the universities of Bonn and Göttingen. In 1825 he changed his name to Christian Johann Heinrich Heine. When his first two books were published, shortly after his graduation in 1826, he abandoned any idea of practicing law. For the next several years Heine traveled widely. In 1831 he settled in Paris, where he married a Frenchwoman, Eugénie Mirat.

Many of Heine's writings were banned in Germany because they were considered radical. In 1845 he contracted a spinal disease. From 1848 until he died on Feb. 17, 1856, in Paris, he was bedridden. During this period Heine wrote some of his most beautiful poetry. Among Heine's volumes of poetry are 'Buch der Lieder' (Book of Songs), published in 1827, and 'Gedichte' (Poems), published in 1853 and 1854.

**HEINLEIN, Robert A.** (1907–88). The American author Robert A. Heinlein helped raise the level of science fiction to a respected form of literary expression. His writing reflected his training in science and technology along with an interest in language, economics, history, and sociology. He won an unprecedented four Hugo science-fiction awards.

Robert Anson Heinlein was born on July 7, 1907, in Butler, Mo. After graduating from the United States Naval Academy in 1929, he served as an officer in the Navy for five years. He spent some time at the University of California at Los Angeles studying mathematics and physics. His first magazine story was published in 1939 and his first novel, 'Rocket Ship Galileo', in 1947. The novel was the basis for his screenplay for the motion picture 'Destination Moon' (1950). His fiction often anticipated scientific and technical advances, such as the atomic bomb and the waterbed. His most popular book was 'Stranger in a Strange Land' (1961), which became a hippie handbook and introduced the verb grok (to know intuitively, totally).

Heinlein's books include 'Beyond This Horizon' (1948), 'Red Planet' (1949), 'Sixth Column' (1949), 'The Puppet Masters' (1951), 'Revolt in 2100' (1953), 'Starman Jones' (1953), 'Tunnel in the Sky' (1955), 'The Menace from Earth' (1959), 'The Moon Is a Harsh Mistress' (1966), 'The Number of the Beast' (1980), 'Expanded Universe' (1980), and 'Friday' (1982). 'Green Hills of Earth' (1951) is a short-story collection. He died in Carmel, Calif., on May 8, 1988.

**HEISENBERG, Werner** (1901–76). For his work on quantum mechanics, the German physicist Werner Heisenberg received the Nobel prize for physics in 1932. He will probably be best remembered, however, for developing the uncertainty (or indeterminacy) principle, the concept that the behavior of subatomic particles can be predicted only on the basis of probability (*see* Uncertainty Principle). Isaac Newton's laws of motion, therefore, cannot be used to predict accurately the behavior of single subatomic particles.

Werner Karl Heisenberg was born on Dec. 5, 1901, in Würzburg. He studied theoretical physics at the University of Munich and received his doctorate in 1923. From there he went to Göttingen to study under Max Born in 1924 and to Copenhagen, Denmark, to work with Niels Bohr. His original quantum theory was published in 1925–26 and his uncertainty principle in 1927. With Bohr he developed the principle of complementarity, a concept of measurement in physics that many physicists, including Albert Einstein, refused to accept.

From 1927 until 1941 Heisenberg was professor of theoretical physics at the University of Leipzig. During World War II he worked with Otto Hahn at the Kaiser Wilhelm Institute for Physics in Berlin on developing a nuclear reactor (*see* Hahn, Otto). Secretly hostile to the Nazi regime, Heisenberg worked to keep Germany from developing effective nuclear weapons. After the war he became director of the Max Planck Institute for Physics. He died in Munich on Feb. 1, 1976.

**HELENA, Mont.** Montana's capital city, Helena, was settled in 1864 by prospectors who had almost given up before they struck gold. They called the gully in which they found the gold Last Chance Gulch.

Helena is in west-central Montana 65 miles (105 kilometers) northeast of Butte and about 12 miles (19 kilometers) west of the course of the Missouri River. To the west rise the Rocky Mountains.

The Capitol was built in 1899. Atop its copper dome stands a small reproduction of the Statue of Liberty. Carroll College, a Roman Catholic institution, is in the city. The museum and art gallery of the Montana Historical Society draw many visitors.

The city is a commercial center for surrounding ranches, farms, and mines. All types of livestock are raised. It also is a center of government activities and has light manufacturing. Tourism is an added source of income, and the Helena National Forest is headquartered here. Adjacent East Helena has smelting and refining works.

In 1875 Helena was made the capital of Montana Territory, and it remained the capital when Montana became a state in 1889. The first rail line reached the city in 1883. Helena has a commission form of government. Population (2000 census), 25,780.

**HELEN OF TROY.** According to Greek legend, Helen of Troy was the most beautiful woman in the world. She was the wife of Menelaus, king of Sparta. Aphrodite, the goddess of love, promised her to Paris, son of King Priam of Troy, to reward Paris for judging Aphrodite the fairest of the goddesses.

During Menelaus' absence, Paris persuaded Helen to flee with him to Troy. Agamemnon, the brother of Menelaus, led an expedition against Troy to recover Helen. This started the Trojan War, in which Paris was killed. When the Greeks finally captured Troy, Menelaus took Helen back to Sparta. The Greek poet Homer told the story of Helen and the Trojan War in his 'Iliad'. (*See also* Homeric Legend; Paris.)

*Helen of Troy is depicted in this detail from 'Paris and Helen', a 1788 oil painting on canvas by Jacques-Louis David. The painting measures 147 cm x 180 cm and is in the Louvre, Paris.*

Giraudon/Art Resource

*Parts of a Helicopter*

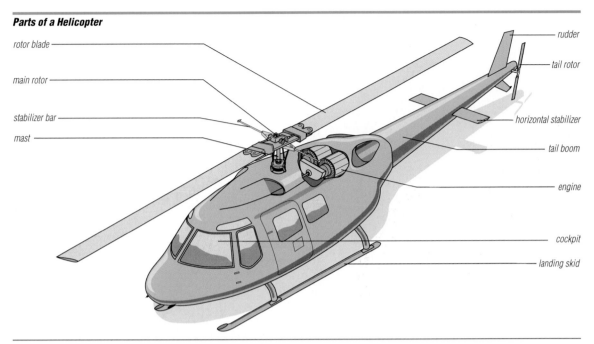

rotor blade

main rotor

stabilizer bar

mast

rudder

tail rotor

horizontal stabilizer

tail boom

engine

cockpit

landing skid

*The helicopter has a rotating wing instead of the fixed wing of the conventional airplane. The pilot makes this versatile flying machine go up, down, forward, backward, and sideways by changing the pitch of the whirling rotor blades.*

# HELICOPTER

The helicopter is one member of the versatile family of airplanes known as vertical takeoff and landing craft (VTOL). In addition to being able to take off and land in a small area without having to use a runway, it can hover in midair and fly forward, backward, or sideways.

Unlike conventional aircraft, the helicopter has a collective pitch stick, which controls upward and downward motion; the cyclic pitch stick, which regulates direction; and a foot pedal, which controls the tail rotor for turning. The parts of the main rotor are shown at the right. It has no fixed wing to sustain it in flight. Instead it depends solely upon rotating blades to provide lift and movement through the air. These blades are called a rotary wing or simply rotor. The blades are hinged to a shaft connected with the plane's engine.

The helicopter rotor is powered by this engine. The rotor of an Autogiro, a craft similar to the helicopter, revolves freely without power. This is called autorotation. In case of engine failure, autorotation is also possible with a helicopter rotor; thus, emergency landings can be made.

The helicopter has several colorful nicknames. Among them are copter, chopper, whirlybird, eggbeater, and flying windmill. Its true name comes from two Greek terms, *helix,* meaning "spiral," and *pteron,* meaning "wing."

### The Helicopter in Flight

The blades of the helicopter rotor are made so that their angle, or pitch, can be changed. An increase in the degree of pitch plus an increase in power from the engine enables the rotor blades to "bite" into the air and lift the helicopter off the ground.

The correct combination of power and pitch is supplied by the collective pitch stick. When the pilot wants to take off, he pulls up on this stick with his left hand. This advances the throttle and sets the rotor blades at the proper angle for the helicopter to rise in the air. To land, the pilot pushes down on the collective pitch stick, and the throttle is retarded and the blades are correctly reset automatically. The correct combination of power and pitch will also enable the craft to hover in the air.

To make the plane go forward, backward, or to the left or right, the main rotor is simply tilted on its shaft (the shaft itself does not tilt) in the direction the pilot wants the craft to go. In addition, each blade of the rotor must change its pitch as it whirls. To accomplish this, the pilot uses an automatic device called the cyclic pitch stick, operated with the pilot's right hand.

### The Importance of the Tail Rotor

A further control of the helicopter in flight is provided by a small propeller at the tail of the fuselage. It is

## Helicopter Controls

instrument panel

throttle

cyclic pitch stick

tail rotor pedals

collective pitch stick

## Parts of the Main Rotor

rotor blade

blade grip

rotor hub

yoke

push-pull tube

mast

stabilizer bar

weight

*The pilot's controls (top) include the instrument panel, the collective pitch stick, which controls upward and downward motion; the cyclic pitch stick, which regulates direction; and a foot pedal, which controls the tail rotor for turning. The parts of the main rotor (bottom) are mounted on top of the helicopter. The rotor is hinged to a shaft connected with the plane's engine.*

powered by the engine which also turns the main rotor. The tail rotor performs an important antitorque function. Torque is the tendency of the fuselage to twist in the opposite direction from that in which the shaft of the main engine is turning, creating a potential loss of control in flight. The tail rotor prevents this tendency. If the torque reaction is to push the fuselage to the right, the tail rotor thrusts to the left and maintains the helicopter on an even course.

The tail rotor also acts as a rudder. The pilot controls it with foot pedals to keep the craft on course.

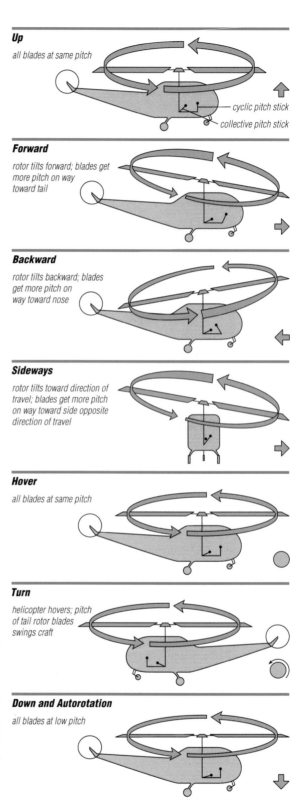

## Up

all blades at same pitch

cyclic pitch stick

collective pitch stick

## Forward

rotor tilts forward; blades get more pitch on way toward tail

## Backward

rotor tilts backward; blades get more pitch on way toward nose

## Sideways

rotor tilts toward direction of travel; blades get more pitch on way toward side opposite direction of travel

## Hover

all blades at same pitch

## Turn

helicopter hovers; pitch of tail rotor blades swings craft

## Down and Autorotation

all blades at low pitch

*Helicopters are maneuvered by changing the pitch, or angle, of the main rotor blades.*

*Some Single Rotor Helicopters*

*Some Multiple Rotor Helicopters*

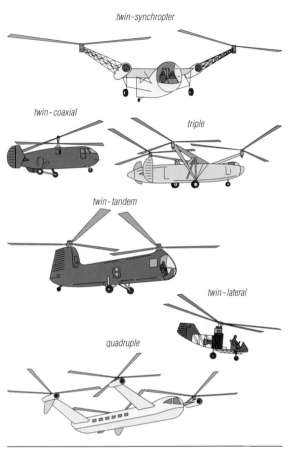

Photos, courtesy of Bell Helicopter Textron, Inc.

*A police helicopter (top), model 206L Long Ranger III, flies over a metropolitan area. Police departments use them for spotting traffic jams and for patrol duty. The V-22 Bell-Boeing (bottom) is a tilt-rotor military craft. Some military helicopters and tilt-rotors are used for rescue and ambulance service, or to carry weapons.*

## Uses of Helicopters

The United States has used helicopters in military operations in both Korea and Vietnam. They perform important tasks in air-sea rescues, patrolling, reconnaissance, the evacuation of the wounded, and the transportation of personnel and equipment into battle. Many new nonmilitary uses for helicopters have been developed from battle-tested ideas.

In several areas, for example, hospitals have built landing pads for helicopter ambulances. Refugees from disasters such as floods, earthquakes, and blizzards are often evacuated by the craft. The Coast Guard uses boat-hulled helicopters for rescues at sea.

The construction industry uses whirlybirds to lift equipment to upper stories of buildings being erected. Heavy construction materials such as steel beams are also raised in this fashion. To install a high television tower a helicopter is often used.

Transportation by helicopter is becoming increasingly popular. Helibuses serve as taxis and as sight-seeing vehicles. Many industrial corporations employ them to fly their personnel and customers from place to place. Petroleum companies use egg beaters as commuter vehicles. One such company transports workers to and from off shore oil-drilling rigs situated 50 miles out in the Gulf of Mexico.

Several police departments have found helicopters particularly effective in spotting and helping to eliminate traffic jams. Police also use them for patrol duty and to track down criminals.

Helicopters are important to the United States Forest Service in combating forest fires. The choppers, however, do not serve merely as vehicles to bring fire fighters to the scene. Downwash produced by the rotors may be directed at the fire. The air stream thus

*A CH-64 Skycrane helicopter (top left) is used to move a house. Such a task is thus performed faster than by truck and does not tie up highway space or clog traffic. The newest helicopter in use by the president of the United States for trips to Camp David and other nearby locations is the Sikorsky VH-60 (bottom left). An S-61 helicopter (top right) is used to ferry passengers between airports and central business districts of cities. The Blackhawk helicopter (bottom right) is used to fight forest fires by spraying flame retardant. The vehicle's maneuverability is well adapted to this dangerous task.*

created blows down on the flames. This confines the blaze temporarily to one place, allowing time for water to be played on the fire. The water is poured from hoses carried in the craft.

Farm work, such as crop seeding, fertilization, dusting, and spraying, is carried out from helicopters. Rotor downwash is also used by fruitgrowers to dry the frost forming on crops.

Ranch owners find that one person in a copter can do the work of from 15 to 18 cowhands in chores that include riding the range, herding cattle, and patroling fences. Pipelines and power lines are checked by inspectors flying in helicopters.

All types of photographs are taken from choppers. Motion-picture producers and newspaper photographers find the helicopter an ideal platform from which to take aerial action shots. Geologists photograph the interiors of volcanoes from the craft. Mapmakers also use aerial photographs in cartography. Helicopters are used to haul many types of cargo. They also serve as towing vehicles. One helicopter towing job, for

example, involved moving a 386-foot-long ship. Air streams from rotors have been used to blow stranded boats from sandbars.

Airline-type helicopter operations have been in service since 1947, when Los Angeles Airways carried the first load of mail. Passenger services linking various areas of the Los Angeles region began in 1954. Later, similar helicopter operations were set up in New York, Chicago, and San Francisco. For many years the demand for helicopter service was not sufficient to make a commercial operation profitable. From 1954 to 1965 the Civil Aeronautics Board subsidized the helicopter lines in the United States. Today helicopter operations exist in most major cities. Helicopter platforms have been installed on or adjacent to municipal buildings, hospitals, and business centers.

### History of the Helicopter

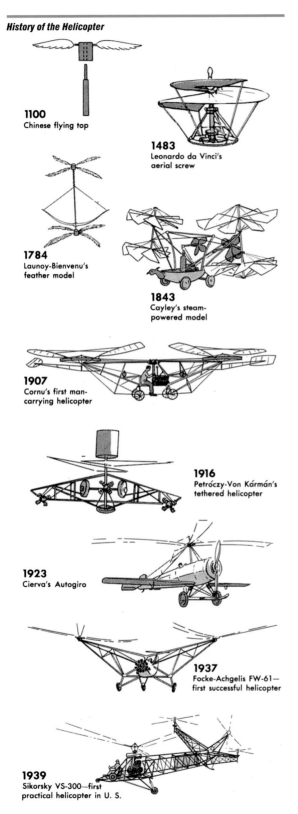

**1100**
Chinese flying top

**1483**
Leonardo da Vinci's
aerial screw

**1784**
Launoy-Bienvenu's
feather model

**1843**
Cayley's steam-
powered model

**1907**
Cornu's first man-
carrying helicopter

**1916**
Petróczy-Von Kármán's
tethered helicopter

**1923**
Cierva's Autogiro

**1937**
Focke-Achgelis FW-61—
first successful helicopter

**1939**
Sikorsky VS-300—first
practical helicopter in U. S.

| **World Helicopter Records** | | | |
|---|---|---|---|
| | Record | Date | Pilot |
| Distance | Around the world First solo flight | 1983 | Dick Smith (Australia) |
| Altitude | 40,820 ft | 1972 | Jean Boulet (France) |
| Speed | 249.08 mph | 1986 | John Egginton (United Kingdom) |

American passenger helicopters fall into three classes. The first carries from 2 to 5 passengers; the second, from 5 to 12 passengers. Both classes are powered by a single engine. The third class can accommodate from 12 to 40 passengers and is designed primarily for use by commercial airlines. It may have more than one engine. The engines on all three classes may be either conventional pistons or gas turbines.

Helicopters were used by the United States in a mine-clearing operation in North Vietnamese harbors after the Vietnam cease-fire of 1973. After the Egyptian-Israeli accord in the Middle East in 1974, American helicopters swept the Suez Canal for mines to help reopen it for traffic.

Soviet helicopters were used in military action in Afghanistan and Ethiopia. The Mi-24 assault helicopter set a speed record of about 230 mph.

**History of Helicopters**

In 1100 the Chinese invented a helicopterlike flying top. Leonardo da Vinci in 1483 designed an aerial screw that was to take off and land vertically. It was never built. A feather model helicopter was constructed by the Frenchmen Launoy and Bienvenu in 1784.

In 1843 Sir George Cayley built a steam-driven helicopter. It rose a few feet but was too heavy to be practical. In 1907 a Frenchman named Paul Cornu built a full-sized helicopter. This device lifted Cornu clear of the ground for several minutes. The machine, however, had not achieved free flight because it was tethered to the ground by cords.

In 1916 two Austrians, Lieut. Stefan Petróczy and Prof. Theodore von Kármán, developed a captive helicopter. It was held aloft by cables anchored to the ground. It remained in the air for about one hour at a 600-foot altitude. Its flight was not officially recognized because it did not carry passengers. In Spain Juan de la Cierva built the first Autogiro in 1923 (*see* Autogiro).

Gerald P. Herrick, a Philadelphian, constructed a "convertaplane" in 1931. This was an airplane equipped with rotors. In flight, the rotors were started up and the airplane was able to land at a steep angle. The German Focke-Achgelis FW-61 was the first successful helicopter. It was built in 1937. In 1938 it remained at an 11,000-foot altitude for about 80 minutes. The first practical flight of a helicopter in the United States took place in 1939, when Igor Sikorsky flew his VS-300.

The world's largest aerial load carrier is the so-called Mil Mi-26. This helicopter is capable of lifting more than 125,000 pounds to 6,560 feet.

In 1982 the record speed for an around-the-world helicopter flight was made by H. Ross Perot, Jr., and J.W. Coburn. They flew the Bell 206L LongRanger II the circumference of the Earth at an average of 34.4 miles per hour. The flight took 29 days, 3 hours, 8 minutes, and 13 seconds to complete.

Robert M. Loebelson

Walter Dawn

*Garden heliotrope* (Heliotropium arborescens)

**HELIOTROPE.** Because the one-sided spikes of its fragrant flowers always seemed to turn toward the sun, the heliotrope got its name from the Greek words *helios,* meaning "sun," and *tropos,* meaning "turn." Wild species of these hairy, many-branched herbs and shrubs are found in many parts of the world. Some species are cultivated in greenhouses and gardens, others are weedy plants. They grow from 1 to 4 feet (0.3 to 1.2 meters) high, with flowers varying in color from blue and purple to pink and even white.

The heliotrope is a genus (*Heliotropium*) of the borage family, Boraginaceae. There are about 250 species. The garden, or cherry-pie, heliotrope (*H. arborescens*) is the most common. The alternate leaves are lance-shaped, and the tiny flowers grow in clustered, five-lobed sprays. A species common in the alkaline and saline areas of the United States is the seaside heliotrope (*H. curassavicum*).

**HELIUM.** Before its presence was known on Earth, helium was identified in the sun. In 1868 a British astronomer, Joseph Norman Lockyer, used spectral analysis to isolate helium in the sun's spectrum. Thus helium got its name from the Greek word *helios,* meaning "sun."

Helium is a colorless, odorless, gaseous element. It is chemically inert; hence it will not burn or react with other materials. Helium has the lowest boiling point of any element. Next to hydrogen, it is the lightest known gas and the second most abundant element in the universe. It is found in great abundance in the stars, where it is synthesized by nuclear fusion of hydrogen. In the Earth's atmosphere, helium is present only in about 1 part per 186,000 because the Earth's gravity is not strong enough to prevent its gradual escape into space. The helium present in the Earth's atmosphere has been generated by the radioactive decay of heavy substances.

Most of the world's helium occurs in natural-gas deposits in the United States. Smaller supplies have been discovered in Canada, South Africa, the Sahara Desert, and elsewhere. Its lightness and nonflammability make helium ideal for use in the inflation of lighter-than-air craft. Because helium's boiling point is close to absolute zero, it is widely used in low-temperature research. It is also vital to the study of superconductivity. Helium is used in arc welding. Deep-sea divers breathe a helium-oxygen mixture to prevent decompression sickness, also called the bends.

**HELL AND HADES.** "Hope not ever to see heaven: I come to lead you to the other shore; into the eternal darkness; into fire and into ice." Dante's 'Inferno', from which the quotation comes, is perhaps the most vivid depiction in literature of the place of eternal punishment for evildoers. Abodes for the dead have formed a part of the religious belief of most peoples. One reason for such belief has been the reluctance to accept the end of human life on Earth as permanent, as the extinction of individual existence.

The names hell and Hades have generally been understood as places of punishment, either eternal or temporary. Ancient cultures often envisioned an abode for the dead as a reward, or as neutral, rather than always as a punishment. In very ancient primitive religions, as well as among American Indians, the dead went to dwell with their ancestors or to a heavenly location with other souls. Ancient Israel conceived of a place called Sheol, a dark and gloomy place, to be sure, but no elements of punishment were attached to it.

The Greek Hades (originally the name of the god who presided over it) did not suggest punishment either. It was a dark subterranean realm or a distant island. The dead were conducted to Hades by the god Hermes. The way was barred, however, by the River Styx. The dead were ferried across the river by the boatman Charon. Eventually, the Greeks added a place called Tartarus, far below Hades, as a place of torment for the wicked. In time Tartarus lost its distinctness and became another name for Hades.

The word hell comes from an Anglo-Saxon root meaning "concealed," and it suggests a place hidden in the hot regions at the Earth's center. In Norse

| Properties of Helium | | |
|---|---|---|
| Symbol . . . . . . . . . . . . . . He | Density in grams per liter | |
| Atomic Number . . . . . . . . . 2 | at 32° F (0° C). . . . . . 0.1785 | |
| Atomic Weight | Boiling Point | |
| . . . . . . . . . . . . . . . . 4.0026 | . . . . . −452.02° F (−268.9° C) | |
| Group in Periodic Table | Melting Point | |
| . . . . . . . . . . . . . . . . . . . . 0 | . . . . . −457.96° F (−272.2° C) | |

mythology Hel was the name of the world of the dead as well as of its goddess. It was especially for evildoers and was distinguished from Valhalla, the place to which those who had fallen in battle went. The ancient Greek myth of Elysium, or the Elysian fields, was similar to Valhalla. It was a dwelling place for heroes on whom the gods had conferred immortality. Eventually it came to mean the abode for all the blessed dead, as opposed to Hades.

The concept of hell as a place of punishment is rooted in the idea of justice. Hell was offered as an answer to the question: If evildoers prosper throughout their lives and are never punished, when will they get what is coming to them? The answer must be: after they die.

The modern Western understanding of hell derives from the latest period in ancient Israel's history, and it was more fully developed by early Christianity. The chief suggestion of such a place in the Hebrew Bible (or Old Testament) is a brief reference in Daniel. The place reserved for the wicked dead was called Gehenna by Jews. Early references depict it as a place of temporary punishment, similar to the Roman Catholic purgatory. By the time Christianity was established, it had become a permanent abode. The torments inflicted there were largely imaginative projections of the worst tortures devised in this world. Eternal fire is the most common punishment, though perpetual cold also has been accepted.

There is no fully developed teaching about hell in the New Testament, though there are frequent mentions of it. Only in the course of later church history was it elaborated into official church doctrine. Today the New Testament statements and their later explanations are taken literally by some Christians, regarded as allegory or myth by some, and denied altogether by others.

Islam has no consistent teaching on hell. It is regarded as permanent in some passages of the Koran and temporary in others. In Hinduism, hell is accepted, but it has no permanent significance. It is but a stage in the long career of the soul. For most Buddhist schools, as well, hell is a transitory phase where sins are purged.

**HELLMAN, Lillian** (1905–84). An American playwright, Lillian Hellman won her first success on Broadway in 1934 with 'The Children's Hour'. Like many of her later plays, it deals with the far-reaching implications of malice and evil. She also wrote scenarios, motion-picture scripts and adaptations, and the book for the 1957 musical 'Candide', for which Leonard Bernstein composed the music.

Lillian Hellman was born in New Orleans, La., on June 20, 1905, but attended school mostly in New York City. There she also went to New York and Columbia universities. In 1925 she married Arthur Kober. They were divorced in 1932. From 1930 to 1932 she read scenarios in Hollywood and then returned to New York City, where she read plays for a theatrical producer. In 1934 she submitted to him 'The Children's Hour', a drama about a child who starts a scandalous

rumor in a girls' school. Her next successful play was 'The Little Foxes' (1939), which tells of life in the South. Both plays are bitter, with cruel characters.

Hellman's wartime plays 'Watch on the Rhine' (1941), which won the New York Drama Critics' Circle Award, and 'The Searching Wind' (1944) are attacks on fascism. Her 'Toys in the Attic', a psychological drama set in New Orleans, was produced in 1960.

Although she was never a Communist, Hellman was blacklisted after refusing to testify against radical friends at House Un-American Activities Committee hearings in 1952. She declared at that time, "I cannot and will not cut my conscience to fit this year's fashions." She later wrote about that experience in 'Scoundrel Time', a work that was published in 1976. She gave up writing for the theater and began her memoirs, 'An Unfinished Woman' (1969) and 'Pentimento' (1973). Hellman died on June 30, 1984, in Martha's Vineyard, Mass.

In her will Hellman established two literary funds. The Lillian Hellman Fund was to be used to advance the arts and sciences. The other, intended to further radical causes, was named for the mystery writer Dashiell Hammett, her companion and critic for 30 years.

**HELMHOLTZ, Hermann von** (1821–94). The law of the conservation of energy was developed by the 19th-century German, Hermann von Helmholtz. This creative and versatile scientist made fundamental contributions to physiology, optics, electrodynamics, mathematics, and meteorology. He believed that all science could be reduced to the laws of classical mechanics, which encompassed matter, force, and energy as the whole of reality.

Hermann Ludwig Ferdinand Helmholtz was born in Prussia (now part of Germany) in Potsdam, on Aug. 31, 1821. His first schooling was at home, where his parents taught him Latin, Greek, French, and other languages as well as the philosophy of Immanuel Kant (see Kant). After graduating from the local gymnasium, or secondary school, he entered the Friedrich Wilhelm Medical Institute in Berlin in 1838. After graduation in 1843 he served as an army doctor for five years.

In 1848 he was appointed assistant at the Anatomical Museum and professor at the Academy of Fine Arts in Berlin. For the rest of his career he did research and taught successively at the Physiological Institute in Königsberg, the University of Bonn, Heidelberg University, and the University of Berlin. He was elevated to the German nobility in 1882. In 1888 he became the first director of the Physico-Technical Institute in Berlin and remained in that post the rest of his life. He died in Berlin on Sept. 8, 1894.

Helmholtz's two most significant publications were 'On the Sensation of Tone as a Physiological Basis for the Theory of Music' (1863) and 'Handbook of Physiological Optics' (1867). His paper "On the Conservation of Force" was issued in 1847. In all his work, ranging from physiology to electrodynamics, he relied on classical mechanics for his reasoning. A decade after his death Albert Einstein would begin publishing the papers that permanently undermined the theories held by Helmholtz.

**HELSINKI, Finland.** Located at the southern tip of the Finnish peninsula, Helsinki is the capital of Finland and the administrative center of Uusimaa province. It is also the leading seaport and industrial city of Finland.

The old center of the city is made up of government buildings, the main building of Helsinki University, and the Great Church, all of which surround Senate Square. The buildings were all designed by architect C.L. Engel and date back to the first half of the 19th century. Examples of modern Finnish architecture are Taivallahti Church, the City Theater, and Finlandia concert hall—the last designed by the noted architect Alvar Aalto. Helsinki is also home to an opera and ballet company, symphony orchestras, and Helsinki University, the largest university in Scandinavia. Helsinki Stadium was built for the 1952 Olympic Games.

Helsinki is surrounded by the natural harbors of the Gulf of Finland. The harbors and excellent railway and road connections to the nation's interior enable Helsinki to handle more than half of Finland's imports. Helsinki's main industries include food and metal processing, printing, textiles, and clothing.

Helsinki was founded in 1550 by King Gustav Vasa of Sweden to compete with Tallinn, a port on the other side of the gulf used to trade with Russian merchants. The city's growth was hindered by a plague in 1710 and devastating fires in 1713 and 1808. In 1809 Finland was ceded to Russia, and in 1812 the capital was moved from Turku to Helsinki. The city was completely reconstructed at this time. Finland gained independence from Russia in 1917 after a brief but violent civil war in Helsinki. Population (2000 estimate), 551,123.

*The Great Church (Helsinki's Lutheran cathedral), completed in 1852, combines Classical and Renaissance styles.*
Sven Samelius

**Ernest Hemingway**
Y. Karsh—Woodfin Camp & Associates

**HEMINGWAY, Ernest** (1899–1961). A writer famous for his terse, direct style, Ernest Hemingway was also known for the way in which his own life mirrored the activities and interests of his characters. Many of his works show man pitted against nature, as in his favorite sports—hunting, fishing, and bullfighting. In others he tells of the experiences of wartime—man against man. The immediate appeal of his best writing probably stems from the fact that he wrote of things he knew intimately and that were important to him.

Ernest Hemingway was born on July 21, 1899, in Oak Park, Ill., a Chicago suburb. His father was a doctor. After high school Hemingway got a job as a reporter on the Kansas City *Star.* During World War I he tried to enlist in the armed forces but was rejected because of an old eye injury. He volunteered as an ambulance driver on the Italian front, and in 1918 he was badly wounded.

After the war he settled in Paris, France, where he began to write fiction. He submitted his work for criticism to the poet Ezra Pound and to Gertrude Stein, a writer who served as friend and adviser to many writers of the time.

The first of many collections of stories, 'In Our Time', published in 1925, did not sell well. His novel 'The Sun Also Rises', which came out a year later, made his name known. It tells of young people in postwar Paris and their search for values in a world that in many ways has lost its meaning.

In 'A Farewell to Arms' (1929), about war on the Italian front, Hemingway tells a love story that is interspersed with scenes of magnificent battle reporting. 'To Have and Have Not' (1937) shows Hemingway's interest in social problems, an interest more fully realized in 'For Whom the Bell Tolls' (1940), set in the Spanish Civil War. In 'Across the River and into the Trees' (1950) an army officer dies while on leave. This novel is generally considered inferior to 'The Old Man and the Sea' (1952), which won a Pulitzer prize in 1953. Hemingway received the Nobel prize for literature in 1954.

Hemingway was a war correspondent in Spain, China, and Europe during World War II. He was married four times and had three sons. Toward the end of his life he suffered from anxiety and depression. He died on July 2, 1961, in his home in Ketchum, Idaho, of a self-inflicted shotgun wound.

**HEMISPHERE.** The Earth resembles a sphere. ("Sphere" comes from the ancient Greek word *sphaira,* meaning "ball.") A sphere can be imagined to be cut in half either horizontally or vertically. Half-spheres, or hemispheres, are the result. This imaginary division into hemispheres is useful in identifying large parts of the globe and in studying aspects of the Earth's motions. (Although it does not affect the use of the word hemisphere, it should be noted that the Earth is not a perfect sphere. It is actually oblate in shape, which means that the polar regions are slightly flattened and the equatorial region bulges slightly.)

Because the Earth is spherical, its cross sections, like any circle, can be divided into 360 degrees. These degrees can be used to measure distance. In order to do this, imaginary lines are drawn around the globe, and degrees are marked on them. Some lines, called parallels, are perpendicular to the Earth's axis (that is, parallel to the equator) and measure latitude, or distances north and south. Other lines, called meridians, can be drawn that connect the north and south poles and measure longitude, or distances east and west.

The parallel that is exactly halfway between the North and South poles is the equator, and it has a value of 0° latitude. The equator divides the Earth into Northern and Southern hemispheres. The Earth's orbit around the sun and the tilt of the Earth's axis affect the seasonal changes in these two hemispheres. Because the Earth's axis is tilted, it is angled with respect to the sun. Thus, during the Earth's orbit around the sun, there are two times of the year when a hemisphere receives the rays of the sun at the highest possible angle or the lowest possible angle. These periods are called solstices. During the solstice that occurs around June 21, the Northern Hemisphere is tilted toward the sun—this corresponds to summer in the Northern Hemisphere. At the same time the Southern Hemisphere is tilted away from the sun and undergoes its winter. During the solstice that occurs around December 21, the Northern Hemisphere tilts away from the sun and undergoes its winter while the Southern Hemisphere tilts toward the sun and undergoes its summer. During the equinoxes, in March and September, neither hemisphere is tilted toward the sun, and both have equal periods of day and night. However, the seasons are still reversed: the Northern Hemisphere's spring occurs during the Southern Hemisphere's autumn.

The equator establishes a Northern and a Southern Hemisphere, but popular misunderstandings still occur. To some Northern Hemisphere residents, many southern localities are thought to be in the Southern Hemisphere when they are actually located north of the equator. Part of South America and more than half of Africa, for example, are north of the equator, even though these continents are frequently thought of as being in the Southern Hemisphere.

The meridians used to measure degrees east and west are all of equal length and all pass through the poles. Every meridian divides the Earth in two. Thus there is no clear natural marker to establish the Eastern

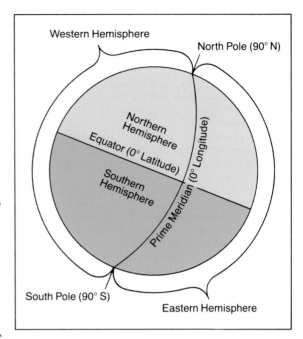

and Western hemispheres. By Eastern or Western Hemisphere is meant a hemisphere on one side of an arbitrarily selected meridian that serves as a baseline. That meridian could pass through any number of cities. An 1884 international agreement, however, established the base, or prime, meridian to be the meridian that passes through Greenwich, England. Since then, by convention, this has been the prime meridian. It is 0° longitude, and all distances east and west are measured from it.

The standard time zones of the Earth are also measured from the Greenwich meridian. Since the Earth rotates approximately 15° of longitude each hour, time zones of 15° intervals were established on either side of the prime meridian. Traveling east of the prime meridian, each time zone is one hour ahead of the zone immediately preceding it. West of the prime meridian each zone is one hour behind the one immediately preceding it. On the opposite side of the globe, at 180°, is the international date line. (In reality time zones are not always uniformly 15° apart because many countries have altered the time zone boundaries within their borders.)

Although the prime meridian is the baseline for all east and west measurements, it is not always considered the boundary line between the Eastern and Western hemispheres. The Western Hemisphere in popular usage includes North and South America—a reflection of the fact that these continents were part of the New World discovered by European explorers beginning in the 15th century. Since these continents are west of Europe, they became known as part of the Western Hemisphere. If the prime meridian is taken as the boundary, parts of Europe and Africa become part of the Western Hemisphere.

**HEMLOCK.** A member of the pine family of trees, the hemlock can be distinguished from other pines by the structure of its branches and needles. Its slender, horizontal branches tend to droop. The needles are short, flat, and blunt-tipped.

There are about ten species of hemlocks native to North America and eastern Asia. They grow to an average height of from 60 to 70 feet (18 to 21 meters). North American hemlocks include the Canadian, found throughout the eastern United States and Canada; the Carolina, common to the southern Alleghenies; the mountain, which grows from Alaska to Montana; and the western, which grows chiefly in Oregon.

Many hemlocks are popular as ornamental evergreens. Others, such as the western hemlock, are timber trees. The bark of the Canadian hemlock contains tannin, used in the tanning industry, and the soft, coarse-grained wood is used in construction.

The name hemlock is also applied to certain poisonous plants of the parsley or carrot family. These include the poison hemlock and the water hemlock.

The scientific name for the Canadian hemlock is *Tsuga canadensis.* The Carolina hemlock is named *T. caroliniana;* the mountain hemlock, *T. Mertensiana;* and the western hemlock, *T. heterophylla.* The scientific name of the poison hemlock is *Conium maculatum.* The water hemlocks compose the genus *Cicuta. (See also* Pine; Tree.)

**HEMP.** For millennia the hemp plant has been cultivated for its strong, durable fiber. It is used for twine, yarn, rope, cable, and string, for artificial sponges, and for coarse fabrics such as sacking and canvas. In Italy it is used to make a fabric similar to linen. The plant is also grown for its seed—used in hempseed oil, paints, soaps, varnishes, and bird feed—and for its leaves and blossoms, which yield the drugs marijuana and hashish.

*Hemp* (Cannabis sativa)

Hemp originated in Central Asia and was cultivated in China as early as 2800 BC. Early in the Christian Era it was grown in the Mediterranean countries of Europe, and its cultivation spread throughout the rest of Europe during the Middle Ages. Today the production of hemp for its fiber is a leading industry in India, Romania, China, Hungary, Poland, and Turkey. It is also grown in North and South America.

The plant is an annual herb with angular, rough stems and alternate deeply lobed leaves. It may grow to 16 feet (5 meters) tall, though plants cultivated for fiber are densely sowed and generally reach heights of only 7 to 10 feet (2 to 3 meters). The flowers are small and greenish yellow; male and female flowers grow on separate plants. The plant's slender woody stalks are hollow except at the tip and base. Hemp fibers come from the inner bark of the stalks. After the stalks are cut, they must ret, or rot, so that the outer bark can be more easily removed. They are either soaked in pools in a process called water retting or left on the ground to absorb rain and dew, which is called dew retting. The stalks are then dried and crushed. A shaking process completes the separation of the fiber from the woody portion. The fiber strands are long—usually more than 6 feet (1.8 meters)—fairly straight, and yellowish, greenish, dark brown, or gray in color.

In warmer regions, the plant may be grown for the production of marijuana or hashish (*see* Drugs). The active ingredient in these drugs is present in all parts of both the male and female plants but is most concentrated in the resin in the flowering tops of the female. In the United States, the hemp plant may be grown only under a government permit.

The scientific name of the hemp plant is *Cannabis sativa.* Although other plant fibers used for cordage have incorrectly been called hemp, only the hemp plant yields true hemp. (*See also* Rope and Twine.)

*These women are cutting hemp stalks and soaking them in a process called water retting. The bark can then be easily removed.*

**HENAN,** or **HONAN.** A province in the north-central part of China, Henan covers an area of 64,500 square miles (167,000 square kilometers). It is bounded by the provinces of Shanxi and Hebei on the north, Shandong and Anhui on the east, Hubei on the south, and Shaanxi on the west. Zhengzhou, its capital since 1954, is located in the north.

Highlands are the principal geographic feature in the west, and the North China Plain forms much of the eastern part. Its principal river, the Huang He, or Yellow River, is subject to occasional disastrous floods. The monsoonal climate has long, hot, humid summers, very cold winters, and uncertain rainfall, causing drought conditions. Wheat is the major crop, and Henan leads all of China in its area of cultivation and production. Millet, sorghum, soybeans, corn, rice, cotton, tobacco, and oilseeds also are grown. Yellow oxen, pigs, sheep, and goats are raised. Henan is one of China's oldest centers of silkworm raising and silk export. Mineral deposits include coal, iron, and lead. Chief industries are tractor assembly, textiles, cigarettes, and food processing. The population is largely rural and is concentrated in the eastern plain with densities as high as 800 to 1,000 persons per square mile (300 to 400 per square kilometer).

Archaeological findings of Neolithic and Shang Bronze Age cultures indicate that Henan was an early center of Chinese civilization. Anyang, Kaifeng, and Luoyang have been national capitals of several Chinese dynasties. Population (2000 estimate), 92,560,000.

**HENNEPIN, Louis** (1626–1701?). A Franciscan missionary, Louis Hennepin was the first explorer to see the upper reaches of the Mississippi River. He also wrote the first published descriptions of the area.

Born on May 12, 1626, in Ath, Belgium, Louis Hennepin joined the Franciscan order in his youth. He preached for a time in the Low Countries. Then in 1675 he went to Canada, traveling on the same ship that carried the sieur de La Salle (*see* La Salle). Hennepin became a missionary to the Indians.

In 1679 Father Hennepin went with La Salle to explore the area around the Great Lakes and the Mississippi River. In 1680, at the site of what is now Peoria, Ill., La Salle turned back to go for fresh supplies. Hennepin and his party, who were to explore the upper Mississippi River, were captured by Sioux Indians. While traveling with the Indians, Hennepin discovered the falls where Minneapolis now stands. He named them St. Anthony Falls, in honor of his patron saint. Rescued in 1681 by the sieur du Lhut (Duluth), Hennepin returned to France. His account of his journeys, 'Description of Louisiana', published in 1683, made him famous. Unfortunately, after the death of La Salle, Hennepin published a book in which he claimed also to have traveled down the Mississippi before La Salle made his memorable journey. This falsehood made people doubt Hennepin's earlier reports. He died in obscurity in Rome, probably in 1701.

**HENRY, Kings of England.** Eight of the kings of England have been named Henry. The first of these, Henry I, was the youngest son of the Norman conqueror, William I. The most recent one was the notorious Henry VIII, who ruled in the 1500s.

**Henry I** (born 1068, ruled 1100–35). The youngest son of William the Conqueror was born in England. His nickname, Beauclerc, which means "good scholar," was given him because of his fine education. He seized the crown in the year 1100, when his brother King William II was killed in a hunting accident and his brother Robert, duke of Normandy, who was next in the line of succession, was absent on a crusade (*see* William, Kings of England).

At his accession Henry I issued the famous Charter of Liberties, which, over a hundred years later, was used as the basis of Magna Carta, the foundation of the liberties of the Anglo-Saxon world. He also favored the church in order to gain its backing against the claims of his brother Robert to the English throne.

The Charter of Liberties helped gain Henry the support of the nobles. He conciliated the English, conquered by his father, by marrying Matilda, who was the daughter of King Malcolm III of Scotland and who was descended from the Anglo-Saxon kings. The support of the common people was assured by the justice he administered through the King's Court.

Henry's only son, William Aetheling, was drowned in 1120 when the *White Ship* sank in the English Channel. According to legend, the king never smiled again. The accident left his daughter Matilda, widow of the Holy Roman emperor Henry V, and his nephew Stephen contestants for the throne at his death.

**Henry II** (born 1133, ruled 1154–89). The grandson of Henry I was the first Plantagenet king of England. His mother was Matilda, daughter of Henry I. His father was Geoffrey of Anjou, whom Matilda married after the death of her first husband, Emperor Henry V. Geoffrey was called Plantagenet for his habit of wearing in his cap a sprig of the broom plant, which in Latin is called *planta genista*.

Henry II was born in Le Mans, France, in March 1133. During his mother's conflict with Stephen for the English throne he was brought to England. Stephen eventually recognized his claim, and Henry became king of England in 1154 after Stephen's death.

Henry II held England and Normandy by his mother's right. From his father he inherited, as French fiefs, the important counties of Anjou, Maine, and Touraine. By his marriage with Eleanor of Aquitaine, whose marriage with the French king Louis VII had been annulled, he acquired Poitou, Guyenne, and Gascony, so that he held most of the British Isles and about half of France.

*Henry I in a miniature from a 14th-century manuscript (Cottonian Claud D11 45 B)*

Henry II reestablished law and order after the anarchy of Stephen's reign. He improved the military service by permitting the barons to pay "shield money," or scutage, in place of serving in the army. With this he hired soldiers who would fight whenever and wherever he wished—an important means of maintaining control over the powerful nobles of the land.

His greatest work was the reform of the law courts. He brought the Curia Regis (King's Court) into every part of England by sending learned judges on circuit through the land to administer the "king's justice." Thus gradually one system of law took the place of the many local customs that had been in use. He also established the grand jury. Now accusations could be brought by a body of representatives of the community against evildoers who were so powerful that no single individual dared accuse them.

The petit jury, also called petty or trial jury, substituted the weighing of evidence and testimony by sworn men for the old superstitious trial by combat or by ordeal. (*See also* Jury System.) Henry even attempted to bring churchmen who committed crimes under the jurisdiction of the king's courts, but the scandal caused by the murder of Archbishop Thomas Becket in the course of this quarrel forced him to give up this reform (*see* Becket).

Henry's last years were embittered by the rebellion of his sons, aided by Philip Augustus of France and by their mother, the unscrupulous Eleanor. The king—old, sick, and discouraged—had to consent to the terms demanded of him. When he saw the name of John, his favorite son, among those of his enemies, he exclaimed, "Now let all things go as they will; I care no more for myself, nor for the world."

Two days later he died, muttering, "Shame, shame on a conquered king." He was succeeded by his son Richard (*see* Richard, Kings of England). After Richard's death, in 1199, John came to the throne (*see* John of England).

**Henry III** (born 1207, ruled 1216–1272). The elder son of King John and grandson of Henry II was a weak and incompetent ruler. He was born in Winchester on Oct. 1, 1207. Until he came of age, in 1227, the government was in the hands of regents.

*Henry IV usurped the throne and held it for 14 years in the face of repeated uprisings and powerful opposition.*

In 1236 Henry married Eleanor of Provence. His extravagance, his lavish gifts to favorites and to his wife's French relatives, and an unsuccessful war in France in 1242 caused mounting opposition to him. In 1258 a group of barons, led by Simon de Montfort, agreed to grant the king money only if he accepted the Provisions of Oxford, a body of reforms to be carried out by a commission of barons.

Henry repudiated the reform measures in 1261. In the Barons' War that followed, King Henry and his son Edward were captured at Lewes in 1264. Edward escaped and rescued his father. After the defeat and death of Simon in 1265, Henry was restored to the throne. Thereafter, however, the gifted and respected Edward was king in all but name. Henry died at Westminster, on Nov. 16, 1272 (*see* Edward, Kings of England; Montfort).

**Henry IV** (born 1366, ruled 1399–1413). Henry of Bolingbroke, alternately known as Henry of Lancaster, was born at Bolingbroke Castle in Lincolnshire, probably in April 1366.

Henry IV was the son of John of Gaunt, duke of Lancaster, and the grandson of King Edward III. He was the founder of the Lancastrian line of English kings. These kings were later to dispute the right to the throne with the York line, also descended from Edward III, in the Wars of the Roses (*see* Roses, Wars of the).

In his youth Henry was distinguished for his prowess in knightly combats. Between 1390 and 1393 he joined the Teutonic Knights in Lithuania and in Prussia. He also visited the Holy Land. In 1398 Richard II banished him from the kingdom (see Richard, Kings of England). When John of Gaunt died the following year, Henry returned to England to claim his father's estates, which Richard had confiscated. With the support of Henry Percy, earl of Northumberland; Percy's son, known as Harry Hotspur; and Ralph Neville, earl of Westmoreland, Henry raised an army and forced the abdication of Richard. Parliament declared him the lawful king.

Henry suppressed an uprising in Wales under Owen Glendower and a revolt in Scotland. There were disputes over his right to the throne, and later the Percys and Neville conspired against him. At Shrewsbury in 1403 they were defeated and Hotspur was killed. Henry died in Westminster Abbey on March 20, 1413, after a five-year illness. He was succeeded by his eldest son, Henry V.

**Henry V** (born 1387, ruled 1413–1422). The eldest son and successor of Henry IV was born at Monmouth in 1387. When he was only 16 years old he was in command of the English forces that defeated the Percys and Neville at Shrewsbury. He helped put down the Welsh revolt, and in 1411 he led an expedition to France. His father's long illness brought him heavy political responsibilities.

These strenuous early years devoted to war and politics contradict the tradition, immortalized by Shakespeare, that "Prince Hal," companion of the fat knight Falstaff, was a riotous madcap. Henry proved to be a forceful king.

Henry put forth again the claim to the French throne, formerly raised by Edward III. He thereby renewed the Hundred Years' War (see Hundred Years' War). By his brilliant victory at Agincourt (1415) he conquered all the northern half of France (see Agincourt, Battle of).

Five years later he married Catherine of Valois, and it was agreed that he should become king of France after the death of her father, the insane Charles VI (see Charles, Kings of France). Henry died of camp fever at Bois de Vincennes, France, in August 1422, leaving as heir to his rights in both kingdoms his infant son Henry, nine months old.

**Henry VI** (born 1421, ruled 1422–1461). One of the most unfortunate of kings was Henry VI. He was born at Windsor Castle on Dec. 6, 1421. He became king of England at the age of nine months and king of France a few weeks later, when his grandfather Charles VI died.

As regent in France, the duke of Bedford for a time maintained and even extended the English holdings. Then Joan of Arc aroused the French, raised the siege of Orléans, and brought the young French Dauphin to Reims Cathedral to be crowned King Charles VII (see Joan of Arc).

Henry was truthful, upright, and just, but he had the strength neither of mind nor of body to rule a kingdom. For long periods he was insane. War and business were never to his liking. He would rather have lived the life of a monk and a scholar.

Bit by bit the English lost the lands which they held in France, until only the city of Calais was left to them

Hans Wild—*Life* © Time Inc.

*In a re-creation of the battle of Agincourt, Henry V's longbowmen barrage their French foe with wave upon wave of arrows. The English victory over the French hastened the end of the heavily armored knight, the military basis of feudalism.*

when the Hundred Years' War ended, in 1453. Meanwhile the misgovernment of Henry's ministers at home led to a rebellion under Jack Cade, in 1450, in which the insurgents took London before they were overpowered and their leaders executed.

Five years later began the bloody Wars of the Roses. Queen Margaret, Henry's French wife, was the real head of the Lancastrian party, and King Henry played only a feeble part. In 1461 he lost his throne to the Yorkists, and Edward IV became king. Henry was restored to the throne in October 1470, but Edward regained it in April 1471. Henry's young son, Prince Edward, was slain after the battle of Tewkesbury in May 1471, and later that month Henry himself was murdered in the Tower of London, where he had been imprisoned. (See also Roses, Wars of the.)

**Henry VII** (born 1457, ruled 1485–1509). The founder of the Tudor monarchy was Henry VII. He was a descendant of Edward III and John of Gaunt through his mother, Margaret Beaufort. His father, Edmund Tudor, was the son of Owen Tudor and Catherine of Valois, the widow of Henry V, and thus a half brother of King Henry VI (see Tudor, House of).

Henry was born at Pembroke Castle, Wales, on Jan. 28, 1457. The murders of Henry VI and Prince Edward in 1471 left him the head of the House of Lancaster. At the battle of Bosworth Field (1485), Richard III, the last Yorkist king, was defeated and killed. Henry became king. He united the houses of Lancaster and York by marrying Elizabeth of York, niece of Richard III. The Wars of the Roses were ended (see Roses, Wars of the).

Henry was the first modern king of England. He established order and security and so gained the support of the rising middle class. He compelled the great nobles to obey the laws by means of his famous Court of Star Chamber. He secured his aims abroad not by war but by treaties and through the marriage alliances of his children.

An efficient system of taxation was introduced, and foreign trade expanded. John Cabot, sailing under the flag of Henry VII, laid the foundation of England's claim to the mainland of North America. Henry died at Richmond in April 1509.

**Henry VIII** (born 1491, ruled 1509–1547). The second son of Henry VII and Elizabeth of York was one of England's strongest and least popular monarchs. He was born at Greenwich on June 28, 1491. The first English ruler to be educated under the influence of the Renaissance, he was a gifted scholar, linguist, composer, and musician. As a youth he was gay and handsome, skilled in all manner of athletic games, but in later life he became coarse and fat. When his elder brother, Arthur, died (1502), he became heir apparent. He succeeded his father on the throne in 1509, and soon thereafter he married Arthur's young widow, Catherine of Aragon. During the first 20 years of his reign he left the shaping of policies largely in the hands of his great counselor, Cardinal Wolsey (*see* Wolsey, Cardinal). By 1527 Henry had made up his mind to get rid of his wife. The only one of Catherine's six children who survived infancy was a sickly girl, the Princess Mary, and it was doubtful whether a woman could succeed to the English throne. Then too, Henry had fallen in love with a lady of the court, Anne Boleyn.

When the pope (Clement VII) would not annul his marriage, Henry turned against Wolsey, deprived him of his office of chancellor, and had him arrested on a charge of treason. He then obtained a divorce through Thomas Cranmer, whom he had made archbishop of Canterbury, and it was soon announced that he had married Anne Boleyn.

The pope was thus defied. All ties that bound the English church to Rome were broken. Appeals to the pope's court were forbidden, all payments to Rome were stopped, and the pope's authority in England was abolished. In 1534 the Act of Supremacy declared Henry himself to be Supreme Head of the Church of England, and anyone who denied this title was guilty of an act of treason. Some changes were also made in the church services, the Bible was translated into English, and printed copies were placed in the churches. The monasteries throughout England were dissolved and their vast lands and goods turned over to the king, who in turn granted those estates to noblemen who would support his policies. In the northern part of the kingdom the people rose in rebellion in behalf of the monks, but the Pilgrimage of Grace, as it was called, was put down.

Although Henry reformed the government of the church, he refused to allow any changes to be made in its doctrines. Before his divorce he had opposed the teachings of Martin Luther in a book that had gained for him from the pope the title Defender of the Faith—a title the monarch of England still bears. After the separation from Rome he persecuted with equal severity the Catholics who adhered to the government of Rome and the Protestants who rejected its doctrines.

Henry was married six times. Anne Boleyn bore the king one child, who became Elizabeth I. Henry soon tired of Anne and had her put to death. A few days

*Henry VIII was painted by Hans Holbein the Younger in 1536. The portrait is in the Galleria Nazionale in Rome.*

later he married a third wife, Jane Seymour. She died in a little more than a year, after having given birth to the future Edward VI.

A marriage was then contracted with a German princess, Anne of Cleves, whom the king had been led to believe to be very beautiful. When he saw her he discovered that he had been tricked, and he promptly divorced this wife and beheaded Thomas Cromwell, the minister who had arranged the marriage. Henry's fifth wife, Catherine Howard, was sent to the block for misconduct. In 1543 he married his sixth wife, the tactful and pious Catherine Parr. Catherine, who survived Henry, lived to marry her fourth husband.

During Henry's reign the union of England and Wales was completed (1536). Ireland was made a kingdom (1541), and Henry became king of Ireland. His wars with Scotland and France remained indecisive in spite of some shallow victories. Although he himself opposed the Reformation, his creation of a national church marked the real beginning of the English Reformation. He died on Jan. 28, 1547, and was buried in St. George's Chapel in Windsor Castle.

**HENRY, Kings of France.** Four kings of France have borne the name Henry. The last and greatest was Henry of Navarre.

**Henry I** (born 1008?, ruled 1031–60). The third of the Capetian line of French monarchs was Henry I. He was the grandson of Hugh Capet and the son of Robert II. His reign was marked by a series of wars with ambitious French nobles. William, duke of Normandy, later known as William the Conqueror, was his contemporary. Henry's attempted invasions of

Brown Brothers

*Henry IV was one of France's ablest and most popular kings. He encouraged agriculture, industry, and exploration.*

Normandy were repelled by William in 1047 and again in 1058. A year before he died he crowned his son, Philip I, as joint king.

**Henry II** (born 1519, ruled 1547–59). The son of Francis I, Henry II married the strong-willed Catherine de' Medici (*see* Medici). In his reign began the persecution of the Huguenots, who were led by Gaspard de Coligny, admiral of France (*see* Coligny). Henry was killed in a tournament. Three of his children came to the French throne—Francis II, Charles IX, and Henry III.

**Henry III** (born 1551, ruled 1574–89). The third son of Henry II and Catherine de' Medici came to the throne after the death of his two older brothers, whose reigns were brief. He was weak and, like his father, was completely dominated by Catherine. He helped her organize the Massacre of St. Bartholomew in 1572 (*see* Huguenots). His assassination, in the course of the Huguenot wars, opened the succession to Henry of Navarre.

**Henry IV** (born 1553, ruled 1589–1610). The founder of the Bourbon line of French kings was the son of Antony of Bourbon and Jeanne d'Albret, queen of Navarre (*see* Bourbon, House of). He was born in Pau, in Béarn, on Dec. 14, 1553. Henry was educated as a Protestant. In 1569, when he was 16 years old, his mother, who was a Huguenot, placed him in the care of the Huguenot leader Coligny (*see* Coligny). Henry escaped the Massacre of St. Bartholomew by letting it be thought that he had renounced the Protestant faith.

Before his death, Henry III, who had no children, had acknowledged Henry of Navarre to be his successor. In addition, Henry of Navarre claimed the throne by right of his descent from King Louis IX (St. Louis) through Louis's son Robert of Clermont. Also,

Henry's wife, Margaret of Valois, was the daughter of Henry II.

Nonetheless, his succession was disputed by the powerful Holy League, which had the backing of King Philip II of Spain. Henry of Navarre was not crowned until he had enforced his claim by resort to arms and had become a Roman Catholic.

The Edict of Nantes, which Henry issued in 1598, gave the Huguenots equal political rights with the Catholics, the right to reside freely anywhere in France, freedom of private worship in their own homes and public worship in certain places (not including the king's court nor within five leagues of Paris), and the government of La Rochelle and a few other strong places as "cities of refuge." This edict remained in force, with some modifications, until 1685, when it was revoked by Louis XIV.

Henry IV also set about restoring the prosperity of the land. He wished, he said, that there should be no peasant in the kingdom so poor that he could not have a chicken in the pot for his Sunday dinner. He encouraged agriculture and manufacturing and built roads to aid commerce. He supported the explorations of Samuel de Champlain in the New World. On May 14, 1610, he was killed by a religious fanatic as he was riding through Paris.

He beautified Paris by building the Hôtel de Ville, the Place Royale, and the Pont Neuf and completing the Tuileries Gardens. He was succeeded by Louis XIII, his son by his second wife, Marie de' Medici.

**HENRY IV** (1050–1106). Of the seven men named Henry who ruled the Holy Roman Empire between 919 and 1313, Henry IV was the most controversial. His conflict with Pope Gregory VII over which of them could appoint high clergy was not resolved until 1122 at the Concordat of Worms, during the reign of Henry's son, Henry V.

Henry IV was born in Goslar, Saxony, on Nov. 11, 1050. He became king of Germany when he was 4 years old. His father, Henry III, died in 1056, and he inherited the kingdoms of Germany, Italy, and Burgundy. His reign was marked by the storm of the Investiture Conflict—whether the pope or emperor should appoint bishops and other high clergy, who at that time were feudal princes and had great power.

In 1076 Henry persuaded the German bishops to renounce obedience to Pope Gregory VII. The pope excommunicated him. Henry's vassals threatened to elect another king, and he was forced to submit. He crossed the Alps into Canossa, Italy, to beg the pope's forgiveness.

After he had stood for three days in the cold, fasting and barefoot, Gregory pardoned him. Meanwhile the German princes elected Rudolph, duke of Swabia, to replace Henry. Civil war continued until 1080, when Rudolph was killed. Gregory had again excommunicated Henry. Henry declared Gregory deposed and set up the antipope Clement III. Henry conquered Rome in 1084, and Clement crowned him Holy Roman emperor.

In 1087 Henry had his eldest son, Conrad, crowned as German king. Conrad later rebelled, and Henry replaced him with his second son, Henry V. In 1104 the young Henry rebelled. In 1105 he imprisoned his father and forced him to abdicate. Henry IV escaped and was building an army when he died on Aug. 7, 1106, in Liège.

**HENRY, Joseph** (1797–1878). One of the first great American scientists after Benjamin Franklin, Joseph Henry was responsible for numerous inventions and discovered several major principles of electromagnetism, including the oscillatory nature of electric discharge and self-inductance, a phenomenon of primary importance in electronic circuitry.

Joseph Henry was born in Albany, N.Y., on Dec. 17, 1797. He came from a poor family and had little schooling. In 1829, while working as a schoolteacher at the Albany Academy, he developed a method greatly increasing the power of an electromagnet. In 1829 he constructed the first electric motor.

Although Michael Faraday is generally given credit for discovering electromagnetic induction in 1831, Henry had observed the phenomenon a year earlier (see Faraday; Electricity). In 1831, before he assisted F.B. Morse in the development of the telegraph, Henry built and successfully operated a telegraph of his own design (see Morse). Henry never patented any of his many devices because he believed that the discoveries of science were for the common benefit of all humanity.

Henry became a professor at the College of New Jersey (later Princeton University) in 1832. He continued his researches and discovered the laws on which the transformer is based. He conducted an experiment that was apparently the first use of radio waves across a distance. He also showed that sunspots radiate less heat than the general solar surface.

In 1846 Henry became the first secretary of the Smithsonian Institution in Washington, D.C., where he initiated a nationwide weather reporting system. He was a primary organizer of the National Academy of Science and its second president. He died in Washington, D.C., on May 13, 1878. In 1892 his name was given to the unit of electrical inductance, the henry.

**HENRY, O.** (1862–1910). Famous for his short stories and a master of the surprise ending, O. Henry is remembered best for such enduring favorites as "The Gift of the Magi" and "The Ransom of Red Chief." The combination of humor and sentiment found in his stories is the basis of their universal appeal.

William Sydney Porter was born in Greensboro, N.C., on Sept. 11, 1862. He was a shy, freckled boy, fond of 'The Arabian Nights' and other books. As a youngster he enjoyed roaming in the fields by himself, drawing cartoons of his friends, and spinning exciting yarns. For a time Porter attended a school kept by his aunt, but for the most part he gained his education through reading and through experience—watching and listening to the people around him. He worked for a time in his uncle's drugstore but soon decided to go to Texas to help on a friend's ranch. There in the Southwest he first tried writing short stories and making up jokes for newspapers.

Porter now began working full time as a journalist. For a year he edited a humorous weekly called *The Rolling Stone.* Then he went to Houston, where he worked as a reporter on the *Houston Daily Post.* Before his marriage Porter had been a teller in the First National Bank of Austin, Tex. In 1896 the authorities in Austin called him back to answer a charge of embezzlement. The affairs of the bank had been handled so loosely that, long before, Porter had protested that it was impossible to make the books balance. If he had stood trial he would probably have been acquitted, but he allowed friends to talk him into fleeing the country. He went to Honduras.

Six months later, having heard that his wife was dying, he returned and gave himself up. By this time the fact that he had fled from justice weighed against him. He was found guilty and spent some three years in the penitentiary.

After his release in 1901 Porter went to Pittsburgh, Pa., where he began using the name O. Henry. The following year he settled in New York City, and there for three years he wrote a story each week for the New York *World*, a newspaper. His stories also began appearing in magazines.

In 1904 he brought out his first collection of stories, 'Cabbages and Kings'. The stories of O. Henry had wide appeal. In many of them he told about the city life he saw around him, but he could also write convincing- ly about the West. He was best at describing ordinary men and women and the touching or funny things they did. Although his writing was enormously popular, popularity did not bring him happiness. Troubled by financial difficulties and alcoholism, his health suffered. O. Henry died in New York City on June 5, 1910.

A master technician in the art of short-story writing, O. Henry often experimented with new ideas for plots. His famous surprise endings give his stories a special zest. Although he wrote for a mass audience and did not intend to be taken too seriously, O. Henry's skill and his novel approach influenced many other writers, both in the United States and abroad.

**HENRY, Patrick** (1736–99). Fearless and eloquent, Patrick Henry became the spokesman of the Southern colonies during the stirring period that led to the American Revolution. His words, which expressed the feelings and hopes of the patriots, helped inspire them to make those dreams into reality.

Patrick Henry was born on May 29, 1736, in Studley, Hanover County, Va. His mother was English. His father, an educated man who worked as a surveyor and county judge, was Scottish. Young Henry's formal education was scanty, and at the age of 15 he entered business. He failed as a farmer and as a storekeeper and turned his attention to the law. Admitted to the bar, he succeeded immediately as a pleader before frontier juries.

In 1763 Henry supported the people against the established church in a case known as the *Parson's Cause.* During the trial he declared in an impassioned speech that a king by vetoing acts of a colonial legislature "degenerates into a tyrant and forfeits all right to his subjects' obedience." This declaration brought him the love of the colonists and a seat in the Virginia House of Burgesses just at the time of the passage of the Stamp Act in 1765.

The older members of the House hesitated, not knowing what course to take in regard to the Stamp Act. Henry introduced a series of resolutions declaring that the British Parliament had no right to tax the American colonies. In the debate that followed, Patrick Henry exclaimed: "Caesar had his Brutus; Charles the First, his Cromwell; and George the Third . . ." Here he was interrupted by loud cries of "Treason! Treason!" from members of the House. Henry paused for just a moment and then coolly finished: "and George the Third may profit by their example. If *this* be treason, make the most of it!" This fiery speech secured the adoption of the resolutions.

In 1774 Henry was sent by Virginia as a delegate to the first Continental Congress. At the second Virginia Convention the next year, he urged the colony to arm its militia. It was in this speech that he uttered the famous words:

*Gentlemen may cry peace! peace! but there is no peace! The war is actually begun! The next gale that sweeps from the North will bring to our ears the clash of resounding arms! Our brethren are already in the field. Is life so dear, or peace so sweet as to be purchased at the price of chains and slavery? Forbid it, Almighty God! I know not what course others may take, but as for me, give me liberty, or give me death.*

Henry also helped draw up Virginia's state constitution in 1776 and was elected first governor of the state. He was reelected twice.

In the Virginia ratification convention of 1788, Henry opposed the adoption of the new Constitution of the United States. He objected to it because it contained no "bill of rights" and because it infringed too much on the rights of the states. He wanted the country to remain a confederation and feared that under the Constitution it would become merely "one great consolidated national government of the people of all the States." Henry's advice to reject the Constitution was not followed, but it was as the result of such opposition that the first ten amendments to the Constitution, popularly known as the Bill of Rights, were adopted.

Henry retired to Red Hill, his plantation near Brookneal, Va. In 1799 he consented to serve again in the Virginia legislative assembly, but on June 6, before he could take his seat, he died of cancer at Red Hill.

**HENRY THE NAVIGATOR** (1394–1460). The founder of the Portuguese empire, Prince Henry of Portugal was a patron of explorers, and he was one of the earliest geographers. In honor of the discoveries he inspired, he came to be called Henry the Navigator.

Henry was born in Oporto on March 4, 1394, the third surviving son of King John I of Portugal. His mother, Philippa, was the daughter of the English duke John of Gaunt.

In 1415 Prince Henry distinguished himself in a campaign in which the Portuguese captured the Moroccan citadel of Ceuta on the African coast across the straits from Gibraltar. While he was in Ceuta he became interested in the continent of Africa and decided to send out expeditions to explore its coasts.

From 1418 the prince sponsored numerous voyages of exploration. The Portuguese explored the islands of the Azores, Madeira, and the Cape Verde Islands, and the African coast as far as present-day Sierra Leone. Prince Henry set up a base near Cape St. Vincent, the southwestern tip of Portugal, not far from the port of Lagos. There, on a rocky promontory called Sagres, Henry created a small court of his own called Vila do Infante. The most brilliant scholars did pioneer work here in navigation, ship design, astronomy, and mapmaking. From Sagres he sent out most of his expeditions. The prince expended his entire fortune on these projects. He was in debt when he died in Vila do Infante on Nov. 13, 1460.

**HENSON, Jim** (1936–90). In adapting the ancient art of puppetry to the modern media of television and motion pictures, Jim Henson brought his puppets to life for children and adults. Henson believed that learning could be fun, and to that end he introduced Kermit the Frog, Bert and Ernie, the Cookie Monster, Big Bird, Miss Piggy, and hundreds of other Muppets—Henson's own term for his invention, a combination of a marionette and a puppet. The Muppets were seen on television's Sesame Street and The Muppet Show in more than 100 countries as well as in such films as 'The Muppet Movie', 'The Great Muppet Caper', and 'The Muppets Take Manhattan'. (*See also* Puppet.)

James Maury Henson was born in Greenville, Miss., on Sept. 24, 1936. The family moved to Hyattsville, Md., when his father was transferred to Washington, D.C. With a little experience in his high school puppet club, Henson got a job as a puppeteer on his own television show, called Sam and Friends.

Beginning in 1969 Henson enjoyed resounding success with the introduction of Sesame Street on public television. Henson continued his success with the television show Fraggle Rock and the cartoon show Jim Henson's Muppet Babies. Henson created puppetlike figures for the movies 'The Dark Crystal', 'Labyrinth', and 'The Witches'. He died of bacterial pneumonia in New York City on May 16, 1990.

**HEPATITIS.** The liver inflammation called hepatitis is usually caused by viral infection or by drugs or alcohol. Its effects vary from a minor flulike illness to liver failure and death. The most common form is acute viral hepatitis, which persists for a few to several weeks. Viral hepatitis that lasts for at least six months is termed chronic. A typical hepatitis attack begins suddenly with fatigue, appetite loss, nausea and vomiting, and fever. Jaundice, a yellowish discoloration of the skin and eyes, may occur about 3 to 10 days later, and the urine may darken. The jaundice normally fades after about two weeks, though the course of recovery varies. Many patients recover fully, but in some cases serious complications and long-term illness may result.

There are seven known hepatitis viruses: A, B, C, D, E, F, and G. The A, E, and F viruses are spread mainly by food or drinking water contaminated with feces from infected individuals. Poor sanitation and overcrowding can aggravate transmission. The hepatitis B, C, D, and G viruses are spread mainly by infected blood and other bodily fluids, commonly through sexual contact or sharing a hypodermic needle. These viruses may also be transmitted through blood transfusions or organ donations. The B and C viruses may be spread from mothers to their newborns at the time of delivery.

Infection caused by the A virus is the most common form of hepatitis worldwide. Type-A hepatitis occurs both as an isolated illness and as an epidemic outbreak. Symptoms normally begin to appear from about 15 to 45 days after exposure to the virus. Most patients with this type of hepatitis recover fully without needing any special treatment.

Type-B hepatitis usually causes a more serious and longer-lasting illness. Permanent liver damage or liver cancer occurs in some cases. The onset of the disease may not occur until 40 days to six months after exposure to the virus. During this period, persons who carry the B virus but do not show symptoms may unknowingly infect others. The symptoms of hepatitis C usually appear from six to nine weeks after exposure. The C virus also can cause serious illness and may greatly increase the risk of liver cancer.

The hepatitis D virus (also known as the delta agent) affects only persons who are also infected with the type-B virus. The D virus causes severe, long-term liver disease. Hepatitis E is similar to type A but its effects are usually more serious and can be fatal. Pregnant women who contract the virus are particularly susceptible to liver failure. The type-F virus was first detected in 1994, and the type-G virus in 1996. The G virus often infects persons who are already infected with the C virus.

The B, C, D, and G viruses can cause chronic hepatitis. In some cases it can be a fairly benign disease. Chronic active hepatitis, however, may result in liver tissue death, cirrhosis of the liver, and eventual liver failure. Alcoholic hepatitis is a complication of long-term alcoholism that can lead to cirrhosis. Autoimmune dysfunction and reactions to certain medications can also lead to chronic hepatitis.

Routine testing of blood donors has greatly reduced the chance of contracting hepatitis from transfusions. Treatment against hepatitis varies. Most cases require no special treatment. Chronic hepatitis B and C are usually treated with drugs, including alpha interferon. Only about half the patients with type-C hepatitis respond to treatment, however. Immune serum globulin can reduce the severity of hepatitis type A if given within two weeks of exposure. Hepatitis B immune globulin may lessen the effects of the B virus and is given to newborns of type-B–infected mothers and to others at risk. Effective vaccines against hepatitis A and hepatitis B have been developed. The vaccine against the B virus also protects against the D virus, since a person cannot be infected with type D without also being infected with type B. (*See also* Liver; Virus.)

**HEPBURN, Katharine** (1907–2003). The title of the biography by Gary Carey, 'Hepburn: Hollywood Yankee' (1983), is an apt description of one of the most distinctive and dynamic American actresses. Katharine Hepburn, in her long stage and motion-picture career, never lost the pungent New England Yankee accent that enriched her performances. She brought to her roles a depth of character, and occasional eccentricity, that set her apart from most leading ladies. She won more Academy awards than any other performer—for 'Morning Glory' (1933), 'Guess Who's Coming to Dinner' (1967), 'The Lion in Winter' (1968), and 'On Golden Pond' (1981).

Katharine Houghton Hepburn was born on May 12, 1907, in Hartford, Conn. She attended Bryn Mawr College, where she appeared in stage productions. After graduation in 1928, she went into show business and had a bit part on Broadway in 'Night Hostess'. After successive plays over the next four years, her role in 'The Warrior's Husband' (1932) won her a motion-picture contract with RKO Studios. Her first film, 'A Bill of Divorcement' (1932), established her as a star, and she appeared in a rapid succession of movies, including 'Little Women' (1933), 'Spitfire' (1934), 'Sylvia Scarlett' (1936), 'Stage Door' (1937), and 'Bringing Up Baby' (1938). After working on the stage in 'Jane Eyre' and 'The Philadelphia Story', she returned to Hollywood to film the latter play, which won the New York Film Critics' award in 1940.

In 1942 Hepburn began her long film association with Spencer Tracy in 'Woman of the Year'. Some of her nine films with him were 'Without Love' (1945), 'State of the Union' (1948), 'Adam's Rib' (1949), and 'Pat and Mike' (1952). Her record 12 Academy award nominations—which stood for over 20 years until it was surpassed by Meryl Streep in 2003—honored her work in 'Alice Adams' (1935), 'The African Queen' (1951), 'The Rainmaker' (1956), and 'Long Day's Journey into Night' (1962), among others. Other stage productions were 'As You Like It' and other Shakespearean plays in the 1950s, 'Coco' (1969), and 'West Side Waltz' (1981). She starred in several television movies in the 1970s, 1980s, and 1990s. Hepburn's final big-screen performance was in 'Love Affair' (1994). She died at her home in Old Saybrook, Conn., on June 29, 2003.

## TINCTURES AND THE ENGLISH MARKS OF CADENCY

| ARGENT<br>(Silver or White)<br>LABEL<br>(First Son) | OR<br>(Gold or Yellow)<br>CRESCENT<br>(Second Son) | AZURE<br>MULLET,<br>or MOLET<br>(Third Son) | GULES<br>(Red)<br>MARTLET<br>(Fourth Son) | VERT<br>(Green)<br>ANNULET<br>(Fifth Son) | PURPURE<br>(Purple)<br>FLEUR-DE-LIS<br>(Sixth Son) | SABLE<br>(Black)<br>ROSE<br>(Seventh Son) | CROSS<br>MOLINE<br>(Eighth Son) | QUATREFOIL,<br>DOUBLE<br>or OCTOFOIL<br>(Ninth Son) |

### THE REFERENCE POINTS OF A SHIELD

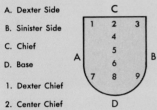

A. Dexter Side
B. Sinister Side
C. Chief
D. Base
1. Dexter Chief
2. Center Chief
3. Sinister Chief
4. Honor Point
5. Fess (Center) Point
6. Nombril (Navel) Point
7. Dexter Base
8. Center Base
9. Sinister Base

### LINES TO DIVIDE SHIELD

Engrailed
Invected
Wavy (Undy)
Embattled (Crenellé)
Indented
Dancetty (Dancetté)
Dovetailed

### HERALDIC FURS

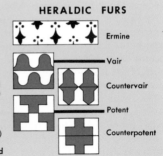

Ermine
Vair
Countervair
Potent
Counterpotent

## FAMILY SHIELDS

1. CHAUCER
2. GREBY
3. HUTSON
4. MURPHY
5. MEEHAN (Meighan)
6. WOODWARD
7. REYNOLDS

8. HAWLEY
9. WASHINGTON
10. PLOWDEN
11. DRUMMOND
12. GILLENTINE
13. CLAPP
14. ELLIOT

**HERALDRY.** In the Middle Ages knights wore armor that completely covered their heads and bodies. There grew up the custom of emblazoning devices on shields and surcoats so that the soldiers could find their commanders and rally around them in the press of battle. The surcoat, a garment worn over the body armor, was the original "coat of arms."

Heraldry gets its name from the heralds who were the official representatives of kings and lords. It was the herald's duty to keep track of family relationships and of the intricate etiquette governing coats of arms.

A complete coat of arms, known as the achievement, includes the shield, also called escutcheon, which is the most important element; the crest; and the motto. The achievement may also be embellished with a helmet; a "torse," or wreath out of which the crest rises above the helmet; and the "mantling," or "lambrequin." This is a scarflike decoration hanging from the helmet. Its two sides are of different colors, so it is doubled over in places to show both surfaces. "Supporters" are used only by royalty, the peerage, and certain orders of knighthood.

*THE ARMS OF SCOTLAND*
**The parts of a coat of arms include (A) crest, (B) crown, (C) helmet, (D) charge, (E) shield, (F) supporter, (G) mantling, or lambrequin, and (H) motto and scroll.**

The "blazon" is the verbal description of a shield. The reference points, colors, and furs are shown above. "Marks of cadency" distinguish the different sons in a family. The "dexter" is the side of the shield at the right of the person wearing it.

The color of the field is always named first; then the principal charge or charges with their location and color; then the secondary charges. For example, the blazon of George Washington's shield (number 9) reads as follows: "Argent, two bars gules, in chief three mullets, of the second." This means: a silver (argent) field, crossed by two red (gules) horizontal bars; in the upper third (chief) are three mullets of the second color mentioned (red). The mullet (the cadency mark of the third son) represents not a star, but the rowel of a spur.

The shield is divided into different areas by a variety of devices illustrated above. There are the "pale" (number 6), "fess" (number 12), "saltire" (number 8), "flanch" (number 2), and "chevron" (numbers 3 and 5). The "bend dexter" (number 14) crosses diagonally from the dexter chief to the sinister base. The "bend sinister," crossing from the sinister chief to the dexter base, is popularly but mistakenly considered a mark of illegitimacy. The outline of the various bars may be straight, wavy (number 11), embattled (number 3), engrailed (number 14), invected (number 8), or dancetty (number 10).

The "charge" is a figure or symbol on the shield. A great variety of charges are used, including geometrical figures, weapons, animals, and plants. A common charge is the lion in various positions: *rampant* (erect on one hind leg); *passant* (walking); *couchant* (lying with the head raised); or *dormant* (asleep). (*See also* Middle Ages.)

**HERBS.** Records of the use of herbs date from ancient Egypt and Biblical times. The Greeks and Romans studied and wrote about herbs and their uses in medicine and cooking. Early physicians used hundreds of herbs to treat a variety of ailments. Herbs were also used to mask unpleasant household odors and to enhance the taste of dull food.

The study and use of herbs continued in Europe. Medieval monasteries became centers of herb collection and cultivation. The herbs were studied for their medical applications and their use in cooking. During the Renaissance, information about herbs was published in books known as herbals.

When the first colonists came to the New World, they brought herbs with them. Colonists soon learned about valuable native herbs from American Indians. Each new wave of immigrants arriving in America brought a new collection of herbal remedies. By the 19th century many home remedies containing herbs were patented and sold. Modern drugs replaced most of these remedies, but many still contain the ingredients derived from herbs.

Herbs grow in temperate regions. They are the aromatic leaves of such plants as marjoram, mint, rosemary, and thyme. Today herbs are used primarily

(Middle row left) David Cavagnaro—Peter Arnold, Inc.; (others) David Leibman

*Some of the common herbs used in foods are (top row, left to right) sage (Salvia Labiatae) pennyroyal mint (Mentha pulegium); (middle row, left to right) thyme (Thymus vulgaris), rosemary (Rosmarinus officinalis);(bottom row, left to right) parsley (Petroselinum crispum), and chicory (Cichorium intybus).*

as seasonings to flavor and enhance food. Other food seasonings are spices, such as black pepper or cinnamon, and aromatic seeds, such as dill or sesame.

They are also used in a variety of products such as soap, shampoo, powder, or cosmetics. Herbal teas, made from many different herbs, are considered by some to be healthful. Many people still use herbs for their medicinal properties. Some modern drugs are refined from ingredients found in herbs.

### Some Common Herbs

**Basil** (*Ocimum basilicum*) is a tropical Old World plant that grows to 24 inches (61 centimeters) in height. Its bushy, egg-shaped leaves curl inward. Whorls of white flowers form at the ends of the stems. The leaves are sweet and fragrant.

**Bay** (*Laurus nobilis*) is a large tree native to the Mediterranean. In cultivation it is a shrub that grows from 3 to 10 feet (91 to 305 centimeters) tall. The dark green, glossy, lance-shaped leaves are used as a very spicy and pungent seasoning.

**Chervil** (*Anthriscus cerefolium*), native to Eurasia, grows to a height of 24 inches (61 centimeters). Its leaves resemble parsley in shape but are finer. White flowers bloom in umbrella-shaped clusters. Chervil tastes somewhat like parsley but has a slight anise flavor that intensifies the taste of other herbs when used in cooking.

**Marjoram** (*Origanum majorana*) is native to North Africa and Asia. It reaches a height of 2 feet (61 centimeters). The slightly fuzzy leaves are oval in shape and are easily confused with those of the oregano. They are mild and sweet.

**Mint,** in botany, includes members of the genus *Mentha,* such as peppermint and spearmint. It is native to Europe and grows to a height of 3 feet (91 centimeters). It is a rapidly spreading plant with lance-shaped leaves, square stems, and spikes of violet flowers. The taste is cooling and is a popular flavoring. The plant has a long history of medicinal applications for many ailments.

**Oregano** (*Origanum vulgare*) is a native of Eurasia and grows to a height of 2 ½ feet (76 centimeters). It is a hardy plant with hairy, oval leaves that are a dull, gray-green in color. Oregano's strong taste and fragrance make it a popular seasoning.

**Parsley** (*Petroselinum crispum*) has two varieties native to Eurasia. They grow to a height of 3 feet (91 centimeters). Both are used for seasoning. Curly parsley, with its tightly curled foliage, is used as a garnish. Italian parsley has flat leaves and a stronger flavor.

**Rosemary** (*Rosmarinus officinalis*) is an evergreen shrub native to the Mediterranean that reaches a height of 2 to 4 feet (61 to 122 centimeters). The narrow leaves have a very fragrant scent that, in the wild, is detectable at great distances. It has many uses medicinally or as a seasoning.

**Sage** (*Salvia officinalis*) is a shrub native to southern Europe. It grows to a height of 2 feet (61 centimeters). The oval, gray-green leaves have a wrinkled surface covered with short, white hairs. Spikes of violet flowers bloom in the summer. Its leaves have a strong flavor.

**Savory.** Summer savory (*Satureia hortensis*) and winter savory (*S. montana*) are native to the Mediterranean. Summer savory grows to a height of 18 inches (46 centimeters) and has narrow, hairy leaves that grow sparsely along the stem. It has a sweet, peppery taste and smell. Winter savory is smaller and wider than summer savory and reaches a height of 12 inches (30 centimeters). The narrow leaves have a sharp, peppery taste.

**Tarragon** (*Artemisia dracunculus*), a shrubby plant native to Eurasia, can reach heights of up to 5 feet (152 centimeters). It has narrow, lance-shaped leaves with white hairs and tiny, round, whitish flowers. Tarragon has a strong, somewhat bitter flavor.

**Thyme** (*Thymus vulgaris*) is native to the Mediterranean and grows to 6 to 15 inches (15 to 38 centimeters) high. It has small, hairy, oval leaves and whorls of lavender flowers along the end of the stem. Thyme is very aromatic and has a sharp, bitter taste.

There are numerous other herbal plants. They include anise, caraway, chamomile, chicory, cumin, dill, fennel, and licorice.

Herbs grow in dry, exposed, and well-drained soil with a lot of sun and low humidity. Manure or compost are often used to promote the formation of oils essential to the cultivation of fragrant and flavorful herbs. Chemical fertilizers, which require a great amount of water, hinder the formation of these oils. Herbs are also grown indoors. Lisa McGowan

**HERCULES.** The strongest and most celebrated of the heroes of classical mythology, Hercules, called Heracles by the Greeks, was the son of the god Zeus and the mortal Alcmene. The goddess Hera, who hated the infant Hercules, sent two serpents to destroy him in his cradle, but Hercules strangled them. As a boy Hercules was trained by the centaur Chiron.

When Hercules was a young man, two maidens came to him. Arete represented virtue; Kakia was vice. Kakia offered Hercules pleasure and riches if he would follow her. Arete offered him only glory for a lifelong struggle against evil. Hercules chose to be guided by Arete.

In a fit of frenzy caused by Hera, Hercules slew his own children. To atone he had to serve his cousin King Eurystheus, who ordered him to perform the tasks known as the 12 labors of Hercules.

The first was the slaying of the Nemean lion. Hercules strangled the animal and wore the lion's skin. He then slew the Hydra, a terrible serpent with nine heads. The third and fourth labors involved the capture of two wild creatures—the Ceryneian stag with golden horns and the wild Erymanthian boar.

For his next labor Hercules had to clean the Augean stables, which had not been cleaned for 30 years. He turned two rivers, the Alpheus and the Peneus, through the stables, finishing the work in a single day. Next he slew the fierce Stymphalian birds, after which he captured the Cretan bull. Then he captured the flesh-eating wild mares of Diomedes, king of Thrace. Hercules killed Diomedes and fed him to the horses. He then had to obtain the belt of Hippolyta, queen of the Amazons. He defeated the Amazons, killed the queen, and took the belt. For his tenth labor Hercules captured the oxen of the monster Geryon, which dwelt on the fabled island Erytheia.

The last two labors were the most difficult. One involved stealing the golden apples guarded by four sister nymphs called the Hesperides. Their father was Atlas, who supported the heavens on his back. To obtain the apples Hercules took Atlas's place while Atlas took the apples. Finally Hercules traveled to Hades, where he captured Cerberus, the many-headed dog who guarded the gates of the underworld. He brought Cerberus to Eurystheus, but the king was so terrified that Hercules had to return to Hades to take the monster back.

Having completed the 12 tasks, Hercules was now free, but he performed other feats. The centaur Nessus tried to carry off Hercules' wife, Deianeira. Hercules shot Nessus with a poisoned arrow. The dying centaur had Deianeira keep some of his blood as a love charm. When Hercules fell in love with another maiden, Deianeira sent him a robe steeped in the blood. Hercules put it on, and poison spread through his body like fire. He fled to Mount Oeta, built a funeral fire, and threw himself on it to die.

Hercules' heroic strength inspired many works of art. A fine example in sculpture is the Farnese Hercules, a copy of an earlier work by the ancient sculptor Lysippus.

**HEREDITY.** The transmission of biological traits from one generation to the next is governed by the process of heredity. Heredity determines certain specific characteristics of plants and animals. Plants inherit traits that affect their physical and metabolic processes. Animals can inherit behavioral, mental, and physical traits. Some traits characteristic of a plant or animal species are generally inherited no matter who the parents are. Other traits, such as human eye color, are specific to individuals, and their inheritance is directly dependent on the genetics of the parents.

The physical key to heredity lies within the nucleus of the cell in structures known as chromosomes. These chromosomes carry smaller units called genes, which contain the hereditary "code." (*See also* Cell.) Each species of plant and animal has a particular number of chromosomes, which are carried in pairs within each cell of the body. When a somatic, or body, cell divides in a process known as mitosis, it produces exact duplicates of each chromosome. Thus the newly formed cells, as well as all of the cells in the body, have exactly the same genes.

Sex cells are different from somatic cells because they divide by a process known as meiosis, which consists of two divisions rather than one (*see* Genetics). The process of meiosis occurs in the sex cells of both males and females and results in the gametes, or germ

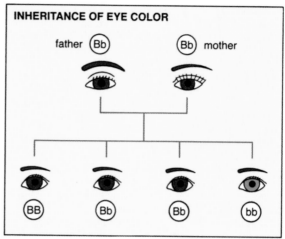

**INHERITANCE OF EYE COLOR**

*If each parent has a dominant brown and a recessive blue gene, there is a one-in-four chance that their child will be blue eyed.*

cells, that are used in fertilization. Each gamete receives one of each chromosome pair from the parent. During fertilization a single male and female gamete unite to form a fertilized egg, or zygote (*see* Embryology). In this way the infant inherits its parents' genes.

Although the genes for each trait are produced in pairs, the expression of the trait in the organism depends on how the two genes are combined. Some genes are dominant, while others are recessive. The presence of one or two dominant genes results in expression of the dominant trait; for example, the gene for brown eyes in humans is dominant over the gene for blue eyes. For the expression of a recessive trait such as blue eyes, however, two recessive genes, inherited independently from the two parents, are required. The translation of genetic information to biological traits is thus a complex process. Many characteristics are influenced by more than one gene. In addition, many genes exist in numerous variations throughout a population. As a result there is a vast potential for variability among hereditary characteristics.

At the microscopic level, the genetic code ultimately determines the purpose of each cell. The process of heredity, however, can be even more finely dissected. Genes transmit the genetic code biochemically; they are composed of deoxyribonucleic acid, or DNA, a complex molecule capable of duplicating itself exactly. It is DNA that is responsible for the replication and transmission of genetic traits at the biochemical level (*see* Genetics).

Ideally, humans have 23 pairs of chromosomes. These chromosomes carry thousands of genes that pass on traits to following generations. Among the common inherited physical traits are straight or curly hair, color blindness, attached or unattached earlobes, and blood type. Mental traits, including some forms of schizophrenia, can also be inherited.

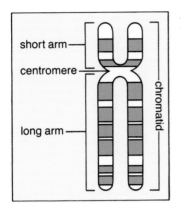

*A chromosome consists of a set of duplicate chromatids that are held together by the centromere and lined with genes, which contain the hereditary code.*

short arm

centromere

long arm

chromatid

Most physical and mental traits are the products of many different genes operating in different ways on various metabolic pathways. Skin color, for example, is controlled by several genes—this is why there is so much variation in skin color not only between different races but also between persons of the same race. Likewise, though a person's intelligence may be hereditarily influenced by the intelligence of the parents, individual intelligence is ultimately the product of a wide variety of genetic combinations and environmental influences.

Heredity is also responsible for many human diseases and disorders. Sometimes a single defective gene can be the cause of the problem, as it is in muscular dystrophy, a widespread disorder characterized by degeneration of the muscles. Likewise phenylketonuria, a metabolic disorder, and sickle-cell anemia, a blood disorder, result from disorders of single genes. (*See also* Genetic Disorders.)

### The History of Heredity Theory

An understanding of the basic process of heredity has been achieved only within the last century. Early theories were clouded by superstition. Ancient Greeks believed that blood was responsible for transmitting traits from one generation to the next. The expression bloodline, referring to particular lineage, stems from this ancient theory.

During the 18th century there were two prominent theories of heredity: ovist and preformationist views. Ovists believed that all traits were carried in the ovaries of the female, and that the male's sperm functioned only to stimulate embryonic development. As a result the mother was held responsible when she did not bear a male child. Preformationists believed that the male's sperm carried tiny, fully developed replicas of the infant and that the female's egg simply provided nourishment for the child before birth.

A theory widely held until the late 19th century was that hereditary traits resulted from a mixing of parental characteristics. Thus a short woman and tall man should have children of medium height. Another theory, now known to be false, was proposed in the 1800s by the French biologist Jean-Baptiste Lamarck.

He suggested that animals acquired traits and passed them on to their offspring. Thus he presumed that giraffes were born with long necks because their parents were constantly stretching their own necks to feed from tall trees.

Modern genetic and heredity theory had its beginnings in 1866, when Gregor Mendel, an Austrian monk, published the results of his crossbreeding experiments with pea plants. He produced plants that were either tall or short, with flowers that were either red or white. From his experiments, Mendel concluded that certain hereditary factors—now called genes—were present in the sex cells of both male and female plants. He reasoned that the combination of these factors in the two sex cells resulted in the traits expressed in the offspring. From his studies, Mendel derived certain basic laws of heredity: hereditary factors do not mix but remain segregated; some factors are dominant, while others are recessive; each member of the parental generation transmits only half of its hereditary factors to each offspring; and different offspring of the same parents receive different sets of hereditary factors. Mendel's work became the foundation for modern genetics.

The infant science of genetics flowered rapidly. By 1902 Walter Sutton of the United States had proposed that chromosomes were the site of Mendel's hereditary factors. In 1910 the American geneticist Thomas Hunt Morgan began his studies of the fruit fly, *Drosophila melanogaster.* Morgan provided evidence not only that genes occur on chromosomes, but also that those genes lying close together on the same chromosome form linkage groups that tend to be inherited together. He further showed that linkage groups often break apart naturally as a result of a phenomenon called crossing over.

During the mid-1900s great advances were made in the understanding of the exact structure and working of genes and DNA, including the deduction of the molecular structure of DNA in 1953 by James Watson and Francis Crick. These developments led to the deciphering of the genetic code of the DNA molecule, which in turn made possible the recombinant DNA techniques that hold immense potential for genetic engineering (*see* Genetic Engineering).

Early in the history of genetic study, there arose a heated debate that is often termed the heredity-environment, or nature-nurture, controversy, a concern among biologists and sociologists regarding the relative roles of heredity versus physical and social surroundings in the total development of an individual. Today it is generally conceded that the genetic background allows certain ranges of expression on which the environment acts to produce individual modification. For example, a trait that is primarily hereditary—skin color in humans—may be modified by environmental influences—suntanning. And conversely, a trait sensitive to environmental modifications—weight in humans—is also genetically conditioned. Thus the development of a trait may be manipulated by environmental changes, and in different environments the carriers of similar genetic traits may develop and behave in different ways.

The most powerful force for changing the number of particular genes within a given population, called gene frequency, is the force of natural selection, first hypothesized by Charles Darwin in the 1800s (*see* Darwin, Charles). Darwin observed that organisms with harmful physical or behavioral variations were more likely to die before they could bear young than those with useful variations. In the language of genetics and heredity, the carriers of some genes may survive more often or be more prolific than the carriers of other genes. Thus certain genes are more efficiently transmitted to succeeding generations than other genes, and the "inferior" genes become less frequent with each successive generation.

When such inequality of the transmission rates of genes is imposed by human will, the result is artificial selection, widely practiced in animal husbandry and agriculture. One of its most impressive successes to date is represented by hybrid corn, which is planted by farmers in order to increase their corn yields. Hybrid corn is the result of artificially crossing inbred corn strains. The hybrid assumes the superior traits of the inbred strains and is more vigorous and productive than the original strains alone.

Modern genetic and heredity studies cover a broad spectrum of phenomena. They include population genetics, the study of genetic patterns within populations; classical genetics, how traits are transmitted and expressed; microbial genetics, the heredity of microorganisms; and molecular genetics, the molecular study of genes and related structures. Knowledge gained from these studies has been applied to the diagnosis, prevention, and treatment of hereditary diseases; to the breeding of plants and animals; and to the development of industrial processes that use microorganisms.

J. Whitfield Gibbons

Lee Boltin

*Hermes, the messenger of the gods, was portrayed in a variety of ways by ancient Greek sculptors. This bronze figurine, 22.8 centimeters high, is in the British Museum.*

**HERMES.** In Greek mythology the god Hermes was considered a subtle schemer. Called Mercurius (Mercury) by the Romans, he was the son of Zeus and Maia, daughter of Atlas. When he was only a few hours old he escaped from his cradle and went out in search of adventures. He stretched cords across a tortoise shell, inventing the lyre.

That evening he stole the oxen of Apollo, god of the sun, hid them in a cave, and killed two of the oxen. When Apollo discovered what had happened, Hermes charmed him by playing on the lyre, and Apollo allowed him to go unpunished. Hermes gave his lyre to Apollo. In return Apollo gave Hermes a magic wand, called the caduceus, which bestowed wealth and prosperity and turned everything it touched into gold. (*See also* Apollo.)

Hermes was the messenger of the gods, and one of his duties was to conduct the ghosts of the dead to the lower world. Among men he became the patron of merchants and the god of eloquence, good fortune, and prudence, as well as cunning, fraud, and theft. He was also the god of the roads and the protector of

travelers. Pillars topped with his image were used as guideposts along roadways. Hermes was often represented as a slender youth, wearing winged sandals, a broad-brimmed hat adorned with two small wings, and holding the caduceus. (*See also* Mythology.)

**HERNIA.** The protrusion of an organ or tissue from the cavity that normally contains it is called a hernia. Hernias, or ruptures, can occur in many parts of the body. Soft abdominal tissue will frequently force its way through or between the abdominal muscles. These muscles normally hold the inner organs and tissues in place. They may become weak or slack, however, and then sudden increases in internal pressure—when a person coughs or lifts a heavy weight, for example—can cause the inner tissues to protrude through the muscles.

Some common types of hernias include an inguinal hernia, when the abdominal organs push through and appear as a bulge in the groin. This constitutes more than four fifths of all hernias and is most common in men. Another common type of hernia is a femoral hernia, a protrusion in the upper inside thigh. This common hernia occurs more often in women. A third type, common in newborn babies, is an umbilical hernia, a protrusion through the navel. This form of hernia usually heals naturally in a few years.

Most hernias can simply be pushed back into the abdomen—such hernias are called reducible. If a hernia cannot be pushed back into place, it is called irreducible. Hernias may become strangulated—that is, the protruding tissue may be so constricted that the circulation of blood within the tissue is cut off. Also, intestinal hernias may become obstructed and the intestinal contents prevented from moving through. These conditions may result in inflammation, infection, and gangrene and, if left untreated, may be fatal within a few hours or days.

**HEROD.** Two kings named Herod are mentioned in the New Testament. The first of these was Herod the Great, king of Judea under the Romans. The second, Herod Antipas, had John the Baptist put to death.

In about 47 BC, Antipater, father of Herod the Great, was appointed governor of Judea, Samaria, and Galilee by Julius Caesar. Herod the Great, also called Herod I, became king in 37 BC and ruled until his death in 4 BC. He was about 73 years old at the time when Jesus was born, and it was Herod who ordered the massacre of the children of Bethlehem.

Herod Antipas, son of Herod the Great, was tetrarch (governor) of Galilee. He questioned Jesus before the crucifixion. Earlier, Herod Antipas had divorced his wife and married his niece, Herodias. When John the Baptist denounced this marriage, Herod had him imprisoned. On Herod's birthday his stepdaughter, Salome, danced before him and his guests. Herod was delighted and told her she might ask for anything she wished. At the urging of her mother, she asked for the head of John the Baptist.

Herod had John executed, and the head was brought to Salome. Salome is not mentioned by name in the Bible. Flavius Josephus, a Jewish historian born about AD 37, tells the story in his book 'The Jewish Antiquities'. The story of Herod and John the Baptist was the subject of an opera by Richard Strauss and a play by Oscar Wilde.

**HERODOTUS** (484?–425? BC). Called the father of history, Herodotus was one of the most widely traveled people of his time. His writings show his interest in both history and geography.

Herodotus was born in Halicarnassus, a Greek colony in Asia Minor. He decided early in life to devote himself to literary pursuits. A frequent visitor to Athens, he was a close friend of Sophocles. He also journeyed to the western shores of the Black Sea, to southern Italy and Egypt, and to the Asian cities of Tyre, Babylon, Ecbatana, Nineveh, and Susa.

Herodotus's great history seeks to combine a general history of the Greeks and non-Greeks with the history of the wars between the Greeks and Persians.

He traces this conflict back to mythical times. Interwoven through the history are descriptions of the people and the countries he visited.

The narrative style of Herodotus is much like that of a storyteller. He includes anecdotes that throw light on the life and manners of the age he describes. His use of historical method—the careful accumulation of data, followed by deciding what conclusions the data support—greatly influenced later historians. (*See also* History; Persian Wars.)

**HERON.** Many of the long-legged wading birds living in the marshes of saltwater lagoons, freshwater lakes, and rivers are herons. Included in the heron family, Ardeidae, are bitterns, boatbills, and egrets. The word egret usually refers to the beautiful white-plumed birds. They are famous for the long plumes, or aigrettes, that are worn by the males during the breeding season.

Herons and egrets are expert fishermen. They stand like statues in the water until their keen eyes discover a fish swimming by. Then, at exactly the right instant, with one sudden jab of the bill, they seize their prey. Sometimes they stalk slowly through the shallow water, lifting each foot clear and setting it down again so gently that no ripple warns the fish or frog.

They live in nearly all parts of North and South America except the polar regions. They range in size from the small green heron to the great blue and the great white herons. A hundred or more birds often live in a single nesting site, or heronry. Their nests are crude platforms of sticks, usually placed in trees. The eggs number from three to six and are white or bluish green. Unlike cranes, with which they are often confused, herons and egrets fly with necks curved back so the head lies between the shoulders.

### The Herons of America

The great blue heron (*Ardea herodias*) ranges throughout the continental United States. It is 42 to 52 inches long. It is slaty blue on the back, wing coverts, and tail, with streaked gray under parts. A long black crest grows from the back of the head.

The green heron (*Butorides virescens*) is common in the eastern United States. A subspecies, Anthony's green heron, lives on the Pacific coast. This bird is 16 to 22 inches long. It has a black crown, reddish-brown neck, green back and wings, and grayish under parts with dark streaks. Unlike most herons, it is a solitary bird. It has a curious trick of "freezing." When it is startled it will fly to a perch and become absolutely rigid, with head and neck pointing skyward in line with the body. This posture, combined with the streaked breast and dark back, enables the bird to blend into the foliage and escape detection.

The great white heron (*Ardea occidentalis*), 48 to 54 inches long, has pure white plumage. It frequents southern Florida and the Florida Keys, where it nests in the mangrove swamps.

The black-crowned night heron (*Nycticorax nycticorax*) breeds throughout the United States

Stephen J. Krasemann—Peter Arnold, Inc.

*The beautiful plumage of the snowy egret nearly caused the bird's extinction. Hunters killed the birds to sell the plumes for women's hats and other decoration.*

and New Jersey and along the Gulf coast through Central America, the West Indies, and South America. The rare reddish egret (*Dichromanassa rufescens*) breeds along the Gulf coast and in southern Florida.

To the egrets, beauty proved a curse, for their feathers were used to adorn hats and dresses. Once found by the tens of thousands, the birds were almost exterminated. Thanks to the Audubon societies, which obtained and enforced protective laws, they are again on the increase. (*See also* Birds.)

**HERPES** *see* **SEXUALLY TRANSMITTED DISEASE.**

**HERRICK, Robert** (1591–1674). A leading Cavalier poet of 17th-century England, Robert Herrick is read for the diversity and perfection of his works, which range from odes and folk songs to epigrams and love lyrics. Herrick excels in the kind of poetry that comes closest to music, by its "concord of sweet sounds," and its precision of outline.

Robert Herrick was born in August 1591 in London. He was one of seven children of Nicholas Herrick, a goldsmith. His father died when he was about a year old, and a wealthy uncle, Sir William Herrick, became his guardian. At 16 young Herrick was apprenticed to the uncle, who was also a goldsmith. Herrick showed more interest in poetry than in learning the trade, so his uncle sent him to Cambridge University. He graduated from Cambridge in 1617 and earned a master's degree there in 1620. In 1623 he became a priest in the Church of England.

Herrick was appointed vicar of Dean Prior, Devonshire, in 1629. Because of his loyalty to Charles

*Robert Herrick*

Culver Pictures, Inc.

mainland, excluding Alaska. It is two feet long. The crown and upper back are black, the lower back, wings, and tail ashy gray. Less common is the yellow-crowned night heron (*Nyctanassa violacea*), which has a more southerly range. The little blue heron (*Florida caerulea*) and the Louisiana heron (*Hydranassa tricolor*) are common in the Southern states from North Carolina to central Texas.

The most beautiful birds of the heron family are the egrets, represented in the United States by three species. The common egret (*Casmerodius alba*) is a white bird 37 to 42 inches long, not to be confused with the larger great white heron. It breeds from southeastern Oregon and Minnesota, Ohio, and New Jersey southward through Mexico and Central and South America. During the nesting season it wears a magnificent train of about 50 straight aigrette plumes that grow from between the shoulder blades and reach beyond the tail. Even more gorgeous is the nuptial dress of the snowy egret (*Egretta thula*), which breeds in northern California, Idaho, Colorado, Oklahoma,

I, he lost the appointment in 1646, when the Commonwealth government came to power. In 1648 he published his only book, 'Hesperides', a collection of 1,400 poems. This volume includes a separate section entitled 'His Noble Numbers', which is made up of religious poetry. Like his friend Ben Jonson, Herrick was inspired by the classical poets. Association with the court musicians of London influenced his poems. At Devonshire he wrote many of his nature poems and perfected his other work. A recurring theme in his poetry is the swift passage of time—reflected, for example, in 'To the Virgins':

> Gather ye rosebuds while ye may,
> Old Time is still aflying,
> And this same flower that smiles today
> Tomorrow will be dying.

Herrick never married. After the restoration of the monarchy he returned to Devonshire in 1662. He died there in October 1674. (*See also* English Literature.)

**HERRING FAMILY.** In AD 240 the Roman historian Solinus wrote that the people of the Hebrides islands, located off Scotland's northwest coast, lived on fish and milk. That fish was herring. Herring and related fishes in the Clupeidae family have been economically significant for hundreds of years to countries bordering the Atlantic and Pacific oceans. In addition to the herring, other commercially valuable fish in this group are shad, menhaden, alewife, and the pilchard, or sardine. (*See also* Fish; Fisheries.)

The 175 species in 46 genera in the herring family all share the same basic physical characteristics. Most are less than 18 inches (46 centimeters) long, but a few, such as the American shad, may reach 30 inches (76 centimeters) in length. All clupeids are plankton feeders. The body is deeply compressed laterally and covered with scales, which form a sharp ridge along the centerline of the belly.

The Atlantic herring (*Clupea harengus*) is abundant off the coasts of North America and Europe. It also lives in the southern Atlantic, but only in the north is it plentiful enough to support commercial fisheries.

The Pacific herring (*C. pallasii*) is widely distributed in the North Pacific from San Diego to Alaska and along the Asian coast from the Kuril Islands south to Japan and Korea. It is a significant part of fisheries in Japan and Russia and is included in the diets of sharks, sea lions, and waterfowl.

One of several species in the genus *Alosa*, the American shad (*A. sapidissima*) is found from the St. Lawrence River south to Florida. Introduced to the Pacific coast several times between 1871 and 1886, it now thrives between Alaska and central California. The shad spends most of its life in the ocean, but in spring it swims up rivers to spawn. Some migrate as far as 300 miles (480 kilometers), where they remain until autumn. Dams and pollution in the rivers have sharply curtailed the commercial shad industry.

The alewife (*A. pseudoharengus*) is another food fish that spawns in fresh water. The alewife population in

*Atlantic herring* (Clupea harengus)

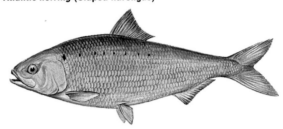

*American shad* (Alosa sapidissima)

*Menhaden* (Brevoortia tyrannus)

*Sardine* (Sardinops caerula)

the St. Lawrence Seaway and Great Lakes multiplied so rapidly in the 1960s that they threatened native fishes by competing for the same food sources. This was remedied in the 1970s with the importation of coho and king salmon, which live on a diet of alewives.

Menhaden (*Brevoortia tyrannus*) lives in warm temperate waters off eastern North and South America. Three other species of menhaden exist off the Atlantic coast of North America. Menhaden is easily caught with a purse seine because it often schools near the surface in shoals of hundreds of thousands. The United States lands seven times as much menhaden as herring. It is used in the manufacture of fertilizer and animal food. Humans do not consume this fat oily fish but it is eaten by many marine animals including swordfish, sharks, whales, and dolphins. Menhaden is preyed upon by bluefishes and striped bass.

Although young herring is canned and sold as sardines, the only true sardines are pilchards. The California pilchard or Pacific sardine (*Sardinops caerula*) is found in waters off south Alaska to Cape San Lucas and throughout the Gulf of California. Pilchards are also found along the Pacific coast of

South America and in waters off New Zealand, Australia, and Japan.

The first cannery for the Pacific sardine was established in 1889. The catch increased steadily until it reached 68 thousand tons between World War I and World War II. But in 1944 the fishery collapsed, probably because of overfishing, and the industry never recovered.

Barbara Katz

**HERSCHEL, William** (1738–1822). The founder of modern stellar astronomy was a German-born organist, William Herschel. His discovery of Uranus in 1781 was the first identification of a planet since ancient times. Herschel developed theories of the structure of nebulas and the evolution of stars, cataloged many binary stars, and made significant modifications in the reflecting telescope. He also proved that the solar system moves through space and discovered infrared radiation.

Friedrich Wilhelm Herschel was born in Hannover, Germany, on Nov. 15, 1738. When he was 21 he moved to England to work as a musician and later taught music, wrote symphonies, and conducted. Herschel made observations of the sun at an early age but was 43 before he became a professional astronomer.

He discovered Uranus with the first reflecting telescope that he built. The discovery brought him an appointment as astronomer for George III, and he was able to spend all his time studying the stars. He was knighted in 1816. Herschel's observations of binary stars demonstrated that gravity governed the stars as well as the solar system. Herschel died in Slough, England, on Aug. 25, 1822.

William Herschel's son, John Herschel, continued his father's study of binary stars and made the first telescopic study of the Southern Hemisphere while at the Cape of Good Hope, South Africa (1834–38). A chemist and physicist, he also made contributions to photography, spectroscopic analysis, and crystallography.

**HERTZ, Heinrich** (1857–94). As the 19th century drew to a close, a number of important discoveries in the field of physics were made. One of them—the discovery of electromagnetic radiation—was the achievement of Heinrich Hertz, a German physicist. Hertz's research paved the way for the development of radio, television, and radar.

Heinrich Rudolf Hertz was born in Hamburg, Germany, on Feb. 22, 1857. His father was a prominent lawyer and legislator. In his youth Heinrich enjoyed building instruments in the family workshop.

Hertz began his college studies at the University of Munich. After a short time he transferred to the University of Berlin, where he received his Doctor of Philosophy degree magna cum laude. In Berlin he was an assistant to Hermann von Helmholtz, one of the foremost physicists of the time. In 1883 Hertz became a lecturer in theoretical physics at the University of Kiel. Two years later he was appointed

professor of physics at Karlsruhe Polytechnic. In 1886 Hertz married Elizabeth Doll, daughter of a Karlsruhe professor; they had two daughters.

In the 1880s physicists were trying to obtain experimental evidence of electromagnetic waves. Their existence had been predicted in 1873 by the mathematical equations of James Clerk Maxwell, a British scientist (*see* Maxwell; Radiation).

In 1887 Hertz tested Maxwell's hypothesis. He used an oscillator made of polished brass knobs, each connected to an induction coil and separated by a tiny gap over which sparks could leap. Hertz reasoned that, if Maxwell's predictions were correct, electromagnetic waves would be transmitted during each series of sparks. To confirm this, Hertz made a simple receiver of looped wire. At the ends of the loop were small knobs separated by a tiny gap. The receiver was placed several yards from the oscillator. According to theory, if electromagnetic waves were spreading from the oscillator sparks, they would induce a current in the loop that would send sparks across the gap. This occurred when Hertz turned on the oscillator, producing the first transmission and reception of electromagnetic waves.

Hertz also noted that electrical conductors reflect the waves and that they can be focused by concave reflectors. He found that nonconductors allow most of the waves to pass through. Another of his discoveries was the photoelectric effect (*see* Electronics, "History"). In 1889 Hertz was appointed professor of physics at the University of Bonn. He died in Bonn on Jan. 1, 1894.

**HERZEN, Aleksandr** (1812–70). The Decembrist revolt of 1825 against Czar Nicholas I of Russia inspired journalist Aleksandr Herzen to devote his life to the overthrow of the old order. His goal was a distinctive Russian form of socialism based on peasant communes. His efforts were a failure in the end, but in his autobiography, 'My Past and Thoughts', published principally from 1861 to 1867, he created one of the finest works of Russian prose.

Aleksandr Ivanovich Herzen was born on April 6, 1812, in Moscow, the illegitimate son of a wealthy nobleman. He attended the University of Moscow from 1829 to 1833. His political theories led to his arrest in 1834, and he was exiled for eight years, working in a provincial government office.

Herzen inherited a considerable fortune upon his father's death in 1846, and he left Russia to live in Europe. From Paris (1846–52), London (1852–65), and Geneva (1865–70) he published his theories, hoping to foment a revolution in Russia. He wavered between hope for governmental reform and radical socialism, eventually losing most of his supporters. For ten years (1857–67) he published a newspaper, *Kolokol* (The Bell), trying to influence government policy in Russia. By 1865 the younger generation of revolutionary exiles in Geneva was no longer interested in his ideas. He devoted his time to his autobiography. He died in Paris on Jan. 21, 1870.

**HERZL, Theodor** (1860–1904). The founder of modern political Zionism was Theodor Herzl. His efforts gave impetus to a 50-year campaign that culminated in the establishment of Israel in 1948. In 1894, as Paris correspondent for a Vienna newspaper, he covered the treason trial of Alfred Dreyfus, a Jewish officer in the French army. The display of anti-Semitism he witnessed swayed him from his conviction that Jews could eliminate anti-Semitism by assimilating into their chosen countries. The only solution, he became convinced, was for a majority of Jews to emigrate to a country of their own.

Theodor Herzl was born on May 2, 1860, in Budapest, Hungary, to well-to-do, middle class parents. As a boy he showed an interest in writing while studying in a scientific secondary school.

In 1884 he earned a doctor of laws degree at the University of Vienna. Soon afterward he abandoned his legal career to become a successful critic, playwright, and essayist. For a number of years he also became a journalist.

In 1896, fired by the experience of the Dreyfus trial, Herzl wrote a brochure called 'The Jewish State'. In it he called for the establishment of a new land for the Jews. To further this goal he convened a series of international Zionist congresses, the first of which was held at Basel, Switzerland, in 1897. These led to the formation of the World Zionist Organization.

Herzl met with many world leaders in his attempts to establish a Jewish state. In lengthy negotiations he sought unsuccessfully to win the Turkish sultan's approval for large-scale Jewish immigration into Palestine. The Zionist congress that met in 1903

rejected a British offer of land for Jewish settlement in Uganda in East Africa. The controversy over the issue discouraged Herzl. Exhausted by his efforts, he died in Edlach, Austria, on July 3, 1904. In 1949 his body was taken to Israel, where Mount Herzl near Jerusalem was established as a tribute to his memory. (*See also* Zionism.)

**HESIOD** (9th century BC). Except for the works of Homer, the epics of Hesiod are the earliest Greek writings to come down to the present. His 'Theogony' relates the myths about the gods, and 'Works and Days' is a book of wisdom literature that traces the decline of humanity from an early golden age.

Hesiod was a native of the village of Ascra in Boeotia, a district in central Greece. Little is known of his life except what he tells in 'Works and Days', in which he criticizes his brother Perses for having made off with the bulk of their inheritance. The poet traveled once to Chalcis on the island of Euboea for a contest of poets. Legend says he was a shepherd until the Muses, inspirers of poetry, endowed him with talent and commanded him to "sing of the race of the blessed gods immortal."

'Theogony' is the earlier of his two books. It relates the history of the gods and of creation, culminating with the triumph of Zeus as the supreme god (*see* Zeus). 'Works and Days' is a more personal narrative. It is addressed to his greedy brother in an attempt to make him change his ways. Hesiod tells of the need for honesty and hard work by using two myths. The first is the story of Pandora, who opened a jar to unleash evils on humanity. Next he traces the decline from a golden age through the silver, bronze, and heroic periods down to his own time.

**HESSE, Hermann** (1877–1962). In the 1960s many of the books written by Hermann Hesse became cult novels for the college-age generation. His emphasis on personal self-realization, youth's search for meaning, and Eastern mysticism gained him a temporary wide following. The novels were written in an earlier period, but something in them appealed to a latter-day young audience. Among his works are 'Beneath the Wheel', published in 1906, 'Demian' (1919), 'Siddhartha' (1922), 'Steppenwolf' (1929), 'Narcissus and Goldmund' (1930), and 'Magister Ludi' (1943). He was awarded the Nobel prize for literature in 1946.

Hesse was born in Calw, Germany, on July 2, 1877. He studied at Maulbronn Seminary to become a missionary but could not adapt himself to the work. In 1904 he became a writer and brought out his first novel, 'Peter Camenzind'. He lived in neutral Switzerland during World War I and became a citizen in 1923. Personal problems led him into psychoanalysis, an experience reflected in 'Demian' about a troubled adolescent who achieves self-awareness. The novel made his reputation. Hesse died in Montagnola, Switzerland, on Aug. 9, 1962.

**Theodor Herzl in 1904**

Courtesy of the Zionist Archives and Library, New York

*Thor Heyerdahl stands next to his craft* **Kon-Tiki.**

**HEYERDAHL, Thor** (born 1914). The Kon-Tiki Museum in Oslo, Norway, contains the primitive ocean-going vessels that Thor Heyerdahl used to prove the possibility of transoceanic contact between ancient, widely separated civilizations. His expeditions were successful, but his theories have not been generally accepted by more academic anthropologists.

Heyerdahl was born in Larvik, Norway, on Oct. 6, 1914. He attended the University of Oslo (1933–36), where he specialized in zoology and geography. A year in the Marquesas Islands in the South Pacific turned his interest to anthropology. Fascinated by the similarity between legends about the Polynesian hero Tiki and the Peruvian leader Kon-Tiki, he set out to prove that an ocean voyage between the west coast of South America and Polynesia could have been made by ancient Indians and that the Polynesians might have originated in South America. In 1947 he and a small crew on the raft *Kon-Tiki* made such a voyage.

In 1970 Heyerdahl succeeded in crossing the Atlantic Ocean from Morocco to Barbados on the *Ra II*, a facsimile of an ancient Egyptian reed boat, to prove that pre-Columbian civilizations of Central America could have been influenced by Egypt. His *Tigris* expedition of 1977 sailed 4,000 miles, from Iraq, across the Arabian Sea to Pakistan, ending in the Red Sea, to prove possible contact by the ancient Sumerians with southwest Asia and the Arabian peninsula. Heyerdahl published his exploits in 'Kon-Tiki' (1950), 'The Ra Expeditions' (1971), and 'The Tigris Expedition' (1979).

**HEZBOLLAH.** The Party of God, or Hezbollah, began as an Islamic terrorist organization in Lebanon in 1981-82 and transformed itself into a freedom-fighting organization/political party in the late 1990s.

Hezbollah was founded with funding from Iran, in an attempt to fight the Israeli occupation of southern Lebanon. Hezbollah fighters reportedly used any means possible to do so, allegedly including the suicide bombings of United States diplomats and military forces in Lebanon, and the kidnapping of Western hostages. As a result of Hezbollah's fight against the Israeli occupation of what Israel calls the Security Zone, Israel promised in the year 2000 to withdraw from southern Lebanon by July of 2000. Hezbollah used other of its monies to win over the Lebanese people by funding schools, hospitals, clinics, and a television station, and by starting up their own political party, which advocated several fairly liberal policies. By the year 2000 they held several seats in parliament. Despite all of these actions, Hezbollah was still on the U.S. State Department's list of terrorist organizations as of 2000.

**HIAWATHA.** Long one of the favorite characters of American folklore, Hiawatha was an American Indian who is best known as the hero of Henry Wadsworth Longfellow's narrative poem, 'The Song of Hiawatha', published in 1855. In Longfellow's poem, Hiawatha is a member of the Ojibwa tribe.

Raised by his grandmother, Nokomis, Hiawatha is able to talk to the animals of the forest and surpasses all the other boys of his tribe in manly skills. He grows up to be a leader of his people, marries the Indian maiden Minnehaha, and acts as a peacemaker among warring tribes.

'The Song of Hiawatha' was inspired largely by Indian legends told by the student of Indian lore Henry Rowe Schoolcraft. Longfellow, like Schoolcraft, confused Hiawatha with the Ojibwa Manabozho. The hero of the poem is thus a composite of tribal legends.

The real Hiawatha was a Mohawk Indian chief who lived in the late 1500s. He was a founder of the Iroquois Confederacy. Tradition credits him with introducing maize and fish oil to his people and with originating picture writing, new navigation techniques, and the practice of medicine.

**HIBERNATION.** Before northern winters begin many birds travel south to warmer climates. Some four-footed animals go southward too. Hardy creatures such as rabbits and foxes stay where they are and live as actively as they do in summertime.

Many animals, however, neither travel southward nor remain active. Instead, they hide in sheltered places and become so quiet that they often seem to be dead. Although it is sometimes said that they "go to sleep" for the winter, they really hibernate.

Many insects hibernate as larvae or grubs. These hide under dead leaves, lie in rotting wood, or burrow into the ground. Most caterpillars (young butterflies and moths) turn into hard-shelled chrysalids or pupae. Often caterpillars lie covered by silky cocoons that they spin.

Mourning cloak butterflies, however, spend the winter as full-grown insects. They hide among logs, under leaves, or in cracks covered by loose bark. On warm winter days the butterflies often crawl out and

*The Eastern American chipmunk* (Tamias striatus) *is dormant for periods of one to eight days, awakening occasionally to eat food that it has stored in its burrow.*

flutter about in the sunshine. Ladybird beetles, or ladybugs, also come out on warm days, but they do not hide alone as butterflies do. Instead they gather in great swarms.

Most freshwater fish remain active all winter, though carp and bass become sluggish and probably do not eat. In the sea, certain flounders and the widemouthed toadfish wriggle into the mud and hibernate under shallow inlets and bays.

American toads push their way down into the ground. Tree frogs hide in hollow trees, but adult green frogs sprawl out under stones in ponds and streams. Their tadpoles lie in soft mud. Snakes find shelter in holes and rocky dens. If these holes or dens are large enough, dozens or even hundreds of snakes may gather and spend the winter in tangled balls. Box turtles burrow into soft ground, while painted turtles dig burrows in the banks of streams. Mud turtles and others bury themselves in mud on the bottoms of ponds.

Before migration was understood, people thought birds hibernated in caves or underwater. After migration was discovered, no birds were thought to hibernate. But in 1946 birds related to whippoorwills were found, apparently hibernating, on a mountain in southern California. There are signs and research data suggesting that other birds may become sluggish or even dormant in winter.

Woodchucks are the best-known hibernators among mammals. They are the "groundhogs" which are said

to come out of their burrows on February 2 but go back for six more weeks of winter if they see their shadows. Actually, woodchucks go into burrows four or five feet (1.2 to 1.5 meters) underground in September or October. There they stay without moving until March. Ground squirrels, jumping mice, and some bats also hibernate, for four to seven months.

Bears are less perfect hibernators. In the southern United States they remain active all through the year. In the North, black bears hibernate when winter comes, but when the cubs are born, their mothers care for them and nurse them. On warm winter days the male bears often wander about. Red squirrels and skunks, among other animals, do the same, and badgers as far south as Iowa hibernate during only the coldest weather.

### Hibernation Differs from Sleep

Such animals seem to spend much of their time dozing or in sleep. Sleeping is very different from hibernation. Sleeping animals relax, but their way of living does not change. True hibernators, however, almost stop living. Many insects, spiders, and snails are frozen solid; some frogs and northern fish are partly frozen. Woodchucks become cooler and cooler, till their bodies are only a little warmer than the air in their burrows. The animals also breathe very slowly, while the beating of their hearts both slows down and becomes irregular. If the weather becomes dangerously cold they "awaken," move about, and raise the

*Mourning cloak butterflies* (Nymphalis antiopa), *unlike most other butterfly species, hibernate as full-grown adults (left). This one was found hibernating alone under a board that had been placed on a leaf. The heart of the bullfrog* (Rana catesbeiana) *slows down so much that the bullfrog becomes partly frozen while hibernating in mud (right).*

temperatures of their bodies. Any that fail to do this freeze to death.

Depending on the species and its habitat, certain kinds of chipmunks take food into their burrows and eat it when they are active on warm winter days. Most put on very little body fat and so rely on this stored food for survival. Almost all animals that hibernate prepare for it during summer by eating large amounts of food, which they convert to thick layers of fat. Woodchucks, ground squirrels, and bears eat so much before hibernation that their bodies become very plump. Even turtles, snakes, and frogs accumulate fat which provides energy for life during the months when they do not eat.

Animals inherit the tendency to hibernate, just as they inherit other characteristics. But this tendency is influenced by other factors, such as cold, the animal's fat stores, and darkness.

Cold is the most important factor encouraging hibernation. Ground squirrels, snakes, insects, and other animals become sluggish as soon as the weather grows chilly, and as it turns colder they become dormant. Skunks, some chipmunks, and badgers also take to their burrows as autumn weather turns cold.

### Fatness Affects Hibernation

Bats hibernate when food becomes scarce, though woodchucks retire to their burrows while it is plentiful. Mountain marmots hibernate during the first autumn snowstorm if they have thick coats of fat. Otherwise they come out after the storm and keep on eating. Ground squirrels that fatten on scraps and gifts of food from people hibernate two to four weeks earlier than others that are not so well fed. The fattest animals remain dormant longest.

Darkness and quiet are very important. Most animals hibernate in dark places and, when the time

comes for them to do so, they try to get away from light. Even insects that normally fly or crawl toward bright light seem to be attracted by dark cracks and corners when autumn comes.

Animals that hibernate in burrows or dens are always sheltered from noise. Therefore, noise does not disturb hibernating ground squirrels and woodchucks. In zoos, which are noisy as well as light, many animals that normally hibernate remain active during the winter.

Estivation differs from hibernation, since it takes place during the summer. In deserts, winter and spring are the times of plentiful food, water, and comfortable temperatures. Summers are dry and very hot, and food often becomes very scarce. Certain desert ground squirrels therefore take to their burrows in June or July and remain there several months. The desert tortoise of the southwestern United States both hibernates and estivates.

Scientists are studying the secrets of hibernation in order to help humans. For example, woodchucks have been used in research on the reduction of body temperature (hypothermia), which is now employed in some types of heart surgery.

Anticipating the problems of astronauts on long journeys to other planets, space scientists are investigating hibernation. Since the process slows such vital functions as heartbeat and breathing rate—without damage to the brain or other parts of the body—induced hibernation could aid space travelers. Less need for oxygen and food would solve storage problems, and the state of coma would alleviate the psychological stress of long confinement in spaceships. Although hibernation cannot be induced by manipulating the environment, injection with brain substances from the ground squirrel has caused other animals to hibernate.

**HIBISCUS.** The largest group of plants in the mallow (Malvaceae) family is the genus *Hibiscus,* which includes about 250 species of herbs, shrubs, and small trees. Some are delicate tropical blooms; others are hardy and grow almost anywhere.

Plants of the *Hibiscus* genus are characterized by large, showy flowers with deep-colored bases. The blossoms may be white, cream, yellow, pink, crimson, magenta, or purple-blue. Some varieties of the hibiscus change from white or yellow in the morning to pink or red in the afternoon.

Among the types cultivated in gardens are the Rose of Sharon (*Hibiscus syriacus*), a tall, late-flowering shrub, and the swamp rose mallow (*H. moscheutos*). Hybrid forms of the swamp rose mallow have been developed to yield more striking flowers.

The pods of another species (*H. esculentus*) are known as okra, or gumbo, and are popular as a food. A fiber plant (*H. cannabinus*) supplies a jute substitute. The herb roselle (*H. sabdariffa*) yields a fruit, similar to the cranberry, that is made into jelly or beverages. The tropical musk mallow, or abelmosk (*H. moschatus*), is valued for its musk-scented seeds, used in perfumes and to flavor coffee.

The origin of the word hibiscus is not certain. In Latin, the word means "marshmallow." Some authorities on the history of flowers trace the name to the ibis, a heronlike marsh bird that is said to feed on certain species of the hibiscus.

**HICKOK, Wild Bill** (1837–76). As a scout, stagecoach driver, and marshal of Midwestern towns, Wild Bill Hickok gained a wide reputation for courage and for his skill with a gun. His deeds—real and legendary—make up some of the most colorful stories of early days on the American frontier.

James Butler Hickok was born in Troy Grove, Ill., on May 27, 1837. In 1855 he fled Illinois after a fight. He worked for a time at farming and later joined General James Lane's Kansas free-state force. Hickok's first experience as a law officer was in Monticello, Kan. He also served as an Indian scout and drove a stagecoach on the Santa Fe and Oregon trails. During the Civil War Hickok was a Union scout.

After the war the cattle business grew, and lawlessness flourished in the Kansas border towns. Hickok became deputy marshal of Fort Riley in 1866 and marshal of Hays City and Abilene in 1869 and 1871, respectively.

In 1872 Hickok joined Buffalo Bill Cody's Wild West Show but left after two years. The lure of gold drew him to the Black Hills of the Dakota Territory. On Aug. 2, 1876, he was shot and killed while playing poker in a saloon at Deadwood. The hand he held—a pair of black eights and a pair of black aces—is now known as the "dead man's hand." (*See also* Calamity Jane.)

**HICKORY.** The most typically American trees are the hickories, particularly the shagbark. From the hard wood of this tree the pioneers made ax handles, wagon wheels and shafts, and other implements. They burned the wood in stoves and smoked meats with it. In the autumn they harvested the hickory nuts. The shagbark and certain other hickories serve these same purposes and many more today. For many of these uses, second-growth hickory is preferred. This is the wood of trees that have sprung up where old hickory groves were cut down and is heavier and stronger than that of old-growth hickories.

The shagbark (*Carya ovata*) grows throughout the eastern half of the United States. It thrives in rich bottomlands but is also found on low hills. It grows very slowly, but when 200 to 300 years old, it may be 80 to 100 feet (24 to 30 meters) tall and 2 to 3 feet (0.6 to 0.9 meter) in diameter.

Three other hickories are also important for their wood. The shellbark hickory (*C. laciniosa*) closely resembles the shagbark; it grows in the Ohio and Mississippi river valleys. The pignut hickory (*C. glabra*) grows on uplands east of the Mississippi. Its wood is sometimes heavier and harder than that of the shagbark, and the nuts are often very bitter. The mockernut hickory (*C. tomentosa*) is like the shagbark in wood and size but has round bark ridges.

Hickories belong to the genus *Carya* or *Hicoria* of the walnut family (Juglandaceae). There are about 18 species, most of them natives of eastern North America. Three species are native to eastern Asia. Those in the United States are classified either as true hickories, valued chiefly for their wood, or as pecan hickories, prized for their nuts (*see* Pecan).

**HICKS, Edward** (1780–1849). A painter of signs and carriages, as well as a popular preacher, Edward Hicks is remembered best as an American primitive painter. He was especially fond of the idea of 'The Peaceable Kingdom', based on the Biblical quotation that begins, "The wolf shall dwell with the lamb . . . " (Isaiah 11:6–9). It is thought that Hicks may have completed as many as 100 versions of this painting, though only about 25 still exist.

Edward Hicks was born in Attleboro (now Langhorne), Pa., on April 4, 1780, during the Revolutionary War. His mother died when he was only a few years old, and Edward was adopted by David and Elizabeth Twining, who were prosperous Quaker farmers. Between the ages of 13 and 20 Hicks worked as an apprentice in a coach maker's shop, and it was there that he learned his trade. In 1803 he joined the Religious Society of Friends, or Quakers.

Hicks became a Quaker minister and was soon much in demand for his sermons. He settled in Newtown, Pa. Here he supported his family by maintaining a shop where he painted signs, carriages, and furniture and also produced the primitive art for which he is known. He died in Newtown on Aug. 23, 1849.

Hicks's favorite subject, 'The Peaceable Kingdom', with its carefully painted animals and children and showing William Penn and the Indians in the distance, seems to express the belief that the Quakers in some way represented the realization of Isaiah's prophecy.

*'Noah's Ark', painted by Edward Hicks when he was 67, is one of the best-known works of folk art in the United States. It is oil on canvas and measures 30½ by 26 ½ inches.*
Philadelphia Museum of Art, bequest of Lisa Norris Elkins (Mrs. William M. Elkins)

His first version of this painting dates from 1830. Other paintings for which he is known are 'The Falls of Niagara', painted about 1835; 'The Residence of David Twining' (1845–48); 'The Cornell Farm' (1848); and 'Noah's Ark', painted just before his death.

**HIDALGO Y COSTILLA, Miguel** (1753–1811). The Father of Mexican Independence, Miguel Hidalgo y Costilla is honored in Mexico as a leader in the revolt against Spain and as a pioneer in economic reforms for the peasants. A priest, he was executed by the Spanish as a traitor. September 16, the day he called the Mexican people to rise up against their Spanish oppressors, is celebrated as Mexico's Independence Day.

Miguel Hidalgo was born on May 8, 1753, near Guanajuato, Mexico, where his father, Cristobel Hidalgo y Costilla, managed a farm. He was the oldest of four sons. The Hidalgo family were Creoles, native Mexicans of Spanish descent. After attending the colleges of St. Francis Xavier and San Nicolás in Valladolid (now Morelia), Hidalgo earned his degree in theology from the National Autonomous University of Mexico. Five years later, in 1778, he became a Roman Catholic priest. He taught theology at San Nicolás and in 1791 became its rector. After service in two other parishes, he went to Dolores (now Dolores Hidalgo) in 1808. There Padre Hidalgo taught Spanish, introduced new farming methods, and started such small industries as pottery and brick making.

The Spanish took harsh measures to prevent Mexican independence. Spanish soldiers destroyed vineyards and silkworms. High taxes, racial discrimination, and slavery caused further unrest. The revolution began on Sept. 16, 1810, when Padre Hidalgo led an army of ragged, untrained peasants against the Spanish. Although they temporarily defeated the Spanish on Oct. 10, 1810, they were finally crushed. Padre Hidalgo was captured on March 21, 1811, and excommunicated. He was executed in Chihuahua on July 31, 1811. (*See also* Mexico; Latin America.)

**HIEROGLYPHICS.** Ancient Egyptians had three different writing systems. The oldest, best known, and most difficult to read is called hieroglyphics. The word, which means "sacred carving," was used by Greeks who saw the script on temple walls and public monuments. The Greeks were somewhat mistaken in their terminology because hieroglyphs were used on gravestones, statues, coffins, vessels, implements, and for all sorts of nonreligious texts—songs, legal documents, and historical inscriptions.

Hieroglyphic writing has two main characteristics: objects are portrayed as ideograms or pictures, and the picture signs have the phonetic, or sound, value of the words represented by the objects. Thus hieroglyphs are not pictures only: they can be spoken, as are words written in an alphabet such as that of English. A written text normally contains three kinds of hieroglyphs: ideograms, which are read as the words they represent; phonograms, which are signs that do not refer to the objects they picture: they simply stand for one or more consonants; and determinatives, which have no phonetic value but help the reader to determine the correct meaning of the text.

Hieroglyphics were established as a writing system by at least 3100 BC. The system remained in use for about 3,500 years. The last known hieroglyphic inscription is dated AD 394. In the earliest period there

Adapted from G. Möller in 'Zeitschrift des Deutschen Vereins für Buchwesen und Schrifttum', ii (1919), 78

| hieroglyphic | | | | hieratic | | | demotic |
|---|---|---|---|---|---|---|---|
| 2700–2600 BC | 2500–2400 BC | c. 1500 BC | 500–100 BC | c. 1900 BC | c. 1300 BC | c. 200 BC | 400–100 BC |

*The hieroglyphics and their hieratic and demotic equivalents give evidence of having evolved over several centuries. The symbols represent, top to bottom, three fox skins tied together, a whip, a harpoon, an adz, a stone jug, a scribe's outfit, and a roll of papyrus tied with a cord.*

were about 700 hieroglyphs. In this first stage of writing only the absolutely necessary symbols were invented. In the second stage of development easier readability was achieved by increasing the number of signs and by using determinatives. After the second stage, a period of about 2,000 years during which the system was essentially unaltered, the number of symbols increased to several thousand. (*See also* Alphabet.)

The other two Egyptian writing systems are hieratic and demotic. These are cursive scripts. Like modern handwriting, they are flowing, and the letters of words are joined. Hieratic (from the Greek *hieratikos*, meaning "priestly") got its name at a time when it was used only for religious texts. Everyday documents, especially government texts, were written in demotic (from the Greek word *dēmotikos*, meaning "for the people").

Both of these writing forms are based on hieroglyphics. Hieratic script was, like hieroglyphics, in use from about 3100 BC. It was originally written in vertical columns and later in horizontal rows from right to left. After 660 BC demotic script replaced hieratic in most ordinary writing, but hieratic remained in use by priests for several more centuries. (*See also* Writing.)

Hieroglyphics were not deciphered until the early 19th century. This was made possible by the discovery of the Rosetta Stone in 1799 by members of Napoleon's expedition to Egypt. This basalt stone, now in the British Museum, contains identical texts in hieroglyphics, demotic, and Greek (for picture*see* Egypt, Ancient). A French linguist and historian, Jean-François Champollion, succeeded in translating the Rosetta Stone in 1822.

**HIKING.** Distance walking for exercise or pleasure is called hiking. The word first came into use around 1809 and is probably derived from the verb "hitch." Hiking is one of the easiest and least expensive ways to get exercise and promote physical fitness.

Many individuals go walking alone on a regular basis, and there are clubs that sponsor group hikes. The Ramblers' Association in Great Britain and the Wilderness Society in the United States are two of the many organizations that encourage hiking by preserving footpaths and by securing rights of way in parkland and forests. The Appalachian Trail Conference has member organizations in 14 states and maintains campsites and a trail more than 2,000 miles (3,200 kilometers) long from Maine to Georgia.

The normal length of a hike is from 7 to 12 miles (11 to 19 kilometers) for half a day and from 12 to 20 miles (19 to 32 kilometers) for a full day. Most American states and European countries have set aside hiking trails in the countryside surrounding densely populated areas.

Hiking, in addition to being a sport in itself, is basic to several other sporting activities. It constitutes a large part of mountain climbing. The most tiring hours of mountaineering are spent on the lower trails, climbing slowly and steadily upward. Backpack camping, hunting, cross-country skiing, and snowshoeing are other sports in which hiking plays a significant role. The ability to walk long distances without tiring also enhances field trips, bird watching, rock collecting, and ordinary sightseeing.

In some countries, notably England, Sweden, and The Netherlands, hiking is used as a test of fitness. In Sweden it was made a national fitness test in the early 1930s. The Nijmegen marches in The Netherlands are organized by the Dutch League of Physical Culture. They are open to people from all parts of the world in civilian and military categories. The test includes four days of consecutive walking over distances up to 35 miles (56 kilometers) each day.

Those who take hiking seriously wear well-made boots or shoes and carry supplies with them—such things as first-aid kits, flashlights, rain gear, accurate topographical maps, food, water, and perhaps a compass. These can be carried in a backpack, leaving the hands free for getting through forests and fields in wilderness areas. Good hikers will adjust their walking to the weather and climate: one does not hike the same way in a hot desert region as along the foothills of a cool, mountainous terrain. Heat exhaustion can be a problem in high-temperature areas, while colder places may induce hypothermia, or an abnormally low body temperature.

As an aid to tourists, many countries publish hiking guides with maps and other information. An informative international guide is the 'Climbers and Hikers Guide to the World's Mountains' by Michael R. Kelsey (Kelsey Publishing Co., 1981). In addition to providing maps for every hiking area, it also contains specialized information on each country and safety tips on various parts of the world.

**HILBERT, David** (1862–1943). The German mathematician David Hilbert reduced Euclidean geometry to a series of axioms. To emphasize the importance of keeping undefined mathematical terms totally abstract he once said, "One must be able to say at all times—instead of points, straight lines, and planes—tables, chairs, and beer mugs." His work with integral equations in 1909 led later in the century to research in functional analysis, the branch of mathematics that studies functions collectively.

Hilbert was born on Jan. 23, 1862, in Königsberg, Prussia (now Kaliningrad, Russia). He received his doctorate from the University of Königsberg in 1884 and remained there as a professor from 1886 to 1895. In 1895 he joined the University of Göttingen and retired in 1930.

A substantial part of Hilbert's fame rests on a list of 23 research problems he presented in 1900 to the International Mathematical Congress in Paris. He surveyed nearly all the mathematics of his day and set forth the problems he thought would be significant for mathematicians in the 20th century. Many of the problems have since been solved, and each solution was a noted event.

He also studied infinite-dimensional space, later called Hilbert space, and contributed to the kinetic theory of gases and the theory of radiation. He received the Mittag-Leffler prize of the Swedish Academy in 1939. Hilbert died in Göttingen on Feb. 14, 1943.

**HILL, James J.** (1838–1916). An empire builder and financier, James J. Hill made a career out of a single great idea. He decided to create a railroad system that would make it possible to tap the resources of the undeveloped Pacific Northwest.

James Jerome Hill was born on Sept. 16, 1838, near Guelph, Ont. He had hoped to become a physician, but he had to discard that plan when he lost the sight in one eye in an accident.

When he was 18 he arrived at the frontier village of St. Paul, Minn. He worked at various jobs—shipping clerk, railroad station agent, and trader. He traveled the wilderness by oxcart, on horseback, and with dog sledges. He saw the agricultural possibilities of the area and learned of the mineral wealth of the Lake Superior region. He was convinced that a railroad through the territory would be a success.

Hill's chance came in 1878. He joined three other men to form a syndicate that purchased the St. Paul and Pacific Railroad. This railroad had never made any profits. It had a valuable right-of-way to the Northwest, but little construction had been done.

In just 15 years Hill had not only turned failure into success but had absorbed many other rail lines into one corporate system. Eventually the line extended to the Canadian border, then westward to the Pacific coast in Washington.

Hill also developed steamship lines on the Great Lakes and on the Pacific coast. He made them a part of what was later the Great Northern Railway system. In 1901 he attempted to merge the Great Northern with the Chicago, Burlington and Quincy and the Northern Pacific, but in 1904 the Supreme Court declared the company to be in violation of antitrust laws and dissolved it. In 1970, however, the three were merged as the Burlington Northern system.

Hill promoted the development of the Northwest by encouraging homesteaders to settle in the new territory. In later years Hill's practical judgment on national problems was eagerly sought. He died on May 29, 1916, in St. Paul.

**HILLARY, Edmund** (born 1919). At 11:30 AM on May 29, 1953, Edmund Hillary and the Nepalese mountaineer Tensing Norkay reached the 29,035-foot (8,850-meter) summit of Mount Everest in the Himalayas. For this achievement Hillary was knighted and Tensing was awarded the George Medal, Great Britain's highest civilian award.

Edmund Percival Hillary was born on July 20, 1919, in Auckland, New Zealand. He started mountain climbing as a teenager in the Southern Alps of New Zealand. During World War II he served in the Royal New Zealand Air Force as a navigator.

Hillary participated in his first expedition to the Himalayas in 1951. The 1953 expedition in which he reached the summit was organized by British Army officer Sir John Hunt. Hillary made several subsequent trips to the Himalayas. He helped build schools and hospitals for the Sherpa people who lived there, and he led efforts to preserve the environment of the region.

From 1955 to 1958 Hillary commanded the New Zealand group of the British Commonwealth Trans-Antarctic Expedition. He reached the South Pole on Jan. 4, 1958. During an Antarctic expedition in 1967 Mount Herschel (10,941 feet; 3,335 meters) was scaled for the first time. Hillary returned to Central Asia in 1977 to lead the first jet-boat expedition up the Ganges River. He climbed the Himalayas to the river's source. His exploits were recounted in 'High Adventure' (1955), 'The Crossing of Antarctica' (1958), and 'No Latitude for Error' (1961). His autobiography, 'Nothing Venture, Nothing Win', was published in 1975.

**HIMALAYAS.** The highest mountain range on Earth, the Himalayas form the northern border of the Indian subcontinent in Asia. The mountains extend in a massive arc for about 1,550 miles (2,500 kilometers) from west to east with more than 30 peaks rising to heights greater than 24,000 feet (7,300 meters) above sea level. These include Mount Everest, the world's highest peak at 29,035 feet (8,850 meters), Kanchenjunga at 28,208 feet (8,598 meters), Makalu at 27,766 feet (8,463 meters), and Dhaulagiri at 26,810 feet (8,172 meters).

Several Indian states and the kingdoms of Nepal and Bhutan lie along the southern slopes of the Himalayas, and the Tibetan Highlands border them in the north. The width of the mountain system varies from 125 to 250 miles (200 to 400 kilometers) from south to north, and the average height is 20,000 feet (6,100 meters). The Himalayas extend over about 229,500 square miles (594,400 square kilometers). India, Nepal, and Bhutan

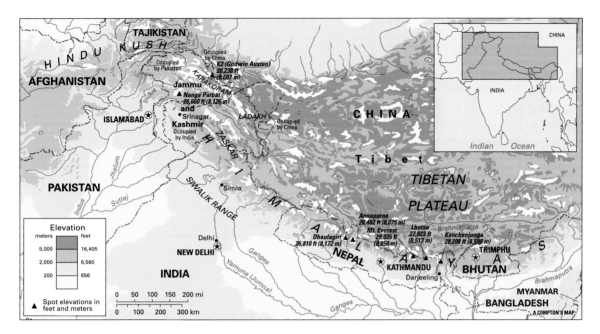

have sovereignty over most of them, but Pakistan occupies part of Kashmir, a region that has been a subject of dispute between India and Pakistan since 1947. China occupies part of the region as well.

The Sanskrit name Himalayas, meaning "abode of snow," truly characterizes the vast permanent snowfields above the snow line. These mountains pose the greatest challenge in the world to mountaineers.

### Physical Characteristics

The most characteristic features of the Himalayas are their great height, complex geologic structure, snowcapped peaks, large valley glaciers, deep river gorges, and rich vegetation. From south to north the Himalayan ranges can be grouped into four parallel belts of varying width.

They are the Outer, or Sub-, Himalayas; the Lesser, or Lower, Himalayas; the Great, or Higher, Himalayas; and the Tethys, or Tibetan, Himalayas. The Karakoram Range in the northwest is also sometimes considered part of the Himalayan system. The mountains can be divided broadly into three regions. The backbone of the system is the Great Himalayas, a single range rising above the snow line with nine of the 14 highest peaks in the world, including Mount Everest (*see* Everest, Mount).

Geologically the Himalayas are relatively young folded mountains and are still undergoing the mountain-building process. Precambrian metamorphic rocks—rocks formed by heat and pressure from 4.6 billion to 570 million years ago—make up much of the structure. The uplift took place in at least three phases. The first phase occurred at the close of the Eocene epoch (about 38 million years ago) when the Great and Tethys Himalayas were uplifted. In the second phase, which occurred in the Miocene epoch (26 million to 7 million years ago), ranges of the Lesser Himalayas were

formed. The final mountain-building phase started at the end of the Tertiary period (about 7 million years ago) when the Siwalik Range, the foothills of the Outer Himalayas, were formed.

The Himalayas act as a great divide and influence the climatic conditions of the Indian subcontinent to the south and of the Central Asian highland to the north. The winter season lasts from October to February, the summer from March to June, and the rainy season from June to September. Climate varies considerably with altitude; the snow line generally lies at about 16,000 feet (4,900 meters) in the Great Himalayas. The annual and daily temperature variation is much greater in the foothills.

The mountain ranges obstruct the cold, dry air from the north into India in winter. They also force the monsoonal winds to give up moisture, causing heavy rain and snow on the Indian side but arid conditions in Tibet. Rainfall decreases from east to west—120 to 60 inches (300 to 150 centimeters). Cherrapunji in Meghalaya State in northeastern India is noted for the world's second highest average annual rainfall of 450 inches (1,140 centimeters).

The Himalayas are drained by 19 major rivers, of which the Indus and the Brahmaputra are the largest. The Jhelum, Chenab, Ravi, Beas, and Sutlej belong to the Indus system; the Yamuna, Ramganga, Kali, Gandak, and Kosi are part of the Ganges system; and the Tista, Raidak, and Manas belong to the Brahmaputra system. Rivers are more numerous and extensive on the southern slopes of the Himalayas and have great potential for producing hydroelectric power. The Bhakra Nangal multipurpose river-valley project, located on the Sutlej River, is one of the most extensive in India. Such major rivers as the Indus, Sutlej, and Brahmaputra have narrow and deep upper valleys that are older than the mountains themselves.

Glaciers cover more than 12,700 square miles (32,900 square kilometers). One of the largest is Gangotri glacier in northern India—20 miles (32 kilometers) long. Glaciers feed most of the upper courses of the rivers, while the middle and lower courses are fed by rain. There are several freshwater lakes as well.

### Plants and Animals

There is great variation in the Himalayan soils. The dark brown soils are well suited for growing fruit trees. The wet, deep, upland soils with high humus content—especially in the Darjeeling and Assam hills—are good for growing tea. Himalayan vegetation is based on altitude and rainfall and can be classified into four groups: tropical evergreen forests of rose chestnut, bamboo, alder, pine, laurel, and palm up to about 3,940 feet (1,200 meters); subtropical deciduous forest with sal, oak, and magnolia up to 7,220 feet (2,200 meters); temperate forests of cedar, birch, hazel, maple, and spruce from 7,220 to 8,860 feet (2,200 to 2,700 meters); and the alpine zone with juniper, rhododendron, mosses, lichens, and several kinds of flowering plants from 8,860 to 11,800 feet (2,700 to 3,600 meters). Alpine meadows are found up to 16,400 feet (5,000 meters).

Elephants, bison, and rhinoceroses inhabit the forested lower slopes of the Outer Himalayas. Snow leopards, brown bears, red pandas, and Tibetan yaks are found above the tree line—above 10,000 feet (3,050 meters). Black bears, langur monkeys, clouded leopards, and goat antelopes live in the foothills. Several animal species, such as the Indian rhinoceros, musk deer, and Kashmir stag, or hangul, were at the point of extinction but are now protected in several national parks and sanctuaries in India. There are catfish in most Himalayan streams, and butterflies are extremely varied and beautiful.

### People and Economy

The people who inhabit the Great and the Tethys Himalayas are primarily of Tibeto-Burman descent, while the Lesser Himalayas are populated by people who trace their roots to Indo-European ancestors. The Gaddis are a hill people who herd sheep and goats. During winter they descend to the lowlands in search of food for their herds, but in summer they return to the higher pastures. The Gujars are also a migrating pastoral people. The major ethnic groups of Nepal are the Newars, Tamangs, Gurangs, Sherpas, and Gurkhas. The Sherpas, who live to the south of Mount Everest, are famous mountaineers. Major Himalayan summer resorts are at Almora, Darjeeling, Mussoorie, Naini Tal, Simla, and Srinagar in India and Murree in Pakistan.

Economic resources abound in the Himalayas, including rich arable land, extensive grasslands and forests, workable mineral deposits, and tremendous potential for easily harnessed hydroelectric power. Terraced cultivation is carried on as high as 8,200 feet (2,500 meters). Rice, corn, wheat, millet, jute, sugarcane, and oilseeds are the major crops. Most of the fruit orchards—producing apples, peaches, pears, and cherries—are in the Kashmir and the Kulu valleys. Rich vineyards on the shores of Dal Lake in Kashmir produce grapes of good quality. Saffron, walnuts, and almonds are also grown in the Vale of Kashmir. Tea gardens abound in the foothills of the Darjeeling district. There are also plantations of cardamom and medicinal herbs. Sheep, goats, and yaks are raised on the rough grazing lands.

Mineral deposits include coal, bauxite, mica, gypsum, sapphires, petroleum, natural gas, chromite, copper, iron ore, borax, sulfur, graphite, lead, and zinc. Some alluvial gold is found in the Indus Valley.

Poor transportation facilities in the Himalayas have acted as a barrier to economic growth. Only in the late 20th century were highways constructed to make the Himalayan region accessible from both north and south. Kathmandu, the capital of Nepal, has an international airport. Srinagar, the summer capital of the Indian-controlled part of Kashmir, has a domestic airport. There are only two narrow-gauge railroads from the northern plains of India into the Lesser Himalayas—one from Kalka to Simla and the other from Siliguri to Darjeeling.

The Himalayas were mapped for the first time in 1590 by a Spanish missionary to the court of the Mughal emperor Akbar. The heights of the Himalayan peaks were first measured correctly in the middle of the 19th century. It was not realized until 1856 that Mount Everest is higher than any other peak in the world. Modern maps of the Himalayas have been prepared by Indian and German geographers and cartographers.

**HINDEMITH, Paul** (1895–1963). The leading German composer of his generation before World War II, Paul Hindemith was also a musical theorist who sought to revitalize tonality as the basis of Western music. A vigorous opponent of the 12-tone school of Arnold Schoenberg, Hindemith formulated a harmonic system based on the enlargement of traditional tonality. His two-volume 'A Concentrated Course in Traditional Harmony', published in 1943 and 1953, was widely used.

Hindemith was born in Hanau, near Frankfurt am Main, on Nov. 16, 1895. He earned his living playing the violin in cafes, dance bands, and theaters. His early works included chamber music written for the Amar-Hindemith Quartet, in which he played the viola, and the song cycle 'Das Marienleben', published in 1923 and radically revised in 1948. He also wrote music for children's games, youth groups, brass bands, and radio plays that was labeled, much to his annoyance, *Gebrauchsmusik*, or "utility music."

Hindemith's major work, 'Mathis der Maler', is an opera about the painter Matthias Grünewald. When the symphony derived from it was performed in 1934 in Berlin, the Nazi cultural authorities banned the opera. Hindemith, who had been professor of composition at the Berlin Hochschule für Musik since 1927, left Germany for Turkey. He taught at the Ankara

Conservatory from 1935 to 1937, Yale University in the United States (1940–53), and the University of Zürich in Switzerland (1951–58).

Hindemith's 'Kammermusik' series, composed from 1922 to 1928 for small, unconventional, astringent groups of instruments, is considered outstanding. Among his other works are 'Symphonic Metamorphosis on Themes of Carl Maria von Weber' (1943), for orchestra, and the opera 'Harmony of the World' (1957; symphonic version, 1952).

**HINDENBURG, Paul von** (1847–1934). In August 1914, soon after the start of World War I, Paul von Hindenburg received a telegram from the German army headquarters. He was asked to take command against the Russians invading from the east. Although he was already 67 years old, he responded, "Am ready." By the end of September he and the chief of staff, General Erich von Ludendorff, had overwhelmingly defeated the Russian forces in the battles of Tannenberg and Masurian Lakes (*see* World War I).

Paul Ludwig Hans Anton von Beneckendorff und von Hindenburg was born in Posen, Germany, on Oct. 2, 1847. At the age of 11 he entered a cadet school. He served in the Seven Weeks' War against Austria in 1866 and in the Franco-Prussian War in 1870–71. After completing his military education, he was placed on the general staff in 1877. He rose to become lieutenant general in 1900. He retired in 1911.

In 1916, two years after his victory over the Russians, he was given chief command of the German armies. The next year his stubborn defense along the Hindenburg Line beat off an Allied drive on the Western front. In 1918 Germany was forced to ask for an armistice.

In 1925 the Conservatives asked Hindenburg to be their candidate as second president of the German Republic. He was elected easily. The former Allies feared that he would attempt to restore the Hohenzollerns to the monarchy, but Hindenburg surprised the world by upholding the Weimar Constitution. He agreed to all policies that would reconcile Germany with its former foes.

In 1932 Hindenburg was reelected president, defeating Adolf Hitler (*see* Hitler). As economic and political conditions grew worse, he finally submitted to Nazi pressure and named Hitler chancellor in 1933. Thereafter Hitler amassed ever greater power, and Hindenburg became virtually inactive. Hindenburg died in Neudeck, Germany, on Aug. 2, 1934. (*See also* Germany, "History.")

**HINDUISM.** The major religion of the Indian subcontinent is Hinduism. The word derives from an ancient Sanskrit term meaning "dwellers by the Indus River," a reference to the location of India's earliest known civilization in what is now Pakistan (*see* Indus Valley Civilization). Apart from animism, from which it may have partly derived, Hinduism is the oldest of the world's religions (*see* Animism). It dates back more

Cathlyn Melloan—EB Inc.

*Hindu worshipers near Varanasi pray and bathe in the waters of the Ganges, considered to be the holiest of rivers.*

than 3,000 years, though its present forms are of more recent origin. Today more than 90 percent of the world's Hindus live in India. Significant minorities may be found in Pakistan and Sri Lanka, and smaller numbers live in Myanmar, South Africa, Trinidad, Europe, and the United States.

Hinduism is so unlike any other religion that it is difficult to define with any precision. It has no founder. Its origins are lost in a very distant past. It does not have one holy book but several. There is no single body of doctrine. Instead there is a great diversity of belief and practice. Many doctrines would be at odds with each other in any other religion. Hinduism, however, has always tended to be inclusive rather than exclusive. There are many sects, cults, theologies, and schools of philosophy, and all of them find a home within Hinduism without persecuting each other or accusing each other of heresy. It is a religion that worships many gods. Yet it also adheres to the view that there is only one God, called Brahman. All other divinities are aspects of the one absolute and unknowable Brahman.

Another distinctive feature of Hinduism is belief in the transmigration of souls, or reincarnation. Associated with this belief is the conviction that all living things are part of the same essence. Individuals pass through cycles of birth and death. This means that an individual soul may return many times in human, animal, or even vegetable form. What a person does in the present life will affect the next life. This is the doctrine of *karman*, the law of cause and effect. The goal of the individual is to escape this cycle, or wheel of birth and rebirth, so that the individual soul, Atman, may eventually become part of the absolute soul, or Brahman.

The caste system of India is another historic characteristic of Hinduism. In its most ancient period Indian society was divided into four classes: priests (or Brahmins), warriors, merchants, and servants. These classes, or castes, have since been subdivided into thousands of subcastes, ranging from the Brahmins at the top to the Untouchables at the bottom. These groups have traditionally been hereditary and have married only among themselves (*see* India, "Caste").

### Origins

The precise origins of Hinduism have so far eluded scholars and other investigators. It is known for certain that there was, from about 2300 to 1500 BC, a highly developed civilization in the Indus Valley and beyond. This civilization had its own religion, which may not have been uniform throughout the extensive land area it covered. Around 1500 BC the Indus Valley was invaded by an Indo-European people called Aryans.

They almost totally transformed Indian civilization, and in so doing they imposed new forms of religion.

The problem in understanding the development of Hinduism is disentangling what may have preceded the Aryan invasion from the religion that was superimposed after 1500 BC. It is probable that much of the Indus Valley religion moved away from Aryan population centers and survived in the countryside. It may have eventually become interwoven with Aryan beliefs and practices to produce historic Hinduism.

The religion of the Aryans was similar in many respects to that of other Indo-European groups. It was a religion of the household, of veneration for ancestors, and of devotion to the world spirit (Brahman). The Aryans had numerous gods, nearly all of whom were male. But the Aryans made no images or pictures of their gods as later Hinduism has done.

Aryan worship was centered around the sacrificial fire at home, while later Hinduism worshiped in temples. The complex ceremony of the Aryans involved ritual sacrifice of animals and the drinking of an inebriating liquor. Hymns were composed for these rituals, and it is in the collections of the hymns, along with incantations and sacrificial formulas, that the nature of the early religion was spelled out. The collections of these are called the Vedas, and it was

*A 19th-century painting from Jaipur (left) shows Vishnu and his ten incarnations: the fish, tortoise, boar, man-lion, dwarf, Rama-with-the-axe, Rama as king, Krishna, Buddha, and Kalkin. An 18th-century Kangra painting (right) depicts Shiva and Ganesa, left, stringing together skulls of the dead while Parvati, right, looks on. Ganesa, their son, is the god first invoked at the beginning of worship or any new undertaking. Nandi the bull, behind the tree, is one of Shiva's chief attendants.*

under their influence that the earliest Hinduism developed. (For the literature of Hinduism, *see* Indian Literature, "The Sanskrit Classics .")

### Vedic Period

Sometime between 1500 and 1200 BC, the period of Aryan conquest and consolidation, the Rig Veda was composed. It is the oldest religious scripture in the world. The Rig Veda is a collection of 1,028 hymns to the gods. Three other collections—the Samaveda, Yajurveda, and Atharvaveda—were added later. These were all composed over a period of several centuries and collected in their present form sometime during the 1st millennium BC.

Between 800 and 600 BC a body of prose writings called the Brahmanas was attached to the Vedas. These contain explanations of the ceremonies mentioned in the Vedas. Even later additions, called the Aranyakas and the Upanishads, presumably written between 600 and 300 BC, were added to this body of literature. All of these texts, along with some later books, became the sacred scripture of Hinduism as it evolved in the second half of the 1st millennium. Of them the Rig Veda is the most revered, though its contents are not much known by most Hindus today.

### From 700 BC to AD 800

The writers of the Vedic hymns seem to have believed in a heaven and hell to which the dead pass, depending on the quality of their earthly lives. Sometime after 600 BC, however, the belief in reincarnation appeared. Although at first confined to small groups of ascetics, it soon spread rapidly throughout India. The doctrine was first expounded in written form in a body of literature called the Upanishads, a term that means "sitting at the foot of a teacher." The purpose of these works is the gaining of a mystical form of knowledge that allows the individual to escape the cycle of rebirths. The Upanishads represent the beginnings of philosophy in India. They are the last stage of interpretation of the Vedas. The Upanishads developed the concept of a single supreme being, Brahman, and they investigated the nature of all reality.

By the time the Buddha appeared in the 6th century BC, the belief in reincarnation was firmly established. From that time Hinduism's main concern became release from the cycle of birth and death instead of making offerings to please or pacify the gods. Sacrifice became infrequent because of an unwillingness to destroy living things. This doctrine of reverence for life, called *ahimsa*, became one of the chief teachings in Jainism (*see* Jainism).

At this same time the primary older gods of the Vedas—named Brahma (not to be confused with Brahman), Indra, Agni, and Varuna—were slowly displaced by newer deities—primarily Vishnu, Shiva, and Shakti—who still have millions of devotees. Many of the earlier gods were absorbed by these three. The Hindu teaching on divine incarnation (gods becoming flesh) made it possible for the older gods to be accepted as incarnate in the newer ones. The religious

development of this period is reflected in two great literary works, the Mahabharata and the Ramayana.

The Mahabharata, or Great Epic of the Bharata Dynasty, is the world's longest poem. It is a mass of legendary material about the struggles for power between two families. It is also an extensive code of conduct (*dharma*) to guide those seeking release from the birth-death cycle. Within the narrative is one of the most famous literary works in the world, the Bhagavadgita, or "The Lord's Song." The book is written in the form of a dialogue between Prince Arjuna and his charioteer, Krishna—an incarnation of Vishnu. The Ramayana, also an epic poem, is about 24,000 couplets long. Its theme is the life of Prince Rama and his adventures.

A few centuries later (perhaps as late as the 10th century AD) another collection of literature, the Puranas, began appearing. These were written in simple poetry, obviously designed for the ordinary reader. They became the scriptures of the common man. Although the Puranas contain a great variety of legendary material, their main purpose was glorifying the gods Vishnu, Shiva, and Brahma. Of the 18 principal Puranas that survive, the most popular is the Bhagavata-Purana on the early life of Krishna.

In the early part of this era, the Hindus generally worshiped without the aids of statues or other images of the gods. By AD 300–650, however, the worship of images in stone temples was firmly established. The worship of female divinities had also become common. The Mother Goddess, most commonly called Shakti, was worshiped in various forms and under differing names. She was the subject of another body of literature called the Tantras. Some animal and human sacrifices were revived by the end of this era, as was the practice of suttee, the burning of a widow on the funeral pyre of her dead husband.

In the period immediately after 550 BC, Buddhism and Jainism emerged, religions centered on the monastic life (*see* Monks and Monasticism). A strong emphasis on the ascetic life in these religions had a profound influence on Hinduism. Asceticism was unknown to the religion of the Vedas, and the priestly class of Brahmins looked down upon it. However, more and more young men became ascetic and gave up the worldly life to become wandering hermits and beggars. Asceticism grew rapidly and has remained a prominent feature of Hinduism.

### From AD 800 to 1800

This 1,000-year era was noted for the division of Hinduism into sects and schools of philosophy, the writing of devotional hymns to the gods, and the influence of Islam in India. By this time the creative vitality of Hinduism had moved to southern India, home of several of the devotional movements collectively called *bhakti*.

Six schools of philosophy emerged during this time. The two most significant were based on the teachings of Sankara and Ramanuja. Sankara was the chief exponent of the Vedanta school of philosophy, from which most of the main currents of modern Hinduism derive. The several schools of Vedanta all believe in the transmigration of souls, the authority of the Vedas, Brahman as the creator of the world, and the responsibility of the individual for his actions.

Sankara taught a doctrine called monism, which means that all things—God, the world, and the individual soul—are basically one in spite of appearances. Ramanuja, the single most influential thinker for devotional Hinduism, was also of the Vedanta school. His teaching differed, however, from Sankara. He believed that God, the soul, and matter are three separate realities. The goal of the soul is to serve God, just as the body is meant to serve the soul. The goal of meditation is the contemplation of God.

An unusual school was founded in the 12th century by Basava. It rejected all forms of image worship, the Vedas, and all caste distinctions. It is probable that Basava's teachings were influenced by Islam.

A similar doctrine was taught by Kabir in the 15th century. He denied image worship, the castes,

asceticism, sacred texts, and pilgrimages. He accepted the doctrine of reincarnation. His God was called Rama, though he accepted the minor gods of Hinduism as having some reality. He was also a hymn writer.

More significant than Hindu schools influenced by Islam was the emergence of Sikhism. It was founded by Kabir's disciple Nanak. Sikhism's theology is basically Hindu, but it took over a number of elements from both Islam and Christianity. It, too, denies the use of images, and it has a form of baptism and a communion meal. In the long run Hinduism probably had a more powerful influence on Muslims living in India than Muslims did on Hinduism.

Hindu devotional literature and hymns honoring Vishnu and Shiva were first written in the Tamil language. Collections appeared as early as the 7th century. The composition of similar hymns in northern languages did not begin for several centuries. By the end of the 17th century, the writing of hymns had ceased, and there were no advances in Hindu thought during the next century. By the time Europeans arrived

*Kapaleeswarar Temple (top) in southern Madras is a very ornate example of Hindu architecture. Done in Dravidian building style, it is devoted to Shiva. Sculptures of Nandi (bottom) guard the Shore Temple at Mahabalipuram, built by the Pallavan king, Rajasimba, and dedicated to Vishnu.*
Cathlyn Melloan—EB Inc.

in large numbers in India, they found a conservative religion steeped in tradition. The chief aim was preserving a rigid social order by means of complex rituals and regulations.

### Modern Hinduism

British colonialism and the arrival of Christian missionaries were the primary influences on Hinduism from the early 19th century. Because of both, Hinduism underwent a revival. By the 20th century it had become so intertwined with the movement for independence that Hinduism and Indian nationalism became virtually synonymous.

While rejecting the doctrines of Christianity, Hinduism was strongly influenced by its social consciousness. A number of influential men launched reform movements that took what was beneficial from the West without compromising basic Hinduism. Rammohan Ray promoted education patterned after that of England, and he called for the prohibition of widow-burning. Dayananda Sarasvati rejected idol worship and the caste system and urged India to adopt Western technology. Narendranath Datta, under the name Vivekananda, founded the Ramakrishna Mission to send out monks to do good works and to promote scholarship. He also carried the message of Hinduism around the world. In the 20th century the major figure in Hindu nationalism was Mahatma Gandhi, who strove successfully to end British colonialism ( *see* Gandhi, Mahatma).

### Gods of Modern Hinduism

Although many divinities may be worshiped, modern Hindus are generally divided into followers of Vishnu, Shiva, or Shakti. Nearly all Hindus look upon one of these as an expression of the ultimate being, the one in charge of the destiny of the universe.

Each group of followers holds the Vedas in high regard, but each also has its own scriptures. In the Bhagavadgita, for example, Vishnu is honored in his incarnation Krishna. Another incarnation, Rama, is the hero of the Ramayana. Vishnu is the protector and preserver of the world, and he is worshiped by many cults in various forms besides Krishna and Rama. The worship of the god is called Vaisnavism. The beginnings of this cult were about the 7th century BC. (*See also* Hare Krishna.)

Shiva, a Sanskrit word meaning "auspicious one," is a more remote god than Vishnu. His worship is called Shivaism. Shiva is a more difficult god to understand than is Vishnu. He is regarded as both destroyer and restorer. Doctrines about Shiva may have merged roles that were once assigned to various earlier gods.

Shiva has a female consort who goes under several names. He is occasionally paired with Shakti, the mother goddess. They and their sons Skanda and Ganesa live on top of Mount Kailasa in the Himalayas. He is depicted in a number of forms—such as a wandering beggar, half man and half female, or a dancer.

Shakti is the mother goddess. Like Shiva, she can be either beneficial or fierce, depending on her form. As Parvati she is depicted as a beautiful woman in middle age. As Kali she is a giantess with black skin, a blood-red tongue, and large tusks.

Kali carries an assortment of weapons and wears a garland of human skulls around her neck. The mother goddess thus stands for all aspects of nature from birth to death.

In addition to the three primary deities, there are several others who are still worshiped. Ganesa, the elephant-headed son of Shiva and Shakti, is prayed to before all undertakings. Lakshmi, the wife of Vishnu, is patroness of wealth. Sarasvati is the goddess of learning and the arts. Hanuman is the monkey-god associated with the adventures of Rama. He appears as the personification of the power of God on Earth. Manasa, the goddess of snakes, is worshiped by peasants in some areas.

Many animals and plants are also regarded as sacred. Most notable is the cow. All cattle are protected, and even among castes that are not vegetarian, beef is not eaten. Monkeys, tree squirrels, and some snakes are also considered holy. Among sacred trees are the banyan and the tulsi. All rivers are considered somewhat holy, but the Ganges in the north of India is the holiest of rivers because it supposedly flows from the head of Shiva. It is the focus of pilgrimage for millions.

People are also sacred according to their station in life. Thus parents are holy to their children and teachers to their students.

### Festivals and Pilgrimages

Temples of any significance hold a festival at least once a year. Festivals are combinations of religious ceremonies, processions of the locally favored god, music, dances, and other forms of celebration. Most festivals are related to the cycles of nature. The New Year celebration, Diwali, takes place with exchanges of gifts, lighting of ceremonial lamps, gambling (a ritual designed to gain luck for the coming year), and fireworks to frighten away spirits of the dead.

Pilgrimages to holy places have been common since the Vedic period. Certain places are considered sacred because of a specific historical event, connection with a legendary figure, the appearance of a god, or location on the bank of a holy river.

Visits to sacred places are supposed to confer some benefit upon the pilgrim—frequently the healing of a dread disease. People who travel to Varanasi (Benares) when death is near hope to be released from the birth-death cycle by dying near the Ganges River. Many shrines organize annual gatherings that are partly religious and partly local fairs.

### Temple Worship

Temples range in size from small village shrines with crude statues to huge complexes—almost small cities—with walls and monumental gates enclosing courtyards, pools for ceremonial bathing, schools, hospitals, and monasteries. Services are not carried out at fixed times as they are in Western religions.

The worship itself is an act of calling forth the god's presence and entertaining the deity as a royal guest. The first act is opening the temple door. For worshipers of Vishnu this symbolizes opening the gates of heaven. For Shiva worshipers it secures the building's protection. Temple visitors may take part in chanting or listening to doctrinal expositions. Images of the gods are honored with gifts of flowers, fruit, or perfumes, and visiting worshipers are given small portions of consecrated food.

In addition to temple worship, there are daily household rites, including an offering of food, often fruit, or flowers to the gods and recitation of the Vedas. Household worship focuses on the transitions in a person's life, such as the rite of passage from childhood to adult responsibility, marriage, or childbirth. Wedding ceremonies are the major household rites, and they have remained quite elaborate, lasting usually up to three days. The traditional funeral method is cremation. Part of the funeral rite is a gift of food to the Brahmins (the priestly class) for the benefit of the deceased.

**HIPPOCRATES** (460?–377? BC). The first name in the history of medicine is Hippocrates, a physician from the island of Cos in ancient Greece. Known as the "Father of Medicine," Hippocrates has long been associated with the Hippocratic Oath, a document he did not write but which sets forth the obligations, ideals, and ethics of physicians. In a modified form the oath is still often required of medical students upon graduation (*see* Medicine).

Very little is known of the life of Hippocrates. He was a contemporary of the philosopher Socrates in the 5th century BC and was mentioned by Plato in two of his Dialogues. He was, in his lifetime, quite well known as a teacher and physician, and he appears to have traveled widely in Greece and Asia Minor, practicing medicine and teaching. There was presumably a medical school on Cos, in which he taught frequently. Hippocrates probably belonged to a family that had produced well-known physicians for many generations. Aristotle says in his 'Politics' that Hippocrates was called "the Great Physician." Hippocrates died at Larissa in Thessaly.

A small body of writings ascribed to Hippocrates has come down to the present. How many he actually wrote will probably never be known. The number of works in ancient times was 70, but only 60 have been preserved. The earliest surviving copy dates from the 10th century AD.

The works differ greatly in their length, in the opinions expressed, and in the types of intended users. Some are for physicians, some for assistants and students, and some for laymen. A few are philosophical. It is generally agreed that the writings made up the medical library at Cos. During the 3rd or 2nd century BC they were shipped to the great library at Alexandria, Egypt. Among the titles are 'Ancient Medicine', 'Regimen in Acute Diseases', 'Wounds of the Head', 'Aphorisms', and 'Epidemics'.

Leonard Lee Rue III

*Hippopotamus* (Hippopotamus amphibius)

**HIPPOPOTAMUS.** An African folk tale describes how God created the hippopotamus and told it to cut grass for the other animals. When the hippo discovered how hot Africa was, however, it asked God if it could stay in the water during the day and cut grass at night when the weather was cool. God agreed, though He was reluctant because He feared the hippo might eat the river's fish. The hippo, however, was as good as its word—it fed only on vegetation.

The name hippopotamus means "river horse," though hippos, as they are also called, are actually related to pigs. The hippopotamus was once found across the African continent. Today, however, because of intensive hunting by Africans, the creature is found only in the river systems of Eastern and Central Africa.

An adult hippopotamus may weigh 4 tons, grow to a length of 12 to 14 feet (3.7 to 4.2 meters), and stand 5 feet (1.5 meters) tall at the shoulder. Next to the elephant, it is one of the largest land mammals. It has a barrel-shaped body and short limbs. The hippo's face is broad and flat, and the ears, nostrils, and protruding eyes are set on the upper surface. Thus they alone may project above water when the animal is submerged. The hippo's incisor and canine teeth are very large and grow continuously as they are worn away; they are prized by Africans for their ivory.

The hippo's thick gray or brown hide is hairless, except for the tip of the tail. The skin contains glands that secrete a protective oily liquid whose red color has led to the popular myth that hippos sweat blood.

The hippo spends its days resting in the water, often in herds of 20 to 40. If disturbed, the hippo may dive for as long as 6 minutes, its ears and nostrils shut tight against the water. It can swim quite fast and can also walk along lake and river bottoms. The hippo rarely wanders far from water, but at night it may travel some distance in search of shore vegetation, sometimes feeding on cultivated crops.

Hippos give birth to a single offspring. The baby will often ride on the mother's back while she swims or floats at the surface. During the breeding season, males often engage in battles, sometimes to the death.

The hippopotamus belongs to the family Hippopotamidae. The scientific name of the common hippo is *Hippopotamus amphibius*. The rare pygmy hippopotamus (*Choeropsis liberiensis*) lives in the streams, wet forests, and swamps of West Africa. It lives alone or in pairs and appears to be less aquatic than its larger relative. Pygmy hippos are 5 to 6 feet (1.5 to 1.8 meters) long, about 3 feet (1 meter) tall, and weigh 350 to 590 pounds (160 to 270 kilograms). ( *See also* Mammal.)

Barbara Katz

**HIROHITO** (1901–89). The longest-reigning monarch of modern times, Hirohito became the emperor of Japan on Dec. 25, 1926. His reign was given the name Showa, meaning "Enlightened Peace." His 60th anniversary on the throne was celebrated in 1986. Tradition says that Hirohito was the 124th direct descendant of the fabled first emperor, Jimmu, and therefore a member of the oldest imperial family in the world. In Japan he was considered sacred and referred to as Tenno Heika, meaning "son of heaven." So significant is the role of the emperor in Japanese society that, when Japan surrendered in World War II, he was allowed to retain his position and title.

Michinomiya Hirohito was born at Aoyama Palace in Tokyo on April 29, 1901. He received his early education at the Peers' School and later attended the Crown Prince's Institute. He studied marine biology, on which he later wrote several books based on research he had done in Sagami Bay. In 1921 he paid a visit to Europe, the first Japanese crown prince to do so. When he returned home he was named prince regent to rule in place of his father, who had retired because of mental illness.

The first 20 years of Hirohito's reign were tumultuous. By the time he became emperor, the military was already in firm control of policy and impelling Japan into a major war. The emperor had grave misgivings about any war with the United States and tried vainly to restrain the army and navy chiefs. In 1945, when Japan was nearing defeat, opinion was divided between those who favored surrender and those who wanted to carry on the war to the bitter end. Hirohito sided with those urging peace. On Aug. 15, 1945, he broadcast on radio his country's surrender.

After the war, there were changes in Hirohito's position. He renounced his divinity. The constitution that had given the emperor supreme authority was rewritten. The new constitution vested sovereignty in the people, and the emperor was designated "symbol of the State and of the unity of the people." He became more accessible, making personal appearances and permitting publication of pictures and stories of himself and his family. In 1959 he permitted his son, Crown Prince Akihito, to marry a commoner. Hirohito died on Jan. 7, 1989, after a long illness. Upon his death Prince Akihito automatically became emperor, and the new reign was given the name Heisei, meaning "Achieving Peace." (*See also* Akihito; Japan.)

**HIROSHIGE** (1797–1858). One of the last great masters of the wood-block print, the Japanese artist Hiroshige had a talent for landscape compositions that was appreciated in the West by the impressionists and postimpressionists. He was born Ando Tokutaro in Edo (now Tokyo), Japan, in 1797. Hiroshige was his professional name. His father was a fire warden, and the son inherited the position. He took up sketching as a child and in 1811 entered the school of master artist Utagawa Toyohiro. He graduated at age 15, and six years later his first work was published.

Hiroshige's artistic life developed through three stages. During his student period, from 1811 to 1830, his work largely imitated that of his elders. From 1830 to 1844 he created his own ideal of landscape design. This is the time of his best work, and he traveled throughout Japan in order to depict as much of his country's beauty as possible in such series as 'Famous Places in Japan' and 'Views of Kyoto'. His finest work is entitled 'Fifty-three Stages on the Tokaido'. During the last phase of his career, from 1844 to 1858, the quality of his work declined because he was very popular and too busy. He died on Oct. 12, 1858, in Edo during a cholera epidemic.

**'View from Satta Peak, Yui', a print by Hiroshige, measures 24.1 by 36.8 centimeters.**
Courtesy of The Art Institute of Chicago, Gift of Miss Katherine S. Buckingham to the Clarence Buckingham Collection, 1925.3518

(Top left) Bruce Roberts—Photo Researchers; (bottom left) Cathlyn Melloan—Tony Stone Worldwide; (right) Nereuda Garcia-Ferraz

*Mexican Americans (top left) in San Antonio, Tex., celebrate a Christmas fiesta. Puerto Ricans in Chicago (bottom left) gather for an outdoor summer music fest. Cubans in Miami (right) wear traditional dress for an outdoor gathering.*

# HISPANIC AMERICANS

In the United States, before there was New England, there was New Spain; and before there was Boston, Mass., there was Santa Fe, N.M. The teaching of American history normally emphasizes the founding and growth of the British colonies in North America, their emergence as an independent nation in 1776, and the development of the United States from east to west. This treatment easily omits the fact that there was significant colonization by Spain of what is now the American Southwest from the 16th century onward. It also tends to ignore, until the Mexican War is mentioned, that the whole Southwest, from Texas westward to California, was a Spanish-speaking territory with its own distinctive heritage, culture, and customs for many decades.

The Spanish-speaking citizens of the United States who were incorporated into the country as a result of the Mexican War are called Mexican Americans. Their numbers have since increased as a result of immigration. Other Spanish-speaking citizens came from Cuba and Puerto Rico, and smaller numbers are immigrants from Central and South America and from the Dominican Republic. Taken together, these people are called Hispanics, or Latinos.

### Portrait of Ethnic Diversity

Hispanics today form the fastest-growing ethnic minority in the United States. As of the 2000 census, they made up about 12.5 percent of the U.S. population and numbered some 35.3 million, representing an increase of more than 50 percent since 1990. The number of Hispanics in the United States continued to grow at such a rapid pace that they became the largest minority group in the nation in 2002, surpassing the African American population for the first time. About 60 percent of Hispanic Americans trace their origins to Mexico.

The term Hispanic is not an ethnic description. It refers to native language and to cultural background. Within the group called Hispanics are peoples of diverse ethnic origins. There are African Americans and American Indians as well as individuals of purely European background whose families have lived in the Americas for generations. And, because of intermarriage, there are descendants who represent a combination of several origins. Hispanics do not necessarily regard themselves as a single group because their attachments are to their specific national origin.

In the case of many Mexican Americans, the national origin is within the United States if their ancestors lived in the Southwest before the Mexican War.

Puerto Ricans enjoy a different status from other Hispanics in that they are citizens of the United States by birth, whether they were born in their homeland or in the United States. They were granted citizenship in 1917. (Puerto Rico became a possession of the United States as a result of the Spanish-American War.) They may therefore go back and forth between the island and the mainland without visas or passports. Mexicans, Cubans, and others must enter the country as immigrants with alien status and must apply for citizenship in the same way as do other immigrants.

Although there are Hispanics in most parts of the United States, some areas have especially large concentrations. Eighty-six percent of Mexican Americans make their homes in five Southwestern states: Texas, California, New Mexico, Arizona, and Colorado.

Texas and California account for more than 50 percent of the total Hispanic population in the United States. About two thirds of Puerto Ricans residing in the United States are in the New York City area, including nearby New Jersey. About 60 percent of Cuban Hispanics reside in Florida, with the heaviest concentration in Dade County (Miami). Another 20 percent are in the New York–New Jersey area, particularly in Union City, N.J. Illinois also has large numbers of Mexican, Puerto Rican, and Cuban Hispanics—mostly in Chicago.

There are two basic reasons for Hispanic immigration to the United States: economic opportunity and escape from political persecution. Very large numbers of Mexicans and Puerto Ricans entered the country to escape poverty and to find a way to make a living. The 20th-century Cuban migration, which began in 1959 when Fidel Castro took over the government of Cuba, was mainly for political reasons.

According to statistics compiled by the United States Department of Commerce, Hispanics are a younger, less affluent, and less educated group than the rest of the population. Their median age is about 23. Sixty-three percent were under age 30 in 1992, and 40 percent were 18 or younger. The median family income was $23,400. This was higher than the median for blacks but lower than the rest of the non-Hispanic median of $35,200. Of the three groups—Mexican Americans, Puerto Ricans, and Cubans—the Puerto Ricans had the lowest incomes and the Cubans the highest. More than 23.4 percent lived below the poverty level in the early 1990s.

### Mexican Americans

Today's Mexican Americans are a product of historical development that began more than four centuries ago, when Spain conquered Mexico and made it a colony. Before that the territory was inhabited exclusively by Indians. The Mexican Americans are, therefore, the second oldest component of American society.

**Historical background.** Mexican American history can be divided into five fairly distinct periods. The first

Dick Rowan—Photo Researchers

*A Mexican American festival in Santa Barbara, Calif., attracts a large non-Hispanic audience to enjoy the music and dancing.*

era, from 1520 until 1809, covers the period from the Spanish conquest until the beginning of the revolt against Spain. It was during these nearly 300 years that the synthesis of Spanish and Indian cultures took place. Early in this period the Southwest of what is now the United States was added to Mexico. (The Spanish administration founded one of the oldest cities in North America, Santa Fe, N.M., in 1610.) The last region to be colonized was California.

During the second era, from 1810 until 1848, the Southwest was part of an independent Mexico. It developed slowly, largely because of the distance between it and the capital of Mexico City. Then in 1846–48 the Mexican War gained the Southwest for the United States. The war was ended by the Treaty of Guadalupe-Hidalgo, in which the United States promised to protect the rights of Mexican Americans in the newly won territories. Most of the treaty's provisions, unfortunately, were not honored by the United States. Huge tracts of land belonging to Mexicans were taken from them by the most dubious legal means or by outright theft. Violence was perpetrated against them, and there was a great deal of economic exploitation. This sad tale of exploitation covers the period from 1849 until 1910, an era of Anglo-American assimilation of the new territory. The Mexican Americans of the Southwest were gradually overwhelmed in numbers by Anglo newcomers from the East. (Anglo is a term used by Hispanics to describe all white non-Hispanic Americans.) (*See also* Mexican War.)

In about 1910 the next era began with the start of massive emigration from Mexico itself. This migration, legal and illegal, has continued to the present. During

*César Chavez (right) founded the United Farm Workers in the 1960s. The union has tried to gain a better standard of living for Mexican American migrant workers (left), who are among the lowest-paid laborers in the United States.*

the early decades, however, the arrival of Mexicans was but a part of the much greater migratory trend that included many immigrants from Europe and the Far East. The Mexican immigration continued steadily until the Great Depression of the 1930s. Then, with the collapse of the United States economy, many immigrants returned to Mexico. Many others were sent back by the United States government. During this period, from 1910 until 1939, Mexican Americans remained largely unassimilated, rural, poor, and Spanish speaking. They were for the most part forgotten Americans amid the crises of the depression and World War II.

The current period began about 1940. In the decades since 1940—and especially since 1960—Mexican Americans have emerged as a distinct and visible social group in the United States. Partly because of the civil rights movement of the 1960s, they asserted themselves and attempted to take what they perceived to be their rightful place in American life. This self-awareness was reinforced by continued migration from Mexico.

During this period the Mexican American population shifted from a basically rural to a mostly urban way of life. As a city-dwelling minority they found themselves sharing the problems of the rest of the urban poor: lack of jobs, second-rate housing, and educational difficulties.

By the early 1990s more than 90 percent of the Mexican Americans, as well as other Hispanics, were living in or near cities. The Los Angeles–Long Beach area has, after Mexico City, more Mexicans than any other city in the Western Hemisphere. There are also sizable communities in Denver, Kansas City, Chicago, Detroit, and New York City. In these and other locations Mexican Americans have begun to seek political and economic power by organizing themselves and registering to vote. In 1985 there were more than 2,100 Mexican American elected officials.

**Migrant laborers.** Farm workers who move from place to place following harvests are called migrant, or migratory, workers (*see* Migrant Labor). In the years

after the American Civil War, Mexicans began crossing into Texas to work the cotton harvests. By the end of World War I they were also working in California on large farms in the Central Valley. Slowly they began to work their way to states farther north as they heard of other crops to be harvested. Many of the migrants returned to Mexico after each season was over, but others stayed to wait for the next season or to look for better-paying jobs.

During World War II much American manpower was lost to the military forces and to defense work, resulting in shortages of farm workers. In July 1942 the governments of the United States and Mexico negotiated an agreement called the Mexican Farm Labor Supply Program. Unofficially it was called the bracero program. (One definition of bracero is "day laborer.") The program continued until 1964, nearly 20 years after the war's end, largely at the insistence of employers who benefited from it. During that period it brought ever greater numbers of Mexicans to states as far away as Minnesota and Wisconsin.

The Mexican government wanted the program continued because of the large amounts of money the braceros sent back to their families, thereby helping the Mexican economy. The braceros favored the program because of the opportunities it offered compared to those in their homeland. Gradually the program lost support, however, and it was terminated by the United States in December 1964.

One advantage of the bracero program was its legality. The United States government kept records of the immigrant workers. After the program ended many undocumented workers kept pouring into the United States, creating the massive problem of illegal aliens.

**Illegal immigration.** The Spanish explorer Francisco Vázquez de Coronado went northward from Mexico and traveled the Southwest in the years 1540–42. He was looking for the fabled (and nonexistent) Seven Cities of Gold—El Dorado. Since the late 19th century millions of Mexicans have retraced his steps on a similar quest. They have been more successful.

The border between Mexico and the United States stretches for 1,950 miles (3,140 kilometers) from near Brownsville, Tex., in the east to Tijuana, Mexico–San Diego, Calif., in the west. It is the longest border in the world separating dire poverty from unparalleled affluence and opportunity. Because Mexico has never been able to develop a working and prosperous economy for all of its citizens, the lure of El Norte (the North) has been powerful.

In the mid-1980s nearly half of the Mexican working population was either unemployed or underemployed. This condition provided an even greater motive to head northward. There were in 1990 an estimated 2 million illegal aliens in the United States, and about 55 percent of them were from Mexico.

Whether this illegal immigration has proved beneficial or harmful to the United States is uncertain. Employers, whether farmers or factory owners, approve the immigration. They insist it does not take jobs from other Americans. They believe that illegal immigrants take only low-paying jobs that Americans do not want anyway. Keeping wages low is beneficial in profits for companies and in consumer prices.

The unionization of migrant workers in the Southwest under the leadership of César Chavez in the 1960s diminished the appeal of migrants for agriculture. Many growers mechanized their harvesting to spare themselves the inconvenience of strikes at those times when the workers are most needed.

Immigration (both legal and illegal) had a significant effect in the Southwest. It created what one author called a "third country," in which characteristics of both Mexico and the United States are blended. It increased the use of the Spanish language. It also revived Mexican culture in the region.

The presence of illegal aliens also put a financial strain on the public services offered by the states. The United States Supreme Court ruled in 1982 that states are required to pay for educating the children of illegal aliens. Many other social services are also available to them at state and local expense. Law enforcement was also burdened, especially with the great increase in drug smuggling across the border. Most illegal drugs, however, are brought in through Florida.

In an attempt to reduce illegal immigration, Congress passed legislation in 1986 that stipulates fines and other penalties for employers who knowingly hire illegal aliens. The bill includes provisions to grant amnesty to illegal aliens who were in the United States prior to Jan. 1, 1982, and to aid farmers who have relied on illegal aliens to harvest their crops.

### Puerto Ricans

Residents of Puerto Rico are not a single ethnic group. They, like other Hispanics, have inherited a mixture of cultures. Puerto Ricans have lived in the mainland United States since at least the 1830s. At that time there was a fairly sizable trade between the island and New York City, but immigration was not large. By the end of the century there were only about 1,500 Puerto Ricans in all of the United States.

The Spanish-American War changed the status of the island by making it a United States possession. In 1917 the Jones Act conferred citizenship on Puerto Ricans, though they had not asked for it. Over the next 23 years several thousand residents moved to the mainland. By 1940 there were nearly 70,000 Puerto Ricans in the mainland United States, mostly in or near New York City.

The great migration began after World War II, and the reasons for it were economic. Puerto Rico, like Mexico, had never been able to develop a growing economy for its residents. Inexpensive airplane fares between San Juan and New York City made it possible for the Puerto Rican immigrant community to more than triple in size by 1950. By 1992 there were about 2.75 million Puerto Ricans on the mainland.

The earliest immigrants settled in the East Harlem section of Manhattan, a region they called El Barrio, meaning "the neighborhood." They moved fairly rapidly into the other four New York City boroughs as well as into upstate New York. In 1970, 64 percent of Puerto Ricans living on the mainland were in New York. By 1980 this figure had dropped to 50 percent, and Puerto Rican enclaves had grown in other major cities—particularly Hartford, Conn.; Philadelphia; Cleveland; Chicago; Los Angeles; and Miami.

Patterns of migration fluctuated in relation to economic conditions in the mainland United States and on the island. During the 1950s an average of 46,000 islanders moved to the mainland annually. During the 1960s this number dropped to 14,000 because economic conditions had improved on the island. During the 1970s, with worsening economic conditions in the United States, more Puerto Ricans returned to the island than came to the mainland. This is not unusual, as there has always been a two-way migration pattern—especially for those born on the island. Many Puerto Ricans prefer living there to living on the mainland, even if they are not as prosperous.

*Illegal immigrants trying to enter the United States are sent back to Mexico. Such scenes take place daily along the border.*
Alon Reininger—Leo de Wys, Inc.

Peter Karas—FPG

*Spanish Harlem in New York City has become home for thousands of Puerto Ricans since the late 1940s.*

Puerto Ricans have also been seasonal, migrant workers along the East Coast and in the Midwest. The sugarcane season on the island is in the winter, while harvesting on the mainland is in the late summer and fall. Thus migrant workers sometimes work at harvests in both places.

In the 1980s a new wave of migration to the mainland began. This one was significantly different from previous ones. Puerto Rico had entered a state of severe economic decline, brought on in part by the recession in the United States proper. Unemployment in Puerto Rico averaged more than 20 percent for several years. For those who were employed, the average per-person income was lower than in any state.

*A Puerto Rican child at the bilingual PRACA day-care center in New York City draws a picture of a boat.*

Jason Lauré

Many who lost their jobs in the 1980s were highly educated professional people and government workers. (One third of the island's workers are government employees.) They began to leave the island in great numbers, creating what many called a "brain drain," the loss of some of the island's most educated residents. Individuals with graduate degrees in such professions as engineering, law, and medicine left the island for jobs on the mainland, and American companies actively recruited new workers from the island.

As with Mexican Americans, Puerto Ricans who come to the mainland tend to be young. The median age is about 22. The families also tend to be larger. Compared with non-Hispanic families, many more Puerto Rican families have five or more children.

Among Hispanics, Puerto Ricans have been less successful economically than Mexicans or Cubans. The more recent migration, however, may change the success rate and income levels of Puerto Ricans. In the early 1990s more than 40 percent were living below the poverty level. Part of the reason for this lack of success can be traced to lower levels of education and a lack of proficiency in the English language. Bilingual education has not generally succeeded in transforming Hispanics into an English-speaking population. Frequently it is used instead for cultural maintenance for perpetuating Spanish.

### Cubans

In January 1959 Fidel Castro overthrew the Cuban dictatorship of Fulgencio Batista. Relations with the United States soon began to deteriorate. Castro confiscated property belonging to American companies, announced his intention of fomenting revolution throughout Latin America, and established close ties with the Soviet Union. In January 1961 President Dwight D. Eisenhower broke diplomatic relations with Cuba. Four months later, in the early months of President John F. Kennedy's administration, about 1,500 anti-Castro Cubans invaded the southwestern coast of Cuba at a place called the Bay of Pigs. This invasion had been planned by the United States Central Intelligence Agency with the help of Cubans who hoped that Castro would be easily overthrown.

The Bay of Pigs invasion was a complete failure. But it did not end the hopes of Cubans in the United States that Castro's regime would be short-lived and that they would soon be able to return to their homeland. The hope of returning still inspires many Cubans to work for Castro's overthrow. They came to the United States as refugees beginning in 1959; the exodus has not ceased since then.

**Historical background.** By 1850 Cuba had developed a thriving worldwide market for its cigars. The cigar business created a small middle class. The growth of this class bred a desire for independence from Spain. A rebellion called the Ten Years War (1868–78) failed, however, and Spanish rule became more oppressive. Thousands of Cubans began leaving the island, and most of them headed for Key West in nearby Florida. As Key West prospered, labor unions from the North came to organize the workers. Strikes nearly ruined the economy, and the cigar manufacturers looked for a more agreeable place to settle.

They chose Tampa, Fla. Vicente Martínez Ybor and associates purchased land near Tampa and set up their cigar businesses. In 1887 Ybor City, as it is now known, was made part of Tampa, and it remains a colorful reminder of its Cuban heritage.

Decades later, during the Great Depression, the cigar business worldwide was hard hit. Many workers left for other parts of the United States, though a substantial core of Cuban Americans remained in Ybor City and nearby.

Today Ybor City has been superseded as a Cuban population center by Little Havana in Miami, Fla. Miami has the oldest and largest concentration of Cubans from the more recent waves of immigration. Florida is a natural destination for Cubans—only 90 miles (145 kilometers) from their homeland and having a similar climate. Apart from these two reasons, Cubans settled in Florida rather than in the more industrial North because it offered greater availability of housing and a larger labor market at the time of their arrival.

The modern migration of Cubans to the United States began in 1959 as Castro's victory seemed imminent. Those who came to the United States were not the poorest segments of society, as had been the case with Mexicans and Puerto Ricans. They were members of the prosperous middle class—shop owners, businesspeople, and professionals who feared the consequences of a Castro takeover. The first Cubans to arrive were those who escaped. Later arrivals for the most part consisted of those allowed to leave by the Cuban government.

During the years 1961 through 1970 a total of 256,769 Cuban immigrants were admitted to the United States. The largest number to arrive in a single year during that decade was 99,312 in 1968. Another 270,000 came during the next decade.

**The Marielitos.** On April 4, 1980, Castro allowed the Peruvian Embassy in Havana to be opened to Cubans who wished to leave the island. Within a few days the number wishing to get away had grown to more than 10,000.

Castro decided on April 20 to open the port of Mariel on Cuba's north coast for those who wanted to go to the United States. In the next five months about 123,000 new Cuban refugees landed in Florida. Among them were about 5,000 hard-core criminals and a larger number of persons who had been held as political prisoners.

The Refugee Act of 1980 drastically reduced the number of Cubans to be allowed into the country. President Jimmy Carter therefore classified the Marielitos as entrants with their status pending. These new arrivals were unlike the previous Cuban immigrants in that they were mostly young, single, adult males. Only a very small number of them could speak any English, and their educational level was generally lower than that of previous arrivals.

UPI/Bettmann

*Cuban boat people arriving illegally in Florida are led away by agents of the United States government.*

They arrived when the United States economy was in a recession, and finding sponsors or jobs for them was difficult. To accommodate these new aliens, President Carter opened processing centers at Eglin Air Force Base in Florida and at military bases in Arkansas, Pennsylvania, and Wisconsin.

The uncertain status of the Marielitos lasted until Oct. 17, 1984, when Congress reenacted the Cuban Refugee Act of 1966. This restored the favorable status Cuban refugees had enjoyed before 1980 and allowed their processing to start within six weeks. By the end of 1985 most of them had received permanent residency status in the United States, which allowed them to apply for citizenship after five years.

**Cuban Americans.** By the early 1990s there were well over 1 million Cuban Americans in the United States. They had come mostly as refugees, which distinguished them from the other large Hispanic groups. Because of their refugee status they were offered help from the federal government that the other groups did not receive. The Cuban Refugee Resettlement Program provided them with financial assistance and help in finding housing.

Cuban Americans live in most major cities in the United States. By far the largest settlement is in south Florida, and the second largest is in and around Union City, N.J. Other Hispanics have tended to disperse themselves around the country. Cubans, by contrast, continue to concentrate in south Florida, where about 60 percent of Cuban Americans lived by 1992.

In contrast to urban Mexican Americans and Puerto Ricans, Cuban Americans are not concentrated in the ghetto neighborhoods of cities. Their prosperity has enabled them to move to the suburbs. Every part of

*Cuban American demonstrators in Miami call attention to the plight of political prisoners held in Cuban jails.*
Bill Andrews—The Miami Herald

Dade County, Fla., has some Cuban population, though the largest concentration is still in the Little Havana area of Miami.

As residents of both city and suburb, Cubans have been more economically successful than other Hispanics. This situation is accounted for by the fact that they were mostly members of the middle class in Cuba (except for the Marielitos), and they have established themselves in business and the professions in the United States. The average family income for Cubans in the mid-1980s was far higher than for other Hispanics, and far fewer Cubans live below the poverty level than do other Hispanics.

Politically, Cuban Americans have tended to be more active than Mexican Americans or Puerto Ricans, though there were strong indications during the 1980s that this trend was changing. Most Hispanics tend to vote with the Democratic party, but Cuban Americans tend to be heavily Republican. Part of the reason for this party affiliation is their greater affluence. Another

reason is their vehement anti-Communism. They persist in their desire to see the Castro government overthrown, and they find more allies within the Republican party. In the 1984 election, for example, it is estimated that 93 percent of Cuban voters supported President Ronald Reagan against his Democratic challenger, Walter Mondale.

**Little Havana.** Cubans succeeded in transforming southern Florida in much the same way that Mexican immigrants changed the border area of the United States and Mexico. Dade County's population is more than 40 percent Cuban. The heartland of this population is within the city of Miami. Little Havana is a 4-square-mile (10-square-kilometer) neighborhood within the city limits of Miami, southeast of the airport and just west of Hialeah. It is a distinctively Cuban city-within-a-city. It is possible for those who live there to exist entirely within the culture they transported from their homeland. Stores, restaurants, schools, churches, theaters—all exist to serve a primarily Spanish-speaking constituency.

As the Cuban population increased and spread beyond Little Havana, cultural influences likewise followed. There are Spanish-language television and radio stations. The *Miami Herald* publishes a daily edition in Spanish.

As many Cubans prospered and left Little Havana, that part of the city changed. Other Hispanics arrived to replace the departed Cubans—immigrants from Nicaragua, Colombia, El Salvador, and other Latin American countries. Within greater Miami in 1990 there were more than 200,000 non-Cuban Hispanics, including the sizable Puerto Rican colony.

### Americanization

Every group of immigrants that has come to the United States has had to deal with the second generation— the children who are born in their new home and who grow up knowing nothing of their parents' native land. Whereas the parents, if they learn English

*A news dealer in Miami's Little Havana, home for thousands of Cubans in the United States, sells Spanish-language papers.*

Barry M. Tenin—Photo Researchers

at all, must make a real effort to do so, the second generation grows up speaking English.

Until programs of bilingual education were instituted, there was no other choice. Although each immigrant group tends to congregate together, the need to learn the new language is prompted by the pressing need of getting involved in the economy: the need to have a job and to support a family.

Members of the second generation do more than learn to speak English well. They also absorb values and ideas that are often foreign to those of their parents. The United States is the homeland for the second generation. Even as the immigrant generation tries to maintain its traditional culture, the second generation brings home a new culture, a new set of traditions that often clash with the values of the parents.

In the case of Hispanic groups, the Americanization process has been uneven. (Americanization primarily means becoming integrated into the economy, being able to take advantage of the opportunities that should be available to everyone.) Mexican communities in the United States are continually augmented by immigration from Mexico. This tends to reinforce traditional cultural patterns, especially the use of Spanish. Puerto Ricans, because they are United States citizens by birth, have found it easy to maintain contact with their native island. This, too, reinforces cultural stability. The Cubans, on the other hand, have not had the privilege of visiting their homeland frequently.

The main barrier to assimilation is not cultural. It is economic. As a second, then a third, generation grows up and moves up the economic ladder, large segments of an originally immigrant society become Americanized. Thus Cuban Americans have made greater strides, in proportion to their numbers, than have Mexican Americans or Puerto Ricans. But as the latter two groups make themselves permanent residents of communities and take part in the political processes, they too improve their situation.

**In politics.** Ileana Ros-Lehtinen became the first Cuban American elected to the United States Congress in 1989; Henry Cisneros was the first Mexican American to become the mayor of a major city (San Antonio, Tex.), in 1981 and was named secretary of housing and urban development by President Clinton in 1992; Raul Castro became the first Mexican American to be elected governor of Arizona (1975); and in 1985 Xavier Suarez became the first Cuban American mayor of Miami. Bob Martinez, the first Hispanic governor of Florida, became the Bush Administration's antidrug leader in March 1991. A Mexican American, Lauro Cavazos, became the first Hispanic named to a Cabinet post when President Reagan appointed him secretary of education in 1988. President Bush appointed Antonia Novello, a native of Puerto Rico, to be Surgeon General of the United States in 1989.

**In entertainment.** Numerous Hispanic Americans have gained fame in the movies and television. These entertainers include Rita Moreno, Anthony Quinn, Linda Ronstadt, Edward James Olmos, Chita Rivera, Jose Ferrer, and Freddie Prinze.

**In athletics.** Hispanic Americans have also excelled in sports. Prominent athletes include golfer Lee Trevino, tennis player Pancho Gonzales, boxer Julio César Chávez, football player Jim Plunkett, and baseball player Keith Hernandez.

**FURTHER RESOURCES FOR HISPANIC AMERICANS**

**Bean, F.D., and Tienda, Marta.** The Hispanic Population of the United States (Russell Sage Foundation, 1988).
**Borjas, G.J.** Friends or Strangers: The Impact of Immigrants on the U.S. Economy (Basic Books, 1990).
**DeFreitas, Gregory.** Inequality at Work: Hispanics in the U.S. Labor Force (Oxford Univ. Press, 1991).
**Garver, Susan, and McGuire, Paula.** Coming to North America from Mexico, Cuba, and Puerto Rico (Delacorte, 1981).
**Kanellos, Nicolàs.** The Hispanic Almanac: From Columbus to Corporate America (Visible Ink, 1994).
**Marvis, B.J.** Contemporary American Success Stories: Famous People of Hispanic Heritage (Mitchell Lane Publishers, 1995).
**Meltzer, Milton.** The Hispanic Americans (Crowell, 1982).
**Moore, J.W., and Pachón, Harry.** Hispanics in the United States (Prentice, 1985).
**Morey, Janet, and Dunn, Wendy.** Famous Hispanic Americans (Dutton Children's Books, 1989).
**Nagel, Rob, and Rose, Sharon, eds.** Hispanic American Biography (UXL, 1995).
**Rogler, L.H.** Migrant in the City (Waterfront, 1984).
**Ryan, Bryan.** Hispanic Writers (Gale Research, 1991).
**Sandoval, Moisés.** On The Move: A History of the Hispanic Church in the United States (Orbis, 1990).
**Telger, Diane, and Kamp, Jim, eds.** Notable Hispanic American Women (Gale Research, 1993).
**Veciana-Suárez, Ana.** Hispanic Media: Impact and Influence (The Media Institute, 1990).

**HISPANIOLA.** The second largest island of the West Indies, Hispaniola is situated between Cuba and Puerto Rico in the Caribbean Sea. It is divided into the Republic of Haiti in the west and the Dominican Republic in the east. (*See also* Dominican Republic; Haiti.)

Covering an area of 29,418 square miles (76,192 square kilometers), it consists of alternate mountain ranges, long valleys, and plains. More than one third of the island lies at elevations higher than 1,500 feet (460 meters), and Pico Duarte at 10,417 feet (3,175 meters) is the highest peak of the West Indies. In contrast to the highlands, the basin of Lago Enriquillo is about 150 feet (46 meters) below sea level. There are frequent earthquakes. The subtropical climate has an average temperature of 79° F (26° C) and an annual rainfall of about 60 inches (150 centimeters).

Mountains are forested with such valuable trees as palms and laurels, and coffee is grown. Sugarcane is grown along the north coast on plantations that were largely established by the French during the 17th century. Other crops include cacao, tobacco, rice, sisal, and cotton. Most of the population is black, and the majority live in rural areas. Agriculture and livestock raising are the chief means of livelihood, but mining is increasingly significant.

The island was inhabited by Arawaks, an American Indian people, before Christopher Columbus landed there in 1492 and named it La Isla Española. During the Spanish colonial period it was also known as Santo Domingo.

*The Oriental Institute, located at the University of Chicago, was founded by James H. Breasted. The museum has a valuable and comprehensive collection of relics, primarily from ancient Egypt.*

Courtesy of the Oriental Institute, University of Chicago

# HISTORY

A sense of the past is a light that illuminates the present and directs attention toward the possibilities of the future. Without an adequate knowledge of history—the written record of events as well as the events themselves—today's events are disconnected occurrences. History is a science—a branch of knowledge that uses specific methods and tools to achieve its goals. To compile a history records are needed. Some of these are written records: government papers, diaries, letters, inscriptions, biographies, and many others. For ancient history, especially of the Middle East and China, there are lists of kings, of wars, and of significant events such as the building of temples or natural disasters. Archaeology uncovers many of these records. The laws promulgated by the Babylonian king Hammurabi (18th century BC) were inscribed on a stone pillar. The pillar, or stela, was discovered in 1901 (*see* Archaeology; Hammurabi).

In the modern period written records are much easier to obtain. Governments and other institutions keep records of nearly everything they do. Sometimes records are discovered by chance. When Germany was defeated in World War II, the fleeing Nazis left behind a huge amount of material documenting the Nazi era. These have been used to reconstruct the history of Germany between 1933 and 1945.

Records today are mostly written or printed on paper. In the past they could be inscribed on stone, written on parchment or papyrus, or drawn on buildings, monuments, or even household pottery or coins. Much has been learned about the reign of the Indian emperor Asoka because of the many edicts he issued. These were inscribed on pillars or rocks at public meeting places around India (*see* Asoka).

The modern science of historiography—history writing—developed as recently as the 19th century. It emerged in Germany, first at the University of Göttingen, then at other schools. Gradually the German influence spread to the rest of Europe and the United States. Behind the German decision to take a methodical and scientific approach to history there lie thousands of years of experience in dealing with history in many quite different societies.

## SENSE OF THE PAST

The Earth, the world of nature, and the universe all have pasts, but they have no history. Nor do individuals have histories, though every person has a past. The written past of an individual is called a biography. Only human societies have histories, based on collective memories from which they reconstruct their pasts. Not all attempts to reconstruct the past have resulted in histories. Before history emerged as a way of recounting past events, there were myth, legend, and epic. Even after ancient societies decided to keep written records, these did not necessarily constitute histories. Often they were no more than lists of kings or accounts of battles.

To be a true history an account of the past must not only retell what happened but must also relate events and people to each other. It must inquire into causes and effects. It must try to discern falsehood in the old records, such as attempts of kings to make themselves look better than they really were. It must also present the evidence on which its findings are based.

### Achievement of Israel

The ancient Greek writer Herodotus has long been known as the father of history. It is a title he was given by the Roman statesman Cicero. Long before Herodotus did his investigations in the 5th century BC, however, a stunning achievement in historical writing had been accomplished in ancient Israel. Most of the historical writings of nearby kingdoms, such as Egypt and Mesopotamia, had been records of events at the time they occurred; they were not researches into the past to discover national origins. This kind of effort was mostly left to writers of epics and the tellers of myths (*see* Epic; Mythology).

Israel, alone in the ancient world, was a nation with a sense of its history. It was a history rooted in a single and unforgettable event—the Exodus (departure) from Egypt under a dynamic leader named Moses. Behind Moses stood other notable personages dating back hundreds of years to Abraham and his descendants. Yet they too were somehow preserved permanently in the folk memory of the nation. (*See also* Abraham; Moses.)

Over a period of centuries Israel compiled what is the first true national history. The documents were preserved in the Hebrew Bible, also called the Old Testament (*see* Bible). The remarkable feature of this history is its inclusion of all the faults and failures, as well as the successes, of the nation over its long history. There was no attempt to color the record to make Israel look good to its descendants or to anyone else. Even the heroes of the narrative are depicted with all of their weaknesses and strengths.

Israel's national history is distinctive for other reasons as well. By the inclusion of a Creation narrative at the beginning, it became the first attempt to construct a universal history, a story that included the whole human race. The story as told in the Hebrew Bible is also an interpretation of history. It asserts that history has both a beginning and a goal. This was in contrast to other societies that looked upon the passing of time as a series of repetitive cycles, much like the passing of the seasons.

In time Israel's history was taken up by Christianity, which both adopted it outright and adapted it to its own uses. Still it remained a universal history and a story that would keep unfolding to the end of time. In the 5th century AD this history was reworked by St. Augustine in his book 'The City of God'. In this book he presents history as a progress toward the kingdom of God. The book is the source of later theories of inevitable progress. Some emphasize a natural progress and improvement in the human condition, while others—especially those inspired by Karl Marx—see history moving through violent revolutions toward a classless society, a heaven on Earth.

### Greek Achievement

When the Greek city-states emerged, they were societies without a past. The previous Cretan and Mycenaean civilizations had been swept away, leaving no trace in the collective memory of the Greeks. What they had were such epic traditions as the books of Homer and accounts of a long-gone age as told in purely mythological and legendary terms by Hesiod (*see* Hesiod; Homeric Legend).

The first historian of any significance in Greece was Hecateus, a native of Asia Minor who lived in the 6th and 5th centuries BC. Only fragments of his 'History' and 'Tour Around the World' have survived. He looked critically at the Greeks' attempts to account for their past and concluded: "The stories of the Greeks are numerous and in my opinion ridiculous."

When Hecateus traveled to Egypt and visited the priests (the official record-keepers), he commented that he was able to trace his ancestry back 16 generations. An Egyptian showed him evidence of the ancestry of their high priests back 345 generations. This overwhelming antiquity impressed him, as it did his successor Herodotus. They determined to inquire into the real origins of the nations they visited. (The word history is derived from the Greek *historia*, meaning "knowledge gained from inquiry.")

Greek historians, especially Herodotus and Thucydides, made at least two significant contributions to the writing of history. They weighed the evidence, attempting to separate the true from the false or fanciful. They also wrote about the recent past. Herodotus dealt with the Persian Wars in his 'History'. Thucydides wrote a history of the Peloponnesian War, an event through which he lived. He says of his research: "With reference to the narrative of events, far from permitting myself to derive it from the first source that came to hand, I did not even trust my own impressions, but it rests partly on what I saw myself, partly on what others saw for me, the accuracy of the report always being tried by the most severe and detailed tests possible." It was this way of dealing with history that was revived by the Germans in the 19th century. (*See also* Herodotus; Thucydides.)

### Chinese Achievement

China produced a mass of historical writings long unequalled by any other country until modern times. In this case, the purpose of history was primarily political. It was meant to serve as a guide for making decisions, in formulating public policies by recalling the way things had previously been done. Confucius (died 479 BC) stressed the need to transcribe all records carefully in order that they be transmitted faithfully to the next generation.

The origins of history writing seem to lie with scribes who kept careful records on the performance of rites honoring ancestors. Kings and emperors had such scribes at court to keep them aware of how things had been done before. These scribes became temple archivists, who eventually had charge of all past records. Slowly there grew a government bureaucracy just for the purpose of keeping records.

The most notable of ancient Chinese historians was Ssu-ma Ch'ien (died 85 BC). He was an astronomer, calendar expert, and grand historian of the imperial court. He authored 'Historical Records', the most significant history of ancient China to the 2nd century BC. In it he brought order to all the complex events of the past, recorded his sources, kept tables of chronology, gave detailed accounts of each Chinese state, and added a collection of biographies. Several centuries later Liu Chih-Chi (661–721) wrote the first treatise in any language on historical method. This was followed in the 11th century by a comprehensive history of China written by Ssu-ma Kuang.

## Some Notable Early Historians

*Some prominent historians are not included below because they are covered in the text of the article or in other articles in Compton's Encyclopedia (see Fact-Index).*

**Bede** (672–735). Usually known as the Venerable Bede, an Anglo-Saxon theologian and historian of the early Middle Ages. Declared a saint in 1899. Best known for his 'Ecclesiastical History of the English People', a vital source of information on the conversion of the Anglo-Saxon tribes.

**Dio Cassius** (150?–235). Roman administrator and historian. His 'Romaika', written in Greek, is the most comprehensive source of information on the last years of the Roman Republic and the early empire. Born in Bithynia in northwestern Asia Minor. Went to Rome about 180 and became a member of the Senate. Served as administrator in several provinces, including Pergamum and Smyrna, Africa, Dalmatia, and Pannonia. His history of Rome began with arrival of legendary Aeneas in Italy and ended during reign of Emperor Alexander Severus.

**Eusebius** (4th century AD). First major historian of Christian church. Fame rests on his 'Ecclesiastical History'. Writing of church history had been difficult before settled conditions of 4th century. Work written and revised several times between 312 and 324. Became bishop of Palestine about 313. Developed theory of Christian empire and wrote flattering 'Life of Constantine'.

**Guicciardini, Francesco** (1483–1540). Statesman and diplomat whose 'The History of Italy' is most valuable work on Italy written during late Renaissance. His earlier 'History of Florence' is major source for history of city after 1494. Served Florence and papacy as diplomat and administrator 1517–34.

**Josephus, Flavius** (37?–100). Joseph ben Matthias, better known as Josephus, was Jewish historian during first century of Roman Empire. Born in Jerusalem, participated unwillingly in revolt against Romans (66–70). Was pardoned by Emperor Vespasian and became partisan of Rome. Served under Titus in Roman siege of Jerusalem in 70. His 'History of the Jewish War' traces Jewish history from 2nd century BC through end of great revolt. 'Antiquities of the Jews' traces their history from creation up to outbreak of revolt in 66. Died in Rome about AD 100.

**Otto of Freising** (1111?–58). His 'Chronicle', covering history of world from Creation until 1146, is one of the most significant historical–philosophical works of Middle Ages. Bishop of Freising in Bavaria from 1138 until death. Half-brother of German king Conrad III and uncle of Frederick I Barbarossa. Another work dealt with Hohenstaufen Dynasty.

**Sallust** (86–34 BC). Roman historian of late Republic and great literary stylist. Politician and soldier. Often accused of corruption and malfeasance. Commanded one of Caesar's legions 49–46. Governor of Numidia 46–44. Author of 'Catiline's War', or 'The Catiline Conspiracy', 'The Jugurthine War', and 'Histories' (of which fragments survive).

**Suetonius** (69?–122?). Biographer and historian whose 'Lives of the Caesars' is filled with revealing and colorful gossip and scandal about lives of first 11 Roman emperors. From 117 to 122 served in various posts under Hadrian. 'Concerning Illustrious Men' contains nearly all that is known about lives of Rome's most eminent authors.

**Varthema, Lodovico de** (1465?–1517). Adventurer and traveler whose account of wanderings in Middle East and Asia earned him great fame in lifetime. Left on journey in 1502. First Christian known to have made Islamic pilgrimage to holy city of Mecca. Traveled through Arabia, India, Central Asia, Burma, Malaysia. Sailed around Africa to return home in 1507. His 'Travels of Lodovico de Varthema' (1510) appeared in English in 1576–77.

### Muslim History Writing

Like Judaism and Christianity, Islam is grounded in historical events, especially the life of Muhammad (*see* Muhammad). Much of Islamic historical writing was written primarily for religious reasons, to inspire the faithful, or as an explanation of legal precedents. Some writers, however, were careful in dealing with their sources, even if all they wrote were essentially biographical sketches of famous men.

By far the greatest of the Muslim writers of history is Ibn Khaldun (1332–1406). His 'Muqaddimah' is only an introduction to his universal history, but he presents a philosophy of history in which he accounts for the rise and fall of civilizations. He formulated general laws that govern the fates of societies, and he established rules for criticizing historical sources in order to get a correct reconstruction of the past. Arnold Toynbee in the 20th century called the 'Muqaddimah' "the greatest work of its kind that has ever yet been created by any mind." (*See also* Ibn Khaldun.)

## MODERN HISTORY

The writing of history during the Middle Ages did not languish entirely, but it made few significant advances. The Renaissance and the Enlightenment, however, brought major changes. Of great significance was learning how to analyze and criticize texts in order to guarantee their authenticity or prove their falsity. This field of textual criticism, called diplomatics, was pioneered in the 17th century by Jean Mabillon. His 'De Re Diplomatica' (1681) is the first formulation of the principles for determining the authenticity and dates of medieval documents. This branch of study has grown dramatically, embracing criticism of all ancient texts, especially those of the Bible.

Another achievement of the age was the secularizing of history—taking it out from under the control of God, the gods, or fate—and telling it simply as the story of human societies. Events and institutions were explained as the result of processes of development, dependent on human decisions and actions. The secularists looked carefully at all the influences that shaped a society. The best-known such history is Edward Gibbon's 'Decline and Fall of the Roman Empire' (1776–88), one of the prose masterpieces in the English language (*see* Gibbon). The leading theorist of this type of history was Giambattista Vico (1668–1744), whose brilliant work was largely ignored until the 20th century.

### German Achievement

It was in Germany, during the late 18th and early 19th centuries, that the bulk of historical writing came to be done by professional historians. For the professionals this was a matter of necessity in order to get good teaching appointments in universities or to consolidate their positions with their colleagues. This abundance of historical writing was aided by a climate of intellectual freedom and an increased tolerance by governments toward historiography.

Governments became willing to open their collections of records to historians. The British Public Record Office was founded in 1838 to give access to large collections of documents. The Vatican archives were opened to historians in 1883 by Pope Leo XIII. Today there are large library collections, both public and private, in many countries for use by historians and other scholars. Among the largest are the Library of Congress in Washington, D.C., and the British Museum in London.

The impetus for historical studies in Germany was provided in the 18th century by Johann Gottfried von Herder. He believed that the historian's task is to reconstruct what has actually happened. All periods and countries are equally deserving of study, according to Herder. He was followed in the 19th century by Leopold von Ranke. He believed that history evolves as the separate development of individuals, peoples, and states. He was especially interested in the continuity of cultural development that results in the nation. His main insistence was on objectivity—to describe how the past really was. Ranke's influence dominated German historiography until after World War I.

Much of German history writing is nationalistic, exalting the German state. This tendency arose from the defeats inflicted upon the German states by Napoleon prior to 1815. The center of the nationalist movement was in Prussia at the University of Berlin (founded in 1809). Eventually it was Prussia that brought about the unification of Germany in 1871, just in time to inflict a major defeat on France. The leader of the movement was Wilhelm von Humboldt. After unification, writers turned their attention to evaluating and praising the new German Empire.

Although the emphasis on nationalism was overdone, it exerted an influence on the growth of national histories in other countries. Jules Michelet, for example, wrote the first history of medieval France based on researches in the French national archives. In England Thomas Babington Macaulay's 'History of England' is a remarkably readable reconstruction of the past. It is considered flawed, however, by his nationalist views (see Macaulay).

### Early American Historiography

Prior to the arrival of German influences, there were several outstanding writers of history in the United States. Only a few are read in the 20th century. George Bancroft was the first American to plan a comprehensive study of the nation's past—from the colonial era through the Revolutionary War. His work, 'History of the United States', was published in ten volumes over a period of 40 years (1834–74). He used a vast number of original sources, including material from European archives. William H. Prescott wrote about Spain's empire in America. The best of his books is 'History of the Conquest of Mexico' (three volumes, 1843). He too used a great number of documentary sources, including material from Spain. Henry Adams, descendant of the second and sixth presidents, wrote 'History of the United States During the Administrations of Thomas

Jefferson and James Madison' (nine volumes, 1889–91). It is still one of the landmarks in American historical writing (see Adams, Henry).

As leading scholars from other nations spent time studying in German universities, the German techniques and methods in history spread throughout Europe and to the United States. The most influential organizer of the new American historiography was undoubtedly Herbert Baxter Adams, who made Johns Hopkins University the center for American historical studies between 1876 and his death in 1901. He was, in addition, a founder of the American Historical Association in 1884.

Woodrow Wilson, later president of the United States, wrote 'A History of the American People' (1902) as an attempt to present a chronicle on a broader base than politics. At the same time James Henry Breasted became one of the world's most eminent Egyptologists and archaeologists. In 1919 he organized the Oriental Institute at the University of Chicago as a repository for Egyptian relics.

The movement for creating a purely American history was launched by Frederick Jackson Turner of the University of Wisconsin in 1893, with his address to the American Historical Association on "The Significance of the Frontier in American History" ( see Frontier, "Meaning of the Frontier"; Turner, Frederick Jackson). Twenty years later Charles A. Beard set forth a new point of view on American history with his 'Economic Interpretation of the Constitution' (1913). In it he presented American history as successive conflicts between groups of economic interests.

### MAKING SENSE OF HISTORY

There are two primary points of view about the historical process, and adherents of neither side can prove their conclusions. One says that history is nothing more than a disordered collection of random happenings. Therefore no meaning can be found in history any more than one can find meaning and purpose in the world of nature.

The opposite point of view, the majority opinion, asserts that there is a design, purpose, or pattern in history. This viewpoint has its origins in the religious traditions of the West—in Judaism, Christianity, and Islam—but primarily in the Bible itself. Religious beliefs have concluded that history is an unfolding of God's plan for the world. Therefore it has purpose. St. Augustine elaborated this thesis in the 5th century, and in the 17th century the French theologian Jacques-Bénigne Bossuet carried the idea further in his 'Discourse on Universal History' (1681). The rise and fall of empires depend, in Bossuet's thought, on the secret designs of Providence.

The scientific discoveries of Isaac Newton changed the way people think about the world. It became possible to regard history as a process set in motion perhaps by God but left mostly to the decisions and actions of humanity. The thinkers of the Enlightenment underscored this, as they looked to humanity itself as the prime mover in history.

## Some Notable Modern Historians

*Some prominent historians are not included below because they are covered in the main text of the article or in other articles in Compton's Encyclopedia (see Fact-Index).*

**Beard, Charles A.** (1874–1948). American historian Charles Austin Beard best known for economic interpretation of development of United States. Graduated from De Pauw University in 1898. Studied at Oxford. First book was 'The Industrial Revolution' (1901). Taught at Columbia University 1904–17. Co-founder of New School for Social Research in 1919. Most noted works: 'An Economic Interpretation of the Constitution of the United States' (1913) and 'Rise of American Civilization' (1927).

**Braudel, Fernand** (1902–85). French historian and one of the great historiographers of 20th century. Studied at Sorbonne in Paris. Taught in Algiers (1924–32), Paris (1932–35), Brazil (1935–37) before joining faculty of École Pratique des Hautes Études in Paris. Served in World War II. First major work was two-volume 'The Mediterranean and the Mediterranean World in the Age of Philip II' (1949). Other outstanding work was three-volume 'Civilization and Capitalism' (1968, 1979).

**Breasted, James Henry** (1865–1935). American historian who founded Oriental Institute in Chicago in 1919. Professor at University of Chicago. Translated and published 'Ancient Records of Egypt' (1906). Author of 'History of Egypt' (1905), 'Ancient Times' (1916), and 'Development of Religion and Thought in Ancient Egypt' (1912).

**Collingwood, Robin George** (1889–1943). English historian and one of leading philosophers of history in 20th century. Studied at Oxford and remained as teacher until retirement in 1941. Leading authority on Roman Britain. Author of 'The Archaeology of Roman Britain' (1930). Philosophical works were 'Religion and Philosophy' (1916), 'Speculum Mentis' (1924), 'Essay on Philosophical Method' (1933), and 'The Idea of History' (1946, after his death).

**Commager, Henry Steele** (born 1902). American historian. Taught at New York University (1926–38), at Columbia (1938–56), and at Amherst College (1956 until retirement in 1971). Co-author of 'Growth of the American Republic' (1930). Wrote 'The American Mind' (1950), 'Freedom, Loyalty, Dissent' (1954), 'Nature and Problems of History' (1965), 'Search for a Usable Past' (1967).

**Mommsen, Theodor** (1817–1903). German historian whose masterpiece was 'The History of Rome' (1854–56, 1885). Awarded Nobel prize for literature in 1902. Wrote 'Roman Constitutional Law' (1871–88), first codification of Roman law, and 'Roman Criminal Law' (1899). His 'Corpus Inscriptionum Latinarum' (Collection of Latin Inscriptions) was first comprehensive collection of its kind. Studied at University of Kiel and in Italy. Active in politics and journalism in Germany during 1840s. Professor at Universities of Leipzig, Zurich, and Breslau.

**Morison, Samuel Eliot** (1887–1976). American historian. Served in United States Navy. Graduated from Harvard University and taught there for 40 years. Books included 'Admiral of the Ocean Sea' (biography of Columbus, 1942), 'John Paul Jones' (1959), 'European Discovery of America' (Northern Voyages, 1971; Southern Voyages, 1974), and 15-volume 'History of United States Naval Operations in World War II' (1947–62).

**Taylor, A.J.P.** (1906–90). English historian whose books concentrated on modern Europe. Graduated from Oxford in 1927. Studied in Vienna. Taught at Manchester University (1930–38) and at Oxford (1938 to retirement). Author of 'Habsburg Monarchy' (1941), 'Course of German History' (1945), 'Struggle for Mastery in Europe' (1954), 'Origins of the Second World War' (1961), and 'English History 1914–1945' (1965).

In the 19th century history was interpreted by the German philosopher G.F.W. Hegel as a process of change caused by action, reaction, and the result, or synthesis, of the two. History cannot be interpreted mechanistically. Humans have freedom, but this freedom can only be fulfilled through overcoming obstacles. History is not a series of smooth transitions but rather progress through struggle and conflict.

A similar view was presented by Karl Marx. History is subject to laws just as nature is. History has a direction. It is governed by economic realities, by the way in which people produce and use wealth. Inevitably classes develop, and these struggle with each other for the control of the means of production. The goal of these conflicts is reached in the classless society, toward which there was an inevitable progress.

Two writers in the 20th century put forward complex and influential philosophies of history: Oswald Spengler and Arnold Toynbee (*see* Spengler; Toynbee). Spengler's pessimistic 'Decline of the West' was published from 1918 to 1922. Coming out as it did under the cloud World War I had cast over Europe, it was widely accepted, though he had actually written it before the war. It describes culture, or civilizations, in biological terms, as though each were a natural organism. Cultures, he believed, are born; they mature, and they die through a process of growth and decay. The problem with this notion is that if cultures are individual biological organisms they cannot influence each other for good or ill. Nevertheless, his thesis agreed well with the disillusionment felt in much of the world after the war.

Toynbee, too, undertook to study the development of civilizations. He rejected the notion that the past can be viewed as a straight line of progress or development. He also disagreed with Spengler's assertion that the West is doomed. Toynbee, in his 12-volume 'Study of History' (1934–61), declares that civilization arose in societies through a response to challenges. If the challenge is too great or too little, there is no significant advance. Hence the Eskimo have not proceeded beyond a rudimentary culture because the challenge of their environment is too great. In the perpetually warm climates societies find the challenge too small. It is in the temperate areas of the world, such as North America and Northern Europe, that humanity has best been able to meet challenges and create high civilizations. (*See also* Civilization.)

### FURTHER RESOURCES FOR HISTORY

**Braudel, Fernand.** On History (Univ. of Chicago Press, 1982).
**Butterfield, Herbert.** The Origins of History (Basic Books, 1981).
**Fitzsimmons, M.A.** The Past Recaptured: Great Historians and the History of History (Notre Dame Press, 1983).
**Hamerow, T.S.** Reflections on History and Historians (Univ. of Wis. Press, 1986).
**Iggers, G.** The German Conception of History (Wesleyan Univ. Press, 1983).
**Kahler, Erich.** Man the Measure (Westview, 1985).
**Renier, G.J.** History: Its Purpose and Method (Mercer Univ. Press, 1982).
**Tuchman, Barbara.** Practicing History (Knopf, 1981).

*Alfred Hitchcock, late in his career, posed before the silhouette of himself that was his trademark. In many of his films he made a fleeting, wordless appearance.*

**HITCHCOCK, Alfred** (1899–1980). The motion picture director Alfred Hitchcock was a master of suspense and horror films. His artistry, often coupled with humorous touches, was such that he himself became as notable as his movie work. He became well known to television audiences through his Alfred Hitchcock Presents, a series that was revived some years after his death.

Hitchcock was born in London, England, on Aug. 13, 1899. He attended St. Ignatius College and the University of London. He began to work in films in 1920. His first directing job was on 'The Pleasure Garden' (1925). His 'Blackmail' (1929) was the first successful British talking picture. After directing such classics as 'The Thirty-nine Steps' (1935) and 'The Lady Vanishes' (1938), he left England for Hollywood, Calif. His first American movie, 'Rebecca' (1940), won an Academy award. He followed this with 'Spellbound' (1945), 'Notorious' (1946), 'Strangers on a Train' (1951), 'Rear Window' (1954), 'Vertigo' (1958), 'North by Northwest' (1959), 'The Birds' (1963), 'Family Plot' (1976), and many more. In 'Psycho' (1960) he raised the horror film to new levels. Hitchcock died in Bel Air, Calif., on April 29, 1980.

**HITLER, Adolf** (1889–1945). The rise of Adolf Hitler to the position of dictator of Germany is the story of a frenzied ambition that plunged the world into the worst war in history. Only an army corporal in World War I, Hitler became Germany's chancellor 15 years later.

He was born on April 20, 1889, in Braunau-am-Inn, Austria, of German descent. His father Alois was the illegitimate son of Maria Anna Schicklgruber. In middle age Alois took the name Hitler from his paternal grandfather. After two wives had died Alois married his foster daughter, Klara Poelzl, a Bavarian, 23 years younger than he. She became Adolf's mother.

Hitler's rambling, emotional autobiography 'Mein Kampf' (My Struggle) reveals his unstable early life. His father, a petty customs official, wanted the boy to study for a government position. But as young Hitler wrote later, "the thought of slaving in an office made me ill . . . not to be master of my own time." Passively defying his father, the self-willed boy filled most of his school hours with daydreams of becoming a painter. His one school interest was history, especially that of the Germans. When his teacher glorified Germany's role, "we would sit there enraptured and often on the verge of tears." From boyhood he was devoted to Wagner's operas that glorified the Teutons' dark and furious mythology.

Failure dogged him. After his father's death, when Adolf was 13, he studied watercolor painting, but accomplished little. After his mother's death, when he was 19, he went to Vienna. There the Academy of Arts rejected him as untalented. Lacking business training, Hitler eked out a living as a laborer in the building trades and by painting cheap postcards. He often slept in parks and ate in free soup kitchens.

These humbling experiences inflamed his discontent. He hated Austria as "a patchwork nation" and looked longingly across the border at energetic, powerful Germany. He wrote, "I was convinced that the State [Austria] was sure to obstruct every really great German and to support . . . everything un-German. . . . I hated the motley collection [in Austria] of Czechs, Ruthenians, Poles, Hungarians, Serbs, Croats, and above all that ever-present fungoid growth—Jews . . . I became a fanatical anti-Semite."

Hitler's hatred of poverty, his rabid devotion to his German heritage, and his loathing of Jews combined to form the seeds of his later political doctrine. He studied the political skill of Vienna's mayor and took special note of that leader's practice of "using all instruments of existing power, and of gaining the favor of influential institutions . . . so he could draw the greatest possible advantages for his own movement from such old-established sources of power." Hitler later applied this technique in Germany.

In 1912 Hitler left "wretched" Vienna for Munich, a "true German town." There he drifted from job to job as carpenter, architect's draftsman, and watercolorist. Always he ranted about his political ideas.

At the outbreak of World War I in 1914, he gave up his Austrian citizenship to enlist in the 16th Bavarian infantry regiment. He would not fight for Austria, "but I was ready to die at any time for my people [Germans]." In his first battle, the Ypres offensive of 1914, he shouted the song 'Deutschland, Deutschland über Alles.' On the Somme in 1916 he was a "front fighter" against British tanks, rose to lance corporal, won the Iron Cross as dispatch runner, and was wounded. In 1917 he fought in the third battle of Ypres.

The armistice found him in a hospital, temporarily blinded by mustard gas and suffering from shock. The news of Germany's defeat agonized him. He believed defeat had been caused by "enemies within," chiefly Jews and Communists.

Now no longer an Austrian citizen and not yet a German citizen, Hitler at the war's end was a man without a country. Bewildered, he remained in the army, stationed in Munich. In the political and economic tempest that swept defeated Germany, Munich became a storm center. Officers of the beaten *Reichswehr* (German army) conspired to win control of Germany. They maintained "informers," one of whom was Adolf Hitler. He was assigned to report on "subversive activities" in Munich's political parties.

This political spying was the turning point of Hitler's life. One night in 1919 he threaded his way through the Herrenstrasse to a bleak little restaurant where a handful of young people sat around a half-broken gas lamp. This little band was the German Workers' party. Guided by "intuition," Hitler joined as its seventh member. He soon took the lead. Then a Reichswehr officer, Capt. Ernest Roehm, saw the party as a possible means of overthrowing the liberal Bavarian republic. Like other officers, Roehm had built one of the private "volunteer" armies, which grew up as arms of the Reichswehr in defiance of the Versailles Treaty. Roehm assigned his arrogant, iron-hard Brown Shirt army to aid the Workers' party. Bulwarked by these armed ruffians, Hitler became the orator of the group.

### Creates the Nazi Party

In 1920 he changed its name to *Nationalsozialistische Deutsche Arbeiterpartei* (National Socialist German Workers' party), abbreviated to *Nazi*. Sneering at the liberal generalities of the various bourgeois parties and hating the Communists, Hitler shouted accusations against the Jews and cried out to the Germans to form an all-powerful national state. His voice, torn and hoarsened by mustard gas, was a hypnotic one.

*Hitler addressed a Nazi party rally (left) in Bad Harzburg, Germany, on Oct. 20, 1931, demanding the resignation of the government. Eight years later, on Nov. 22, 1939, as chancellor of Germany in the first months of World War II, he spoke to a gathering of old comrades at the Buergerbrau beer hall (right), where a bomb exploded shortly after he had left.*

His speeches kindled the anger of rivals, especially the Communists, and they tried to break up his meetings. They were prevented from doing so by the brutal Nazis.

The flamboyant spirit of the growing Nazi party now began to attract the varied restless men who were to become its core. They included chiefly Alfred Rosenberg, Russian-born engineer and "philosopher," anti-Jew, and anti-Christian; Rudolf Hess, Egyptian-born mathematician and geographer; Hermann Goering, Bavarian combat pilot; Gen. Erich von Ludendorff, war hero; and Maj. Gen. Franz von Epp, Bavarian infantry commander. All helped to persuade Communist-fearing German industrialists to give money to the party, for Hitler assured them that "we combat only Jewish international capital."

An established Munich journal, *Völkischer Beobachter* (National Observer) was bought to spread Nazi influence. For his followers Hitler adopted the ancient swastika (hooked cross) as the party emblem and designed the Nazi red banner with the black swastika. He saluted his comrades with raised stiff arm and was greeted by the word *Heil!*

### From "Beer Hall Putsch" to Prison

By 1923 the Nazis had grown strong enough in Munich to try to seize the government. They started the "Beer Hall Putsch," so-called because Hitler and his henchmen tried to take over the reins of government at a meeting that was held in a beer hall. The attempt failed. Hitler was convicted of treason and sentenced to five years in prison. The Bavarian

government commuted the term to eight months. While in prison Hitler, aided by the loyal Rudolf Hess, began 'Mein Kampf'.

Emerging from prison in 1924, Hitler once again seemed destined to failure. The government had banned the Nazi party, and only a handful of the members clung together. For months Hitler took little interest. At length Roehm, Hess, and a newcomer—a small, lame enthusiast named Joseph Paul Goebbels—spurred him back to leadership. Accepting, Hitler said, "I shall need seven years before the movement is on top again."

### Industrialists Help Rebuild Nazi Party

He was right. The years 1924–28 were prosperous for Germany, and revolutions do not flourish on prosperity. From 1925 to 1927 Hitler was even forbidden to speak publicly in either Bavaria or Saxony. Then a world-wide depression plunged Germany again into poverty and unemployment, and the Nazis began to gain votes. By 1930 Hitler had the support of many industrialists and the military caste. In 1933 President Paul von Hindenburg appointed him chancellor. The history section in the article Germany traces the steps by which Hitler became dictator and instigator of World War II. (*See also* World War II.)

Believing himself on the road to world conquest, in 1941 Hitler made himself Personal Commander of the Army and, in 1942, Supreme War Lord. However, on July 20, 1944, a group of officers, dismayed by his "intuitive" military failures, set off a bomb in his office. He escaped with only a nervous shock.

### The Legend of "Hitler the Superman"

Nazi propaganda had made of Hitler a symbol of strength and national virtue. He had won German citizenship in 1930 only by the scheming of Nazi

*Adolf Hitler in military uniform.*

AP/Wide World

henchmen, yet he was hailed as the ideal German leader. His indecisions were cloaked as "intuition." Despite his hours and even days of brooding inertia, he was pictured as a man of intense action. He became idolized by young Germans, whom he had betrayed by his creed, "the entire work of education is branding the race feeling into the hearts and brains of youth."

Covering his unsavory and cruel character, propaganda built a legend of his ascetic habits and selfless devotion to Germany. Some of this legend vanished when his long, secret association with Eva Braun was revealed. He married her in April 1945, just before he committed suicide in the ruined Reichschancellery. Hitler was declared dead officially Oct. 25, 1956, after his remains had been definitely identified.

**HITTITES.** Four thousand years ago the warrior Hittites of Asia Minor rose to world power. For more than a thousand years they ruled most of the region now in modern Turkey and Syria. Their empire rivaled in size and strength the two other world powers of the time, Egypt and the Assyro-Babylonian empires of Mesopotamia.

About a thousand years before the Christian Era their empire fell and their civilization passed into oblivion. Only their name remained, kept in man's memory by scattered references in the Old Testament.

The story of the Hittites, nearly all that is known of it, has been recovered within a single lifetime. Most of it has been pieced together since World War I. The chief source of information is the royal library of 10,000 clay tablets discovered in 1906 and later, in the ruins of the ancient Hittite capital Khattushash, near Bogaz Koi in Turkey, about 90 miles (145 kilometers) east of Ankara.

These tablets are in cuneiform writing, and most of them, though in Babylonian spelling, are in the Hittite language. For years Hugo Winckler, the German archaeologist who made the find, and other scholars labored vainly to get a clue to this unknown tongue. One day an Austrian professor, Friedrich Hrozny, found in the same sentence with the Babylonian word-sign for bread, the Hittite word *wadar* spelled out. He thought this might be the same as our "water." Other words seemed to have the same roots as the Latin "*aqua*" (water) and our "eat." Working from these slight clues, by 1915 he was able to announce that he had solved the riddle, and that Hittite is an Indo-European language, related to our own. But the translation of the tablets took another ten years.

From these and other documents, and from the remains of their great fortified cities, it is now known that the Hittites were wild tribesmen when, not long after 3000 BC, they swept down from the north with horse and chariot and bronze daggers. They found it easy to conquer the farmers and herdsmen of Asia Minor, who were skilled only in the arts of peace and had no means of transport faster or more powerful than the donkey. It was almost 2000 BC, however, before the Hittite dominions were united into an empire by a king named Labarna. A later king pushed

*A Hittite warrior (top), from about 1000BC, was depicted in a wall relief from the outer citadel gate in Zincirli, Turkey. Two superb lions (bottom) were dug up near Antioch in Turkey.*

*The Hittites were superb artisans, as can be seen from a finely crafted gold cup (top left) found in Mycenae and now housed in the National Museum in Athens. Clay documents were sealed in clay envelopes (top right). At the top of a relief (bottom) showing a Hittite prince hunting deer can be seen an example of Hittite hieroglyphics, not deciphered until the 1930s.*

the Hittite power into Syria and Mesopotamia. This empire lasted until 1650 BC. A still more powerful one arose in 1450 BC.

If the basis of the old empire had been the horse, that of the new was iron. The Hittites appear to have been the first to use iron. For a time their mines on the Black Sea represented the world supply.

Later the Hittite domain broke up into city kingdoms (1050–850 BC), and these finally collapsed before the Acheans, who came in a new wave of Indo-European invasion like that from which the Hittite empire had sprung. The Hittites continued to be famous soldiers, however. Uriah the Hittite was a captain in David's army.

In the fertile fringes of their rugged country the ancient Hittites planted barley, wheat, grapes, and olives. Beekeeping was their sugar industry. They raised horses, cattle, sheep, and goats. Their shoes,

turned up like a ski, were invented for use in snowy mountain passes. Loom weights and spindle whorls found in great numbers show that they manufactured cloth. Beautiful cups, jars, and pitchers indicate their interest in graceful and original forms and in convenient contrivances. The Hittites were also famous workers in metals. Their business methods were Babylonian, and for buying and selling they too used the weighed pieces of silver from which the Greeks got the idea for coins. Caravan routes led from town to town. Big game abounded, and hunting was the sport of king and commoner.

The Hittite state was a military organization. Daily life was closely regulated by law. The price of plowed field and vineyard, of cattle and their hides, was fixed. So were the wages of free man and slave. Punishments for breaches of the law were mild, but crimes such as murder and theft were made prohibitively expensive by heavy fines.

The Hittites contributed to Western civilization by acting as middlemen for the older cultures of the East. They passed on to the Greeks ideas that influenced their art, their religion, and their business. Hittite mines supplied the iron that put new implements in the hands of the Mediterranean peoples and brought the Bronze Age to a close. Above all, Hittites contributed by holding with a firm hand the bridge between Asia and Europe while Western culture was in its early stages. Asian despots might have throttled European civilization in its infancy, had it not been for that millennium of Hittite supremacy.

Richard Cummins/Corbis

*Hobart is Tasmania's capital, largest city, and chief commercial center. With a fine deepwater port, it is also a transportation hub.*

## HOBART, Australia.

Australia's southernmost city, Hobart is the capital of the island-state of Tasmania. Its metropolitan area is home to some two fifths of the state's residents. The city lies on the Derwent River Estuary, about 12 miles (19 kilometers) from the southeastern coast of the island. The often snow-covered Mount Wellington rises 4,167 feet (1,270 meters) in the west, and Mount Nelson overlooks the city from the south. The city has a mild-to-cool climate with an annual average temperature of 54° F (12° C).

Hobart has retained many of its historic—mostly sandstone—buildings, such as the Anglesea Barracks (1811), St. George's Church (1838), the Theatre Royal (1837; partly rebuilt), and Australia's oldest Jewish synagogue (mid-1840s). The city is home to the University of Tasmania and the state library, symphony orchestra, and museum and art gallery. Every December yachts race hundreds of miles south from Sydney, on the mainland, to Hobart.

Hobart is the commercial center of Tasmania. The city's economy depends largely on services, including health care, government, retail trade, education, banking, and business activities. Manufacturing is also important. Local factories produce processed fruits and other foods, automobile parts, wood and paper products, printed materials, and metal parts. A center of transport, the city has an excellent deepwater port and air, rail, and highway links.

Hobart is Australia's second oldest state capital, after Sydney. The British founded Hobart as a colony in 1804. In the 1800s it grew as a supply port for seal hunters and whaling ships. It officially became a city in 1842. Population (2001 census), metropolitan area, 191,169.

**HOBBES, Thomas** (1588–1679). The English political theorist Thomas Hobbes lived during the decades when kingly absolutism in Europe was drawing to a close and sentiments for popular democracy were emerging. In his book 'Leviathan' (1651) he provided the formula for an ideal state in which all citizens would live together under terms of a social contract. To keep everyone from exercising too much freedom, however, there would be an absolute monarch.

Hobbes was born in Westport in Wiltshire, England, on April 5, 1588. He graduated from Oxford University in 1608 and became a classical scholar and mathematician before taking an interest in the study of politics. His first work was a translation of Thucydides' history of the Peloponnesian War (1629). His fascination with mathematics began at age 40, when he read Euclid's 'Elements'.

His study of geometry and physics led him to plan a three-volume work on the physical world, the human body, and citizenship. As events were progressing toward civil war in England, he wrote the third volume first under the title 'The Elements of Law, Natural and Politic' (1640). The political crisis in England caused him to flee into exile in Paris, where he remained until 1651.

Hobbes enjoyed royal favor and security from his enemies beginning in 1660, when Charles II came to the throne. Hobbes had earlier tutored Charles in mathematics. He was briefly threatened with charges of heresy, but the king protected him. He continued writing and publishing almost up to the day of his death. He published a translation of Homer's 'Odyssey' in 1675 and of the 'Iliad' in 1676. Hobbes died in Derbyshire on Dec. 4, 1679.

**HOBBY, Oveta Culp** (1905–95). During World War II Oveta Culp Hobby served as director of the newly formed U.S. Women's Army Corps (WAC). In 1953 she was appointed secretary of the new Department of Health, Education, and Welfare (HEW, now Health and Human Services), the second woman to hold a Cabinet position in the U.S. federal government.

Oveta Culp was born on Jan. 19, 1905, in Killeen, Tex. She attended Mary Hardin-Baylor College and the University of Texas law school. For six years, from 1925 to 1931, she worked as parliamentarian for the Texas legislature. In 1931 she married William P. Hobby, publisher of the *Houston Post*, and after her marriage she became an integral part of the newspaper's operation. Except for her years in government work, she remained with the newspaper until her retirement in 1965. In 1941 Hobby went to Washington to head the women's division of the War Department's Bureau of Public Relations. The next year she was appointed to supervise the WAC. She supported Dwight D. Eisenhower for the presidency in 1952. After his election she was appointed administrator of the Federal Security Agency, which became HEW in 1953. She remained as secretary of the department until 1955. Hobby died in Houston on Aug. 16, 1995.

*Learning to paint early in life may lay the foundation for a hobby pursued in later years.*
© Erika Stone—Peter Arnold, Inc.

# HOBBY

In the 16th century a favorite toy for children of all ages was the hobbyhorse. In appearance a hobbyhorse could be as simple as a stick, or it could have a decorated wooden framework with an imitation horse's head attached. Whether simple or elaborate, children used them for the games of the time involving war and knighthood, much as children in the early part of the 20th century played cowboys and Indians. In time the popularity of the hobbyhorse declined, but the pleasure of doing something outside the routine activities of daily life had brought a new word into the language, the word hobby, which is a shortened form of hobbyhorse.

Hobbies today include a vast range of activities. The definition that best covers all these activities is probably constructive leisure-time activities. This definition excludes games and sports, and it leaves out purely spectator activities like watching television. It also excludes schooling and work done to make a living. A hobby, like playing with a hobbyhorse, is an activity apart from the ordinary routines of life. It should encourage the use of creativity and imagination and bring the reward of learning. Some hobbies bring monetary rewards as well.

## HISTORICAL BACKGROUND

Before the 20th century, hobbies were something that only wealthy people had the time and money to enjoy. The present-day interest in hobbies throughout the world is the product of more free time for far more people, resulting from shortened working hours and greater prosperity.

Some popular hobbies are as old as civilization. These include such activities as music, dance, literature, painting, sculpture, carving and whittling, weaving, raising pets, astrology, and the making of pottery, baskets, beadwork, kites, toys, leather goods, dolls, hunting decoys, fishing lures, jewelry, and miniatures or models.

Rulers in ancient times often collected valuable objects, rare manuscripts, and art treasures. The monasteries of the Middle Ages maintained libraries to store the valuable documents and art works that they collected and produced. Later, individuals who were well educated and had a broad range of interests made field trips and traveled to other countries, bringing back fossils, plants, artifacts, and other objects. Such people also built up extensive personal libraries and collections.

During the second half of the 19th century the Arts and Crafts Movement in England appeared as a reaction to the Industrial Revolution and prompted a great popular interest in handicrafts through its magazine, appropriately named *The Hobby Horse* (see Handicrafts). There were public exhibitions of handicrafts in England between 1888 and 1896, followed by similar expositions in Boston and Chicago in 1897.

## KINDS OF HOBBIES

Hobbies are either consciously chosen, or they arise from an individual's interests, skills, daily work, tastes, ambitions, or past schooling. Stamp or coin collecting are examples of hobbies based on deliberate choice. Making model airplanes can be something to do for a pastime, or it might develop as a result of service in an air force or as an airline pilot. Designing computer programs is apt to be a hobby based on work experience or schooling.

All hobbies involve activity, but some involve more than others. Collecting—whether of antiques, coins, or first editions of books—is relatively passive compared to doing one's own paintings or making furniture. Whatever the activity level, all types can require high levels of expertise.

There are vast amounts of information available for hobbyists who want to learn more about their specialty or who need instruction. Most towns and cities have hobby shops and handicraft stores that sell kits, books, and magazines. There are books about hobbies in general as well as works on specific hobbies. There is a magazine for every hobby. Among the dozens of magazines available are: *Antiques and Collecting Hobbies; Aviation Postcard Collector; Book Collecting World; British Model Soldier Society Bulletin; Classic Car; Collectors World; Crafts; Dime Novel Roundup; Engineering in Miniature; Flying Models; Jewelry Making, Gems, and Minerals; Miniature Collector; National Hobby News;* and *Craft and Needlework Age.*

There have traditionally been four types of hobbies—those relating to history, nature, handicrafts, and the arts. Recently, with advances in electronics, many individuals have made computer use a hobby, while others use videocassette cameras to make their own movies. There can be considerable overlap between some types, especially between hobbies relating to the arts and those that have to do with the past. Scrimshaw, for instance, is an art, but it is also a kind of memorabilia relating to 19th-century sailing. Many hobbies require both collecting and creating.

### HOBBIES IN THE ARTS

The arts covered in this section are painting, sculpture, music, and literature. They may be the most challenging areas for hobbyists to work in, and perhaps for this reason they are less popular than nature, historical, or handicraft hobbies.

### Painting, Decoupage, and Sculpture

Amateur artists have included such well-known personalities as British Prime Minister Winston Churchill, President Dwight D. Eisenhower, singer Tony Bennett, actor Anthony Quinn, and comedians Red Skelton and Phyllis Diller. They are described as amateurs because they did not make their living by painting. The quality of their work was often highly professional. Churchill had a retrospective show of his work at New York City's Metropolitan Museum of Art, and the works of the others have also been publicly displayed. One of the best-known amateur artists in the 20th-century United States was a retired farm woman named Anna Mary Robertson Moses, who painted under the name Grandma Moses. Although she had no formal art training, her paintings were critically acclaimed and have been exhibited throughout the United States and Europe.

For beginners there are kits packaged with materials and instructions. Some kits are for painting by numbers—actually a hobby closer to handicraft than doing original art. There are also kits for decoupage, collage, the making of mobiles, wood-block printing, and other art forms. Many communities offer courses for both adults and children who want to learn painting. Senior citizen centers often have art courses for retired people. Many colleges accept part-time art students, and night-school courses are often available as well.

Decoupage, an art form that originated in France during the 17th century, involves cutting out designs and patterned materials and fastening them permanently to some surface. One of the appeals of decoupage is the ability to turn plain but useful items into appealing works of folk art (*see* Folk Art).

Collage, a 20th-century offshoot of decoupage, uses the techniques of decoupage within the limits of a frame to create a piece of artwork. Pablo Picasso was one of the first painters to use the technique, combining paints with other materials on canvas.

**Weaving is a skill that younger children can turn into a hobby to make useful household objects.**
J. Berndt—Stock, Boston

Amateur sculptors also can find kits of materials and instructions. Beginners usually start with clay before going on to materials such as stone or wood. Some hobbyists use other, untraditional materials, including soap, scrap metal, wax, vegetables, or bread dough, to make sculptures.

### Music and Theater

Hobbyists make of music both a pastime and sometimes a second vocation. They may learn to play a musical instrument for pleasure, but there are many opportunities for people with sufficient talent to participate in chamber music concerts, community orchestras, or other groups. Singers join choral organizations or form duets, quartets, or other small groups for public performances. The well-known barbershop quartets are made up largely of individuals who enjoy music as a hobby. Some popular rock music groups got their start by playing together in high school as a hobby. Some hobbyists collect musical instruments, sheet music, or recordings.

Community theaters offer an outlet for amateurs of diverse talents. Besides acting, there is need for set designers and builders, lighting specialists, costumers, directors, and stage managers. Some theater groups—especially in Europe—stage annual pageants, Christmas plays, or Passion plays. The actors who appear in the Passion play at Oberammergau, Germany, are well-trained amateurs who must occupy themselves with other work during the ten years between performances. In addition to taking an active part in productions, people may make a hobby of attending performances, collecting playbills, and reading plays.

### Writing

Writing is a common task of daily life, but many people who feel they have no talent for other arts are able to express themselves better with words. Some amateur writers have been able to become professionals after selling stories to publishers. Others are satisfied to become accomplished letter writers. Community newspapers often depend on amateur writers for weekly columns. In New York State the Kingston *Daily Freeman* has run outstanding articles on forgotten industries of the past contributed by nonprofessional writers. (*See also* Writing, Creative.)

## HOBBIES RELATING TO THE PAST

President Harry Truman and Prime Minister Winston Churchill were amateur historians. Churchill, in fact, almost gained the status of a professional through his books on the world wars and the English-speaking peoples. Many individuals find out more about their nation's past by traveling to scenes of battles or other historic events or by visiting historic places. Quite often hobbyists who are interested in history decide to collect antiques, coins, stamps, and memorabilia. (For coin and stamp collecting, *see* Coins; Stamp.)

### Antiques

Collecting antiques can be expensive, but it may also be profitable. A genuine antique, defined as an object 100 or more years old, can be expensive to purchase. It can also increase in value and be worth much more than the original purchase price if the collector later decides to sell it. Many countries permit antiques to be imported duty free as art objects. Under the Florence agreement of 1952, sponsored by the United Nations Educational, Scientific, and Cultural Organization, antiques were included in the definition of cultural materials.

Antique collecting is an ancient hobby, dating back to the period when temple treasures were preserved in Greece and Rome. Interest in learning about and preserving a nation's past are common motives for starting a collection. The search for antiques often

*Playing an instrument in a school orchestra or band can lead to a career or a musical hobby.*
Alan Felix—FPG International

involves travel, and vacation itineraries are planned as antique-hunting expeditions. So lucrative has antique collecting become that some unscrupulous individuals have gone into the business of manufacturing fake antiques (*see* Counterfeiting and Forgery).

As collecting has become widespread, regular antique shows have been established in many cities. There are publications and price lists indicating items that are currently popular and those that are expected to be in demand in the future.

## Memorabilia

Objects that bring to mind the past are called memorabilia or mementos. People may collect such objects because of nostalgia, sentiment, a desire to have reminders of a way of life that has passed, or special interest in a historical event, such as the American Civil War. Collectible items of a specific era may include postcards, newspapers, books, political campaign buttons, musical recordings, road maps, license plates, household utensils, photographs, travel souvenirs, old mail-order catalogs, toys, player-piano rolls, comic books, figurines and dolls, and old almanacs. All of these items may be of value, and offers to buy or sell them may be found in collector and hobby magazines.

Personal memorabilia collected by an individual are called souvenirs. They normally represent memories of places visited. Souvenirs of some trips are general in that they recall visits to countries or cities. Others recollect a special occasion such as a world fair. Souvenirs include color slides, photographs, postcards, picture books, local artwork or crafts, plates, coffee or beer mugs, items of clothing—almost anything acquired to remember a travel experience.

**Military history** has attracted a large number of enthusiasts. In the United States the Civil War of 1861–65 has more devotees than any similar period in American history. Famous battlefields, such as Gettysburg and Vicksburg, draw thousands of visitors each year. The number of collectible items from the war include old weapons, uniforms, Confederate stamps and coins, photographs, toy soldiers, and information about President Abraham Lincoln and other leaders of the time. In Europe the Napoleonic era is a favorite period for collectors and students. Some military hobbyists may focus on one country's wars by collecting uniforms and weapons from each conflict, though this can be a very expensive and time-consuming pastime.

**Transportation history** provides a great variety of memorabilia. Among the more expensive and durable items are models of past railroad trains, ships, automobiles, carriages, stagecoaches, urban trolley cars, steamboats, and early airplanes. Other mementos include travel posters, advertisements, route maps, timetables, and furnishings and fixtures from actual vehicles or vessels.

One of the most attractive examples of seafaring memorabilia is scrimshaw—engravings scribed in walrus tusks or the bones or teeth of whales. The etched portion was usually inked or rubbed with pigment to bring out the design. Scrimshaw, created mostly by American or British whalers, was usually done with either a jackknife or a sail needle. Examples date from as early as the 17th century, but the art reached its peak during the years from 1830 to 1850.

**Sports enthusiasts** collect a great variety of memorabilia, including game programs, autographed pictures of players or teams, team emblems and pennants, uniforms and caps, and autographed footballs or baseballs. Among the least expensive and most popular of sports items are baseball cards. As many as 3 billion of these cards are printed annually, and they are very popular with children. For decades gum manufacturers have offered them in bubble-gum packages. Early in the 20th century, baseball cards were sold with tobacco products. Advances in photographic technology have made possible the printing of baseball cards that contain more than one image, depending on how the card is held to the light. So prevalent is the hobby that it has its own publication, *Baseball Card Monthly*. Complete sets of baseball cards increase in value, so that sets from the early 1980s were valued at several hundred dollars a few years later.

## NATURE HOBBIES

The observation of nature is humanity's oldest pastime. From it have emerged the natural sciences as well as a variety of hobbies. In the late 20th century, concern for preservation of the environment led many people to study ecology and to use their time to protect or develop nature preserves. Nature itself provides a wide range of subjects for study—trees, flowers, shrubs, birds, insects, reptiles, amphibians, mammals, minerals, and fossils. Cities and suburbs foster nature study by building zoos and aquariums and by laying out nature trails, parks, and animal sanctuaries. Elsewhere nature has cooperated by creating its own plant and animal sanctuaries in marshes, swamps, forests, and other natural habitats.

Nature hobbies are mainly of two types: activities, such as gardening or bird-watching, and collecting. A nature hobby can also be combined with another interest such as photography.

### Gardening

In the British Isles and other parts of Europe private gardening has long been an avocation of large numbers of city and town dwellers. The English garden is famous around the world for its variety and beauty. In North America the movement to the suburbs since 1950 has provided many families with space to add attractive gardens to their property.

A good garden is well arranged. The trees, flowers, and shrubs work together to create an effect of diversity within unity. Such a garden may include a space to grow fruits and vegetables. Trees, shrubs, and other plants are chosen and placed to make the garden as attractive as possible throughout the growing season. City dwellers, who usually have less space, may have

to confine their gardening to tiny backyard plots, flower boxes, terraces, or even rooftops. A building may even have trees growing on the roof. (*See also* Garden and Gardening; Houseplant.)

### Bird-watching

As a result of concern over the environment, people are starting to learn more about its components: animals and plant life. The presence or absence of different kinds of birds is an indicator of the health or deterioration of an environment. A good bird-watcher must be able to identify species of birds and note the particulars of their habitats. The amount of equipment required is small: a pair of binoculars, a field guide to birds, a notebook and pencil, and perhaps a camera. The best times for bird-watching are early in the morning when the birds start feeding or late in the afternoon when they are almost ready to roost for the night.

### Indoor Observation Enclosures

Examples of animal and vegetable life, in addition to rocks and minerals, are common collectibles. Some specimens are displayed as curiosities or for their scientific interest. Others, like dried flowers, can be used in seasonal arrangements.

**Habitat boxes.** Plants and animals live together in communities, or habitats. An interesting way to study plant and animal communities is to make a habitat box. A field trip can be the occasion to gather stones, pebbles, and plant materials. Dried weeds make better plant material for inclusion in a box than do flowers, which soon fade and die. Models of birds and animals can be made from clay or papier-mâché, or they may be cut out and mounted on cardboard. The sides and back of the box should be painted with some scene. Methods for achieving realistic effects are limited only by the imagination of the builder.

**Terrariums.** Whereas a habitat box is a static, unchanging display, a terrarium houses living plants and animals. If animals are provided with the proper cages and food, they can live a relatively normal life in confined surroundings.

The terrarium is a glass-sided box with a movable lid used to house land and amphibious animals or insects in their natural plant surroundings. Snakes, frogs, toads, chameleons, lizards, newts, snails, turtles, and other small animals may be kept in a terrarium. Some animals must, of course, be kept separate from others.

A terrarium may range from a glass jar containing a few water plants and insect larvae to the size of a furniture packing case. Terrariums 3 to 4 feet (1 to 1.3 meters) in length permit the association of woodland, bog, desert, or meadow plants with appropriate animal life.

A straight-sided glass tank makes the best terrarium. The size of the tank depends on the number of inhabitants. A satisfactory small tank measures 12 inches high, 18 inches long, and 13 inches deep (30 by 45 by 33 centimeters). Such tanks can be purchased at pet shops that carry tropical fish. It is also possible to make a tank at home by taping together the edges of four pieces of glass and setting the glass in a plaster of Paris cast in a large tray. Aquarium cement on the inside joints will make the tank waterproof. A hinged lid completes the box.

A gravel base inside the terrarium will help drain excess moisture and keep the topsoil from getting soggy. Gravel should be well washed to remove impurities. For a woodland garden about 2 inches (5 centimeters) of humus soil should cover the gravel. A bog garden requires the acid soil that may be found around swamps and peat bogs. In a desert terrarium the base should be covered with 3 or 4 inches (7 to 10 centimeters) of a sandy potting mixture. Different soil bases can be purchased from greenhouses.

*Gardening can become a nearly full-time hobby during the growing season. Roses (left), the overall favorite perennial, need special care. A vegetable garden (right) also needs to be tended frequently to keep out weeds and insect pests and to gather crops as they ripen.*

The soil should be contoured. Hills and valleys have more eye appeal than flat surfaces. Lichen-covered rocks lend variety to the landscape and provide resting and sunning places for some animals and hiding places for others (*see* Lichen). A mossy tree branch can be used by snakes and lizards for climbing, and a small pool is agreeable even to desert animals.

The plants in the terrarium may include ferns, club mosses, evergreen seedlings, and such flowers as wood sorrel, violets, and bluets. In a bog garden a pitcher plant or a sundew can be used. The plants should be surrounded with sphagnum moss.

The gravel base should be kept moist, but not so much so that the soil becomes soggy. For a drier interior the lid can be raised or removed to let moisture escape. The terrarium should receive only an hour or two of direct sunlight daily. Temperatures ranging from 60° F to 75° F (15° C to 24° C) are preferable.

Careful study about the animals inside the terrarium will provide information about the foods they need. Earthworms are the most useful all-around food. They can be collected in large numbers after a rain and stored in a damp place in a box of soil. Worms can survive indefinitely on a diet of beef suet or hard-boiled eggs. Lizards, frogs, toads, and salamanders may be enticed to eat raw chopped beef or liver if it is moved in front of them on the end of a toothpick or straw. Some pet stores will sell live insects for feeding

*Bird-watchers in Florida's Everglades National Park encounter a great diversity of wildlife to photograph.*
Rod Planck Photography

the animals in terrariums and aquariums. (*See also* Ant; Aquarium, "The Home Aquarium .")

**Observation beehive.** An observation beehive must be purchased from a bee supply house. No amateur should attempt to capture these well-armed insects. The hive stands on a windowsill and has an opening to the outdoors. It requires no attention. The side facing indoors is of glass, making it possible to watch the bees build hive cells, feed and care for larvae, and store honey. The hive may be brought indoors during the winter and its inmates fed with water and honey. (*See also* Bee.)

### Insect Collections

Young future biologists often make a hobby of insect collecting. The steps in making such a collection are finding the insects, killing them properly, and mounting them.

Insects must be caught carefully in order not to damage their appearance. Some can be easily caught by hand. Others may require a net (butterflies, for example), and some can be trapped. Soil-dwelling insects can be shaken from a square foot of sod. It takes more time and care to catch those that come out only at night. Some of these may be attracted to a light, while others can be lured by the right bait—sweet foods, syrup, molasses, or meat. Water bugs can be caught with fine-meshed nets.

Insects must be killed in order to be preserved. With the exception of moths and butterflies, most insects can be killed by dropping them into a 70 percent solution of alcohol. To prevent discoloration, soft-bodied larvae and pupae are killed in boiling water. Specialists kill moths, butterflies, and some other adult insects in cyanide bottles, or "killing jars." Cyanide is a deadly poison and should be used only under careful supervision. Amateurs may use a jar containing cotton moistened with carbon tetrachloride or ethyl acetate. It is desirable to have two killing jars, one for moths and

butterflies and another for all other types of insects. The scales from butterfly and moth wings rub off easily and cling to anything they touch.

After the insects are dead they should be removed from the bottle and pinned at once or stored in cellophane envelopes for future mounting. It is a good idea to mount them as soon as possible, however, while the tissues are still flexible enough that the wings may be spread for display purposes.

For more effective display and easier handling, adult insects of all but the smallest species are mounted with a rustproof pin forced directly through the body of the insect. Species less than half an inch (1.3 centimeters) long should be glued at the side of the thorax to the tips of cardboard triangles. The triangles can then be mounted on boards or in display boxes.

If an insect has dried out it must be moistened to make it relax, or the brittle appendages will break off. Any large, tightly covered crock or jar containing a deep layer of wet sand can serve as a relaxing chamber. A few drops of carbolic acid (phenol) should be added to the sand to prevent the growth of fungus molds, and there should be a platform to keep the specimens from contact with the sand. One to three days in the relaxer is ample time for most insects.

The wings of butterflies, moths, dragonflies, and damselflies are usually spread on specially constructed boards and allowed to dry for about a week. They will then retain their position.

The cork-bottomed display or storage boxes in which insects are pinned should be as airtight as possible to prevent mold. The display boxes should contain the fumes of paradichlorobenzene (PDB), the crystals of which can be purchased from a pharmacist. The fumes discourage museum pests, such as book lice or carpet beetles, which will devour the specimens. Attractive mounts can be made by embedding the insects in a clear plastic, a material that can be obtained from biological supply houses.

*Butterflies must be carefully mounted with pins after their wings have been spread and allowed to dry.*
© William E. Ferguson

*Seashells are attractive by themselves, and they can also be used to make other decorative items, such as a mobile.*
Cathlyn Melloan—EB Inc.

### Other Collectibles

In addition to plants and animals, an interesting variety of other things can be gathered out of doors. These include rocks, minerals, gemstones, and seashells. Collecting rocks and minerals is an inexpensive hobby. Finding gemstones can be both rewarding and profitable. Finding good seashells is more of a challenge, because it is necessary to live near the kind of shore where they can be found or else to travel there. Few of the beaches frequented by tourists have many interesting shells.

A rock is a hardened mass made up of more than one mineral. A mineral is a chemical element or a chemical compound in a crystal structure. There are about 2,000 varieties of minerals. Rocks and minerals,

*The ready availability of rocks in streams or on dry land makes collecting them one of the easiest hobbies to enjoy.*

Mike Mazzaschi—Stock, Boston

though unevenly distributed, are probably the most plentiful substances on Earth. Some localities may have as many as 75 to 100 different varieties of minerals, while other areas will have only five or ten. There are books such as 'A Field Guide to Minerals' to help collectors get started. There are also collectors' clubs and museums that display mineral collections. ( *See also* Rock; Minerals.)

Collectors who work with gemstones are called lapidaries, from the Latin *lapis* meaning "stone." Many of the minerals capable of being cut into gemstones are from the quartz family—amethyst, agate, carnelian, and jasper, for example. The western section of North America is the most likely region in which to find good gemstone minerals. If the collector is simply going to gather and keep gem-quality minerals, the only expense is getting to where they may be found. If the lapidarian intends to cut, grind, and polish the stones for sale, the cost of equipment can be high. (*See also* Jewelry and Gems.)

Scientific estimates suggest that there are about 75,000 known species of seashells ( *see* Shell). One of the basic appeals of shells, apart from their beauty, is that they are plentiful in some localities and may usually be obtained without much cost. In busy tourist areas shells are more likely to be gathered by local residents and sold at high prices. Experienced collectors search for shells at low tide, when they have the entire area between tides to explore. Shells of animals that live in deeper waters have attracted many skin divers to the hobby of shell collecting. Once collected, shells can be used to make trays, jewelry, and picture frames.

Other collectible items found in nature are fossils and artifacts of past civilizations. Finding these things requires a more extensive and complicated search than gathering rocks or shells because it is necessary to know where to look. In the case of coins, pottery, or other man-made artifacts, one must be where a civilization once existed. Those who know best how to find good locations are archaeologists. Closely related

William Franklin McMahon

*Leathercraft is a versatile hobby because leather can be worked in many different ways to produce a variety of useful items.*

to searching for items from a past civilization is the treasure hunt, which may involve an undersea venture to look for a sunken ship with a valuable cargo (*see* Treasure Hunting). This, too, is an expensive and time-consuming effort and may involve risk.

## HANDICRAFT HOBBIES

Making things by hand, the way nearly everything was made before the Industrial Revolution, has attracted uncounted devotees. To make an object gives the satisfaction of having created something, and it allows for the exercise of individual artistry and talent. Handicrafts include carving and whittling, weaving, embroidery, needlework, ceramics, puppetry, wood-working, basketry, and more. The making of models is covered in the article Models and Model Building.

For nearly every kind of craft there are kits available in hobby shops or craft centers. There are kits for painting by numbers, for making mosaics, and for crafts using plastics, leather, textiles, metal, cork, clay, beads and sequins, ribbon, wool, yard goods, and laces. There are patterned goods for needlepoint. The sciences are represented by kits for chemistry, biology, physics, astronomy, and the Earth sciences.

Some hobbyists refuse to use kits. Instead, they welcome the challenge of taking discarded materials—rags, old newspapers, tin cans, or junk—and making them into something attractive and useful. (*See also* Needlework; Pottery and Porcelain.)

## MECHANICAL AND ELECTRONIC HOBBIES

Many hobbies benefit from the use of equipment, and for others—computers, for example—the equipment itself becomes the focal point of the hobby. For some scientific hobbies, such as amateur astronomy or meteorology, there is a definite need for adequate equipment. (*See also* Astronomy, Amateur .)

### Photography

A camera is often taken along on nature hikes or on bird-watching expeditions to obtain photographs. But photography itself is also a popular hobby, one that can require a great deal of expensive equipment.

*Woodworking can be learned in school. As a hobby it offers unlimited scope for creativity in making furniture and other household items.*

Porterfield-Chickering/Photo Researchers

Gretchen Garner

**By painting a design on clear glass it is possible to create the effect of a small stained-glass window.**

The amateur photographer has enormous resources at his disposal to help him learn his craft. There are camera shops, books, magazines, newspaper columns, and exhibitions of photographs. Many of the world's finest photographers have published volumes of their work. Today's cameras have automatic devices that relieve the picture taker of any thoughts other than concentrating on his subject.

Photography as an art form derives from an understanding of every phase of the hobby—from using the right camera, lighting, and film, to the developing process. A camera club or advice from an experienced photographer can speed the learning process.

Some hobbyists work only in black and white, while others insist on color. Some photographers want only slides, while many make only prints. An amateur photographer who does all aspects of the work must have equipment for developing, cropping, printing, and enlarging. Subject matter is as variable as the interests of the photographer.

Making motion pictures has been simplified by the development of the videocassette camera. It is now possible for an individual to make home movies, with sound, and avoid the need to have them developed. The cassette can be placed directly into a videocassette recorder (VCR) and played through a television set. A VCR camera can be used by travelers who want to take motion pictures of places they visit, instead of bothering with still prints or colored slides. It is also useful for filming special events such as weddings and anniversaries. (*See also* Photography.)

## Amateur Weather Forecasting

The study of weather and weather forecasting is called meteorology (*see* Meteorology). Amateur meteorologists often give valuable information about local conditions to professional weather forecasters on radio or television. Weather forecasts are based on sky conditions and cloud cover, temperature, humidity, barometric readings of air pressure, and wind direction.

To observe sky conditions and types of clouds takes no equipment, only a knowledge of clouds (*see* Cloud). Measuring temperature requires some equipment, but it need not be expensive. The only item that has to be purchased is a thermometer. It is possible to buy thermometers that record both outdoor and indoor temperatures. There is also a type of thermometer that records maximum and minimum temperatures for the day. A thermometer must be placed in a shaded location, because it is intended to record the temperature of the air, not the heat of the sun.

A barometer records air pressure and is the most vital instrument in weather forecasting. Changes in air pressure indicate changes in weather patterns (*see* Atmosphere; Barometer). It is possible to make one's own jar barometer to give a general indication of air pressure. It will not, however, be as accurate as one bought in a store.

A jar barometer is made by covering the top of a pint jar with a tightly stretched balloon tied with a string around the jar's neck. One end of a straw is

**The young nature photographer with an inexpensive camera can get good pictures with proper film and care about lighting.**

Don Smetzer—CLICK/Chicago

then glued to the top of the balloon. The other end of the straw should have its end cut to a point somewhat like the end of a fountain pen. A card marked with parallel lines is placed next to the pointed end of the straw so that the point almost touches the lines. Air pressure on the balloon will cause the straw to rise or fall. A barometric record can be kept by marking the location of the straw's point each day on the card.

Wind direction is indicated by a weather vane. This is another instrument that can be homemade. A simple one has the appearance of an arrow mounted on a base. A stick of wood half an inch (1.27 centimeters) square and 12 inches (30.48 centimeters) long with a hole drilled in the center is the main part of the weather vane. A cardboard or wooden pointer fits into a slit at one end of the stick, and a "feather" of light wood or cardboard is attached in a slit at the other end. The feather must be larger than the pointer so it will catch the wind. Next, a washer is placed over the hole in the stick and a loose-fitting nail dropped through it. A short piece of metal tubing is placed over the lower end of the nail before the nail is pounded into a wooden, stationary mounting. When the wind blows, the stick pivots the nail until the pointer faces into the wind. (*See also* Wind.)

A rain gauge is simply a jar with measurement indicators on the outside, much like a measuring cup. A narrow vessel such as an olive jar can be marked on the outside to show fractions of an inch. A tin can may also be used. It is not necessary to make measurements on the can. Rainfall can be measured by dipping a ruler into the can. Rain gauges should be placed about waist high off the ground in an unobstructed area.

Humidity, the amount of moisture in the air, is measured with a hygrometer. A very simple type consists of two thermometers mounted next to each other. One is an ordinary thermometer that measures

air temperature regardless of humidity. The other has a wet bulb attached at the bottom. The reading on the wet bulb thermometer will be the lower of the two because the wet bulb is cooled by evaporation. The difference between the two readings can be used to calculate humidity.

### Ham Radio

Amateur radio operators who broadcast over short-wave frequencies are called ham radio operators. The origin of the term is unknown. Ham radio is noncommercial, two-way transmission in which messages are sent by Morse code or by voice.

Interest in amateur broadcasting arose as soon as the radio was invented by Guglielmo Marconi (*see* Radio). Because amateur broadcasts interfered with low-wave transmission of commercial and military communication, the United States government instituted controls in 1911. Ham radio enthusiasts were limited to the use of short-wave frequencies, which at the time was deemed to have limited potential.

After World War I, however, amateurs became active in experimenting, and by 1923 some operators achieved successful transatlantic transmission over short waves. Over the years amateur radio operators have provided emergency communication during natural and other disasters. After the great Mexico City earthquake of September 1985, ham operators helped get information about survivors to relatives in the United States. Amateurs are now able to use communications satellites to assist in broadcasting.

Amateur radio operators in the United States are subject to international and federal regulation. There are six classes of licenses. Competence in the use of International Morse Code and a knowledge of radio theory and regulation are required to obtain advanced-level licenses. There are restrictions on the power of transmitters, and some frequencies must be shared with regard for the needs of others.

The unlicensed amateur starts with a receiver to listen in on transmissions. A headset allows better reception than does a radio speaker. An antenna can be a wire strung outside a window or an expensive piece of equipment on the roof. Ham radio equipment can be purchased at electronics stores. Listening in gives the beginner the chance to learn how transmitting is done and a chance to practice Morse Code. Before broadcasting, an amateur must obtain a license. In the United States application is made to the Federal Communications Commission in Washington, D.C. In Canada amateur radio broadcasters are regulated by the Department of Transportation and in Great Britain by the Department of Trade. There are a number of handbooks to guide beginners who are preparing to take a licensing examination.

After obtaining a license the ham operator needs a transmitter. Kits for building them can be bought from electronics stores, or one can buy a ready-made model. Other necessary equipment includes maps of the world, an international time-zone clock or a time-conversion table, and a log book to record broadcast

*Today's technology affords children the chance to build electrical equipment from spare parts or from kits.*

Patricia Hollander Gross—Stock, Boston

activity. The log book is a government requirement. An amateur should also have printed cards giving his name, address, and station call letters. There are local radio clubs to assist members, and ham operators may also join the American Radio Relay League to get technical information and its useful magazine.

### Computer Hobbyists

Great advances in hardware—more powerful micro-processors, color monitors, and better printers—as well as a much greater diversity of software have combined to make personal computers far more appealing and functional for professionals and amateurs alike. In 1980 the average home computer carried only 16K RAM—somewhat more than 16,000 bytes of Random Access Memory. Ten years later, personal computers were on the market with 4 megabytes of RAM and more. Hard discs with huge memory capacities were also becoming more common. (*See also* Computer.)

Another improvement took place when International Business Machines (IBM) launched its series of personal computers. The popularity of these machines helped enforce, or standardize, software compatibility. Computers made by other companies started using the same operating system as the IBM personal computers so that they could run the same programs. In 1987 the introduction by IBM of a new line of computers—System 2—with another operating system was expected to force another round of compatibility adjustments among manufacturers.

Computer hobbyists— or hackers, as they are often called—engage in many of the same activities as computer professionals. They operate software such as word processing, accounting, and graphics programs. They design their own programs, a far more difficult task when done without the aid of an easily readable computer language such as BASIC. Computers can also be used to do such things as design models and track weather, thus becoming a help with other hobbies. They are also valuable for record keeping.

To help the amateur make better use of his computer there are a number of monthly magazines, including *Byte, Personal Computing,* and *PC World.* And there are hundreds of different books on all aspects of programming and technology.

Other information on hobbies can be found in the 'Reader's Digest Crafts and Hobbies' (published by Reader's Digest Association in 1981).

**HO CHI MINH** (1890–1969). As founder of the Indo-Chinese Communist party in 1930 and president of North Vietnam from 1945 to 1969, Ho Chi Minh led the longest and most costly 20th-century war against colonialism. His whole adult life was devoted to ending French and, later, American domination of Vietnam. His goals were achieved in 1975, six years after his death, when the last Americans left South Vietnam (*see* Vietnam War).

Ho was born Nguyen Tat Thanh on May 19, 1890, in Hoang Tru, Vietnam (then known in the West as French Indochina). He attended school in Hue during

Marc Riboud—Magnum

*Ho Chi Minh in 1968 saw the start of peace negotiations with the United States, but his death probably lengthened the war.*

his teen years, worked as a schoolmaster for a time, and went to a technical school in Saigon. In 1911 he went to work on ocean freighters, which took him around Africa and as far as Boston and New York City. After two years in London (1915–17) he moved to Paris and remained there until 1923. While in Paris he became a socialist and organized a group of Vietnamese living there in a protest against French colonial policy.

Inspired by the successful Communist revolution in Russia, he went to Moscow in 1924 and took part in the fifth Congress of the Communist International. His anticolonial views kept him from returning to Vietnam until the end of World War II. Much of his time was spent in China, where he organized the Indo-Chinese Communist party on Feb. 3, 1930. It was in about 1940 that he began to use the name Ho Chi Minh, meaning "he who enlightens."

In 1941 Ho and his comrades formed the League for the Independence of Vietnam, or Vietminh. By 1945 the Japanese had overrun Vietnam and defeated the French, and later in the year the Japanese were defeated by the United States. Ho immediately sought the cooperation of the United States in preventing the return of colonial rule, and on Sept. 2, 1945, he proclaimed the independence of Vietnam.

This proclamation was premature: two Indochina wars were fought before Vietnam became independent. Ho's main contribution during the wars was keeping both the Soviet Union and China from gaining too great an influence in Vietnam. Although his death was reported on Sept. 3, 1969, in Hanoi, the Vietnamese Communist party disclosed in 1989 that Ho had actually died on September 2, Vietnam's National Day.

**HO CHI MINH CITY, Vietnam.** Formerly known as Saigon, Ho Chi Minh City is the chief port and leading city of Vietnam. Located 50 miles (80 kilometers) from the South China Sea, the city is on the Saigon, or Dongnai, River to the north of the Mekong Delta. With the city of Cholon, where most industries are located, it forms a single metropolitan area.

The city plan—with broad avenues, shopping centers, and large public buildings—reflects its earlier French domination. There are some high-rise office buildings and large supermarkets. A cathedral (1883) and two Buddhist pagodas (both 18th-century) are architectural landmarks. The majority of the inhabitants are Vietnamese, but there are large numbers of immigrant Chinese who live mostly in and around the Cholon area.

After the Communists took control in 1975, Saigon lost its administrative function as a capital city. The elegant Cercle Sportif—a former center of social life for Westerners—was made a people's museum, and the opera house was converted to a national theater. The University of Saigon—Vietnam's oldest university, founded in 1917—and the Buddhist University of Van Hanh were merged to form the National Ho Chi Minh University. Other notable institutions are the National School of Finance, the Institute of Agricultural Research, the Archaeological Research Institute, the National Scientific Research Council of Vietnam, the National Library II, and the City Museum. Many public gardens, cinemas, and open-air theatrical troupes provide the city's main relaxations.

The hot and humid monsoonal climate provides about 78 inches (198 centimeters) of annual rainfall,

*Soldiers stand near a Buddhist temple in Ho Chi Minh City. The bicycle is a favored mode of transport.*

A. Keler—Sygma

mostly between June and September, and the annual average temperature is 79° F (26° C). Rice, sugarcane, and rubber are raised in the surrounding area. The city is a major fishing center. Principal exports are rubber, fish, and forest products; chief imports are textiles, medicines, and food items.

Ho Chi Minh City is the major manufacturing and distribution center of southern Vietnam. Industries include shipbuilding, leather tanning, metalworking, aircraft repair, woodworking and sawmilling, and the manufacture of textiles, rubber, soap, varnish, chemicals, machinery, bicycles, and sewing machines. Food-processing industries include fruit packing, brewing and distilling, rice milling, sugar refining, and oilseed, fish, tea, and coffee processing. Small-scale cottage industries are common. After the Communist takeover in 1975, new industries with emphasis on self-sufficiency were established. Such traditional handicrafts as furniture, carpets, lacquer paintings, art pieces in ivory and bronze, pottery, and woven articles are exported by a state-run agency.

The city's port handles most of southern Vietnam's shipping, and there is a naval base near the port. The Tan Son Nhut International Airport serves both domestic and international flights and is a major military base. A number of highways connect the city with the rest of the country. It is linked by canals to the Mekong River and is served by an extensive waterway system.

The area now occupied by Ho Chi Minh City was long part of the Kingdom of Cambodia. The Vietnamese first occupied the region in the 1670s. French traders and missionaries settled here during the early part of the 19th century, and in 1859 the French captured the city. Saigon became the capital of the French protectorate of Cochinchina from 1862 to 1954 and later of all French Indochina. As the capital of Cochinchina Saigon was transformed into a major port city and a metropolitan center of beautiful villas, public buildings, and well-paved, tree-lined streets. Saigon-Cholon was one of Asia's fast-growing cities during and after World War II.

Saigon was occupied by the Japanese from 1940 to 1945, but the city was largely unaffected by World War II. After the war a nationalist revolt against French rule wracked the country. In 1954 the Communist-led Vietminh forces won a victory in the north. The country was divided at the 17th parallel into North and South Vietnam, and Saigon became the capital of South Vietnam (Republic of Vietnam). Some 900,000 non-Communists fled southward and settled around the Saigon area. These refugees greatly influenced the city's cultural and political life. Saigon was the headquarters of the United States military operations during the Vietnam War of the 1960s and early 1970s. The city went through many changes as a result of the war, and sections of it were destroyed. Saigon was captured by North Vietnamese troops on April 30, 1975, and was renamed in 1976 in honor of Ho Chi Minh, one of Vietnam's most influential Communist leaders. Population (1999 estimate), 4,549,000.

**FIELD HOCKEY FIELD**

**HOCKEY, FIELD.** The modern game of field hockey, whether for men or women, is played by two 11-member teams using sticks with a crook at the striking end. The object is to hit a ball into the opponent's goal. The playing field is 100 yards long and 60 yards wide, and the most common playing surface is grass. However, all international matches are required to be played on artificial turf. The goals at each end are 7 feet high and 12 feet wide, and the shooting circle is a semicircle centered on and 16 yards from the goal. The stick has one flat and one rounded side, and the ball must be hit with the flat side. The ball is made of solid plastic, weighs from 5 ½ to 5 ¾ ounces, and measures from 8 ¹³⁄₁₆ to 9 ¼ inches in circumference.

Each team's 11 players include five forwards, three halfbacks, two fullbacks, and a goalkeeper. The goalkeeper wears heavy padding, but the other players usually wear no protective gear. There are two 35-minute halves with a five-minute intermission between the halves.

Play begins with a passback, or face-off, which also begins play after each goal and after the five-minute intermission. To passback, two opposing team members face each other in the center of the field. They alternately tap the ground and each other's stick three times and then try to gain control of the ball and hit it to a teammate.

Goals can be scored only from within the shooting circle and must go through the goalposts and under the crossbar that forms the top of the goal. Each goal is worth one point. Players use the stick to dribble, pass, and hit the ball. Only the goalkeeper may use hands or body to stop the ball. No time-outs are allowed unless there is an injury. In some countries, including the United States, a substitution rule may be agreed upon before the game. In this case, either team may call time-out to substitute players.

Unique to the game of field hockey is the obstruction rule. In virtually every other sport, shielding the ball with one's body is an integral part of the game strategy.

In field hockey, however, this is not allowed. All players must have an equal chance to gain control of the ball as it is dribbled and passed down the field.

If the ball is hit out-of-bounds, the team that last touched it loses possession of the ball. A player from the opposing team places the ball on the sideline at the spot at which it crossed the sideline and then hits the ball back into the field of play. Fouls include raising the stick above the shoulder; undercutting the ball to lift it; interference with the stick; and, for all players except the goalkeeper, hitting the ball with the hands or stopping it with the feet or body. The usual penalty for a foul is a free hit for the opposing team. A free hit is made by a member of the opposing team from a penalty corner, a point on the goal line at least 10 yards from the goal. All players must be outside the shooting circle before the free hit is played.

A game very much like field hockey was played thousands of years ago in ancient Egypt and Persia. Since the 19th century, associations have been formed to make decisions regarding rules and regulations. The first field hockey club, Blackheath, located southeast of London, was founded before 1861. Standardized rules were adopted in London in 1875, and in 1886 the Hockey Association added the shooting circle around each goal. British soldiers brought the game to countries in Asia, and today India and Pakistan have some of the world's finest teams. Women began playing organized field hockey during the second half of the 19th century, and for a time it was considered the only proper team sport for women.

Men's field hockey has been included in the Olympic Games since 1908. Women's hockey became an Olympic event in 1980. Other tournaments include the Champion's Cup, Asian Games, European Cup, Women's World Cup, and Pan-American Games. On April 1, 1993, the separate governing bodies of national men's and women's field hockey in the United States merged to form the sole governing body, the United States Field Hockey Association.

Karen Collins and Dr. Judith Davidson

*With elegance and precision, the Great (Wayne) Gretzky redefined standards for conduct and performance on the ice. At age 28 he broke the 1,850-point career scoring record.*

**HOCKEY, ICE.** The fastest of all team sports, ice hockey has been described as a combination of "blood, sweat, and beauty." With an increased focus on the bloodshed, descriptions of professional hockey games today are more likely to include words like "goon," "mayhem," and "degenerate." Stiffer penalties have not discouraged the players from using their basic equipment of sticks and skates as weapons, and this brutality has diminished the abstract beauty of the sport. Still, for a game in which bare-knuckle brawls have become the essence, one of the prestigious prizes is a trophy for the "most gentlemanly player."

Even without the violence, ice hockey is a rugged game that demands superbly conditioned athletes. Even without the deliberate fouls, serious injuries can result from the sheer speed of the action on the ice. More than any other team sport, ice hockey is a game of motion: even when the action is whistled to a stop, the momentum keeps flowing. The basic plays of the game are repeated endlessly, but the players are never able to skate in quite the same patterns and the sequences of their moves keep changing.

### History of Ice Hockey

The sport of ice hockey evolved from the casual games played on makeshift ice skates in Northern Europe during the Middle Ages (*see* Skates and Skating).

...............................................

*This article was contributed by Bob Verdi, Sports Columnist, Chicago Tribune; former Managing Editor, Hockey Digest; former member Board of Directors, Professional Hockey Writers Association.*

Similar to field hockey, it involves hitting an object with sticks between two goalposts (*see* Hockey, Field). Probably the first ice hockey players were North American Indians who used field tools that were curved at the lower end. The French word for the similarly shaped shepherd's crook, *hoquet,* was attached by French explorers who watched the Indians' improvised ball-and-stick games.

A crude form of ice hockey was introduced in Canada's frozen harbors by British troops in the mid-19th century. The exact locale of the first formal hockey game is debatable because three Canadian cities—Halifax, Kingston, and Montreal—all have reasonable claims to pioneering the sport. It is believed that some form of the game was being played in Kingston, in what is now Ontario, as early as 1830; however, it was a McGill University student from Halifax, N.S., who organized the first recorded game. The game was played in about 1875 between two teams of McGill students on the Montreal campus. The first official hockey league was a four-club unit formed ten years later in Kingston.

Although the original game called for nine men on each side, the number of team players involved could vary from one community to another. Soon a committee met in Montreal to establish regulations for seven-man teams. The positions agreed upon were goalkeeper, two defensemen, three forwards, and a rover who alternated between offense and defense. The National Hockey Association, formed in 1909, eliminated the rover, which meant that east-west championship games alternated between the six- and seven-man styles for a time. Until the mid-1920s teams were sometimes forced to play with fewer than three skaters on the ice because of penalties. The rules and equipment were improvised gradually whenever problems cropped up and as rougher play made certain types of injuries more common. The creation in 1893 of a status symbol, the Stanley Cup—then awarded to Canada's best amateur hockey team—gave some credibility to the sport.

### Playing Area and Equipment

Ice hockey is a particularly low-scoring game in which the team that hits the most pucks into its opponent's goal wins. The goals are located at each end of the hockey rink, an enclosed rectangular ice surface with rounded corners. The standard size of the rink is shown by the diagram on the opposite page, though there may be slight variations. It is surrounded by wooden walls—sideboards and endboards that stand about three or four feet above the surface of the ice. Some of the roughest hockey action occurs when players are slammed into the boards. To protect the spectators, rinks usually have glass extending from the top of these boards. The glass also keeps the skaters, as well as the pucks, within the playing area.

Each goal has a cage framed by two vertical posts four feet high and a horizontal bar six feet long across the top. Stretching from the posts to the ice level is a white net that encloses the sides and back and forms the cage into which the pucks are shot. The only time a

**NHL ICE HOCKEY RINK**

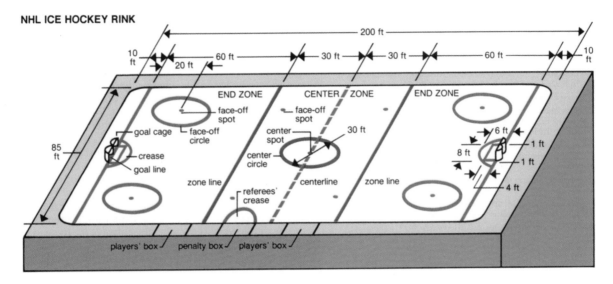

goal can be scored is when the puck completely crosses the goal line—a 2-inch-wide red border that extends between the vertical goalposts.

The puck is a disklike object made of black vulcanized rubber, 3 inches in diameter and 1 inch thick, with a weight of about 6 ounces. The puck may move at speeds of more than 100 miles per hour.

The rink is divided into three zones. Drawn 60 feet from each goal line is a zone line, or blue line, extending across the width of the rink and up the sideboards. Exactly between the two blue lines, at the middle of the rink, is the centerline, or red line. The ice surface between the blue lines is the center, or neutral, zone. A team's defensive zone is that area from the nearest blue line toward the goal that it is defending. Its attacking zone is the surface from the blue line on the other side of the red line toward the goal that its opponent is defending. The ice surface also includes markings for face-offs. A face-off is used to start or restart play whenever it has been stopped. It is initiated by one of the three officials (usually one referee and two linesmen), who drops the puck between two players, one from each team. In all, there are nine face-off spots, each one foot in diameter. Four of these are between the blue lines, and the other five are those enclosed by the face-off circles. One face-off circle, or area, 30 feet in diameter, is directly in center ice (neutral zone), and four other face-off circles are on either side of the goal cage in both defending zones.

The primary tool of the hockey player is the wooden stick used to maneuver the puck about the ice. In professional hockey the length from the bottom, or heel, of the stick to the top cannot exceed 55 inches, and the length from the heel to the outward end, or toe, of its blade cannot exceed 12½ inches.

### How the Game Is Played

A hockey game is divided into three periods of 20 minutes each. Most levels of the sport also provide for an overtime period if the score is tied. Eliminated from

regular season play during World War II, overtime periods were reintroduced by the National Hockey league for the 1983–84 season.

Hockey teams usually carry 18 to 20 players and use most of them. Included are three forward lines and at least two pairs of defensemen, all of whom rotate about every two minutes. Most teams will carry two goalkeepers, or goaltenders (usually called goalies), but generally one plays for an entire game. His only rest comes when play is stopped, when the puck is at the other end of the rink, or during intermission.

Unlike most other sports, ice hockey does not require that changes in personnel be made only when there is a stoppage in play. Substitutions often occur on the fly. Because action may proceed continuously for a period of several minutes, a player may skate over to his bench just off the ice surface and immediately be replaced by a teammate who plays the same position.

| National Hockey League | | | |
|---|---|---|---|
| **Western Conference** | | **Eastern Conference** | |
| **Pacific Division** | | **Atlantic Division** | |
| Anaheim | Mighty Ducks | New Jersey | Devils |
| Dallas | Stars | New York | Islanders |
| Los Angeles | Kings | New York | Rangers |
| Phoenix | Coyotes | Philadelphia | Flyers |
| San Jose | Sharks | Pittsburgh | Penguins |
| **Central Division** | | **Northeast Division** | |
| Chicago | Blackhawks | Boston | Bruins |
| Columbus | Blue Jackets | Buffalo | Sabres |
| Detroit | Red Wings | Montreal | Canadiens |
| Nashville | Predators | Ottawa | Senators |
| St. Louis | Blues | Toronto | Maple Leafs |
| **Northwest Division** | | **Southeast Division** | |
| Calgary | Flames | Atlanta | Thrashers |
| Colorado | Avalanche | Carolina | Hurricanes |
| Edmonton | Oilers | Florida | Panthers |
| Minnesota | Wild | Tampa Bay | Lightning |
| Vancouver | Canucks | Washington | Capitals |

## Ice Hockey Terms

**Art Ross Trophy.** Awarded since 1947 to the scoring leader in honor of the innovative coach-manager-player (not a high scorer himself) who established professional hockey in Boston and designed the modern puck and nets.

**board check.** To bodycheck an opponent into the boards.

**bodycheck.** To block the puck carrier (or an opponent going for the puck) by hitting him from the front or side (and above the knees) with the upper part of the body.

**breakaway.** Drive in which one or more offensive players are moving in on the goal with fewer defenders than attackers.

**charging.** Taking more than two strides before running into an opponent.

**cross-check.** To hit an opponent illegally with the stick held by both hands in front of the body.

**Hart Memorial Trophy.** Awarded since 1923 to the most valuable player in honor of Cecil Hart, Montreal manager-coach.

**hat trick.** Scoring of three goals by an individual player in a single game.

**head-man.** To pass the puck to a teammate closer to the opponent's goal during a rush.

**high-sticking.** Carrying the stick above the permissible height or injuring an opponent with a high stick.

**icing.** Shooting a puck from within the defensive zone (half in pro play) of the ice across the opponents' goal line, when play is picked up by an opponent other than the goalie.

**interference.** Checking or hampering an opponent who is not in possession of the puck or is not attempting to gain possession.

**Lady Byng Memorial Trophy.** Awarded since 1925 to the player who combines high skills with gentlemanly play (usually measured by a low penalty-minute total) in honor of the wife of a Canadian governor-general.

**offside pass.** Illegal pass made from the defensive zone to a player in the neutral zone across the red line.

**penalty.** Suspension for foul play for two (minor penalty), five (major penalty), or ten (misconduct penalty) minutes or for the remainder of the game (match penalty).

**penalty killer.** Player assigned by a shorthanded team to defend against the power play.

**penalty shot.** Unhindered shot at the goal (defended only by the goalie), awarded for certain infractions by the opponent. The puck is dead after the shot.

**poke check.** Hitting the puck away from the puck carrier by poking, hooking, or sweeping the puck free.

**power play.** Situation in which one team has more players on the ice than the other (because of a penalty) and attacks.

**slap pass.** A pass deflected on to another player without gaining full control of the puck.

**slap shot.** Hard, swinging stroke in which the stick blade hits the ice just behind the puck.

**slashing.** Swinging the stick at an opponent.

**spearing.** Jabbing an opponent with the point of the stick blade or the head of the stick.

**standup goalie.** A goalkeeper who attempts to stop most shots while standing up, rather than by dropping to the ice.

**Stanley Cup.** Championship trophy first donated by Frederick Arthur, Lord Stanley of Preston, governor-general of Canada.

**Vezina Trophy.** Awarded to the top goaltender in honor of Georges Vezina, a standup goalie with Montreal.

The hazards of changing personnel on the fly are twofold: it must be done at just the right time, or the opponent will take advantage of the temporary shortage in manpower; and, if confusion occurs upon switching players, a team may end up with too many players on the ice and be given a penalty.

The last line of defense, the goalie is entrusted with keeping the puck out of his team's net. With his stick (which is somewhat thicker than the other players' sticks) he steers a puck to a teammate or away from a foe. Directly in front of his net, the goalie stands in the crease, an area four feet by eight feet drawn on the ice and into which the opposition is not supposed to enter. If a player on the other team scores a goal while in this crease—provided that he has not been thrust into the area by a member of the defending team—the goal is disallowed. The goalie must always try to keep his eye on the puck, a task that is made even more arduous when players congregate around his net. Protected by special safety equipment and extra padding, he has to handle all types of shots—short, long, and those from different angles—that hurtle at his body. He may block these with any part of his equipment, or he may glove them and hold on, stopping play. (The goalkeeper is the only player allowed to catch the puck in the glove.)

The goalie's most immediate assistance is provided by his two defensemen, who are positioned on either side of him. In front of the two defensemen are the three forwards—the left wing, center, and right wing. Although defensemen frequently become involved directly in their team's offensive aspect of the game, their primary duties are to limit the number of shots on their goal and to break up scoring threats.

The three forwards are primarily interested in scoring. They do most of the penetration into the opponent's defensive zone and attempt most of their team's shots on the other team's goal. The center is often a clever stick handler with the major assignment of providing the puck for the two wings. Forward lines whose members are working well together usually pass the puck back and forth several times until they achieve an opening for a good shot. Although the forwards concentrate on offense, they are also depended on to check, or guard, the opposition. Normally the center on one team is responsible for checking the other team's center, while the left wings line up against the right wings of the opposing team.

A game starts with a face-off at the center-ice face-off circle. The opposing centers try to gain possession of the puck or direct it to a teammate as it is dropped by the referee. Either by passing the puck to a teammate in a better position, or by carrying the puck himself, a player for the team in possession strives continually for a pattern that will produce the best possible shot on the opponent's net. The better shots a team takes, the better chance it has of scoring.

There are limits on how a team may send the puck into an opponent's territory, and one of hockey's most important penalties—the offside penalty—is used to enforce these limits. A player may not pass the puck

Mike Powell—Allsport USA

*Teams from the Soviet Union dominated international ice hockey for decades. Shown here in action against the United States, the Soviets won their 7th Olympic gold medal in 1988.*

over two lines (either blue line and the red line) to a teammate, nor may a player precede the puck over the blue line into the opposition's territory. In either case, offside is whistled by an official; play is halted and then resumed with a face-off outside the guilty club's attacking zone. It is the position of the player's skates that determines whether he is offside. Only if both of his skates have completely crossed the line in question (red or blue) is a player judged to be in the zone where he is headed.

The administration of ice hockey penalties makes the game one of the few sports in which a team is deprived of a player after a transgression. The most prevalent penalty is the two-minute minor, which is assessed for such transgressions as holding, tripping, charging, elbowing, hooking, slashing, and interference. When a referee spots such an infraction, he will whistle the offender off the ice and send him to a penalty box or bench where the player sits during the time of his infraction. Penalties incurred by a goalie are served by a teammate. The player's team may not replace him on the ice, and until his time has expired he may only leave the penalty box when his club, while shorthanded, is scored against.

When a player is charged with a major penalty, he must serve the full time (five minutes), no matter how often his club is scored against. Major penalties are given for fighting with or injuring an opponent. If a player is guilty of insubordination to an official he receives a ten-minute misconduct penalty. Misconduct suspensions may be given for abusive language, extended fighting, a second major penalty, or failure to proceed to the penalty box. When a player is benched for misconduct, his team does not have to play shorthanded. In extreme cases—for example, for joining a fight in progress—a player may receive an automatic game misconduct or match penalty, meaning he is expelled from the game.

As penalty minutes per game nearly doubled during the 1980s, many critics of the sport felt that lawlessness was taking over the NHL. The introduction of mandatory suspensions for major stick-related penalties

---

## Some NHL Champion Players

*Some prominent persons are not included below because they are covered in the main text of this article or in other articles in Compton's Encyclopedia ( seeFact-Index).*

**Howe, Gordie** (Mr. Hockey) (born 1928). Born in Floral, Sask. Right wing, Detroit Red Wings 1946–71. With effortless style and devastating elbows, became six-time winner of Art Ross and Hart trophies. First Hall of Famer to play after retirement, joined sons, Mark and Marty, on WHA's Houston Aeros. Scored 1,000th goal with New England (Hartford) Whalers 1977.

**Lemieux, Mario** (born 1965). Born in Montreal, Que. Center, Pittsburgh Penguins 1984–. In 1988–89 season set NHL record for shorthanded goals (13), became his team's all-time leader in assists.

**Mikita, Stan** (born 1940). Born Stanislav Gvoth in Czechoslovakia, to Canada in 1948. Center, Chicago Blackhawks 1959–80. One of hockey's "dirtiest" players for seven seasons, cleaned up image to become only player to win Triple Crown (three major trophies in one season, 1966–67, repeated 1967–68).

**Orr, Bobby** (born 1948). Born in Parry Sound, Ont. Defenseman, Boston Bruins 1966–76. Inaugurated rushing style for defensemen. First major player to employ an agent. Set defense records for goals (46), assists (102), and points (139). Blackhawks coach 1976–77. Damaged knees forced retirement.

**Richard, Maurice** (The Rocket) (1921–2000). Born in Montreal, Que. Forward, Montreal Canadiens 1942–60. Ambidextrous and hot-tempered, first player to score 50 goals (50-game season). Suspension from 1955 play-offs for hitting an official ignited a riot. Slashed Achilles tendon ended injury-plagued career.

**Vezina, Georges** (Chicoutimi Cucumber) (1888–1926). Born in Chicoutimi, Que. Goalie, Montreal Canadiens 1910–25. Allowed an overall average of only 3.45 goals per game in the maskless era that limited goalies to standup play. Never missed a game until 1925–26 season, when he was felled by tuberculosis.

---

had little effect on the total number of fighting penalties. As a result multigame suspensions increased, in frequency and in length. Stiff penalties in the late 1980s ranged from 20 games (for flipping the skates from under an official) to 15 games (for vicious cross-checking) to 12 games (for a deliberate attack on an opponent in revenge for the earlier elbowing of a teammate, who was knocked unconscious).

### Professional Hockey

After the failure of a project for an International Hockey Hall of Fame in Kingston, the most popular candidate for the birthplace of the sport, the NHL Hall of Fame was established in 1961 at Toronto. Although the NHL was established in 1917, there were still only six franchises a half century later—teams in Montreal, Toronto, Detroit, Chicago, New York, and Boston. In the peak period of 1926–31 there had been a ten-team circuit. The advent of golden superstars like Bobby Hull and Bobby Orr helped popularize the game in the United States (*see* Hull). In 1967 the NHL added franchises in Los Angeles, Oakland, Minnesota, Philadelphia, Pittsburgh, and St. Louis. Another expansion in 1970 added Buffalo and Vancouver. By

1974 the league had two nine-team conferences, each with two divisions.

The success of the NHL encouraged a rival league, the World Hockey Association (WHA), to begin operation in the 1972–73 season. The WHA lured about 60 players from the NHL. The WHA, which originally consisted of 12 teams, expanded to 14 in 1974. The league was realigned in 1976, again with 12 teams, but cut back in 1977 and again in 1978. At the end of the 1978–79 season, four of the remaining six WHA teams were merged into the NHL. The other two WHA teams were disbanded, leaving the NHL as the only professional league in North America. There are several minor leagues as well.

With the addition of the former WHA clubs the NHL opened the 1979–80 season with a record 21 teams. The league experienced growth and reorganization during the 1990s, and by the early 21st century it consisted of two 15-team conferences, each with three divisions. The Eastern Conference is split into Atlantic, Northeast, and Southeast divisions. The Western Conference consists of the Central, Northwest, and Pacific divisions. Each team plays an 82-game regular-season schedule that extends from the beginning of October into the first week of April. At the end of the season the top teams in each division engage in playoffs, and the overall winner receives the Stanley Cup.

In the 1980s a few unsuccessful attempts were made to arrange a world championship between the European hockey champion and the North American (Stanley Cup) winner. Under the International Ice Hockey Federation, many countries compete for the world title. In Olympic competition the Soviet Union dominated the event from the 1950s to the 1980s. Players from the former Soviet Union, competing in the 1992 Winter Olympics as the Unified Team, again won the Gold medal. United States teams won in 1960 and 1980. (For Stanley Cup winners, *see* Hockey in Fact-Index.)

**FURTHER RESOURCES FOR ICE HOCKEY**

**Diamond, Dan, and McGoey, Peter.** Hockey, the Illustrated History (Doubleday, 1985).
**Fischler, Stan, and Fischler, S.W.** The Hockey Encyclopedia: The Complete Record of Professional Ice Hockey (Macmillan, 1983).
**Nelson, R.G.** Bobby Hull's Hockey Made Easy (Beaufort, 1984).
**Palmer, Guy.** Hockey Drill Book (Leisure Press, 1984).
**Rosenthal, Bert.** Wayne Gretzky: The Great Gretzky (Childrens, 1983).
**Wayne, Bennett, ed.** Hockey Hotshots (Garrard, 1977).

**HODGKIN, Dorothy Crowfoot** (1910–94). The English chemist Dorothy Crowfoot Hodgkin was awarded the Nobel prize for chemistry in 1964 for her work in determining the structure of vitamin $B_{12}$. In 1948 she and her colleagues made the first X-ray diffraction photograph of the vitamin. Until then normal chemical methods had revealed little of the structure of the central part of the molecule, at the heart of which is a cobalt atom. The atomic arrangement of the compound was eventually determined through the techniques that Hodgkin helped develop.

Dorothy Mary Crowfoot was born on May 12, 1910, in Cairo, Egypt. She studied in England at the Sir John Leman School and at Somerville College, Oxford. While at Oxford she studied X rays of complicated macromolecules. In 1934 she and a colleague at Cambridge University made the first X-ray diffraction photograph of the protein pepsin. She returned to Somerville College later in 1934 as a tutor in chemistry. In 1937 she married Thomas Hodgkin, a lecturer and writer. From 1942 to 1949 she worked on a structural analysis of penicillin.

Hodgkin became a fellow of the Royal Society in 1947, professor of the Royal Society at Oxford University (1960–77), and a member of the Order of Merit in 1965. She spent the early 1960s in Africa at the University of Ghana, where her husband directed the Institute of African Studies. She was appointed chancellor of Bristol University in 1970 and an honorary fellow there in 1988. She was also a fellow of Wolfson College, Oxford (1977–83). Hodgkin died on July 29, 1994, in Shipston-on-Stour, Warwickshire, England.

**HOFFMANN, E.T.A.** (1776–1822). 'The Tales of Hoffmann', an opera in which the grotesque undersides of a poet's nature haunt his memories of love, was inspired by the German author E.T.A. Hoffmann. The French composer Jacques Offenbach wrote his only grand opera as a tribute to Hoffmann's humorous Märchen (folktale) style. Hoffmann mixed his fantasy world of the macabre with the real world. He was also a lawyer, composer, music critic, and caricaturist.

Ernst Theodor Wilhelm Hoffmann was born in Königsberg, Prussia (now Kaliningrad, Russia), on Jan. 24, 1776. Later in life, to honor the memory of the composer Wolfgang Amadeus Mozart, he changed the Wilhelm in his name to Amadeus and has been known simply as E.T.A. Hoffmann.

After Hoffmann studied law at the local university, he finished his schooling at Glogau and Berlin. In 1800 he became a law officer in Prussia's Polish provinces and began to compose music, mainly operas. When the Prussian government was dissolved in 1806, he went to Bamberg as a conductor, music director, and theater designer. He left Bamberg in 1813 and lived briefly in Dresden and Leipzig before taking a position in the court of appeals in Berlin. Hoffmann divided his time between legal work and his music and stories until his death in Berlin on June 25, 1822.

Best known for the supernatural and sinister characters in his short stories, Hoffmann himself was the central character of the Offenbach opera (1881). Other noted composers who adapted his tales were Richard Wagner, in 'Die Meistersinger von Nürnberg' (1868); Paul Hindemith, in 'Cardillac' (1926); Peter Ilich Tchaikovsky, in 'The Nutcracker Suite' (1892); and Léo Delibes, in 'Coppélia' (1870). One of his recurring characters, a conductor-composer named Johannes Kreisler, inspired Robert Schumann's piano pieces 'Kreisleriana' (1838). A "fragmentary biography" of the character appeared in one of Hoffmann's two novels, which was an "autobiography" based on a tomcat.

*'Fantasia in Blue', painted in oil on canvas by Hans Hofmann in 1954, measures 132 by 152 centimeters.*

**HOFMANN, Hans** (1880–1966). The German-born painter Hans Hofmann was one of the principal inspirations for the style called abstract expressionism. He was also one of the most influential art teachers of the 20th century.

Hans Hofmann was born in Weissenberg, Germany, on March 21, 1880. He grew up in Munich, where he studied architecture before taking up painting in 1898. From 1904 to 1914 he studied in Paris, where he experimented with increasingly abstract styles of painting.

From 1915 to 1931 Hofmann directed his own school in Munich before moving to the United States. After teaching for a year in California and New York City, he opened the Hans Hofmann School of Fine Arts in New York. It quickly became one of the most prestigious art schools in the United States.

Although he had exhibited often in Europe, his first American show was not until 1944. In 1957 a major retrospective of his paintings was held at the Whitney Museum of American Art in New York. In 1958 he gave up the school to devote full time to his own painting. Another significant exhibit took place at the Museum of Modern Art in 1963. Late in life he had become as celebrated for his art as he was for his teaching. Hofmann died in New York City on Feb. 17, 1966.

**HOG** *see* **PIG.**

**HOGARTH, William** (1697–1764). The English painter and engraver William Hogarth was primarily a humorist and satirist. His best-known works include several series of popular satiric engravings in which he ridiculed the viciousness and folly that he saw in the world around him.

William Hogarth was born in London, England, on Nov. 10, 1697. His father, Richard Hogarth, was a schoolteacher. At an early age young Hogarth showed artistic talent and was apprenticed to an engraver in London. In 1720 he left his master and set up shop for himself. He studied painting with Sir James Thornhill and married Thornhill's daughter, Jane, in 1729.

Hogarth's fame began in 1731 with the appearance of a series of six pictures called 'A Harlot's Progress'. Other series followed, including 'A Rake's Progress' (1735) and 'Marriage à la Mode' (1745). Editions of these engravings sold well. Hogarth managed to get a law passed, called the Hogarth Act, that protected an artist's copyright and kept others from selling copies.

In 1734 he reopened his drawing school, and it became an arena for artistic discussion and experiment. In 1740 he turned again to painting portraits. His own self-portrait was done in 1745 as an artistic manifesto. By the late 1740s he was executing inexpensive prints, such as 'Gin Lane', for the general public.

Hogarth, who has been called a master of caricature, contributed greatly to the development of technique in this field. Unlike modern caricaturists, however, Hogarth did not ridicule individuals by exaggerating their conspicuous features. Instead he made fun of humanity as a whole, satirizing its weaknesses, pretensions, and vices.

In his own day many critics considered Hogarth's work to be vulgar and inferior. Now he is placed high in the history of English art. He is respected for his originality, his superb rendering of costume and setting, and for the accuracy of his vision, his humor, and the humanness of his characters.

Hogarth died in London on Oct. 26, 1764. He was buried in Chiswick churchyard where his friends erected a tomb to him in 1771. Nearby is Hogarth's summer home, which became a museum in 1902.

*'The Countess's Morning Levée', an oil painting by Hogarth in a series done in 1743–45, measures 90 by 69 centimeters.*

**HOHENSTAUFEN DYNASTY.** The ruling house, or dynasty, of the Holy Roman Empire and Germany for more than 100 years was named Hohenstaufen (*see* Germany, "History"; Holy Roman Empire). More accurately, the name is Staufen, from the castle built by the family's founder, Count Frederick, in the Swabian Jura Mountains.

The dynasty ruled from 1138 until 1254 with the exception of the years 1208 to 1212. Frederick I (died 1105) married Agnes, the daughter of Emperor Henry IV. They had two sons, Frederick and Conrad, who became heirs of their uncle Henry V.

When Henry V died he was briefly succeeded by Lothair III. The Staufen family rebelled against Lothair, and on his death in 1137 Conrad became Conrad III, German king and Holy Roman emperor. Subsequent Hohenstaufen rulers were Frederick I Barbarossa (Holy Roman emperor 1155–90), Henry VI (Holy Roman emperor 1190–97), Philip of Swabia (king 1198–1208), Frederick II (king 1212–50, emperor from 1220), and Conrad IV (king 1237–54). The last illegitimate son of Frederick II, Enzio, died in 1272, and the Hohenstaufen line came to an end.

**HOHENZOLLERN DYNASTY.** One of the most prominent ruling houses in the history of Europe, the Hohenzollern Dynasty played a major role in the history of Germany from the late Middle Ages until the end of World War I. The first known ancestor of the family was Burchard I, who was count of Zollern in the 11th century. By the third and fourth generations after Burchard, two branches of the family had formed. One, the Zollern-Hohenberg, became extinct by 1486. The other, originally the counts of Nuremberg, survived into the 20th century. The Nuremberg branch was further divided about 1200 into the Franconian and Swabian lines.

The Franconian branch moved into prominence when Frederick VI (1371–1440) was appointed elector of Brandenburg in 1415 as Frederick I. This territory in the northeastern lowlands of Germany was the nucleus on which the kingdom of Prussia was built. It was in 1701 that Frederick III of Brandenburg was given the title "king in Prussia." The title was changed to "king of Prussia" in 1772, when Frederick the Great obtained it (*see* Frederick the Great). The Prussian kings retained their title as electors of Brandenburg until the Holy Roman Empire was dissolved by Napoleon I in 1806 (*see* Germany, "History"; Holy Roman Empire).

Subsequent rulers of Prussia were Frederick William II (ruled 1786–97), Frederick William III (ruled 1797–1840), Frederick William IV (ruled 1840–61), William I (ruled 1861–88), Frederick III (ruled 1888), and William II (ruled 1888–1918). During the reign of William I, Germany was united by the military might of Prussia, and the Franco-Prussian War was fought. Under William II (more commonly known as Kaiser Wilhelm II) Germany fought and lost World War I. William II abdicated in the last days of the war and went into exile in The Netherlands. This ended the German sovereignty of the Hohenzollerns. The Swabian branch of the family remained in power longer. Ferdinand became king of Romania in 1914, and his descendants ruled there until 1947.

**HOJO FAMILY.** The governing power of Japan from 1199 until 1333 was in the hands of neither the emperors nor the military rulers called shoguns. It was exercised instead by successive members of the Hojo family, who acted as regents for the shoguns. The emperors at this time had very little power. Until 1868 Japan was, except for a brief interval, governed by shoguns. It was the death of the shogun Yoritomo Minamoto in 1199 that allowed his assistant Tokimasa Hojo, the first known member of the Hojo family, to become guardian of the new shogun and effective ruler of the country. Tokimasa Hojo died in 1215. His successors were Yoshitoki (died 1224), Yasutoki (died 1242), Tsunetoki (died 1246), Tokiyori (died 1263), Tokimune (died 1284), Sadatoki (died 1311), and Takatoki (died 1333).

With Tokimasa Hojo the regent came to control the law, military system, and revenues of Japan. He made sure that the regency was monopolized by his family and made hereditary. This assumption of power was not difficult because the military class did not wish to relinquish the benefits of peace and stability achieved by the Hojos.

The final consolidation of Hojo power came in 1221, when the emperor urged the warlord of western Japan to rebel. The revolt failed, and the Hojos confiscated thousands of estates and parceled them out to landless adherents and friends. The first three Hojo regencies were the high point of strong government by the family and its associates. The emperors lived in forced retirement from the seats of authority, but their revenues, property, and ceremonials were protected. The Buddhist clergy were kept in line by a scrupulous auditing of their accounts. Peasants were protected in their freedom and land holdings, and Hojo retainers were kept prosperous and away from the court, thus minimizing the likelihood of conspiracies.

Tokimune's was the last strong and stable Hojo regency. For most of his time in office and for ten years afterward, China, under Kublai Khan, attempted to subjugate Japan. The costs of a successful defense greatly strained the resources of the Hojos and their vassals. (*See also* Kublai Khan.)

The ninth and last of the Hojo regents was Takatoki, a weak and dissolute individual who left conduct of the government in the hands of incompetent friends. In 1331, in a quarrel over the succession of emperors, Takatoki exiled the emperor. He escaped and waged war against the regent.

The revolt succeeded to the point that Takatoki committed suicide on July 4, 1333. Nevertheless, the strength of the civil government installed by the Hojos proved too strong to be undone. The emperor's attempt to restore imperial rule lasted only a short time. A new shogun, Takauji Ashikaga, gained control of the government in 1338.

*'The Merchant Georg Gisze of Danzig', painted by Hans Holbein the Younger in 1532, is in Berlin's Staatliche Museen.*

**HOLBEIN FAMILY.** An influential German family of artists of the late 15th and early 16th centuries was the Holbein family. Its most famous member, Hans the Younger, is best known for the realistic portraits he painted of the court of King Henry VIII of England. Other painters in the family were Hans the Younger's father, Hans the Elder; uncle, Sigmund; and brother, Ambrosius.

**Hans Holbein the Elder** (1465?–1524). Born in Augsburg, Bavaria, the elder Holbein, like his brother Sigmund, painted richly colored religious works in the late Gothic style. In addition to the altar paintings that are his principal works, he designed church windows and also made a number of portrait drawings that foreshadow the work of his famous son. His later paintings show the transition from the late Gothic to the Renaissance style. He died in Isenheim, Alsace.

**Hans Holbein the Younger** (1497–1543). Born in Augsburg, Bavaria, Hans received his first lessons in art from his father. In 1515 the younger Holbein went to Basel, Switzerland, with his brother, Ambrosius. Among the many scholars living in Basel at that time was the famous Dutch humanist Erasmus, who befriended the young artist and asked him to illustrate his satire, 'Encomium Moriae' (The Praise of Folly). Holbein also illustrated other books, including Martin Luther's German translation of the Bible. In addition he painted pictures and portraits and, like his father, designed stained-glass windows. He also created designs for a series of 41 woodcuts called 'The Dance of Death'.

About 1525 the factional strife that accompanied the Reformation made Basel a difficult place for an artist to work. In 1526 Holbein, carrying a letter of introduction

from Erasmus to the English statesman and author Sir Thomas More, set out for London. He met with a favorable reception in England and stayed there for two years. In 1528 he returned to Basel, where he painted portraits and murals for the town hall. In 1532 he left his wife and children there and traveled once again to London.

In England, where he became court painter to Henry VIII, Holbein was known chiefly as a painter of portraits. His services were much in demand. The more than 100 miniature and full-size portraits he completed at Henry's court provide a remarkable document of that colorful period. An old account of his services at court relates that he painted the portrait of the king, "life size, so well that everyone who looks is astonished, since it seems to live as if it moved its head and limbs." In spite of their richness of detail, Holbein's portraits provide remarkably little insight into the personality and character of the people he painted.

Holbein also found time to perform numerous services for Henry. He designed the king's state robes and made drawings that were the basis of all kinds of items used by the royal household, from buttons to bridles to bookbindings. In 1539, when Henry was thinking of marrying Anne of Cleves, he sent Holbein to paint her portrait (*see* Painting). In 1543 Holbein was in London working on another portrait of the king when he died, a victim of the plague.

**HÖLDERLIN, Friedrich** (1770–1843). After more than a century of obscurity, the lyric poetry of Friedrich Hölderlin came to be recognized as some of the finest writing in the German language. He succeeded in transferring the forms of classical Greek verse into German, something that had not been done before. He also sought to reconcile the Christian faith with the religious spirit of ancient Greece.

Hölderlin was born in Lauffen am Neckar, Germany, on March 20, 1770. Because of his family's poverty, he was sent to theological schools—candidates for the ministry received a free education. Upon graduation from the University of Tübingen in 1793, he decided against the ministry and got a job as a tutor through his friend, the writer Friedrich Schiller. This was the first of several tutorial positions he held over the next several years. During one of them he fell deeply in love, and the breaking off of the relationship in 1798 seemed to unhinge him mentally. This sorrow, combined with his incredible poverty, drove him into a permanent insanity by 1807, when he was working as librarian for Frederick V of Hesse-Homburg. He was confined to a carpenter's house in Tübingen for the last 36 years of his life. He died on June 7, 1843.

Hölderlin's writing was done between 1793 and 1807. His major work was an uncompleted two-volume novel, 'Hyperion', published in 1797 and 1799, the story of a disillusioned fighter for the liberation of Greece. His 'Death of Empedocles' also remained unfinished. The verse translations of Sophocles' dramas (1804) are unparalleled in any language.

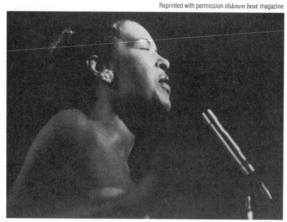

*Billie Holiday in 1958*

**HOLIDAY, Billie** (1915–59). Lady Day, as she was usually called, was the finest jazz singer of her generation, and in the opinion of her followers and many critics she was the greatest jazz singer of the 20th century. The autobiography (1956) of Billie Holiday, written in collaboration with William Dufty, and the movie (1972) made from it, was called 'Lady Sings the Blues'. The title is less a reflection of her music than of her unhappy childhood and the struggle against heroin addiction later in her life. Although Holiday received no professional training, her singing was sophisticated and her diction and phrasing were dramatically intense.

Billie Holiday was born Eleanora Fagan on April 7, 1915, in Baltimore, Md. Her parents were unwed teenagers, Sadie Fagan and Clarence Holiday. Her father was a professional guitarist. Young Holiday made her singing debut in 1931 in obscure Harlem nightclubs. Her first recording session, with accompaniment by Benny Goodman, was held in 1933. She was not widely recognized until 1935, but her early recordings are now regarded as jazz masterpieces.

Although she was still singing in 1958, Holiday's best years were from 1936 to 1943, when her professional and private relationship with saxophonist Lester Young created some of the finest recorded examples of the interplay between vocal and instrumental music. (It was Young who first called her Lady Day.) She appeared in concert with Duke Ellington, Count Basie, Fletcher Henderson, Benny Goodman, Chick Webb, Artie Shaw, and others. Among the compositions associated with her are 'Strange Fruit', 'Fine and Mellow', 'Yesterday's', 'God Bless the Child', 'Don't Explain', 'Lover Man', and 'Gloomy Sunday'. Holiday died in New York City on July 17, 1959. (*See also* Jazz.)

**HOLIDAYS** *see* **FESTIVALS AND HOLIDAYS.**

**HOLINESS MOVEMENT.** John Wesley, the founder of Methodism, believed that human perfection was possible within an individual's lifetime. This perfection, called holiness, was not a human achievement, however, but a gift from God. Wesley believed that if God could forgive sin, He could also transform the individual into a saint to lead a perfect and unflawed life. (*See also* Methodism; Wesley, John.)

This quest for individual perfection originated early in the history of Christianity. It is based on a number of isolated statements in the Bible's New Testament. In the Gospel according to Matthew, 5:48, for example, Jesus is quoted as saying: "Be perfect therefore, as your heavenly father is perfect." Many different sects, dating from the Roman Empire to colonial America, held such a belief. The modern holiness movement, however, owes its origins to Wesley and his followers within the Methodist denomination. The main early development and growth of the holiness movement was in the British colonies of North America. Within Methodism itself the doctrine concerning holiness was not unanimously accepted, and during the decades after the American Revolution emphasis on it was minimal. In the 1830s a revived interest was prompted by the monthly magazine *Guide to Christian Perfection*. Some Methodists became convinced that the emphasis on personal holiness was a chief doctrine of their denomination.

In 1843 about two dozen clergymen and 6,000 members withdrew from the Methodist Episcopal church and formed the Wesleyan Methodist church. This group merged with the Pilgrim Holiness church in 1968 to form the Wesleyan church. In 1860, as the controversy within Methodism over the holiness issue continued, another body of Methodists formed the Free Methodist Church of North America.

Members of other Protestant denominations who favored the holiness movement tended to retain their individual church memberships. They sought fellowship with other like-minded Christians in revival meetings and such organizations as the National Association for the Promotion of Holiness, founded in 1867 in New Jersey.

Separatism, however, was not long in coming. Between 1880 and 1916 several different organizations were founded. The Church of God, headquartered in Anderson, Ind., was one of the earliest. Other associations also use the Church of God name, and most of them are holiness groups. In 1887 the Christian and Missionary Alliance was founded by a Presbyterian clergyman in New York City. A group with origins in Methodism is the Church of the Nazarene, formed by the merger of two holiness groups in 1895. This is one of the largest of the holiness associations. The movement was not confined to the United States. In England, home of Methodism, the Emmanuel Holiness church was founded in 1916. It is one of several such associations in Great Britain.

**HOLISTIC MEDICINE.** The concept of holism was introduced by the South African prime minister and philosopher Jan Christian Smuts in 1925 as an alternative to the prevailing analytical and reductive way of scientific thinking. In Smuts's theory of holism the whole organism and its systems are greater than the sum of their parts.

The holistic (sometimes spelled wholistic) philosophy has expanded into the field of medicine. There are three basic aspects of the holistic approach to medicine. First, it emphasizes disease prevention by placing responsibility with the individual patient as self-healer—to use his own resources to promote health, prevent illness, and encourage healing. Holistic medicine also considers the patient as an individual and unique person, not as a symptom-bearing organism. Finally, holistic practitioners attempt to make use of the many available diagnosis, treatment, and health methods, including both alternative and standard medical methods. Holistic health practitioners view the use of standard medical practices as only one of many ways in which to achieve well-being.

In the last decade the holistic health movement has witnessed an increase in popularity and acceptance. With this has come some criticism of medical quacks who use the holistic philosophy as a front for medical practices deemed unacceptable by holistic practitioners. While the holistic approach to medicine is undergoing development and change, it is still based upon the early concept of holism first presented by Smuts.

### Holistic Medical Practices

Holistic medicine does not have one widely used diagnostic procedure or treatment because it is primarily an attitude about health and healing. Thus, traditional physicians, nurses, specialists, and other health-care professionals may consider themselves holistic practitioners. Holistic medicine addresses not only the whole person, but also the person's environment and involves various healing and health-promoting practices. Holistic practitioners believe that patients should be active participants in their own health care since all individuals are believed to have the capacity—mental, emotional, social, spiritual, and physical—to heal themselves.

Many other health practices concerned with the whole person are not in themselves necessarily holistic medical practices. For example, while acupuncture involves care for the entire body, it does not include other treatments sometimes considered in holistic treatment. Acupuncture may be one of many techniques considered in holistic medical treatment. Others include biofeedback, meditation, modern fluid replacement, ancient energy balance, and surgery (*see* Acupuncture; Biofeedback; Medicine; Surgery; Therapy). Some other methods used in holistic medicine are psychic healing, hypnosis, and various Eastern spiritual and physical disciplines ( *see* Hypnosis).

Holistic diagnosis may include standard laboratory tests or other diagnostic methods. The interrelated physical, mental, and spiritual capabilities in the whole person are major health determinants. A practitioner may, for example, watch the way patients stand, sit, and walk, as well as look for the physical expression of an emotional state. Health-care treatments are usually provided in the context of the patient's culture, family, and community.

Although many holistic practitioners make use of available technical equipment and statistical analysis, the emphasis is on each patient's genetic, biological, and psychosocial strength and uniqueness. Holistic practice is designed to mobilize the individual's self-healing capacity.

Surgical or medical intervention is not disputed in holistic medical practice. Rather, the emphasis is on preventive self-care and self-education.

In recent years concern has risen over the settings in which health care takes place. As a result, alternatives to hospital care emerged for childbirth deliveries and long-term confinement for the terminally ill (*see* Hospice). Since hospital settings often overwhelm and intimidate, many holistic health-care facilities have been located outside but near conventional hospitals. With this proximity arrangement, specialized hospital personnel and technology are readily available in life-threatening situations.

Holistic medicine views health as a positive state, not as the absence of disease. Such a positive approach to treating existing diseases is currently being used by many researchers and physicians. This positive-attitude approach to medical care has been used in cancer therapy by having patients think differently and positively about chemotherapy and radiation therapy.

The use of touching is another major element of holistic medicine. Many body therapies, including massage, chiropractic manipulation, and rolfing, or systematic massage, are based on physical contact. These touch-oriented therapies are based on a holistic approach to human functioning. Touch is used to promote greater relaxation, to improve body alignment and functioning, or to enhance sensory awareness.

Another holistic health therapy called psychotherapeutic body work was first developed by Wilhelm Reich. It has greatly influenced the field of bioenergetics. Once an illness has been identified, it is viewed both as a misfortune and an opportunity for discovery. Holistic medicine emphasizes the idea that psychosocial stresses, such as unemployment, divorce, or death of a close relative or friend, may contribute to ill health (*see* Stress).

In recent years a variety of traditionally trained medical professionals has examined the ideals and documented benefits of holistic medicine. Others still criticize the fragmentation of the holistic medical movement and blame it for promoting medical quackery. Others, calling for physicians as consolers and healers as well as technologically trained practitioners, embrace the humanistic approach offered by holistic medicine.

**HOLLY.** During the Christmas season, many people of North America and Europe decorate their homes with wreaths and sprays of holly. The bright red berries and dark green prickly leaves provide a traditional note of Christmas color.

There are about 400 species of holly shrubs and trees in the temperate and tropical regions of North and South America and Asia. Many, but not all, are evergreens. The leaves of some species are dried and used to make tealike beverages.

The chief North American species, known as American holly, grows naturally along the Atlantic coast and in the Southern states. These trees grow to 50 feet (15 meters) in height. The wood is used for interior finishing and cabinetry. European, or English, holly is frequently cultivated as a garden shrub in the United States and England. In Europe the wood is used for veneers and inlays. Kashi holly grows in Japan and China and is used for decoration during the Chinese New Year. The young shoots are sometimes eaten.

The scientific name of the American holly is *Ilex opaca;* of the European holly, *I. aquifolium;* of the Kashi holly, *I. chinensis.*

**HOLLYHOCK.** A native of Asia Minor, the hollyhock had spread west to the Middle East by the 11th century. In the 17th century Pilgrims carried the hollyhock to North America. Since these early times the plant has been widely cultivated for its handsome flowers.

The earliest hollyhocks had single blossoms. They were probably rose-pink, shading into red and white. Today magnificent double hollyhocks have been cultivated, and colors range from yellow to purple and maroon. Hollyhocks love the sun but will grow in partial shade. They are herbaceous plants, mostly perennial, of the mallow family. About 60 species grow from the Eastern Mediterranean regions to central Asia.

The hollyhock belongs to the genus **Alcea**. The most widely known is **A. rosea**, which has been cultivated and naturalized in most parts of the world. The hollyhock's flowers, about 3 inches (8 centimeters) across, grow on short peduncles from the stalk. There are five large, wedge-shaped petals and numerous stamens. The stalk is thick and hairy and grows as tall as 9 feet (2.7 meters). The leaves have five to seven lobes and are rough, rounded, and heart-shaped.

**HOLMES, Oliver Wendell** (1809–94). One of the most famous American writers of his day, Oliver Wendell Holmes was also a surgeon, teacher, and lecturer. Although he wrote several novels, two biographies, and a number of familiar poems, he is probably best known for a series of essays that first appeared in *Atlantic Monthly*. These were subsequently published in a series of volumes collectively referred to as the "Breakfast-Table" books.

Holmes was born on Aug. 29, 1809, in Cambridge, Mass., where his father was a clergyman. The elder Holmes was also a Harvard professor and a historian. Holmes received his early education in Cambridge and at Phillips Academy in Andover. He attended Harvard College, graduating in 1829. His fame as a writer began in 1830 with his poem 'Old Ironsides'. The popular sentiment aroused by this poem saved the frigate *Constitution* from destruction.

After he graduated from Harvard Holmes studied law, then medicine, in Boston and in Europe. He

received an M.D. degree at Harvard in 1836. That same year he also published his 'Poems', which contained the amusing poem 'My Aunt' and the humorous-pathetic 'Last Leaf'. Holmes's verses became so popular that he has been called the poet laureate of Boston.

Holmes won a Boylston prize for a medical essay in 1836 and two more in 1837. He was appointed professor of anatomy at Dartmouth College in 1838. In 1840 Holmes married Amelia Lee Jackson. They had three children, one of whom became a famous justice of the Supreme Court (*see* Holmes, Oliver Wendell, Jr.).

Until 1857 Holmes concentrated on teaching and on writing medical articles. 'The Contagiousness of Puerperal Fever', which appeared in 1843, is probably the most noteworthy of these. In 1847 he was appointed anatomy professor at Harvard. From then until 1853 he also served as dean of the Harvard medical school.

In 1857 Holmes's career as a popular writer got fully under way. That year James Russell Lowell brought out the first issue of the *Atlantic Monthly* and chose Holmes to be the prose writer for publication. Here began the series of essays that later appeared in book form as 'The Autocrat of the Breakfast-Table', published in 1858; 'The Professor of the Breakfast-Table' (1860); and 'The Poet at the Breakfast-Table' (1872). The last of this series, called 'Over the Teacups', appeared in 1891.

As a writer and lecturer Holmes was greatly loved for his wit, wisdom, and charm. In spite of his remarkable and wide-ranging talents, he was never guilty of talking down to his audiences. Holmes died on Oct. 7, 1894, in his home in Boston.

**HOLMES, Oliver Wendell, Jr.** (1841–1935). One of the most famous justices of the Supreme Court of the United States, Oliver Wendell Holmes, Jr., was known as "the great dissenter." He was called this because often when the court handed down a decision Holmes delivered a minority opinion, or dissent.

Holmes was born in Boston on March 8, 1841. His father was Oliver Wendell Holmes (*see* Holmes, Oliver Wendell). His mother was a daughter of a justice of the Massachusetts Supreme Court. Young Holmes was educated in private grammar schools and at Harvard College.

At the start of the Civil War, during his senior year at Harvard, Holmes enlisted as a private in the Union Army. He was called to active service as a lieutenant after his graduation, and during the war he was wounded three times. He returned to Harvard to continue his law studies and was admitted to the bar in 1867. He joined a law firm and also taught law at Harvard. In 1872 he married Fanny Bowditch Dixwell, the daughter of his Latin school headmaster.

In 1881 Holmes wrote 'The Common Law', which is regarded as a classic legal text. In 1882 he was appointed a justice of the Massachusetts Supreme Court. In 1902 President Theodore Roosevelt appointed him an associate justice of the United States Supreme Court. He served until he was almost 91 years old.

EB Inc.

*Oliver Wendell Holmes, Jr.*

Justice Holmes believed the law should change to meet altering social conditions. He condemned child labor as uncivilized and upheld the right of strikers to form orderly picket lines. Holmes felt that even people whose beliefs might be considered dangerous were entitled to the protection of the law and that granted by the Constitution. He was not a radical in politics, however.

In retirement Holmes decided against writing a book, believing that his many opinions and dissents adequately reflected his views. He spent his time reading and enjoying nature. Holmes died on March 6, 1935, in Washington, D.C. He was buried with military honors in Arlington National Cemetery on what would have been his 94th birthday.

**HOLMIUM** *see* Fact-Index.

**HOLOCAUST.** The killing of millions of people by Nazi Germany during World War II is referred to as the Holocaust, though the term is most commonly used to describe the fate of Europe's Jews. While Roma (Gypsies), Slavs, homosexuals, and others also were singled out for obliteration, the Nazis' various policies for exterminating the Jews were the most deliberate and calculated, and the primary goal of the Nazi regime was the extermination of all the Jews in Europe. This purpose was nearly fulfilled. Out of an estimated 9.5 million Jews living in Europe before the war, about 6 million were killed. In addition, millions of Poles and Russians were also killed.

Only in Denmark were heroic national efforts made to save the Jewish population in spite of the German occupation. Most Danish Jews were sent to neutral Sweden to live out the war. Other efforts to save the Jews were made by individuals, such as the Swedish businessman Raoul Wallenberg, and by institutions. (*See also* Genocide; Wallenberg.)

Adolf Hitler's persecution of Jews began as soon as the Nazis came to power in 1933. A strident anti-Semitism had always been part of his party platform (*see* Hitler). Hitler's policies later found eager support in other European nations as well, where centuries of deeply ingrained Christian anti-Semitism erupted into violence under cover of war. Beginning in April 1933, Jewish businesses were boycotted and vandalized. Jews were driven from their jobs in government and universities. During a meeting of the Nazi party in Nuremberg in September 1935 laws—known as the Nuremberg Laws—were developed to further aid in the discrimination of Jews. These laws were later modified to include Roma, who were the only group other than the Jews to be targeted for the gas chambers. Jews lost their citizenship and were forbidden to intermarry with other Germans. They became nonpersons in their own country with no claim to rights of any kind. Many fled to other European nations, to Palestine, or to the United States, but emigration was often problematic.

On Nov. 9–10, 1938, the Night of Broken Glass (*Kristallnacht* in German), nearly every synagogue in Germany was destroyed or damaged along with many other Jewish institutions. There followed the rounding up of thousands of Jews to be imprisoned in concentration camps. Their wealth and property were confiscated.

Although these outrages were reported around the world, there was almost no organized opposition to what was happening. This silence meant, to Hitler, tacit approval of his policies.

By late 1941, after the invasion of the Soviet Union, the overwhelming mass of European Jewry had been brought under German domination. Many Jews had been forced into ghettos, overcrowded, guarded urban areas, where disease was rampant and resources in short supply. It was sometime near this point in the war that the Nazi leaders began their "final solution" to what they called the Jewish problem. An earlier plan to ship all Jews to the island of Madagascar was rejected as impracticable.

The Wannsee Conference met on Jan. 20, 1942, in a suburb of Berlin. Fifteen Nazis, headed by Reinhard Heydrich, made plans for the final solution. All Jews were to be evacuated to camps in Eastern Europe. Many would be killed outright, while others would endure slave labor and meager rations until they died. Before or after they were killed, they were stripped of every potentially valuable possession—clothing, eyeglasses, jewelry, gold teeth, and hair.

At the first extermination camp, Chelmno, built in occupied Poland in late 1941, victims were killed in mobile gas vans. In other camps, such as Belzec, Sobibor, and Treblinka, completed in 1942, the Nazis found that the most effective method of exterminating people was in specially constructed gas chambers. After the gassing the bodies were then moved to nearby furnaces to be burned. The Nazis had little trouble recruiting help from among the citizens of occupied countries to staff the camps.

The largest extermination camp was Auschwitz II-Birkenau. At its peak, as many as 8,000 Jews were killed there daily. Killings were also carried out by mobile death squads, called *Einsatzgruppen* ("deployment groups"), which traveled from town to town gathering and murdering large numbers of people, including entire families of men, women, and children.

Organizing such a massive undertaking seriously detracted from Germany's war effort. It required the cooperation of the government bureaucracy, the military, industry, and the railroads. There were frequent shortages of trains to transport troops because of the thousands of people being shipped eastward to the camps. By 1945, when it was obvious that Germany was losing the war, this goal rather than the war itself had become paramount.

Although both Allied and Jewish leaders in the United States knew of the exterminations, Jewish efforts to have the Allies bomb the death camps were unsuccessful. When the war ended and Allied troops entered Germany and Eastern Europe, news of the Holocaust had a shattering effect upon the world, but especially upon a German public already disheartened by defeat. Pictures of the camps were sometimes too gruesome to be published. The damage suffered by the Jews of Europe could never be repaired.

The trials of those who committed Nazi war crimes began after the war's end. An international tribunal tried 22 high-ranking Nazi officials for war crimes and crimes against humanity at a series of trials held in Nuremberg in 1945–46. Later trials targeted additional perpetrators, including judges, concentration camp commanders, and military officers. The search for additional perpetrators continued during the remainder of the 20th century and resulted in several high-profile trials.

**HOLOGRAPHY.** Photography was once considered the best means of recording visual information, but with the development of holography in the 1960s, the simple, two-dimensional images of photographs were surpassed. Holography is a technique by which the image of a three dimensional object is recorded on film so that upon reconstruction, or playback, the constructed image of the object is three dimensional. The term hologram comes from the Greek words *holos*, meaning "whole," and *gram*, meaning "writing." Each portion of the hologram stores an encoded message about the whole object.

Creating the common hologram involves the use of two beams of light originating from a single laser. This laser light is of a single frequency (monochromatic) and forms waves that are in phase with one another (coherent). The light beam originating from the laser is split by a partially reflective mirror. The narrow beams are redirected by mirrors and expanded by lens-and-pinhole arrangements. One beam, called the object beam, illuminates the surface of the object. The light then scatters and reflects onto the film. The other beam, called the reference beam, strikes the film directly. These two beams interact on the film, producing an interference pattern of closely spaced lines, called a complex diffraction grating. This film of the pattern is the hologram.

To view the hologram the film is developed and the viewer looks through it, using the same laser light source to illuminate the film. The relative position of the light source with respect to the film image is the same as the original object-light source relationship. The image of the object in the film appears as a three-dimensional form in space. The visual effect of a hologram is similar to looking through a window (the holographic film) at an object. Some holograms are recorded with the object close to the film. This decreases the coherence requirement for reconstruction and allows viewing with ordinary light. A complex two-step process can also be used in encoding any hologram to allow it to be viewed in ordinary light.

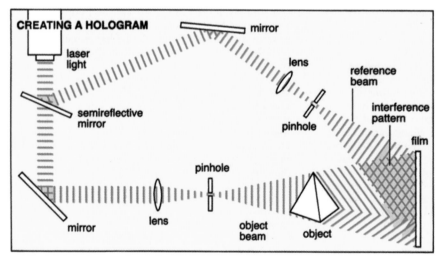

**CREATING A HOLOGRAM**

mirror

laser light

lens

reference beam

semireflective mirror

interference pattern

pinhole

film

pinhole

mirror

lens

object beam

object

*The interaction of light waves from two laser beams forms the actual hologram—a swirling interference pattern recorded on film. The process begins when a laser beam is split by a semitransparent mirror into an object beam and a reference beam. Both are redirected by mirrors with the object beam being sent to the object. A three-dimensional image is formed when a laser beam is directed through the hologram.*

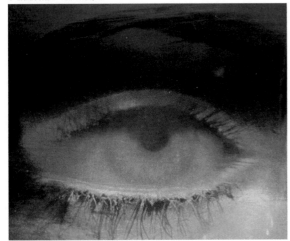

*A close-up of a white light commercial hologram.*

Unlike ordinary photography, where only the wavelength and light intensity are recorded, the holographic process records both the amplitude and the phase relationships of light reflected from the object. Phase information is important if a small change in location or deformation of an object is to be noted. Two or more successive holograms taken of the same body before and after deformation allow the change in shape to be viewed. This technique, called holographic interferometry, can be used to watch a part vibrate or to see minute deformations caused by various loads. Holography is also used to visualize flows and as a means of non-destructive testing to locate cracks in structural components.

Holography has many applications. In holographic microscopy, for example, an entire region of an object is recorded for subsequent detailed analysis. Holography is also used in the development of optical elements, such as scanners, filters, and diffraction gratings. Displays, ranging from advertising to airplane cockpit views, use holography to give the "depth" feeling of a real object. Holograms are also used in production or process controls to monitor small changes in physical parameters. Holographic records are sometimes digitized and stored for subsequent use by an image digitizing system connected to computers. Superimposing two or more holograms is often used as a security measure. Some holograms embedded in credit cards show a different object, depending on the angle of view. This impedes the forging of such cards.

Modern industrial holography uses optical fiber cables and bundles to simplify the optical set-ups and to permit holographic interference measurements to be performed on surfaces that are remote or inaccessible to normal view. Special holographic cameras are commercially available to produce images in a few seconds.

The fundamental concept of holographic recording was first described in 1948 by Hungarian-born Dennis Gabor to improve the resolving power of electron microscopes. It was not until lasers were developed in the early 1960s, however, that the first quality holographic image was produced using a strong coherent light source. Subsequent improvements of holography followed the development of lasers and related technologies. (*See also* Laser and Maser; Photography.)

John A. Gilbert

**HOLY GRAIL.** One of the most significant and interesting components of the legends about King Arthur concerns an object called the Holy Grail (*see* Arthurian Legend). The word grail seems to be derived from *graal,* a word still used in France to refer to a wide- mouthed cup. In the legend's most predominant forms, the Holy Grail is identified with the cup used by Jesus Christ at the Last Supper.

In the legends the Holy Grail is the object of a search, and finding it symbolizes a kind of mystical union with God. When and how the legend originated is unknown. It appeared in several pieces of literature during the late Middle Ages—from the 12th through the 15th century. The earliest known book to deal with it as a holy object is 'Le Conte du Graal' (The Story of the Grail, also known as the Tale of Perceval) by Chrétien de Troyes, a French poet of the 12th century. In it Chrétien unites the religious quest for the Grail with a number of knightly adventures.

In the story Perceval is a knight of childlike innocence. His adventure consists of visiting the castle of the wounded Fisher King, where he sees a myster-ious dish—the Grail. Having previously been scolded for asking too many questions, he refrains from saying anything about the Grail. His failure to ask a question prevents the Fisher King from being healed of his wounds. Afterward Perceval sets off in search of the Grail and learns the real meaning of chivalry, or knighthood, and its connections with Christianity.

In later versions of the book, Perceval is replaced by Sir Gawain, who goes in search of the lance that had pierced Christ's side at the crucifixion. In a 13th-century treatment of the story by Wolfram von Eschenbach, the Grail is a precious stone that has fallen from heaven, not a cup. Wolfram's story became the basis for Richard Wagner's last opera, 'Parsifal' (1882).

The Grail story is given an explicitly Christian interpretation in the work of Robert de Borron written around the end of the 12th century. He wrote an early history of the Grail in his 'Joseph of Arimathea', based on a figure described in the New Testament as present at the crucifixion. Borron identifies the Grail as the cup used at the Last Supper. The Grail is eventually brought to Western Europe, where it is connected with the founding of the Round Table by King Arthur's father, Uther Pendragon.

The version of the Holy Grail legend that had the widest influence in romances of the late Middle Ages was written by Sir Thomas Malory (died 1470?). His book is 'Morte d'Arthur' (Death of Arthur). In the story King Arthur has been told that a seat at the Round Table will someday be filled by a knight who seeks and finds the Holy Grail. A stone is found with a sword embedded in it, but no knight is able to draw the sword from the stone until Sir Galahad, son of Sir Lancelot, is brought to the Round Table. He alone is able to remove the sword. Arthur and his knights then set out on the quest.

The Grail represents not a search for salvation but a vision of God as the reward for a pure life. Lancelot, because of his adultery with Queen Guinevere, only sees the Grail in a dream. Perceval, having committed but one sin, is permitted to see it in visions. Only to Galahad is it given to look into the Grail itself and to behold mysteries that no other human can imagine. After his vision Galahad dies, and the other knights return to Camelot. Knights who do not seek divine help in their pursuit fail completely in their quest.

**HOLY ROMAN EMPIRE.** From Christmas Day in AD 800 until Aug. 6, 1806, there existed in Europe a peculiar political institution called the Holy Roman Empire. The name of the empire as it is known today did not come into general use until 1254. It has truly been said that this political arrangement was not holy, or Roman, or an empire. Any holiness attached to it came from the claims of the popes in their attempts to assert religious control in Europe. It was Roman to the extent that it tried to revive, without success, the political authority of the Roman Empire in the West as a countermeasure to the Byzantine Empire in the East. It was an empire in the loosest sense of the word—at no time was it able to consolidate unchallenged political control over the vast territories it pretended to rule. There was no central government, no unity of language, no common system of law, no sense of common loyalty among the many states within it. Over the centuries the empire's boundaries shifted and shrank drastically.

### Origins

The original Roman Empire ended in Italy and Western Europe in AD 476, when the last emperor—Romulus Augustulus—was deposed. Political power passed to Constantinople (now Istanbul), the capital of the Byzantine Empire. Theoretically Constantinople included all of Europe in its domain. Realistically, however, this proved impossible, as barbarian kingdoms were established throughout Western Europe. The only figure in the West who had any claim to universal authority was the pope in Rome, and he was legally bishop of Rome, confirmed in his position by the Byzantine emperor.

By the 8th century, Byzantine control of Italy had vanished. The Lombard kingdom of northern Italy had driven out the emperor's representative in Ravenna in 751. There were also strong religious differences between the pope and the church in Constantinople—differences that would lead to a complete break in 1054. Confronted with this situation, the Roman popes sought political protection from the only people who would give it—the kings of the Franks, the strongest power north of the Alps. In 754 the Frankish king Pepin the Short invaded Italy and conquered the Lombard kingdom. Two years later he

assigned the former Byzantine territory around Ravenna to the pope. This was the birth of the Papal States of Italy, which would endure until the unification of Italy in the 19th century.

This close cooperation between popes and the Frankish kings would have far-reaching consequences. It laid the basis for centuries of conflict between emperors and popes over who had the supreme authority in Europe. According to the popes, the empire was the political arm of the church. The emperors, on the other hand, saw themselves as directly responsible to God, and they relied on conquest and control for their power.

There is little doubt that the popes hoped to become the successors of emperors in the West. Since this was politically impossible, the next best solution was to assert religious control by means of political institutions. On Dec. 25, 800, Pope Leo III crowned Charlemagne emperor during a service at St. Peter's Basilica in Rome (*see* Charlemagne). The act was illegal, because popes never had the right to crown emperors. The crowning did nothing for Charlemagne. He was as before king of the Franks and Lombards and the most powerful monarch in Europe. The main practical outcome of Leo's act was to complete the separation between East and West. It thereby set up a rivalry with Constantinople, a rivalry in which neither side had a real advantage. Most significantly the coronation involved the new emperor and his successors in the political pretensions of the papacy.

### Charlemagne's Empire

The empire lasted as long as it did because the idea was politically and religiously appealing to the peoples and rulers of Europe. It did not endure unbroken, however. Charlemagne's kingdom did not remain whole very long after his death. His domains were fragmented by his successors. The last of his descendants to hold the title of emperor was Charles III the Fat (881–87). From 888 France, Germany, and Italy were separate states (though not unified nations by any means). A succession of emperors, mostly nominees of the popes, followed Charles. With the death of the last of these in 924, the powerful Roman family of the Crescentii abolished the title of emperor in Italy—at least for a time.

### Rise of the Germanic Empire

The imperial title had died temporarily in Italy, but it persisted north of the Alps. It was a notion of empire that had nothing to do with Rome. By the middle of the 10th century there were two Frankish kingdoms—east and west. The West Kingdom was composed largely of today's France. The East Frankish Kingdom was Germanic. From this time the Holy Roman Empire was to be basically Germanic, though it maintained pretensions of rule over greater territory, including Italy. In the German lands the kings were Saxon, not Frankish.

Otto I (died 973) was the first of the Saxon kings powerful enough to assert control over Germany and

Italy. He was crowned emperor by Pope John XII in 962. Although he held the title, he made no pretense of governing the East Frankish lands. From his reign the empire was to be a union of German states and northern Italy.

Otto I did not claim the title of Roman emperor, but his descendants did. Otto II did so to proclaim his rivalry with the emperor at Constantinople. Otto III (ruled 983–1002) made Rome his capital. He felt himself to be the political power by which Christian domination would spread throughout Europe. Popes were subject to him and his successors down to Henry III (1039–56). By that time effective rule over Germany and Italy together had become impracticable. Distance alone made it difficult.

### Reassertion of Papal Power

For more than 200 years, from 1056 until 1273, the popes made a political comeback. Some very strong-minded individuals were elected pope—among them, Gregory VII and Innocent III were the most notable. They wasted no time in refuting the pretensions of the emperors to control the church.

It was the Investiture Controversy that brought matters to a head. At issue was the question whether political figures, such as emperors and kings, had the right to appoint bishops and heads of monasteries and to invest them with the symbols of their office. At the heart of the issue was the place of the emperor in Christian society, especially his relationship with the papacy. It was Pope Gregory VII (pope 1073–85) who initiated the controversy in 1076 by stating that only the pope had the right to crown emperors, just as it was his right to appoint bishops and other church officials. The controversy was brought to a close in 1122 by an agreement between Pope Calixtus II and Emperor Henry V, but future popes revived the issue as they saw fit.

The era of the Hohenstaufen emperors (1138–1254, except for the years 1198–1214) was a time of almost unceasing conflict between popes and emperors (*see* Hohenstaufen Dynasty). The greatest of these, Frederick I Barbarossa, added the word holy to the name of his empire to balance the claims of the Holy Church. He emphasized continuity with the past, going back to the days of Charlemagne. His rights as emperor, he determined, were not based on the deed of Leo III but on the territorial conquest of the Franks. Lawyers for the emperors argued against the popes, saying that "he who is chosen by the election of the princes alone is the true emperor." (The emperors were generally chosen by this time through an election held by German princes.)

The conflicts with the popes drew the Hohenstaufen emperors into Italian politics. The temptation to control Italy, and thus Rome, was persistent. Henry VI married the heiress to Sicily, and the Norman Kingdom of Sicily was used to restore imperial power in Italy. The popes reacted vigorously to this threat. They found allies in their opposition to the emperors, and by 1245 it was possible to depose Frederick II. His death in 1250 effectively ended the Holy Roman Empire of the Middle Ages. Over the next two decades the imperial structure fell apart in Italy.

### Hapsburg Rulers

If most of Italy was lost, the empire maintained itself north of the Alps in Germany for several centuries. It became little more than a coalition of German states, each with its own ruler. When Rudolf I of the House of Hapsburg became German king in 1273, he was the head of a federation of German princes. He abandoned all claims to the center and south of Italy and retained only nominal title to the north. (The north of Italy was not entirely free of Hapsburg domination until after World War I.) After him only four emperors were crowned by a pope or his delegate. The last was Charles V, a Hapsburg who was also king of Spain.

By the end of the Middle Ages, any hope of reviving anything like a real empire in Europe had become impossible. France and Spain were the most powerful kingdoms in Europe. Both were contending for control of the continent. The weak and disunited German states were in no position to establish any kind of control, even within their own boundaries. (Germany did not become united until 1870.) Charles IV therefore set out to make the empire a solely German institution. By an agreement with Pope Clement V, he abandoned Italy. He went to Rome for his coronation on April 5, 1355. He then refashioned the empire into the Holy Roman Empire of the German Nation.

From then the empire was essentially part of the history of Germany. A few emperors, notably Charles V, entertained a larger vision of power, but there was no way for him to unite his Spanish and Austrian possessions with Germany as long as France stood in the way. (*See also* Germany, "History.")

The 16th-century Reformation in the church further divided the weak empire. Germany was split into two religious camps, and the emperor was little more than the head of a religious faction. The electors, the real heads of the German states, were entrenched by virtue of championing either Roman Catholicism or Lutheranism.

The Thirty Years' War, originally a religious conflict, devastated Germany and further weakened what little reality the empire had left. No emperor afterward ever tried to establish a central authority. (*See also* Thirty Years' War.)

The end came with Napoleon. For several centuries France had been intending to annex at least the fringes of the empire. It had never happened. When Napoleon carried his wars eastward, however, he was resolved to terminate the reign of Emperor Francis II (later Francis I of Austria). The emperor saw what was coming, and he resigned his title on Aug. 6, 1806. The empire ceased to exist as a political reality. It persisted for some time as an ideal. It was used as an inspiration for the German Empire of 1870 and more so by Adolf Hitler's Third Reich (Empire) in the 1930s. (For list of emperors *see* Holy Roman Emperors table in Fact-Index.)

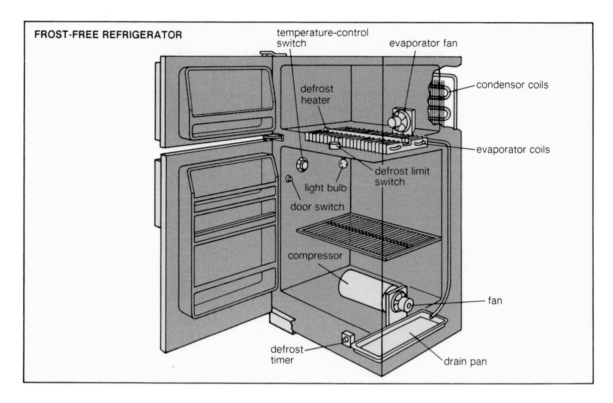

FROST-FREE REFRIGERATOR

temperature-control switch

evaporator fan

condensor coils

defrost heater

evaporator coils

defrost limit switch

light bulb

door switch

compressor

fan

defrost timer

drain pan

## HOME APPLIANCES

**HOME APPLIANCES.** Devices operated by electricity or gas and found in the home are called home appliances. Excluded from consideration in this article are sewing machines and electrically operated tools, such as saws, drills, lathes, and other workshop equipment (*see* Sewing; Tools).

The variety of home appliances has greatly increased during the 20th century. Originally only a few simple utensils, such as pots and pans, stoves, cutlery, and ice boxes were found in the home. With the disappearance of domestic servants, home appliances were designed to ease the work load in the home. Many, like vacuum cleaners or microwave ovens, are chosen for their labor-saving or time-saving capabilities; others are purchased for their convenience.

Home appliances can be divided into several categories. These are kitchen equipment; laundry equipment; cleaning equipment; entertainment-center equipment; and appliances used for heating and cooling as well as for water softening. Through the use of computers and microchips, it is now possible to design fully automated homes. All appliances are interconnected and under the control of one computer.

### Kitchen Equipment

Large kitchen appliances include refrigerators, freezers, ranges and ovens, dishwashers, trash compactors, and waste-disposal units. Some, such as freezers, may be kept outside the kitchen because of lack of space. Refrigerators often contain freezer compartments as well as ice-making machines.

Refrigerators and freezers generally operate on a compression system of cooling. In a frost-free refrigerator, refrigerant gas is compressed by a compressor and transmitted to condenser coils where it is pressurized, cooled, and liquefied. In liquid form, the refrigerant then passes through an expansion valve and returns to a gaseous state in the evaporator coils. The refrigerant absorbs heat as it changes from a liquid to a gas, and the temperature of the inside of the refrigerator is lowered. The condenser fan forces heat into the room, and the evaporator fan circulates the cooled air in the freezer compartment. During defrosting, the defrost heater melts any ice that has accumulated on the evaporator coils. It is turned on by the defrost timer and turned off by the defrost limit switch. The defrost water drains into a pan beneath the refrigerator.

Food-waste disposers, or garbage grinders, are designed to pulverize most types of food waste. Certain items, however, such as grease, bones, corn husks, and paper, can damage the disposal unit. The garbage grinder is fitted into a sink drain so that, with a continuous flow of cold water, the waste may be flushed into the sewage system as it is ground. The unit contains steel knives that rotate at high speed inside the food-waste container. The motor is started by an electric switch near the sink or by an internal switch that is tripped by the flow of cold water.

Microwave ovens convert electric energy into microwave energy to heat or cook foods quickly. Some microwave ovens are easily portable; others are heavy and relatively stationary. Electricity passes through a magnetron tube to produce microwaves. The microwaves are then channeled to a slow rotating fan, which distributes them into a metal oven cavity. The waves bounce off the top, bottom, and sides of the cavity to penetrate the food evenly.

Outdoor grills may also be included among larger kitchen appliances. Some grills are permanently installed and are operated with gas; others can be moved easily and use charcoal briquettes for cooking.

Small appliances run by electricity fall into two categories: heating units and motor-driven units. Electrically heated devices are based on the fact that as electricity flows through a substance, the resistance offered by the material creates heat. The amount of resistance depends on the material used. In the toaster, the heating elements are usually made of nichrome wire. When the lever is pressed down, it lowers the bread on the carriage. This action closes a keeper-release switch. The color-control knob sets the position of the switch, which is connected to a bimetallic arm. As the temperature rises, this arm bends and trips the switch. The keeper release then disengages the solenoid and keeper, the heating elements turn off, and the carriage pops up. The lift arm is connected to a piston chamber that slowly raises the toast. Other electrically heated devices are coffeemakers, roasters, frying pans, broilers, hot plates, popcorn poppers, waffle irons, and egg cookers.

Small motor-driven appliances include food processors, blenders, juicers, can openers (with knife sharpener attachments), ice crushers, beaters and mixers, coffee grinders, ice-cream makers, exhaust fans, and countertop refrigerators.

### Laundry Equipment

The appliances used for laundering are washing machines, dryers, and irons. Washing machines are normally powered by electricity. Dryers, which contain heating units, use either electricity or natural gas. In modern, fully automatic washing machines, the laundry is placed in the tub, the current switched on, and the controls are adjusted. Once the washing and rinsing cycles are completed and the spin-dry process has removed excess water from the laundry, the machine turns off automatically.

The automatic dryer, by heating and tumbling the laundry, evaporates the remaining water from the articles in a predetermined amount of time. Dryers are usually controlled with temperature settings for normal, delicate, and permanent-press fabrics.

The final laundering stage is ironing—the removal of fabric creases by the application of heat and moisture under pressure. The electric hand iron is used in most homes. It has temperature settings for different kinds of fabrics and often a small reservoir of water, which is heated to produce steam. Some irons have automatic shut-off controls for safety.

### Cleaning Equipment

Although various implements and materials are used in the home for cleaning, the standard appliances are a

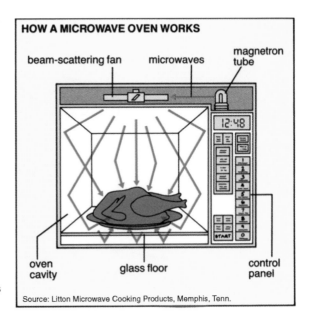

**HOW A MICROWAVE OVEN WORKS**

beam-scattering fan · microwaves · magnetron tube · 12:48 · oven cavity · glass floor · control panel

Source: Litton Microwave Cooking Products, Memphis, Tenn.

carpet sweeper and vacuum cleaner. Some homeowners also possess rug cleaners and floor polishers. For outside the house there are power lawn mowers, weed cutters, hedge trimmers, and snow blowers. Electrically operated paint sprayers also belong to this category. Most of these are motor-driven appliances. Lawn-mower and snow-remover motors are powered by electricity or gasoline.

Vacuum cleaners are of two types: canister and upright. The canister type consists of a metal—or plastic—cylinder that holds the motor, the fan, and the bag that collects the dirt. A flexible hose with a nozzle is attached to the canister. Different removable nozzles are available to vacuum carpets, bare floors, furniture, and draperies.

The upright vacuum cleaner has a long handle and is pushed on wheels. The motor, fan, and a rotating cylindrical brush are located in one compartment. When the vacuum cleaner is switched on, the brush rotates by a belt, and air is drawn over it by the fan to carry dirt from the carpet and into a bag suspended from the handle. Some upright cleaners have attachments for other types of vacuuming.

Rug and carpet cleaners, powered by electricity, use concentrated liquid detergents added to water in a small tank. The detergents are applied to the rug and scrubbed with a brush until the lather has disappeared. When the rug is dry it is vacuumed to remove leftover dirt and detergent.

Floor polishers look like upright vacuum cleaners. Instead of a rotating cylindrical brush, a floor polisher has from one to three disk-shaped brushes that have long, stiff bristles and spin at a high speed. The heat created by the friction of the brushes melts the wax into the floor and gives a high polish. Steel-wool pads or sandpaper disks are attached for prewax floor cleaning and felt disks are used for high-luster polishing.

**PARTS OF A TOASTER**

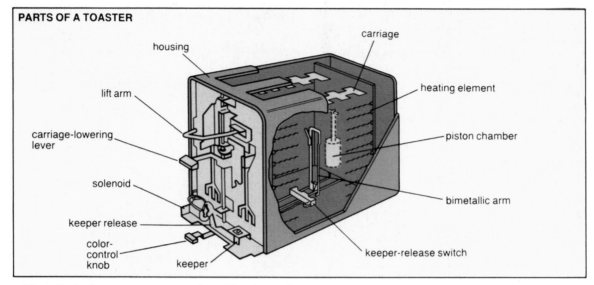

The cylinder lawn mower, invented in 1830, changed little until after World War II, when power mowers were introduced. About the same time, the motor-powered snow remover began to replace snow shovels. Some power lawn mowers still use cylinder-mounted blades, but most have rotary blades. Snow removers either blow the snow off to one side or propel it with blades.

**Heating and Cooling Equipment**

Within a home, air temperature and quality are controlled or modified by a number of appliances. Large systems designed to heat, cool, and ventilate the home generally are not considered home appliances (*see* Air Conditioning; Heating and Ventilating). An electric space heater, on the other hand, is similar to a toaster. The heated coils are exposed to a room to radiate heat. Some space heaters are fueled by kerosene or a similar petroleum derivative.

Temperature in a building is controlled by a small appliance called a thermostat. Thermostats, with built-in thermometers, regulate the heat output of a furnace through a system of relays, valves, and switches. The thermostat generates electrical signals when the temperature rises above or falls below the desired level. It usually controls the flow of fuel to the heating unit. Thermostats are also used to regulate central air-conditioning units.

Small air-conditioning-units, installed in windows or built into outside walls, operate on the same principle as a compression-type refrigerator. Air is drawn through a filter to remove dust, smoke, and pollen. It then passes over the cooling coils, causing some condensation, thereby dehumidifying the air as well as cooling it. The condenser fan directs excess moisture onto the condensing coils, where it either evaporates or is channeled into a drain outside the house. Heat from the condenser is dissipated outside the house, while cool air is blown by a fan through vents into a room. (*See also* Air Conditioning.)

**Humidifiers and Dehumidifiers**

Air quality is also modified by smaller appliances such as fans, humidifiers, dehumidifiers, and air purifiers. Most of these are motor-driven, electrically powered appliances. Electric fans circulate indoor air for cooling and ventilation or to control humidity (*see* Fan, Electric).

Humidifiers put moisture into the air. Because cold air holds less moisture than warm air, when outdoor temperatures drop, inside humidity falls as well. A humidifier is basically a water tank containing a drum or a wheel with an attached water-retaining material. As the drum rotates, it picks up water. A fan, blowing through the drum, sends moisture-laden air into a room. Some homes have central humidifying systems.

A dehumidifier is similar to a refrigerator. It contains a small refrigeration system with a compressor. A fan pulls in air, which passes over cooling coils, causing water vapor to condense. The condensed water drips down into a pan, which must be emptied regularly. Some units contain a humidistat that turns off the compressor when a desired level of humidity is reached. Dehumidifiers are meant to operate during warm weather, when humidity is high. Unless they contain a deicing unit, they will not work well at a temperature of less than 65° F (18° C), because the water will freeze on the coils.

**Air Purifiers**

There are three kinds of air purifiers: fan-filter systems, electrostatic precipitators, and negative-ion generators. Most of the less expensive cleaners on the market are of the fan-filter type. Air is drawn into the appliance by a fan, and the impurities are trapped in a filter.

Electrostatic precipitators draw in air with a fan. The air passes an electrode that gives particles in the air an electrical charge. Then the air passes a collector plate with an opposite charge, and the particles are drawn off and stick to the plate. This kind of air purifier can be installed as part of a forced-air heating system in a home.

Negative-ion generators have proved to be the best room air purifiers. These appliances put electrons into the air. The electrons turn air molecules into negative ions, which give particles a negative charge. The particles then tend to adhere to surfaces, such as walls and ceilings.

### Water Softeners

Water hardness (the presence of too many minerals) can be reduced by filters attached to faucets; by portable, motor-driven appliances that circulate water through a filter system; or by mechanical softeners. The mechanical softener is the largest and most expensive type. It is hooked into the water-intake part of the plumbing system and removes minerals by a process called ion exchange. A tanklike container holds a quantity of beadlike ion-exchange resins. These have an affinity for the calcium and magnesium ions that make water hard. If water containing calcium and magnesium ions passes over a bed of resin containing a concentration of sodium ions, the calcium and magnesium will combine chemically with the resins. The sodium ions will be released into the water. For water with a high iron content, special filters are needed.

### Smoke and Ionization Detectors

A smoke detector is a small appliance that has come into common use since the 1970s. There are two types of these fire-detection devices: ionization and photoelectric. An ionization detector is based upon the principle that radiation increases the ability of air to conduct electricity. Radioactive material within the detector ionizes the air, causing a weak electrical current to flow through the smoke chamber. When smoke enters the chamber, it interrupts the electrical flow, causing the alarm to go off.

The other type of detector contains a tiny lamp and a photocell. Smoke entering the chamber scatters or reflects light from the lamp. The photocell senses the light and sets off a current of electricity, setting off the alarm. Some smoke detectors may also contain a heat-sensing device, normally a strip of metal that will melt at a specific high temperature.

Smoke detectors are installed on ceilings because heat and smoke rise within a room. They operate on batteries or on household electricity. Those that use household electricity may be plug-in units, or they may be installed directly into the wiring. The disadvantage of battery-powered units is that batteries may wear out without the homeowner realizing it. Plug-in and wiring-installed units are inoperable during power failures. (*See also* Safety.)

### Entertainment Centers

Radios, television sets, and phonographs have generally been placed in any room where they are to be used—normally in living rooms but also in bedrooms, dens, recreation rooms, and even kitchens. There are now radios that can be hung in showers.

There has been a recent trend to create entertainment centers in homes. This means setting aside one room to contain one or more television sets; videocassette recorders; a stereo set with radio, tape deck, and several speakers; storage space for phonograph records, tapes, and videocassettes; and perhaps a computer and printer.

### Automated Homes

Also called the "intelligent home," an automated house is an appliance-controlled dwelling made possible by computers, microchips, television, voice synthesis, and solid-state circuitry.

As envisaged by General Electric, American Telephone and Telegraph, and other companies currently designing them, all the appliances in such a home are interconnected. They respond to voice commands, and they are able to communicate with each other. A dishwasher, for instance, could relay a message to the water heater to produce more hot water. The whole electrical system of the home is centrally controlled by a computer and activated by a telephone. A homeowner can relay commands from a distant computer or telephone to his house. Light and heat levels are adjusted automatically. Repairmen can be called automatically if some appliance breaks down. The chief obstacle to building automated homes is not technological; it is the high cost of the equipment.

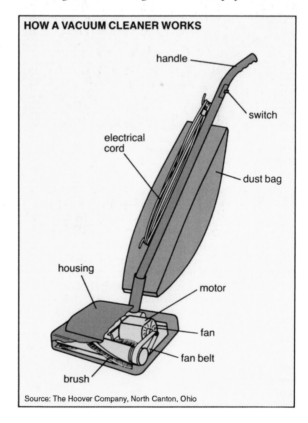

**HOW A VACUUM CLEANER WORKS**

handle

switch

electrical cord

dust bag

housing

motor

fan

fan belt

brush

Source: The Hoover Company, North Canton, Ohio

*In a nutrition class at Duke University's Fitness Center, a large mirror has been placed above the table to allow students to view what the instructors are doing.*

# HOME ECONOMICS

Within a school curriculum, the study of home economics is sometimes described as life education. Because much of an individual's life has traditionally centered upon the home and the family, home economics has been largely concerned with learning how to deal with the problems and challenges of homemaking. A basic knowledge of home economics helps a person make up a workable household budget, plan and prepare nutritious meals, choose a fabric for draperies, and care for a small child.

*This article was contributed by Anna M. Gorman, Professor of Home Economics, Oklahoma State University, Stillwater.*

In recent years the scope of home economics has broadened considerably. It now includes areas of national and international interest. Today's home economist may, for example, be engaged in developing foods for space flights, providing answers to the nutritional problems of underdeveloped nations, or setting up national classifications for textiles.

The study of home economics encompasses a wide variety of subjects, including foods and nutrition; clothing and textiles; housing, home equipment, and home management; family economics; child development; and family relations. Home economists are often required to have academic preparation in such related areas as chemistry, physics, sociology, psychology, and design.

## Home Economics Education

Home economics courses serve different purposes at different levels of education. In elementary and junior high school, home economics students acquire homemaking information and skills that are helpful in daily life. In high school, students are introduced to all the areas of home economics and to the occupations related to home economics. In community colleges, home economics students concentrate on either technical training or on the first two years of preparation for a professional career. At the college or university level, home economics majors prepare themselves for a choice of careers in home economics.

In the secondary schools, home economics courses often include units on foods and nutrition, clothing and textiles, child development, housing and interior design, family and consumer economics, and management. Individualized problem-solving instruction and project-centered techniques are often used. For example, a student might help a community organization redecorate its recreation room in conjunction with a unit on interior design.

The Vocational Education Act of 1963 played a vital role in making home economics education more widely available. It provided federal funds for programs in secondary schools, area vocational schools, and community colleges to prepare students for vocations in fields related to home economics. Persons who received this vocational training could become, for example, food service workers, child care assistants, or fashion designers.

Students who plan to become professional home economists usually major in a specific field, such as dietetics or textile chemistry, within a college or school of home economics. Majoring in home economics education provides the necessary background for students who wish to teach home economics. Internships and graduate degrees may be required for home economists entering certain fields.

## PROFESSIONS IN HOME ECONOMICS

One important decision a student must make after enrolling in a college or school of home economics is the choice of a major. This choice will determine what home economics profession the student will be qualified to enter after graduation. Home economics majors in such colleges or schools usually include foods and nutrition, art and design, housing and equipment, clothing, textiles, merchandising, family economics, home management, child development, family relations, and education. Each of these fields offers a variety of professional opportunities.

### Dietetics and Nutrition

A home economist with a major in foods and nutrition can choose from among a number of careers. The most common professions of home economists are in the fields of dietetics, nutrition, food service, and test-kitchen research. These professions require educational backgrounds that include a study of the principles of food and cookery, quantity food preparation, management training, and related sciences such as chemistry and bacteriology.

Dietitians plan menus for hospitals, schools, restaurants, airlines, and other organizations that provide food service for large numbers of people. The hospital dietitian may work in therapeutic dietetics, making up special diets in cooperation with the medical staff of the hospital. The hospital dietitian may also conduct classes for patients who must become familiar with their special dietary needs and restrictions. In addition to the Bachelor of Science degree in home economics, the dietitian is required to complete a year's internship at a restaurant or hospital that has been approved by the American Dietetic Association.

Nutritionists are dietitians who teach people what they should eat in order to maintain good health (*see* Food and Nutrition). Nutritionists may work with public health agencies or for food or pharmaceutical companies. The nutritionist with a food or pharmaceutical company keeps up with developments in nutrition and explains to the sales staff how the company's products can fill nutritional needs.

Food service managers supervise large-volume feeding operations. They might be employed by motels, hotels, or restaurant chains. They might also be in charge of school lunch programs or of food service for a branch or division of the armed forces. The food service manager usually directs a staff of assistants and oversees food and equipment purchases and the taking of inventories.

Home economists engaged in test-kitchen research may be responsible for developing new food products or improving existing ones. Home economists in test kitchens may also create and test recipes and provide information on food preparation. Test kitchens are operated by magazines and newspapers, advertising and public relations agencies, companies that process foods, and agencies of the federal government.

### Clothing and Textiles

Many professions in home economics are related to clothing and textiles. The clothing and textiles major with a fine arts background may find a career as a dress or fabric designer. Clothing designers are usually

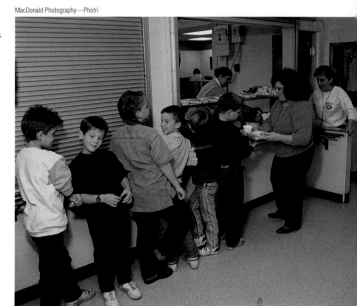

*Grade-school students line up for lunch in a school cafeteria. One of the many careers open to home economists is diet management in school lunchrooms.*

employed by garment or pattern manufacturers; textile designers usually work for fabric mills. ( *See also* Clothing; Dress Design; Garment Industry.)

The clothing and textiles major with a background in economics or business organization might join the sales staff of a company that manufactures textiles, patterns, or sewing notions such as thread, zippers, trim, or yarn. Other possibilities are positions in department or clothing stores, which would include those of buyer, merchandise manager, and fashion coordinator.

The home economists who enter professions involving clothing, textiles, or fashion must have a background in textile chemistry, fashion history, pattern design, and other related subjects. A sense of fashion and an aptitude for sales are also considered valuable assets.

### Housing

The housing field, like the clothing and textile industries, has many opportunities for the home economist with a flair for design or business. Interior designers help clients furnish their homes and solve problems in the use of living space and furnishings. They also tell their clients what furnishings and accessories are available and which of these are good values. An interior designer may be self-employed or may work for a firm that specializes in interior design or architecture. Interior designers are also employed by retail stores, furniture and drapery manufacturers, and trade associations. ( *See also* Interior Design.)

Some home economists become executive housekeepers. They manage such institutions as hospitals, hotels, and dormitories. They are responsible for keeping such establishments clean, orderly, attractive, and safe. To do this, executive housekeepers direct a

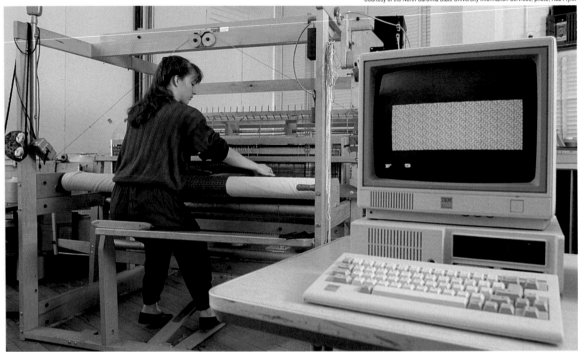

*A textile design student at North Carolina State University College of Textiles demonstrates weaving a design sample on acomputerized dobby loom, a type of loom used in industrial processes.*

staff of assistants, prepare budgets and reports, and order and receive supplies.

Home equipment specialists are often employed by public utilities or by the manufacturers of household appliances such as washing machines and clothes dryers. They work to acquaint the public with the products their company sells and to produce goodwill for the company. In order to answer inquiries from people who use or are interested in buying household appliances, they need to know what equipment is available and how it is operated.

The home equipment specialist is trained in household physics, food preparation, nutrition, quantity cooking, demonstration methods, kitchen design, and public speaking. A basic knowledge of advertising, salesmanship, business organization, and labor problems is also needed.

### Research

Research is being conducted in all areas of home economics. A home economist engaged in research may study, for example, variations in the texture, tenderness, and juiciness of a freeze-dried chicken or the effectiveness of fluorescent whiteners in a laundry detergent. Research home economists may work for colleges and universities, private companies, independent research and testing organizations, or government agencies. The United States Department of Agriculture employs research home economists with specialties in such fields as family economics, nutrition, and textiles. Home economics research requires an ability to work with precision, thoroughness, and

imagination. Most home economics researchers hold a doctoral degree.

### Welfare Work and Child Development

Home economists of varying backgrounds may engage in social work or welfare work with agencies that offer aid to people who cannot adequately care for themselves. Such home economists may help social workers plan corrective measures when money management, diet, or housekeeping standards need to be improved. They may also serve caseworkers by setting up standards and guidelines to help appraise various types of family problems.

The child welfare worker deals with children who have problems—particularly children who need to be placed in homes away from their parents and children who have broken the law. The child welfare worker helps solve problems involving such children by reviewing family records, conducting interviews, visiting homes, and providing information.

Child development is another field associated with home economics. Child development jobs usually involve working with groups of children who attend day-care centers, nursery schools, community centers, Head Start programs, or kindergartens. The duties of the preschool teacher may include reading stories, supervising play and creative expression periods, and serving lunch. Because preschools stress emotional and social adjustment rather than formal learning, the teacher needs to see that the children interact well. A background in child development or family relations is essential (*see* Child Development).

*A home economist, working as a food stylist in a public relations department, tries to create a "perfect" muffin for a photograph that will appear in an advertisement.*

Kenji Kerins

### Teaching

The home economics teacher needs a broad home economics background covering all the content areas of home economics, including family relations and child development, interior design, household economics and management, clothing and textiles, and foods and nutrition. Prospective teachers are also required to take science, humanities, and social science courses as well as education courses and student teaching. In some states, the entry level home economics teacher has a team of educators who assist him or her to become a certified teacher.

The home economists of the Federal Extension Service are also engaged in home economics education. The programs are designed to bring new information and research findings to people throughout the United States. Most counties of the nation are served by an extension home economist. These extension home economists receive a constant stream of information from the nation's land-grant colleges and from many departments of the federal government.

This information is channeled in many ways to the people in the community. The extension home economist organizes programs for professionals, writes columns for newspapers and magazines, conducts radio and television programs, and works with local extension clubs. These home economists are involved in programs in nutrition education, care of children and the elderly, family financial management, building family strengths, alcohol traffic safety, and leadership development in public policy. Although extension programs were originally developed for rural families, they are now also provided for large urban communities.

Another type of extension home economist is the youth adviser who works with leaders of 4-H clubs and other youth organizations. The youth adviser makes the latest findings in the field of child development available to all people who work with children (*see* Youth Organizations).

The consumer marketing agents also do extension work. These agents serve producers, retailers, and consumers alike. They check supermarket food prices regularly. After analyzing their data, they tell people—usually through the communications media—which foods are most plentiful and the best buys.

Extension workers may have a variety of backgrounds in home economics. Some have a general home economics background similar to that of home economics teachers; others have majors in specific fields of home economics.

### Communications

The home economist with a specialized background and a major in journalism may often find a position in communications. Positions on newspapers and magazines, in public relations and advertising agencies, trade associations, and television and radio stations are available to home economists.

Newspapers often have specific sections devoted to areas such as food or home improvement, and these are staffed by editors and writers who have a broad knowledge of foods, clothing, fashion, or home furnishings. Magazines are usually more specialized than newspapers, and many deal more directly with homemaking topics. Home economists in editorial work must be able to organize their subject matter logically and to write in a clear and interesting manner. (*See also* Magazine and Journal; Newspaper.)

Public relations and advertising agencies also offer a variety of positions to home economists. The job of persons with a background in home economics who do public relations work for public relations agencies, trade associations, or manufacturers is primarily to bring favorable information about products to the public. Home economists in public relations also supply articles, photographs, films, and other product information to the news media. It is necessary that this information be presented as interestingly as possible so that it will be used. The job of home economists who work in advertising is similar to that of home economists in public relations, with one exception: the home economist in advertising works for a client who has already purchased space or time in the media to present information about his or her product (*see* Advertising).

The food stylist is a home economist in the communications field who prepares food for photographs and films that may be used in advertisements or articles. The food must look appetizing and be able to hold up under hot photographic lights.

A trade association is supported by the manufacturers or producers within an industry. The purpose of a trade association is to promote the industry and its products. Most food and textile associations, such as the National Dairy Council and the National Cotton Council, employ home economists to do promotional, educational, or public relations work.

## HISTORY OF HOME ECONOMICS EDUCATION

The study of home economics began in the United States after the American Revolution. In colonial America, as in the Old World, a young woman received instruction in homemaking and child care primarily at home. But in the 19th century a number of forces helped create a favorable climate for the introduction of home economics as a field of study in schools. Among the most significant were a spirit of humanitarianism, faith in education, and a belief in the equal rights of women.

The early American's confidence in a person's ability to shape his or her environment through education led to the founding of colleges that taught occupational skills. When women began to share in higher education, the household arts became a part of the curriculum as both a cultural and a professional field of study.

The first institutions to provide a foundation for the growth of home economics education were the land-grant colleges and universities established by the Morrill Act of 1862. These land-grant institutions sought "to promote the liberal and practical education of the industrial classes." They offered technical courses that were related to the lives of their students. Some of these courses were especially designed to serve the needs of women students.

By 1890, domestic science courses were being offered widely in American public high schools, as well as in colleges and universities. These courses included instruction in cooking, sewing, millinery, laundering, home decoration, home sanitation, home hygiene, and home nursing. The teaching of domestic science in the secondary schools led to a demand for the training of home economics teachers in the colleges. However, the major emphasis on home management remained until the early part of the 20th century.

In 1899 Ellen H. Richards, an instructor of sanitary chemistry at the Massachusetts Institute of Technology, helped organize a conference of persons interested in the application of science to household problems. The conference, held at Lake Placid, N.Y., was attended by specialists in chemistry, biology, economics, psychology, and sociology. Out of that and subsequent meetings at Lake Placid grew the American Home Economics Association, founded in 1909.

The members of the American Home Economics Association were dedicated to the improvement of living conditions in the home and the community, and they worked to win acceptance for home economics education. Their efforts were aided greatly by the passage of the Vocational Education Act of 1917, which provided federal funds to pay the salaries of home economics teachers as well as teachers of agricultural, trade, and industrial subjects. By 1920, 6,000 high schools in the United States were offering courses in home economics. As the social sciences developed, some of their findings were incorporated into the home economics curriculum. The original emphasis on food, clothing, and shelter was broadened to include such topics as human relationships. By 1935, home economics educators were being urged to glean from "all fields of knowledge, all lines of activity" whatever might serve to improve families and family life.

As the scope of home economics training broadened, the variety of professions in home economics increased. On the university level, home economics training became more and more specialized. On the secondary school level, the focus of home economics education changed from "how to do it" to "why it is done." Overall, the study of home economics has been influenced by the changing quality of modern life. Today, home economics students are no longer taught merely how to cook and sew but also how to buy the food they prepare and fabrics for the clothing they make. In fact, a large number of home economics courses place greater emphasis on consumer education than on homemaking skills. Moreover, home economics appears to be moving away from areas of concern only to the individual or the family and toward problems of national and international concern, such as overpopulation, urban poverty, and the development of emerging nations.

### FURTHER RESOURCES FOR HOME ECONOMICS

**Abendroth, R.B.** Changes and Choices, Personal Development and Relationships (Goodheart, 1986).
**Campbell, S.R.** The Confident Consumer (Goodheart, 1982).
**Draper, Henry.** The Caring Parent (Bennett, 1983).
**Hahn, James and Lynn.** Exploring a Career in Home Economics (Rosen, 1981).
**Kowtaluk, Helen and Kopan, A.O.** Food for Today, rev. ed. (Bennett, 1986).
**Liddell, L.A.** Clothes and Your Appearance (Goodheart, 1985).
**Parker, F.J.** Home Economics: An Introduction to a Dynamic Profession, 3rd ed. (Macmillan, 1987).
**Ryder, Verdene.** Contemporary Living (Goodheart, 1987).
**Thompson, P.J. and Faiola-Priest, Theodora.** Lifeplans (South-Western, 1987).

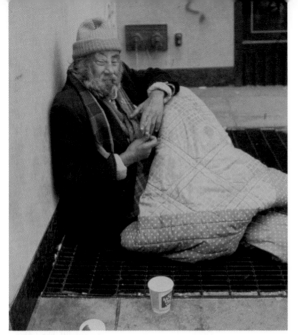

© Erika Stone—Peter Arnold, Inc.

*A homeless man living on the streets has counterparts in all major U.S. cities.*

**HOMELESSNESS.** Few social problems have increased so suddenly or been dramatized so effectively as the plight of the homeless in the 1980s and 1990s. Once an invisible people who could easily be ignored, the homeless are now recognized everywhere on the streets and in the public facilities of major cities. There are bag ladies who roam the streets carrying what is left of their possessions in shopping bags or grocery carts. There are disoriented men curled up on benches, in stairwells, or alongside walls. There are children—some runaways and some throwaways—scrounging for food and shelter.

The number of homeless people in underdeveloped societies in the mid-1980s was estimated by the United Nations (UN) to be more than 100 million. The so-called "new" homeless live in the developed, industrialized nations of Europe, North America, and East Asia. Accurate statistics have been impossible to verify, in part because of the conflicting viewpoints on the subject of homelessness. Politicians, lawyers, and others who become advocates for the homeless have said that there are from 2 to 3 million homeless in the United States alone. Others who have studied the problem from a less sympathetic point of view suggest that the number is closer to 300,000.

One reason for statistical uncertainty is the composition of the homeless population. Some families suffer temporary poverty because of loss of a job. Unable to afford rent or mortgage payments, they may temporarily join the ranks of the homeless for a period of days or weeks (or they may live with relatives). Once another job is found, the family can usually afford shelter once more.

The number of those who are truly homeless consists of possibly 3 percent or less of the very poor. Their most common characteristic is poverty, though some work at least part-time, while others receive various kinds of welfare payments. The makeup of the homeless population, according to a 1987 study by the United States Conference of Mayors, indicated the following breakdown: 56 percent single men, 15 percent single women, and 28 percent in families—usually one-parent families. As a group, the homeless tend to be young, mostly under the age of 40.

The National Institute of Mental Health has estimated that one third of the homeless in the 1980s were former mental patients who had been discharged under deinstitutionalization programs. Many of the homeless are also addicted to drugs or alcohol or both. Some are victims of structural unemployment—temporary, but massive, changes in an economy. Others become homeless when the eligibility rules for assistance change or when the supply of low-rent housing runs out. Some members of the homeless population are voluntary in the sense that they leave intolerable situations within their former homes. Battered wives and abused or neglected children become runaways, living on the streets or in shelters opened by charities. In Japan many men reportedly have dropped out of the economy voluntarily for such reasons as stress, old age, indifference, or to escape family problems.

Government responses to the problem have varied. Canada and the United States have no laws on homelessness, but government agencies provide funds to operate shelters and soup kitchens. England has a Homeless Persons Act, enacted in 1977, that requires local authorities to house the homeless. In an attempt to improve housing for the poor, the UN declared 1987 the International Year of Shelter for the Homeless.

**HOMEOPATHY.** A system of medical treatment, homeopathy is based on the principle that "likes are cured by likes." According to this law of similars, drugs that cause disease symptoms in healthy individuals can also be used to cure illnesses that produce the same symptoms in sick individuals.

Homeopathic physicians study each patient to choose the remedy that will treat the disorder creating the symptoms. Patients are highly sensitive to the selected remedies and are given the substances in very small doses. According to homeopathic theory, these substances act by stimulating the body's natural defenses and recuperative powers. Before any substance is used as a homeopathic remedy, its effects are tested by administering various doses to healthy persons and recording the symptoms that arise.

Homeopathy was founded in the 1790s by the German physician Samuel Hahnemann. He developed the law of similars by testing various substances on himself. Hahnemann published the principles of homeopathy in 'Organon of the Rational Art of Healing', published in 1810, and taught his homeopathic methods to other physicians. Homeopathy's initial popularity in the United States led to the founding of the American Institute of Homeopathy in 1844.

In general, homeopathy has not found great acceptance by the medical profession in the 20th century. It has been criticized because it focuses on symptoms, while neglecting to search out the underlying causes of disease. Homeopathy continues to have many adherents, however. Some countries, such as England, Sri Lanka, Pakistan, and Brazil, encourage the use of homeopathy. The International Foundation for Homeopathy was founded in 1978. (*See also* Drugs; Holistic Medicine.)

**HOMER, Winslow** (1836–1910). One of the greatest of American painters, Winslow Homer is best known for his watercolors and oil paintings of the sea. These paintings often have great dramatic effect because of the way they show man's powerlessness in the face of the unfeeling forces of nature.

Homer was born on Feb. 24, 1836, in Boston, Mass. When he was 6 his family moved to nearby Cambridge, where he became fond of outdoor life. His mother, an amateur artist, encouraged his interest in art, and at 19 he was apprenticed to a lithographer in Boston. He quickly developed skill in line drawing, and two years later he opened a studio.

In 1859 he moved to New York City, where he worked as an illustrator. His first big assignment was to sketch Abraham Lincoln's presidential inauguration for *Harper's Weekly*. During the Civil War Homer was an artist-correspondent. He also began exhibiting some of his paintings at the National Academy of Design. Homer turned some of his Army-life sketches into oils. Encouraged by the reception they received, he gave up illustrating. His first paintings told a story, usually of some everyday occurrence. Art critics of the time were unimpressed. Today these story paintings, though generally considered to be inferior to his later

work, serve as valuable records of 19th-century life. Homer's most familiar paintings include 'Snap the Whip', which dates from 1872, 'Fog Warning' (1885), and 'The Gulf Stream' (1899).

Homer spent 1881 and 1882 in Tynemouth on the coast of northeastern England. When he returned to the United States, he settled in Prout's Neck on the coast of Maine. There he did some of his finest work. Aside from frequent trips—to the Adirondacks, Florida, and the Caribbean—he lived there for the rest of his life. Homer never married. He died in Prout's Neck on Sept. 29, 1910. (*See also* Painting.)

**HOMERIC LEGEND.** Apart from the historical writings of ancient Israel, the two major pieces of epic literature in Western civilization are the 'Iliad' and the 'Odyssey', two books ascribed to the ancient Greek poet Homer. These two works represent a brilliant retelling of myths and legends. For the Greeks of the 7th century BC, however, these books were their history. Their past had been obliterated by the destruction of Mycenaean Civilization (*see* Greece, Ancient). The tales that came down to the Greeks from Homer and other storytellers were regarded by them as authentic narratives of a past they could not otherwise recover.

The individual who has traditionally been credited with putting the ancient Greek legends into writing is Homer. About him nothing certain is known. The later historian Herodotus (5th century BC) said that Homer was a Greek from Ionia on the west coast of Asia Minor. He was perhaps a native of the island of Chios and supposedly lived around 850 BC. Other historians place him closer to 750 BC.

*'Fog Warning' (1885), an oil on canvas, is one of the most famous of all Winslow Homer's works. It shows a fisherman off the Grand Banks of Newfoundland pitting his strength against a turbulent sea.*

Museum of Fine Arts, Boston

*Homer sang the tales of Troy and of the voyage of Odysseus to the Greeks before the stories were written down in poetic form.*

Nawrocki Stock Photo

Tradition depicts Homer as a blind minstrel wandering from place to place reciting poems that had come down to him from a very old oral tradition. Many scholars believe that the books as they exist today were not written by a single person and were not put in writing until centuries after they took their present form. It is probable that much of the epic tradition of the two books was formed in the 200 or 300 years before an alphabet reached Greece in the 9th or 8th century BC. If so, it is possible that Homer used earlier writings to help him, or he could have dictated his poems to someone else because of his blindness or because he was illiterate.

### Background to the 'Iliad'

The 'Iliad' is a summary in verse of what was apparently a very long war conducted against Troy by the Greeks. As in much myth, there is a kernel of reality behind it. That there was such a war is quite likely. It would have made sense for predecessors of the ancient Greeks to conduct a war against the city in order to gain control of the Dardanelles, the water passage between the Mediterranean and Black seas. Had Troy, located near this waterway, been a hostile power, the destruction of it might have enabled the Greeks to colonize the west coast of Asia Minor. The war probably took place sometime between 1250 and 1185 BC.

For many centuries it was believed that the 'Iliad' was a piece of imaginative and inventive fiction. In 1870, however, the German scholar Heinrich Schliemann began excavations at the place where Troy was believed to have stood.

He satisfied himself, and eventually the rest of the world, that there had actually been a war fought there. The excavations revealed that several cities had stood on the spot before the one Homer celebrated. (*See also* Schliemann.)

Altogether, Schliemann and his successors found the ruins of nine cities built atop one another over a period of 3,500 years. Homer's Troy was the seventh city. Ruins of its great walls, 16 feet (5 meters) thick, and flanking towers still remained.

### Story of the 'Iliad'

The 'Iliad' is an amazing tale of heroes and heroines, gods and goddesses. But most of all it is the story of Achilles, of his anger and determination, and of his slaying of the Trojan hero Hector.

The purpose of the war was to recover the most beautiful woman in the world, Helen. She was the wife of Menelaus, king of Sparta. But she had been carried off to Troy by Paris, son of King Priam of Troy. Menelaus, naturally, swore vengeance. He called upon the kings and princes of Greece to help him. Among those who responded were Achilles, Ajax, Diomedes, Odysseus, and Nestor. Agamemnon, king of Mycenae and brother of Menelaus, was chosen commander in chief.

After two years of preparation, the Greek fleet of more than 1,000 ships and an army of 100,000 men assembled at the port of Aulis in northeastern Greece. Hence the saying that Helen had the face that launched 1,000 ships.

The fleet was detained at Aulis by a calm sea. Seeking the reason for the delay, they were told by a soothsayer that Agamemnon had killed a stag sacred to the goddess Artemis (or Diana). The wrath of the goddess could only be appeased by the sacrifice of the offender's daughter.

Agamemnon was forced to consent. His daughter Iphigenia was led to an altar. The goddess relented at the last minute and snatched Iphigenia away, leaving a deer in her place. Iphigenia became a priestess in the temple of Artemis at Tauris.

With the anger of Artemis appeased, the wind proved favorable and the fleet set sail. They arrived to find the Trojans well prepared. King Priam was too old to fight. He had assembled supplies for a long siege, however, and formed alliances with neighboring

*Some of the main participants in the Trojan War were, left to right, Agamemnon, Achilles, Nestor, Odysseus, Diomedes, Paris, and Menelaus.*
Historical Pictures Service, Chicago

princes and chieftains. The city was also protected by impenetrable walls. Its defenders included Hector, Aeneas (of whom the Roman poet Virgil wrote much later), Sarpedon, and other warriors.

For more than nine years the Greeks besieged Troy unsuccessfully. Then Achilles quarreled with Agamemnon and refused to take further part in the conflict. It was the slaying of his friend Patroclus about two thirds of the way through the book that brought Achilles back to the action. He killed Hector in battle, but later he was himself killed—driving the Greeks to despair of ever winning.

It was then that the crafty Odysseus stepped forward with a stratagem. Aided by the goddess Athena, he planned the construction of a huge wooden horse with enough room to contain 100 warriors. Secretly the best warriors were hidden inside. Then the rest of the Greeks boarded ship as though to sail home in defeat. The Trojans thought the horse was a peace offering to Athena. One of the Trojan priests, Laocoön, warned against "Greeks, even bearing gifts." Cassandra, daughter of King Priam, also predicted disaster. She had been given the gift of prophecy but had then been cursed—her prophecies, though always true, would never be believed. Their warnings were shouted down, and a breach in the wall was made to allow the horse to be dragged in.

As the Trojans slept that night, the Greek warriors emerged and signaled the waiting ships to bring back the rest of the Greeks to Troy. Soon thousands of Greeks were swarming into the city. By morning only a mass of ruins remained. Nearly all the inhabitants were slain. Helen returned to her husband, and the Greeks sailed for home. The one whose voyage home took the longest was Odysseus. The adventures of his return trip were told in the second Homeric epic.

### The 'Odyssey'

Odysseus, who was later called Ulysses by the Romans, was king of Ithaca, a small island on the west coast of Greece. When summoned to join his fellow chieftains in the war against Troy, he could not bear to leave his young wife, Penelope, and their son, Telemachus. He therefore pretended to be insane. To convince everyone of his madness, he plowed the sand along the seashore as though it were a field. But Prince Palamedes, who came for him, recognized this as a trick. To prove it, Palamedes placed little Telemachus in the path of the plow. When Odysseus quickly turned the plow aside to avoid striking his son, all saw that his madness was a pretense. So Odysseus fitted 12 ships and went to Troy.

By the war's end he had been away from home for

*Achilles drags the body of slain Hector before the walls of Troy, while the goddess Athena looks on.*
Historical Pictures Service, Chicago

ten years. He filled his ships with treasure taken from the Trojans and set sail. Ordinarily the trip from Troy to Ithaca would have taken only a short time. The Greek gods, however, decided that it should take Odysseus ten years to reach his wife and son. During those years he and his men endured a series of hazardous and remarkable adventures.

Soon after leaving Troy the ships ran into a raging storm. For nine days the winds drove the ships past Ithaca and far off course. On the tenth day they reached the island of the Lotus-Eaters. When a party of men went ashore, they ate of the lotus plants. This magic food made them forget all longing for home. Odysseus had them dragged back to the ships, and again they set sail. They arrived at the island of the Cyclopes, a race of fierce one-eyed giants (*see* Cyclops). Odysseus set out with 12 men to explore the island. They entered the cave of Polyphemus, the most ferocious of the Cyclopes. He kept them prisoners and devoured six of the men. While the giant slept, Odysseus stole his staff and sharpened it. With this weapon, heated red-hot, he burned out the giant's eye. Odysseus and his men escaped by tying themselves to the bellies of some sheep let out to pasture.

Their next stop was at the Aeolian Isle, a peaceful land where Aeolus, Keeper of the Winds, lived. When they left after a month of relaxation, Aeolus gave them a favorable wind to speed them on their way. The other winds he bound into a leather bag and put on board Odysseus' ship.

The ships sailed smoothly for nine days until Ithaca was in sight. While Odysseus was sleeping his men determined to open the leather bag because they believed it was filled with gold. Upon doing so, the winds were released. They drove the ships back to the Aeolian Isle. This time, however, they were not welcomed. Aeolus believed that men so unlucky must be hated by the gods.

A week later the ships beached at the island of the Laestrygones, a country of cannibals. Huge men hurled rocks and destroyed 11 of the ships. The crews of all 11 ships perished. Only Odysseus and his ship's crew survived to continue their journey.

Their next stopping place was the island home of Circe, the enchantress. She cast a spell on Odysseus' men, changing them into swine. Odysseus himself was protected by an herb given to him by Hermes, messenger of the gods. When Circe realized he was protected by Hermes, she changed the swine back into men and prevailed upon them all to remain for a year at her palace.

When they decided to leave, she said they must first journey to Hades, the dwelling place of the dead (*see* Hell and Hades). When they reached Hades, Odysseus met many of his departed comrades, including Achilles. He and his companions were told that many perils still awaited them. There was a chance of reaching home. If they were to do so, however, they must curb their greed when they came to the place where the sun-god Helios pastured his herds. If a single beast were harmed, they would all be doomed.

*The monumental wooden horse was cleverly devised by Odysseus as a means of getting Greek warriors into Troy.*

As they continued their journey, they were forced to sail past the dwelling place of the Sirens, sea nymphs whose singing lured men to certain death. To prevent this from happening, Odysseus had his men put wax in their ears. He had himself tied to the mast so he could listen to the singing.

Once this danger was bypassed, a more ominous one lay ahead. The ship had to sail between Scylla and Charybdis. On one side of a narrow strait Charybdis pulled everything nearby into a vast whirlpool. On the other side Scylla, a six-headed monster, waited to devour anyone who passed by. The ship succeeded in getting through with a burst of speed but not before losing six sailors to the jaws of Scylla.

Those who survived reached the pleasant Isle of the Sun, where Helios pastured his animals. Odysseus wished to sail past it, but the men feared the night seas. They disembarked and were held there for a month by strong winds. As their food supply ran out,

*Odysseus bids farewell to his wife Penelope and infant son Telemachus, as his faithful dog Argos lies nearby.*

the sailors decided they had to kill one of the animals. While Odysseus slept they did so. They were able to sail away without problems, leading them to think they had escaped the wrath of Helios. But Zeus, highest of the gods, replied to the sun-god's request for vengeance by sending a hurricane. It destroyed the ship and crew, leaving Odysseus alone in the sea, clinging to the mast. Ten days later he was carried ashore on the island of Calypso. She kept him prisoner for seven years before he was released through the aid of Athena and Hermes. He made a raft, and after a series of other adventures he finally reached Ithaca.

His problems were not over. He had been gone for 20 years, and no one believed he could still be alive. It was dangerous for him to make himself known because several men were waiting to wed Penelope and gain the kingship. Athena changed Odysseus' appearance and hid in a cave his treasure that he had brought with him from his last stopping place.

Penelope's suitors were staying at the palace, wasting the kingdom's wealth and trying to make the queen choose among them. Telemachus, the son and heir to the throne, had grown up and spent his time vainly trying to rid the palace of the suitors. Penelope herself put them off by a ruse. She insisted she could not marry anyone until she had finished weaving a shroud for Laertes, the aged father of Odysseus, who was near death. What she wove by day she unraveled each night, so the cloth was never finished. Servants finally gave away her secret to the suitors, however, and they hounded her for an answer.

Odysseus meanwhile found shelter in the hut of his former swineherd. There Telemachus appeared, having escaped the plan of the suitors to kill him. Odysseus revealed himself to his son, and together they plotted what they would do. Telemachus returned to the

**The blinded Polyphemus hurls a rock at Odysseus' ship and misses, as the crew derides him from the deck.**

Drawing by Steele Savage

Drawing by Steele Savage

**The disguised Odysseus triumphs over Penelope's suitors by driving an arrow through the blades of 12 axes.**

palace, bringing along Odysseus disguised as a beggar. No one recognized Odysseus except his nurse and his aged dog Argos, but the animal was too weak and soon died.

Penelope did not recognize her husband, but she made him welcome and prepared a room for him. She had by this time decided finally to choose one of the suitors. She decided to make the choice on the basis of a contest among them. The next evening she brought out the great bow Odysseus had left at home, along with its quiver full of arrows. She announced she would marry the man who could drive an arrow through holes in the blades of 12 axes set in a row.

Many tried, but none could even bend the bow. Odysseus, still clothed as a beggar, stepped forward and asked to test his strength. The suitors thought the idea ridiculous, but Telemachus gave him the bow. Snatching an arrow, he sent it flying straight through the 12 axe blades. After Odysseus had shown who he was, he and Telemachus killed all the suitors. The kingdom of Ithaca was restored to him.

### Analysis of the 'Odyssey'

Although set within the circumstances of the Trojan War, the 'Odyssey' is a far different book. With the 'Iliad', from the book itself as well as the archaeological excavations that support it, it is reasonable to infer a real historical event as background. With the 'Odyssey' such an assumption is impossible.

The book is a tale of adventure at sea and of homecoming after a long absence. These two themes have pervaded Western literature ever since the Homeric epic was written, and the story may well have proved a popular one well before Greek history began. The story could just as well have stood on its own without any relation to the conflict of the Greeks with Troy.

The vividly fictional characteristics of the story have not prevented critics, past and present, from seeking to place it in a specific geographic context. Hesiod, who wrote later than Homer, believed that Odysseus and his ships sailed around in the general area of Italy and Sicily, to the west of Ithaca. Later analysts tried to set the wanderings within the Mediterranean Sea generally, while others suggested the Atlantic Ocean as more likely.

The ancient astronomer Eratosthenes (2nd century BC) regarded all such speculations as foolish. For him the world of Odysseus was a completely imaginary one. Indications of this are found within the text itself. Some of the hero's wanderings could well have been based on the even older story of Jason and his Argonauts, who sailed east in search of the golden fleece. It is quite likely that several ancient legends were woven into one continuous epic.

**HOMOSEXUALITY** *see* **SEXUALITY.**

**HONDURAS.** The Republic of Honduras occupies a prominent pivotal position in the seven-country Central America land bridge that connects North and South America. Stretching 175 miles (282 kilometers) across the isthmus from the Caribbean Sea to the Gulf of Fonseca on the Pacific Ocean, Honduras borders Guatemala on the northwest, El Salvador on the southwest, and Nicaragua on the southeast. In area Honduras, with more than 43,000 square miles (112,000 square kilometers), is the second largest country in Central America, only a bit smaller than neighboring Nicaragua.

### Land and Climate

Throughout western and central Honduras rugged mountains of moderate height, reaching 9,000 feet (2,750 meters) above sea level in a few places, are interspersed with many upland valleys. The mountain ranges are generally from west to east, but some valleys trend northward and southward, as around the 112,000-acre (45,000-hectare) Comayagua Valley of central Honduras. These well-watered zones of little slope have been the most favored sites of human settlement in both aboriginal and modern times.

Temperatures in Honduras are not as high as might be expected from its tropical location only 15 to 16 degrees north of the equator. Near the lowland coastal plains the onshore winds are a moderating influence,

. . . . . . . . . . . . . . . . . . . . . . . . . . . . . . . . . . . . . . . . . .

*This article was contributed by William V. Davidson, Associate Professor of Geography and Anthropology, Louisiana State University, Baton Rouge, and author of 'Historical Geography of the Bay Islands, Honduras' (1974).*

H. Kanus—Shostal Associates

*Most Hondurans live in rural areas, such as the village of San Antonio de Oriente in the department of Francisco Morazán.*

and the increased elevation of the mountainous interior brings cooler temperatures.

The seasons are expressed not so much according to temperatures, as in most of North America, but more according to the distribution of rainfall throughout the year. Between January and May the *verano,* or dry period, occurs, and *invierno,* the wet season, extends from June to December. In the Pacific coast lowland *departamentos,* or departments, of Choluteca and Valle, droughts are occasionally severe.

Winds normally flow over the country from the east and northeast toward west—the famous Trade Winds renowned for their consistency of direction. The strongest winds, those coming with the Caribbean hurricanes, are not a yearly threat, but on occasion a disastrous tropical storm strikes the offshore islands and adjacent mainland lowlands. Fifi, the worst hurricane, passed over the length of the north coast in the fall of 1974, blowing down the banana plants and producing floods and mudslides that destroyed the town of Choloma and left multitudes homeless.

Almost all of the major rivers flow into the Caribbean Sea, reflecting the distribution of the highest mountains in the west and the origins of the moisture-laden winds from the east coast. They are the Ulúa, Aguán, Negro, Platano, Patuca, and, on the Nicaragua border, the Río Coco, the largest in Central America. The downstream portions of these rivers are navigable to shallow-draft vessels, but upstream from the first rapids only dugout canoes can be used for local travel and commerce. Lake Yojoa, a large highland lake 10 miles (16 kilometers) long, is remarkable for its beautiful mountain landscapes and world-class largemouth bass.

Honduras can be partitioned into three grand regions according to physical geography, population composition, and local attitude. The largest of these subdivisions is the western and central highlands, where Spanish-speaking people of Indian-Spanish heritage comprise the bulk of the population. A second large zone in the east is Costa de Mosquitos, or Mosquito Coast, also known as La Mosquitia, which is a region of pine savannas, coastal lowlands, and shallow lagoons. The small population is primarily Indian and they are speakers of creole English. A third region is La Costa Norte, the north coast, including the Islas de la Bahía (Bay Islands) just offshore. Minority cultures make up a considerable proportion of the population. They include the Garífuna (Black Caribs), the English-speaking Bay Islanders, whose ancestors once occupied the Cayman Islands, and the black English creoles, who have worked the coastal banana plantations.

In spite of serious deforestation from the mid-1960s, Honduras remains a wooded land. The central and western highlands are pine covered, and the eastern lowlands and the north coast grow tropical hardwoods. A vibrant forest products industry and the desire to clear lands for pasture often produce conflicts over developments; a government agency oversees the exploitation and conservation of this renewable resource.

As might be expected in such a lush tropical environment, variation in habitats, as well as plant and animal communities, is enormous. The lands surrounding the mouth and lower course of the Platano River in Mosquitia are designated as a UNESCO Biosphere Reserve, a protected refuge for an unusually diverse plant and animal community.

## People

Among themselves Hondurans are known affectionately as *catrachos*. Generally they live concentrated in the central and western upland valleys and along La Costa Norte. Population decreases to the south and east. Almost half of the people live in rural settlements.

The largest urban centers are the capital, Tegucigalpa; San Pedro Sula, the center of the industrial and commercial agriculture complex of the lower Ulúa Valley; La Ceiba, home of the former Standard Fruit Company; and Choluteca, the focus of activities in southern Honduras.

More than four fifths of the people are mestizos—Spanish-speaking persons of Indian-Spanish heritage. Roughly 5 percent are Amerindians. While many remnants of the native cultures still exist, very few Honduran Indians retain their original languages.

Afro- and Anglo-Antilleans who migrated to Honduras more than 100 years ago from Caribbean islands occupy the north coast and the Bay Islands. The largest component of this community are the Garífuna, or Black Caribs, who live in coastal villages.

In the 1970s and 1980s a new population—approximately 50,000 "legal" refugees—arrived in Honduras to escape the civil unrest in surrounding countries. Most were housed by the United Nations in camps relatively near the borders, but numerous uncounted "illegal" refugees scattered throughout the country. More than 20,000 Salvadoran mestizos lived in four camps in western Honduras; a similar number of Miskito and Sumu Indians from Nicaragua settled in eastern Honduras.

Roman Catholicism is the predominant religion of Honduras. Ornate churches, some dating from the early colonial period, are often found in sparsely settled rural areas.

## Economy

The country is normally regarded as the poorest in Central America, but the annual per capita income of about 1,400 lempiras (700 United States dollars) does not reflect the value of the large amount of foodstuffs produced for immediate consumption by the farmer and his family. Honduras was once considered the most typical of the so-called "banana republics" in which foreign investors, especially those associated with large American-owned fruit companies, often attempted to direct the internal affairs of the country. During the first half of the 20th century, bananas by far dominated the export economy. Today agricultural production is more diversified. Foreign fruit companies no longer own and operate the plantations or manage the docks and railways. The north coast towns of Tela, La Ceiba, and Trujillo, which grew because of the fruit company investments and transshipments of bananas, no longer provide the only outlets to shipping abroad. Today Puerto Cortés is the site of a large new port that serves as the Caribbean terminus of the transisthmian route across the country. Honduras still produces more bananas than any of its Central American neighbors, but coffee, cattle, sugarcane, lumber, tobacco, and seafoods are significant contributors to regional economies.

Small-scale agriculture in corn (maize), beans, and rice has long been the major economic activity, but the trend is toward more crop diversification and commercialization. Industrialization has also begun. The leading products are soft drinks, beer, cement, cooking oil, light textiles, seafood, and rum.

Tourism has great potential for producing much-desired foreign capital. The clear, warm Caribbean waters are ideal for sport diving, and the coral-sand beaches and climate contribute to a setting favorable for international tourism. The famous Mayan ruins at Copán, which date from the Classic period of AD 300 to 900, and the well-preserved colonial fort at Omoa attract many visitors.

### History and Government

Honduras was first brought to the attention of Europeans in 1502 during the fourth and last voyage of Christopher Columbus. He sailed along the north coast and made at least two stops to meet the Indians and to take possession of the land for the Spanish crown. After inspecting the Islas de la Bahía and stopping at the large protected bay at Trujillo, the little fleet of four ships sailed around the eastern shore into more favorable weather. The exclamation "Gracias a Diós!" (Thanks to God) is now the name of the easternmost cape in Honduras.

Hernando Cortez, Pedro de Alvarado, and Francisco Montejo were among the early colonial administrators who directed the conquest and settlement by Europeans. The ports of Trujillo and Puerto Caballos were the first centers. As the Spaniards penetrated the interior and subjugated the native Indians, regional towns of Spaniards grew at San Pedro, Gracias, Choluteca, Olancho, and Comayagua, the colonial capital. After the first century more than 100 Spanish-controlled villages had been formed for the purposes of religious conversion and economic tribute. Most of the natives, however, had died. They had no immunities to Old World diseases.

Spain organized colonial Honduras primarily for the exportation of gold and silver, but indigo, sarsaparilla, and dyewoods also found their way into European markets. During the 17th and 18th centuries English, French, and Dutch pirates had occasional successes in stealing the colonial produce of the Spaniards.

Emerging from the domination of the Spanish in 1821 and withstanding the internal wars of the 1830s, Honduras became a country that is only now escaping the cycle of frequent disruptive changes in national government. After 1821 the country averaged almost one presidential change per year. The United States has often been criticized for interfering in its political affairs.

The Honduran army has played a dominant role in the selection of civilian leadership. In the 1980s, however, the armed forces allowed civilian politicians to dominate the government. In 1981 the Liberal party candidate, Roberto Suazo Córdova, was elected president. The election of 1985 was peaceful, remained unusually democratic, and brought José Azcona, also a Liberal candidate, to the presidency.

Political stability was a critical factor in the completion of such development projects as the El Cajon hydroelectric dam in central Honduras, the opening of new agricultural lands in the lower Aguán Valley, a land entitlement program under the agrarian reform agency, a road-building program, and the construction of rural schoolhouses.

In March 1988 the United States sent troops to Honduras after it was reported that Nicaraguan forces

---

### Facts About Honduras

**Official Name.** Republic of Honduras.

**Capital.** Tegucigalpa.

**Area.** 43,433 square miles (112,492 square kilometers).

**Population** (2002 estimate). 6,561,000; 151.1 persons per square mile (58.3 persons per square kilometer); 53.7 percent urban, 46.3 percent rural (2001 estimate).

**Major Language.** Spanish (official).

**Major Religion.** Roman Catholicism.

**Literacy.** 72.7 percent.

**Highest Peak.** Las Minas.

**Major Rivers.** Patuca, Ulúa.

**Form of Government.** Republic.

**Chief of State and Head of Government.** President.

**Legislature.** National Assembly; consists of 128 members elected for four-year terms.

**Voting Qualification.** Age 18.

**Political Divisions.** 18 departments.

**Major Cities** (2000 estimate). Tegucigalpa (metropolitan area, 1,037,600); San Pedro Sula (471,000); El Progreso (109,400); La Ceiba (107,200); Choluteca (96,900).

**Chief Manufactured and Mined Products.** Gypsum, salt, zinc, lead, gold, food products, wearing apparel, beverages, nonmetallic mineral products, wood products, consumer chemicals.

**Chief Agricultural Products.** *Crops*—sugarcane, bananas, palm oil, corn (maize), plantains, coffee, oranges, cantaloupes, sorghum, pineapples. *Livestock*—cattle, pigs, chickens.

**Flag.** *Colors*—White and blue (*see* Flags of the World).

**Monetary Unit.** 1 Honduran lempira = 100 centavos.

had crossed into Honduras. The American troops held training exercises but saw no military action. In presidential elections held in November 1989, Rafael Leonardo Callejas of the National party defeated the ruling Liberal party's candidate; he took office on Jan. 27, 1990. For the previous eight years Honduras had been a sanctuary for Nicaraguan rebels opposed to the Sandinista government in that country. The victory of the opposition in Nicaragua's 1990 elections eased the way for the dismantling of the rebel bases in Honduras. Carlos Roberto Reina of the Liberal party became president in 1994. During his tenure and that of his successor, Carlos Flores, the police and military were placed under civilian control. Flores was succeeded in 2002 by Ricardo Maduro. In 2003 the government pledged to investigate the murders of more than 1,500 street children that had occurred over the previous five years. Human rights groups alleged that the deaths were a result of actions by paramilitary death squads. Population (2002 estimate), 6,561,000.

### FURTHER RESOURCES FOR HONDURAS

**Berryman, Phillip.** Inside Central America (Pantheon, 1985).
**Haynes, Tricia.** Let's Visit Honduras (Chelsea House, 1988).
**Newson, Linda.** The Cost of Conquest (Westview, 1986).
**Peckenham, Nancy, and Street, Annie, eds.** Honduras: Portrait of a Captive Nation (Praeger, 1985).

**HONEY.** In ancient times, honey was called the nectar of the gods and was mankind's principal sweetener. Honey consists almost entirely of sugars, but it also contains a number of minerals, B-complex vitamins, and amino acids.

Honey is a syrupy food produced by bees from plant nectar, a kind of sweet sap secreted by flowers. Honey is easily assimilated in the human body because it has been predigested: bees temporarily store the nectar in a special part of their stomachs, where it is partially di- gested. The bees' digestive fluids contain enzymes that transform the nectar into honey. Bees later regurgitate the honey into the cells of their honeycomb, where the honey dries and thickens. To produce about 1 pound (0.5 kilogram) of honey requires 25,000 trips between the hive and flowers. A pound of honey contains the essence of about 2 million flowers. (*See also* Bee.)

The color and flavor of the honey are determined by the flowers from which the nectar is taken. For example, honey made from alfalfa is amber with a distinctive, minty flavor, whereas honey from buckwheat is the color of molasses and strongly flavored. In the United States most commercial honey comes from clover, buckwheat, alfalfa, and orange.

Honey is most often served in its natural state like jam or jelly. It is also widely used in baked goods and candies. It is generally marketed in one of three forms. Comb honey is honey in the comb as it is stored by the bees. Chunk honey is bottled with small chunks of the comb. Extracted honey is liquid honey that has been removed from the comb by centrifuge.

**HONEYSUCKLE.** There are more than 150 species of honeysuckles found throughout the Northern Hemisphere. They are usually deciduous, sometimes more or less evergreen, and may be climbers, tall bushes, or trailers. Most have two-lipped flowers and red, orange, or black berries.

Birds and insects relish the honeysuckle's colorful, juicy berries, and the sweetly fragrant flowers have made many of the climbing species long-standing favorites in the garden. The shrubs and trailers are used for beds, borders, and ground cover.

The trumpet honeysuckle is a popular climber in eastern North America and the hardiest of the climbing species. It has orange-scarlet flowers with yellow centers and bears red fruit. The tatarian honeysuckle, one of the most common bush species, reaches a height of 10 feet (3 meters). In late spring it is covered with rose-pink or white blossoms and in the fall with bright red berries. It is native to Southeastern Europe and Siberia. Italian woodbine, or sweet honeysuckle, is native to Eurasia but has been naturalized in the Eastern United States. Its purple-white flowers are pollinated mostly by hawk moths because the tubes are too long for most other insects to reach the nectar. The fruit is a red-orange berry.

The scientific name of the trumpet honeysuckle is *Lonicera sempervirens*. The tatarian honeysuckle is *L. tatarica*; the Italian woodbine, *L. caprifolium*.

**HONG KONG.** Located on the southeast coast of China at the mouth of the Pearl River delta 80 miles (130 kilometers) southeast of Canton, Hong Kong is centered around one of the world's largest natural deepwater harbors. The congested metropolis is actually several cities that are part of a territory measuring 424 square miles (1,098 square kilometers)—Hong Kong Island, the Kowloon peninsula, and the New Territories. The New Territories in turn make up the larger peninsula from which Kowloon extends and more than 230 surrounding islands. Tall mountains rise from the sea and create a topography of rugged beauty and dramatic vistas.

The heart of the metropolis is the capital on Hong Kong Island, Victoria, which climbs almost vertical streets halfway up Victoria Peak. Rising to a height of 1,825 feet (556 meters), the top of the peak has most of the territory's few detached houses and mansions. The island shelters the harbor from the South China Sea. Major government buildings and the headquarters of banks and powerful hongs, or commercial trading houses, are located at the foot of the peak in Central Hong Kong Island—on land largely reclaimed from the harbor. The major commercial center is the city of Kowloon directly across the harbor. Most industrial property is in skyscraper "new towns" in the New

Territories to the north. Except for the huge island of Lantau, most of the remaining islands are small and sparsely populated. A few have bedroom communities with inhabitants who ferry to work on Hong Kong or Kowloon. A large floating population of boat dwellers dock in the territory's typhoon shelters.

Steep terrain has forced about 90 percent of Hong Kong's population to congregate in just 15 percent of the land area, creating one of the highest population densities in the world. With no place to expand but upward, it has some of the world's tallest buildings outside New York City. Much of the territory, however, is uninhabited government parkland, and some of it is still wild. It has many snakes, and the bird population on Hong Kong Island includes a large community of escaped domestic parakeets and their offspring.

Hong Kong's tropical latitude produces high temperatures most of the year and a short, mild winter. Spring is extremely wet, often causing dangerous landslides and floods. Autumn is extremely dry. The most significant weather event is the typhoon season of late summer.

## People

The major spurt in Hong Kong's population growth was in the late 1970s, when it swelled from about 4 million to 5 million. This was the result of an influx both from China and from Vietnam following the fall of Saigon in 1975. With little room left and diminishing public resources, the government severely restricted immigration in 1980. By 1990 there were more than 56,000 Vietnamese in Hong Kong; only about 12,000 were considered refugees, awaiting resettlement in a third country. A program of forced repatriation to Vietnam began in 1991.

More than nine tenths of Hong Kong's population is Chinese—mostly Cantonese. Former Shanghai businessmen, boat people, fishermen, and New Territories farmers represent other Chinese ethnic groups. Britons make up a narrow majority of the non-Chinese, followed by Indians and Americans. The Cantonese dialect of Chinese and English are official languages.

Buddhism and Taoism are the most popular religions in Hong Kong, which has more than 600 Buddhist and Taoist temples. There is a large minority of Christians, both Protestant and Roman Catholic, and a small minority of Muslims, most of whom are Chinese. There are also small Hindu, Sikh, and Jewish communities.

## Economy

Hong Kong's international significance accelerated in the second half of the 20th century—not only from the explosive growth of its industry but also from the reemergence of China as a participant in world trade and politics. It is strategically positioned at the center of the most rapidly growing area of the world—the Pacific rim. A philosophy of free trade and minimal taxes and regulations attracted investment from around the world. Its location in respect to the trading day made it the center of world trading while London and New York City sleep. It is also the gateway for trade with the

most populous nation on Earth. China depends on the territory to provide the bulk of its foreign exchange and investment.

Hong Kong has no substantial natural resources, and much of what it needs is imported. A large share of its income is from services it provides as a transshipment and warehousing gateway between China and Southeast Asia and the rest of the world. Industry is essential to Hong Kong's role as a key exporter. Among the most important goods produced are printed materials, textiles and clothing, foods, machinery, transport equipment, metal products, and electronics. Hong Kong is one of the world's largest exporters of watches and clocks. Key imports include machinery, consumer goods, food products, and mineral fuels. China, Japan, Taiwan, and the United States are Hong Kong's most important trade partners.

While industry dominated the economic base prior to the 1980s, today services are becoming an increasingly important sector. Hong Kong is the shopping, eating, fashion, and entertainment mecca of Asia. It is the movie capital of the world, with more feature films and videos produced in the territory than anywhere else.

Hong Kong is one of the world's busiest shipping centers and is upgrading its port facilities with a new airport and container port on an island in the harbor. More than 12,000 oceangoing vessels call at the port each year. These and hundreds of Chinese sampans, sailing junks, ferryboats, hydrofoils, and pleasure craft create a bustling and exciting atmosphere.

## Government and History

Hong Kong is a Special Administrative Region of the People's Republic of China under the principle "one country, two systems." Under the Basic Law, the constitution adopted for Hong Kong in 1990, the former British colony enjoys a capitalist economy, a free port, a separate customs territory, and its own currency and finances. A chief executive heads the Executive Council, which is responsible for enforcing laws passed by the 60-member Legislative Council. China manages Hong Kong's foreign and military policy but has promised not to impose socialism before 2047.

There is archaeological evidence of settlement as early as the 3rd century BC. A few rural Chinese villages in the New Territories have been inhabited since the 11th century. Before the British flag was placed on Hong Kong Island in 1841 by merchant-adventurers expelled from Canton, the island harbored only a few Chinese pirates, vagabonds, and stonecutters.

The Chinese were forced to cede the island to the British in 1842 following their defeat in the First Opium War. According to one legend, the Chinese named the settlement Heung Keung, or "Fragrant Harbor," because of the scent of Indian opium that hovered in the air from the British clipper ships waiting to make their run up the Pearl River to Canton. Beginning with the Taiping Rebellion in 1850, Hong Kong grew rapidly. Civil wars and economic and social changes in China drove various waves of refugees into the territory. At the end of the Second Opium War in 1860, the British forced the Chinese to cede part of the Kowloon peninsula. In 1899 the British took a 99-year lease on the New Territories. China always considered the agreements to be "unequal treaties."

The events of the 1930s and 1940s played havoc with the population of Hong Kong. Nearly 880,000 people lived there in 1931. Chinese refugees nearly doubled that number after Japan occupied Canton in 1938, just before the outbreak of World War II. Three years later, in 1941, Japan occupied Hong Kong and arranged mass deportation because of food shortages. Japanese occupation and Allied bombing decimated Hong Kong's population, which dropped to about 600,000 by the end of the war. The population once again rebounded after the British resumed control of the territory following the conclusion of World War II.

The Communist victory in mainland China in 1949 drove more refugees into Hong Kong, and it became the base for Western "China watchers." Many Chinese lost their lives trying to swim over the border through shark-infested Mirs Bay. By the mid-1950s the colony had some 2.2 million people.

Hong Kong did not have enough housing or jobs for so many people. A public housing program, introduced after a fire left 53,000 squatters homeless in 1953, expanded to accomodate about half the population before the end of the century. The economy, previously dependent on the port, diversified with the construction of textile and other factories. Labor unrest in 1967 erupted into riots instigated by proponents of the Cultural Revolution in China.

With the death of Mao Zedong in 1976, the new Chinese government moved to negotiate a peaceful solution to the "unequal treaties" problem and to arrange a return of the territory to China's jurisdiction at the expiration in 1997 of Britain's 99-year lease of the New Territories. Under the Sino-British Agreement ratified on May 27, 1985, Britain agreed to return sovereignty in Hong Kong to China on July 1, 1997. China agreed to maintain the same form of government and personal freedoms, but the violent suppression of the democracy movement in Beijing in June 1989 ended the perception that China would exert only minimal authority after the 1997 transfer of power. Thousands of educated professionals were emigrating at a rate of 1,000 a week in 1990, mostly to the United States, Canada, and Australia. In an effort to keep key jobholders in place, Britain offered full passports to 50,000 Hong Kong families to provide them legal refuge in 1997 if they needed it. China, however, announced it would not recognize the British passports. The British government also took measures to strengthen laws concerning democratic processes and basic human rights in the country, leading to the ratification of a new constitution, called the Basic Law, in 1990. In 1991 Hong Kong held its first direct elections for the Legislative Council in 150 years of British rule. Pro-democracy forces won most of the contested seats.

In December 1996 a selection committee approved by the Chinese government chose the shipping magnate Tung Chee-hwa to become Hong Kong' first executive when the British governor stepped down in July 1997. Tung raised concerns in Hong Kong when he announced in February 1997 that certain rights—such as the right of assembly—guaranteed by laws passed by the British government would be repealed or amended once the transfer of power had been completed. During the power-transfer ceremony on June 30, 1997, Chinese President Jiang Zemin expressed his commitment to maintaining Hong Kong's continued economic, legislative, and judicial autonomy. Subsequent legislative elections were deemed fair and open by international observers. In 2002 Tung was elected to a second term as chief executive by an 800-member election committee. In 2003 Hong Kong experienced one of the earliest outbreaks of SARS (Severe Acute Respiratory Syndrome). More than 1,700 people were stricken, and approximately 300 died within nine months. Population (2002 estimate), 6,785,000.

*Francine Modderno*

**HONOLULU, Hawaii.** The capital and largest city of Hawaii is the port city of Honolulu, located on the southeastern coast of the island of Oahu. The city of Honolulu spreads for about 10 miles (16 kilometers) along the shores of Oahu and for 4 miles (6 kilometers) inland across a narrow plain to the foothills of the Koolau Range. This range is an extinct volcanic chain whose spurs reach almost to the seashore. Among its features are the craters Koko Head, Diamond Head, and Punchbowl. The renowned Waikiki Beach is lined with hotels. The beach is crescent-shaped and stretches from the Ala Wai Canal to the peak of Diamond Head. Millions of tourists visit Honolulu each year.

A walking tour of downtown Honolulu can include the modern Capitol, which has a large art collection; Washington Place, a mansion built in 1846 and now the residence of Hawaii's governors; and the only royal palace in the United States—Iolani Palace, now a museum but a former legislative seat and royal residence.

The Bishop Museum has extensive collections of Polynesian art and artifacts. As the cultural center of Hawaii, Honolulu also is home to the Honolulu Academy of Arts and Waikiki Aquarium. Aloha Stadium hosts the football Pro Bowl each January. Honolulu is also the seat of the University of Hawaii in Manoa Valley. Other educational institutions include Chaminade and Hawaii Pacific universities, the Colleges of Honolulu and Kapiolani, and the Kamehameha schools for children of Hawaiian descent. At nearby Pearl Harbor is a huge United States Navy base, where visitors come to pay tribute to the 1,100 Americans buried at the USS *Arizona* Memorial.

Honolulu is a regular port of call for freight and passenger ships. Overseas air service operates through Honolulu International Airport.

© Craig Aurness—Westlight

*At the eastern edge of Honolulu, the 642-foot Koko Head looms behind Hanauma Bay, a body of water formed in an extinct volcano.*

Much of Hawaii's industry is centered in the city-county of Honolulu. Many of the manufactured products are for the local market to lessen dependence on imports. The principal sources of income besides tourism and military spending are agricultural crops and sportswear. The city's port and international airport handle the exports from pineapple canneries, sugar refineries, and clothing factories as well as the steel, aluminum, petroleum, cement, and dairying industries.

Honolulu was first settled by Polynesians centuries ago and given its name, which means "protected bay." Legend indicates that settlement may have occurred as early as AD 500. The site did not enter recorded Western history, however, until Nov. 21, 1794, when the harbor was discovered by Capt. William Brown of the British ship *Butterworth*.

During the mid-1800s the city flourished as a trading and supply port for the whaling industry. King Kamehameha III moved his court there in 1845, and it became the official capital in 1850.

When the Territory of Hawaii was organized by the United States in 1900, Honolulu was made the capital. In December 1941 the city and the Pearl Harbor naval complex a few miles to the west were attacked by the Japanese. The city was in a strategic position in both World War II and the Korean War as well as throughout the war in Vietnam. After Hawaii became the 50th state in 1959, Honolulu experienced both residential and industrial expansion.

Honolulu's mayor-council form of government also controls Honolulu County, which covers the entire island of Oahu as well as some small islands and reefs in the northwestern Hawaiian Islands. Population (2000 census), 371,657.

**HOOF.** The hard covering that protects the toes of many animals is called a hoof. Because all hoofed animals walk on the tips of their toes, they require a strong, firm, insensitive surface to bear the weight of their bodies. Hooves help them walk and run on hard ground. In animals such as the horse and antelope, hooves are an adaptation for fast running and lend the animal both speed and endurance. The sharp hooves of some animals are also used for defense.

Hooves are made of keratin, or horn, a fibrous protein that is produced by the outer layer of the skin. Hooves are actually very similar to the nails and claws of other mammals: they are made of the same material, they occur in approximately the same place—at the tip of the leg, toe, or finger—and cover only the upper surface, and they have the same evolutionary origin. (*See also* Evolution.) Hooves grow from the base, or attached end. They continue to grow throughout the animal's life, just as nails and claws do, but their length is controlled by wear. Only the cells at the base of the hoof are living.

The hoof consists of two parts. The broad, hard, upper portion is called the unguis; it completely surrounds the end of the toe, extending down and forming a rim around the bottom of the hoof. A somewhat softer plate, called the subunguis, covers the bottom of the toe and is extensively developed in hoofed animals to form a tough pad. (In humans the subunguis is only a small ridge under the tip of the nail.) Horseshoes are nailed to the hard unguis to protect the horse's hooves against breaking and splitting (*see* Horse).

Mammals with hooves are called ungulates. There are nearly 1,000 different forms of ungulates. They are divided into two principal groups: those with an even number of toes and those with an odd number. The even-toed animals have an even number of toes on all their feet. They include pigs, hippopotamuses, cattle, deer, camels, goats, antelope, and sheep. Two-toed ungulates are often called cloven-hoofed because each toe is covered by a separate hoof, so that their hooves appear to be split, or cloven. The odd-toed animals have an odd number of toes on each of their hind feet. They include horses, asses, and zebras, which have a single solid hoof on each foot. Other odd-toed ungulates, such as tapirs and rhinoceroses, have three toes on each foot, each covered by a separate hoof.

A variety of diseases and conditions may afflict the hoof. By far the most familiar is hoof-and-mouth disease (also called foot-and-mouth disease and aftosa). This is a highly contagious and fatal viral disease affecting practically all even-toed mammals, including cattle, sheep, goats, pigs, and deer. Only the horse is resistant to this infection. The disease is characterized by the formation of painful fluid-filled blisters on the tongue, lips, and other tissues of the mouth and on parts of the body where the skin is thin, as on the udder and teats, and around the hoof. (*See also* Mammal; Zoology.)

**HOOKWORM** *see* **WORM.**

**31st President of the United States
(1874–1964; president, 1929–33)**

# HERBERT HOOVER

When United States voters elected Herbert Hoover 31st president in 1928, the country was enjoying an industrial and financial boom. Within seven months of his taking office, however, the country was swallowed up in a depression that swept the entire world. He devised emergency measures in both the domestic and the foreign fields. Conditions, however, grew worse steadily until by the end of his term more than 12 million people were unemployed. Blamed for the hard times, he was defeated in the 1932 election.

Herbert Clark Hoover was born in West Branch, Iowa, on Aug. 10, 1874. The Hoovers were Quakers of Swiss origin who had lived in America since 1740. His parents, Jesse Hoover, a blacksmith and farm implement dealer, and Huldah Minthorn Hoover, died before he was ten years of age. He and his brother and sister were welcomed into the homes of relatives.

Hoover's 'Memoirs' describes a typical country childhood. It relates happy memories of Aunt Millie's fine cooking, of coasting, shooting wild turkeys, trapping rabbits, and fishing with a hook and worm. Once he and his cousins made a mowing machine from an old saw and other odds and ends. The machine did not last long after they hitched it to a calf. On a visit to his Uncle Laban Miles, government agent for the Osage nation in Indian Territory, he learned campfire cooking and other outdoor skills from Indian playmates.

In 1884 he went to Newberg, Ore., to live with his uncle, Dr. John Minthorn. Herbert attended the Quaker academy in which his uncle taught. When he was nearly 15, the Minthorns moved to Salem. He worked as office boy in the land-settlement business of his uncle and attended night school. A prospecting trip with a mining engineer inspired the youth to study engineering. He determined to attend the new Leland Stanford Jr. University (now Stanford University) at Palo Alto, Calif. He was one of the first to enroll in 1891.

## He Becomes an Engineer

He worked his way through college by operating a newspaper route and a laundry agency, and doing clerical work in the department of geology. He managed to find time to play on the freshman baseball nine and to help organize student activities. He worked on geological surveys in the summer.

A favorite story deals with his job as disbursing officer for a United States Geological Survey party. When a pack mule was found dead, the rules required Hoover and two witnesses to investigate the cause of death. They found a loose hind shoe caught in the animal's neck halter. So they reported that it had broken its neck while scratching its head with a hind foot. The bureau in Washington refused to accept this "tall story," and charged the party $60 for the lost animal. From that time on Hoover watched mules to confirm the fact that they could scratch their heads with a hind foot.

When Hoover was graduated in 1895, engineering jobs were scarce. He found work pushing a car in a gold mine. For this he received $2.00 a day for a ten-hour night shift seven days a week. He next got work in an engineer's office by offering to do typing. Once hired, he proved his ability on jobs in Colorado, New Mixico, and Arizona.

He received his first great chance before he was 24, when his employer recommended him to a British engineering firm. He introduced American mining methods in the hot, dry Coolgardie gold fields of Western Australia for them. One mine whose purchase he recommended produced 55 million dollars in gold during the next 50 years.

### Marriage and Life in China

When he was offered a position organizing a national department of mines and railways in China, he cabled Lou Henry, his Stanford sweetheart, proposing immediate marriage. They sailed for China on their wedding day, Feb. 10, 1899. In Asia Hoover's exploring journeys took him into Manchuria and Mongolia. The Chinese were disappointed that no vast gold veins were discovered, but Hoover found immense coal fields and valuable industrial minerals.

When the Boxer Rebellion broke out, the Hoovers were among the 200 foreigners who were besieged in Tientsin (now Tianjin) for a month. Hoover helped

## Time Line of Presidents, Events, and Periods

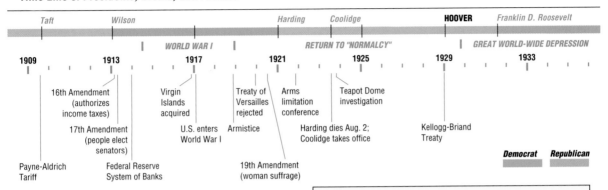

| Taft | Wilson | | Harding | Coolidge | **HOOVER** | Franklin D. Roosevelt |

| | WORLD WAR I | | RETURN TO "NORMALCY" | | GREAT WORLD-WIDE DEPRESSION |

1909     1913     1917     1921     1925     1929     1933

16th Amendment
(authorizes
income taxes)

Virgin
Islands
acquired

Treaty of
Versailles
rejected

Arms
limitation
conference

Teapot Dome
investigation

17th Amendment
(people elect
senators)

U.S. enters
World War I

Armistice

Harding dies Aug. 2;
Coolidge takes office

Kellogg-Briand
Treaty

Payne-Aldrich
Tariff

Federal Reserve
System of Banks

19th Amendment
(woman suffrage)

Democrat     Republican

---

**HOOVER'S ADMINISTRATION 1929–33**

Federal Farm Board created (1929).
Financial crisis and beginning of depression (1929).
Naval Treaty of London (1930).
Hawley-Smoot Tariff Act (1930).
Veterans' Administration formed (1930).
Soldiers' Bonus Bill passed (1931).
German and Interallied Moratorium Agreement (1931).
Reconstruction Finance Corporation created and other relief measures passed (1932).
20th Amendment adopted (1933).

---

UPI/Bettmann

*At high-school age Herbert Hoover worked as an office boy in his uncle's firm. He made up lost schooling in two months of tutoring to pass the Stanford entrance examinations.*

strengthen fortifications and procure food and pure water. His wife served as a volunteer nurse.

### Worldwide Engineering Exploits

Hoover was a partner in a British engineering firm from 1902 to 1908. He traveled all over the world to work out engineering problems in the mines his company managed. The properties included coal mines in China, Wales, and the Transvaal; a tin mine in Cornwall; and gold mines in Western Australia, New Zealand, South Africa, and West Africa. There were also copper mines in Queensland and Canada, a lead-silver mine in Nevada, and a turquoise mine in the Sinai Peninsula of Egypt. His wife and children shared the hardships and adventures of these journeys. The Hoovers' sons were born in London—Herbert, Jr., on Aug. 4, 1903, and Allan on July 17, 1907.

In 1908 Hoover opened his own engineering firm, with offices in New York City, San Francisco, London, Petrograd, and Paris. The firm served as technical adviser and as reorganizer of failing companies.

In his leisure time, he wrote the textbook 'Principles of Mining', which was used for many years in college classrooms. Assisted by Mrs. Hoover he translated Agricola's medieval Latin treatise on mining, 'De Re Metallica'. (The couple had studied geology together in college.) Hoover's technical achievements were many and notable. His work brought him handsome fees and interests in profitable mines.

### Public Service in World War I

When World War I broke out Hoover was in London seeking exhibits for the Panama-Pacific Exposition. At the request of the American ambassador, he undertook to help 200,000 stranded American tourists return home. His organization cashed checks, made reservations, and raised funds.

Next Hoover was persuaded to undertake the task of Belgian relief. The German armies had occupied Belgium and northern France. In the grip of the Allied blockade, these countries faced starvation. Hoover turned his business duties over to others and gave his entire time to the relief project.

The first task was to overcome the objections of both the Germans and the Allies. Then Hoover and his colleagues organized the Commission for Relief in Belgium. They sought and obtained funds from charitable people everywhere and from the governments of France, England, and the United States. By the end of the war the Commission had sent a total of 5 million tons of food and clothing to occupied Belgium and France. After the United States broke with Germany, Hoover turned the work over to Dutch and Spanish neutrals.

## Major World Events During Hoover's Administration

**London.** *Conference on Naval Armament, 1930*

**Germany.** *War debt and reparations settlements:
Young plan, 1929; debt moratorium, 1931;
Lausanne Conference, 1932.*

**Germany.** *Hitler made chancellor, 1933*

**Spain.** *Spanish republic founded, 1931*

**Japan-Manchuria.** *Japan occupies Manchuria, 1931*

**Peru-Chile.** *Tacna-Arica settlement, 1929*

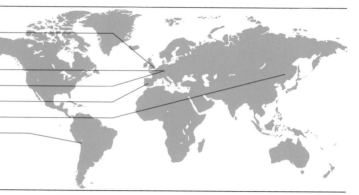

UPI/Bettmann

*In this family group, Allan, right, Herbert, Jr., and his wife,
Margaret, stand behind their parents. Herbert, Jr.'s, babies,
Peggy-Ann and Herbert III, were beloved White House children.*

Hoover drew no salary for his years of work and paid his own expenses. Later, even as president, he continued to live on his private means. He used his salary to hire able associates or for public or charitable purposes. He kept none for himself.

### Food Administrator and Economic Councilor

When the United States entered the war President Woodrow Wilson appointed Hoover food administrator. Fourteen million families pledged themselves to his program for producing and saving food. The word Hooverize was coined to mean "saving, substituting, practicing self-denial, and thus helping win the war."

At the end of the war Hoover was named head of the Supreme Economic Council by the Peace Conference. He directed the distribution of food to the starving peoples of Europe. His organization helped to open railroad traffic, administered fuel supplies, fought typhus epidemics, and started the wheels of commerce. Hoover headed the American Relief Organization, which provided meals for undernourished children. In three years between 14 and 16 million children were restored to strength and health. At Hoover's suggestion the Friends Service Committee (Quakers) carried on this work in Germany. He continued to extend the relief work, assisting over 30 countries, including the Soviet Union in the famine of 1921.

### Work as Secretary of Commerce

Hoover served as secretary of commerce from 1921 to 1928, in the administrations of Presidents Harding and Coolidge. He greatly expanded the activities of the department. Called "consulting engineer to the nation," he sought to increase national efficiency. Under him the Bureau of Standards adopted standards and sizes for hundreds of items. He reorganized the Bureau of Foreign and Domestic Commerce to provide businesses with information on export opportunities. In a continued drive to improve the use of water resources he laid the groundwork for irrigation and power developments in the Colorado and Columbia rivers and in California. He pushed flood control and navigation improvement in the Mississippi system. These projects were expanded during his term as president.

Hoover worked out the principles and methods of public ownership and control of wave channels for radio broadcasting. He helped establish government aid and regulation of civil aviation.

### Election to the Presidency

Hoover was nominated for the presidency on the first ballot at the Republican convention in Kansas City, Mo., in 1928. Charles Curtis of Kansas received the vice-presidential nomination. The party promised to maintain prosperity, to assist the farmer, and to make stronger attempts to enforce the prohibition amendment and law in general.

The Democrats made an issue of the scandals of the Harding administration (*see* Harding). They nominated Gov. Alfred E. Smith of New York, an avowed wet and a Roman Catholic. The South, largely Protestant and

*Grant Wood painted Hoover's old home in West Branch, Iowa, as it looked when he was president. Later Mrs. Hoover had it restored to its original form—a tiny three-room cottage. A birthplace society maintains house and grounds as a park.*

dry, turned against Smith. He carried only eight states. Three of every five votes went to Hoover in this his first candidacy for elective office.

When the new president took office the country was riding the crest of a wave of prosperity. Recounting the economic progress of the decade Hoover had called attention to a 45 per cent increase in national income and a 25 per cent increase in production and consumption, with an 8 per cent growth in population. He pointed to 3,500,000 new homes, 9,000,000 houses equipped with electricity, 6,000,000 more telephones, 7,000,000 radio sets, and 14,000,000 additional automobiles. He told of an 11 per cent increase in grade-school enrollment; 66 per cent more students in the high schools; and 75 per cent more in institutions of higher learning. He expressed the hope that "we shall soon with the help of God be in sight of the day when poverty will be banished from this nation."

### Foreign Relations and Fact-Finding Boards

Hoover's seven years in the Cabinet had permitted him to see the needs of the government and to shape his policies. His years abroad had given him a world outlook. To develop good neighbor relations with Latin America, he and Mrs. Hoover paid a visit to the Latin capitals on the battleship *Maryland* before his inauguration. Following this trip Hoover helped to settle the long-standing Tacna-Arica dispute between Peru and Chile. He later withdrew all the troops which had been stationed in the Latin American countries to protect United States interests.

The president's scientific training called for a thorough study of any problem he faced, so he appointed many fact-finding commissions. The Wickersham commission studied law enforcement. It recommended a stricter enforcement of prohibition and opposed repeal of the 18th Amendment.

Public opinion turned against prohibition during Hoover's administration. At the end of his term the 21st Amendment, repealing the 18th, went to the states for ratification.

An important commission on social and economic trends analyzed the great changes in the American economy since World War I. A study of the organization of government offices preceded numerous changes to improve efficiency. The Veterans' Bureau and the Bureau of Pensions, for example, were reorganized and merged.

### Farm Aid and Tariff Revision

Hoover tried hard to carry out his campaign promises. He signed the Agricultural Marketing Act in June 1929 to keep promises of farm aid, although he did not believe in supporting commodity prices. American farmers had not shared the widespread prosperity of the 1920s. Sales and prices of farm products had fallen. Many farmers had lost their land by mortgage foreclosure, and two fifths of the farms were operated by tenants.

Under the marketing act, a Federal Farm Board was furnished with a 500-million-dollar revolving fund to establish marketing co-operatives. They lent money to farmer members, who pledged their crops as security. The co-operatives could hold products off the market to await a price rise. The depression made this plan unworkable, for prices quickly fell below the loan rate. When the federal government bought the holdings of the co-operatives to maintain prices, crops increased. Prices continued to fall.

Tariff revision had been promised as an aid to farmers. The Hawley-Smoot Tariff Act of 1930 failed to serve this purpose. Its rates were the highest in history. Foreign nations raised their tariffs to create export balances for debt payments.

### Financial Panic Sets Off Great Depression

The stock-market crash of October 1929 is usually regarded as the beginning of the Great Depression, though there had been a slump in industry earlier. Prices of securities had reached their high point in September, as people in all walks of life had begun speculating on a continuously rising market. Many bought "on margin" (*see* Stock Market). Their investments were wiped out as stock prices fell. Despite occasional rallies, the market continued downward throughout Hoover's term. In 1932, for example, stocks sold at about 10 percent of their 1929 value.

The market collapse was the signal for a widespread economic breakdown. Trade fell off as credit tightened, and people with cash feared to spend it. Overstocked merchants and manufacturers were forced to close down or to discharge employees. Workers displaced by new laborsaving machinery swelled the army of the unemployed. Widespread bank failures took the savings of hundreds of thousands. Mortgage foreclosures swept away people's businesses and

UPI/Bettmann

*Hoover enjoyed fishing off the Florida coast and angling for trout in the Rapidan River at his Blue Ridge summer camp.*

homes. A severe drought occurred in 1930 and added to the suffering of Middle Western farmers. The unemployed were forced to turn to public or private charity when their savings were gone.

### Hoover's Attack on the Depression

At first leaders believed that the slump was temporary. Hoover quickly called meetings of key men in industry and received assurances that they would avoid laying off labor and cutting wages. He urged the states to create jobs through public works. He encouraged drives by local community chests and other charities. He took the position that direct aid to the unemployed was the duty of the localities and of private charities. Federal relief, he felt, would be subject to political control and graft, while a direct dole would weaken individual initiative.

It was his belief that the economic system could best be quickened by expanding credit. Thus businessmen could start activities that would improve trade and employment. His critics called this aid to the men at the top the "trickle down" system. They expressed doubt that the unemployed at the bottom could wait for the remedy to work a cure.

In 1932 banks were on the verge of collapse and unemployment was approaching 25 percent. At Hoover's urging, Congress created the Reconstruction Finance Corporation (RFC) to lend money to banks, loan associations, insurance companies, and railroads. During his term the RFC lent more than 2 billion dollars.

### Emergency Relief Laws and Public Works

The Emergency Relief Act of 1932 provided for RFC loans to states for use in direct relief. The act also permitted Federal Reserve Banks to lend to small businesses. Home Loan Banks were established in 1932, and the capital of Federal Land Banks was gradually increased.

Hoover at first looked to public works construction to supply jobs. More was spent on public works in his term than in the preceding 36 years. Later he decided that the number of jobs provided by nonproductive public works was too small for their high cost. He opposed the congressmen's "pork barrel" bills and recommended loans for projects that could later pay for themselves. Congress authorized loans for such projects—after it was too late to help employment in his term.

### Relations with Congress and the Public

In the elections of 1930, Democrats captured the House of Representatives. The Senate was made up of 48 Republicans, 47 Democrats, and one Farmer-Labor party man. Republicans of the liberal wing failed to support the president. Hoover had trouble getting Congress to pass his legislation.

Congress rejected Hoover's measures to reform the banking system and the stock exchange. The Senate's inquiry relative to the need for this legislation, however, uncovered scandals in the securities market that weakened public confidence.

Hoover had difficulty dealing with Congress because he had not developed the skills of the professional politician. Somewhat shy, President Hoover was not completely at ease in public and lacked the magnetic power to charm and persuade.

His position on the Soldiers' Bonus Bill made him unpopular with veterans' groups. This bill, which raised the maximum loans on veterans' insurance certificates to 50 per cent of the face value, was passed over his veto. In 1932 he aroused resentment by ordering out of Washington the "bonus army" which had come to demand immediate payment of the bonus. He called out federal troops under Gen. Douglas MacArthur to burn their camp and then to send them home.

### European Collapse and the Moratorium

After 1931 Hoover saw the deepening depression as part of a world depression having its origin in Europe. He took international leadership in efforts to prevent ruin when banks failed in Austria and Germany and their economies collapsed. He asked the nations to agree to a one-year moratorium on intergovernmental debts. Agreement came too late to save the sagging foreign economies. Great Britain was forced to stop gold payments in September and other nations soon followed. Foreign trade slumped and American farm prices tumbled further.

Hoover sought international co-operation in other matters. In 1930 he called the London Conference on

UPI/Bettmann

*Hoover accepts an honorary doctorate from Lille University, commending his World War I relief work in Belgium and France. He had been given 80 honorary degrees by his 80th birthday.*

UPI/Bettmann

*Herbert Hoover addresses the Republican national convention of 1948 in Philadelphia, Pa.*

Naval Armament. Here the nations agreed to limit the size and number of war vessels. He sent a delegation to the League of Nations disarmament conference in 1932. He was organizing a world economic conference when his term ended.

### Defeat in 1932

The depression continued to deepen as the election campaign of 1932 got under way. There were more huge business failures, some of them scandalous, involving banks and utilities companies. An estimated 12 to 13 million people were unemployed.

Hoover and Curtis were renominated by the Republicans. The Democrats named Gov. Franklin D. Roosevelt of New York, with John N. Garner of Texas as vice-president (*see* Roosevelt, Franklin Delano). American voters made Hoover the scapegoat for their troubles. He was crushingly defeated.

No administration had begun more happily than Hoover's. None ended in such despair. More and more banks closed. States declared bank "holidays" to save the remainder. The lame duck session of Congress was dismal. The Democratic house put off remedial legislation. Hoover tried to find a basis on which the president-elect would cooperate with him; but Roosevelt refused to become involved in the president's policies. The 20th (Lame Duck) Amendment was proclaimed in effect February 6. It advanced the date for the meeting of a new Congress to the January 3 following its election, and the president's inauguration date from March 4 to January 20.

### Hoover as Elder Statesman

Retiring to his home in Palo Alto, Calif., on the campus of Stanford University, Hoover made little comment on public affairs for two years. Then in books, articles, and speeches he criticized Roosevelt's New Deal as socialistic. After 1939 he frequently differed with the administration's policies on the war and on peace aims. In 1940 he offered a plan for food distribution in occupied countries. The British refused a test of the plan in Belgium on the grounds that this country was a base for Nazi attacks on Britain. Poland and Finland named him director of American relief efforts on their behalf. The Hoover Institution on War, Revolution, and Peace houses priceless historical records. It was built in Stanford in 1940.

In 1946, as honorary chairman of the Famine Emergency Committee, he flew to Europe, Asia, and South America to survey food needs and supplies. In 1948 President Truman appointed him to recommend changes that would make federal agencies more efficient and economical. His money-saving changes included the creation of the General Services Administration to centralize buying and distribution of government supplies. Hoover served as elder statesman and adviser to the Eisenhower Administration and headed a new economy commission. In 1962 the Herbert Hoover Presidential Library in West Branch, Iowa, was dedicated.

Hoover died in New York City on Oct. 20, 1964, at the age of 90. He was buried near his birthplace in West Branch. (For Hoover's Cabinet and Supreme Court appointments *see* Fact-Index.)

**FURTHER RESOURCES FOR HERBERT C. HOOVER**

**Clinton, Susan.** Herbert Hoover: 31st President of the United States (Childrens, 1988).
**Hilton, Suzanne.** The World of Young Herbert Hoover (Walker, 1987).
**Kane, J.N.** Facts About the Presidents: A Compilation of Biographical and Historical Information, 5th ed. (Wilson, 1990).
**Nash, G.H.** The Life of Herbert Hoover, 2 vols. (Norton, 1983–88).
**Smith, R.N.** An Uncommon Man: The Triumph of Herbert Hoover (High Plains, 1990).

**HOOVER, J. Edgar** (1895–1972). For nearly half a century J. Edgar Hoover was one of the most powerful officials in the federal government of the United States. As head of the Federal Bureau of Investigation (FBI) from 1924 until his death in 1972, he was the nation's chief law-enforcement officer. His intimate knowledge about politicians and government operations made him a man to be feared by elected officials, and none of the eight presidents under whom he served dared fire him.

John Edgar Hoover was born on Jan. 1, 1895, in Washington, D.C. He graduated from George Washington University in 1916 and earned a Master of Laws degree in 1917. In 1919 he became assistant to Attorney General A. Mitchell Palmer in the Department of Justice. It was Palmer who instigated the post–World War I "red scare," an anti-Communist hysteria that led to the deportation of many aliens. Hoover was put in charge of the deportations. In 1921 Hoover became assistant director of the department's Bureau of Investigation (as the FBI was called until 1935). He became director of the bureau in 1924.

Hoover made the FBI one of the world's most effective law-enforcement agencies. He established its vast fingerprint file, crime laboratory, and training academy. He enhanced the FBI's fame by apprehending many gangsters, bank robbers, and other lawbreakers. After World War II he waged a relentless fight against internal subversion. By the 1970s Hoover was often criticized for his authoritarian methods. He died in Washington, D.C., on May 2, 1972.

**HOOVER DAM** *see* DAM.

**HOPE, Bob** (1903–2003). By 1940 Bob Hope was a well-known comedian in vaudeville, on Broadway, and in a popular radio show. In 1940 he teamed with Bing Crosby and Dorothy Lamour to film 'The Road to Singapore', the movie that established him as a Hollywood celebrity. It was followed by many other films.

Leslie Townes Hope was born on May 29, 1903, near London, England. His family emigrated to the United States four years later and settled in Cleveland, Ohio. After high school he tried amateur boxing before entering show business. He made his Broadway debut in 'The Sidewalks of New York' in 1927. The next year he developed a comedy monologue routine and took the name Bob Hope.

His first major stage roles were in 'Ballyhoo' (1932) and 'Roberta' (1933). He started in radio in 1935 and got his own show in 1938. In his motion-picture debut in 'The Big Broadcast of 1938' Hope sang 'Thanks for the Memory', which became his theme song.

Early in World War II he assembled troupes of show-business personalities to entertain United States armed forces personnel around the world, even in combat zones. These undertakings and many others earned him numerous humanitarian honors and gave him a world reputation exceeded by few people in the

*Bob Hope entertains American service personnel during the Christmas season of 1970 at Camp Eagle in Vietnam, about 420 miles (675 kilometers) north of Saigon.*
AP/Wide World

20th century. He received a People to People award from President Dwight D. Eisenhower, a Congressional Gold Medal from President John F. Kennedy, and the Medal of Freedom from President Lyndon Johnson. In 1998 he was made an honorary knight by the queen of England.

Tours to entertain servicemen continued through the Korean and Vietnam wars, and as late as 1983 he went to Lebanon to entertain American service personnel stationed there. His book 'I Never Left Home' (1944) told of the early tours. Hope's television debut was in 1950, and he continued to appear on television for more than 35 years, mostly in specials. He died in Toluca Lake, Calif., on July 27, 2003, at the age of 100.

**HOPKINS, Anthony** (born 1937). The classically trained and highly regarded Welsh actor Anthony Hopkins worked steadily in films and on stage for three decades before achieving popular stardom. His work ranged from biographical roles to Shakespeare to period dramas, but it was as the unnerving, psychopathic Hannibal Lecter in the film 'The Silence of the Lambs' (1991) that he achieved his breakthrough with a mass audience.

Anthony Hopkins was born in Port Talbot, Wales, on Dec. 31, 1937, the only child of Richard Hopkins, a baker, and his wife, Muriel. Anthony attended Cowbridge Grammar School. He did not do well academically, but his proficiency at the piano won him a scholarship to the Cardiff College of Music and Drama in Cardiff, where he studied for two years. After spending two years in the military and working in a steel foundry, Hopkins joined the Manchester Library Theatre as an assistant stage manager. From there he went to the Nottingham Repertory Company and decided to pursue formal training as an actor.

He was awarded a scholarship to the Royal Academy of Dramatic Art and graduated two years later, in 1963.

He joined the Phoenix Theatre in Leicester, then went on to the Liverpool Playhouse and the Hornchurch Repertory Company. In 1965 he was invited to audition for Sir Laurence Olivier, the director of the National Theatre at the Old Vic. Hopkins was a member of the National from 1966 to 1973, starting in supporting roles but eventually playing Coriolanus and Macbeth.

Hopkins made his film debut in 1967, playing Richard the Lion-Hearted in 'The Lion in Winter'. From that time on he made at least one film for theatrical release or for television almost every year, and at times as many as six in a year. He continued his stage work, in 1974 going to Broadway to play Dr. Dysart in the National Theatre production of 'Equus'. He lived in the United States for ten years, doing mostly film and television work. He won two Emmy awards, one for his portrayal of Bruno Hauptmann in 'The Lindbergh Kidnapping Case' (1976) and the other for playing Hitler in a 1980 production. During this period he made the Hollywood fright films 'Audrey Rose' (1977) and 'Magic' (1978), as well as playing Dr. Frederick Treves in 'The Elephant Man' (1980).

Hopkins returned to the London stage and the National Theatre in 1985 in 'Pravda', then starred as Shakespeare's King Lear (1986) and Antony (1987). In 1989 he starred in the West End production of 'M Butterfly'. He continued to make films, notably 'The Bounty' (1984) and '84 Charing Cross Road' (1986), but he had his most popular success beginning in 1991 with 'The Silence of the Lambs', for which he won the Academy award for best actor. Hopkins won more acclaim with his work in 'Howards End' and 'Bram Stoker's Dracula' (1992) and in 'The Remains of the Day' and 'Shadowlands' (1993). His later films included 'Legends of the Fall' (1994), 'Nixon' (1995), and 'Surviving Picasso' (1995). Hopkins was awarded a C.B.E. (Commander, Order of the British Empire) in 1987 and was knighted in January 1993.

**HOPKINS, Frederick Gowland** (1861–1947). The British biochemist Frederick Gowland Hopkins received (with Christiaan Eijkman) the Nobel prize for physiology or medicine in 1929 for contributions to the understanding of human health and nutrition. He discovered vitamins, which are essential in animal diets to maintain health.

Hopkins was born on June 20, 1861, in Eastbourne, East Sussex, England. In 1888 he began his medical studies at Guy's Hospital in London. After earning a degree in medicine at the University of London in 1894 he took a position on the staff of the hospital's medical school. In 1899 he was asked to join a new school of physiology at Cambridge University and stayed until 1943.

Early in his research Hopkins realized that biochemists lacked an accurate knowledge of proteins. In 1901 he and an associate discovered the amino acid tryptophan and isolated it from protein. (Amino acids are the building blocks of protein.) From 1906 to 1907 he demonstrated that tryptophan and certain other amino acids cannot be manufactured from other

nutrients by animals but must be supplied in the diet. He found that no animal can live on a mixture of pure protein, fat, and carbohydrate; certain "accessory substances," later called vitamins, were needed. In 1907 he and Sir Walter Fletcher laid the foundation for the modern understanding of muscular contraction with the discovery that working muscle accumulates lactic acid. In 1922 he isolated the tripeptide (three amino acids linked in sequence) glutathione from living tissue and showed its role in oxidation in cells. Hopkins was knighted in 1925 and was president of the Royal Society of London in 1931. He died in Cambridge on May 16, 1947.

**HOPKINS, Gerard Manley** (1844–89). The collected poetry of Gerard Manley Hopkins was not published until 1918, nearly 30 years after his death. Even then his work was not well received, but a second edition in 1930 won a host of readers. Thereafter his poems were recognized as some of the most original, powerful, and influential literary accomplishments of the 19th century.

Hopkins was born on July 28, 1844, in Stratford, England. He won a poetry prize at the Highgate grammar school and was awarded a grant to study at Balliol College, Oxford. While at Oxford he was converted to Roman Catholicism. In 1868 he joined the Jesuit order and burned his early poetry, determined to write no more verse. While studying theology at St. Beuno's College in Wales, he learned the Welsh language and was impressed by its literary qualities. The death of five nuns in a shipwreck in 1875 impelled him to write the long poem 'The Wreck of the Deutschland', the first of many outstanding compositions written over the next 14 years.

Hopkins became a priest in 1877 and served parishes in London, Oxford, Liverpool, and Glasgow. After teaching at Stonyhurst College he was appointed professor of classics in 1884 at University College in Dublin. He died there of typhoid fever on June 8, 1889. His friend Robert Bridges, later poet laureate, published the first edition of his poetry.

**HOPPER, Edward** (1882–1967). The American painter Edward Hopper used bright colors to depict ordinary scenes from everyday life. His paintings were done in such a way as to create a somber, melancholy mood. Snapshotlike compositions such as 'Nighthawks' (1942) use the eerie light of an all-night diner to isolate the customers and foster an inescapable sense of loneliness.

Hopper was born in Nyack, N.Y., on July 22, 1882. In 1899 he went to New York City to study at the New York School of Art. He was trained primarily as an illustrator, but between 1901 and 1906 he studied painting under Robert Henri, the realist painter and leader of the Ashcan School of realism. Three trips to Europe in the years 1906 to 1910 exposed Hopper to the experimentation going on in France, but the new ideas did not influence him. Apart from summers in New England, he lived in New York City.

Although he exhibited at the Armory Show of 1913 in New York City, Hopper devoted most of his time to

'Nighthawks', an oil on canvas painting by Edward Hopper, was completed in 1942. It measures 144 by 76.2 centimeters.
Courtesy of The Art Institute of Chicago, Friends of American Art Collection, 1942.51

advertising and illustrative etchings until 1924. He then took up painting full time.

Like other artists of the Ashcan School, Hopper depicted commonplace scenes from city life. His subjects included city streets, roadside lunch counters, Victorian homes, New England cottages, barren apartments, and theater interiors. All exhibit a pervasive calm with no hint of urban congestion. Among his works were 'House by the Railroad' (1925), 'Early Sunday Morning' (1930), 'Room in Brooklyn' (1932), and 'Second Story Sunlight' (1960).

Hopper's first one-man show was in 1920. Later in life he had major retrospective shows at the Museum of Modern Art and the Whitney Museum of American Art in New York City. He died in New York City on May 15, 1967.

**HOPS.** When the green, conelike blossom clusters of hop vines take on a yellow tinge and rustle like paper flowers, hop growers rush to pick them. The value of a harvest depends upon gathering the flower-fruit at just the right time. The yellowish aromatic resins and oils contained in the fruit deteriorate rapidly. These substances give hops their commercial value.

The principal use of hops is in making beer and other malt beverages. The aromatic and slightly bitter hops were originally used to mask the sweet taste of beer. Later it was found that beer flavored with hops kept its quality longer.

The hop vine is a perennial climber. Each year it produces several twisting stems that reach a length of about 20 to 40 feet (6 to 12 meters). The vines do not grow horizontally but cling to upright poles or wire. Hop vines always twist in a clockwise helix.

The most valuable hop plants are hybrids, which means that their own seeds do not produce plants that are like wild hops; therefore, hop plants must be propagated by root cuttings or by the planting of hybrid seedlings. Although there are both male and female plants, the best hops come from fields where only female plants are grown. This prevents seed production, which would detract from the value of the

fruit. Hops are harvested in August and then dried in special kilns. Drying temperatures reach nearly 150° F (66° C). Sulfur is usually burned beneath the kilns in order to keep the hops green.

Areas of the Czech Republic, Germany, Japan, and Great Britain are noted for the excellence of their hops. After the brewing process, hop cones are used to make fertilizer. (*See also* Beer and Brewing.)

The hop belongs to the hemp family, Cannabaceae. Its leaves, with three to seven lobes, are heart-shaped. The flowers grow in panicles. The scientific name of the European hop is *Humulus lupulus*.

**HORACE** (65–8 BC). Quintus Horatius Flaccus, commonly known as Horace, was the great lyric poet of Rome during the age of Augustus. Of his writings there have come down to the present 121 lyric poems and 41 verse essays. His major works are 'Odes', 'Epodes', 'Secular Hymn', 'Epistles', 'Satires', and 'Ars Poetica' (Art of Poetry). Much of his writing is devoted to praising the reign of Augustus and the changes wrought in the Roman state by the emperor.

Horace was born on Dec. 8, 65 BC in Venusia in what is now southeastern Italy. He studied in Rome before going to Athens in about 46 BC. While he was in Greece, Julius Caesar was assassinated, and civil war broke out between his slayers on one side and Octavian (the future Augustus) and Mark Antony on the other. Octavian was the eventual victor in the strife, and though he had sided with the opposition, Horace was pardoned in Rome. In about 39 BC he was appointed a treasury clerk. He lived in Rome and at a villa about 22 miles (35 kilometers) away.

The first ten poems of 'Satires' were published in 35 BC. 'Epodes' and a second set of eight 'Satires' came out in 30–29 BC. The first 'Odes', 88 short poems in three books, were issued in 23 BC. The first 'Epistles' were published in 20 BC, and more of them appeared in the years 17–14 BC. In 17 BC he composed 'Secular Hymn', and the next year he completed a fourth book of 'Odes'. 'Ars Poetica' was part of the 'Epistles'. Horace died in Rome on Nov. 27, 8 BC.

## Where Hormones Are Made

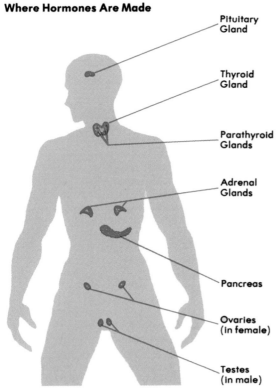

Pituitary Gland

Thyroid Gland

Parathyroid Glands

Adrenal Glands

Pancreas

Ovaries (in female)

Testes (in male)

*The endocrine glands shown above are among the most important. Hormones secreted by these ductless glands are chemical messengers that signal the start or stop of many key body functions.*

# HORMONES

The body has a special information system that relies on chemical messengers called hormones. These organic chemicals are made in ductless endocrine glands that pour their hormones into the blood. In most cases, the hormones then float to target organs where they turn biochemical reactions on or off.

The major endocrine glands are the pituitary, the thyroid, the parathyroids, the pancreas, the adrenals, and the ovaries and testes. Their hormones will be discussed in this article. Hormones are also made in the stomach, the small intestine, and the kidneys. The pineal and the thymus glands possibly make them, too. The placenta of pregnant mammals has an endocrine function. It can make pituitary and ovarian hormones as well as a special one of its own.

Many living things produce hormones. Insects, for example, have hormones that speed up as well as stop growth at different stages of their life cycle. By maintaining a proper balance of these hormones, an

. . . . . . . . . . . . . . . . . . . . . . . . . . . . . . . . . . . . . . . . . . . . . . . . . . . .

*This article was contributed by Choh Hao Li, late Professor and Director, Laboratory of Molecular Endocrinology, University of California, San Francisco.*

insect develops in the appropriate way. Ecdysome is an insect hormone. It influences molting and metamorphosis (*see* Insect).

Plants produce hormones, also. One of the best-known plant hormones is indoleacetic acid. It promotes rooting and growth.

### The Pituitary Controls Other Glands

The pituitary gland (also called the hypophysis) is a small, oval structure under the brain. It has two parts—the anterior lobe (adenohypophysis) and the posterior lobe (neurohypophysis). In some animals, the adenohypophysis includes an intermediate lobe.

The pituitary influences the activity of many other endocrine glands. Most of its hormones are made in its anterior lobe. Hence, the anterior pituitary is usually called the "master" gland of the body. Its products are growth hormone (GH), prolactin, adrenocorticotropic hormone (ACTH), lipotropic hormone (LPH), thyroid-stimulating hormone (TSH), follicle-stimulating hormone (FSH), interstitial cell-stimulating hormone (ICSH), and melanocyte-stimulating hormone (MSH). Chemically, the anterior pituitary hormones are either polypeptides or more complex proteins (*see* Protein). The posterior lobe does not produce hormones but merely stores two hormones made in the hypothalamus of the brain. They are vasopressin and oxytocin. Chemically, they are cyclic polypeptides.

Nearly all the anterior pituitary hormones act on specific tissues. Growth hormone, an exception, affects the body's overall growth processes. It also aids other hormones in their work. Prolactin controls the development, growth, and milk production of the mammary glands. ACTH stimulates the adrenal glands to produce steroid hormones. TSH prompts the thyroid gland to produce thyroxine. FSH and ICSH together induce the gonads—ovaries and testes—to make sex hormones. MSH acts on the melanocytes in the skin to render changes in pigmentation. LPH mobilizes lipid, or fat, from fatty tissue.

The pituitary must secrete the correct amount of GH for normal early growth. If a shortage occurs, an infant becomes a dwarf. This disorder, however, can be corrected by injection of monkey GH or human growth hormone (HGH). By contrast, if the pituitary produces too much GH in early life, an infant becomes a giant. And if the gland becomes overactive in adult life, a person develops acromegaly, an enlargement of the jaw and the extremities. The pituitary must then be removed by surgery.

Vasopressin from the posterior pituitary raises blood pressure by its action on blood vessels. It is sometimes called antidiuretic hormone because it helps the body retain water. It prevents the kidneys from producing too much urine, a condition called diuresis. Without vasopressin, a person develops diabetes insipidus and may excrete up to 30 liters (about 30 quarts) of urine a day. Oxytocin initiates birth by causing muscle contraction in the uterus. It also induces milk flow from the mother's breasts and controls postpartum bleeding (*see* Reproductive System).

## What Hormones Do

| Endocrine Gland | Hormone Output | Function of Hormone |
|---|---|---|
| Anterior pituitary (and intermediate pituitary, in some animals) (adenohypophysis) | Growth hormone (GH) | Influences nitrogen storage for muscle building |
| | Thyroid-stimulating hormone (TSH) | Controls hormonal activity of thyroid gland |
| | Adrenocorticotropic hormone (ACTH) | Controls hormonal activity of adrenal gland cortex |
| | Follicle-stimulating hormone (FSH) | Ripens egg follicles in ovaries; triggers sperm formation in testes |
| | Interstitial cell-stimulating hormone (ICSH) | With FSH, causes ripe follicles to release eggs; causes sperm to develop fully |
| | Prolactin | Triggers mammary gland growth and milk production |
| | Lipotropic hormone (LPH) | Affects metabolism of fats in liver |
| | Melanocyte-stimulating hormone (MSH) | Controls distribution of melanin, a dark pigment, in cells called melanocytes |
| Posterior pituitary (neurohypophysis) | Vasopressin | Raises blood pressure; restricts urine flow |
| | Oxytocin | Contracts muscles of uterus to aid birth |
| Thyroid | Thyroxine | Controls iodine incorporation and suppresses goiters; regulates growth and tissue development in young |
| | Triiodothyronine | |
| | Thyrocalcitonin | Maintains healthy bones |
| Parathyroids | Parathyroid hormone | Controls calcium concentrations in blood to prevent severe muscle spasms |
| Adrenal cortex | Adrenal steroids (a) Glucocorticoids (b) Mineralocorticoids | When activated by ACTH, (a) affect manufacture and use of sugar; (b) maintain salt balances in the body |
| Adrenal medulla | Epinephrine (adrenaline) | In stress raises blood pressure, speeds heartbeat, makes liver give up glycogen |
| | Norepinephrine (noradrenaline) | Slows heartbeat, reduces brain blood flow, maintains normal circulation |
| Pancreas (islets of Langerhans) | Insulin | Inhibits liver sugar output when blood levels are either normal or high; aids passage of sugar into muscles |
| | Glucagon | Raises level of blood sugar |
| Ovary | Estrogen | Promotes growth of uterus and body features of adult female |
| | Progesterone | Prepares uterus wall for implantation of fertilized egg; stops egg release during pregnancy |
| Testis | Testosterone | Promotes body features of adult male |

## The Thyroid Gland Regulates Body Energy

The thyroid gland lies on both sides of the trachea in the neck. Its two lobes connected by an isthmus resemble the letter H. The average adult thyroid gland weighs about 1 ounce (30 grams). Under the constant direction of TSH, the thyroid converts iodine in food into thyroxine, an amino acid derivative, and small amounts of chemically similar triiodothyronine. They regulate both the rate at which food is burned for body energy and the expression of thyroid hormone-sensitive genes.

Sometimes the thyroid becomes overactive and produces excess thyroxine, a condition called hyperthyroidism. A hyperthyroid person is nervous, wastes energy, and becomes irritable easily. The disorder is treated with radioisotopes or by surgery ( *see* Nuclear Energy). On the other hand, lack of thyroid hormone, or hypothyroidism, can arise either from a defective gland or from foods that upset thyroid processes. A young hypothyroid sufferer becomes a cretin, whose physical and mental growth is greatly stunted. Thyroxine treatment usually corrects cretinism when caught in time.

The thyroid gland also makes a polypeptide hormone called thyrocalcitonin, which controls the body's calcium level. It works in conjunction with parathyroid hormone made by the four tiny parathyroid glands imbedded in the thyroid and vitamin D in food to help develop and maintain healthy bones.

Basal metabolic rate (BMR) is the medical measurement of thyroid activity. By regulating BMR the thyroid controls energy output and enables humans and other animals to adapt to environmental changes, such as hot and cold weather.

## The Pancreas and Diabetes

The pancreas plays a vital role by producing two important polypeptide hormones—insulin and glucagon. They are made in a part of the pancreas called the islets of Langerhans.

Insulin affects nearly every cell in the body because it is involved in the metabolism of carbohydrates, fats, and proteins. Lack of insulin causes diabetes mellitus, a common but potentially fatal ailment (*see* Diabetes). Diabetics have too much glucose, a sugar, in the blood. Without insulin an untreated diabetic's tissues cannot get the glucose from the blood for their energy needs. As a result, the diabetic becomes weak. Other complications occur, such as hyperacidity and dehydration from excessive loss of water in the urine. Thirst increases. The sufferer can die if the cells fail to replenish their lost energy and become exhausted. Fortunately insulin injections can correct diabetes. In milder forms of the disease the pancreas makes insulin but does not release enough. Certain nonprotein drugs, however, can coax the pancreas to release life-sustaining amounts of the hormone. Diabetes can easily be discovered by a glucose-tolerance test. A diabetic will have high blood-sugar levels long after drinking a glucose solution. Hyperinsulinism is another

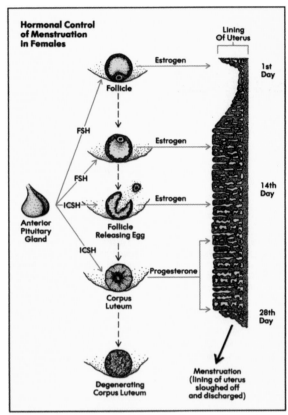

*Menstruation is regulated by FSH, ICSH, estrogen, and progesterone. They build up the lining of the uterus to prepare for pregnancy. If pregnancy does not occur, the lining is sloughed off and a new cycle begins. Each cycle takes on the average about 28 days.*

dangerous pancreatic disorder. Too much insulin can result in weakness, anxiety, depression, and even serious convulsions and collapse. Glucose treatment or surgery generally remedy this problem.

Glucagon, the other pancreatic hormone, tends to raise the blood-sugar level. Both glucagon and insulin work together to help maintain the normal level of glucose in the blood so that the body always has a constant and even supply.

## The Adrenal Glands Essential for Life

The vital adrenal glands lie on top of the kidneys. Each gland consists of an outer cortex and an inner medulla. Each region produces hormones that are chemically different (*see* Gland).

The adrenal cortex, under the control of ACTH, produces steroid hormones. The cortical steroids fall into two classes—the glucocorticoids and the mineralocorticoids. Each in a varying degree affects vital food metabolism and mineral balance. Cortisol, a glucocorticoid, is used medically to stop inflammation. It is also given to transplant patients to prevent their bodies from rejecting newly transplanted tissue. Addison's disease is an adrenal cortex deficiency. It results in low blood pressure, weakness, low body temperature, and sodium loss. Cortisol and sodium

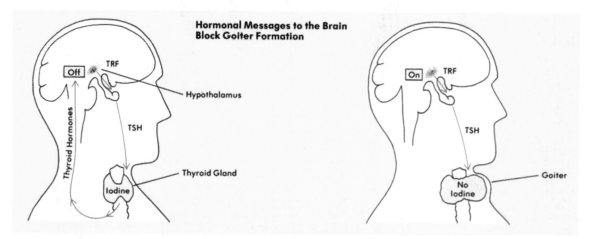

**Hormonal Messages to the Brain Block Goiter Formation**

*Feedback regulates hormone production in the thyroid. When the brain's hypothalamus releases TRF (thyrotropin-releasing factor), the anterior pituitary gland releases TSH. In turn, TSH prompts the thyroid to make its own hormones. When enough thyroid hormones get to the brain, it stops releasing TRF. But without enough iodine, the thyroid does not make enough hormones. Hence, the hypothalamus is not "turned off." The overtaxed cells of the thyroid then form a bulging neck goiter.*

chloride are used to treat it. An overactive adrenal cortex in women, however, results in hirsutism, an excess of body hair.

The adrenal medulla produces epinephrine (adrenaline) and norepinephrine (noradrenaline). Epinephrine triggers the body responses needed when a person experiences fear, shock, cold, or fatigue. Both hormones raise blood pressure and heartbeat. Under their influence, glycogen in the body is converted to glucose for additional energy.

**Hormones and Reproduction**

The hormones that guide reproductive processes come from the anterior pituitary and the gonads. During pregnancy, the placenta also makes hormones.

The sex and the form of a developing fetus are affected by events that take place in the woman's womb. Even though a fetus's sex is determined genetically, the proper hormones must be available for the fetus to develop the appropriate sex organs. Its gonads are fairly inactive at birth, but gradual changes take place each day for years until puberty. Then, changes in the pattern of FSH and ICSH stimulate the gonads to produce their hormones.

When FSH and ICSH act on the testes, sperm cells develop. Mature sperm usually form in boys by the age of 16. Testosterone, the major male hormone, plays a part in sperm formation. It also affects male secondary sexual characteristics and development of the male accessory sex organs—the prostate gland and the seminal vesicles. When FSH and ICSH act on an ovary, an egg develops in an ovarian follicle. Under the influence of FSH and then ICSH, the follicle ripens until it bursts and releases an egg. The egg then moves down one of the two oviducts for possible fertilization by a sperm. Meanwhile, the ruptured follicle changes into a corpus luteum. This tiny structure then produces progesterone, a steroid hormone needed for

maintaining pregnancy. If fertilization does not occur, the corpus luteum degenerates.

Progesterone and estrogen are the female sex hormones. They control the secondary sexual characteristics, such as body form and voice pitch, as well as development of the uterus, vagina, and other female accessory sex organs. They are also responsible for the monthly female "period," or menstrual cycle. Although irregularities occur, about once a month in the female body estrogen and then progesterone build up and maintain the uterine lining in preparation for pregnancy. If the egg released in about mid-cycle is not fertilized, the uterine lining is sloughed off, menstruation occurs, and the cycle begins again. This cycle continues until menopause, when the ovaries no longer function. If fertilization occurs, however, the built-up lining is retained. Estrogen and progesterone then prepare a place in the uterine wall where the fertilized egg can lodge and develop into a fetus. The placenta develops and starts to produce hormones. As the fetus grows, prolactin from the woman's pituitary prepares her breasts for milk production and flow.

**Feedback Control of Hormone Secretion**

The pituitary gland coordinates the activity of the endocrine glands to ensure a hormone balance. A regulatory feedback control system—a push-pull type of operation—controls pituitary output. For example, the pituitary hormones FSH and ICSH act on the gonads to produce their respective steroid hormones. When the concentration of these steroids reaches a certain level in the blood, they act on the pituitary to cut off any further supply of FSH and ICSH. As soon as the gonadal hormone level falls, FSH and ICSH output is automatically turned on again. The brain plays a key part in the feedback operation. It produces chemical compounds that signal the pituitary to secrete hormones. The gonadal hormones, for example, work by stimulating the brain to either inhibit or activate production of releasing factors. The nervous and endocrine systems become integrated through this process. As a result, the body is assured of a balance of necessary hormones. Brain-thyroid and brain-adrenal feedback systems also exist (*see* Biofeedback).

According to the receptor theory of hormone selectivity, hormone-sensitive tissues have a trapping mechanism, or receptor, that picks up a needed hormone as blood flows through the tissue. Receptors exist for steroid, polypeptide, and protein hormones. Once the receptor traps a hormone from the blood, it initiates the production of second messengers, including cAMP (cyclic adenosine monophosphate), and cGMP (cyclic guanosine monophosphate). The second messengers regulate intracellular and cell-to-cell reactions.

### Commercial and Medical Uses of Hormones

Doctors can correct hormone deficiencies by giving their patients the needed hormones. Hypopituitary patients suffering from dwarfism, for example, are given HGH. Diabetics receive insulin.

Oral contraception, one method of birth control, combines the use of natural ovarian hormones with slightly modified synthetic ones. Birth control pills use estrogen and progesterone to inhibit ovulation and thus prevent pregnancy. (*See also* Birth Control.)

Sometimes a couple cannot have children because the woman's ovaries are malfunctioning or the man's testes cannot produce sperm. These problems may be corrected with FSH and ICSH from human pituitaries. Human chorionic gonadotropin, a hormone produced solely by the placenta, has also been used. Hormone therapy for female infertility, however, has sometimes led to overstimulation of the ovaries and thus to multiple births (*See also* Fertility and Infertility; Multiple Birth.)

Estrogen may be given to postmenopausal women to prevent or treat osteoporosis, a bone disorder marked by a decrease in bone mass and a higher risk of bone fractures. Estrogen supplements may also be used to relieve the discomforts of menopause and to treat ovarian disease and certain other conditions. The application of estrogen is declining, however, because it has been linked with a number of serious health risks, including several forms of cancer and tumors.

By analyzing the chemical structures of natural hormones, scientists are able to synthesize artificial substitutes to meet a growing medical demand. Steroid hormones are not as hard to synthesize as are the more complex polypeptide and protein hormones. However, advances led to the laboratory synthesis of ACTH, insulin, thyrocalcitonin, oxytocin, and vasopressin. Polypeptide and protein hormones are made up of amino acids that must be strung together in a particular order. At first scientists made hormones by building up the components several pieces at a time and finally linking them in order. Later, the solid-phase method was devised. In this procedure, the hormone's tail-end amino acid is attached to a resin or other substance and then the amino-acid sequence is hooked up in reverse order until the head end of the hormone molecule is reached. In the final step, the completed chain is freed from the resin matrix. This technique can be automated. Thus a great deal of synthetic hormone can be made at a fast rate. Recombinant DNA methods have led to great advances in the manufacture of such proteins as insulin and HGH.

Recombinant DNA also has been used in the food industry. In the late 20th century scientists found that bovine growth hormone, or bovine somatotropin (BST), injected into cattle greatly increased milk and meat production. The United States Food and Drug Administration in 1993 approved the use of bioengineered BST in cattle intended for human consumption. The decision was endorsed by many medical and health organizations, but it was opposed by consumer, environmental, and animal-rights groups. The concerns of these groups ranged from food safety to the effects of synthetic hormones on the animals themselves. Use of growth hormones, whether synthetically or naturally derived, in food animals is banned in Canada and the European Union. (*See also* Biochemistry; Disease, Human; Drugs; Organic Chemistry; Steroids.)

**HORN** *see* **WIND INSTRUMENTS.**

**HORNET** *see* **WASP.**

**HORNEY, Karen** (1885–1952). The German-born psychoanalyst Karen Horney stressed social and environmental factors as determining individual personality traits and causing neuroses and personality disorders. In this she departed from the approach of Sigmund Freud, objecting to his concepts of libido, death instinct, and penis envy.

Horney was born Karen Danielsen in Hamburg, Germany, on Sept. 16, 1885. She received her medical degree from the University of Berlin in 1912 and trained in psychoanalysis with an associate of Freud named Karl Abraham. From 1915 to 1920 she did outpatient and clinical work at Berlin hospitals, and for the next 12 years she held a private practice and taught at the Berlin Psychoanalytic Institute.

After coming to the United States in 1932 she became associate director of the Chicago Institute for Psychoanalysis. She moved to New York City in 1934 to teach at the New School for Social Research and returned to private practice. She died in New York City on Dec. 4, 1952.

In her early books, 'The Neurotic Personality of Our Time' (1937) and 'New Ways in Psychoanalysis' (1939), Horney argued that Freud's idea of penis envy treated female psychology as an offshoot of male psychology. She also believed that the infant's basic anxiety regarding isolation and helplessness was a main cause of later neurosis. The ways in which a child copes with anxiety eventually can give rise to persistent and irrational needs. Two of her later books were 'Our Inner Conflicts' (1945) and 'Neurosis and Human Growth' (1950).

**HOROWITZ, Vladimir** (1903–89). In 1986 the Russian-born concert pianist Vladimir Horowitz capped a career of more than 60 years with a triumphant return to the concert stage in his native land. He had made his debut in Khar'kov, Ukraine, in 1922. Throughout his highly paid career Horowitz was noted for his technique, his almost orchestral sound, and his dynamic range.

Horowitz was born in Berdichev, Russia, on Oct. 1, 1903. Trained at the conservatory at Kiev, he became an accomplished pianist but preferred composing his own music to performing. After his family lost most of its possessions in the Russian Revolution, he began giving piano recitals in exchange for food and clothing. His success as a pianist in the new Soviet Union was assured by a series of 23 recitals in Leningrad in 1924. In these he performed a total of more than 200 works. In 1925 he went on a concert tour of Europe. He made his American debut in 1928. In 1933 he married the daughter of conductor Arturo Toscanini. Seven years later, after the outbreak of World War II in Europe, they settled in the United States, and in 1944 he became a United States citizen. He was awarded the Medal of Freedom in 1986.

Although he abandoned the concert stage four times (1936–38, 1953–65, 1968–74, and 1983–85), Horowitz continued making records. Always an electrifying showman, he was also featured in a film documentary entitled 'Vladimir Horowitz: the Last Romantic'. His last public performances were in Europe in 1987. He died in New York City on Nov. 5, 1989.

**HORROR STORY.** "During the whole of a dull, dark and soundless day in the autumn of the year, when the clouds hung oppressively low in the heavens, I had been passing alone, on horseback, through a singularly dreary tract of country; and at length found myself, as the shades of the evening drew on, within view of the melancholy House of Usher." Thus Edgar Allan Poe opened his story of "The Fall of the House of Usher" in 1839. In this beautifully crafted sentence he captured so much that is essential to the horror story—darkness, ominous solitude, foreboding calm, apprehension and uncertainty, and a deep feeling of melancholy that could soon turn to fear.

Many kinds of fiction are self-explanatory: mysteries, Westerns, love stories, spy thrillers, and science fiction define themselves by the terms used to name them. The horror story is less easily defined, perhaps because other types of fiction so often use the trappings of terror to enhance their plots. Charles Dickens used the vehicle of an old-fashioned ghost story to tell 'A Christmas Carol', but that book is not a horror story. Nor does a Grimm brothers fairy tale such as "Hänsel and Gretel," with its child-devouring witch, belong to the genre.

The nature of the horror story is best indicated by the title of the 1990s television series Tales from the Darkside. Human beings have always acknowledged that there is evil in the world and a dark side to human nature that cannot be explained except perhaps in religious terms. This evil may be imagined as having an almost unlimited power to inspire anxiety, fear, dread, and terror in addition to doing actual physical and mental harm.

In the tale of horror quite ordinary people are confronted by something unknown and fearful, which can be neither understood nor explained in reasonable terms. It is the emphasis on the unreasonable that lies at the heart of horror stories.

This kind of literature arose in the 18th century at the start of a movement called Romanticism. The movement was a reaction against a rational, ordered world in which humanity was basically good and everything could be explained scientifically. The literary type that inspired the horror story is Gothic fiction, tales of evil, often set in sinister medieval surroundings (see Gothic Fiction). This original kind of horror fiction has persisted to the present. An early 20th-century master of the type was H.P. Lovecraft, most of whose stories appeared in the magazine Weird Tales. A more recent writer was Stephen King, author of 'Carrie' (1974), 'The Shining' (1977), 'Pet Sematary' (1984), 'Misery' (1987), and 'Rose Madder' (1995) ( see King, Stephen).

**Vampires and werewolves.** Much horror literature is grounded in superstition, fear of demons, and the dread of death. No single tale brings all of these elements together so well as the vampire legend, an ancient folk superstition (see Folklore). The vampire is described as "undead," an entombed individual who rises each night to feed on the blood of the living. In literature its best representation is 'Dracula' (1897) by Bram Stoker. The legend was retold in 'Interview with the Vampire' (1976) by Anne Rice. The Dracula story was eagerly taken up by Hollywood in the 1931 film that starred Bela Lugosi, and numerous movies on the theme have been made since.

Similar to the vampire legend is the story of the werewolf, the human being under a curse who turns into a half man, half wolf—presumably when the moon is full. This creature prowls around, devouring animals, people, or corpses, but he returns to human form by day. As with Dracula, the werewolf became a popular subject for movies, beginning with 'The Werewolf of London' (1935) and the 'Wolfman' films of the 1940s. According to one superstition the werewolf, after being killed, turns into a vampire.

The belief that the dead can return to haunt and harm the living has long been an element of fiction. Ghost stories are at least as old as the Bible: in the Old Testament, King Saul calls up the ghost of Samuel to foretell the outcome of a battle. In Shakespeare's 'Hamlet', the ghost of the slain king provides the information from which Hamlet plots revenge for his father's murder. One of the masters of the modern ghost story was Ambrose Bierce, some of whose stories were collected in 'Ghost and Horror Stories of Ambrose Bierce' (1964). A variation on the ghost theme is the haunted house, about which hundreds of stories have been written. The series of 'Amityville Horror' books by John G. Jones belongs in this category.

Culver Pictures, Inc.

*Lon Chaney, Jr. (left), played the lead in 'The Mummy's Tomb' (1942). The Chicago stage production of 'Little Shop of Horrors' (right), featured Gene Weygandt, left, and Malcolm Rothman.*

Between the vampires and the ghosts are creatures called the living dead and zombies who return from the grave to devour the living. Hollywood celebrated this story in 'Night of the Living Dead' (1968) and other films. In literature one of the best examples is the intriguing book 'The Beast with Five Fingers' (1928; film version 1946) by W.F. Harvey. It is the story of a severed hand that goes on living after its owner dies. The movie 'Friday the 13th' (1980) and its sequels also used the revived corpse as villain. In the 1986 film 'Trick or Treat', a dead rock music star is called back to life.

Stories about the devil and lesser demons date at least as far back as the Middle Ages, when the Christian church tried to instill fear in the hearts of believers about the consequences of sin. In 20th-century literature the devil plays a central role in William Blatty's novel 'The Exorcist' (1971) and in Ira Levin's novel of Satanism, 'Rosemary's Baby' (1967). Both were made into motion pictures. David Seltzer's 'The Omen' (1976) about a child-demon was originally a screenplay.

**Monsters,** human and not quite human, have long been popular with fans of horror fiction. Undoubtedly the favorite monster is that created by Victor Frankenstein in Mary Shelley's novel 'Frankenstein' (1818). Hollywood discovered Frankenstein in 1931 with the classic film starring Boris Karloff. The movie version and its sequels are in striking contrast to Shelley's intent, because she tells a moral tale about rejection and suffering. The monster is inherently good until spurned by the rest of humanity.

A more genuine monster novel is Robert Louis Stevenson's 'Strange Case of Dr. Jekyll and Mr. Hyde' (1886) in which a physician, through drinking a self-concocted potion, becomes a monster. In 'The Phantom of the Opera' the monster is entirely human, wearing a mask to hide his deformed features. The first movie version in 1925 starred Lon Chaney, Sr. It was

remade in 1943 and 1961, and in 1986 it became a stage production in London, England.

Another variety of monster, the animal-like creature with a human mind, was created primarily for films. 'Godzilla' (1956) in Japan and 'The Fly' (1958, 1986) in the United States are examples. A science-fiction adaptation of the monster theme appears in 'Alien' (1979) and its 1986 sequel.

Many stories do not require monsters of any kind—only depraved human beings. One of the earliest films of this type is 'Freaks' (1932). The movie 'Night of the Hunter' (1955) is thoroughly frightening without the use of legendary creatures, as is 'Halloween' (1978) and its sequels. 'Magic' (1978) uses a ventriloquist's dummy as the killer in a psychological horror story.

**Television.** The possibilities that are open to the writer of horror stories are limited only by the imagination. Television has presented a number of series in which every facet of horror and mystery were explored. Best known to viewers are Alfred Hitchcock Presents (1955–62; changed to The Alfred Hitchcock Hour, 1962–64; and revived in 1985); Rod Serling's two programs The Twilight Zone (1959–65; revived in 1985) and Night Gallery (1970–73); and Boris Karloff's Thriller (1960–62). Other popular television series were Ghost Story, hosted by Sebastian Cabot; Lights Out (originally a radio series by Arch Obler); The Invaders; One Step Beyond (later, Next Step Beyond); Outer Limits; and Tales of the Unexpected. British television presented Mystery and Imagination and The Hammer House of Horror.

The use of horror as a comedy vehicle was tried in the cult movie 'Rocky Horror Picture Show' (1975); the film and stage play 'Little Shop of Horrors' (film 1960, 1986; play 1982), about a man-eating plant; such slapstick movies as 'Abbott and Costello Meet Frankenstein' (1947); and the vampire spoof 'Love at First Bite' (1979). Comedy-horror shows on television were The Munsters and The Addams Family.

# HORSE

*Imperiously he leaps, he neighs, he bounds, . . .*
*His ears up-prick'd; his braided hanging mane*
*Upon his compass'd crest now stand on end;*
*His nostrils drink the air, and forth again,*
*As from a furnace, vapours doth he send; . . .*
*Sometimes he trots, as if he told the steps,*
*With gentle majesty and modest pride;*
*Anon he rears upright, curvets, and leaps,*
*As who should say, "Lo, thus my strength is tried."*

             *William Shakespeare: 'Venus and Adonis'*

. . . . . . . . . . . . . . . . . . . . . . . . . . . . . . . . . . . . . . . . . .

*Contributors for this article include Margaret Cabell Self, author of 'The Horseman's Encyclopedia' and many other books about horses and horsemanship, and Albert M. Lane, Livestock Specialist, University of Arizona School of Agriculture. The section "Evolution of the Horse" was critically reviewed by George Gaylord Simpson, Late Professor of Geology, University of Arizona. The horse breed illustrations, done by Harry Michaels, were especially commissioned for Compton's Encyclopedia.*

Of all the animals, the horse has probably most closely shared in human adventures and has been most intimately allied with human progress. For thousands of years, the horse has participated in the pleasures, the dangers, and the hard work that have marked human life. Perhaps because of this long relationship, the horse holds a special place in mankind's affection.

No one knows exactly when people and horses first became companions. Some historians believe that probably people hunted early horses as they did other game animals. Drawings, engravings, and sculptures of horses that date back many thousands of years may have been made by hunters and medicine men as offerings to the gods for a good hunt. Then perhaps people recognized the advantage of the horse's fleetness, tamed the horse, and used it to pursue other animals for food. When food became scarce in one area, the horse helped people move and settle in other areas that were more productive.

Gradually people found more and more uses for the horse and became increasingly dependent upon it. As this dependence grew, the horse became a partner in human life. It shared the dangers of war, the satisfactions of peace, the pomp and splendors of knighthood, and the sufferings and privations of exploring and settling new lands and wresting a living from the soil. The horse also made possible many pleasures. It carried people in hunting fields, in polo matches, and in races. It drew the wagons for circuses and traveling players, then often performed in the acts they presented. Pride in this magnificent beast has prompted people to show it off in horse shows, and admiration for the animal's beauty and grace have inspired its portrayal in art and literature.

Until the early 1900s the horse was an integral part of everyday life. Then machines began to perform many of the jobs that horses had done, and the population of horses—especially in Europe and North America—dropped drastically. For example, in 1915 there were more than 21 million horses in the United States, but by 1955 their number had dropped to only a little more than 3 million. Although no census has been taken since the late 1950s, a special survey published in 1966 indicated that there had been a great increase in the population of light horses. It is conjectured that this increase results from the growing interest in riding for pleasure and in breeding fine horses.

### THE ANATOMY OF THE HORSE

The horse is a beautiful and utilitarian beast. Both its beauty and its utility result from the relationship among all its body parts in form and in function. The general shape and appearance of a horse is called conformation. Conformation includes the form and proportion of various parts of the animal's body and the way they fit together to give overall balance and structural smoothness. Thus balance or proportion of the horse's body is important because each part has a functional relationship to the rest of the parts.

Although breeders have developed horses of many different colors, sizes, and special attributes, all of the animals have a "horselike" appearance. In general, the horse is a relatively large animal that weighs about 1,000 pounds or more. It stands about 5½ feet high at the shoulder and is about 9 feet long from the tip of its nose to its tail. It has a long, muscular neck; a large chest; a rather straight back; and powerful hindquarters. Its legs are strong and comparatively slender. In motion, the hind legs provide the propelling force and the front legs act primarily as supports.

---

**Scientific Classification**

**Phylum:** Chordata      **Family:** Equidae
**Subphylum:** Vertebrata     **Genus:** *Equus*
**Class:** Mammalia     **Species:** *E. caballus*
**Order:** Perissodactyla

Horses are in the order of odd-toed hoofed animals, Perissodactyla, and belong to the horse family, Equidae. All modern horses are genus *Equus*, species *E. caballus*. For information about other members of the horse family, *see* the articles Ass and Zebra.

---

### PREVIEW

*The article Horse is divided into the following sections and subsections:*

## Horse Terms

**aid.** The signal or command given to a horse by the rider indicating what the horse is to do. **Natural aids** are conveyed by the rider's hands, legs, voice, back, and weight distribution. **Artificial aids** include spurs, whip, and martingale.

**bit.** The metal part of the bridle that fits into the horse's mouth under the tongue. The reins are attached to it.

**cadence.** The rhythm of a horse's gait. Each gait has its own beat. The walk, for example, is a slow one-two-three-four; the trot, a fast one-two, one-two.

**cold blood.** All horses are considered to have cold blood except Thoroughbreds and Arabian breeds. The phrase implies that the horse is unexcitable, a calm and phlegmatic type.

**collection.** The gathering together by the horse of all its forces to be ready to move at any gait in any direction immediately upon demand of the rider. All gaits have an extended and collected form. Collected gaits—such as the slow canter—give the horse more elevation but less forward movement.

**colt.** A male horse between the age of weaning and 4 years old.

**dressage.** Specially designed training and exercises that make the horse supple, collected, balanced, and responsive to aids.

**filly.** A female horse between the age of weaning and 4 years old.

**foal.** A male or female horse between birth and weaning. Used as a verb, the word means "to give birth."

**gait.** The way and sequence in which a horse places its feet on the ground to obtain forward motion.

**gelding.** An altered male horse.

**hand.** The scale of measurement for a horse's height. Height is measured from the highest point of the withers to the ground. A hand is equal to 4 inches, and fractions of a hand are given in inches. In the figure 15.2 hands, for example, the horse is 15 hands or 60 inches high, plus 2 inches, or a total of 62 inches.

**haute école.** The "high school" of horse training; the special training in performing difficult movements especially as practiced by the Lipizzan horses and riders at the Spanish Riding School in Vienna.

**hot blood.** All Thoroughbreds and Arabian breeds are considered to have hot blood. The phrase implies that the horse is spirited and eager and has a delicate head and fine coat.

**mare.** A female horse that is more than 4 years old.

**mudder.** Horse that runs well on a wet, sloppy racetrack.

**seat.** The position of a horseman in the saddle. The position differs with the type of riding that is done and the type of horse that is ridden.

**stallion.** An unaltered male horse that is more than 4 years old.

**tack.** Stable gear. Tack, derived from tackle, includes all the horse's equipment for riding—such as saddle, bridle, and halter.

**tack-up.** To saddle and bridle a horse.

**yearling.** A young male or female horse during the year between its first and second birthdays.

## Famous Horses

**Black Beauty.** The horse that is the main character in a book of the same name written by Anna Sewell to call attention to common abuses of the animal in the 19th century.

**Bucephalus.** The favorite mount of Alexander the Great during his Asian conquests, and in whose honor Alexander named a city in Persia.

**Bulle Rock.** First thoroughbred to be imported from England to America (1730).

**Byerly Turk.** One of the three stallions on which the Thoroughbred line of racehorses was founded.

**Ching Chui.** One of the six famous war-horses of the Chinese Emperor T'ai Tsung, who died in AD 637. His tomb was decorated with statues of his war-horses, and a poem commemorated the victorious battle in which each took part.

**Copenhagen.** The favorite mount of the Duke of Wellington, who rode this famous charger in the battle of Waterloo.

**Darley Arabian.** One of the three stallions on which the Thoroughbred line of racehorses was founded.

**Flicka.** A main character in the well-known novel 'My Friend Flicka' by Mary O'Hara.

**Godolphin Barb**, or **Godolphin Arabian.** One of the three stallions on which the Thoroughbred line of horses was founded.

**Iroquois.** The first American-bred horse to win the English Derby.

**Justin Morgan.** Foundation sire of the Morgan breed, one of the best-known breeds of road horse in America.

**Marengo.** The favorite mount of Napoleon, on which the emperor was mounted at Waterloo.

**Nelson.** General George Washington's charger, which was present at Valley Forge and Yorktown and remained with the first president at Mount Vernon.

**Pegasus.** The winged horse of Greek mythology who carried the thunderbolt of Zeus and for whom a constellation is named.

**Rakush.** The mount of Rustam, the chief hero of the Persian epic poem 'Shah Namah', or Book of Kings, in which Rakush was reputed to be the best warhorse in the world and largely responsible for his master's successful exploits.

**Rosinante.** The ugly horse that carried Don Quixote on his bumbling adventures in Cervantes' tale 'Don Quixote'.

**Sleepy Tom.** Although blind, this horse became the outstanding pacer of the world, racing at top speed with only the voice and signals of his trainer as guides.

**Sultan.** Sometimes called Ivan, this horse was the favorite mount of William Cody (Buffalo Bill) and was often used in his Wild West shows.

**Traveller.** The favorite mount and almost inseparable companion of Gen. Robert E. Lee. Traveller was with Lee from Appomattox to Richmond and went with him to Lexington when Lee became president of Washington College there.

**Trojan Horse.** The huge wooden horse in whose hollow body Greek soldiers hid to gain entry into the city of Troy to conquer it. The story is told in Homer's 'Iliad'.

## The Horse's Head and Body

The horse's head and neck make up about two fifths of the total length of the animal. The head is held naturally at about a 45 degree angle to the neck. The head and neck act as a counterbalance as the center of gravity shifts when the animal is in motion.

The ears are proportionate to the head, neither too small nor so large that they look mulish. They are held upright and turned forward when the horse is alert. The horse can move his ears freely to pick up sounds from various directions.

The eyes are larger than those of any other land animal, and the horse has excellent long-range vision both at night and in the daytime. Each eye can see things above and below, behind as well as in front. A horse's eyes see things separately. An object may be seen first with one eye, then with the other. Stationary objects, especially small ones, seen in this way seem to jump, and the horse may become frightened. Sometimes to keep the animal from being startled horsemen put pads called blinders, or blinkers, near the horse's eyes to limit vision.

The nose has wide, flaring nostrils. A horse must get all its air through its nasal passages. It does not get extra breath through its mouth as do cows, dogs, sheep, and many other kinds of domestic animals. Even on a very hot day, or when the horse has been racing or working hard, it never pants with its tongue out. The reason for this probably is that a horse's soft palate forms a musclelike curtain that separates the mouth cavity from the breathing passages except when the horse is swallowing.

The horse has large jaws, and the teeth are large and strong. A mature male horse has 40 teeth, a mature female has 36. The front teeth, or incisors, are separated from the rear teeth, molars or grinders, by a wide and sensitive space, or bar. The bar forms the space into which the bit fits. Male horses also have two extra teeth called tushes. Horsemen examine a horse's teeth to estimate the animal's age. The teeth grow longer and at a more oblique angle with age, and the surfaces wear away.

The horse's body is large and sleek. The wide chest contains the huge lungs and heart that are necessary equipment for an animal that must have great endurance for running or enormous power for pulling loads. The back is strong, well muscled, and rigid enough to provide the legs with freedom to move easily. A back that curves downward at the center is called swayback; one that curves upward is called roach, or hog, back.

## The Horse's Legs and Feet

The legs are long, strong, and comparatively slender. The front legs support weight, help maintain body balance and stability, and contribute to the forward movement of the animal. The part of the leg called the knee by horsemen is comparable to the wrist joint in man. The hind legs are heavily muscled to provide the propelling force in running and the pushing force for

---

*DO YOU KNOW*

1. Why does a horse not pant even after a long race on a hot day?
2. Why do some horses wear "blinders"?
3. How can a horse's age be judged?

pulling a heavy load. The central point for these forces lies in the hock joint, and this joint bears the burden for all forward movement. It is comparable to the ankle joint in man.

A horse's foot is really a single toe, and the hoof is a thick toenail. The tip of the toe bone fits within the hoof, and the heel angles upward. The bone is so porous that it looks somewhat like pumice stone. The toe bone and two other bones make up the horse's foot. All fit within and are protected by the hoof.

The hoof is a boxlike part made up of the same kind of material as that in a man's fingernail. The part of the hoof that we see when the horse's feet are on the ground is the wall. The wall protects the front and sides of the foot. It is longest and thickest in the front and decreases toward the back of the foot. Horseshoes are put on the underpart of the wall to help protect it from extensive wear. The shoes must be changed and the hoofs trimmed once a month. A hoof grows about one-third inch in four weeks.

When the horse's foot is raised, the sole and the frog can be seen. The sole covers most of the undersurface of the foot and is arched to protect the bones and soft parts of the foot above it. The frog is a soft elastic section shaped like a triangle with its base at the heel and its apex pointing forward. It is a shock absorber, cushioning the jarring impact that occurs every time the animal's foot comes in contact with the ground.

## A HORSE'S LIFE HISTORY

Foals may be born at any time of the year. But many horse breeders prefer that birth take place in the springtime. Foals born in winter need more stable room as well as more food and care than do those born in milder weather. Foals born in spring can roam outdoors and nibble grass to supplement their diet. No matter what time of the year a foal is born, however, its first birthday is recorded as being the first day of January after its birth. So, New Year's Day is the official birthday of every horse.

### The Birth of a Foal

The gestation period—the length of time a mare carries the foal inside her body—is usually 11 to 12 months. The actual birth process takes only a short time—usually about 15 to 30 minutes. Normally a foal is born with its front feet first. One leg is extended; the other leg is slightly bent; and the head is thrust between the two legs. The newborn foal rests quietly for about 10 or 15 minutes, then tries to get up and is soon able to stand. Within a few hours after birth the foal is able to frisk about quite well on its gangly legs.

## The Parts of a Horse

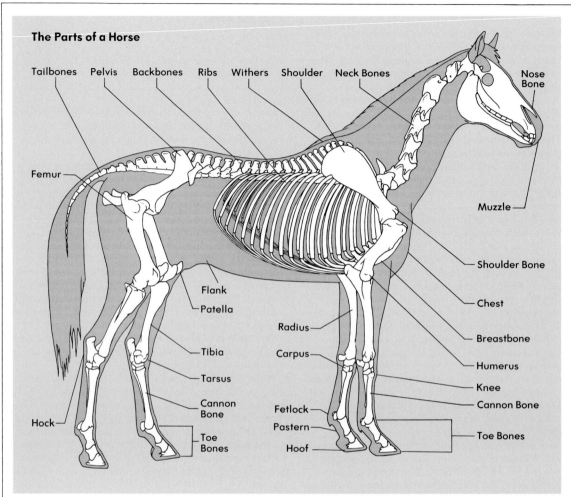

Tailbones    Pelvis    Backbones    Ribs    Withers    Shoulder    Neck Bones

Nose Bone

Femur

Muzzle

Flank

Patella

Shoulder Bone

Chest

Radius

Breastbone

Tibia

Carpus

Humerus

Tarsus

Knee

Cannon Bone

Cannon Bone

Hock

Fetlock

Pastern

Toe Bones

Toe Bones

Hoof

### Teeth of a Horse

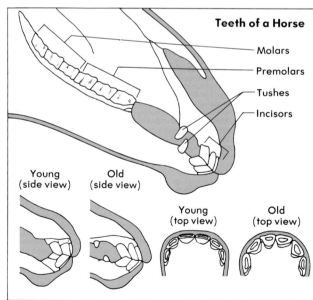

Molars

Premolars

Tushes

Incisors

Young (side view)    Old (side view)    Young (top view)    Old (top view)

### Foot of a Horse

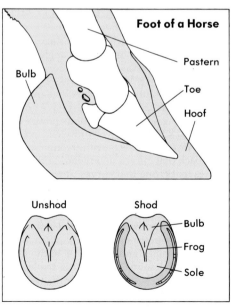

Pastern

Bulb

Toe

Hoof

Unshod    Shod

Bulb

Frog

Sole

*The foal lying next to its mother is only a few minutes old. Foals are born with their eyes open and with a full coat of hair. Both the mother and the newborn foal rest for a little while after the birth, but soon get up and move about.*

The legs of a newborn foal are almost as long as those of the mare, and grow only slightly during the horse's lifetime. The rest of the animal's body develops and the muscles of the legs become large and strong, but the big bones of the legs remain about the same size. Though it usually has grown to full height several years before, a horse is considered to be mature at seven years of age.

### The Young Horse

A newborn foal begins to nurse as soon as it can stand up after birth. For the first six months of its life it depends mostly on the mare's milk and on grain supplied by its owner for nourishment. It begins to supplement its diet by nibbling grass and clover, sometimes spreading its long legs wide somewhat like a giraffe. By the time the foal is six months old, it has grown enough to make grazing easier. Then it is weaned, or taken away from the mare. The process of weaning is begun by moving the mare to a new stall, away from the foal, so that the separation is final. If

> **DO YOU KNOW**
>
> 1. When is the official birthday of a horse?
> 2. How soon after birth can a foal walk?
> 3. At what age does a horse's training begin?

the foal sees, hears, or smells the mare again, the process must be started over.

Within a week or ten days after birth, a foal has two upper and two lower incisor teeth. At a year old, it has six upper teeth and six lower ones. All of these are milk teeth, much shorter and smaller than the permanent ones. The horse begins to get its permanent teeth when it is about 2½ years old, but does not have all of them until it is about five years old. It is then said to have a "full mouth."

### The Training of a Horse

A horse's training begins almost immediately after it is born. Trainers handle the foal and brush its thick, fuzzy coat frequently. By the time the animal is a

*Przewalski's horse (top) is the only kind of true wild horse that survived into the 1900s. It was believed to be extinct in the wild, but small herds of these horses have been sighted in remote areas of Mongolia. The tarpan (bottom), a wild horse of southern Russia, became extinct in the middle 1800s. In a unique experiment, scientists bred horses with tarpan characteristics and in a kind of backward evolution developed a breed of tarpan.*

month old, it has learned to wear a halter. As a yearling, it learns to respond to reins, and at two years old it is saddle-trained. When it is three, the colt begins specialized training for whatever career has been chosen for it—perhaps as a riding horse, polo horse, circus horse, or racehorse. But usually it is not required to do exhaustive work until it is about five years old.

One year of a horse's life is equal to about three years of a man's life. Seven years of a horse's life would be comparable to 21 years in a man's life. Horses cease to be useful for most kinds of work when they are about 23 or 24 years old, though they still may be able to do certain kinds of light work. The life span of a horse is considered to be 25 to 30 years, but some horses may live to be 40 or more.

## THE HORSE BREEDS

The animal we know today as the horse is the result of centuries of selective breeding. By careful selection breeders throughout history have developed various kinds of horses with a wide variety of characteristics to suit many different needs. The Great Horse of the Middle Ages, for example, was bred for size and strength to carry a heavily armored knight and his weapons into battle. The massive horses of such breeds are often called "cold blooded." The Arabs bred lithe desert horses that were small and swift. These animals are often referred to as "hot blooded." Cross-breeding of hot blooded and cold blooded

### Horse Breeds

| Ponies (Weight range 450–850 lbs) | Height Range (in hands) | Color Range | Light Horses (Weight range 800–1,300 lbs) | Height Range (in hands) | Color Range |
|---|---|---|---|---|---|
| Hackney | 14.2 or under | Black, brown, bay, chestnut | American Saddle Horse | 15.0–16.0 | Black, bay, chestnut, gray |
| Shetland | 11.2 or under | Any solid color or pinto | Hackney | 14.2–16.0 | Black, brown, bay, chestnut |
| Welsh | 11.0–14.0 | Any solid color | Appaloosa | 14.0–15.2 | Distinctive patterned spotting |
| **Heavy Horses (Weight range 1,350–2,200 lbs)** | | | Standardbred | 15.0–16.2 | Most solid colors |
| | | | Arabian | 14.1–15.1 | All solid colors |
| | | | Palomino | 14.0–17.0 | Golden |
| | | | Mustang | 13.2–15.0 | Any color |
| Belgian | 15.3–17.0 | Chestnut, roan | Morgan | 14.1–15.1 | Bay, chestnut |
| Cleveland Bay | 16.0–17.0 | Bay | Lipizzan | 15.1–16.1 | Gray (white), chestnut, bay, roan |
| Percheron | 16.0–17.0 | Gray, black | | | |
| Clydesdale | 16.0–16.2 | Bay, brown | | | |
| Shire | 17.0–17.1 | Black, bay, brown, roan, gray | Tennessee Walking Horse | 15.0–16.0 | Any solid color |
| German Coach | 15.2–16.3 | Black | Quarter Horse | 14.3–15.1 | Any solid color |
| Suffolk | 15.2–16.2 | Chestnut | Thoroughbred | 15.0–16.0 | Any solid color |

**Hackney Pony**

**Shetland Pony**

**Welsh Pony**

**Belgian**

Cleveland Bay

Percheron

Clydesdale

Shire

German Coach

Suffolk

**American Saddle Horse**

**Hackney**

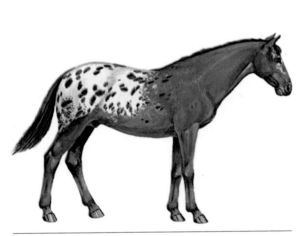

**Appaloosa**

**Standardbred**

**Arabian**

**Mustang**

**Palomino**

**Morgan**

**Lippizaner**

**Tennessee Walking Horse**

**Quarter Horse**

**Thoroughbred**

star

stripe

blaze

snip

*The color of a horse's coat and the animal's markings are often used in descriptions. Some of the coat colors are shown in the drawings at the left, and some of the face markings are shown in the drawings above. Markings may also appear on the legs. A horse keeps its markings for life, and they are often used as a means for identification.*

*The colors shown above in column one, from top to bottom, are: dappled gray, dun, brown. In column two the colors are, top to bottom: strawberry roan, chestnut, and skewbald, a type of Pinto horse. In column three, top to bottom, the colors are: palomino, bay, and black.*

horses for certain characteristics produced breeds ranging from riding horses to draft horses.

The Thoroughbred is considered by many to be the highpoint of elegance and fine selective breeding. Many persons mistakenly apply the name Thoroughbred to any purebred horse. But a Thoroughbred is a distinct breed of running horses that traces its ancestry through the male line directly back to three Eastern stallions: the Byerly Turk, the Darley Arabian, and the Godolphin Barb (or Godolphin Arabian). These horses had been imported into England before 1750 and were used by breeders to develop the famous Thoroughbred racing horse.

For convenience the breeds of horses are often divided into three major groups: (1) ponies, (2) heavy, or draft, horses, and (3) light horses. The color drawings on the following pages of this article show horses in these three groups.

### Color and Markings of the Horse

A person buying a horse for pleasure riding may choose the animal for the color and markings entirely according to individual taste. Horse breeders, however, consider color an important point in judging the value of a horse. Some breeds are required to have certain colors and patterns in order to be registered. Registries for such breeds as the Appaloosa and Pinto, for example, may not accept horses with undesirable colors or patterns.

Color is one of the most conspicuous features of a horse and is often the basis for description, such as bay, chestnut, or gray. These colors, however, differ somewhat from the usual conception of the color. Common colors used for horses include the following:

**Black.** All hairs are completely black, with no lighter color appearing.

**Brown.** All hairs are brown, but may be so dark they look black to most people. The true color shows in hairs around the nose and eyes or wherever the coat is thin.

**Bay.** Hairs may be brown but show auburn or red shades; mane, tail, and stockings are black.

**Chestnut.** Hairs are the same colors as the bay, but mane, tail, and stockings are the coat color or lighter.

**Dun.** Hairs are dull grayish-yellow or dull grayish-gold, but mane and tail are black.

Horses of many different breeds add to the enjoyment of leisure time. Children and adults thrill to the tricks of a circus horse, the strength of a rodeo horse, or the skill of a polo pony. Thoroughbreds, trotters, and jumpers provide entertainment for thousands of people. But perhaps the greatest pleasure a horse gives to people is when they are together on a quiet country lane.

Walter Chandoha

C.J. Bucher Publishers, Ltd.

Frank Verticchio

U.S. Trotting Association

Artstreet

Farrell Grehan—Photo Researchers

Ray Woolfe, Jr.

A Lipizzan horse (below) performs a spectacular courbette with ease and grace at the Spanish Riding School in Vienna, Austria. The horse's saddle and bridle are traditional, and the costume worn by the rider has remained almost unchanged for the last two hundred years. A troupe of Lipizzans (left) execute the measured paces of a quadrille at the Maple Leaf Gardens in Toronto, Ont. The meticulous precision of horses and riders as they move through the intricate patterns of the performance results from their rigorous training for perfection.
Photo Researchers; photos, (below) Jerry Cooke, (top) Thomas D. Lowes

**Gray.** Hairs are black or brown at birth, but lighten with age and may be almost white at maturity.

**Palomino.** Hairs are gold or yellow, but mane and tail are white.

**Roan.** Strawberry roans have a chestnut body color with white hairs interspersed. Blue roans have a black or brown body color with white hairs interspersed.

White face markings and leg markings may occur on horses of any coat color. The markings of the Appaloosa and Pinto horses, however, are distinctive. Appaloosa horses are often called "spotted horses." They may have light coat patterns with dark spots or dark coat patterns with light spots. Pinto or paint horses have coats with large, splashy patterns. Brown and white patterns are called skewbald, and black and white ones are piebald.

### The Lipizzan

Many people consider the Lipizzan, or Lipizzaner, the most beautiful of all horses, the royalty of the horse breeds. Anyone who sees these magnificent animals cannot help but be impressed by their grace and dignity.

Perhaps the best known horses in the world are the Lipizzans of the Spanish Riding School of Vienna. Here, perfectly trained horses perform difficult movements on and above the ground with the seemingly effortless grace of ballet dancers. These are not the artificial actions that are sometimes learned by horses for the circus or trick-riding rings. All the feats are based on the natural movements of a horse, those done by a playful horse frisking about in high spirits in an open

pasture. Years of careful training perfect each of the movements done by the Lipizzan.

"Lipizzan" is almost synonymous with "white horse" in the minds of many people, and it is true that those chosen for performance at the Spanish Riding School are white. But some Lipizzans may be chestnut, bay, or roan. Even the white horses are not born white. All are dark at birth and become white only at about the age of 4 years or as late as 10 years.

Lipizzans mature much more slowly than do other breeds of horses. For the first four years of the colt's life it runs free with the herd. Then a trainer, who has been specially trained, is chosen for the colt. He assumes complete responsibility for its care and training, and no one else is allowed to touch it.

Schooling for the Lipizzan begins with a two-year initial training period. Usually only stallions are chosen. For the first three months, horse and trainer work on the rudiments of discipline, and the horse learns to trust the trainer completely. Schooling for the remainder of the two years consists chiefly of exercises that keep the stallion flexible and supple. When the Lipizzan is 6 years old, training for performing figures begins. For the next two years the horse undergoes intensive individual schooling that will make him a star performer in the riding school. He will learn to balance perfectly on his hind legs in the levade, be stately in a cadenced quadrille, leap high above the ground in a courbette, and soar suspended in space in the capriole. For about the next 20 years, the Lipizzan's life consists almost entirely of practice and performance. When the horse can no longer perform in the show ring, he becomes an instructor, teaching fledgling riders who hope to become masters of this special art of horsemanship.

## THE GAITS OF THE HORSE

A horse's gait is the way in which the animal moves its legs and places its hoofs to obtain forward movement. There are various kinds of gaits. Each produces a different kind of ride for the horseman, and each may be used for a different purpose. Each gait also has a specific cadence or rhythmic beat. The cadence is the rhythm of the sound heard when the horse's hoofs strike the ground.

The horse has three natural gaits. These are the walk, the trot, and the gallop—all of which are illustrated and described in detail above. The canter, furthermore, is a collected or restrained form of the gallop. It gives greater "lift" but less forward motion to the horse than does the gallop. Other kinds of gaits are known as artificial gaits, which are usually variations of the natural gaits. Artificial gaits are obtained by selective breeding or by special training of certain breeds of horses.

The rack and the slow gait are artificial gaits. The slow gait has several forms including the fox trot, the broken pace, the running walk, and the amble. The rack is a fast gait.

Sometimes horsemen speak of five-gaited horses or three-gaited horses. Although many horses can be

taught to perform either gait, the American saddle horse and the Tennessee walking horse are exceptional at performing these gaits. The five-gaited American saddle horse can do a walk, a trot, a canter, one of the slow gaits, and a rack. The three-gaited Tennessee walking horse has a flat-footed walk, a running walk, and a slow canter.

These artificial gaits were developed by Southern planters in colonial times. They give a smoother ride for the horseman than either the trot or pace, and the rider can spend longer hours in the saddle. The rack is, however, tiring for the horse. A western horse's gaits include a walk, a slow gait, and a lope, which is a form of the canter.

## HORSEMANSHIP—THE ART OF RIDING

Almost everyone has seen at the movies or on television graceful riders on saddle horses cantering along bridle paths or cowboys seated with careless ease on mustangs loping off into the sunset. It looks quite easy. But in the art of riding, as in any other kind of art, it takes an enormous amount of practice and patience to become a master. The thrill of being a disciplined rider on a disciplined horse, however, is well worth the effort.

An observant movie and television viewer will have noted that the equipment of the horse on the bridle path was different from that of the mustang. The novice rider will need to know something about a horse's equipment before he can use it. A horse's gear is called tack, which includes the saddle and the bridle. It is possible to ride a horse without either saddle or bridle, and sometimes student riders are required to do this to develop balance and confidence. For most riding, however, gear is used.

The tack for riding includes, in addition to the saddle and bridle, a halter, lead shank (a rope with a clip on the end) and, if the climate is cold, a stable blanket. The purpose of tack is to provide the rider with a means by which he can control the horse and also to provide him with a seat on the horse's back.

There are basically two major classes of tack—English and western—and there are many varieties in each of the classes. Horsemen choose their tack carefully to suit the type of riding they do. The choice will also depend upon how the horse is trained.

### Some Types of Saddles

Many varieties of saddles have been developed, but all are built in basically the same way. The frame, often called the tree, of the saddle is made of wood, steel, or a combination of the two. The rigid frame is well padded and covered with leather. One or more wide straps called girths are attached. A girth passes under the horse's body and is fastened to the opposite side. A leather strap for the stirrup is suspended from each side of the saddle. The flap, a wide, flat piece of leather, hangs between the stirrup strap and the horse's side.

Saddles are contoured on the underside to fit a horse's back and on the top side to fit the rider's body. A saddle should be properly fitted to the horse so a

**THE WALK.** *The walk is a four-beat gait and the slowest of the three natural gaits of the horse. In this gait, both legs on one side move, then both legs on the other side move. The feet are lifted only a short distance and then usually are placed flat on the ground. The gait has an even cadence and gives a smooth ride with no feeling of jogging. The illustrations for this and the other gaits are keyed to show red for right legs and green for left. The hoof prints show the placement of the hoofs in each position.*

**THE TROT.** *The trot is a two-beat gait. In the trot, diagonal pairs of legs move: left front and right rear; right front and left rear. The feet are lifted a little higher than in the walk and come down with the tip of the hoof striking the ground first. The gait gives the rider a slight feeling of jogging. When the speed increases to a fast trot, the jogging also increases and the rider then posts, lifting himself slightly out of the saddle with each jog.*

**THE GALLOP.** *The gallop, the fastest of the horse's three natural gaits, is a three-beat gait. The first beat is made by a hind foot. The second beat is made by the other hind foot coming down at the same time as the front foot diagonally across from it. The third beat is made by the other front foot. Then a period of suspension occurs when all four feet are off the ground. The series begins again when the first hind foot strikes the ground again for the first beat. A slow, restrained gallop is called a canter.*

rider's weight is centered on the horse but not directly on the withers and the spine.

English saddles are often called flat saddles because they are so gently contoured that the rider's seat is almost flat. There are three basic types of flat saddles: (1) the forward seat or jumping saddle, (2) the modified forward saddle, and (3) the dressage saddle. The forward seat or jumping saddle has flaps that extend well forward over the horse's shoulders. This saddle is preferred by many riders for open jumping. In the modified forward saddle the flaps do not extend quite so far forward as they do on the jumping saddle. This saddle is used for ordinary riding, for jumping, and for hunting. The dressage saddle has a deeper seat than do the other saddles.

The western saddle has a deep seat, a high pommel from which the saddle horn rises, and a high, fanlike cantle. Rings and rawhide saddle strings are attached to hold a cowboy's equipment. There are several different types of western saddles including parade saddles,

cutting saddles, and roping saddles. Each is designed for the special use its name implies. Western saddles have little padding, so a heavy blanket or thick pad is usually placed under them.

### Bridles—The Horse's Headgear

The bridle includes all the equipment a horse wears on his head: the bits, curb chains, crownpiece and browband, cheekpiece, and reins. There are several different kinds of bridles.

English bridles are known by the type of bit used. The snaffle bit and the pelham bit are the most common. The snaffle is a simple, jointed bit that works on the corners of the horse's mouth. The pelham has two sets of rings for the reins and fits on the bars of the horse's mouth. Many horses used for hunting and jumping wear snaffle bridles with running martingales. The reins run through the martingale and the bit and act on the bars instead of on the corners of the mouth.

## English Saddle

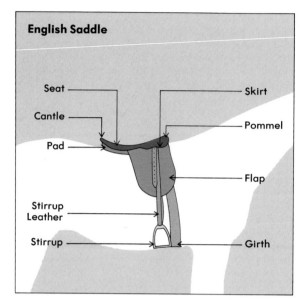

Seat — — Skirt

Cantle — — Pommel

Pad —

— Flap

Stirrup Leather

Stirrup — — Girth

## Western Saddle

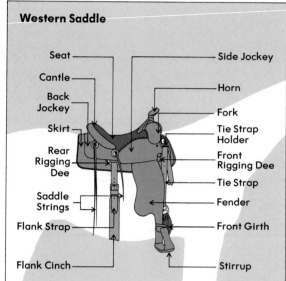

Seat — — Side Jockey

Cantle — — Horn

Back Jockey

— Fork

Skirt — — Tie Strap Holder

Rear Rigging Dee — — Front Rigging Dee

— Tie Strap

Saddle Strings — — Fender

Flank Strap — — Front Girth

Flank Cinch — — Stirrup

The western bridle usually is fitted with some type of curb bit. The western curb bit, however, has longer shanks than the English and has no curb chain.

### The Art of Riding

A novice soon learns that one of the basic skills in the art of riding is balance. A horseman stays on his mount by balance, not by gripping his mount with his legs or by using the reins as lifelines. To achieve and maintain his balance, the rider's center of gravity must be directly over that of the horse. The horse's center of gravity is in direct line with the girth of the saddle when the horse is standing still.

### The Rider's Position

Horsemen call a rider's position on the horse his "seat." The rider sits erect in the deepest part of the saddle, which is over the stirrup leathers. In the flat saddle, the knees are bent and pushed ahead of the stirrup leathers. This places the angle of the thigh parallel to the angle of the horse's shoulder blade. When properly seated, a rider's ear, hip, and heel are in line, and the tip of the toe is directly under the point of the knee. His arms are relaxed but held so that a straight line could be drawn from the tip of the elbow along the forehand, wrists, and reins to the horse's bit. Illustrations with this article show the position of the rider on the horse at various gaits.

### Communication and Control

A horse trained for riding has been taught the "language of the aids." A rider must also learn this language so he can communicate with his mount. There are two kinds of aids—natural and artificial. The natural aids include the voice, the action of the hands on the reins, the use of the legs and heels, the use of the back, and the distribution of the rider's weight. The artificial aids include the whip, the spur, and

various types of equipment such as side reins and martingales.

The reins are one line of communication. A horse is trained to go in the direction of the tension put on the rein. Although a skilled horseman uses the reins for many effects, the novice uses them for two basic ones: (1) to direct, and (2) to lead. If the rider carries his right rein slightly to the right and pulls back (direct) or to the side (lead), the horse turns in the direction of the pull. If the rider pulls both reins straight back, the horse slows down or stops. Every rider must learn to keep very light contact on the horse's mouth through a stretched rein. A slight increase of tension directs the horse, and immediate relaxation of tension when the horse begins to respond is the horse's reward for obedience. Continued tension punishes the animal and may confuse him.

The reins indicate the direction of movement (turn, go forward, or back), but the leg aids indicate that motion should start. The horse moves away from the pressure of a leg or heel. When a rider applies pressure only with his left leg, the horse moves his haunches to the right. When pressure is applied with both legs, the horse begins to move forward.

The rider uses his weight to help the horse keep in balance and also to indicate a change of direction. A rider on a well-trained horse has only to step down in one stirrup and the horse will turn in that direction. When a rider shifts his weight backward slightly the horse will slow down. The rider uses his voice to encourage, to praise, or to admonish his mount.

### Mounting and Dismounting

Illustrations with this article explain the four phases for mounting a horse properly. In dismounting the procedures are reversed. When the rider swings his right foot back over the horse he bears his weight on his hands, brings his feet together, then kicks his left

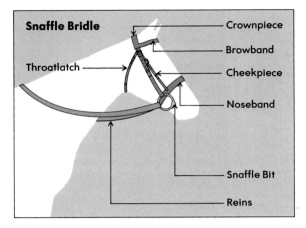

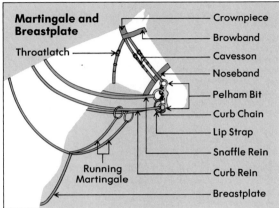

foot out of the stirrup. He drops to the ground, turning slightly so that he lands facing the front of the horse. He then transfers the reins to his right hand.

### The Western Seat

Western riding is primarily a working form of riding, and the horses are differently trained. The horse works on a loose rein, and the rider holds the reins in one hand and directs the horse with a neck rein. Horses used for western-type riding are especially trained to respond to neck reining. When the rider wishes to go to the right, he moves the hand holding the reins to the right. The horse feels the touch of the left rein on his neck and turns in the opposite direction—to the right. The touch of the right rein brings a move to the left.

The western rider sits deeply and firmly in the saddle. His aids are his weight and his legs. The stirrup straps are longer than those of a flat saddle, and the horseman rides with his knees only slightly bent. He maintains his center of gravity over the horse, however, and his feet are not pushed forward.

### CARING FOR A HORSE

The horse, like any other kind of animal, responds to proper care and good treatment. Caring for a horse requires considerable time and patience, however, and only persons who are willing to expend the time and have adequate space should consider keeping a horse at home. Many horsemen who enjoy owning their own mounts keep them at professional boarding stables to ensure proper care.

### Housing a Horse

The minimum size box stall for a horse is ten feet by ten feet. Stalls must be large enough so that the horse can lie down and get up without injuring itself and can turn around comfortably. They also must have areas where bedding, feed, hay, and equipment can be stored. The walls of the stall should be constructed of two-inch-thick oak boards to the height of five feet. Above this, heavy wire or lighter boards can be used. The flooring can be of clay, sand, or cinders. At least

three inches of bedding should be spread on the floor. Bedding soaks up moisture and provides the horse with a clean, dry bed.

Mangers, racks, or other containers for hay and grain should be placed on the walls at heights that are convenient for the horse to reach. Water should be available day and night.

One of the most time-consuming of all the chores necessary for the proper care of a horse is cleaning the stable. The stall and bedding must be cleaned daily. The bedding must be removed and replaced periodically.

### Feeding a Horse

The amount and kind of feed a horse needs depends upon the size of the animal, his condition, and the kind of work that is demanded of him. For a pastured horse, the grass he nibbles may provide sufficient food. But most horses, especially working horses, need supplementary feed for energy.

Feed consists of hay supplemented by grain rations. Hay is a substitute for the pasture grass. Grain is a concentrated food and is given in small amounts several times a day. Water is also an important part of the horse's diet, but grain swells when wet so the water should always be given first. Many horsemen follow the routine of small but frequent feedings in this sequence: water, hay, grain.

### Grooming a Horse

A horse should be thoroughly groomed at least once a day. A well-groomed horse looks attractive, but grooming has a far more important function. It improves the animal's circulation and helps tone the muscles. So, vigorous grooming is necessary.

Grooming tools include a cloth, a brush of rough straw, a soft body brush, a rubber or plastic currycomb, and a hoof-pick. All parts of the horse's body must be groomed. The cloth is used first to remove surface dust and dirt. The soft brush cleans the face and lower legs where the hair is short. The currycomb and rough brush are used where the hair is long. The horse's feet need special care to prevent

*To mount a horse, the rider stands at the horse's left side and either faces the rear or faces the shoulder. She gathers the reins in her left hand and places her hand on the neck, sliding her hand down to shorten the reins.*

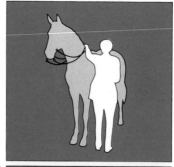

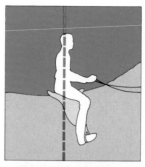

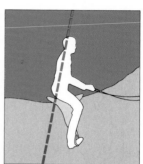

*Still holding the reins, and grasping the horse's mane in her left hand, the rider uses her right hand to steady the stirrup while she puts the left toe of her boot in it. Then she moves her right hand to grasp the cantle of either an English saddle or a western saddle.*

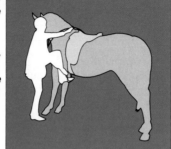

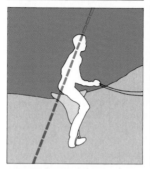

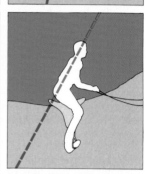

*The rider springs upward from the ball of her right foot, turns slightly to face the animal, and straightens her knees so that she is standing on the ball of her left foot in the stirrup, the right foot next to it, but bearing most of her weight on her hands on the horse's back.*

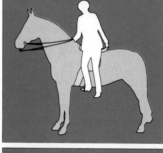

WALK (top left). *In the illustrations above, the dotted line represents the angle of the rider's body. In each position, he holds his back straight, shoulders back.*
TROT (top right). *For the trot, the rider leans forward slightly, making sure that there is no weight on the buttocks.*
CANTER (bottom left). *In the canter, the rider's body and arms are inclined forward a little more than during the trot.*
GALLOP (bottom right). *During the gallop, the rider's body leans even farther forward, and his arms are even more extended than in the canter.*

*The rider then leans on her left arm and moves her right hand from the cantle to either the pommel of an English saddle or the horn of a western saddle. She swings her fully extended right leg over the horse's back and rump. She then settles lightly into the saddle and places her right foot in the right stirrup.*

infections. They should be cleaned every day and each time the horse is ridden. A hoof-pick is used to pick out hard materials such as packed manure and stones that collect under the foot.

Grooming gives the horseman an opportunity to closely inspect all parts of the horse's body for any cuts, abrasions, or signs of disease. The stable should be equipped with first-aid articles. Home remedies can be used to treat superficial cuts and abrasions, but a veterinarian should be called to treat any other kind of injury or disease.

### Saddling and Bridling a Horse

An important part of a horse's care is proper saddling and bridling. To put on the bridle, slip it over the horse's nose, guide the bit into the mouth, and slide the crownpiece over the ears. Adjust the noseband and browband. Fasten the throatlatch and the curb chain. Be sure that all parts of the bridle lie flat and are neither too loose nor too tight. To put on the saddle, lay it on the withers and slide it back into place. Attach the girth or cinch evenly on both sides. The girth should be neither too loose nor too tight. To test for proper fit, slip a hand between the body of the horse and the girth just below the saddle, then slide it down to the bottom. It should feel tight only where it passes under the horse. On western saddles with two

*The properly mounted rider sits easily in the saddle with her head up, back straight, and shoulders well back. Her legs hang comfortably. The balls of her feet are in the stirrups, the heels are held down, and the toes are turned slightly outward.*

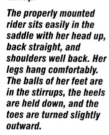

cinches, the forward cinch is made very snug, the rear one less so. Cinches are fitted tighter than girths because of the work the horse does.

## EVOLUTION OF THE HORSE

Horses have a long and interesting history on Earth, and the study of their complex evolutionary development probably constitutes one of the most extensive and intensive searches done by scientists. As a result, the evolutionary story of the horse is perhaps the most complete of that of any of Earth's animals.

Geologists believe that the first humans appeared on Earth about 2 million years ago—a very long time in terms of the way we count time, but like a fraction of a second in terms of geologic time. Horses appeared on Earth long before people—about 60 million years ago, at or shortly before the beginning of the Eocene epoch of Earth's history. This fact has been so well established that fossils of these animals found in rock strata are used by scientists to date the rocks. These early horses lived on both the European and the North American continents. Evidence of possible ancestors in older rocks in North America, however, leads scientists to believe that probably the animals originated on that continent.

### Eohippus—The Dawn Horse

The modern horse with its sleek coat, straight back, proudly arching neck, and long legs bears little resemblance to its ancient ancestors. This small ancestor was only about the size of an adult fox. In fact, when the first bones of these animals were found in 1838 and 1839, they were believed to be the bones of ancient monkeys or of the harelike animals called hyraxes or conies. The animal was given the scientific name *Hyracotherium* because of its resemblance to the hyrax; however, the genus name more commonly used for the animal is *Eohippus.*

The name *Eohippus* comes from two Greek words: *eos,* meaning "dawn," and *hippos,* meaning "horse." The name also reflects the fact that *Eohippus* occurs in the Eocene—the "dawn" portion of the most recent epoch of geologic time. *Eohippus* was an active and abundant animal, and many fossils have been found. However, almost all are fragmentary, and finding a complete skeleton is rare. For this reason, only a few skeletons have been reconstructed and mounted.

There were several different species of *Eohippus,* and they varied greatly in size. The smallest were about 10 inches high at the shoulder, and the largest were more than 20 inches high.

The body of *Eohippus* looked almost like that of a rabbit. The hindquarters were high, and the the arched back sloped downward toward the neck and head. The animal had a long, stout tail, which bears no resemblance to that of the modern horse. Modern horses have short tails; the whisk of hairs that grow from the tip make them appear long.

The head of this ancient animal was shaped almost like that of a dog. The snout was more pointed than broad as in that of the modern horse. The large eyes

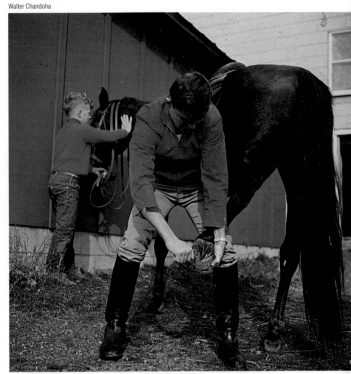
Walter Chandoha

*Grooming a horse thoroughly at least once a day is important for the animal's health and appearance. The feet need special care, and a hoof-pick is used to remove hard materials that collect under each foot.*

were set midway between the front and the back of the skull. The teeth were simple. The cheek teeth had a few cusps, more like our own molars than like the large, strong, heavily ridged teeth of the horse today.

The feet of *Eohippus* added to its doglike appearance. The front feet had four toes, and the hind feet had three. Each toe ended in its own small hoof. Tough pads, much like those of a dog, bore the animal's weight.

*Eohippus* was well equipped to live in the world of its time. The small animal had short legs that were not built for speed, but it probably was fast for its size. Its light weight and spreading toes kept it from sinking into the soft earth.

### Mesohippus—The Middle Horse

*Mesohippus* probably is the best known fossil horse. Buried and preserved bones of these animals are abundant, especially in the Badlands of South Dakota. *Mesohippus* lived about 35 million years ago, during the Oligocene epoch of geologic time.

Unlike *Eohippus; Mesohippus* looked much like a small modern horse. Although there were smaller and larger species, *Mesohippus* averaged about 24 inches. The body was longer than that of *Eohippus,* and the back less arched but still not the straight, rigid back of the modern horse.

The head of *Mesohippus* had a more "horsy" appearance although the face was still slender and

*The series of drawings shown at the top are reconstructions that show what scientists believe horses may have looked like at each of four major stages of their evolution. They range from the small, doglike "dawn horse" of the Eocene epoch through the almost modern looking horse of the Pliocene epoch. The color box at the top left corner is a key to the locator map on the far right.*

*The series of drawings shown at the bottom right are reconstructions of skeletons and foot bones from remains that have been found. They show the basic changes that took place as the horse developed over the ages. The locator map on the far right shows the areas in which scientists have found remains of each kind of horse.*

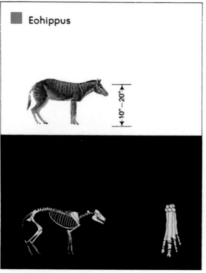
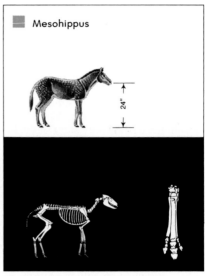

■ Eohippus

■ Mesohippus

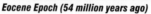

**Eocene Epoch (54 million years ago)**   **Oligocene Epoch (38 million years ago)**

almost snoutlike. The jaws were still shallow, but the typical horse muzzle probably had begun to develop. The eyes were positioned farther back on the head than in *Eohippus.* The teeth were larger and stronger than those of *Eohippus.* Also, a little gap was beginning to form behind the front teeth where today the horse has a large gap into which the bit fits.

The legs of *Mesohippus* were longer and more slender, but each foot still had several toes. Now, however, there were only three toes on the front feet as well as on the back feet. As in *Eohippus,* the center toe was the largest, and there were pads on the feet and between the toes.

### Merychippus—The Transformation Horse

Some of the most radical and rapid changes in the evolution of the horse took place during the Miocene epoch of geologic time. Perhaps the most important were the changes in the structure of the teeth, which made it possible for horses to become grazers (grass eaters) rather than browsers (leaf eaters) as *Eohippus* and *Mesohippus* had been. By the middle of the Miocene—which began about 26,000,000 years ago—*Merychippus* had molar teeth with high crowns. The teeth were covered with a strong bonelike substance called cement. Such teeth could grind the coarse grasses into edible masses for the animal.

*Merychippus* also showed other changes, somewhat less dramatic than those of the teeth. The animal grew about 40–42 inches high—as large as many modern ponies. It had a long muzzle, deep jaws, and eyes quite far back on the head. The body and leg proportions were not exactly the same in all species of *Merychippus.* Some were stocky, others slender. But in general, changes that had taken place in the legs and feet made these parts appear more nearly like those of horses today. Certain bones of the leg grew together,

making each leg rigid but highly effective for carrying weight and for a more efficient forward motion. The feet still had three toes, but the weight of the animal was carried on a greatly enlarged and strongly hoofed central toe. The side toes were short and small, and the foot pads had disappeared.

### Pliohippus—The One-Toed Grazing Horse

Several groups of horses descended from *Merychippus.* One of these was *Pliohippus,* a horse of the Pliocene epoch. The modern horse, *Equus,* is a direct descendant of *Pliohippus.* Although, again, there are variations among some species, generally *Pliohippus* closely resembles the horse of today. *Pliohippus* had only one hoofed toe. The others became slivers of bone (splints) that even in modern horses grow along the cannon bone of the leg. Differences between *Pliohippus* and the modern *Equus* lie mostly in the refinement of the details of the animals' anatomy, which are used by scientists to separate them.

### THE HORSE IN HISTORY

Man's association with the horse probably began more than 4,000 years ago. In the beginning this association was not a companionable one. Prehistorians believe that man hunted horses as a game animal.

No one knows exactly when or where man first tamed the horse. Some scientists believe that the first horses may have been domesticated in the area of present day Turkestan, probably long before 2000 BC. The horse worked for man as a draft animal for at least 1,000 years before the art of riding developed. However, some groups of nomads probably had small herds of these animals and rode them. When Greek traders first saw these mounted men in the Black Sea region, they believed them to be a strange animal, half horse and half man. The Greeks called them centaurs

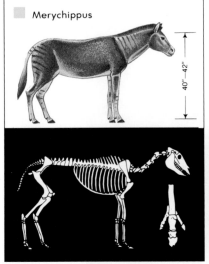

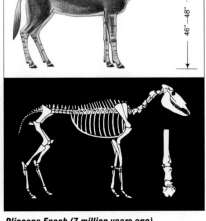

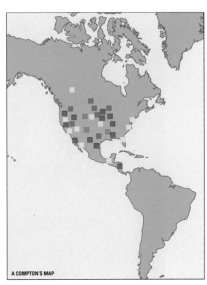

*Miocene Epoch (26 million years ago)*     *Pliocene Epoch (7 million years ago)*     *Fossil Location*

and developed many fables about these unusual beasts.

### Horses in the Ancient World

War horses and chariots were used by the Mitanni in Syria and the Hittites in Anatolia by about 1600 BC. A remarkable book, the earliest known work devoted exclusively to horses, was written by a Mitanni horseman hired by a Hittite king. The clay tablets that comprise the book give detailed directions for the care and training of chariot horses.

In about 1700 BC the Hyksos from Syria and Palestine introduced domesticated horses into Egypt. By the 1500s BC, the Egyptians used horse-drawn vehicles, but few Egyptians rode horses. By 1000 BC the use of horses had spread westward from Egypt.

The Greeks viewed the horse as a heroic symbol, a wonder beast ridden by great warriors and by the gods. The Romans made great use of the horse, and vehicles carrying freight or passengers clattered over the streets of Rome. By 45 BC, all vehicles had been banned from within the city, and in other cities they were allowed only at night. Presumably the reason for this ban was because the vehicles endangered pedestrians and caused traffic jams.

As the use of horses spread throughout the ancient world, breeding programs were established to produce animals with special qualities to suit specific purposes. For example, a large, heavy horse was needed to carry an armored soldier into battle, but a small, light horse could be used for riding and racing. Generations of cross-breeding made pure strains rare.

### Horses in the Medieval World

During the Middle Ages, experimentation in breeding horses continued. The growth of international trade increased the need for a reasonable means for the overland transportation of goods. Sturdy pack horses were desired to carry merchandise between towns and into the countryside. Large, strong draft horses were in demand for use in teams to draw carts of bulk merchandise over long distances. In addition, horses for the business of knighthood had to be developed. A well-equipped knight needed at least four different types of horses: (1) a charger, (2) a palfrey, (3) a courser, and (4) a battle horse.

### Horses in American Conquest and Exploration

European explorers brought horses to the New World—the first in the Americas since the native horses had died out about 8,500 years before. The Spanish had royal horse farms operating in Jamaica by 1515, and Francisco Pizarro obtained horses from these farms for his expeditions to Peru. Stock farms in Cuba supplied horses to Hernando Cortez for the invasion of Mexico in 1519. Horses carried the Spanish explorers and colonizers in their push through southwestern and western North America.

The westward movement from eastern North America is usually symbolized by the covered wagon. Many of the wagons were drawn by oxen, but mounted explorers usually preceded them, and mounted scouts accompanied them. After the West began to open up, the wagons were replaced by stagecoaches that carried passengers and mail.

Until the early 1900s, horses supplied much of the transportation and much of the power for vehicles.

---

**DO YOU KNOW**

1. What is a centaur?
2. What ancient city probably had traffic jams?
3. Who wrote the first known book about horses?

*A glazed earthenware horse (above) of the T'ang Dynasty (AD 618–907) shows that the Chinese of that time had a great knowledge of crossbreeding. They developed a sinewy but sturdy horse suitable for pulling heavy loads as well as for riding. The sculpture shows a padded saddle and other trappings for riding at that time. Charlemagne, a ruler of Western Europe (768–814), is depicted on his horse (bottom right) in a bronze sculpture by an unknown artist.*

Horses pulled the first railroad cars. In the cities, horses drew the garbage wagons, milk carts, and fire engines. On the farms, ranches, and plantations, they powered the plows and harvesting machines. Today, the automobile, truck, and tractor have largely replaced the horse, although the performance capability of these vehicles is still evaluated in horsepower.

**Horses in Sport**

The horse has long been a source of recreation for humans. The Persians were playing polo long before 600 BC. The ancient Greeks hunted wild boar and mountain lion on horseback. The ancient Romans conducted horse shows, which included chariot racing as well as trick riding. The English of the 1100s enjoyed thoroughbred racing and fox hunting. Circuses and rodeos still draw thousands of spectators.

As the horse became less important in warfare, as a beast of burden, and as a means of transportation because of increased mechanization, it became more important in sport. In the United States, after a drop in the horse population during the early 1900s, the number of horses bred and registered gradually increased. Today horses are used for pleasure riding, racing, hunting, and polo. Horse show competitions of various kinds are also popular. Many persons vie for

*A horse and knight of Prato, Italy, are shown dressed for a tournament in this detail from a manuscript of the 1300s. Strong horses were needed to carry knights in full armor. Here, the armor is covered by a surcoat, whose design identifies the knight.*

*A modern Belgian farmer still uses a horse-drawn farm implement as farmers have done for centuries.*

top honors at rodeos, pony club rallies, and 4-H club meets as well as at the traditional horse shows. Although the use of the workhorse has gradually dwindled, the need of the horse as a companion in recreation continues to increase.

### THE HORSE IN THE ARTS

The horse has played an enormously important part in the daily life of man since prehistoric times. So it is not surprising to find that the horse has been a favored subject for artists in every field throughout history. Even in prehistoric times, hunters scratched pictures of horses on the walls of caves. These drawings, some of which date back to about 18,000 BC, vividly depict in simple lines the animation and action of the animals. The cave artists also succeeded in showing the distinguishing characteristics of the wild horse such as the short body, thick neck with heavy head and upright mane, and short but graceful legs.

The Assyrians, whose land lay between the Tigris and Euphrates rivers, were very interested in horses. Relief sculptures carved in stone depict the deeds of their warriors. Sophisticated and detailed carvings in the stone ruins of the ancient city of Calah in Iraq show Assyrian war chariots.

Egyptians decorated their tombs with spindle-legged stylized horses. Those shown on tombs were often many times larger than life size. A small wooden statuette of a horse and rider, carved about 1500 BC, was found inside a tomb. The sculptured horse is much more graceful than those shown in the drawings by artists of this period.

The beauty and form of the horse seems to have inspired artists of almost every culture. We find Japanese screens, Russian icons, ancient Persian tapestries, and 16th-century East Indian miniatures showing the horse in action—some in warfare and others in such sports as polo and lion and tiger hunting.

Perhaps the most famous and beautiful sculptures of all time are those of the horses that form part of a frieze around the Parthenon in Athens. These sculptures, done by the Greek sculptor Phidias about 447 BC, express the Greek idea of perfection. They show young men riding bareback on graceful horses that are portrayed at all gaits as well as at the halt or performing dressage movements.

Throughout the world, there are statues of history's famous military men, always mounted with the charger at the levade, or prancing with arched neck. In Italy, the museums and public squares of cities and towns are filled with statues of mounted and unmounted horses. Some of these date back to the 1st century BC. In Venice, Andrea del Verrocchio's monument to the military leader Bartolommeo Colleoni, done in the late 1400s, shows the artist's ability to portray in bronze the strength and straining energy of a military horse.

During the Middle Ages, tapestries were a popular art form. Many of the castles of Europe used tapestries not only as a decoration but as a practical measure to help cover the stone walls and keep out the cold. The tapestry scenes often included horses. Perhaps one of the best known is the Bayeux Tapestry, thought by some to have been designed by Queen Matilda to honor the success of her husband, William the Conqueror, when he invaded England in 1066. Two hundred horses are embroidered into this work of art.

During the 1500s and 1600s Dutch, Flemish, and Spanish painters were interested in portraying the horse in sports. Sporting prints became extremely popular in England during the 18th and 19th centuries when many artists produced racing and hunting scenes. Many American artists used horses as subjects in some of their art. Among these were Frederick Remington, who is famous for his portrayals of pioneer life in the American West.

*Albrecht Dürer's engraving of the great European horse of the 1500s, shows the tremendous power of these animals, which enabled them to carry a knight in full armor.*

*Painting of a horse, below, was done by a prehistoric artist on the walls of Naiux cave in southern France. The simple line drawing clearly shows the characteristics of the animal.*

The mythology of almost every Western culture includes the horse as an important character. For example, in Greek mythology the sun god, Apollo, crossed the heavens each day in a chariot drawn by fiery steeds. Another famous Greek horse was Bellerophon's flying horse Pegasus, who was placed among the stars. Norse myths tell the story of the hero Sigurd, who rides a brave stallion through a wall of magic fire to rescue the heroine Brynhild. This same story occurs in German mythology and became the basis for Richard Wagner's opera "Siegfried."

The grace and beauty of the horse has inspired many poets. William Shakespeare's famous poem "Venus and Adonis" paints superb word pictures of a stallion and a filly. Lines from this poem appear under the photograph at the beginning of this article. Another poet, John Masefield, created two masterpieces describing the horse in sports. His "Reynard the Fox" tells of the thrills of a hunt, and "Right Royal" portrays the excitement of a horse race.

Novelists, too, have been inspired by the strength and spirit of this animal. Books about horses in fact and fiction are extremely popular with readers of all ages and many appear every year. At the end of this article is a list of some of the fine books that have been written about horses.

*Marino Marini, an Italian artist, includes a horse in most of his works, (right) including the bronze 'Horse and Rider'.*

*Toulouse-Lautrec's painting 'The Ringmaster' (below) captures the excitement of a circus horse's performance.*

Reprinted by permission from C.W. Anderson (© 1936), 'Billy and Blaze' (The Macmillan Co.)

From Marguerite Henry, 'King of the Wind' (© 1948 Rand McNally & Co.), illustrated by Wesley Dennis

Illustration © 1945 by The Viking Press, Inc., from John Steinbeck, 'The Red Pony,' illustrated by Wesley Dennis (reprinted by permission of the publisher)

## *The Horse in Literature*

### FICTION

**Anderson, C.W.** Billy and Blaze (Macmillan, 1936). The first of the excellent Blaze stories for young horse lovers. Billy receives a horse for his birthday and names it for the marking on its face. Illustrated by the author. Others in the series include 'Blaze and the Gypsies' (1937) and 'Blaze and Thunderbolt' (1955).

**Bagnold, Enid.** National Velvet (Morrow, 1949). A famous novel about a girl who races her beloved horse in the Grand National. Illustrated by Paul Brown.

**Farley, Walter.** The Black Stallion (Random, 1941). The first of a popular series about a wild horse and its racehorse descendants. See also 'Son of the Black Stallion' (1947) and 'The Blood Bay Colt' (1950).

**Henry, Marguerite.** King of the Wind (Rand, 1948). A Newbery-winning story about the sire of a long line of Arabian thoroughbreds, including Man o' War. Illustrated by Wesley Dennis. Also by Mrs. Henry are 'Misty of Chincoteague' (1947), 'Brighty of the Grand Canyon' (1953), and 'White Stallion of Lipizza' (1964).

**James, Will.** Smoky (Scribner, 1926). Written in cowboy dialect, this story tells of a horse that becomes a killer after being mistreated. Illustrated by the author and winner of the Newbery Medal in 1927.

**O'Hara, Mary.** My Friend Flicka (Lippincott, 1941). The first of a trilogy, which includes 'Thunderhead' (1943) and 'Green Grass of Wyoming' (1946), written for adults but enjoyed by children. A story of a boy's love for his colt, with fine descriptions of Wyoming.

**Rounds, Glen.** The Blind Colt (Holiday, 1941). A tender story of a boy's devotion to a mustang marked for death.

**Sewell, Anna.** Black Beauty (Pendulum, 1973). Written as a protest in 1877 when there was much cruelty to horses, this sentimental story is still enjoyed by young readers.

**Steinbeck, John.** The Red Pony (Viking Press, 1959). A 1937 short novel by a Nobel prize laureate tells of Jody's discovery of the meaning of life when his pony dies. Illustrated by Wesley Dennis.

### NONFICTION

**Amaral, Anthony.** Movie Horses (Bobbs, 1967). Describes how horses are trained for motion picture scenes.

**Anderson, C.W.** Complete Book of Horses and Horsemanship (Macmillan, 1973). Covers the history, breeds, and care of the horse. Illustrated by the author.

**Brady, Irene.** America's Horses and Ponies (Houghton, 1969). Describes popular American breeds.

**Haines, Francis.** Horses in America (Crowell, 1971). A fascinating history of the role of the horse.

**Henry, Marguerite.** Album of Horses (Rand, 1951). Contains little-known facts about 20 breeds of horses. Illustrated by Wesley Dennis.

**Henry, Marguerite.** All About Horses (Random, 1967). The characteristics, breeds, and history of the horse are surveyed for younger readers.

**Hofsinde, Robert.** The Indian and His Horse (Morrow, 1960). Describes the effect of the horse on the life of the American Indian.

**Ryden, Hope.** America's Last Wild Horses (Dutton, 1970). A natural history of the wild horses whose existence is now threatened.

**Self, M.C.** At the Horse Show with Margaret Cabell Self (A. S. Barnes, 1966). The principles of showing a horse, show jumping, and gaits.

**Self, M.C.** The Complete Book of Horses & Ponies (McGraw, 1963). Anatomy, breeds, care, and riding.

**Simpson, G.G.** Horses: the Story of the Horse Family in the Modern World and Through Sixty Million Years of History (Oxford, 1951). Describes the evolution of the horse for older readers.

**Slaughter, Jean.** Pony Care (Knopf, 1961). A helpful guide to the daily care of ponies.

**Sullivan, George.** Better Horseback Riding for Boys and Girls (Dodd, 1969). Illustrated instructions for the beginner from leading a horse to tacking up.

**Zuelke, Ruth.** The Horse in Art (Lerner Publications, 1965). Examines the style of artists who used horses as subjects.

Tony Triolo—Sports Illustrated
*Seattle Slew, on the right near the rail, ridden by jockey Jean Cruquet, wins the Belmont Stakes in 1977.*
*The horse thus gained the last victory needed for horse racing's Triple Crown.*

**HORSE RACING.** The sport of kings, as horse racing is often called, is one of the oldest and most universal spectator sports. It is called the sport of kings because the ownership of horses was traditionally limited to the wealthiest members of society—royalty and nobility. Modern racing was established in England by King Charles II, who was an ardent patron of the sport throughout his reign.

The earliest written manual on the care, feeding, and training of horses dates from about 1500 BC in Asia Minor. There is a full description of a chariot race in Homer's 'Iliad', which is dated about the 9th or 8th century BC. Both chariot and bareback (mounted) horse races were held at the Olympic Games from 740 to 700 BC. The type of race called the steeplechase dates back at least to the 5th century BC.

Wagering, or betting, has always played a major role in racing. Today's wagering takes two forms: bookmaking and pari-mutuel betting. Bookmaking is a gambling practice of determining odds and receiving and paying off bets. The practice is legal in England and illegal in the United States, except for a few states. Pari-mutuel betting was introduced in France by businessman Pierre Oller about 1870. Most such betting takes place at tracks, though some places have off-track betting. Players buy tickets on the horses they back, and winners receive payoffs from a pool of all bets. Modern pari-mutuel betting uses computers or other devices called totalizers. These calculate the betting pools and the odds on each horse.

Today there are four kinds of horse races. These races are Thoroughbred horse racing, quarter-horse racing, harness racing, and the steeplechase. They are distinguished by the types of horses, the equipment, the way the races are run, and the terrain on which they are run.

### Thoroughbred Racing

A Thoroughbred race is run on a flat course, either of grass, or turf, or dirt. In England races are run exclusively on grass. In the United States, oval shaped dirt tracks predominate, most commonly 1 mile (1.6 kilometers) in circumference, but in other countries tracks may be irregular in shape. England's Ascot course is a rounded triangle. Many American tracks have a grass oval inside the outer dirt track.

Thoroughbred racing includes such world-famous events as the Belmont Stakes, which began in 1867, the Kentucky Derby (1875), and the Preakness Stakes (1873) in the United States (collectively called the Triple Crown); England's Gold Cup at the Royal Ascot (1807) and the Derby at Epsom Downs (1780); and the French Prix de l'Arc de Triomphe (1920).

The race gets its name from the kind of horse used. The Thoroughbred is a breed of horse developed in England for racing and jumping. Although the origin of the breed may be traced back to stocks of Arab and Barb horses brought to England in about the 3rd century, the immediate source according to tradition (in the female line) was 43 or more mares imported early in the 17th century.

In the male line, modern Thoroughbreds trace their ancestry to only three stallions: the Byerly Turk, the Darley Arabian, and the Godolphin Barb—all of the late 17th and early 18th centuries. By coincidence, the male line of each of these three survives through single male descendants: Matchem (1748–81), King Herod (1758–80), and Eclipse (1764–89). Today the descendants of Eclipse make up the vast majority of Thoroughbreds.

Thoroughbreds have slim bodies, delicate heads, broad chests, and short backs. They average 64 inches (163 centimeters) in height (measured as 16 hands for horses) and weigh about 1,000 pounds (450 kilograms). Apart from racing, Thoroughbreds may be used for hunting, polo, and riding. They are registered in 'The General Stud Book' of the English Jockey Club (organized about 1750) and in the studbooks of clubs in other countries.

The earliest races in England were match contests between two, or at most three, horses. Pressure by the public eventually produced events with larger fields of

© Cappy Jackson Photos

***Local Kid, ridden by Charles Fenwick, Jr., clears a jump on the way toward winning the British Grand National steeplechase. Bewleys Hill, right, is ridden by Dixon Stroud, Jr.***

runners. The early races were 4-mile (6.4-kilometer) heats, with two heats needed for a win. A rider's skill and judgment were not so vital in gaining a victory. But as dash, or one-heat, racing became the rule, the rider's ability to gain a few feet became vital.

The length of a course varies, depending on the specific race and on the custom of the country in which it is run. The Royal Ascot Gold Cup race is over a 2½-mile (4-kilometer) course, while some of the other classic races run at Ascot are only 1 ½ miles (2.4 kilometers). The most common distance for American races became ¾ mile (1.2 kilometers). Races in the United States are dominated by the commercial aspect of the sport. Hence, it is the speed of the horse that is emphasized. In England, speed and stamina are both considered significant.

In Thoroughbred racing the term handicap is used to signify the adjustment of the weight the horse carries in relation to its age and sex. A 2-year-old horse may begin racing in the spring with a greater weight allowance that may progressively drop as the season advances. Sex allowances are from 3 to 5 pounds (1.4 to 2.3 kilograms) less for female horses than for males. Weight penalties or allowances may also be adjusted on the basis of a horse's past performance. Handicapping seeks to give all the horses racing an equal chance of winning.

Although Thoroughbreds reach their peak racing ability at age 5, 3 years is generally considered the classic racing age. Larger purses have increased stake fees (fees charged owners who wish to race their horses). This fact plus the money to be made through breeding fees and the sale of horses have combined to diminish the number of races available for horses beyond the age of 4. There are, however, some notable exceptions to this trend. Among them are the Sydney Cup in Australia, the Queen Elizabeth Stakes in England, the Prix de l'Arc de Triomphe in Paris, and the Emperor's Cup in Japan.

The race procedure begins when the jockeys, as the riders are called, weigh in and report to the paddock

for instructions from the trainers. (The paddock is the section at the track where horses are saddled.) An official is present to verify the identity of the horses. After the jockeys mount, they parade the horses past the stewards for inspection.

When the race is to start, the horses are led to the starting gate, which is electrically operated at most tracks. As the race is being run, the stewards and patrol judges, aided by a motion-picture patrol, look for rule violations. The finish is photographed by a special camera, and if the race is very close the film must be developed before final results are announced. In North America, horses are timed to the nearest one fifth of a second, while in most countries they are timed to the nearest one hundredth of a second.

The result of the race is not official, however, until the jockeys weigh in and the horses are checked for carrying the proper weight. Rule infractions claimed by jockeys must be examined by the judges. Saliva and urine samples are taken from the horses to detect prohibited substances. Winning horses have been disqualified for having been injected with drugs.

The governance of racing varies from nation to nation. In England the Jockey Club is the regulatory agency for long-term policy. Overall control of the sport is in the hands of the Joint Racing Board, composed of members of the Jockey Club and members of the Horserace Betting Levy Board appointed by the government. In the United States the sport is regulated by state racing commissions. In a few other nations the government owns the tracks and horses.

### Quarter-Horse Racing

Quarter-horse racing is an event for racing horses at great speed over short distances on straightaway courses. The distance was originally ¼ mile (0.4 kilometer). The sport originated in North America shortly after the founding of Jamestown in 1607. Although the horses were long acknowledged to be a distinct type, the registration of quarter horses as a breed did not begin until the founding of the American

Quarter Horse Registry in 1940. It is now the largest horse registry in the world.

Modern quarter-horse racing is conducted at about 100 tracks in North America. The rules and procedures are nearly the same as for Thoroughbred racing, but the races themselves are different. Quarter-horse races are run on straight tracks, for distances that vary from 220 to 660 yards (200 to 600 meters). Vying for position along the rail thus plays no part in this kind of race. The large number of entries and the short distances combine to produce a large number of photo finishes. The races are timed to the nearest one hundredth of a second, in contrast to Thoroughbred races in North America.

### Harness Racing

An ancient form of racing involved horses pulling chariots. The modern equivalent is harness racing. The horses pull drivers seated in light, two-wheeled vehicles, called sulkies, around oval-shaped dirt tracks. Most of the races are a mile in length. (For picture *see* Horse.) The horses used are trotters of different breeds. In Holland, where modern harness racing originated in the 16th century, Dutch Fresian horses were common trotters. In Russia, Count Grigory Orlov developed a powerful breed called the Orlov trotter from his stallion Barss. The Norfolk Trotter emerged as a breed in England in about 1750. The American Standardbred was established as a breed in 1879. The current strain of Standardbreds is descended from Hambletonian 10, foaled in 1849. This stallion sired 1,331 males and females between 1851 and 1875. All American Standardbreds and many trotters in other countries are descended from him.

In racing, the horses are of two kinds, differentiated by gait. Pacers move both legs on one side of the body at the same time. Trotters stride with their left front and right rear legs moving forward at the same time, then the right front and left rear together.

The sulky evolved from a single-seat pleasure vehicle. Sulkies once weighed about 125 pounds (56 kilograms), but their weight has been progressively reduced. Today many are little more than a U-shaped light metal shaft fastened to a narrow seat, and most weigh less than 25 pounds (11 kilograms).

### The Steeplechase

The steeplechase, which involves jumping over a variety of obstacles, is, for the horse, the most arduous and dangerous of races. (For picture *see* Horse.) The race's name is derived from contests over natural terrain in which church steeples served as landmarks. The Greek author Xenophon referred to this kind of racing as early as the 5th century BC. It was long a favorite sport of cavalry officers.

Today the most famous such race is the Grand National at Aintree in Lancashire, England. It is a handicap race, with weights ranging up to 175 pounds (79 kilograms). The course covers a distance of 4 miles and 856 yards (7,180 meters) and has 30 obstacles. The number of entrants is quite large—as many as 66 have started at one time. Many of the starters do not finish the race. Other well-known races are the Irish Sweepstakes and the Grand Steeplechase of Paris. The American Grand National was first run at Belmont Park in New York in 1899.

In contrast to Thoroughbred racing, large mature horses are preferred; and stamina is as necessary as speed. Racing through age 10 is not uncommon. Many of the horses are half-breds, a term loosely applied to any horse that is not a pure Thoroughbred.

**HORSESHOE PITCHING.** The modern game of horseshoe pitching is more popular in Canada and the United States than elsewhere. It was introduced into North America during colonial times. The National Horseshoe Pitchers Association of America—the governing body of the sport since 1926—sponsors national and international tournaments annually.

The game may be played by two or four persons. The only equipment consists of horseshoes and two iron or steel stakes embedded in the ground. The horseshoes weigh 2 ½ pounds (1 kilogram). They are 7 ½ inches (19 centimeters) long and 7 inches (18 centimeters) wide at the greatest width. The space between the calks, or ends, of the shoe is 3 ½ inches (9 centimeters). The iron stakes are 40 feet (12 meters) apart, extend 14 inches (36 centimeters) from the level of the ground, and are inclined 3 inches (7.6 centimeters) toward each other.

If there are two players, each pitches two shoes from a pitching box 6 feet (1.8 meters) square, which has one of the stakes in its center. The pitching by both players from one side is called an inning. Both players then cross to the opposite pitching box and pitch from it. If there are four players, one member of each team pitches from each box.

Regulation games are played to a score of 50 points. Scoring is done after each inning. One point is given for each shoe 6 inches (15 centimeters) or less from the stake and closer to it than an opponent's. A ringer (shoe that encloses the stake) counts three points. Two shoes equidistant from the stake or two ringers, if thrown by opposing players, cancel out each other. A horseshoe leaning against the stake counts one point.

**HOSIERY.** Knitted items of clothing called hosiery are designed to be worn on the feet and legs, inside shoes or boots. The word is derived from the Old English *hosa*, which means a covering for the leg. In the United States and most other countries hosiery refers to stockings, socks, panty hose, and tights. In Great Britain hosiery includes machine-knitted garments of all types.

While stockings and socks come in pairs, one for each leg, panty hose and tights are single garments in which the separate legs of the hose are joined at the waist. (Tights may also refer to a neck-to-toe garment.) Although identical in concept, tights and panty hose have quite different histories. Tights were originally worn by men, beginning in the late Middle Ages. Noblemen wore tights of silk or velvet, often in bright colors and sometimes with each leg of a different color. Tights are still worn by ballet performers. Panty hose did not enter the hosiery market until the early 1960s. These two-legged items for women replaced pairs of one-legged stockings that attached to a garter belt.

The term full-fashioned is used to describe women's stockings that fit tightly to the leg. Originally these were knit on a type of straight-bar machine invented by William Cotton in 1864 in England. After knitting, they were seamed, because it was impossible to make well-fitting hose without a seam at the back. Since about 1960 most women who wear hose have worn seamless nylon stockings. Seamless stockings are made on a circular machine. The earliest seamless stockings were essentially straight knitted tubes that did not fit as well as full-fashioned stockings. The tube shape was caused by the fact that circular knitting machines cannot drop stitches to narrow the stocking. The thermoplastic qualities of nylon were used later to form a permanent shape in the tube, thus contributing to a preference for the seamless over the seamed, full-fashioned stockings.

The fit of hosiery has been improved by the adoption of stretch fabrics. A special process changes nylon or dacron filaments into a fluffy yarn that stretches. Such fabrics have made possible the manufacture of one-size-fits-all stockings for men and women. Hosiery can be made in any size to fit any shape of leg. Some stretch stockings are called support hose. They are worn by individuals who stand or walk a great deal or for medical reasons. The top of men's socks may be either regular rib or elastic. Elastic tops are made in part with rubber threads.

Apart from nylon and other synthetic fabrics used to make sheer stockings for women, cotton and wool are also used. Cotton is used mainly for children's and men's socks. Wool is popular for sports hosiery.

The terms denier and gauge are used to describe the fineness and weight of hosiery. Denier is the thickness of the thread. The lower the denier, the finer the yarn; 20 denier is finer than 30 denier, for example. Gauge refers to the number of loops, or stitches, in every 1 ½ inches (3.8 centimeters) in a row of knitting. If the gauge is 51, for instance, the stockings have 51 stitches every 1 ½ inches (3.8 centimeters).

The earliest known leg and foot coverings were not knitted. The ancient Greek poet Hesiod used the term *piloi*, probably referring to matted animal hair worn as a lining inside shoes. The Romans used a form of leg covering made from strips of woven cloth or leather and wrapped them around their legs. The forerunners of modern stockings were called *udones* by later Romans. These were made from woven fabric, skins, or felt and pulled on over the feet.

Hand-knitted fabrics have been made for many centuries. Knitted socks discovered in Egyptian tombs have been dated between the 3rd and 6th centuries AD. The first knitting machine was invented in England by William Lee, a clergyman, in 1589. This device became the prototype of all mechanical means of knitting for hundreds of years (*see* Knitting). Lee's brother improved the machine and helped bring about the mechanical knitting industry. The industry in North America was started in the 17th century with a machine that had been smuggled out of England. (English law forbade the exporting of machinery to the colonies to prevent the start of colonial manufacturing, which would create competition for English industries.)

The first significant modification of the knitting machine was made by Jebediah Strutt in 1758, when he introduced rib knitting. The general principles of knitting embodied in Lee's original machine remain incorporated into most modern knitting technology.

**HOSPICE.** Institutions designed to relieve the physical and emotional suffering of the dying are called hospices. The term hospice is derived from the same Latin word from which come "hospital" and "hospitality." In the Middle Ages hospices were places of refuge that provided rest and refreshment to travelers, not unlike inns or hotels. Today, hospices offer an alternative form of care for terminally ill patients. They also provide emotional support for the patients' relatives.

Hospice care emerged as an alternative to hospital confinement for several reasons. The primary one is probably the very high cost of keeping terminally ill patients alive indefinitely through the use of respirators and other means.

Second, aggressive life-prolonging measures, usually undertaken in intensive care units, frequently do nothing more than add to the discomfort and isolation of dying persons. Hospices, while staffed with physicians, nurses, and other medical personnel, create a home-like and sympathetic environment dedicated to making the last days of the dying as pleasant as possible. Hospice care is also much less expensive than a hospital stay. In the United States, Medicare provides some financial support for hospice care, and in Great Britain hospice care is subsidized by the National Health Service.

More than 90 percent of hospice patients suffer from cancer. Therefore, the first priority is the alleviation of pain through the use of analgesics, tranquilizers, and a variety of physical therapies. Hospices emphasize the prevention of pain through vigilant monitoring and by the careful dispensing of painkillers. In the United States there are hospices to care for patients with AIDS (acquired immunodeficiency syndrome), normally a terminal condition, which reached epidemic proportions in the 1980s.

The modern hospice movement began in England with the founding of St. Christopher's Hospice at Sydenham, near London, by Cicely Saunders in 1967. The movement came to the United States in 1975, after Saunders lectured on the subject at Yale University in Connecticut. There were about 1,400 hospices in the United States in the mid-1980s. A useful book on the subject is 'Hospice Programs and Public Policy' edited by Paul Torrens (American Hospital Publishing, Inc., 1985).

© 1987 E. Alan McGee, Atlanta

*Good Samaritan Hospital in Lexington, Ky., was founded in 1888. It is one of the leading health-care institutions in the United States. It established Kentucky's first cancer clinic in 1940.*

# HOSPITAL

A hospital is a place where pregnant, sick, or injured people can go for many kinds of medical attention and treatment. A hospital always contains beds for patients who require care for many days or even longer. Large hospitals have many special departments with highly trained doctors and nurses, as well as specialized machines and other equipment for diagnosing and treating sickness.

Hospitals and the practice of medicine are related. The earliest known hospitals were built by Hindus in present-day Sri Lanka during the 5th century BC. The first hospital in the Western Hemisphere was built in Santo Domingo, on the island of Hispaniola, in about 1503. Some 20 years later in Mexico City, Hernando Cortez built a hospital that is now the oldest hospital still in existence in the Western Hemisphere. The first solely medical hospital in the United States—the Pennsylvania Hospital—was established in Philadelphia in 1751, although poorhouses that provided some medical care had been founded earlier in other cities. There are about 6,600 hospitals in the

. . . . . . . . . . . . . . . . . . . . . . . . . . . . . . . . . . . . . . . . . . . .

*This article was contributed by Dr. Charles A. Sanders, General Director, Massachusetts General Hospital (Boston). It was reviewed by Martin S. Bander and Michelle E. Marcella, News and Public Affairs, Massachusetts General Hospital.*

United States. Some are chronic institutions where people with long-term problems, such as those caused by stroke, are cared for. Most are acute institutions, however, where patients usually remain for a few days to a few weeks at a time. Most hospitals are nonprofit institutions, although others are operated by their owners for financial profit and are known as proprietary institutions. More than one fourth of the hospitals in the United States are operated either by a local government, a state, or a federal agency, such as the Veterans Administration.

A general hospital is one capable of treating many diseases. Other kinds concentrate on a single disease or clientele. For example, there are hospitals devoted solely to treating cancer or arthritis patients. There are maternity hospitals for delivering babies, children's hospitals for treating disorders of the young, and geriatric hospitals for the aged.

A teaching hospital is usually linked with a medical school. In a teaching hospital, a medical student can see how experienced doctors care for the sick. After graduating from medical school, the young doctor, under the guidance of experienced physicians, actually treats patients in a hospital, first as an intern and later as a resident. The length of a residency program increases for those who train for specialties, subspecialties, and surgical specialties; subspecialties generally require the most years of training (*see* Medicine). These training programs benefit both trainee and patients: the young doctor gains experience, and the patient gets around-the-clock medical care.

Teaching hospitals, frequently called referral centers because their patients are referred from other hospitals, generally specialize in the diagnosis and treatment of complicated diseases. Nonteaching hospitals, usually called community hospitals because their patients come from the surrounding community, usually deal with more common disorders. A teaching hospital may also be a community hospital for the area it serves. Because a hospital can serve so many purposes, it can be a general, nongovernmental, nonprofit, and community hospital, all at the same time.

## Major Departments

Hospitals contain specialty areas where certain kinds of medical services are offered. Most of these sections are called departments.

**Nursing.** The nursing department is one of the most important in a hospital. A nurse in a centrally located nursing station is always only seconds away from any patient needing urgent medical attention.

Nurses chart basic information about the patient's condition, such as temperature, pulse, and blood pressure. Nurses report important changes in the patient's condition to doctors and then carry out the doctor's orders for correcting the situation if the doctor's presence is not required. Increasingly, nurses have taken on additional responsibility. (*See also* Nursing.)

**Surgery.** Some injuries or other disorders can best be corrected only through surgery (*see* Surgery). Major surgery is usually performed in a hospital operating room, though minor surgery may be performed in the office of a physician who has a private practice.

A typical operating room contains a tiltable operating table, bright overhead light, and instrument stands. It also has a suction machine to draw off mucus or remove fluids from an open wound; a preparation table for gauze pads and antiseptics; and a stand that holds sponges, or special pieces of gauze, used during an operation. Certain operating rooms are specially set up for unique types of surgery. When open-heart surgery is done, for example, the operating room must have a heart-lung machine to take over the jobs of those immobilized organs.

Anyone undergoing surgery is anesthetized, or made insensitive to pain. General anesthesia causes temporary unconsciousness or semi-consciousness, and local anesthesia causes a temporary loss of feeling in a specific region of the body. For many centuries before the advent of ether, alcohol was often ingested before surgery to cause a general decrease in bodily feeling, or numbness. Ether, however, is generally considered to be the first anesthetic. Since it was discovered that ether causes liver damage, other substances, such as sleep-producing general anesthetics, have come into common use. Pleasant-smelling anesthetic gases,

*A nurse wearing rubber gloves prepares to insert an intravenous feeding or medicinal tube into a patient's hand. The gloves are a precaution against catching or passing on a disease.*

administered through a face mask, put the patient into a deep sleep. The surgeon can then operate on any portion of the patient without inflicting pain. A spinal anesthetic is another type. When a spinal anesthetic is given, a liquid anesthetic is injected into the patient's spinal canal. Nerves from the point of injection downward toward the feet are temporarily paralyzed, and feeling in the body areas they serve is deadened. Intravenous anesthetics, still another type, are injected into a vein. Intravenous anesthetics are fast-acting and sometimes can induce sleep in a few seconds. They and spinal anesthetics can be used together to produce light sleep and pain insensitivity. Other methods of inducing anesthesia are also available, thereby permitting an anesthetist a wide selection of liquid and gaseous drugs for a particular patient's needs. Improved surgical techniques, effective ways of preventing infection, and modern anesthetics have made the operating room increasingly safe for the patient. (*See also* Anesthesia; Medicine; Surgery.)

After surgery a patient is taken to a recovery room until the patient awakens. There, the patient's overall condition is monitored carefully by skilled nurses for several hours. The recovery room may be large enough to hold several postoperative patients at the same time. Lifesaving emergency equipment is there for the rare times that it is needed. For the patient, however, the recovery room is frequently only a blurred memory.

From the recovery room a critically ill patient might be sent to an intensive care unit. These units are available for seriously ill patients whether or not they have had surgery. The intensive care unit is run by specially trained doctors and nurses who have an array of advanced electronic equipment at hand. Monitors constantly record such vital information as breathing and heartbeat. A nurse watching a display screen or hearing an alarm can rapidly provide aid if trouble is detected. Intensive care units are found in many hospitals. Large teaching hospitals have many such units. They might have one for patients with burns, for example, one for those with heart conditions, one for

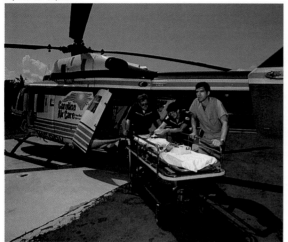

*A Medivac team in Chapel Hill, N.C., rushes an injured child from the unit's helicopter to a hospital emergency room. Helicopters are used in such cases because of their speed.*

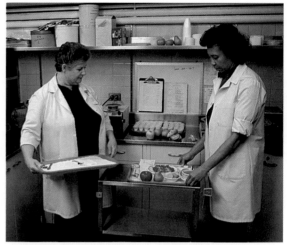

*A dietitian inspects a meal before it is delivered to a patient. Patients, especially diabetics, often require special diets. Patients undergoing surgery or testing may also need a diet change.*

patients with brain or central nervous system disorders, and so on. (*See also* Bioengineering.)

**Obstetrics and gynecology.** The obstetrics and gynecology department tends to the health of female patients in general as well as newborn babies and their mothers. Years ago childbirth was much more hazardous than it is today. Modern obstetrical care has improved the survival rates of pregnant women and newborns who are at risk of a poor outcome. Much of the improvement results from special care that pregnant women may receive during the pregnancy. Special prenatal care includes proper diet, special exercises, and education about pregnancy and childbirth. Many fathers attend birthing classes to learn how to ease the woman's burdens during pregnancy and birth. If a fetus is at high risk for an inherited disorder, specialists can, by a method called amniocentesis, draw off some of the fluid surrounding the fetus inside the mother and analyze cells in the fluid for signs of inherited disorders. Another test, called chorionic villus sampling (CVS), involves taking a sample of tissue from the membrane that surrounds the fetus inside the uterus. This allows for more detailed testing of the fetus's genetic material. Surgeons have treated fetuses in the woman's uterus. Surgeons are also developing ways to remove a fetus, treat it, and return it to the uterus for the remainder of fetal development. Other ways of diagnosing obstetrical disorders include the use of ultrasonic, or high-frequency sound, devices and thermographic devices that find problems by means of unusual heat patterns in the woman's body. (*S also* Pregnancy and Birth; Ultrasound.)

A baby may be delivered in a special kind of operating room called a delivery room or in a more homelike birthing room. The operating room delivery table puts the woman in the best position for the health care professional to supervise the birth process. Some hospitals permit others, such as the father, in the delivery room to comfort the woman giving birth or to coach her through the birth process. In some hospitals nurse-midwives instead of physicians care for women during uncomplicated pregnancies and then, barring any problems, supervise the birth.

After a baby is born it is placed in the hospital nursery, or it may stay in the mother's room. If the baby is ill or has a very low birth weight, the protective environment of an isolette—an infection-free cubicle with controlled oxygen, heat, and humidity—is required until the baby's condition improves and the lungs have developed properly. Critical illness in a newborn requires the specialized care of a newborn intensive care unit.

**Emergency care.** Hospital emergency rooms are set up for treating injuries and illnesses that require prompt action. Lifesaving equipment is always available there. In large hospitals, emergency rooms have doctors in many branches of medicine on call. For example, a cardiologist would be summoned for someone suffering a heart attack, or an orthopedic surgeon would be called to tend a serious bone fracture. Emergency patients with minor ailments are treated and released, but those with more serious problems might be admitted into the hospital. (*See also* Trauma Center.)

Many hospitals maintain outpatient units where patients can seek treatment for chronic illnesses without hospital confinement. The larger hospitals tend to have specialty clinics for a variety of problems, such as skin diseases, nerve disorders, or orthopedic maladies.

Hospital emergency rooms have served a growing number of people whose disorders ordinarily do not require immediate attention. Many people, especially those in low-income sections of large cities, find it difficult to get affordable medical care when they need it and therefore go to emergency rooms with minor illnesses, including colds. As a result, the emergency departments are frequently overcrowded.

*The duration of a hospital stay is normally filled with a variety of medical and administrative procedures. Except for people who are taken to the emergency room, admission (top left) is by appointment and under a physician's orders. The patient is first weighed and measured (top right). Then a nurse goes through the common routine of taking the patient's temperature (bottom left). Once admitted to her room, the patient undergoes further testing and monitoring prior to any surgery. A nurse listens to the patient's heart with a stethoscope (bottom right). Blood pressure will be noted, and blood samples may also be taken.*

**X-Ray department.** A medical specialist called a radiologist uses X rays and other forms of energy to determine conditions inside the body. X-ray and other images are taken in the hospital radiology department. Another kind of specialist, called a neuroradiologist, uses X-ray or nuclear techniques to diagnose and treat diseases of the brain and central nervous system. Also, radiation generated by powerful machines in the radiation medicine department is used by radiation oncologists to treat certain diseases, particularly cancer. (*See also* Diagnosis; Radiation; X Rays.)

**Nutrition.** Hospitalized persons often need special foods, which are prepared by the hospital's dietetics department. A dietitian is trained to tailor a meal to the needs of each patient. Diabetics, for example, need sugar-free, balanced diets, while heart patients need low-salt diets. Also, the dietetics service must put considerable effort into planning and preparing meals for all other patients. Imagination must be used to avoid monotonous meals and to stimulate the appetites of sick persons.

**Corrective therapy.** Hospitals usually have allied health-care specialists called therapists. A physical therapist may help improve a patient's injured or diseased body parts by means of massage and whirlpool baths or by teaching the patient how to do special exercises.

An occupational therapist helps train or retrain a disabled person for work. A respiratory therapist helps patients with breathing problems. A recreational therapist designs and supervises interesting activities to help relieve the boredom of long hospital stays. (*See also* Medicine; Therapy.)

**Pediatrics.** Sick children requiring hospitalization are treated in the pediatrics department. There they are cared for by specially trained pediatric nurses or even nurse-practitioners who have received extra instruction in caring for sick children. Many hospitals have playrooms for children. A recreation director may supervise play, or a volunteer worker might be responsible for the playroom.

Some hospitals provide sleeping facilities for a parent so that he or she can be near the hospitalized child and provide a measure of care. In this way the child is spared some of the anxiety and fear of being sick among strangers. To help allay fears, some pediatric services encourage children to visit the hospital before they are admitted for treatment.

**Other departments.** Large hospitals usually have a number of specialized medical departments, such as a dermatology department for skin diseases, a neurology department for brain and central nervous system disorders, a psychiatry department for mental illnesses, and a cardiology department for heart disease. Personnel in the pathology department study tissue specimens to help diagnose disease or determine causes of death (*see* Medicine). The hospital's blood bank collects, stores, and dispenses blood (*see* Blood). The rehabilitation medicine department helps paralyzed patients and those with other limb problems (*see*

*A hospital stay can be frightening for a child. Many hospitals now try to make the stay as easy and comfortable as possible. A girl whose tonsils are to be removed (top left) settles in her room with her favorite teddy bear. Her mother stays and reads with her. The next morning, with her mother still attending, the patient is prepared for the operation (top right). After the surgery, the patient stays in a recovery room before being returned to her own room and bed (bottom left). With the recovery well under way, the patient is released from the hospital anywhere from a few hours to a day or two later (bottom right).*

Disease, Human) gain the skills required for life outside the hospital.

If a hospital is to run smoothly it must have a medical records department where each patient's medical information is filed. A hospital must also have a housekeeping department responsible for keeping the hospital clean and a maintenance department for keeping the hospital in good repair. And to ensure smooth functioning, a hospital also has an administrative group responsible for the overall operation of the institution.

**Admitting and billing processes.** A patient is admitted to a hospital for overnight stay only on the recommendation of a physician who has admitting privileges at that institution. The hospital admitting office does the necessary paperwork and finds out if the incoming patient has some form of health insurance.

Costs for inpatients, or those who must stay in the hospital, are generally of two types—room rates and ancillary, or additional, services. Private rooms cost more than semiprivate rooms, which accommodate two to four persons. Wards, which usually contain four or more persons, are the least expensive. The most expensive rooms are intensive care units, because they have a high ratio of doctors and nurses to patients and more elaborate and therefore more costly equipment.

The room rate makes up about one third to two thirds of a patient's hospital bill. Included in the room rate are the costs of nursing care, food, housekeeping,

fuel and utilities, equipment sterilization, and staff doctors hired by the hospital, among others. Ancillary charges include costs for medications, laboratory tests, X rays, physical therapy, operating room use, blood, braces, dentures, and casts, when any of these are needed.

### Special Problems of Hospitals

Because hospitals must house and treat the sick, hospitals have problems unlike those of other places of accommodation. A major problem a hospital must cope with is the natural dislike people have of being away from home when sick.

Hospital costs can be a major problem if they are allowed to grow at a fast rate. One major reason for large increases in the cost of health care has been the granting of higher salaries and wages to hospital personnel, who for years were among the lowest paid workers in the health care industry. A second reason for rising hospital costs has been the demand for more services by medical consumers. Yet another reason has been the growing cost of medical technology and treatment. A single diagnostic device, for example, may cost hundreds of thousands of dollars. Hospital administrators cannot always justify spending money on a new device that may be outmoded within a year. Yet in some cases a particular machine, such as a magnetic resonance imaging (MRI) device, is so useful that not having one could not be justified. To reduce the costs of operation and to deflect the expense of having

The Containerized Hospital Emergency Mobile (CHEM) has a variety of uses. In less developed countries it can bring vital medical care to people in remote areas. It can also take medical assistance to rural parts of industrialized nations. A CHEM can serve as an operating room or an emergency room. The unit is often used in preventive-medicine programs for health screening.
Courtesy of Kennedy Medical Offices

machinery date quickly, hospitals in a given area may share use of expensive, high technology devices.

**Telling the hospital's story.** Surgery and unusual procedures and tests can be especially frightening to people who have no idea of what the processes entail. Therefore many hospitals have public relations departments that prepare pamphlets that explain hospital routine. Handbooks that summarize admitting and discharge procedures and tell about events in between are often given to incoming patients. Some hospitals provide pamphlets or booklets about special services, such as blood dispensing, open-heart surgery, or intensive care. In addition, hospital personnel try to explain procedures whenever possible.

Before an operation, for instance, an anesthetist may discuss with the patient the type of anesthetic to be used. Or a nurse or a doctor may warn about the sounds a testing machine makes. A hospital worker may tell whether or not a test will be uncomfortable. Since pain and discomfort are natural worries, a patient can often be reassured when a doctor discusses what will happen during some medical procedure. Sometimes a visit to the operating room or a talk with another patient who has undergone the same procedure can be reassuring, too.

**Disaster plans.** When a major disaster occurs, a hospital may have to treat many more patients than it ordinarily would. Most hospitals have disaster plans ready for such emergencies. A doctor called a triage officer quickly determines how seriously a victim is hurt. The doctor then has the injured person moved to an appropriate area for treatment according to a priority of need. The most seriously injured are attended first. In a major disaster, many persons might require hospitalization. A hospital should therefore have a plan ready to evacuate some of its patients if it

is already full. Certain members of the medical staff must decide which patients are well enough to go home or to be treated as outpatients. Others might be moved to nursing homes or extended-care facilities.

**Neighborhood health clinics.** In some countries health care is delivered relatively equally to all citizens; however, that is not the case in the United States. People in rural areas and in low-income neighborhoods of large cities tend to have access to fewer physicians than do people who live in other areas. In addition, most doctors do not make house calls, even though sick people might have difficulty getting to the doctor's office. Unable to get adequate health care in their own neighborhoods, patients may make frequent use of hospital emergency rooms, often with ailments that do not require urgent attention. Hospitals in medically underserved areas, therefore, have been crowded with a growing number of outpatients and have been finding it increasingly difficult to serve them all. Although adding more physicians to emergency room staffs would seem to be a way of reducing the patient load, many hospitals cannot afford more doctors, cannot provide extra space for more examining rooms, or cannot risk the cost of added full-time staff because emergency room patient loads are unpredictably variable.

To upgrade health-care delivery in their communities, many urban hospitals have established neighborhood health clinics. There, people living in underserved communities can get medical care. Often the neighborhood clinics are miniature versions of clinics in teaching hospitals. Many hospital services are available at the neighborhood clinic, but when patients need special testing or treatment, they are sent to the hospital. In some cases the people of the community run the clinics. In others there is joint hospital-community control. Still others are administered entirely by hospitals or by doctors. Because these clinics tend to lose money, physicians often volunteer their time and the federal government or other sources usually provide some of the funds required for the operation.

**Renovation and expansion needs.** Construction costs run high when a hospital must expand or renovate. The high costs are a reflection of the special, more expensive building designs specific to hospitals. The construction design, for example, must include such items as ramps for wheelchairs, rail supports for certain patients, reinforced floors for heavy equipment, thick walls for radiation safety, research laboratories, and operating rooms fitted with anti-infection devices.

To cut costs, hospital builders sometimes erect the outer shell of the building and then finish the interior as a need develops. This is practical only when administrators know the hospital will need expansion over a period of years. As a result, the major part of the structure is built at current construction rates rather than at future, usually higher, ones.

**Health insurance.** Less than one half of the United States population has some form of health insurance (*see* Health Insurance). Health insurance, including Medicare and Medicaid—federally sponsored programs for the elderly and the poor—and other kinds of insurance protection have given these people the means to seek a variety of hospital services when needed.

Some authorities believe that treatment of many more persons on an outpatient basis would reduce, to some extent, the higher costs of hospitalization. Some also believe that a greater emphasis on preventive medicine would eventually stabilize or even reduce hospital costs. In response to rising costs, alternative health-care systems have arisen in the form of for-profit, investor-owned hospitals and prepaid group practices, such as health maintenance organizations, or HMOs (*see* Health Maintenance Organization).

In the United States, even with federal participation under Medicare and Medicaid, insurance payment for health-care services is considerably less advanced than it is in other parts of the world. In Europe, in particular, such financial support tends to come from government, and only a small percentage of the costs of hospital operation needs to be covered by payments made directly by patients. Details vary somewhat from country to country.

However, citizens in countries such as Sweden must pay high taxes to cover medical care, and citizens of other nations with broad-coverage health care tend to have long waits for nonemergency care. (*See also* Health Agencies; Hospice.)

---

**FURTHER RESOURCES FOR HOSPITAL**

**Howe, James.** The Hospital Book (Morrow Junior Books, 1994).
**Inlander, C.B.** A Consumer Guide to Surviving Your Hospital Stay (Outlet, 1993).
**Milstein, L.B.** Giving Comfort (Viking Penguin, 1994).
**Sigel, Lois.** New Careers in Hospitals (Rosen Group, 1990).
**Snook, I.D.** Hospitals (Aspen, 1991).

**HOSTEL.** The words hostel and hotel are both derived from the Old French word *ostel,* meaning "inn," but both are originally rooted in the Latin *hospes,* meaning "guest" (as are hospital and hospice). Today the common term is youth hostel, referring to supervised, dormitory-like shelters that provide inexpensive overnight accommodations for traveling young people. Many serve meals as well, or they have kitchens in which guests can prepare their own meals.

The primary advantage of hostels is expense: staying at one costs far less than it does at most commercial hotels. Guests usually make their own beds and do other light work to maintain the hostel in partial exchange for using the facilities.

Hostels can be found in many countries, especially throughout Europe. They are situated both in cities and in rural areas. Those in the countryside are normally placed at intervals so visitors can hike or bicycle from one to another within a day's time. The earliest hostels were founded, in fact, to serve as resting places for hikers. At some hostels a time limit is imposed on the length of stay.

The youth hostel movement was a by-product of the generation gap in Germany early in the 20th century. In 1896 a 21-year-old student at Berlin University, Hermann Hoffmann, started a small self-improvement group. The study group often hiked through nearby woods. In 1901 several members of the group drew up a constitution, turned the organization into a hiking society, and took the name *Wandervögel,* meaning "migratory birds."

The organization rapidly attracted thousands of youth from all over Germany—young people who were disenchanted with the values and discipline of the older generation and who wanted to set out on new paths for themselves. Although not a political movement, the *Wandervögel* devoted themselves to all things German—folklore, folk music, and exaltation of their nation. In the early years bands of these youth hiked around Germany, usually sleeping outdoors. In 1910 the first hostel was opened to accommodate them, and others soon followed. The idea quickly spread to Switzerland and The Netherlands, and then to the rest of Europe.

World War I interrupted the development of the hostel movement, but it resumed shortly afterward, when numerous other youth groups were formed. In 1930 the Youth Hostels Association of Great Britain was founded. An international conference in 1932 led to the establishment of the International Youth Hostel Federation. This organization has its headquarters at Welwyn Garden City in Hertfordshire, England. There are affiliates in 70 countries, including American Youth Hostels, which was founded in the United States in 1934. The federation publishes handbooks and guides, and national affiliates also have their publications. The American Youth Hostels staff publishes an annual book called 'Hostelling North America: A Guide to Hostels in Canada and the United States'. Such general travel books as the Fodor and Michelin guides also list hostels by location.

*The lobby and first floor restaurant of the Hyatt Regency Chicago Hotel are enclosed by glass, making possible a green and landscaped environment with plenty of sunlight.*

**HOTEL AND MOTEL.** The travel industry represents one of the largest components of the world economy. Within it, the hotel and motel industry plays a central role in the housing and feeding of people away from home. The word hotel is derived from the French word meaning "inn," and that, in turn, comes from the Latin *hospes,* meaning "guest." Motel is simply a contraction of the words motor and hotel. The term came into common use in the 1920s, indicating an establishment that provided parking for cars as well as food and lodging. Today many hotels have parking facilities and many motels have become so large that the distinction has become almost meaningless. (*See also* Travel and Tourism.)

### Classification by Type

In the mid-1980s there were about 9 million hotel rooms in the world, including about 2.6 million in the United States. Hotels normally fall into one of five categories: transient, residential, resort, motel, and convention center. Considering the enormous growth of the hotel industry since World War II, however, these classifications are becoming blurred. The term transient, for instance, represents the dominant kind of hotel—a place offering lodging and meals to business travelers or tourists who stay a limited number of days. This definition fits resort hotels, convention centers, and motels as well, though these three types have other distinguishing characteristics.

A residential hotel is basically an apartment building for permanent guests. It offers maid service, a dining room, probably a cocktail lounge, and meal service in rooms. Residential hotels are usually located in cities, and they range from the very luxurious to quite plain accommodations.

Resort hotels are usually located in scenic, recreational, or historic sites away from large cities. They are built on lakeshores, seashores, in mountain areas, at health spas, and in other locations that tend to attract tourists. Some of the most popular resort complexes are in Florida, on Caribbean islands, along the east and west coasts of Mexico, in the Hawaiian Islands, and along the coasts of the Mediterranean and Black seas. There are, in addition, the famous health resorts, such as Baden Baden in Germany and Hot Springs, Ark., in the United States. (These were the original resorts.) Ski resorts, such as those in Switzerland, Austria, Italy, and, in the United States, in the West, and New England, operate primarily during the winter months. Resorts in warm climates, on the other hand, generally remain open all year long.

Although the word motel is still in use, the terms motor lodge, motor inn, and motor hotel have become more common. These have been traditionally situated away from central city areas and near highways and highway interchanges, making them especially convenient for people who travel by car. The first motels originated in the United States during the 1920s, and they were usually operated by a husband and wife team. They were found in rural areas and offered primarily lodging, though some of them had small diners or coffee shops. By 1950, when automobile travel had become the chief mode of family travel, the number of motels began to increase dramatically.

In 1952 Holiday Inns, Incorporated, was founded in Memphis, Tenn., as a motel chain. By the 1980s it had become the world's largest hotel chain, with well over 1,700 properties in more than 50 countries. The expansion of Holiday Inns from motels into full-fledged hotels was followed by a similar development in other motel chains and helped blur the distinction between motels and hotels. Though motels are more common in North America than elsewhere, there has been a significant increase in motel building in Europe, Japan, and the Caribbean Basin since the 1960s.

The modern motor hotel no longer depends solely on automobile travel for location. Many are now situated within or near major airports. They often serve as convention and exhibition centers. They also are convenient for business travelers, relieving them of the need of traveling to the central city to conduct their business.

Convention centers are large buildings, or complexes of buildings, which usually contain a hotel. The purpose of these centers is to provide ample space for major exhibitions or convention space for large gatherings. Some centers are large enough to include a sports arena, theaters, shops, and a recreation area in addition to a hotel, restaurants, and convention space.

### Classification by Quality

Accommodations for travelers vary a great deal in quality. In this case, quality refers to the number and kinds of services offered. The stratification of hotels is more evident in Europe than the United States. In Europe, hotels are rated according to their services, and the more services offered, the higher the cost of staying at the hotel. Top-rated, or five-star, hotels are the most luxurious hotels—establishments such as the Mandarin in Hong Kong, the Ritz in Paris, or the Cipriani in Venice.

The modern luxury hotel did not originate in the United States, but the pattern for its modern development was established there. Such hotels are virtually small, self-contained villages, offering nearly every conceivable amenity to travelers. Among their services are restaurants, cocktail lounges, breakfast rooms, laundry and dry cleaning facilities, exercise rooms, 24-hour room service, pharmacies, news-stands, small shops, swimming pools, private meeting rooms, exhibition space, car rental offices, travel bureaus, and more. In places where gambling is allowed, the hotels contain large casinos. In Las Vegas and Atlantic City there are large showrooms, or theaters, as well.

Below the five-star rating the hotels diminish the number of services as well as the cost of accommodations, though the quality of many four-star hotels is often so high it is difficult to distinguish them from luxury hotels. On the European continent, as the number of stars decreases, the number of services also decreases. But establishments that offer less, and consequently cost less, are still very acceptable places for tourists to stay.

Many inexpensive European hotels are family-operated and maintain a high quality in the services they do offer. Even small bed-and-breakfast hotels make efforts to help tourists in every way

Rene Burri—Magnum

*Rooms at the luxurious Ritz Hotel in Paris are lavishly furnished in continental styles.*

possible. European hotels, especially in France, usually have a staff member called a concierge. This individual, who normally speaks several languages, is available to help guests arrange tours, obtain theater and restaurant reservations, handle luggage, and provide many other types of assistance. In the British Isles, North America, and the Far East similar levels of quality in inexpensive hotels are not necessarily maintained.

### Reservation Systems

Before travel became one of the world's leading industries, getting a room for the night away from home was no more difficult than walking into a hotel and asking for it. Today this is much less true, especially for the more expensive hotels in cities that host large conventions and exhibitions. To get into a resort hotel without a reservation is almost impossible, unless one arrives off season.

Reservations can be made in a variety of ways. The hotel can be called directly; a hotel chain's toll-free telephone number can be called; a travel agent can be used; or an airline can be asked to make the reservation. In 1965 Holiday Inns introduced the hotel

*The Sheraton Hotel resort at Cancún, Mexico, is—like many resorts—virtually a self-contained village. The pools and cabana are in the foreground, while the Gulf of Mexico is behind the hotel at the top of the picture.*

Robert Frerck—Odyssey Productions

industry's first computerized reservation system. Hotel chains maintain their own computer systems; independent hotels usually have agents take care of bookings for them.

### History

There were inns throughout the ancient civilized world, strategically placed to accommodate merchants, military personnel, government officials, and others whose work forced them to travel. During the early Middle Ages, when travel was infrequent and unsafe, hospitality was often dispensed by religious orders.

Beginning in about the 12th century inn standards rose steadily as local economies improved. By 1589 there was a traveler's guide defining the differences between the various kinds of accommodations available. When Marco Polo ventured to China in the 13th century, he found an extensive system of relay houses for travelers and way stations for the Mongol postal service. By the end of the Middle Ages there were inns throughout Europe and in the Islamic countries. The Industrial Revolution stimulated inn building, especially in England, whose inns became a standard for the rest of the world.

The first hotels in North America were Atlantic seaport inns and converted farmhouses along stagecoach routes. When canals and railroads were built in the 19th century, the wayside inn gave way to larger hotels built along the rights-of-way. As cities grew, new hotels were constructed in the business centers and theater districts. By 1800 the United States already had the largest hotels in the world, and this trend toward large size continued into the 20th century.

As travel for pleasure gained popularity in Europe, luxury and resort hotels were built in many countries. Some of the first resort hotels were built along the French and Italian rivieras, from Marseilles to Pisa. The Savoy Hotel in London set new standards of luxury when it opened in 1889 by having its own electricity, theater, private chapel, laundry, and printing press. The hotel was managed by César Ritz, who opened his own luxury hotel in Paris in 1898.

**HOUDINI, Harry** (1874–1926). One of the best-recognized names in magic is that of Harry Houdini. His ability to skillfully free himself from ropes, chains, locks, and handcuffs made him world famous, and he was billed in theaters as "The Elusive American." He was a master of the escape act.

Born Erik Weisz in Budapest, Hungary, on March 24, 1874, he was brought to the United States as an infant. The family first settled in Appleton, Wis., then moved to New York City, where the father, Rabbi Samuel Weiss (the Americanized spelling of the name), made a meager living as a teacher.

Taking his stage name from a famous French magician, Jean-Eugène Robert-Houdin, young Harry set out to become a professional magician (see Magic). With a friend, who was later replaced by Harry's brother Theodore (known as Dash), he formed a team

known as The Houdini Brothers, and they performed escape acts.

While working at Coney Island in New York, Harry met and married Wilhelmina Beatrice Rahner. Bess, as she was known, served as his assistant for several years. Houdini and his wife changed their act several times, at one point performing as spirit mediums. Never extremely effective with magic and conjuring, Houdini became a master of the escape stunt.

Following a highly successful tour of England in 1900, Houdini's act was solidly booked in the United States. He gave his stunts frightening, mysterious-sounding names like Metamorphosis, the Chinese Water Torture Cell, and Buried Alive. Onstage he might be tied hand and foot and nailed into a packing case, or submerged in a giant milk can filled with water. Between shows, he might be wrapped in a hospital straitjacket and suspended upside down high above the street, only to free himself in minutes.

Later in life, after several international tours, Harry Houdini made a number of motion pictures and toured as a lecturer exposing the tricks of psychics and spiritualists. He died on Halloween 1926 in Detroit, Mich., after his appendix ruptured. He is buried in Machpelah Cemetery in Queens, N.Y.

James Randi

**FURTHER RESOURCES FOR HARRY HOUDINI**

**Brandon, Ruth.** The Life and Many Deaths of Harry Houdini (Random, 1993).
**Kellock, Harold.** Houdini: The Life Story (From the Recollections and Documents of Beatrice Houdini) (Harcourt, 1928).
**Randi, James, and Sugar, Ber Randolph.** Houdini: His Life and Art (Grossett, 1976).
**Williams, Beryl, and Epstein, Samuel.** The Great Houdini (Amereon, Ltd., n.d.).

**HOUSEPLANT.** Any plant adapted for growing indoors is a houseplant. The most common houseplants are members of exotic species that flourish naturally only in warm climates. Once having been domesticated, however, they are able to survive in home environments even in fairly cold parts of the world. Houseplants are found in homes, offices, and indoor public spaces. They are grown from seeds or cuttings or purchased as seedlings or full-grown plants.

The practice of growing plants indoors was known in ancient times. The Romans were the first to use special indoor growing areas to speed up plant growth. Houseplants did not become widely popular until after the 17th century. In 1608 an English authority on agriculture, Sir Hugh Platt, published 'The Garden of Eden', which discussed how plants might be grown indoors. Not long afterward, many previously unknown species brought back to Europe from the tropics by explorers who sailed on voyages of discovery could be found in newly built greenhouses and conservatories.

Home environments are usually different from a plant's native land. Two factors determine the success of the huge number of species grown today as houseplants. It is essential that houseplants be easy to care for, and they must be able to tolerate the fairly low

*Ferns and other houseplants add a great deal of color and life to well-lighted rooms in a house or apartment.*

levels of light and humidity found in most homes. Attractiveness also plays an obvious role—houseplants are favored either because of their foliage or the flowers they produce.

Among the foliage plants, two popular varieties are the philodendrons and begonias. Jade plants are called leaf succulents, because they store water in their fleshy leaves. Other succulents that are popular as houseplants are the cacti. They are found in a multitude of bizarre shapes and often combine pretty blossoms with unusually formed spines. Some common houseplants have the appearance of small trees, such as the rubber trees and palms. Other popular houseplants are the ferns and ivies (*see* Cactus; Fern; Ivy; Palm).

Because they require greater attention and a more precisely controlled environment, flowering plants are generally less successful in the home than are foliage plants. But there are some notable exceptions, the most famous being the many varieties of the African violet.

Other popular flowering plants include impatiens, hibiscus, and geraniums, which do well in sunny windows. Although most orchids must be grown in greenhouses, there are a few that will thrive in the home. Some houseplants yield edible fruit, such as small oranges, lemons, tomatoes, and peppers.

### Conditions for Growth

Many houseplants can tolerate improper care to a certain extent. However, overwatering, overfeeding, insufficient light, drafts, or lack of air circulation can deter growth or make a plant susceptible to disease. (*See also* Plant.)

**Light.** All plants need some bright light each day, though it need not be direct. The bright light and intense heat of the sun streaming in a window can scorch most houseplants. In the Northern Hemisphere houseplants prefer filtered, indirect light from an east-, west-, or north-facing window. Artificial light is also used combined with natural light, or in its place.

Among the common houseplants that require shade are the asparagus fern, baby's tears, bird's nest fern, grape ivy, palm, peperomia, philodendron, prayer plant, rubber plant, snake plant, and Swedish ivy. Houseplants that need bright light are the African violet, aloe, cactus, coleus, cyclamen, spider plant, and wandering jew.

**Temperature and humidity.** Most houseplants will do well at temperatures of 65° to 75° F (18° to 24° C), the range found in most homes. Plants will tolerate a minor temperature drop at night when thermostats are routinely lowered. Houseplants also require a humid environment not usually found indoors. Daily spraying or placement of the plants in a tray of damp pebbles increases the humidity.

**Water.** Watering must be adjusted to the needs of the plant, the size of its container, the composition of its soil, and the temperature and humidity of the room. Most plants go through a dormancy period during the winter and need less water than they do the rest of the year. Overwatering is usually fatal.

**Soil.** The potting soil used for houseplants is usually a mixture of soil, peat and sand, vermiculite, or perlite. Some mixtures are soilless, containing mostly peat. Peat mixtures lack nutrients necessary for successful plant growth and are supplemented regularly. Unlike garden soil, potting mixtures are sterile and allow better drainage and air circulation around the roots.

**Nutrients.** Houseplants need regular feeding when they are actively growing because the nutrients in their containers are gradually used up. The nutrients vital to all plant growth—nitrogen, phosphorus, and potassium—are contained in fertilizers or plant food that can be added to the soil. In addition, nutrients can be sprayed onto a plant's leaves, a practice that stimulates foliage growth.

**Pest control.** Pests are less of a problem indoors, but houseplants are always susceptible to pest infestation. Pests and disease are brought into the home on new plants or in the air. Infestation is controlled by washing the plant with various liquids, ranging from alcohol to soapy water, or with commercial insecticides. (*See also* Fertilizer.)

### Containers

Houseplants are displayed in a variety of containers, usually made of clay or plastic. Most have a drainage hole and a saucer to catch the excess water. Trailing plants are often planted in a hanging container so the leaves can fall over the sides. Standing window boxes or tiered stands of wood or other material are also used.

Lisa McGowan

*A home in the suburbs, a goal of many families, has increased dramatically in value.*

# HOUSING

The provision of housing is a basic function of every human society. Everyone needs housing of some kind. A housing unit, or home, is the place where people carry on the private activities of their lives. Home is where people eat and sleep, where they store their belongings, where they can mingle undisturbed with members of their families. Although homes may be used as offices, stores, or workshops, a home is a place where goods and services are consumed rather than produced.

## THE NEED FOR HOUSING

Housing units differ in many respects. Some are owned by their occupants; some are rented. Some units are separate buildings; some are apartments. The number and sizes of rooms in housing units vary greatly, as does the quality of cooking, plumbing, and heating facilities.

Housing standards vary in different societies. In the United States, for example, it is thought that there should be at least one room for each member of a family. But this social-cultural standard is peculiar to the United States, for there is no clear evidence that

................................................

*This article was contributed by Wallace F. Smith, Professor of Business Administration, University of California at Berkeley.*

having less than one room for each member of a family is in any way harmful to its well-being. The American view that a bathroom should be available exclusively to just one family is far from universal.

### Households

In 2000 there were about 105 million households in the United States. A household is defined by the Bureau of the Census as a person or a group of persons living in a separate housing unit. A family consisting of a husband, a wife, and the children who live with them constitutes a household. A person living alone also constitutes a household—unless he or she lives in a transient hotel or in a furnished room in someone else's housing unit.

Two unrelated persons sharing an apartment count as one household. So does a widowed or divorced person with children to care for. Household is a more inclusive term than family, and the number of households is more useful than the number of families as a gauge of the need for housing.

A household may be large or small, rich or poor, young or old, urban or rural, white-collar or blue-collar, and so on. Different kinds of households tend to have different housing needs and wants.

Demographic and geographic changes affect the number of households. Such demographic changes include those that occur as individuals are born, grow into adulthood, marry, have children, become old, and die. Divorce, separation, and institutionalization (entry into a retirement home, for example) are other demographic changes that have a bearing on the number of households. Geographic changes that influence the number of households are those that occur as individuals move out of one residence and into another.

The demographic events related to the need for housing occur approximately as follows in the life cycle of a typical American man or woman:

|  | Age | |
|---|---|---|
|  | Man | Woman |
| Leave parents' home. . . . . . . . . . . | 21 | 21 |
| Marry. . . . . . . . . . . . . . . . . . . . . . | 25 | 23 |
| First child born. . . . . . . . . . . . . . | 26 | 24 |
| First child enters school. . . . . . . . . | 31 | 29 |
| Last child born . . . . . . . . . . . . . . . | 32 | 30 |
| Last child leaves home . . . . . . . . . | 52 | 50 |
| Husband dies. . . . . . . . . . . . . . . . . | 71 | 69 |
| Widow dies . . . . . . . . . . . . . . . . . | — | 78 |

In a life cycle typical of many Americans, a young person has an apartment for a few years and then marries someone who may or may not still live with his or her parents. The new couple often needs an apartment larger than the one either previously had and probably a still larger dwelling after their first child is born. When the child is about 5 years old, the parents may move closer to an elementary school. This is often when they first become homeowners. After the last child leaves home, the family home is an "empty nest," usually larger than the middle-aged couple needs. At some point, perhaps upon retirement, the couple may sell the house and move into an apartment, condominium, or retirement village. After her husband dies, the elderly widow maintains housing for herself.

Yearly changes in the number of households stem largely from the changing needs generated by the life cycles of the population as a whole. The number of households 10 or 20 years ahead can be predicted with considerable accuracy because individuals tend to follow the traditional life cycle fairly closely. Projections indicate that in the year 2010 the total number of households in the United States will be between 113 million and 115 million. These projections take into account such factors as the number of people delaying marriage, the divorce rate, and the number of elderly people.

Geographic shifts in the location of households are reflected in the movement of households from the farm to the city, from one city to another, from the city to the suburbs, and from one city neighborhood to another. The average household in the United States moves about every five years. This average includes young apartment dwellers who move once a year or oftener and home-owning widows who have lived in the same house for 50 years or more.

**Number of Households* in the United States**

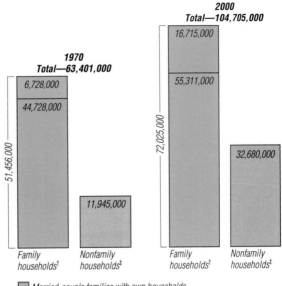

Married-couple families with own households

Other family households

**Married Couples in the United States Without Their Own Households***
*(percent of all married couples)*

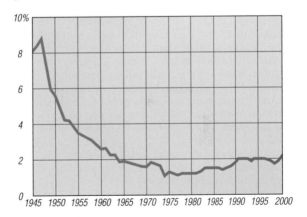

*A household comprises all persons living in the same housing unit.
†A family household consists of the householder (formerly "household head") and all other persons in the household related to the householder.
‡A nonfamily household is a person living alone or a householder living with nonrelatives only.
Source: Bureau of the Census, U.S. Dept. of Commerce

Many rural counties and even entire predominantly rural states have had a net loss of population through out-migration to urban areas. This has resulted largely from the declining importance of the family farm and the attraction of job opportunities in the cities. At the same time, many large cities have lost population to their suburban areas, which as a result have shown enormous increases in the number of households. However, metropolitan areas as a whole—central cities plus suburbs—have grown rapidly, too.

**Occupancy of Housing Units in the United States** (in millions)

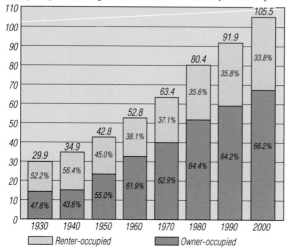

☐ Renter-occupied    ■ Owner-occupied

Source: Bureau of the Census, U.S. Dept. of Commerce

**Age of Occupied Housing Units in the United States**

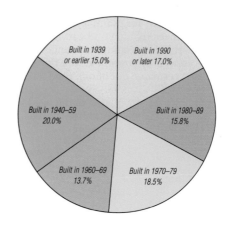

Source: Bureau of the Census, U.S. Dept. of Commerce

## Housing Standards

When people are asked what kind of housing they need or want, the question evokes a variety of answers: "four bedrooms"; "lots of storage space"; "close to my work"; "low rent"; "a quiet neighborhood"; "a big yard"; "a scenic view"; and so on. To most people, housing quality obviously means more than simply shelter.

**Floor area.** "Is it big enough?" is perhaps the first question a family asks when it looks at a new house or apartment. A family might want, for example, a master bedroom for the husband and wife, a separate bedroom for the younger children of each sex, a separate bedroom for each child over 12, a bedroom for a grandparent or a guest, large closets, an extra half-bathroom, a dining room or a kitchen with a good-sized eating area, a large living room, a family or recreation room, a den or library, a patio, a two-car garage, and so on. Since most families would like to have as much space as they can afford, space expectations have risen as incomes have risen.

**Floor plan.** The layout of a dwelling can contribute to its desirability. But preferences in floor plans change. Up to the 1930s it was considered essential to have a separate dining room. Afterward, a dining area adjoining the living room and kitchen was regarded as adequate. The desired kitchen size tended to shrink when the kitchen was displaced by the living room or the recreation room as the informal center of family life; however, since the 1980s large kitchens have become more popular. Walk-in closets and dressing rooms between the master bedroom and bathroom have become fashionable. Many people prefer to have the front door open into an entrance hallway, however small, rather than directly into the living room. Bathrooms are generally away from the front entrance. Two- or even three-story houses are as acceptable as ranch houses and bi- or tri-levels.

**Equipment.** Families in the United States expect their homes to have electrical wiring sufficient for lighting and many appliances; a system of hot and cold running water; a central heating system suitable to the climate; a sink, a range, a refrigerator, and cabinets in the kitchen; a bathtub and shower, a flush toilet, and a sink unit in the bathroom; and an automatic washer and dryer in the laundry room. As time goes by, more and more items once considered luxuries—such as wall-to-wall carpeting, central air conditioning, a dishwasher, and a garbage-disposal unit—are built into new homes and apartments.

**Interior finish.** Ceilings in the United States have generally been lowered to a height of about 8 feet (2.4 meters). At the same time, a feeling of spaciousness has been preserved by increasing window areas, enlarging living rooms, and using lighter interior wall colors. Carefully joined, easy-to-clean walls and ceilings are preferred. Wallpaper and wood or plywood paneling are popular decorating options. Kitchen and bathroom floors are being covered with linoleum or tile, and tiled kitchen and bathroom walls have become increasingly common. The floors of other rooms are usually hardwood or covered with permanent carpeting, though asphalt tile flooring is also widely used, especially for family rooms.

**Exterior design.** A single-family house on its own lot is the type of dwelling preferred by most families in the United States. Row houses are traditional in some cities, and apartment buildings containing up to a hundred or more separate dwelling units are especially common in the central districts of large cities. In such multifamily buildings the common areas—hallways, elevators, garages, basements—are important aspects of livability. Families in the United States generally favor traditional housing forms. Few are willing to live in experimental dwellings, such as plastic bubbles or geodesic domes. "A house should

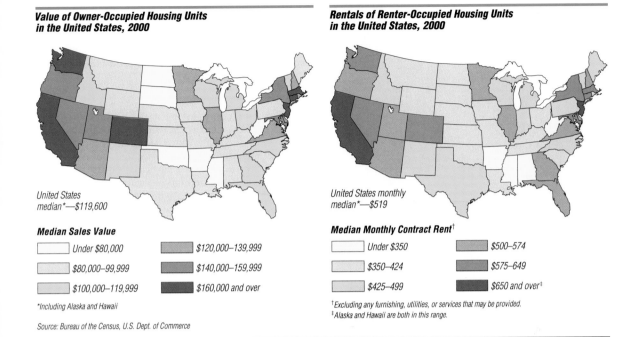

**Value of Owner-Occupied Housing Units in the United States, 2000**

United States median*—$119,600

**Median Sales Value**

| | |
|---|---|
| Under $80,000 | $120,000–139,999 |
| $80,000–99,999 | $140,000–159,999 |
| $100,000–119,999 | $160,000 and over |

*Including Alaska and Hawaii

Source: Bureau of the Census, U.S. Dept. of Commerce

**Rentals of Renter-Occupied Housing Units in the United States, 2000**

United States monthly median*—$519

**Median Monthly Contract Rent†**

| | |
|---|---|
| Under $350 | $500–574 |
| $350–424 | $575–649 |
| $425–499 | $650 and over‡ |

†Excluding any furnishing, utilities, or services that may be provided.
‡Alaska and Hawaii are both in this range.

---

look like a house" is what Americans seem to be saying to the architects.

**Structural condition.** Housing is expected to be durable and solidly constructed. Some older structures, however, may have roofs that sag or leak, cracked foundations and walls, floors that are not level, and doors that do not fit their frames. Wind and rain may get through the window frames.

Wooden structural elements, such as floor joists and rafters, may be rotted or pest infested. Work done by a previous occupant—do-it-yourself wiring or plumbing, for example—may be unattractive or even dangerous. Multiple layers of paint may conceal the original materials and finish. Some of these defects are immediately visible, but others may be discovered only after occupancy.

**The house lot.** A single-family house usually occupies no more than one third of the lot on which it stands. By tradition and usually by law, a house is set well back from the street, making it necessary for the homeowner to maintain a front yard or garden. The backyard is generally used for recreation and relaxation. Apartment dwellers normally have no private open space, but there may be yards or patios that they can share with other occupants of their building. Row houses and town houses usually have small yards or patios at the rear.

**Accessibility.** A vital feature of any dwelling is its accessibility to the occupant's place of work and to stores, schools, homes of friends and relatives, and other frequently visited places. Accessibility is determined not only by distance from the dwelling but also by the time and cost of the journey. Homes are therefore judged in part by their nearness to

expressways and paved roads and to rail and bus transportation. Most persons in the United States live less than an hour's commuting time from their jobs.

**Neighborhood.** Homeseekers are often greatly concerned about the quality and the appearance of neighboring dwellings as well as the dwelling that they are considering purchasing. They are generally also concerned about the race, ethnic background, and social or economic class of their prospective neighbors.

In most nations housing standards are markedly below those of the United States. In Mexico in 1991 one fifth of houses had no piped water supply and two fifths of houses had no sewerage. Japan topped the United States, France, West Germany, and the United Kingdom in 1987 in new dwellings but was last among them in residential buildings per 1,000 people and floor area per building. Crowded housing conditions even exist in such other affluent countries as Sweden. Only in relatively few nations are central heating and automatic hot water systems installed in all new buildings.

Housing in the United States is generally of better quality and in greater supply than that of other countries. The main question, however, is whether its housing needs are being met at a rate which its own people consider reasonable. Also important is whether each family has at least the minimum quality of housing necessary for health, comfort, and self-respect.

**The Choice of Housing**

The quality of housing available to an individual, a couple, or a larger family ultimately depends on the ability to pay. The choice of a home is determined largely by income and assets and by the proportion of

*Multistory walk-up apartment buildings in Boston, Mass., are typical of dwellings in high-density areas of the older large cities in the United States.*

## THE PROVISION OF HOUSING

The supply of housing in the United States consists of buildings that have been erected during many decades of construction. This large supply of used housing is known as the housing inventory.

### The Housing Market

The housing inventory is a major national resource. But the size of the housing inventory is not the only measure of its adequacy. Much of the inventory is old and deteriorated, inconveniently located, out of fashion, and unsuited to the particular needs of people who happen to be in the market for housing. Even if sufficient housing of adequate quality is available, does this mean that a family seeking a home will be able to obtain the housing unit that best meets its needs? And when a family's housing needs change, will it be able to move to a more suitable dwelling?

These questions are generally answered in the business-motivated marketplace. But the matching of households with housing units in this way sometimes produces unsatisfactory results. A low-income family, for example, may be compelled to live in a crowded or dilapidated dwelling. A widow may live alone in an

*Town houses, such as these in Chicago, Ill., offer more privacy than apartments and make more economical use of high-priced city land than detached, single-family houses.*

them available for housing. Incomes vary considerably, not only among different households but also for the same household at various stages of its life cycle. The assets of most homeseekers consist mainly of savings and equity, or the money they can realize from the sale of the house they already live in. They may also have insurance policies and investments easily converted to cash. Several thousand dollars is usually needed for a down payment (the initial payment). The balance of the purchase price is met by securing a loan known as a mortgage.

A young family seeking to buy a home usually has such limited funds that its first house (or condominium) is relatively inexpensive. But as the mortgage loan is gradually repaid, equity grows so that it can be used as the down payment on a better house. On average, homeowners move on to a better house about six years after buying their first house. A family's assets may be used to keep up payments on the house during periods of temporary unemployment or in retirement or widowhood.

Housing costs for the homeowner generally include mortgage payments, property taxes, and the cost of repairs and utilities. For the renter, they generally include rental payments and the cost of some utilities. A rule of thumb in the United States is that a family should pay no more than 25 percent of its income for housing. Most American households actually spend between 15 and 20 percent. Retired persons and widows, however, often spend more than 30 percent, and well-to-do persons may spend less than 10 percent.

*The "For Sale" signs on the lawn of a suburban condo complex inform prospective buyers where to call for information. Most sales are made through real estate brokers, who receive a commission when the property is sold.*
© Jeff Greenberg—Peter Arnold, Inc.

eight-room house while a family of six is put up in a two-room motel unit by a welfare agency. A black family may be barred from buying a vacant home that it wants and can afford because the home is in a white neighborhood.

The housing inventory of the United States totaled 119 million units in 2001, according to the census of housing. All but three million were year-round dwelling units. About 82 million, or almost 69 percent, were in one-unit structures, and 28 million, or almost 24 percent, were in structures of two or more units. The remainder were mobile homes or trailers. Housing units vary greatly in age, number of rooms, structural condition, equipment, and location. However, the choices available to a family looking for a home are largely limited to the city in which it makes its living.

The local housing market operates by means of a network of information that enables owners of dwellings to find out who is looking for housing and enables home-seeking families to find out which housing units are for sale or for rent. A principal means of communication is a classified ad in the local newspaper. Another is a "For Rent" or "For Sale" sign placed on the property where people looking for housing can see it.

Properties for sale or for rent may be listed with a local real estate broker. The broker receives a commission—usually 6 percent of the sale price—when he sells a property. Most home sales are made through brokers, but apartment rentals are generally arranged in other ways. In many cases homeseekers come to the broker's office. Because individual brokers may not have a suitable property for such prospective buyers, they often exchange listings with other brokers and split the commissions with them.

After a property owner and a prospective buyer or renter are brought together, the selling price or rental terms are negotiated, and the necessary legal documents are prepared. The real estate broker usually helps arrange mortgage financing and fire insurance for the home buyer. He may also make arrangements for title insurance—a guarantee against loss if the seller's title to the property proves defective—and structural inspection reports. Normally, the various deposits required and the documents concerned with the transaction are held by an escrow agent, a licensed neutral third party, until the transaction has been completed. Usually, the escrow agent also completes the official closing statement which settles accounts between the home buyer and the home seller.

The seller usually pays the broker's commission. But the closing costs to the buyer—the cash he must provide for title insurance, prepaid property taxes, fire insurance, and various fees—are usually substantial. The buyer must have at least several hundred dollars in ready cash. Also, the down payment may amount to several thousands of dollars, even though it is often made with a second mortgage or with proceeds from the sale of another house. With government-financed mortgage loans that are nearly equal to the full selling price, down payments are quite low.

Renting an apartment is much simpler than buying a house. There is no mortgage to arrange, no need to prorate property taxes or insurance payments between the old and the new tenant, and, in most cases, no need to enter the transaction in public records as must be done when a building is sold. But a cash deposit as security against damage to the property and prepayment of rent for one or two months may be required. In such cases a new tenant, like a home buyer, may need a substantial amount of ready cash.

Prospective home buyers or their mortgage lenders often have a professional appraiser estimate the value of a home that has been offered for sale. The appraiser

**One of Moscow's apartment complexes, Krylatskoye, is a self-sufficient area with its own schools, stores, and recreation zones.**
TASS/Sovfoto

estimates the fair market value of the property and identifies major structural or legal defects. For his services, he gets a flat fee that does not depend on either the selling price or the completion of the sale. If a home has obvious structural defects—a crack in the foundation, for example—or seems to be in need of major remodeling, the prospective home buyer may consult an architect, an engineer, or a contractor as well as an appraiser.

In most instances the exact amount it will cost to lease an apartment is easily determined. The selling price of a home, however, tells the buyer little about how much the house will actually cost him in the long run. A large part of his monthly housing expenses

will go for mortgage interest and property taxes. To find out what his costs will be, the home buyer must carefully translate into approximate monthly charges the interest rate and the repayment term of the loan, the value of the property as assessed for tax purposes, and the local property tax rate. Favorable federal income tax provisions affecting homeowners must also be taken into consideration. For example, homeowners may deduct mortgage interest and property tax payments in determining their taxable income. A change in the value of a property during the period of ownership may affect the ultimate money cost of housing—through increased taxes, for example—but such changes are difficult to forecast.

**Number of New Housing Units Started in the United States (in millions)***

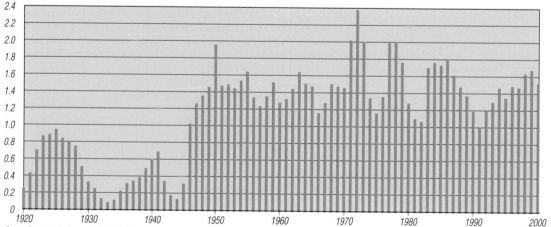

Source: Bureau of the Census, U.S. Dept. of Commerce

*Farm housing units were excluded before 1959. Entries before 1991 may include both privately owned and publicly owned housing units. Entries after 1990 are for privately owned housing units only.

### Types of New Privately Owned Housing Units Started in the United States
(in percent of total)

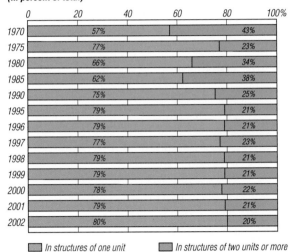

| | In structures of one unit | In structures of two units or more |
|---|---|---|
| 1970 | 57% | 43% |
| 1975 | 77% | 23% |
| 1980 | 66% | 34% |
| 1985 | 62% | 38% |
| 1990 | 75% | 25% |
| 1995 | 79% | 21% |
| 1996 | 79% | 21% |
| 1997 | 77% | 23% |
| 1998 | 79% | 21% |
| 1999 | 79% | 21% |
| 2000 | 78% | 22% |
| 2001 | 79% | 21% |
| 2002 | 80% | 20% |

☐ In structures of one unit ☐ In structures of two units or more

Source: Bureau of the Census, U.S. Dept. of Commerce

### Mobile Homes Shipped to Dealers in the United States
(in thousands)

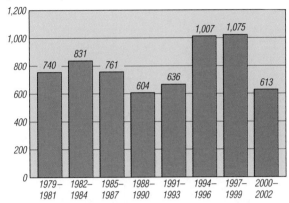

| Period | Thousands |
|---|---|
| 1979–1981 | 740 |
| 1982–1984 | 831 |
| 1985–1987 | 761 |
| 1988–1990 | 604 |
| 1991–1993 | 636 |
| 1994–1996 | 1,007 |
| 1997–1999 | 1,075 |
| 2000–2002 | 613 |

Sources: Bureau of the Census; U.S. Dept. of Housing and Urban Development; Institute for Building Technology and Safety; Manufactured Housing Institute

## Home Financing

Home buyers rarely can or want to put up the cash for the full cost of a house or other home. Most must borrow a large part of the purchase price, pledging the house and lot and the down payment as security. Mortgage financing is therefore necessary to the functioning of the housing market in the United States. It is provided on generally similar terms by several types of financial institutions nationwide. The typical home-mortgage loan in the United States is written for a term of about 30 years and provides about 80 percent of the purchase price. In most cases the buyer must pay a loan fee, often expressed as "points," or a percentage of the amount of the loan. The mortgage contract generally requires the lender to make uniform monthly payments which will amortize, or pay off, the loan by the end of the term. The fixed interest rate charged reflects the market conditions for money at the time the mortgage was written. In 1946 the interest rate was about 5 percent; in 1982 it peaked at 15 percent but went down in the late 1980s. A minor increase in the rate of interest results in a large increase in the monthly cost of owning a home. Over the term of a mortgage, interest payments can be greater than the purchase price. Interest rates on adjustable-rate mortgages vary with the market. These mortgages became increasingly popular into the 1990s, as did 10-percent rather than 20-percent down payments.

Savings and loan associations specialize almost completely in mortgage finance for owner-occupied housing. They lend money that has been deposited in savings accounts. Commercial banks and mutual savings banks also invest savings deposits in real estate mortgages. Life insurance companies make loans from their insurance policy premium-payment reserves. A significant number of mortgages are held by private individuals. Mortgage lenders consider whether an applicant has a good enough credit record and income to meet the monthly payments.

If a homeowner fails to make the monthly mortgage payments, the loan may be foreclosed. This means that the house will be sold to satisfy the debt and that the would-be homeowner will lose the house and any equity that has built up in it. In times of unemployment the foreclosure rate rises. However, a foreclosure sale in a community hard hit by unemployment may bring in less than the outstanding indebtedness, resulting in a financial loss to the lender. A lending institution may therefore be reluctant to foreclose and may try to work out a new payment schedule instead.

Homeowners can borrow additional money to reduce the cash down payment at the time of purchase or for personal expenses later on by placing a second mortgage against the property. In case of foreclosure the holder of the second mortgage gets paid after the holder of the first mortgage. Because of the greater risk to the lender, the interest rate on a second mortgage is higher.

Although home ownership is a well-established tradition in many nations other than the United States, in some of these nations the housing market is very different. In Japan, for example, mortgage credit institutions for buying homes are virtually nonexistent, and the high price of land has led to 100-year mortgages. In Italy, France, and Germany, rental housing in urban areas is often financed by large business concerns. With the help of the United Nations and other international agencies, Zimbabwe's government has offered home-ownership financing to low-income people.

Real estate brokers outside the United States are more likely to handle housing rentals than housing sales and are reluctant to exchange market information. Appraisal practices are highly developed

in Great Britain but are almost unknown in many other countries. Until the 1980s in Communist countries there was no private ownership of income-producing property. Cooperative housing, however, was encouraged by government loans and subsidies.

An increasing number of apartments in the United States are owned by their occupants as cooperatives or condominiums. A cooperative is a multiple-dwelling project owned in common by its residents; a condominium is a multiple-dwelling project whose separate units are individually owned. The market for apartments in some areas is limited mostly to households without children.

New apartment buildings are sometimes financed by insurance companies or pension funds. Most are built by developers for sale to such groups as syndicates, which are partnerships of investors. Like buyers of single-family houses, investors in apartment buildings usually secure mortgage loans to pay most of the purchase price. For their investment the owners receive rental income and such advantages as reduced federal taxes on their personal income from other sources. Even more than buyers of single-family houses, they depend on the expert advice of appraisers, brokers, lawyers, property management firms, and accountants.

### Housebuilding

The construction of new housing units in the United States averages about 1.4 million per year. A family may buy a lot and hire an architect to design and supervise the construction of a house. Most new houses, however, are built in groups of 5 to 100 or more by business firms that first buy the land and lay out the streets and water and sewer lines. The houses are on separate lots and of generally similar design. The completed houses are sold to the public.

These speculative developers, or merchant builders, ordinarily subcontract much of the construction work to specialized firms of carpenters, masons, plumbers, electricians, glaziers, and other craftsmen. The work is coordinated by a general contractor, and the entire venture is financed by a short-term construction mortgage. Most housing developers operate on a small scale and have little working capital. Thus the volume of housebuilding for the entire nation depends largely on the funds developers are able to obtain from financial institutions.

The housebuilding process is often described as old-fashioned and inefficient. Craftsmen assemble each house separately on its own lot, using materials not far removed from their natural state. Much hand labor is required, and assembly-line techniques are rarely used. The cost of finished housing might be significantly reduced if whole houses or major components of houses—such as plumbing systems, walls, or roofs—were mass-produced in factories and quickly assembled at the homesite.

Housebuilding technology in the United States has made some advances in recent years. Factory-made components, such as aluminum window sashes and plywood wall panels, have come into wider use, and spray and roller painting have largely replaced brush painting. In the early 1970s the United States government was encouraging private industry to invest in factory-built housing. This included the building of boxlike modular units that could be stacked in various ways to form complete houses and apartments.

Justin Wager

*This building, which includes both a shop and apartments, is typical of many business streets. Most housing in the United States, however, is in separate residential structures.*

Europeans have had much experience with prefabricated and factory-built housing. Cost savings due to large-scale production of such housing have been realized, for example, in Great Britain, Italy, Sweden, and France. Prefabrication was especially emphasized in the Soviet Union and Eastern Europe, and by the 1990s interest had grown in Japan.

Manufactured (or mobile) homes compose the major part of the factory-built housing supply in the United States. Such homes have increased in size and improved in comfort since trailers pulled by automobiles first appeared in the late 1920s. They are also cheaper than conventional homes; however, since manufactured homes must usually be paid for in 15 years instead of 30, the difference in monthly payments between the two styles often is not great. The space on which a manufactured home stands must be rented. Unlike a conventional house and lot, a manufactured home usually depreciates in value much as a new car does. Average annual production in the

United States decreased from 336,000 in the mid-1990s to about 200,000 in the early 21st century.

## HOUSING: A COMPLEX PROBLEM

"The need for affordable housing" became a refrain heard throughout the world by the closing decades of the 20th century. Estimates of the number of homeless people in the United States alone ranged up to 3 million by the late 1980s (*see* Homelessness). Public housing's woes included decreased federal spending on construction and increased drug-related violence (*see* "The Government's Role" and "Housing Future Generations" in this article).

Even for middle- and upper-income groups, the cost of shelter became a primary concern, particularly as home prices increased much more rapidly than did incomes. From 1975 to 1985 the median value of all homes increased by 125 percent; however, the median family income of married-couple renters aged 25 to 29 (a prime home-buying group) increased by only 80 percent. In Canada, where conventional mortgages typically require a 25-percent down payment, average resale prices for homes shot up by 121 percent during the 1980s. The Canadian Mortgage and Housing Corporation offered terms on a 10-percent down payment and in 1989 announced plans that allowed first-time buyers to put only 5 percent down.

### The Quality of Housing

Houses and apartment buildings need continual maintenance and repairs, or even substantial modernization. As structures age, however, their owners tend to lose interest in maintaining them, and the structures deteriorate. The rate of deterioration is likely to be greater if neighboring buildings are also

*Row houses—a continuous group of houses with shared sidewalls—were an early version of town houses. These row houses were built in Philadelphia in about 1920.*

Free Library of Philadelphia

Components, Inc.

*The floor of this prefabricated house is placed on basement walls that have already been installed (top). Then the sidewalls are dropped into place (bottom).*

neglected. If a building is in a run-down area, lending institutions are reluctant to lend money for repairs.

By 2001, the housing inventory of the United States totaled about 116 million year-round units (occupied and vacant). A primary indicator of housing quality is plumbing, once considered a leading problem in the country. Substandard plumbing lacks one or more of the following: hot and cold piped water, a private flush toilet, or a private bathtub or shower. The percentage of occupied units nationwide with substandard plumbing has decreased from 45 in 1940, to 17 in 1960, to 0.6 in 2000. In some areas, however, at least 0.9 percent of homes lacked standard facilities—notably in the South and the states of Alaska, Arizona, New Mexico, Hawaii, and Maine.

Another measure of housing is the number of vacant units, which in 2001 accounted for 8.2 percent of all year-round units. Why are they not used to house families living in substandard units? One reason is that some of these units are not near enough to the families that need them. The rent or asking price for many vacant standard units may be beyond the financial means of inadequately housed families, who usually have low incomes. The normal rent-to-income ratio ranges between 22 and 28 percent. The vacant units may also be too small for many households. Racial discrimination has barred many from moving into suitable houses or apartments. A vacancy rate of about 5 percent allows households to shop around for better housing.

One reason for the decline of inner-city neighborhoods is that most of them were laid out a century or more ago, long before the advent of today's heavy automobile and truck traffic. Noisy and cluttered streets have induced families that could afford it to move to the quieter suburbs. Although the central city remains a magnet for suburban commuters, their property and sales taxes and their civic interests are mostly commanded by the suburbs. Faced with higher welfare, education, and other service costs for an increasingly low-income population, the old central city is sometimes forced to cut its public services. Since the 1980s, however, many metropolitan area populations began to grow, reversing a trend of the 1970s.

## Disparities and Discrimination

The burden of overcrowded and substandard housing in the United States is disproportionately greater for nonwhite families than for white families. In 2000, 1.1 percent of blacks and 1.5 percent of Hispanic householders lived in dwellings lacking complete plumbing facilities, contrasted with 0.4 percent of whites. Grouped together, 4.4 percent of American Indian, Eskimo, and Aleut peoples had substandard plumbing. How crowded or spacious a dwelling is can indicate the quality of housing. In 2000 housing units with a black householder averaged 2.74 persons per housing unit. For householders of Hispanic origin the number was 3.62. The averages for some immigrant

**Substandard\* Plumbing in the United States**
*(percent of all occupied housing units)*

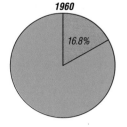

1960

16.8%

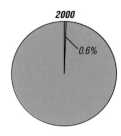

2000

0.6%

*\*Lacking private toilet, private bath or shower, or hot running water.*
*In 1990 the requirement for private facilities was dropped.*
*Source: Bureau of the Census, U.S. Dept. of Commerce*

groups, including Cambodians and Vietnamese, were even higher. These compare with 2.43 for housing units with a white householder.

Hispanic American households encounter other housing problems comparable to those of black households. For example, both groups have lower ownership rates, income levels, and amount of savings or investments than the population as a whole. In 2000, 13 percent of black households and 7 percent of Hispanic households lived in public or subsidized housing, in contrast to 4 percent of all householders. As late as the 1970s some American Indians lived in one- or two-room log cabins with outside privies. They drew water from wells and streams. Most of the dwellings had no electricity and no organized waste-disposal system.

Much inferior housing is found in the segregated black neighborhoods of the nation's large cities. Prior to 1948, when the United States Supreme Court ruled that restrictive covenants, or racial exclusion clauses, in real estate deeds were not enforceable, nonwhites could be legally barred from buying or renting housing in many neighborhoods. Into the 1990s, in a practice called redlining (as if a red line were drawn around areas), realtors and private sellers prevented minority buyers from seeing houses they were qualified to buy. Although many open-housing laws have been passed, the nation's cities and suburbs remain largely segregated.

One reason for this was the widespread belief among whites that, if black families moved into an all-white neighborhood, property values would fall. Although numerous studies show this belief to be ill founded, it remains a principal basis for segregation. Ironically, "white flight" can be part of a self-fulfilling prophecy as the white families leaving—not the minorities arriving—can adversely affect the housing market.

Residential segregation by race is in part a by-product of segregation by income. Slums and other old districts of the central cities generally contain the oldest and least desirable housing. But it is housing that low-income, largely nonwhite, families can afford, while more affluent, largely white, families can move out to newer and better housing in outlying areas.

Many white families moved to the suburbs to get away from black and other minority families that were moving into inner-city neighborhoods. They expected their new suburban communities to remain racially segregated. Racial integration can be effectively discouraged by zoning new residential land at very low densities, for example, by requiring a minimum lot size of as much as one acre per house. This makes the cost of housing in such areas too high for low-income families, including the great majority of nonwhites. Suburban communities have in many cases also barred the construction of subsidized low-cost housing.

Economic and racial segregation in housing has been accompanied by a gradual movement from the cities to the suburbs of manufacturing plants employing large numbers of nonwhite blue-collar workers. Thus more and more of the jobs on which low-income and nonwhite families rely are being moved farther away from the housing available to them.

Nonwhite and other minority families find it more difficult to get mortgage loans because their incomes are generally lower than those of whites. Also, in the past, lending institutions set up credit restrictions based on race. Thus, even minority families with incomes sufficient to meet the necessary mortgage payments could find it difficult to buy a new home.

### The High Cost of Construction

If the cost of constructing new housing could be lowered, a larger supply of adequate housing might become available. High costs may be due in part to technological backwardness in the housebuilding industry. They may also be due to over-rigorous requirements of local building codes and zoning laws, to practices of the building-trades labor unions, and to increasing land costs and financing expenses.

Local building codes set minimum standards for the materials and methods used in housing construction. Originally introduced to provide protection against shoddy workmanship and unsafe housing, such restrictions have lost some of their validity as building materials and methods have improved. For example, in many cities in the United States the use of plastic pipe in drainage systems is prohibited, though such pipe is often an adequate substitute for more costly metal pipe. Moreover, since building codes differ somewhat from city to city, they make it difficult for companies to produce standardized building materials for a national market and thus to cut costs through the savings of large-scale production. For these and other reasons the effect of building codes has been to make housing more costly than it need be. Fortunately, building-code reform is progressing.

*Farmhouses much like this one are scattered throughout the Midwest. The air conditioner and TV antenna show that, like most American farm homes, it has access to electric power.*

Chicago Housing and Urban Development Office

U.S. Dept. of Agriculture; photo, Jack Schneider

*This shack is home for a poor family in a rural area of the southern United States. Substandard housing is common in some regions.*

Building-trades unions may stretch out the time a job takes to protect their members from early layoffs. For example, painters' unions may insist that the sizes of paintbrushes be limited, or electricians' unions may require that prefabricated electrical components be taken apart and then reassembled at the building site.

Zoning laws often limit the number of houses a builder can construct on an acre of land. Since land is expensive, the builder's unit costs are higher when a zoning law limits the number of houses to, say, only two per acre. Builders might be able to increase the supply of low-cost housing if they could buy large tracts of inexpensive land on the suburban fringes of metropolitan areas. But such land is often held off the market by owners who expect it to increase in value.

High land costs interfere especially with the reconstruction of central city areas. Unless the land in such areas is used intensively— by erecting tall apartment buildings on it—the land cost per housing unit is very high. Central city land is expensive because of the greater competition for its use. This is mainly because of its closeness to the principal shopping and office districts of a metropolitan area. People who live in central areas spend less on transportation if they work or shop in the central city. This saving is translated into high land values. Central city land is also expensive because it is expected that offices and stores, which tend to bring in more revenue than housing, or high-rise luxury apartment buildings will replace the close-in, run-down residential and commercial areas. Still another reason for high land prices in the central area of a city is that almost all land there is already built on. To construct new buildings, old but still rentable buildings have to be demolished.

Low-income families who live in central city areas generally derive little benefit from either their close-in location or the increase in the value of the land on which their homes are situated. Few slum families are

property owners, so the increase in land value does not benefit them. It is in fact detrimental, because it quickly leads to increased rents. Moreover, many of these families have industrial or service jobs in outlying areas. So they are faced with high transportation costs as well as excessive rents.

The amount of money that lending institutions have available for housebuilding loans depends on the rate at which consumers and businesses throughout the economy are saving money. It also depends on the extent of competing demands for loans from other sectors of the economy, such as government or manufacturing. When, for example, there is a rise in manufacturing investment or when government borrowing rises because of increased military spending, a smaller share of total savings is available for home building. But when there is a slump in other investments, more funds are available for home building. Thus the level of housing construction tends to rise when economic activity as a whole falls and to fall when it rises. As a result, there is a fluctuating demand for the services of home-building firms and the craftsmen they employ. Sometimes the housing industry has more work than it can handle; at other times it is affected by widespread unemployment.

Consequently, families looking for housing are sometimes confronted with few choices and high prices, while at other times under different circumstances numerous bargains are available. But family housing needs do not fluctuate with the level of housebuilding activity. On the contrary, there is a greater market demand for new housing when general business conditions are good and home construction is in its typical downswing.

### Housing in Rural Areas; Housing for the Elderly

About one fifth of the homes in the United States are in rural areas. A high proportion of rural housing is substandard. Thousands of dilapidated farmhouses have been abandoned by families moving to better homes in the cities. Rural housing in general is older and in worse condition than urban housing because the market for rural housing is disappearing. Thus, there is little financial incentive to repair, modernize, or replace worn-out rural structures.

The families of sharecroppers, migrant farmers, or farmers with unprofitable landholdings are among those that have the most severe housing problems. Many of them live in shanties with leaking roofs, without running water or indoor toilets, and without electricity. The public services available to them, such as roads and schools, are often very poor. The solution to the housing problems of many of these families lies in moving to the city. For those whose prospects as farmers seem more promising, however, "self-help" housing is a possible solution. In a self-help program several families share the labor of building new homes for themselves, thus earning a so-called sweat equity. Such programs are often guided by volunteer building experts, and some financial help is obtainable from the Farm Service Agency, a federal program. Many elderly

**Sales of New and Existing One-Family Houses in the United States** *(in thousands)*

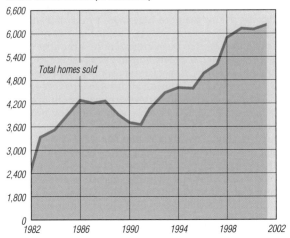

Sources: U.S. Dept. of Housing and Urban Development; U.S. League of Savings Institutions

**Public Housing in the United States***

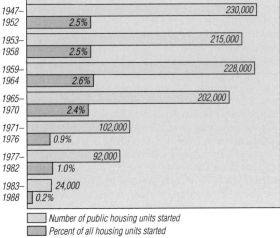

*Reporting of this statistic ended in 1989.
Source: Bureau of the Census, U.S. Dept. of Commerce

people are also very poor, dependent on meager savings and pensions or assistance from their children. Of every 100 persons in the United States over age 64 in 2000, approximately 57 were women. Of these, 26 were widows. About 40 percent of elderly women and 17 percent of elderly men lived alone. The incomes of about 11.8 percent of women over 65 were below the poverty level as defined by the federal government. Many elderly people live with their children, usually out of necessity.

Elderly homeowners with fixed incomes are often unable to pay mounting property taxes or rising maintenance costs. The gradual disappearance of familiar stores and other facilities in the neighborhood where they may have lived for many decades makes it difficult for elderly persons to shop, to obtain medical and social services, and to find congenial company.

Elderly people have special housing needs. It is better for them to live in elevator or single-story buildings without stairs to climb. They find it less taxing and less dangerous if shelves and cabinets are not too high and electrical outlets are not too low. Since elderly persons are less able to smell smoke or escaping gas or to hear fire warnings, they need housing where the dangers of fire and gas leaks are minimized. Higher room temperatures and nonslip flooring are also desirable in dwellings for the elderly.

### Housing Problems Outside the United States

The housing problems in other nations differ from those of the United States. During World War II one fourth of the housing supply in western Germany was destroyed. In 1950 there were only 10 million dwellings for a population of 15 million households. Many Japanese cities were leveled by air raids.

In developing countries, such as Kenya, Indonesia, and the Philippines, impoverished rural families migrate by the hundreds of thousands to find work in

the busy cities, where little or no housing is available. As a result, thousands of makeshift, unsanitary shelters are being thrown up in areas without streets and water-supply or sewage-disposal systems.

By the 1980s lack of housing units and poor construction plagued the Soviet Union and many Eastern European countries. An earthquake in Armenia in 1988 left over 500,000 homeless; two years later only a few buildings had been replaced. Before the breakup of the Soviet Union, authorities estimated that the country needed 40 million new units by the year 2000. In 1990 families who went through official channels in Moscow had to wait eight to ten years for an apartment. The post-Soviet period has not seen the disappearance of such housing shortages.

### THE GOVERNMENT'S ROLE

All levels of government in the United States—federal, state, and local—are actively concerned with housing. On the federal level, agencies and programs were established to influence the supply of mortgage money for the purchase and construction of housing. The first major step was the creation in 1932 of the Federal Home Loan Bank System. It consisted of semipublic banks that extended short-term credits to savings and loan associations. At the same time, the federal government began to charter new savings and loan associations. Only the states had previously granted such charters. In some states, where supervision had been inadequate, families had lost their savings when mismanaged associations went bankrupt. In 1934 the Federal Savings and Loan Insurance Corporation began offering depositors in both federal- and state-chartered associations insurance against the loss of their savings.

The Home Owners' Loan Corporation was established in 1933. It provided cash to banks that, as a result of heavy withdrawals of savings during the depression, were unable to extend the home mortgages of borrowers who had lost their jobs. Such government help for mortgage refinancing, amounting to more than 3 billion dollars, lowered the monthly payments by stretching out the term of the loan. Sometimes payments were deferred altogether for many months.

Under a public housing program established in 1937, the federal government paid the interest and principal on mortgages sold to investors by city government agencies to finance the construction of housing for low-income families. The kind of housing that local housing authorities could build, the rules for selecting tenants, and the formulas for setting rents were determined primarily by the federal government. Rents were based on the occupant family's income. If the occupant family's income rose, so did its rent. If income rose above a certain maximum, which varied with family size, the family had to move out. A family was

not admitted to public housing in the first place if its income was above this maximum. By the late 1980s there were approximately 1.5 million public housing units, about 1.6 percent of the nation's total housing inventory.

Public housing has been criticized for a number of reasons. One is that public housing projects are exempt from local property taxes. Despite some payments in lieu of taxes by local housing authorities, the loss of a local tax base has led many property owners to oppose public housing. Moreover, since public housing projects are usually large and institutional in appearance, their occupants can be clearly identified as recipients of a public subsidy. In addition a disproportionate number of the occupants of public housing are blacks, who tend to be concentrated in their own projects. This has made it appear that the federal government was sponsoring racially segregated housing. Furthermore, rising

---

## Major Federal Housing Laws and Agencies in the United States

**Federal Home Loan Bank System.** Created in 1932. A system of 12 regional banks, supervised by the Federal Home Loan Bank Board. Provides short-term credit to member savings and loan associations.

**Home Owners' Loan Corporation (HOLC).** Created in 1933. Refinanced residential mortgages in areas of economic distress. Gave more time to pay off loans. Dissolved in 1953.

**National Housing Act.** Passed in 1934. Created the Federal Housing Administration (FHA), which insures private mortgage loans on residential property and, by thus protecting lenders against loss, encourages the use of long-term mortgages with high loan-to-value ratios.

**United States Housing Act of 1937.** Created the United States Housing Authority (renamed the Federal Public Housing Administration in 1942 and the Public Housing Administration in 1947). Subsidized the building of low-rent public housing by local authorities.

**Federal National Mortgage Association (FNMA, or "Fannie Mae").** Created in 1948 (became a private organization in 1968). Provides a secondary market for FHA and Veterans Administration (VA) home mortgage loans by standing ready to purchase such loans from financial institutions.

**Servicemen's Readjustment Act of 1944 (the GI "Bill of Rights").** Established the Veterans Administration program guaranteeing home mortgage loans extended to veterans.

**Farmers Home Administration.** Created in 1946 (absorbed into the Farm Service Agency in 1994). Made loans and grants for construction and repair of farm homes.

**Housing Act of 1949.** Created the Urban Redevelopment Agency and gave it the authority to subsidize three fourths of the cost of local slum clearance and urban renewal. Under the act, "primarily residential" and "blighted" urban areas could be condemned, cleared of buildings, and sold for private redevelopment.

**Housing Act of 1954.** Modified urban redevelopment and renewal activities by requiring communities to adopt code enforcement, relocation, and other measures that would prevent the further spread of urban blight. Established new FHA mortgage insurance programs to help relocate slum residents and to encourage new urban construction.

**Housing Act of 1964.** Liberalized FHA procedures to speed the processing of FHA-insured mortgages. Set up a low-interest housing-rehabilitation loan program.

**Housing and Urban Development Act of 1965.** Established the Cabinet-level Department of Housing and Urban Development (HUD). HUD was formed from the Housing and Home Finance

Agency (HHFA) and incorporated the Federal Housing Administration, the Federal National Mortgage Association, the Public Housing Administration, the Urban Renewal Administration, and the Community Facilities Administration.

**Demonstration Cities and Metropolitan Development Act of 1966.** Created the Model Cities Program to coordinate health, education, welfare, housing, and employment programs for revitalizing urban communities. Provided financial incentives for coordinated metropolitan area planning. Established a loan guarantee program to encourage the development of "New Communities."

**Housing and Urban Development Act of 1968.** Created the Government National Mortgage Association (GNMA, or "Ginnie Mae") which took over certain FHA mortgage subsidy functions from the FNMA. Established new housing subsidy programs that reduced the cost of housing loans, liberalized FHA loan programs to encourage mortgage lending in high-rise neighborhoods, extended guarantees and grants to developers of New Communities, and liberalized grants for public housing and for housing rehabilitation.

**Housing and Urban Development Act of 1970.** Authorized greater outlays for housing subsidy programs and additional funds for rent supplements to moderate-income households. Created a Community Development Corporation to encourage "new towns."

**Emergency Home Finance Act of 1970.** Authorized the Home Loan Bank System to reduce interest rates on home mortgages by means of a federal subsidy. Established mechanisms for a secondary market in conventional mortgages. Created a special interest subsidy program for low- and moderate-income housing.

**Equal Credit Opportunity Act.** Passed in 1974. Prohibited discrimination in credit transactions, such as applying for a mortgage loan, on the basis of sex or marital status.

**Housing and Community Development Act of 1974.** Liberalized the types and amounts of loans a savings association may make.

**Housing and Community Development Act of 1977.** Liberalized savings association lending limits. Required regulatory agencies to consider an institution's record of serving the credit needs of its community when evaluating applications such as those for new facilities and mergers.

**National Affordable Housing Act of 1990.** Authorized block grants to state and local governments for construction and rehabilitation of public housing. Funded Homeownership and Opportunity for People Everywhere (HOPE) program to help poor residents buy their public housing units.

operating costs combined with fixed rent ceilings have brought some local housing authorities close to bankruptcy despite the large federal subsidies they receive.

Several steps were taken by the late 1960s to upgrade public housing. Smaller, privately built structures were added to the public housing inventory, partly to cut costly delays in construction and partly to make public housing resemble unsubsidized housing. Efforts were made to scatter these smaller buildings in middle-income neighborhoods. Local housing authorities were also allowed to lease privately owned housing units, paying rents determined by the market, and then to sublease them to low-income families at lower rents. Leased housing had been well received because it neither removes properties from the tax rolls nor competes with private housing.

Since the early 1960s an increasing number of public housing units have been made available to elderly persons and have even been specially designed to meet their needs. By 1988 more than one quarter of all occupied public housing units in the United States were occupied by elderly couples or individuals.

The Federal Housing Administration (FHA) was established in 1934. Essentially a government insurance agency, the FHA collects premiums from mortgage borrowers and uses them to make good the losses incurred by lenders because of mortgage foreclosures. In this way, financial institutions are encouraged to make more housing loans than they might otherwise. In return for this protection, lenders are required to offer loans to home buyers on far more generous terms than were customary before 1934. Under the basic FHA program, a family could secure a loan for 97 percent of the purchase price of a home. The loan could be repaid over a period of up to 30 years at an interest rate usually lower than that required for an uninsured loan. In 1944 the Veterans Administration (VA) offered a program similar to that of the FHA.

Both the FHA and VA programs greatly stimulated home building and home ownership after World War II. These programs, designed to facilitate home ownership, accounted for the rapid development of suburban tracts outside most major cities after 1945. Less use was made of FHA mortgage insurance for the construction of apartment buildings, partially because a mild form of rent control was imposed on the completed apartments. FHA mortgage insurance proved so effective in stimulating home building that similar FHA programs were established for the construction of homes for the elderly, for the development of mobile-home parks, and for the encouragement of cooperative and condominium housing.

Less than 25 percent of all home loans in the United States were made under the FHA and VA programs in the late 1980s. Their impact had been very great by the 1960s, however, because conventional loan terms, except for interest rates, and appraisal procedures became similar to those recommended by the FHA.

The repair and remodeling of homes has been facilitated by a separate FHA loan-insurance program. Similar to a personal loan but more acceptable to the lender because it is insured, such home-repair loans have attracted many millions of borrowers.

Mortgage insurance by itself does not make housing cheaper. But the FHA also subsidizes new housing for low-income and moderate-income families. One method is to write a mortgage loan with an interest rate below the market rate. The loan is then purchased by the Federal National Mortgage Association (FNMA). The FNMA, or "Fannie Mae," established in 1938 as a federal agency and since 1968 a private corporation, absorbs the difference between the

---

## Housing Terms

**building code.** A local law that specifies the type of building materials and construction permitted.

**closing costs.** Cash in addition to the down payment which the buyer of property is required to provide at the time of purchase to cover fees, taxes, title insurance, fire insurance, etc.

**dilapidated housing unit.** A housing unit that is dangerous to the health, safety, or well-being of the occupants due to critical or widespread defects.

**down payment.** The cash or its equivalent given for the purchase of property; equals the purchase price less the amount borrowed.

**equity.** The legal ownership of property; also, the value of property less liens against it.

**escrow.** The deposit of funds and documents with a third party while a transaction is being negotiated or completed.

**gentrification.** The movement of middle- and upper-income people into a deteriorating or recently renewed city area, forcing out low-income occupants.

**household.** A person or group of persons occupying a separate housing unit.

**housing code.** A local law that specifies illegal forms of use and occupancy in buildings intended for human habitation.

**housing unit.** A house, apartment, room, or group of rooms having separate cooking facilities or entrance and intended for occupancy by one household.

**mobile home.** A factory-built dwelling assembled on a wheeled chassis and capable of being moved from one location to another; also called **manufactured home.**

**mortgage.** A pledge of housing or other property as security for a debt; also, the loan obtained with such security.

**rehabilitation.** The repair and modernization of obsolete or substandard dwellings.

**relocation.** The finding of acceptable housing for persons displaced by urban renewal or other programs.

**rent control, rent stabilization.** Restriction by state or local government of the amount of rent that landlords can charge their tenants.

**substandard housing unit.** A housing unit that is dilapidated or lacks private sanitary facilities.

**urban renewal.** A federal program for the rehabilitation of slum dwellings or for the removal of slums to make land available for other uses.

**zoning.** A local law that limits the uses to which land parcels in various areas may be put.

*The natural beauty of the land was preserved and a variety of housing types were provided by the developers of Columbia, Md., a New Community between Baltimore and Washington, D.C.*
The Rouse Co.

contract and market rates of interest. Special FHA loan insurance has also been made available to nonprofit sponsors of low-cost housing projects in an effort to get housing produced at lower cost.

The Housing and Urban Development Act of 1968 set up new programs that allowed the FHA to insure mortgages for houses and apartment buildings on which the interest rate paid by the occupant or developer could be as low as 1 percent. The FHA also administers the Rent Supplement program, under which low-income tenants living in privately owned apartments pay 30 percent of their income toward the rent, with a government check to the owner making up the difference.

The FNMA and the Government National Mortgage Association ("Ginnie Mae"), created in 1968 as a counterpart to "Fannie Mae," assist the housing industry by purchasing FHA and VA mortgages whenever lenders need the funds tied up in mortgages. This encourages lenders to make mortgage loans and provides them with a means to expand their lending power when their local housing markets are growing. In 1970 the purchase and sale of existing mortgages was extended to include noninsured conventional mortgages.

Urban renewal legislation was first enacted in the United States in 1949. A city could buy slum properties, demolish the buildings, and resell the cleared land at a loss to groups which promised to construct modern, well-planned buildings on it. Unlike slum-clearance programs in other nations, urban renewal was not a means of providing standard housing for slum dwellers. Occupants of the slums slated for destruction were helped with moving costs, but they had to find some other place to live. The resulting relocation problem gave rise to much criticism of urban renewal, particularly where luxury housing or office buildings

were built on the cleared land. In the Housing Act of 1964, greater emphasis was given to the rehabilitation of existing dwellings and to the provision of land for public or nonprofit housing.

The Model Cities Program of 1966 sought to solve the education, employment, welfare, and health problems of slum dwellers as well as their housing problems. The program sought to coordinate and make the best use possible of existing federal, state, and local government programs. One difficulty that was encountered by the program was ensuring adequate participation in planning and administration by the slum residents themselves.

A principal objective of the Housing and Urban Development Act of 1968 was to encourage the creation of "New Communities." In other nations, notably Great Britain with its "New Towns," entire new cities had been built after World War II to reduce urban congestion. Some land developers in the United States laid out similar self-contained communities, designed for 100,000 or more people, such as Columbia, Md., and Lake Havasu City, Ariz. But even the largest developers did not have sufficient financial resources for projects of such size. Under the 1968 housing act, the federal government undertook to guarantee the bonds being marketed to raise funds for these new communities. In return, the developers were to agree to certain standards. These standards required that economic and planning studies be made before development was undertaken and encouraged the developers to provide housing for nearly all income groups and for a variety of family sizes.

Federal spending on housing was dramatically reduced under President Reagan; the net budget authority for public housing and subsidized rentals dropped from about 28 billion dollars in 1980 to about 9 billion dollars in 1989, despite an increase in

*This subdivision in Las Vegas, Nev., shows identical housing.*

poverty-level households. During the same period the Department of Housing and Urban Development (HUD) was wracked by political favoritism, fraud, and misuse of funds totaling as much as 4 billion dollars. Both trends were reversed starting in 1989 under HUD secretary Jack Kemp and led to 1990 legislation funding construction, rehabilitation, and tenant ownership of public housing.

Housing production and home ownership in the United States have been greatly affected by federal income tax laws. An apartment-building construction boom in the late 1950s and early 1960s was caused in part by a temporary income tax provision that allowed investors to write off new buildings at a very rapid rate. The Tax Reform Act of 1986 provided unlimited deductions for mortgages on first and second mortgages and a tax credit for owners of low-income housing projects.

The licensing and regulatory powers of state governments also affect real estate and housing activities. Land developers are required, for example, to supply adequate drainage, water, and electricity in new housing tracts. Architects, building contractors, and real estate brokers must be licensed so as to protect the public against careless or deceptive land developers. In addition, state agencies closely supervise savings and loan associations, the real estate activities of banks and insurance companies, and the efforts of corporations, trusts, or syndicates to attract investors into real estate.

Many states have housing programs similar to those of the federal government. California, for example, sold bonds and relent the proceeds to qualified veterans for the purchase of homes. New York's Urban Development Corporation can raise money, receive federal subsidies, and acquire land for housebuilding.

Cities regulate the pattern of land use—such as the number of housing units per acre and the number of parking places per housing unit—by means of zoning laws. Local building codes prohibit the use of nonresidential structures for housing and limit the number of occupants per housing unit. Often, however, zoning laws do not allow land to be used for low-income housing, and building and housing codes are laxly enforced.

The programs of other governments have sought to stimulate new housing. West Germany used tax incentives to encourage private investment in housing. Great Britain has developed its New Towns and fostered, since 1980, tenant ownership of public housing. The Japanese government built complexes of high-rise apartment buildings for middle-income families, a great departure from the nation's traditional one-story house-and-garden homes. In Hong Kong, high-rise buildings erected by the government rehoused thousands of families who had been living in shacks, though by the 1980s immigration made the squatter problem worse than before.

### HOUSING FUTURE GENERATIONS

A nation can improve its housing inventory to a certain extent if it spends less on other things. In this way, more elaborate and durable houses can be built, and obsolete housing can be replaced more rapidly. But any substantial diversion of a nation's resources into housing would decrease the funds available for investment in other areas, such as new factories. This might slow the nation's economic growth rate—a difficult prospect for any government to face.

Housing construction in the United States absorbs about 4 percent of the gross national product—the total output of all goods and services. This percentage emerges from the normal operations of the marketplace and from the spending patterns of households.

But the marketplace may understate the effective demand as well as the need for housing. Left to the operations of the marketplace, available housing resources may not be used to best advantage. Into the 1990s the number of homeless was increased as whole city neighborhoods were "gentrified"—transformed by middle- and upper-income buyers who displace low-income residents in the process of renovation and upscaling. Some elderly homeowners, caught between their fixed pensions and the rising cost of living, are inclined to neglect needed home repairs. Landlords can profitably defer maintenance if their tenants have difficulty in finding other places to live. Individual property owners may decide not to repair their property if most of the other houses on their streets look shabby.

The strong tradition of the single-family house has discouraged the building of well-designed multistory buildings, as are found in many European cities, that would economize on outlays for land and utilities without sacrificing basic housing amenities. Traditional practices in housing finance deny many households the opportunity to become homeowners. Minority or youthful households are often unable to qualify for mortgage loans because their credit records—marred perhaps by defaults or collection problems due to unemployment—do not measure up to customary financial standards even when their income prospects are good.

The savings and loan crisis of the early 1990s and the resulting bailout took their toll on the housing market. The affects included a prolonging of the real estate slump that began in the late 1980s, interest rates on mortgages and home-equity loans that were higher than they otherwise would have been, and the end of 5-percent down payments permitted by some savings and loan associations in the 1980s.

Local property taxes also tend to discourage housing construction and home improvements. In many communities the tax on housing is equivalent to a sales tax of 20 to 30 percent. The purchase of a home is expensive and difficult partly because the complexities of real estate law and finance necessitate the services of skilled advisers. Computers may eventually be used to match up houses for sale with prospective buyers. They can also estimate the price at which a home will sell far faster and more accurately than traditional methods can.

Many families in the United States occupy more than one housing unit. The second unit may be a mobile home or a cabin in the mountains for vacations, or a condominium apartment in the city for the convenience of the executive whose family lives in a distant suburb. The number of second homes in the United States was about 2 million in 1980. In addition, for 250,000 dollars a person could buy one custom-built dwelling or two standard dwellings. So a high level of housing construction does not automatically insure that the housing problem as a whole is being solved.

A fundamental issue in the United States is the proper role of government in meeting the nation's housing needs. Into the 1960s this role was primarily regulatory and indirect, performed through such devices as local building codes, wartime rent controls, and FHA mortgage insurance. By the 1970s several types of government subsidies had been introduced—such as below-market interest rates and rent supplements.

Starting in the 1980s, because of decreased federal funds, many United States cities were forced to increase their roles in providing housing. Local and federal officials also joined hands with private developers and nonprofit organizations in such cities as New York, Chicago, and Boston. In the San Francisco Bay Area the nonprofit Bridge Housing Corporation by 1989 had built over 3,000 units in mixed-income developments. Portions of New York's South Bronx—long considered a wasteland—have been reclaimed with single- and multifamily dwellings. Bickerdike Redevelopment in Chicago's Humboldt Park neighborhood used federal and private seed money to renovate and build low-income townhouses. Among the provisions of the National Affordable Housing Act of 1990 are funds to help tenants of public housing buy their own units, increasing their pride of ownership as well as their economic prospects. (*See also* Building Construction; City; Real Estate Industry; Savings and Loan Association; Shelter.)

---

**FURTHER RESOURCES FOR HOUSING**

**Adkins, Jan.** How a House Happens (Walker, 1983).
**Barton, Byron.** Building a House (Greenwillow, 1981).
**Bauer, Catherine.** Modern Housing (Ayer, 1974).
**Boldy, Duncan and Heumann, Leonard.** Housing for the Elderly: Planning and Policy Formation in Western Europe and North America (St. Martin, 1982).
**Burns, Grant.** Affordable Housing: A Resource Guide to Alternative and Factory-Built Homes, New Technologies, and the Owner-Builder Option (McFarland, 1989).
**Cosby, R.L. and Flynn, Terri., eds.** Housing for Older Adults: Options and Answers (National Counsel on Aging, 1986).
**Davis, Bertha.** America's Housing Crisis (Watts, 1990).
**Drakakis-Smith, David.** Urbanization, Housing and the Development Process (St. Martin, 1980).
**Smith, W.F.** Housing: The Social and Economic Elements (Univ. of Calif. Press, 1970).
**Solomon, A.P.** Housing the Urban Poor (MIT Press, 1974).
**Van Vliet, Willem and others.** Housing Needs and Policy Approaches: Trends in Thirteen Countries (Duke Univ. Press, 1985).

(*See also* bibliographies for **Architecture; Building Construction; Shelter.**)

**HOUSMAN, A.E.** (1859–1936). One of England's finest and most popular lyric poets, A.E. Housman was for most of his life a classical scholar and Latin professor. He led a quiet, secluded life and never married.

Alfred Edward Housman was born in Fockbury, Worcestershire, England, on March 26, 1859. His father was a lawyer; his mother died when he was still a child. His brother Laurence was a writer and illustrator. Laurence Housman's best-known work is his play 'Victoria Regina'.

Housman went to school in nearby Bromsgrove and then studied at St. John's College, Oxford. He left college and worked for ten years as a clerk in the Patent Office in London. In 1892, after a long period of intensive study of Greek and Roman classics, he was appointed professor of Latin at University College, London. In 1911 Housman became professor of Latin at Trinity College, Cambridge. He held this post for the rest of his life. His reputation as a scholar was based on his editions of the Roman authors Manilius, Juvenal, and Lucan. When the commonsense methods he used to resolve editorial questions drew criticism, his sarcastic wit proved a good defensive weapon.

'A Shropshire Lad', his first volume of poems, was published in 1896. It was 26 years before he published a second, 'Last Poems'. Another volume, 'More Poems', was published shortly after his death by his brother Laurence. Housman's poetry is noted for its simple, direct style and its melancholy tone, which reflects the gloomy outlook he held on life. He died in Cambridge on April 30, 1936.

**HOUSTON, Sam** (1793–1863). The commander of the army that won the battle of San Jacinto—and Texas' independence—Sam Houston was twice elected president of the Republic of Texas. He also served Tennessee as United States congressman and governor. When Texas became a state, he served it as United States senator and governor.

Samuel Houston was born in Rockbridge County, Va., on March 2, 1793. His father, Maj. Sam Houston, fought in the American Revolution. After Major Houston died in 1807, his widow moved the family to a frontier farm in the Tennessee wilderness.

Although young Houston did not like school, he did a great deal of reading on his own. When he was 16 he got a job in a village store. He did not like storekeeping any more than he did school, and he soon ran away to live with the neighboring Cherokee Indians. Their chief, Oolooteka, adopted Houston as his own son, and he lived with the Cherokees for nearly three years.

Houston returned home and opened a log-cabin school. Soon, however, he volunteered for duty in the War of 1812. He served under Andrew Jackson against the Creek Indians. A good soldier, he was promoted to the rank of lieutenant. In 1814 he was wounded at Horseshoe Bend, Ala.

By this time Houston was 21 and had reached his full height of 6 feet 2 inches. Jackson liked his young officer and after the war helped him get a position as

Library of Congress

*Sam Houston, military hero and governor of Texas, was photographed by Mathew Brady, the noted photographer.*

subagent for the Cherokee Indians. Houston retained his commission until 1818. He resigned from the Army because the secretary of war, John Calhoun, reprimanded him when he went to Calhoun's office dressed in Indian clothes.

Houston returned to Tennessee and studied law. In his first year of practice he was elected district attorney. Houston was an expert stump speaker and made a striking figure wearing either Indian clothing, which he often did, or more ordinary clothes. Again aided by Jackson he was appointed major general of the Tennessee militia in 1821. Two years later he was elected to Congress and reelected in 1825. He was 34 years old when he became governor.

In 1829 Houston married. His marriage soon ended in divorce, and he resigned his office and gave up his campaign for reelection. When the Cherokees were moved to Arkansas, he followed. He traded with them and was their adviser. Several times he went to Washington, D.C., to fight for their rights. During this period he visited Texas. There he became interested in the Texans' demand for separation from Mexico.

Texas declared its independence in March 1836 (*see* Texas). When the Mexican general Santa Anna marched northward to put down the revolt, the Texans raised an army to defend themselves. Houston was named commander in chief. On April 21 Houston's forces, though outnumbered, attacked and defeated the Mexicans at San Jacinto. Santa Anna was captured. Texas had won its independence.

Houston was elected president of the new republic in 1836. After two years as president he served a term in the Texas congress and then in 1841 became president again. Meanwhile, in 1840 he had married Margaret Lea of Alabama. They had eight children.

Houston worked hard to have the United States annex Texas. He succeeded in 1845. The annexation brought on the Mexican War. Houston refused a general's commission but served as senator from the new state. He was elected governor in 1859.

The onset of the American Civil War caused difficulties for Houston. He tried to prevent the secession of Texas, and when he refused to swear allegiance to the Confederacy he was deposed as governor in 1861. He died on July 26, 1863.

**HOUSTON, Tex.** The fourth most populous city in the nation and the largest in Texas, Houston is the home of the world's largest man-made ship channel and the nation's third busiest seaport. As the site of the Johnson Space Center, or Mission Control, "Houston" was the first word spoken from the surface of the moon.

Sprawling more than 1,800 square miles (4,700 square kilometers) on the coastal plain 50 miles (80 kilometers) from the Gulf of Mexico, Houston is the major industrial and commercial hub of Texas and the Southwest. The youngest of the nation's four largest cities, Houston was founded in 1836 and grew rapidly, in part from the city's emergence as the center of Texas's petroleum and petrochemical industries.

As the international price of oil neared $40 per barrel in 1981, Houston's central business district along the banks of Buffalo Bayou—with all its shiny ultramodern high rises—became a model of Sunbelt growth. During those years Houston was considered by many a boomtown. Oil was the staple of the Houston economy, and money and opportunities flowed with the petroleum.

When the price of oil began to drop in the mid-1980s, Houston fell on hard times. Economists believed the key to Houston's financial future was diversification. Strides in medical, space, and other nonenergy industries assure that never again will Houston be a one-industry town.

### Physical Description

An early brochure designed to lure settlers depicted the new city as being surrounded by rolling hills and mountains. That was before the advent of truth in advertising laws. Houston is almost completely flat and lies only 40 feet (12 meters) above sea level. The seat of Harris County, Houston actually lies in three counties: Harris, Fort Bend, and Montgomery. Harris

. . . . . . . . . . . . . . . . . . . . . . . . . . . . . . . . . . . . . . . . . . . . . . . . .

*This article was contributed by Gail Gilchriest, columnist for the* Houston Post *and former managing editor,* Houstonian.

County alone contains part or all of 32 incorporated suburbs.

Heat and humidity are a part of life in semitropical Houston, as expected at such an altitude and close proximity to the gulf. Rainfall is frequent, averaging about 45 inches (114 centimeters) annually. Summers are oppressive—there are about 90 days per year with temperatures of 90° F (32° C) or higher. All offices and public buildings are air-conditioned, as are all but the poorest homes. Houston winters, on the other hand, are extremely mild and average only about 20 days per year with temperatures below freezing.

From Allen's Landing on the banks of Buffalo Bayou where the city began, Houston sprawls across the plain as far as one can see. The downtown business area near the bayou is compact. Most skyscrapers were built after 1960. Among notable landmarks in downtown Houston are Philip Johnson's postmodern Republic Bank Center and the 75-story Texas Commerce Tower, with its colorful Joan Miró sculpture in front.

A 45-mile (72-kilometer) traffic loop belts the central city. Within the Loop major commercial developments include Greenway Plaza (an urban office park), the Astrodomain (Astrodome stadium, Astrohall, Astroarena, and Astroworld amusement park), and the Texas Medical Center (32 medical institutions). Just outside the Loop the Galleria-Post Oak shopping area is known for its exclusive department stores and specialty shops. Transco Tower, the world's tallest building outside a central business district, stands 901 feet (275 meters) tall and is near the Galleria. It is visible from all parts of the city.

Southwest of downtown is the National Aeronautics and Space Administration (NASA). East of downtown the Houston Ship Channel extends 50 miles (80 kilometers) from the turning basin at its western end to the gulf. The channel is lined with the many petrochemical plants and petroleum refineries that make Houston one of the country's major manufacturing centers.

### People

Houston is the largest city in both the South and Southwest, and its population has doubled every 20 years since 1900. According to the 1980 census the median age in Harris County is 27.5 years, and there are 2.62 persons per household.

In 1985 Houston had one of the highest median family incomes of any metropolitan area in the South, but the cost of living was below average for United States cities of more than 500,000 people. The fall in the price of oil, however, caused an unemployment rate in 1986 of 10 percent.

Newcomers make up a large proportion of the population. During the years of high oil prices and rapid growth, many immigrants from Mexico, Vietnam, and South American countries joined people from other parts of the United States in migrating to the "land of easy money." By the end of the 1980s, Houston's unbounded growth slowed, but many newcomers remained.

*The elaborate highway network that carries traffic in and out of Houston provides a good view of the city's skyscrapers. Much new construction took place after 1973, when the oil boom began.*

African Americans make up about 25 percent of the population; many live within the Loop in the central city. Some 37 percent of the city's residents are Hispanics, who live predominantly north of downtown and along the banks of the ship channel. Many Vietnamese, who arrived in Houston in the late 1970s, live and work downtown.

Houston led the nation in new home construction in the 1970s, but many Houstonians live in apartment complexes or condominiums scattered all over the city. The affluent white population reside in the mansions and large homes of River Oaks and Memorial. Middle-class single-family dwellings are found in the inner-city neighborhoods surrounding Rice University and Hermann Park and in the suburbs.

### Culture, Education, and Recreation

From the rapid influx of educated white-collar workers in the 1970s and 1980s, Houston enjoyed a cultural boom that paralleled the city's phenomenal growth. The 3,000-seat Jesse H. Jones Hall in the heart of downtown houses the Houston Symphony Orchestra. In 1987 the $72 million Wortham Theatre Center opened as the home of the Houston Grand Opera and Houston Ballet. The center has two performance halls: the 2,200-seat Brown Theater and the 1,100-seat Cullen Theater, both equipped for television broadcasts. Each summer all the major performing arts groups give free performances in Hermann Park's Miller Outdoor Theatre. From the Spring Opera Festival to the Shakespeare Festival, the opening of the Miller Theatre's season signals the coming of summer.

In the Montrose area not far from downtown are clustered the city's museums. The Houston Museum of Fine Arts is the city's oldest and largest. Across the street the Lillie and Hugh Roy Cullen Sculpture Garden and Glassell School of Art are also part of the Museum of Fine Arts complex. The Contemporary Arts Museum specializes in modern and avant-garde exhibitions, and the Menil Collection Museum houses the extensive private collection of Jean and Dominique de Menil. The Rothko Chapel, near the Menil Collection Museum, is an ecumenical center for religious, intercultural, and civil rights activities and is filled with abstract canvases by Mark Rothko. It is also a project of the de Menil family.

The Museum of Natural History and Burke Baker Planetarium in Hermann Park have exhibits devoted to space science, energy, petroleum science, chemistry, medicine, gems and minerals, communications, and more. The park is one of 260 in the city and also features a botanical garden, an 18-hole municipal golf course, equestrian trails and stable, and a zoo. Memorial park near downtown has a 3-mile (5-kilometer) lighted jogging track and other athletic facilities.

In 2000 the Houston Astros baseball team moved from the Astrodome to a new ballpark. Houston's new football team, the Texans, debuted at Reliant Stadium in 2002. Basketball's Houston Rockets compete at the Summit.

*A sculpture by Joan Miró, the Spanish artist, stands in the plaza in front of the Texas Commerce Tower in Houston (left). A Saturn V three-stage rocket (right) is on display at the Johnson Space Center. Saturn rockets were used in the Apollo program that sent astronauts to the moon.*

Houston's public schools form the seventh largest district in the nation with 241 schools. More than 100,000 students are enrolled in 27 institutions of higher learning, which include Rice University, the University of Houston, and Texas Southern University.

### Economy

The high volume of outgoing cargoes of crude petroleum and petroleum products makes the Port of Houston third among United States ports in annual commerce and is a major factor in Houston's continuing economic vitality. Since 1901, the year Spindletop started the booming petroleum industry in Texas, Houston's economy has been largely built on oil and petrochemicals. Several major companies—including Exxon, Tenneco, and Pennzoil—are based in Houston and employ thousands of workers. Here is roughly 8 percent of all refinery production in the United States. To serve the petroleum refining and exploration industries, Houston is also one of the leading producers of field equipment for both onshore and offshore petroleum exploration and retrieval.

The Texas Medical Center, organized in 1943, is a fine health-care facility and a multimillion dollar part of Houston's economy. In the mid-1980s the center's 32 institutions employed 52,000 people. It also educated more than 14,000 students and treated more than 2 million patients each year.

Built in 1962, the $761 million Johnson Space Center is a focal point of NASA's manned spaceflight program. It houses NASA's space shuttle operations and is the

lead installation for development of the space station. In addition to the government's space interests, there are several private corporations exploring the commercialization of space.

### History and Government

Houston's history has been shaped by a succession of get-rich-quick schemes. Perhaps the earliest of these was the short-lived but lucrative trade with Indians started by shipwrecked Spanish sailor Álvar Núñez Cabeza de Vaca in 1528 (*see* Cabeza de Vaca). The real-estate empire of New York brothers John and Augustus Allen in 1836 was the second and led to the city's founding. The Allens named their new community Houston in honor of their friend and hero General Sam Houston. The same year the Allens arrived, General Houston won Texas's independence from Mexico by defeating Gen. Santa Anna and his troops on the banks of the San Jacinto River only a few miles from the site of the new settlement. Rather optimistically and prophetically, the Allen brothers advertised that Houston would be "beyond all doubt, the great interior commercial emporium of Texas."

Houston was the capital of Texas from 1837 until 1839 and again in 1842. In 1846, when the Lone Star of the Republic of Texas flag was lowered and Texas became the 28th star on Old Glory, Austin became the permanent capital of the state.

The narrow Buffalo Bayou was a barely navigable waterway but nevertheless something of a port from 1837. In 1853 its use increased dramatically when

Walter Frerck—Odyssey Productions

*The Houston Ship Channel, completed in 1914, has made the city one of the major ports in the United States. Some of the area's many petrochemical plants lie alongside the channel.*

another group of get-rich-quick Houstonians inaugurated the first area railroad. Rail service enabled the shipment of goods to and from Galveston, where seagoing vessels docked.

In spite of the yellow fever epidemics that swept the city in 1839 and 1867 and a fire that gutted the major business district in 1859, Houston grew. By 1870 many of Houston's 9,382 residents were involved in the lucrative cotton trade, and telegraph and rail links to the rest of the nation were in place. The first free public schools were started in 1876. Electric street lights were introduced in the 1880s and streetcars in 1891.

At the turn of the century a group of local businessmen called on Congress for funds to build a ship channel to the gulf. No more than a deep ditch in the beginning, the waterway was not completed until 1914. The destruction of Galveston's deepwater port by the hurricane of 1900 and the discovery of oil at Spindletop in 1901, however, made the new Port of Houston a fortuitous undertaking.

Houston's early economy was based on agriculture, specifically cotton. With the discovery of petroleum in Beaumont, and at Humble and Sour Lake, oil slowly became the mainstay of Houston's economy.

Houston has a mayor-council form of government in which the mayor and 14 council members (five elected at large and nine from single-member districts) serve as the legislative body. These officials and the city controller are elected for two-year terms. A county judge and four commissioners, serving four-year terms, perform the principal administrative and legislative function for Harris County. Population, city (2000 census), 1,953,631; metropolitan area, 4,177,646.

**FURTHER RESOURCES FOR HOUSTON**

**Davenport, J.C.** Houston (Texas Monthly, 1985).
**Kaplan, David.** Roundup: A Texas Kid's Companion (Texas Monthly, 1983).
**Latham, J.L.** Sam Houston: Hero of Texas (Garrard, 1965).
**Milburn, Douglas.** Houston, a Self-Portrait (Herring, 1986).
**Miller, Ray.** Ray Miller's Houston (Cordovan, 1985).

**HOWARD, John** (1726–90). The John Howard Association in the United States perpetuates both the name and the work of the 18th-century English prison reformer. Howard was a man of considerable wealth who devoted much of his time and money to worthy causes. Apart from prison reform he promoted public health by seeking the means to prevent the spread of contagious diseases. Ironically he died on Jan. 20, 1790, of camp fever (probably typhoid) contracted in Kherson, Russia.

John Howard was born on Sept. 2, 1726, probably in Hackney, England. He inherited his father's wealth in 1742 and traveled extensively in Europe. In 1773 he became sheriff in Bedfordshire, where he saw firsthand wretched prison conditions. In 1774 and again in 1779 he persuaded Parliament to pass legislation to improve the lives of prisoners and to aid in prison reform. The 1774 act abolished discharge fees that prisoners had to pay when released, and it required justices to look after the health of inmates. The 1779 law ordered the building of penitentiary houses for the reform of prisoners.

Howard spent the last years of his life studying means of preventing the plague. It was on a trip visiting military hospitals in Russia that he died.

The Bettmann Archive

*Elias Howe completed his first sewing machine in 1845 and took it to England to demonstrate it to manufacturers.*

**HOWE, Elias** (1819–67). Before Elias Howe invented the sewing machine, the fastest sewing possible was only about 50 stitches per minute. Howe's invention stitched five times faster than that. It eventually helped to establish mass production of clothing and other sewn goods.

Elias Howe was born in Spencer, Mass., on July 9, 1819. While still small, he worked on his father's farm and gristmill. When he was 16 he went to Lowell, where he worked in a factory making cotton-weaving machinery, and he later moved to Cambridge. He married in 1841.

Around the same year, Howe heard of the need for a machine that could sew. The problem fascinated him, and he spent all his spare time during the next five years developing a practical sewing machine. First he tried using a needle that was pointed at both ends, with an eye in the middle. It was a failure. Then he conceived of a machine that made a lockstitch. Howe left his job to work on his invention. Unable to support his wife and three children, he decided to move them into his father's home. Shortly thereafter he interested a friend, George Fisher, in his machine. Fisher invited the Howe family into his home and gave Howe money to continue with his work. Howe completed his first successful sewing machine in 1845.

In 1846 Howe was granted a patent for his invention. The machine was ill received in the United States because people feared it might displace those employed in hand sewing. Howe sold the English rights for about 1,250 dollars. He then went to London to adapt the machine to the buyer's special needs, but his salary was small, and he later returned to the United States destitute. Upon his arrival, he found his wife dying. While he had been abroad, sewing machines were being widely manufactured and sold in the United States in flagrant violation of his patent. After much litigation, his rights were finally established in 1854. From then until the time that his patent expired, he received royalties on all sewing machines produced in the country. (*See also* Sewing.) Howe died on Oct. 3, 1867, in Brooklyn, N.Y.

**HOWELLS, William Dean** (1837–1920). Writer and critic William Dean Howells was for many years regarded as the dean of American literature. He was a magazine editor who wrote numerous novels in addition to farces and comedies, essays, criticism, and poems. He used his considerable influence to promote the school of realism in American fiction.

Howells was born in Martin's Ferry, Ohio, on March 1, 1837. His father traveled around Ohio working as a printer and journalist. When young Howells was 9 he began to set type in his father's shop. He did not attend high school or college, but he studied foreign languages and literature at home. Between 1856 and 1861 he worked on the *Ohio State Journal* in Columbus as a reporter and editor. In 1860 he published a book of poems. It was a campaign biography of Abraham Lincoln, however, that really launched Howells's career. He used the money he made from that project to go to New England, where he met such writers as James Russell Lowell and Ralph Waldo Emerson. In 1861 Lincoln, having become president, named Howells consul at Venice. In 1862 Howells married his Columbus sweetheart, Elinor G. Mead, in Paris. They had two daughters and a son.

After returning to the United States in 1865, he worked in Boston as assistant editor of the *Atlantic Monthly.* In 1871 he became editor in chief. That same year he published his first novel, 'Their Wedding Journey'. Howells left the *Atlantic* in 1881 to devote himself to writing. In 1891 he moved to New York City and for a few months was editor of *Cosmopolitan Magazine.* Later he went to *Harper's Monthly,* where from 1900 until his death he conducted 'The Editor's Easy Chair', a review of contemporary life and letters. He was the first president of the American Academy of Arts and Letters. His best-known novels include 'A Foregone Conclusion', published in 1875; 'The Lady of Aroostook' (1879); 'The Rise of Silas Lapham' (1885); 'Indian Summer' (1886); and 'A Hazard of New Fortunes' (1889). He died on May 11, 1920, in New York City. (*See also* American Literature.)

**HUANG HE, or HWANG HO (YELLOW RIVER).** Chinese historians routinely refer to the Huang He as the cradle of Chinese civilization. Such a description is quite appropriate given that the Huang He and its tributaries such as the Wei, Fen, and Wuding have served as the backdrop for many significant events in China's long and remarkable history. The earliest capitals of the dynastic era, Luoyang and Anyang, were located along the Wei, the Huang He's major tributary. The river system and its valleys have played an integral part in the history of China for more than 3,000 years; control of the river and its drainage area provided the great surplus of grain required for China's military and political expansion beginning in the Ch'in Dynasty (221–206 BC).

The Huang He, or Yellow River, gets its name from the extremely high volume of windblown silt, or loess, that enters the river in its middle reaches as it cuts through the Loess Plateau. It is this loess that gives the river its color and its name. As an indicator of the terrible devastation resulting from the river overflowing its levees, the river has also been known alternatively as "China's sorrow" or the "river of tears." Because of the ever-present threat of flooding, only two of China's largest cities, Lanzhou and Kaifeng, have ever developed along its banks.

The Huang is China's second longest river, with a length of 2,900 miles (4,700 kilometers). Given the length of the river and the relatively large drainage area of the river and its tributaries, the actual annual runoff is slight compared to that of the Yangtze, China's longest river. The course of the river can be divided into two distinct sections—the mountainous upper reaches and the plains portion, which is often subdivided into the middle and lower basins. The headwaters of the river lie within the Kunlun Mountains, located in China's far west. The middle basin includes the course of the river through the Ordos desert and the Loess Plateau. In this section the Wei and the Fen join the Huang. The lower basin, beginning in northern Henan Province, encompasses the great North China Plain, which extends to the sea, interrupted only by the hills of Shandong Province. Over the centuries, the mouth of the river, on the Yellow Sea, has moved many times by as much as 500 miles (800 kilometers) to points north and south of the Shandong Peninsula. The Hai and Huai rivers, also important rivers in northern coastal China, are actually distributaries of the Huang (*see* China).

The system of levees that now covers virtually all of the lower reaches of the river was begun prior to the 6th century BC. During the Warring States period (481–221 BC), states often used dikes to divert floodwaters and bring destruction on their neighbors. During periods of flooding, water can inundate hundreds of miles of low-lying agricultural land and bring ruin on the inhabitants. Along many portions of the lower basin, the bed of the river is far above the surrounding agricultural plains. This condition developed due to the centuries of levee building and levee raising required because of the high rates of silt deposition on the bed of the river. In China's history, extensive flooding has occurred countless times, and several of the most terrible floods, with their ensuing famines, have been responsible for the deaths of more than a million persons at a time. After the southern levee of the river failed in Hunan Province in 1887, more than 2 million died from drowning, starvation, or the epidemics that followed.

Central to all problems of flooding and water management along the Huang He has been the great load of silt carried by the river. The river has the highest recorded silt load of any major river in the world, with every cubic foot of water carrying more

than 2 pounds (0.9 kilogram) of silt. The high silt load has limited the utility of the water for power generation, urban consumption, and industrial uses; it also limits the length of the river that can be navigated by large ships down to the lower reach of the river below Kaifeng.

In the late 20th century, a massive construction project that would divert water from the Yangtze to the North China Plain was initiated. This extremely expensive and ambitious project was developed because the water available to the region from the Huang He and its distributaries had fallen far short of the water supply required by this growing urban-industrial region.

Gregory Veeck

**HUBEI,** or **HUPEI.** One of China's 22 provinces, Hubei is located on the upper reaches of the Yangtze River. It is bounded on the north by mountains and the province of Henan; on the east by Anhui; on the south by Jiangxi and Hunan; and on the west by Sichuan and Shaanxi in another mountainous region. The capital and only major city in the province, Wuhan, is a network of three cities: Hankow, Hanyang, and Wuchang. Hubei covers an area of 72,400 square miles (187,500 square kilometers).

Hubei is subject to severe flooding when the Yangtze rises. Its short winters can be harsh, and its summers are long, hot, and oppressive. Except for Wuhan, most of the province has a rural population. Hubei is located between the primarily wheat-producing north and the rice-producing south. Both grains are grown in Hubei in addition to corn (maize) and cotton. Wuhan specializes in iron and steel industries. For more than 2,000 years the Yangtze and its tributary, the Han, have been the center of Hubei's transportation and communication. Navigation of these rivers has helped bring technological advances from Hubei's cities to more rural areas. As the cities built museums, libraries, and sports complexes, the rural districts opened stores and community facilities.

Until 1661 Hubei and Hunan, its neighbor to the south, formed a single province. The Taiping Rebellion brought fierce battles to Hubei, and the 1911 revolution that toppled the Ch'ing (Manchu) Dynasty began here. During the Sino-Japanese War in 1937–45, Hubei was heavily bombed. Population (2000 estimate), 60,280,000.

**HUDSON, Henry** (1575?–1611). Because of the thriving trade in spices and silk between the Far East and Europe, Henry Hudson and other explorers made a number of difficult and dangerous voyages searching for a northeast or northwest passage. Such a passage—a shortcut northward from the east coast of Europe and thence either eastward over the top of Europe and Asia or westward over the top of North America—would provide a shorter, quicker way to the Pacific. Hudson tried both routes. Although he did not succeed, his four voyages added greatly to knowledge of the Arctic and North America.

Little is known of Hudson before 1607, when he undertook the first of two voyages for the English Muscovy Company. He sailed to Greenland and searched vainly for a passage through the polar ice barrier around Spitsbergen. On a second voyage, in 1608, Hudson reached Novaya Zemlya, islands north of Russia, but again he was turned back by ice.

The next year, in command of the *Half Moon* for the Dutch East India Company, Hudson sailed to America. He explored the inlets southward along the coast to southern Virginia, probing for a passage across the continent. He then turned northward and entered the Hudson River, named after him, sailing upstream as far as the present site of Albany.

A group of Englishmen backed Hudson's fourth voyage in 1610–11. With the *Discovery* and a crew of 25 men, Hudson sailed into what is now Hudson Bay and explored the east coast to its southernmost reach in James Bay. After a winter caught in the ice, the *Discovery* sailed northward. Again it was icebound. Most of the crew mutinied. In June 1611 Hudson, his son, and seven sick men were forced into a small boat and left to freeze or starve. The mutineers headed home, but several of their leaders were killed by Inuit. The rest reached England, where they were tried for mutiny but found not guilty.

**HUDSON BAY.** In northeastern Canada lies the vast inland sea known as Hudson Bay. The area of Hudson Bay proper is 316,000 square miles (818,000 square kilometers), and its deepest point is 846 feet (258 meters). More broadly defined, Hudson Bay includes James Bay, Foxe Basin, Hudson Strait, and Ungava Bay. This area's total size is 480,000 square miles (1,240,000 square kilometers) with a maximum depth of 2,846 feet (867 meters). Rivers flowing into Hudson Bay include the Churchill, Nelson, and Attawapiskat.

The eastern and northeastern shores of the bay along Quebec are lined with high bluffs. Hudson Bay is also bounded by the Northwest Territories and by Manitoba and Ontario to the south. It is connected with the Atlantic Ocean to the east by Hudson Strait and with Foxe Basin to the north by Foxe Channel. Through Foxe Basin the waters of Hudson Bay reach the Arctic Ocean. Of the bay's many islands, Southampton is the largest.

Much of the shore is covered with birch, willow, and aspen trees, though trees cannot grow much to the north of Churchill, Man. Walrus, dolphins, and killer whales live in the northern part of the saltwater bay, and polar bears hunt seals on the ice of the bay. Caribou, musk oxen, fur-bearing animals, and game birds are plentiful, and fish include halibut, cod, and salmon. Inuit and American Indians live by hunting, fishing, and trapping. For many years, during the summer a Hudson's Bay Company ship carried supplies to trading posts along the shores and picked up furs. The bay does not freeze but is filled with drifting ice for nine months of the year.

The Canadian government has designated the whole Hudson Bay Basin a "closed sea" for conservation purposes. Churchill on the west shore is the largest town in the area. Hudson Strait was entered by the Cabots in 1498 (*see* Cabot, John and Sebastian). Hudson Bay was first explored by Henry Hudson in 1610 (*see* Hudson, Henry).

**HUDSON RIVER.** An inspiration to storytellers, artists, and American history buffs, the Hudson River has played a strategic role in the growth of the United States. The harbor at its mouth helped New York City become one of the world's largest cities.

Rising in lakes of the Adirondack Mountains in northeastern New York State, the Hudson is at first narrow, winding, and rock-obstructed. The river flows southeastward to Corinth and then northeastward to Hudson Falls. Most of its route from there is southward until it empties into New York Bay at the Battery at the southern tip of Manhattan Island in New York City, 306 miles (492 kilometers) from its source. It winds through wooded hills and descends over falls and rapids, passes by the American Revolution battlegrounds of Saratoga, and then is joined from the west by its chief tributary, the Mohawk. Downstream from Albany, the Hudson broadens and is bordered by many towns and large estates of the Catskill Mountains. Farther down, the river flows past the United States Military Academy at West Point.

The Hudson forms the border between New York and New Jersey, and in New York City it is lined by docks and wharves. The river is navigable all year to Albany, and for eight months barge traffic can reach the Great Lakes. Major products shipped on the Hudson include sand, gravel, petroleum, coal, and lignite. At Stony Point, the river widens to form the Tappan Zee. The Palisades, a wall of rock reaching 500 feet (150 meters) high, extend along the western bank into New Jersey. This area inspired stories by Washington Irving as well as the Hudson River School of landscape painting and architecture.

The river was explored in 1609 by Henry Hudson. Because it furnishes the only deep waterway open to large vessels through the Atlantic Highlands, it greatly aided the early commercial and industrial development of New York. An early attempt at steam navigation was made by Robert Fulton in 1807. In the 19th century the Erie, Delaware and Hudson, and Champlain canals linked the river to the Great Lakes.

**HUDSON'S BAY COMPANY.** For more than 300 years the Hudson's Bay Company fur-trading stations lay scattered over the vast northern regions of Canada. Most of their stores—formerly referred to as trading posts—were located along the shores of Hudson Bay, James Bay, and the Arctic Ocean and throughout the western interior.

The early history of this company and its rivals is closely tied to the history of northwestern Canada. In the 1600s two French traders, Pierre Esprit de Radisson and Médart Chouart, sieur de Groseilliers, bought a fortune in furs from the Indians only to have most of them confiscated by government officials in Quebec. Enraged at the refusal of the French court to hear their appeals, they went to England, where they told King Charles II of the riches to be won in Canada.

The king was fascinated by their accounts, and in 1670 he granted a charter to his cousin, Prince Rupert of Bavaria, and 17 associates. The charter created the "Governor and Company of Adventurers of England trading into Hudson's Bay" and gave them sole rights of trade in the lands drained by rivers and streams flowing into Hudson Bay. At the time no one realized the vast extent of Rupert's Land, as the territory was then called. It covered Ontario; Quebec, north of the Laurentian Mountains and west of Labrador; all of Manitoba; most of Saskatchewan; and the southern half of Alberta. In 1821, when the company absorbed the rival North West Company, its vast holdings reached into what is now the northwestern United States and up to the Arctic Ocean. (*See also* Fur Trade.)

The Hudson's Bay Company owned the land and governed the people living on it. By the Deed of Surrender of 1869, it sold its chartered lands to the new Dominion of Canada in return for farmland in the western prairies. The company subsequently sold all of its land, but it retained some mineral rights.

About the time of World War I the Hudson's Bay Company began to expand its wholesale and retail activities to operate large modern department stores in major cities and suburban areas. In 1970 it received supplemental charters as a Canadian company, and its headquarters were transferred from London to Canada. In 1987 its Arctic stores were sold to a Canadian competitor, and in 1991 the company stopped selling furs in its stores because they were no longer profitable. Today the company's main business activities are investments in real estate and in petroleum and natural-gas production.

**HUGHES, Charles Evans** (1862–1948). The 11th chief justice of the United States, Charles Evans Hughes also served as secretary of state, governor of the state of New York, and judge of the World Court. Few Americans have held so many significant positions.

Hughes was born on April 11, 1862, in Glens Falls, N.Y. Hughes received a bachelor's degree from Brown University at the age of 19 and a degree in law from Columbia University three years later. Admitted to the bar that same year, he soon became known in New York City as a skilled lawyer. From 1891 through 1893 he taught law at Cornell University.

Hughes attracted attention in 1905 by successfully investigating utility rates in New York. He then probed the state's scandal-ridden insurance industry. Most of his recommendations later were made law. As Republican governor of New York from 1907 through 1910, Hughes pushed reforms—including increased regulation of public utilities, an anti–racetrack-gambling law, and a direct-primary law—through the state legislature. He resigned as governor in 1910 when President William Howard Taft appointed him to the United States Supreme Court. He left the court in 1916 to run on the Republican ticket against President Woodrow Wilson but lost by a narrow margin.

During World War I Hughes headed the draft-appeals board in New York. In 1918 Wilson asked him to investigate charges of fraud in the building of Army and Navy aircraft. During this period Hughes frequently pleaded as an attorney before his former colleagues on the Supreme Court. From 1921 to 1925 he was secretary of state under Presidents Warren G. Harding and Calvin Coolidge. He was appointed to the Permanent Court of Arbitration at The Hague in 1926 and in 1928 became a judge of the World Court.

In 1930 Hughes was renamed to the Supreme Court, this time as chief justice, by President Herbert Hoover. He usually sided with the court's liberal wing in interpreting President Franklin D. Roosevelt's New Deal measures. Hughes retired in 1941 and died in Osterville, Mass., on Aug. 27, 1948.

**HUGHES, Howard** (1905–76). A mania for privacy inspired more public interest in Howard Hughes than did his public career as industrialist, aviator, and motion picture producer. Hughes was an introvert who, in 1950, went into complete seclusion and conducted all of his business through a close circle of associates. In his final years he moved furtively from one place to another—Las Vegas, Nev., the Bahamas, Nicaragua, Mexico, England, and Canada—taking elaborate precautions to ensure complete privacy and security in luxury hotels. He eventually became deeply disturbed. He was on an airplane en route from Mexico to Texas when he died on April 5, 1976.

Howard Robard Hughes was born in Houston, Tex., on Dec. 24, 1905. He studied at the California Institute of Technology and at Rice Institute of Technology in Houston. When he was 17 his father died, and he took over the Hughes Tool Company. In 1926 he used his

*Howard Hughes sits in his plane in 1936, ready to take off on a speed flight. At that time he held the transcontinental record.*

AP/Wide World

wealth to move to Hollywood and become a movie producer. Among his films were 'Hell's Angels' (1930), 'The Front Page' (1931), 'Scarface' (1932), and the controversial 'The Outlaw' (1941), featuring Jane Russell. He also introduced Jean Harlow and Paul Muni to the screen. He controlled RKO Pictures Corporation from 1948 until 1957, except for a brief period in 1953–54.

Hughes was also founder of the Hughes Aircraft Company. As a pilot he set a number of speed records, including a flight around the world in 91 hours and 14 minutes in July 1938. He designed and built an eight-engine flying boat, now called the *Spruce Goose,* to carry 750 passengers. From 1959 until 1966 he controlled Trans World Airlines and was a major stockholder in Northeast Airlines (1962–64). In the late 1960s he became a land and hotel owner in Las Vegas, where he spent some of his last years.

**HUGHES, Langston** (1902–67). Known during his lifetime as "the poet laureate of Harlem," Langston Hughes also worked as a journalist, dramatist, and children's author. His poems, which tell of the joys and miseries of the ordinary black man in America, have been widely translated.

James Langston Hughes was born on Feb. 1, 1902, in Joplin, Mo. When he was still a baby his parents separated, and his father went to Mexico. Hughes grew up and went to school in Lawrence, Kan., where his grandmother helped rear him. After she died he and his mother lived in Lincoln, Ill., for a time and then moved to Cleveland, Ohio. In Cleveland Hughes attended Central High School, where he was on the track team and wrote poems for the school magazine. After graduating he went to Mexico for a year or so to be with his father. In 1921 he enrolled at Columbia University in New York City, but he was so lonely and unhappy that he left after a year.

He worked at various jobs, including that of seaman, traveling to Africa and Europe. His first book of poetry, 'The Weary Blues', published in 1926, made him known among literary people. In 1925 he had shown some of his poems to Vachel Lindsay, who commented favorably on his work. He went to Lincoln University in Oxford, Pa., on a scholarship and received his B.A. degree there in 1929.

From then on Hughes earned his living as a writer, portraying African American life with idiomatic realism. 'Not Without Laughter', a novel published in 1930, won the Harmon gold medal for literature. A book of poems for children, 'The Dream Keeper', came out in 1932. In 1934 appeared 'The Ways of White Folks', a collection of short stories. His play 'Mulatto' opened on Broadway in 1935. He wrote the lyrics for 'Street Scene', a 1947 opera by Kurt Weill. Hughes also lectured in schools and colleges, where he talked with black youth who had literary ability and encouraged them to write.

In the 1950s and 1960s Hughes's work included a volume of poetry, 'Montage of a Dream Deferred', published in 1951; of short stories, 'Laughing to Keep

***Langston Hughes***
Archive Photos

from Crying' (1952); and a children's picture book titled 'Black Misery' (1969), which wryly illustrates growing up African American in the United States. Hughes died in New York City on May 22, 1967.

**HUGHES, Samuel** (1853–1921). As Canada's minister of militia and defense at the start of World War I in 1914, Samuel Hughes raised and equipped for overseas service a large part of the 600,000 Canadians who took part in that conflict.

Samuel Hughes was born in Darlington, Canada West (now Ontario), on Jan. 8, 1853. He enlisted in the militia at the age of 13. When he was 17 he won a medal for service against the invading Fenians, people of Irish descent who lived in the United States and who wanted to overthrow the British government in Canada. Hughes was educated at the Toronto Normal School and the University of Toronto. He taught school from 1875 to 1885. In 1885 he took up newspaper work and until 1897 he worked as editor and owner of the Lindsay, Ont., *Warder.*

In 1892 he was elected to the dominion House of Commons, and from that time on he played a prominent part in public affairs. Hughes strongly advocated that Canada should assist Great Britain in time of war. During the Boer War he offered his assistance in raising troops and also served in the intelligence and transportation departments.

From his youth Hughes displayed a special interest in military affairs and rose in rank from private in the voluntary militia to lieutenant general. His knowledge and experience in both politics and the military fitted him for the office of minister of militia, to which he was appointed in 1911. Hughes was a splendid organizer, and in 1915 the British government created him Knight Commander of the Bath for his contribution to the war effort. Despite this, others in the government considered him rash and arbitrary, and his administration of the militia office was the subject of bitter criticism. These attacks led to his resignation in 1916. Hughes died in Lindsay on Aug. 24, 1921.

**Victor Hugo**
Felix Nadar—© Archives
Photographiques, Paris/S.P.A.D.E.M.

**HUGO, Victor** (1802–85). The great French novelist and poet Victor Hugo created two of the most famous characters in literature—Jean Valjean, the ex-convict hero of 'Les Misérables', and the hunchback Quasimodo in 'The Hunchback of Notre Dame'. Known for the vast range and immense quantity of his output, Hugo was able during much of his long life to write as many as 100 lines of verse or 20 pages of prose each day.

Victor-Marie Hugo was born in Besançon on Feb. 26, 1802, the son of an officer in Napoleon's army. Hugo's father and mother did not get along, and most of his early years were spent in Paris, where his mother preferred to live. Hugo and his two brothers knew their father from occasional visits as a grand man in a splendid uniform.

In preparatory school, Hugo began to write. He won poetry prizes and wrote for a literary magazine he helped found. In 1821 the magazine failed. Hugo's mother died the same year. After a period of extreme poverty, Hugo was awarded an annual pension by Louis XVIII for his 'Miscellaneous Odes and Poems', published in 1822. He then married his childhood sweetheart, Adèle Foucher.

Between 1822 and 1832 Hugo established himself as a major literary figure in France. He wrote poetry, novels, and plays and became a leader in the Romantic movement. (*See also* French Literature.)

In 1830 his play 'Hernani' was a spectacular success. By shattering the artificial rules that had previously governed the writing of French drama, Hugo brought new freedom to the French stage. His novel 'Notre Dame de Paris' was published in 1831. Translated as 'The Hunchback of Notre Dame', it became vastly popular in many countries. In 1832 his play 'Le Roi s'amuse', or 'The King's Diversion', on which Giuseppe Verdi later based his opera 'Rigoletto', was staged. Like so many of Hugo's works, 'The Hunchback of Notre Dame' and 'The King's Diversion' were criticisms of social and political injustice. Another reason for writing the plays was to provide parts for the young actress Juliette Negroni, who became his mistress in 1833 and was to be his companion for the rest of her life.

In 1841 Hugo was elected to the French Academy, and in 1849 he became a member of the National Assembly. An outspoken political opponent of Napoleon III, Hugo had to flee France in 1851.

He remained in exile until 1870. During that time he wrote some of his finest works. In 1862 appeared 'Les Misérables', one of the most popular novels of all time. Hugo's wife died in 1868, and Negroni moved into his home.

After the fall of the empire in 1870, Hugo returned to Paris. There he lived the rest of his life as a literary idol. Huge crowds turned out to celebrate his 80th birthday. Hugo died in Paris on May 22, 1885, and is buried in the Panthéon.

**HUGUENOTS.** A persecuted minority in France during most of the period from the early 1500s until 1789, the French Protestants were given the name Huguenots in the time of the Reformation. The word may come from the German word *Eidgenossen,* or "confederates," a term once applied to Swiss Protestants.

In their struggles for religious freedom, the Huguenots were driven to become a political party and even a "state within the state," headed by some of the greatest French nobles. By the middle of the 16th century, the Huguenots by their numbers and influence had aroused the fears of the Catholic party and the powerful family of Guise.

Eight separate religious wars followed. The first war began with an attack by the duke of Guise and his followers on a congregation of Huguenots assembled for worship in a barn. A period of peace that followed the third war was broken in 1572 by the massacre of St. Bartholomew's Day, the most dreadful of the many crimes that marked this era of religious and civil warfare (*see* Coligny, Gaspard de; Reformation).

The Huguenot wars ended in 1598, when Henry IV—who had been a Huguenot but who had agreed to conform to the Roman Catholic church—issued the Edict of Nantes. The edict gave the French Protestants political rights, religious freedom, and the possession of certain fortified towns (*see* Henry, Kings of France). Despite the edict, the Huguenots were still harassed and persecuted from time to time, and when Louis XIV revoked the Edict of Nantes in 1685, all protection of law was withdrawn from the Huguenots. Although they were forbidden to leave France, hundreds of thousands fled. They carried French arts, manufactures, and culture to England, Germany, the Netherlands, and the British colonies of North America.

The famous opera 'Les Huguenots' by Giacomo Meyerbeer uses the tragic times of the Huguenot persecutions for its plot. Its hero and heroine are killed in the massacre of St. Bartholomew's Day.

**HULL, Bobby** (born 1939). During a professional career that lasted from 1957 until his retirement in 1981, Bobby Hull was one of the highest-scoring players in ice hockey. In the 1959–60 season he led the National Hockey League (NHL) with 39 goals. In the 1961–62 season he matched a previous record of 50 goals, and in

**Bobby Hull**
Courtesy of Winnipeg Jets
Hockey Club

1965–66 he established a new record with 54 goals, 43 assists, and 97 points. In his 1974–75 season, while with the Winnipeg Jets in Manitoba, he scored 77 goals.

Robert Marvin Hull was born on Jan. 3, 1939, in Point Anne, Ont. By age 12 he was playing organized hockey on a team with his father. He dropped out of St. Catherine's Collegiate School in Ontario to join the Chicago Blackhawks in 1957 and remained with the team until 1972. He then moved to the World Hockey Association (WHA) in Canada and played for the Winnipeg Jets until 1979. His last season was with the Hartford Whalers of the NHL.

While with the NHL, Hull had five seasons in which he scored 50 or more goals, and he had four such seasons with the WHA. His NHL totals were 609 goals, 555 assists, and 1,164 points. In the WHA he had 303 goals, 335 assists, and 638 points. Among his awards were the Art Ross Trophy for highest scorer, which he won in 1960, 1962, and 1966, and the Hart Trophy for most valuable player (1965 and 1966). ( *See also* Hockey, Ice.)

**HUMANE SOCIETIES.** Animals help people in many ways. They do work like plowing, herding, or pulling wagons. Domesticated animals such as dogs and even monkeys can help perform everyday tasks for people who have physical impairments. Wild and farm animals provide food and hides or pelts. Scientists use laboratory animals to study diseases and how to treat them. Humane societies were organized to make sure that the animals used in these ways do not suffer unnecessary pain.

Organized protection for animals began in England in the early 19th century. In 1822 Richard Martin, an Irish member of Parliament, worked to pass an act to prevent the cruel treatment of cattle. Two years later a Society for the Prevention of Cruelty to Animals was formed to enforce the Martin act and to help other animals. After 1835, when Queen Victoria became a patroness of the society, its influence grew, and humane societies were formed in many parts of the world.

Henry Bergh, an American who became interested in the work of the British society while in London, founded the Society for the Prevention of Cruelty to Animals in the United States. It was incorporated in 1866 by the legislature of the state of New York. In 1874 Bergh founded the New York Society for the Prevention of Cruelty to Children, probably the first organized movement for the protection of children in the United States. In 1877 the American Humane Association was formed to protect both children and animals. Many organizations now have the specific aim of protecting children—and others—from various kinds of abuse (*see* Child Abuse).

Defenders of Wildlife (formerly Defenders of Furbearers) was founded in 1947 in Washington, D.C., to develop painless methods of capturing and killing furbearing and other animals. Humane groups aided in the passage of a humane slaughtering law by the United States Congress in 1958. The law set up standards for butchering animals as painlessly as possible. Related work is done by wildlife societies, which seek to protect wild animals (*see* Endangered Species). Humane societies also provide animal shelters and hospitals, conduct educational campaigns on the care of pets, and promote laws to protect animals.

**HUMAN GENOME PROJECT.** Also called the Human Genome Initiative, the Human Genome Project is an international effort launched in 1988 by the National Institutes of Health and the Department of Energy to sequence and then decode all the genes on the 46 chromosomes of humans. The United States, Canada, Japan, Germany, Great Britain, France, and Italy are all taking part in the project. Corporations such as Celera Genomics, Human Genome Sciences, and Incyte have also been working to sequence the human genome. On June 26, 2000, both the Human Genome Project and Celera Genomics jointly announced the completion of the initial sequencing of the human genome. This landmark of scientific achievement represented the completion of the first stage of the project. Results published by both groups in February 2001 declared that the human genome actually contains only about 30,000 to 40,000 genes, much fewer than originally thought. By April 2003 researchers had sequenced 99 percent of the human genome's gene-containing regions, and the sequencing was completed to an accuracy of 99.99 percent.

Sequencing the human genome involved laying out the entire genetic code embedded in human DNA. In this portion of the process, scientists worked at spelling out the approximately 3.1 billion chemical "letters" that make up human DNA. This genetic "alphabet" consists of 4 letters: A, C, G, and T. Each letter represents a different chemical called a base. "A" stands for adenine; "C," for cytosine; "G," for guanine; and "T," for thymine. Different sequences of these letters make up different genes. Each gene produces a specific protein. (*See also* DNA.)

The step after sequencing is decoding, figuring out what the sequence of letters means. After that, scientists must determine which part of the sequence fits on which human gene and what each gene does. These last three steps may take decades to complete, though the sequencing process was completed years before expected. The hope is that this work will help in the development of drugs that work at the genetic level, or that it may allow for the actual replacement of defective genes with normal ones. Some headway has already been made in the areas of skin cancer, diabetes, Alzheimer's disease, migraines, and narcolepsy. (*See also* Cell; Evolution; Genetics; Protein.)

**HUMANISM.** "Man is the measure of all things," said the Greek philosopher Protagoras in the 5th century BC. This statement serves to clarify the two primary definitions of humanism. First of all, humanism was a movement that arose during the 14th century in Italy. The time in which humanism flourished was called the Renaissance, which means "rebirth" (*see* Renaissance).

Humanism was, in fact, the essence of the Renaissance. It involved a revival of study of the ancient Latin and Greek authors in order to learn about them for their own sake, to see them in their proper historical context. It involved trying to see what the ancient authors had actually meant, uninfluenced by specifically Christian interpretations of them.

Second, humanism became a point of view that asserted human dignity and values, and as such it survives today. Like the 17th-century Enlightenment, humanism expressed a confidence—perhaps even an overconfidence—in humanity's ability to exert control over nature or to shape society according to its needs and desires. (*See also* Enlightenment.)

In the late 20th century the term secular humanism became prominent, especially in the United States. Some religious leaders denounce any attitude that rejects religion while promoting purely human goals and values. In a sense, however, all humanism is secular in that it separates the worldly or temporal from the spiritual or eternal.

**The new knowledge.** Humanism derives from the Latin word *humanitas*. The word obviously means "humanity," but in relation to humanism it signifies more. For the Roman statesman Cicero, *humanitas* meant cultivation of the mind, a certain kind of broad education needed to function adequately in society. Such an education was designed to allow people to explore the whole range of knowledge, including the sciences and mathematics, in order to develop their full potential. Today the word humanities signifies this type of education.

For the Italian Renaissance humanists, the humanities consisted primarily of studying the ancient, pre-Christian authors. It also meant using the knowledge they gained to promote the development of human capacities, to open new possibilities for mankind. One of the new directions was exploration of the natural world by science. Ancient scientific texts spurred the scholars of the Renaissance to rethink the world and the universe, to reject notions that had become official doctrines in the church, and to look in new directions with new methods. Hence there occurred the birth of modern science and mathematics in the work of such men as Galileo, Copernicus, and Leonardo da Vinci.

**Historical perspective.** Humanism arose in the cities of northern Italy—in Florence, Venice, Pisa, Milan, Rome, and others—just as they were becoming potent economic forces. As they gained economic strength, they wanted to govern themselves and to be free from control by the religious and governmental authorities that had developed during the Middle Ages. Traditional institutions were seen as obstacles to economic progress and to the emergence and testing of new ideas.

Neither religion nor God was rejected by the humanists. Their goal was to remove religion as a prime dominating and obstructive force in their lives and to establish it as one of several institutions in society. Religion was seen to have a valid civil function: it no longer pointed only toward heaven as mankind's ultimate goal; it opened the possibility of happiness and prosperity on Earth by exalting work, creativity, and political participation.

This attitude toward religion helped breed tolerance among humanists. Because they believed in the unity of all truth, they regarded diverse religious points of view as expressions of that one truth. This spirit of tolerance was not highly regarded by the churches, however. It took several centuries of conflict and effort, culminating in the Enlightenment, before the idea of general religious tolerance became widely accepted. (*See also* Church and State.)

**The northern humanists.** Neither the Renaissance nor humanism was confined to Italy. By the 15th century it had spread north of the Alps. Originally those who wanted a humanist education had to travel to the universities of Italy, but by the end of the 15th century such cities as Antwerp, London, Paris, and Augsburg were becoming humanist centers.

It has often been mistakenly stated that humanism north of Italy was of a specifically Christian type. It is true that there was, under the leadership of Erasmus of Rotterdam, a great emphasis on study of Biblical texts and the message of the New Testament (*see* Erasmus, Desiderius). It is also true, however, that the tools with which to study the Biblical texts in Greek and Hebrew were not available earlier than the late 15th century. This groundwork had been laid primarily by the Italian humanists. When the Bible texts were more fully understood, they were used to urge reform in the church and a new commitment to Christian living throughout Europe. It can nevertheless be said of the northern Renaissance that, once Christian humanism took root there, it had greater influence than it did in Italy. The revival of interest in the Bible soon merged with a number of complex political and social issues to launch the Reformation of the 16th century (*see* Reformation).

*The Olduvai Gorge, in northern Tanzania, is one of the world's richest archaeological sites for the study of human origins. Containing deposits close to 2 million years old, Olduvai has yielded important specimens of human ancestors and a record of hominid habitation over millions of years.*

# HUMAN ORIGINS

In the 4th century BC, the Greek philosopher Plato somewhat flippantly defined "man" as an erect and featherless biped. Subsequently Diogenes the Cynic, in an equally flippant fashion, displayed a plucked chicken and declared, "Here is Plato's man." Plato's student, Aristotle, also was concerned with verbal definitions and distinctions, but he went on to describe the natural world in a matter-of-fact fashion that has earned him recognition as the founder of the biological sciences. In his work on biology, he avoided the effort to treat biological entities by the use of rigid formal logic, and, though he made some inevitable errors in fact, his pragmatic approach has served as a model for biological observation ever since.

From long before the time of the ancient Greeks, human beings were generally recognized as members of the animal world. Much later, in the middle of the 19th century, Charles Darwin, in his brilliant book 'On the Origin of Species by Means of Natural Selection' (1859), forced the world to face the fact that all the living creatures of the world had almost certainly descended from a common ancestor. He further developed that view in his work 'The Descent of Man'

(1871), in which he specifically stated that humankind ultimately shared a common origin with the rest of animate nature (*see* Darwin, Charles). At the time when Darwin was writing, there was only the most rudimentary sort of a fossil record to support his view, and he was further hindered by the use of the term man to stand for the human species as a whole. As that word suggests, there was a tendency to conceive of males as typifying the human condition. Obviously, females are of equal importance to the survival of the human species, and, somewhat belatedly, the field of biological anthropology has come to realize that males and females require equal attention if the phenomenon of humankind and how it emerged from its nonhuman predecessors is ever to be understood.

It came as something of a surprise when scientists determined that human beings share almost 99 percent of their genetic material with chimpanzees. This led one scientific journalist to refer to humans as "the third chimpanzee." Despite all that is held in common, however, the differences are crucial and allow humans to be allotted their own genus and species, *Homo sapiens*. Human feet have lost their grasping capabilities and clearly reflect the fact that humans are characteristically bipedal while chimpanzees and all of their other relatives are characteristically quadrupedal as well as being more clearly adapted to tree-climbing as part of their normal way of life. Humans also lack

. . . . . . . . . . . . . . . . . . . . . . . . . . . . . . . . . . . . .

*This article was written by C. Loring Brace, Professor of Anthropology and Curator, Museum of Anthropology, University of Michigan.*

the fur coat that all other primates possess, and, relative to body size, human brains are nearly three times as large as those of the apes.

Finally, all human groups are completely dependent on the use of language, without which they could not survive, and there is nothing comparable among their nearest nonhuman kin. The learning of previous generations is passed on by linguistic means, and new insights and experiences by individuals can become the property of the group as a whole when these are verbally transmitted. This clearly is a key to human survival, and it is a uniquely human attribute. That body of verbally transmitted learning and traditions is referred to as culture.

Humans live in a culturally conditioned world to such an extent that it can be referred to as a cultural ecological niche. This is the arena in which the survival of the human species is played out. The occupants of the cultural ecological niche impose a series of selective pressures on each other as they use language and other aspects of culture to their advantage. In general, those who have trouble learning the rudiments of language will have less chance for survival. The cultural ecological niche puts a premium on those portions of the brain associated with linguistic capability. One would expect, then, that the evidence for the increasing complexity of the prehistoric cultural record would be linked to an increase in brain size of the associated prehistoric hominids. This is indeed the case.

Researchers can assess brain size and the form of limbs and feet of prehistoric specimens to see what they can tell us about the course of human development. It is much less easy, however, to tell such things as whether or not the prehistoric creatures in question had lost their fur coatings yet or whether they had developed the capacity for articulate speech. The soft tissues of the body do not generally survive the process of decomposition. Although the archaeological and anatomical record does provide us with some indirect clues by which the answers to such questions can be suggested, those answers are only tentative.

Evidence from East African fossils indicates that erect-walking bipedalism began at least 3.5 million years ago, substantially before there was any significant expansion of brain size over anthropoid ape

*A trail of hominid footprints was found in a Pliocene deposit at Laetoli, northern Tanzania. Several australopithecines walked across ash fallen from a nearby volcano. The prints show that bipedal walking had developed by about 3.7 to 3.5 million years ago.*

levels. This was also a million years before the earliest known use of stone tools. At the same time, however, the canine teeth had ceased to project above the level of the other members of the row the way they do in virtually all nonhuman relatives. This may indicate that the canine teeth were no longer being used for defensive or aggressive purposes and that they were being replaced in this capacity by handheld implements made of perishable materials. Even though actual tools have not been discovered, it seems unlikely that a relatively slow-moving terrestrial biped lacking defensively enlarged canine teeth could have survived without them. (*See also* Teeth and Gums.)

## THE STUDY OF ANCIENT HUMANS

Prehuman bipeds predated stone tools, which appeared approximately 2.5 million years ago. Their distribution and ways of life are known only from rare discoveries of usually incomplete skeletal remains. In most instances, their discovery was the work of paleontologists as a somewhat incidental by-product of their efforts at recovering the much more abundant skeletal remains of various kinds of prehistoric mammals (see Skeleton). Stone tools, however, do not dissolve and disappear the way bones often do. After their makers had discarded them, they continued to exist as witnesses to the activities of the early hominids—a term used for creatures that are more than just apes and which includes everything from prehuman bipeds up to contemporary human beings. Actual hominid skeletal remains are quite rare, but once stone tools begin to appear in the archaeological record, the areas occupied by toolmakers can be traced through the time writing begins and prehistory proper comes to an end.

The task of discovering the extent and form of prehistoric tools is the focus of archaeology. Since the records for prehistoric human existence are found underground, the most fundamental archaeological procedure is excavation—the essence of the archaeological dig. This is not a random procedure. Local residents, farmers, or workers who happen upon prehistoric tools will often alert archaeologists to an area of promise for systematic investigation. Overlying soil is removed, with care being taken to note its natural layers and the exact position of each object and artifact discovered in the process. The coordinates of each item are recorded so that the archaeologist later can try to determine how the various pieces came to be located where they were found, which can lead to understanding of the activities of the original makers. An essential part of the procedure is to collect information that can be used to establish a time level in the past when the hominid activities took place.

### Estimating the Age of Finds

In the 19th century, attempts to establish the age of archaeological items that predate the beginning of written records were frequently inaccurate. Geologists provided estimates of how long it would probably take for layers of silt of a given thickness to accumulate in lake basins and river beds by the processes of wind- and rain-driven erosion of adjacent highlands. There was a lot of guesswork involved, and, though the geologists successfully established rough orders of magnitude, anything more precise required the use of techniques that simply were not available until well into the 20th century.

Right after the end of World War II, in a spin-off of the nuclear technology that had been part of the effort to create the atomic bomb, Willard F. Libby developed the radiocarbon, or carbon-14, dating technique. Carbon is one of the essential elements in all living matter, and a set proportion of the carbon incorporated in living tissue is radioactive and decays at a known rate. When an organism dies, no new carbon is taken up by any of its tissues. Not only do the soft parts decay and disappear, but the carbon-14 decays at a regular rate. The proportion of radioactive carbon-14 atoms to nonradioactive carbon-12 atoms can tell the analyst how long it has been since the tissue being analyzed belonged to a living creature. As radioactive elements go, carbon-14 decays relatively rapidly, and the technique ceases to give reliable indications of age for anything much older than 40,000 or 50,000 years. (See also Archaeology; Radioactivity; Radiocarbon Dating.)

During the 1950s, geophysicists explored the use of other radioactive elements for similar purposes. The first method to yield successful results was the potassium-argon (K/Ar) technique, which can accurately date materials ranging from hundreds of thousands to millions of years old. There was still a gap, however, between the oldest radiocarbon dates and the youngest potassium-argon dates, and it was during just that period of time that some of the more crucial events in human evolution took place. Subsequently, the investigation of the proportions between the radioactive isotopes of elements such as protactinium, rubidium, strontium, thorium, and uranium and their stable end products helped provide a check for the K/Ar estimates and also helped fill in some of the remaining blanks.

The assessment of the magnetic polarity of various prehistoric strata has also been useful in dating material. When the products of volcanic eruptions such as lava cool and crystallize, the crystals behave like tiny magnetized particles which align themselves according to the Earth's north-south axis—the Earth being a gigantic magnet with the North being the negative pole. Periodically in the past, however, the North and South poles have reversed themselves, with the North Pole spending a period as the positive pole. This does not seem to have affected conditions for the living world, but it does mean that the materials from volcanoes that erupted during such periods will have a reversed polarity. Careful work, especially on ocean-floor drilling cores, has enabled geologists to build up a picture of polarity reversals throughout the geological past. There are long periods of normal and equally long periods of reversed polarity with many irregularly spaced normal and reversed intervals that occur within them. While a reversed or normal period is not automatically dated without having a reliable radiometric assessment of the layer in question, the pattern does allow us to place given sequences in relation to each other. This has helped establish relative dates for strata that cannot themselves be dated directly.

More recently, the trapped electron charge in certain kinds of crystals has been measured to give an estimate of the length of time since the crystal was deposited at that particular location. This is the basis for the tech- niques called electron-spin, or paramagnetic, resonance (ESR, or EPR) and thermoluminescence (TL) dating procedures. Low levels of radioactivity from surround- ing sediments get trapped in crystalline material such as tooth enamel or carbonate deposits that accumulate in cave sediments. By checking for the amount of naturally occurring radiation in the surrounding sediments, geophysicists can produce measurements of the trapped signal that are direct indicators of how long the crystal in question has been in that particular deposit. These techniques work well for ages that range from a few thousand up to more than a million years. This is the time period during which many of the crucial events of human evolution were taking place.

## THE TIME SPAN OF HUMAN EVOLUTION

The earliest hominids identified so far were found in Africa and date from the Pliocene epoch, which began about 7 million years ago and ended just less than 2 million years ago. The succeeding period, the Pleistocene epoch, began just under 2 million years ago and ended about 10,000 years ago, at which time it gave way to the Holocene, or Recent, epoch. The Pleistocene has sometimes been referred to as the Ice Age, but it was not just a single period of unrelieved glaciation (*see* Ice Age). Older scientific studies describe four glacial onsets, but it is now widely accepted that glacial intensification has occurred at intervals of about 100,000 years for the past million years and more. Approximately a dozen periods of global cooling can be identified during which the areas that are now the north temperate zone experienced varying degrees of glaciation. (*See also* Earth, "The Earth Through Time.")

Human beings are derived from tropical primates, and to this day humans retain the physiological characteristics of tropical mammals. Survival, even in the temperate zone, would not be possible without the aid of such cultural elements as artificially constructed shelter, clothing, and heat. Until culture had developed to the point where it could provide such assistance, the earliest hominids were restricted to residence in the tropics. Although the anatomical evidence—bipedalism and reduced canine tooth size—suggests that tools of a perishable nature must

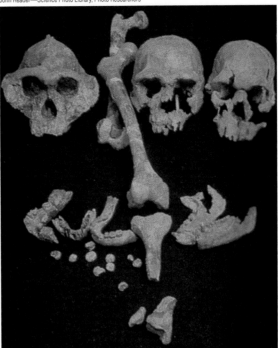

*Three hominid species existed contemporaneously at East Turkana, Kenya, about 1.5 million years ago. H. "habilis," H. erectus, and A. robustus were found in the same geological deposits in the 1970s and 1980s.*

have been used by the first known hominids 4 million years ago, the first recognizable stone tools appear in African deposits late in the Pliocene epoch about 2.5 million years ago.

### Distribution of Early Hominids

The locus, or site, of human emergence was clearly in Africa. Humankind's closest relatives, the chimpanzee and the gorilla, are African, and it is accepted by many that humans and chimpanzees shared a common African ancestor perhaps 5 million years ago, before the Pliocene epoch began. Our own bipedal ancestor is known from skeletal fragments at least 4 million years old found in East Africa in northern Kenya and Tanzania. Skeletal fragments of those early bipeds dating from 3 to 4 million years ago have been found from central Ethiopia all the way down to South Africa.

It was announced in 1996 that French paleontologists digging in a dried lake bed in the Central African nation of Chad had discovered remains of a hominid they believed represented a new species. The scientists said that the hominid, *Australopithecus bahrelghazalia,* lived between 3 million and 3.5 million years ago. The discovery promised to challenge the conventional thinking about the location of the origin of human ancestors. The new find in the Chad desert was made 1,500 miles (2,400 kilometers) to the west of contemporary hominid fossils unearthed in Ethiopia.

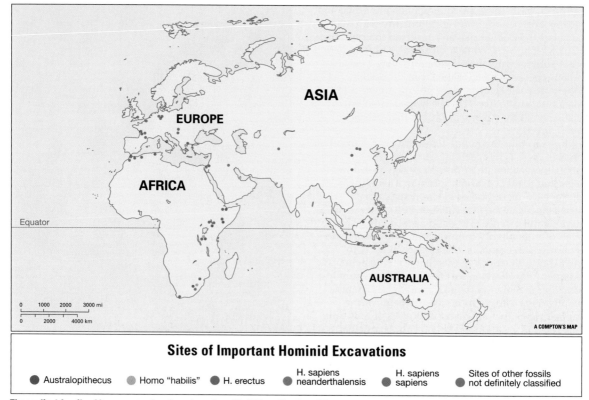

## Sites of Important Hominid Excavations

● Australopithecus    ● Homo "habilis"    ● H. erectus    ● H. sapiens neanderthalensis    ● H. sapiens sapiens    ● Sites of other fossils not definitely classified

*The earliest fossils of human ancestors have been found in Africa. About a million years ago, members of the genus Homo began populating the rest of the Old World.*

The distribution of those who used stone tools beginning 2.5 million years ago can be traced from the tools they left behind, and these are found throughout the plains country of Africa, from its southern tip up through the grasslands of East Africa and across the northern edge of the continent to the Atlantic shores of northwest Africa. Evidently, human ancestors were adapted to living in relatively open country. Neither their bones nor their tools have been found in areas that were covered with tropical forests.

At some time during the Lower Pleistocene, between 2 and 1 million years ago, the distribution of stone tools spilled out of Africa, and it is clear that their makers had moved out into the tropics of the rest of the Old World. The only possible land route out of Africa is via the connection between Egypt and the Middle East, and it is not surprising that the earliest dated evidence for tools outside of Africa should be from Israel. These tools, from the site of 'Ubeidiya, date from about 1.4 million years ago, and their form is almost exactly the same as that of tools found in Olduvai Gorge in Tanzania that date from the same period. Tools dating from later periods are found in some quantity throughout the Indian subcontinent and over into Southeast Asia. Although there are dating problems, slightly more recent tools have been found in Europe and in China, indicating that their makers had extended their range up into the temperate zone

both eastward and westward. There is reason to suspect, however, that human occupation in the temperate zone was only intermittent and that each time there was an intensification of glacial conditions the temperate-zone toolmakers failed to survive. The ensuing postglaciation return of the hominids to the temperate areas then represented renewed colonization from the population that continued to maintain itself throughout the tropics of the Old World.

There are two schools of thought concerning the locus of the origin of modern human form. One holds that modern human form was a unique African contribution, and that after it arose in Africa it then spread throughout the world and extinguished the earlier hominids that had been living there ever since their initial spread from Africa early in the Pleistocene. Within this school of thought there are differences of opinion on just when that spread of modern human form took place. Some place it several hundred thousand years ago, while others see it as having taken place between 100,000 and 50,000 years ago.

The second school of thought notes that the archaeological evidence supports only one major movement out of Africa in the early Pleistocene. In this view, modern human form emerged more or less simultaneously throughout the whole area occupied across the Old World as a consequence of the effects of cultural innovations that were spread from one group to another and which effectively changed the nature of impinging selective forces throughout the range of human occupation. In this view, the modern African form developed in Africa from non-modern African antecedents; the modern Asian form emerged from preceding non-modern Asians; and the modern European form came from the transformation of non-modern European ancestors.

## EMERGENCE OF HUMAN FORM

### The Problem of Names

The name hominid is used for everything that is not properly an anthropoid ape right up to and including modern human beings. The term is useful since it is doubtful that most people would think of the earliest representatives as fully human if living examples were encountered in the world of today. Although they walked on two feet, there is reason to suspect that they still maintained a chimpanzee-like fur coat and that they retained climbing capabilities that have long since been lost in the human line; it is also most doubtful that they possessed anything that would be recognized as a language. On the other hand, they had features that pushed them in a human direction to an extent not found in any living apes. Not only were they bipedal, but they almost certainly depended on the use of tools for their survival, which means that they had the rudiments of culture to an extent not true for any living nonhumans in the world today.

The first representative of these early hominids to have been discovered was examined by the anthropologist Raymond A. Dart in South Africa in 1924, and he named it *Australopithecus* (meaning "southern ape") *africanus*. The specimen was an immature skull, face, and jaw, and, though there is still a question as to what it would have looked like had it grown to maturity, this name has been used for many of its contemporaries of more than 2.5 million years ago. Some of its contemporaries display aspects of difference—relatively larger jaws and teeth, for example—that have led to their recognition as separate species. Many professionals, however, feel that they still belong to the same genus—*Australopithecus*. For this reason, the whole range of early hominids, from the time of their first appearance well back in the Pliocene up to the onset of the Pleistocene nearly 2 million years ago, have been referred to as australopithecines.

Late in the stretch of time encompassing the australopithecines there are clear signs that differentiation was becoming more apparent, and an adaptation was gradually emerging that would come to be recognized as a true human being deserving of recognition as a member of the genus *Homo*. Various fossil fragments from the time between the first appearance of stone tools and the appearance of the first unequivocal member of that genus, *H. erectus*, somewhat earlier than 1.5 million years ago have been classified as, or referred to, the genus *Homo*. Many tentative specific, or species, names have been offered, and the one that is most widely referred to is *H.*

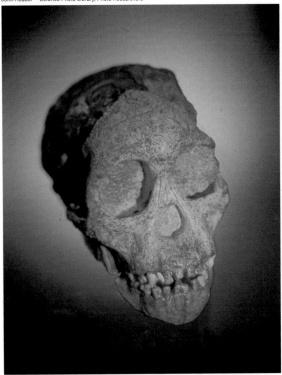

*The type specimen of A. africanus was found near Taung, South Africa, in 1924. The specimen, described by Raymond Dart in 1925, consists of the partial skull of a juvenile and is sometimes referred to as the Taung baby. Not until 1940 did discoveries elsewhere confirm that australopithecines were hominids.*

"*habilis,*" though there is no agreement on just what specimens actually belong to that species. (The use of quotation marks around terms of nomenclature indicates that there is some doubt about whether the name was properly proposed or whether it can be properly applied to the specimens in question.)

By 1.6 million years ago, it is clear that one hominid line had achieved a brain size double that of australopithecines, or somewhat more than two thirds of the modern average. Tooth size had dropped markedly from the australopithecine range down to the top of, and somewhat above, the modern range; and the hints of an ancillary climbing adaptation had disappeared. Clearly this is a true if primitive human being, and this is what is recognized by the species designation *H. erectus*. Although there is evidence to show that cerebral reorganization had taken place in the speech-control center of the brain, there are reasons to doubt that *erectus* possessed what we would recognize as language. This is the reason *erectus* is recognized as specifically distinct from *H. sapiens*.

By the time modern levels of brain size had been reached about 200,000 years ago, there are aspects of the archaeological record that lead scientists to suspect that the rudiments of speech had also been developed. This is the point where it is legitimate to use the specific designation *H. sapiens*. However, these archaic

*Two types of australopithecine are often proposed. The gracile type is represented by the top skull, A. africanus, found at Sterkfontein, South Africa. The bottom skull, that of the robust type, A. robustus, was found at Swartkrans, South Africa.*

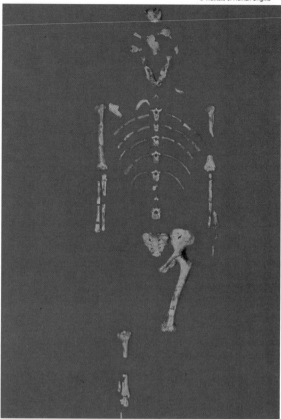

*A remarkably complete australopithecine skeleton was discovered at Hadar, Ethiopia. The skeleton, that of a female about 3 feet 7 inches (1 meter) tall, was nicknamed "Lucy"and belongs to A. afarensis. Lucy's pelvis indicates that the species had an upright gait.*

representatives of *H. sapiens* differ from the preceding *H. erectus* only in the possession of modern levels of brain size. All the other features of the dentition and aspects of skeletal and muscular robustness can hardly be distinguished from the comparable features of *H. erectus*. Some specialists use the term Neanderthal to refer to this configuration of modern levels of brain in a hominid that has retained Middle Pleistocene levels of robustness in the rest of the body.

The emergence of fully modern form was the result of a series of reductions in the face, jaws, and teeth, and in separate reductions in the postcranial levels of muscularity and skeletal reinforcement. Fully modern human form is classified as *H. sapiens sapiens*. The separate trajectories, or lines of development, of dentofacial and postcranial reductions were responses to cultural adaptations that arose in different parts of the world at different times. Eventually these reductions spread to all human populations.

### Australopithecines

Creatures that are recognized as australopithecines are known from specimens that date from as early as 4 million to perhaps as recently as 1 million years ago. From 4 million to 2.5 million years ago, there is no evidence for stone tools, though there is reason to believe that australopithecines relied on implements of a perishable nature for their survival. All of the evidence known so far comes from Africa, and the earliest specimens have been found in East Africa from central Ethiopia to Tanzania.

From the anatomy of the pelvis, leg, and foot, it is evident that the australopithecines were erect-walking

bipeds and not quadrupeds. The hands, then, were freed from regular duties in locomotion. However, the anatomy of the hand, wrist, shoulder, and chest suggests that australopithecines retained a climbing capability that was later lost. It is possible that they continued to use trees as places of refuge at night.

Although the canine teeth had ceased to project beyond the level of the others in the tooth row, australopithecine molars were actually larger than those of anthropoid apes of comparable body size. The lack of projection of the canine teeth has been taken as evidence that defense was relegated to tools held in hands that were no longer used for locomotor purposes. The large size of the molars suggests that the diet included items that had a higher grit content than the diet of apes like chimpanzees. It is possible that australopithecines were competing with baboons for the available resources of the African grasslands, since baboons also have relatively large teeth in proportion to their body size. Access to edible roots and tubers could have been aided by the use of hand-wielded digging sticks, and it has been suggested that such implements might well have doubled as defensive implements.

All the available indications suggest that the

*The first known stone tools, those of the Oldowan industry, may be associated with Homo "habilis" and date from 2.5 to 1.5 million years ago. The basic technique of the Oldowan, or chopping-tool, industry is the striking of flakes from both sides of a stone core.*

australopithecines started as grassland gatherers. Male body size was twice that of females, a degree of sexual dimorphism that is more comparable to that found in the gorilla than in chimpanzees or humans. This suggests a social system in which one or a few dominant males monopolized sexual access to females within the group.

By 2.5 million years ago, the addition of stone tools to the cultural repertoire signals the beginning of a major shift in adaptation. For a long time, archaeologists focused on what they called the pebble tools themselves, but there is now reason to suspect that those were principally blanks from which the real tools were struck. The actual tools used were the flakes that were removed from those pebble cores, and the flakes were used until the edges became dull, at which time a fresh flake was detached for use. From the quantities of flakes found in association with processed animal skeletons, it appears that the flakes were used as butchering implements. And from the circumstances surrounding the location and positioning of the skeletons in question, it seems likely that the australopithecines were scavenging the carcasses of large animals—such as hippopotamuses and elephants—that had died of natural causes or been killed by predators.

There were at least two major categories of australopithecine: one with very large teeth and heavy jaw muscles, referred to as "robust" australopithecines, and another called "gracile" australopithecines. The main difference, in fact, is in the size of the jaws and teeth but, beyond that, there is no appreciable difference in body size between the robusts and the graciles. Sexual dimorphism was pronounced in both groups. The evidence suggests that the large-toothed robust australopithecines concentrated strictly on plant foods with high abrasive content, while the gracile ones

selected from a wider range of edible resources. The number and arrangement of small openings for blood vessels in the skulls of gracile australopithecines indicate the development of a surface circulation mechanism involving the skin on the outside of the skull that would keep the brain from overheating during strenuous activity. This mechanism is even more well-developed in the ensuing *H. erectus* and *H. sapiens*, and it suggests that the gracile australopithecines were beginning to adjust to the pressures of hunting activities pursued in the heat of the day. The increased capacity for dissipating heat, as indicated by the development of this kind of circulation to vessels in the skin, suggests that selective forces may have been at work to begin to reduce the fur coat normally present on terrestrial mammals.

### Homo "habilis"

The various specimens referred to as *H. "habilis"* are largely known from East African collections belonging to the period between the last known gracile australopithecines and the first clear-cut representatives of *H. erectus* approximately 2 million years ago. Quite obviously a major change was taking place in hominid adaptation. Robust australopithecines continued without change and eventually became extinct after *H. erectus* was firmly established, though it is not known whether *erectus* played any role in the disappearance of the robust australopithecines.

The transformation of a gracile australopithecine into a recognizable representative of *H. erectus* required a doubling of brain size and a major reduction in the size of the molars. During the period that contains those specimens sometimes referred to as *H. "habilis,"* all sorts of combinations occur. There are specimens that have enlarged if not fully *erectus*-size brains but that retain fully australopithecine-size teeth, and there are specimens where there has been no brain expansion at all and yet tooth reduction is down to *erectus* levels. There are also many intermediate specimens. Adding to the confusion is a proliferation of names applied to the same specimens. One of the most convincing specimens to bear the name *H. "habilis"* has also been called *A. "habilis"* by one distinguished authority and *Pithecanthropus rudolfensis* by another.

There is no doubt that there was a transition going on between 2 and 1.6 million years ago. The problem is to identify which specimens should be classified together and what they should be called. The confusion has left many specialists quite uncomfortable, which is why the term *"habilis"* is often left in quotation marks.

### Homo erectus

By 1.6 million years ago, the confusion is resolved, and two obvious hominids can be identified: one is a surviving strain of robust australopithecine, and the other is *H. erectus*. For that time period, demonstrable *H. erectus* specimens are known only from Africa. The tools with which they are associated are distributed throughout the grasslands of the continent from the southern tip up through the plains of East Africa, north

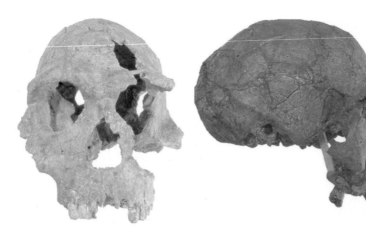

*A skull belonging to H. "habilis" (left) was found at Koobi Fora, near Lake Turkana in Kenya. The face is long, broad, and flat with australopithecine-like cheekbones. H. "habilis" used tools and was widely distributed in Africa. H. erectus (right), from the same site, was the first human type to spread out of Africa, reaching Asia. The browridges are prominent, but the face is less projecting than that of H. "habilis," and the brain is markedly larger.*

Photos, John Reader—Science Photo Library, Photo Researchers

to the Mediterranean, and west to the Atlantic coast. Actual specimens are known from Olduvai Gorge in Tanzania, East Turkana and Nariokotome in Kenya, and Swartkrans in South Africa.

By 1 million years ago, there was only one hominid left—*H. erectus*—and it was distributed throughout the tropics of the Old World from Africa through the Indian subcontinent and on into Southeast Asia. The fossil remains are rare and fragmentary, but the area of occupation is indicated by the distribution of the tools that were the products of *erectus'* manufacturing activities. The stone tools were apparently used for butchering hunted animals, and the indications are that *H. erectus* was engaged in the systematic hunting of game in addition to continuing the collecting activities that had characterized the subsistence of the earlier hominids. *H. erectus* had effectively become one of what has been called the "large-carnivore guild," and it was the successful exploitation of the hunting way of life that allowed them to spread out of Africa and throughout the Old World tropics. During interglacial episodes throughout the latter half of the Lower Pleistocene and much of the Middle Pleistocene (750,000 to about 120,000 years ago), *H. erectus* made temporary incursions into temperate latitudes at both the eastern and western extremities of the Old World.

The tools that are most commonly associated with the manufacturing activities of *H. erectus* are the ovate, bifacial Acheulean hand axes, named after Saint-Acheul, France, the site where they were first identified in the 1840s. However, other evidence suggests that those bifacial tools had not been developed before the *erectus* hunters spread out of Africa. If, as suspected, their function was in severing the major joints of the animals hunted, the hand axes were more an adjunct than a basic component of hunting technology. In any case, hunters at the *erectus* stage had spread all the way to the Far East before bifacial tools were invented. These were slowly adopted and spread among the inhabitants from Europe through India, but they never reached the eastern edge of *erectus* habitation.

The physical differences between *H. erectus* and modern humans are most evident in the head. Brain size ranges from just over half the modern human average up to the lower reaches of the modern human range; tooth size is about 50 percent larger than that of present-day people living in the north temperate zone; and cranial reinforcements such as browridges include the most strongly developed of any in the course of hominid evolution. From the neck on down, however, differences are more those of degree than of kind. Long-bone shaft thickness is greater than that found in living humans, and there is pronounced evidence for muscularity and joint reinforcement. Sexual dimorphism is considerably less than in australopithecines but more marked than in present-day humans. Otherwise, such things as stature and proportions of limb length are essentially the same as they are today.

### Homo sapiens

The one thing necessary to convert *H. erectus* into *H. sapiens* was the expansion of the brain to modern levels—that is, the increase from an average of about 1,000 cubic centimeters (61 cubic inches) to somewhere in the neighborhood of 1,350 cubic centimeters (82.4 cubic inches). Complicating this assessment is the fact that brain size is proportional to body size in any given group, and that *erectus* brain size increased from less than 900 cubic centimeters (55 cubic inches) in the late Lower Pleistocene to 1,200 cubic centimeters (73 cubic inches) and more in the Middle Pleistocene.

When all is taken into account, it appears that modern levels of relative brain size were reached sometime between 250,000 and 200,000 years ago, in the late Middle Pleistocene. The people in which this can first be observed were no taller, on the average, than humans living today, but they were distinctly more robust. These people have been called Neanderthals, or *H. sapiens neanderthalensis*. The first such specimen was discovered in the German valley called the Neanderthal in 1856. Neanderthal brain size was actually near 1,500 cubic centimeters (91 cubic inches), but, because Neanderthals were bulkier than humans living today, the proportion of the brain to the body was essentially the same as it is today.

*The Acheulean, Mousterian, and Solutrean toolmaking industries represent three phases in human cultural development. The Acheulean (top left) was dominant among* **H. erectus** *populations in Africa, Western Europe, and Southwest Asia. Its characteristic tool is the hand ax, which could be used for digging, cutting, and scraping. The Acheulean tradition lasted from 1.5 million years ago in Africa to 100,000 years ago in Europe. The Mousterian (top right) is linked with Neanderthal populations in Europe, Western Asia, and Northern Africa beginning about 70,000 years ago. The Mousterian assemblage varied regionally; it contained points and scrapers, and the edges of the objects were toothed. The Solutrean (bottom) belongs to the Upper Paleolithic in France and Spain, about 21,000 to 17,000 years ago, and is characterized by thin, leaf-shaped points retouched over the entire surface. The Solutrean was the dominant industry of Western Europe during the last glaciation, when Northern and Central Europe were apparently abandoned.*

For many years, scientists believed that Neanderthals were the direct ancestors of modern humans. However, in 1997, a landmark study of DNA extracted from the 1856 fossil produced strong evidence to suggest that this was not the case. The scientists compared the DNA sequence of a region of the fossil mitochondrial genome with the sequence of a comparable region in the mitochondrial DNA of modern humans. The results indicated a threefold difference between the sequences of modern humans and Neanderthals. Furthermore, the type of differences, as well as their locations in the sequences, suggest it is highly unlikely that Neanderthals contributed to the modern human mitochondrial gene pool. The scientists further calculated that, while Neanderthals and modern humans did indeed share a common ancestor, the two lineages diverged between 550,000 and 690,000 years ago; the first known Neanderthal is placed at approximately 300,000 years ago, while the first modern humans are believed to have evolved around 200,000 years ago.

After the brain–body ratio reached its modern proportions, relative brain size stabilized in all human populations and has remained the same ever since. It is clear that major behavioral changes are indicated by the archaeological record. For the first time, there is evidence for regional differentiation in the style of making stone tools. At first, the areas of shared stylistic similarities are relatively large: all of Western

Europe, for example. Subsequently, these regionally restricted areas of shared style elements become smaller and more clearly defined. Although the implications cannot be proven, it may be significant that the regions within which shared styles were maintained are strikingly similar in extent to what are separate language areas for human populations today.

This is probably as close as researchers shall ever get to obtaining evidence for the origin of language as we know it. With language, the innovations of the brightest members of a group can be transmitted to all other members.

### Technology and Modern Form

About 10,000 years ago, after the attainment of modern levels of intellectual and linguistic capacity, the remaining changes that produced modern physical form were all in the nature of reductions from Middle Pleistocene levels of robustness. Unlike the achievement of modern mental capabilities, however, the various aspects of robustness reduction pursued different trajectories in different parts of the world. These trajectories were related to the development of particular aspects of technology in particular places. These technologies in turn changed the nature of the imposition of selective forces for their inventors and for those who subsequently received the inventions.

Two examples of how the development of technology affects the imposition of selective forces

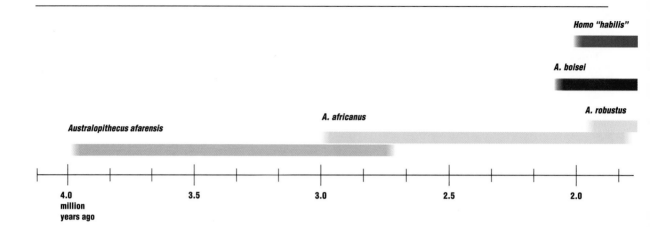

Homo "habilis"

A. boisei

A. robustus

A. africanus

Australopithecus afarensis

4.0
million
years ago

3.5

3.0

2.5

2.0

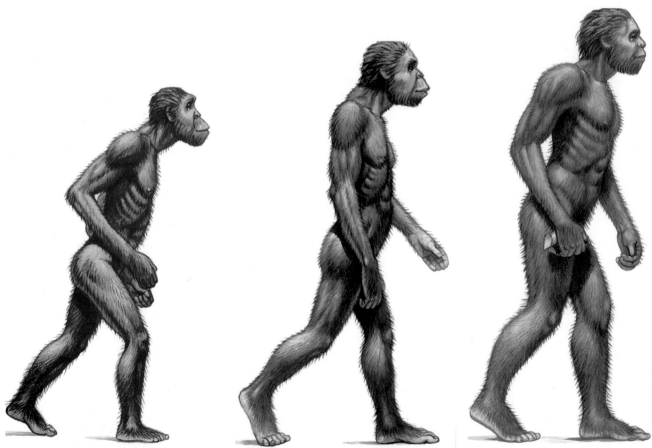

*Hominid fossil evidence stretches back at least 4 million years, and various species have been identified at sites around the world. A. afarensis (left) was a small, bipedal, apelike hominid that inhabited East Africa. Another australopithecine, A. africanus (center), is known from South African sites and, like afarensis, is thought to have subsisted on a herbivorous diet. The earliest recognized members of the genus Homo belong to the species H. "habilis" (right). First identified by Louis Leakey at Olduvai Gorge, Tanzania, H. "habilis" is also known from elsewhere in Africa.*

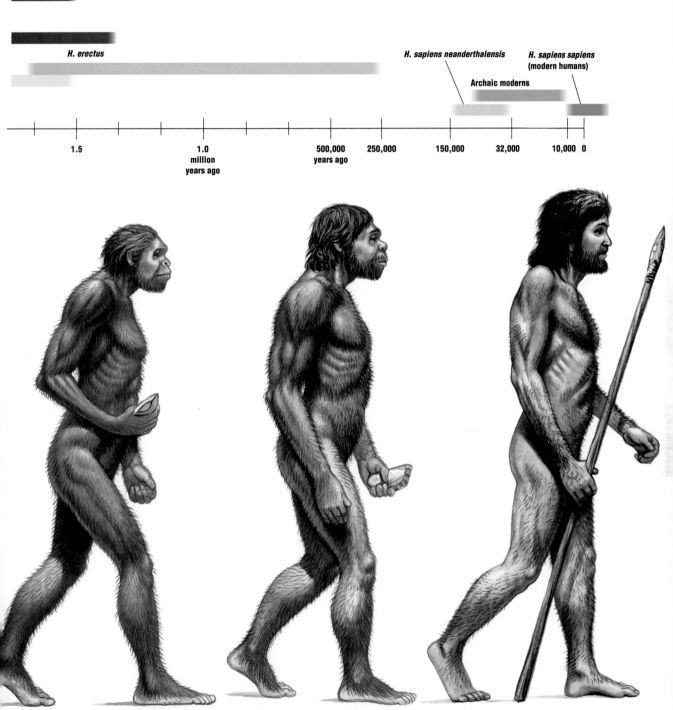

H. erectus (left) appeared in East Africa about 1.6 million years ago and eventually spread across Asia. H. erectus showed increased brain capacity over that of H. "habilis." H. sapiens neanderthalensis (center) is well known from Europe and Asia, but the Neanderthals disappear from the fossil record after about 35,000 years ago in Europe. By that time, most of the Old World was occupied by modern forms of H. sapiens, such as those found at Cro-Magnon, France (right). The questions remain as to what happened to the Neanderthals and where modern H. sapiens originated.

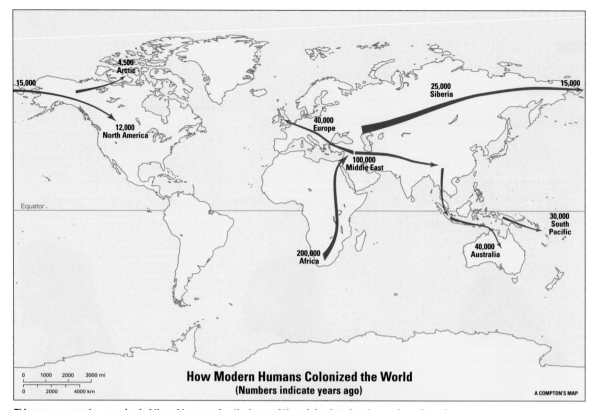

**How Modern Humans Colonized the World**
(Numbers indicate years ago)

A COMPTON'S MAP

*This map represents one school of thought concerning the locus of the origin of modern human form. H. sapiens emerged in southeastern Africa by about 200,000 years ago. Modern humans appeared outside Africa for the first time about 100,000 years ago. By 70,000 years ago, they had reached East Asia; by 50,000 years ago, Australia; by 40,000 years ago, Europe; and by 25,000 years ago, Siberia. The most reliable evidence indicates that humans did not cross into North America earlier than 15,000 years ago.*

have been particularly important to the shaping of human form. First is the control of fire and its use for food preparation. While there are claims for the hominid control of fire going back into the Pliocene, the undisputed evidence for the continuous and necessary use of fire goes back only as far as the late Middle Pleistocene, just about the time at which *H. sapiens* can first be recognized. It was the control of fire that allowed people to remain in the western part of the north temperate zone—ranging from the Middle East to the Atlantic shore of Europe—during the next-to-last glaciation somewhat more than 200,000 years ago.

Fire not only provided necessary warmth for physiologically tropical beings in a glacial climate, but it was also essential to thaw food that had become frozen between the time that the game was killed and the time that it could be consumed. For the first time, cooking was obligatory. This not only made eating frozen food possible, it meant that the total amount of chewing over the course of an individual's life was reduced from previous levels. The relaxation of selective forces allowed mutations to accumulate, and, because most mutations lead to a reduction of the structure that the mutated genes modify, the consequence was the reduction of jaw and tooth size for

the descendants of those who first cooked their food simply in order to make it ingestible. The consequence of this is that modern human dentofacial reduction has proceeded furthest among the inhabitants of the north temperate zone and particularly among those who continue to live in that stretch from the Middle East to Western Europe where obligatory cooking can first be identified.

Cooking and facial reduction probably first developed among the northern Neanderthals, and their African contemporaries produced an innovation—the spear—that led to the modification of the body from the neck down. The stone tools used by the Neanderthals in Europe, the Middle East, and Africa have been referred to as Mousterian tools after the site of Le Moustier in France where they were first identified in the 1860s. Hand axes continued to be made, often of a much more refined type than those of the earlier Pleistocene, but the Mousterian industry is characterized by a proliferation of points and scrapers made from flakes. The scrapers in the north were clearly for the preparation of animal skins for clothing.

In Africa, long, elegantly prepared flakes were part of the assemblage of Mousterian tools. These are called Levalloisian flakes, after the Paris suburb where they

## Human Origins Terms

**anthropoid.** A member of the classification that includes gibbons, orangutans, chimpanzees, and gorillas in addition to humans and their ancestors. The anthropoid apes are the nearest living relations to humans.

**bifacial.** Shaped on both faces; for example, a stone tool such as a hand ax of the Lower Paleolithic.

**biomass.** The amount of living matter in a given area or habitat, especially that available as a source of energy to organisms in the habitat.

**bipedal.** Habitually walking on two legs. Many animals walk on two legs—for example, birds—but only hominoids have pelvis and legs adapted for the support and propulsion of the body in the erect position. Chimpanzees, gorillas, and others besides humans are frequently bipedal. Humans, however, are the only ones that are habitually bipedal—that is, while humans can climb trees and employ other forms of locomotion, the human body is specifically adapted for upright locomotion on the ground. The adaptation of bipedalism was an important development in human evolution. (See also **erect posture**.)

**browridge.** Bony arch above the eye socket. Heavier and joined together to form a single arch above the nose in primitive humans; much reduced and separated in modern humans. Heavy single arch present in gorillas, Homo erectus, and, to a lesser extent, Neanderthals.

**canine tooth.** The conical, pointed tooth located between the lateral incisor and the first premolar.

**core.** Stone from which flakes are struck during the process of making stone tools.

**dentofacial.** Term used in describing the characteristics of the teeth, jaws, and face.

**erect posture.** Erection of the trunk. All primates have the ability to walk in the upright position—with the trunk held erect—though many are habitually quadrupedal when walking or in the resting position, and the structure of their bodies is adapted accordingly. Humans and their ancestors are the only primates whose body structure is adapted for maintaining the habitually erect posture while both standing and walking.

**flake tool.** A stone tool made from a piece of stone detached from the core by striking it off. Two examples are hand axes and scrapers.

**gracile.** Small, lightly built.

**hominid.** Member of the family Hominidae, the zoological classification in which humans and their ancestors belong. Included are prehumans such as australopithecines. Not included are the living great apes (gibbon, orangutan, chimpanzee, and gorilla), or anthropoid apes, of the family Pongidae.

**hominoid.** Member of the primate family, the superfamily Hominoidea, which includes humans, the apes, and their extinct relatives.

**Pliocene.** The youngest epoch of the Tertiary period, from about 7 million to about 2 million years ago, immediately preceding the Pleistocene epoch. Name means 'most recent.' Human and ape evolutionary branches were separate at this time.

**Pleistocene.** The earlier epoch of the Quaternary period, beginning about 2 million years ago. Sometimes considered to date up to the present, though the period termed the Holocene is usually considered to have begun about 10,000 years ago and to continue up to the present. Characterized by unstable global climate (this is the period of the Ice Ages). Modern humans appeared in the Late Pleistocene.

**point.** Tool thought to have been used for a spear or projectile. Would be fastened to a shaft for use as an arrowhead, for example. Points of both stone and bone have been found.

**postcranial.** Term for the bones of the body other than the cranium, or skull, and jaw.

**primate.** Member of the zoological order that includes lemurs, bushbabies, Old and New World monkeys, apes, and humans. Primate order is recognizable as far back as 70 million years ago.

**quadrupedal.** Habitually walking on four limbs. Compare with **bipedal**.

**robust.** Large, heavily built.

**scraper.** A flake tool thought to have been used for either cleaning skins (side scraper) or woodworking (end scraper or steep scraper).

**sexual dimorphism.** Physical differences—such as those of shape, size, or color—between the males and females of a species.

**strata** (singular: **stratum**). Layers of geological or archaeological material deposited over time. Strata, and the materials within them, can often be classified and dated when the sequence of geological or archaeological events can be reconstructed. The sequence of deposits is called its stratigraphy.

**temperate zone.** Geographic regions between the tropic of Cancer and the Arctic Circle and between the tropic of Capricorn and the Antarctic Circle. Temperate zone climate is characterized by cool or cold winters and warm or hot summers.

**tropic zone.** Geographic region between the Tropic of Cancer and the Tropic of Capricorn; the equatorial zone.

**type site.** Usually, the site at which a stone-tool industry was first discovered. Sometimes means the site containing artifacts that best represent the style.

---

were first identified at the beginning of the 1930s. Levalloisian flakes were not important in European Mousterian assemblages, but they were quite common in the African equivalent of the Mousterian, the Middle Stone Age, or Mesolithic, which goes back to about 200,000 years ago. Experimental testing has shown that the fracture patterns observed on many of the African Levalloisian flakes could only have been produced by their use as projectile points.

It would appear that the thrown spear as an adjunct to hunting activities was initially an African innovation. For the first time, the hunter did not literally have to come to grips with his prey and could impale it from a distance. The consequence was the relaxation of selective forces maintaining Middle Pleistocene levels of muscularity and robustness in the body below the neck. Reduction in postcranial

robustness then appeared for the first time among Africans towards the end of the Middle Pleistocene. Representatives of these actually got as far north as Israel, where they appear at the site of Qafzeh early in the Late Pleistocene about 100,000 years ago. While the Qafzeh people had a relatively modern appearance, the regular use of fire for cooking had not yet penetrated into sub-Saharan Africa, so the African representatives at Qafzeh had unreduced Middle Pleistocene levels of jaw and tooth size.

Eventually, cooking technology spread southward, and jaw and tooth reduction proceeded in a fashion parallel to what had been going on in the north for the previous 100,000 years or more. Projectile technology was adopted by the people of the north, and, in comparable fashion, the result was the reduction in the previous levels of arm and shoulder robustness over

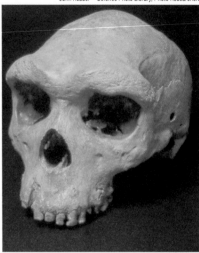

*A precursor to modern humans known as Rhodesia man (top) is from Kabwe, Rhodesia (now Zambia). The skull, about 125,000 years old, has been classified as* **H. rhodesiensis,** *a name that would denote its status as a separate species, and as* **H. sapiens rhodesiensis,** *which would place it in a subspecies of* **H. sapiens.** *It is believed to be an intermediate form between late* **H. erectus** *and early* **H. sapiens.** *(Bottom) The skull of a Neanderthal found at La Ferrassie, France, and that of an anatomically modern human from Cro-Magnon, France, are of similar antiquity.*

the course of time. These aspects of technology spread independently into other parts of the world, and the consequences for their adopters proceeded in a predictable manner. As a result, no population in the world today retains a fully Middle Pleistocene level of robustness in either its dentition or its chest and shoulder morphology; that is, there is no living human population that would qualify for the designation Neanderthal.

There is one other technology that led to a reduction of robustness and muscularity even more effectively than the use of projectiles: the invention and application of string. Nooses, snares, and nets not only allowed the capture of prey without the previously necessary levels of exertion, but they also gave people access to a huge biomass (the quantity of living matter available within a habitat) that had formerly been unavailable. Flocks of birds, schools of fish, and rabbit-size mammals represent an enormous food resource. After the end of the Mousterian—the technological complex usually associated with the Neanderthals—people of the ensuing Upper Paleolithic did not at first see much of a change in their way of life. In the latter part of the Upper Paleolithic, starting somewhat more than 20,000 years ago, the use of a string-based technology changed the nature of expectable dietary resources, and one of the immediate consequences was a dramatic increase in human population size and density.

The earliest evidence of art created by humans also dates from this period. The dramatic polychrome paintings of game animals on the walls of caves in southern France and Spain provide evidence that the realm of human visual imagery was every bit as well developed 15,000 to 20,000 years ago as it is today. It was just good fortune that led to the preservation and discovery of these galleries of prehistoric art, and there is no reason to think that contemporaries of those remarkable artists elsewhere throughout the Old World were not every bit as talented. Circumstances just did not favor the survival of their creations.

## POSTGLACIAL LIFE

The last glaciation of the Pleistocene came to an end between 10,000 and 12,000 years ago, and the disappearance of the ice sheets coincided with the first entry of humans into the Western Hemisphere—the New World—by way of what was then dry land connecting Siberia and Alaska (*see* Indians, American). Already at that time, people in various parts of the world were experimenting with new methods of subsistence. Technology was used to prepare and process certain plants that previously would not have been of much value for human consumption. Grains and legumes—such as beans and peas—require modification by heat before they can be digested by human beings, and, even before the invention of heat-proof clay containers, people had discovered that milling grains into meal allowed the grains to be cooked in the form of wafers or loaves. This opened up a vast realm of dietary resources and prepared the way for the enormous expansion of human populations that began after the Pleistocene had ended.

The focus on the collection of plant foods led naturally to efforts to assist the propagation and growth of those plants, and the shift was under way towards full-scale farming—agriculture. This led to the development of settled farming communities. This signaled an end to the nomadism of the Pleistocene hunting and gathering way of life. (*See also* City; Civilization.)

It should be noted that, with only a tiny and dwindling number of exceptions, the vast majority of the peoples of the world today are sustained by the products of agriculture. Even the few who can still be called hunter-gatherers practice a sophisticated post-Pleistocene or Middle Stone Age kind of foraging. Only a very few small contemporary human populations are pursuing the kind of subsistence

John Reader—Science Photo Library, Photo Researchers

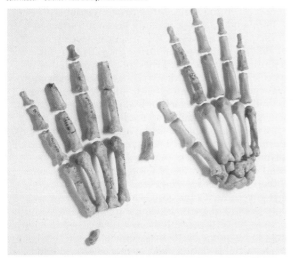

*A comparison of* A. afarensis *and modern hand bones shows that, even 3 million years ago, hominid hands were probably as dexterous as those of modern humans. Some australopithecine bones have been included with the modern ones, emphasizing the only slight changes in the structure of the hominid hand through time.*

strategy that human ancestors followed from the time that *H. erectus* spread out of Africa more than a million years ago to the end of the Pleistocene just over 10,000 years ago. And those few populations are subject to the same kind of selective forces that affected *H. erectus*. In this sense, virtually no modern human group is biologically adapted to its current way of life.

The increase in population density and the proximity to domesticated animals that were the consequences of a farming way of life greatly increased the spread of communicable diseases. Peoples with several thousand years of agricultural background—that is, nearly all people alive today—have developed a degree of immunity or resistance to many diseases. However, there have been few visible changes in human form that have arisen as a consequence of the development of a settled, agriculturally supported way of living.

There is one change, however, that does merit mention. The application of heat to frozen foods back in the Pleistocene had reduced the selective forces maintaining prehistoric levels of jaw and tooth size, but the invention of pottery eliminated those selective forces entirely. The result was that the descendants of the first humans to invent and use pottery have undergone more dental reduction than any of the other people in the world. The modern form of the human chewing machinery, then, is the result of the only really significant visible biological change to have occurred since the appearance of agriculture about 10,000 years ago. Scientists may predict that the technological aids that are now virtually universal will lead to other types of morphological reduction. It takes at least 10,000 years, however, for the consequences of new technology to become evident in such physical changes. The prediction of specific changes, therefore, cannot properly be regarded as science because they are not in the realm of the verifiable.

## A Possible Common Ancestor of Monkeys and Humans

In 2000 scientists made an announcement about the 1995 discovery of *Eosimias*, or 'dawn monkey,' which lived 45 million years ago. *Eosimias* was a nocturnal animal, which weighed only a few ounces as an adult and was small enough to fit in a human palm. Analysis of the *Eosimias* ankle and foot bones show that the bones have features of both prosimians, or lower primates, such as lemurs and bush babies, and anthropoids, or higher primates, such as monkeys and humans. In fact, *Eosimias* might be the first species on the anthropoid branch of the evolutionary tree. If that is the case, that would make it the common ancestor of gibbons, orangutans, gorillas, chimpanzees, and humans.

### FURTHER RESOURCES FOR HUMAN ORIGINS

**Books for Young People**

**Sita, Lisa.** Human Biology and Evolution (Thomson Learning, 1995).

**Warburton, Lois.** Human Origins: Tracing Humanity's Evolution (Lucent Books, 1992).

**Willis, Delta.** The Leakey Family: Leaders in the Search for Human Origins (Facts on File, 1992).

**Books for Adults**

**Brace, C.L.** The Stages of Human Evolution, 5th ed. (Prentice, 1995).

**Caird, Rod.** Ape Man: The Story of Human Evolution (Macmillan, 1994).

**Campbell, B.G., and Loy, J.D.** Humankind Emerging, 7th ed. (HarperCollins, 1995).

**Cavalli-Sforza, L.L., and Cavalli-Sforza, Francesco.** The Great Human Diasporas (Addison-Wesley, 1994). **Foley, Robert.** Humans Before Humanity (Blackwell, 1995).

**Howells, William.** Getting Here: The Story of Human Evolution (Compass Press, 1993).

**Jones, Steve, and others, eds.** The Cambridge Encyclopedia of Human Evolution (Cambridge Univ. Press, 1994).

**Leakey, Richard.** The Origin of Humankind (Basic Books, 1994).

**Leakey, Richard.** Origins Reconsidered: In Search of What Makes Us Human (Doubleday, 1992).

**Leakey, Richard, and Lewin, Roger.** Origins: What New Discoveries Real About the Emergence of Our Species and Its Possible Future (Viking Penguin, 1991).

**Lewin, Roger.** The Origin of Modern Humans: A Scientific American Library Volume (W.H. Freeman, 1995).

**Rasmussen, D.T., and Schopf.** The Origin and Evolution of Humans and Humanness (Jones and Bartlett, Inc., 1993).

**Ridley, Matt.** The Origins of Virtue (Viking, 1997).

**Schick, K.D., and Toth, Nicholas.** Making Silent Stones Speak: Human Evolution and the Dawn of Technology (Simon and Schuster, 1993).

**Shreeve, James.** The Neandertal Enigma: Solving the Mystery of Modern Human Origins (William Morrow, 1995).

**Staski, Edward, and Marks, Jonathan.** Evolutionary Anthropology: An Introduction to Physical Anthropology and Archaeology (Harcourt Brace, 1992).

**Tattersall, Ian.** The Fossil Trail: How We Know What We Think We Know About Human Evolution (Oxford Univ. Press, 1995).

**Tattersall, Ian.** The Human Odyssey: Four Million Years of Human Evolution (Prentice, 1993).

**Van Riper, A.B.** Men Among the Mammoths: Victorian Science and the Discovery of Human Evolution (Univ. of Chicago Press, 1993).

(*See also* Further Resources for Anthropology; Archaeology; Evolution.)

**HUMAN RIGHTS.** A right may be defined as something to which an individual has a just claim. The American Declaration of Independence states that "all men . . . are endowed by their Creator with certain unalienable Rights, that among these are Life, Liberty, and the pursuit of Happiness." This is a brief statement about human rights in contrast to civil rights. Human rights are those that individuals have by virtue of their existence as human beings. The right to life itself and the basic necessities of food and clothing may be considered fundamental human rights.

Civil, or legal, rights are those granted by a government. The right to vote at age 18 is a civil right, not a human right (*see* Civil Rights). In the course of the 19th and 20th centuries there was a broadening of the concept of human rights to include many rights formerly regarded as civil.

### Historical Background

The term human rights came into common use only after World War II. It was made current by the United Nations Universal Declaration of Human Rights, published in 1948. As a term human rights replaced natural rights, a very old concept, and the related phrase rights of man, which did not necessarily include the rights of women.

Most scholars trace the origin of the concept of natural rights to ancient Greek and Roman thought. In the literature and philosophy of both Greece and Rome there are abundant statements acknowledging laws of the gods and of nature, and such laws were understood to take precedence over laws made by the state.

The human-rights concept, however, can actually be traced to an earlier period. The Hebrew Bible (called the Old Testament by Christians) relates the story of ancient Israel, and in it are abundant inferences about human rights. There is no well-developed statement on the issue, but there are significant scattered passages that give clear evidence of a point of view at least as advanced as Greek and Roman philosophy. The Ten Commandments, by the prohibition of murder and theft, give implicit recognition of the right to life and property. This recognition is considerably broadened by later elaboration of the laws and by the passionate discourses on justice by such prophets as Amos.

If the concept of human rights is very old, the general recognition of their validity is not. Throughout most of history, governments failed to accept the notion that people have rights independent of the state. This is called statism, and it implies the supremacy of the state in all matters pertaining to the lives of subjects. Statism is still a potent concept in the 20th century. Germany under Adolf Hitler and the Soviet Union during the rule of Joseph Stalin are prime examples, and there are other equally valid instances that still exist.

The modern development of the human-rights concept began during the late Middle Ages in the period called the Renaissance, when resistance to political and economic tyranny began to surface in Europe. (For a survey of the historical development, *see* Bill of Rights.) It was during the 17th and 18th centuries, a period called the Enlightenment, that specific attention was drawn by scientific discoveries to the workings of natural law. This, in turn, seemed to imply the existence of natural rights with which the state should not be allowed to interfere.

By the time of the American and French revolutions, a complete turnaround had taken place in the relationship of governments to human rights. The point of view elaborated by the American Founding Fathers, as well as by the French revolutionaries, is that government's purpose is to protect and defend rights, not to dispense or exploit them. James Madison went so far as to assert that "as a man is said to have a right to his property, he may equally be said to have a property in his rights." And further, "Government is instituted to protect property of every sort." The Declaration of the Rights of Man and of the Citizen (France, 1789) states that, "Men are born and remain free and equal in rights," and "The aim of every political association is the preservation of the natural and inprescriptible rights of man."

Such advanced views of human rights were not without their critics. From the end of the 18th century through the third decade of the 20th, outspoken and influential theorists attacked the human-rights concept. Edmund Burke in England denounced what he called "the monstrous fiction" of human equality. Philosopher Jeremy Bentham stated that only imaginary rights can be derived from a law of nature. These thinkers were joined, in the course of 100 years, by Bentham's disciple John Stuart Mill, the French political theorist Joseph de Meistre, the German jurist Friedrich Karl von Svaigny, the Austrian philosopher Ludwig Wittgenstein, and others. By 1894 the British writer F.H. Bradley could exalt the concept of statism by saying: "The rights of the individual today are not worth consideration. . . . The welfare of the community is the end and is the ultimate standard."

The critics, however, were going against the tide of history. In the United States and many parts of Europe, there was distinct progress in the development of human rights. These instances might not have been sufficient without the laboratory of human rights abuse that Nazi Germany provided for all the world to see. The appalling crimes against humanity, most evident in the extermination of millions of people in concentration camps, horrified the civilized world and helped bring human rights to their present level of acceptance (*see* Genocide; Holocaust).

### Definitions of Rights

The general acceptance of human rights led to a widespread agreement on certain fundamental assumptions about them: (1) If a right is affirmed as a human right rather than a civil right, it is understood to be universal, something that applies to all human beings everywhere. (2) Rights are understood to represent individual and group demands for the sharing of political and economic power. (3) It is agreed that human rights are not always absolute: they may be limited or restrained for the sake of the common good or to secure the rights of others. (4) Human rights is not an umbrella term to cover all personal desires. (5) The concept of rights often implies related obligations. Thomas Jefferson noted that eternal vigilance is the price of liberty. Therefore, if individuals would maintain their freedom, their duty is to guard against political, religious, and social activities that may restrict their rights and the rights of others.

Acceptance of fundamental assumptions has not lessened disagreement on which rights can be classified as human rights. Historically the debate has been carried on about three categories: individual, social, and collective. Individual rights refers to the basic rights to life and liberty mentioned in the Declaration of Independence. Social rights broadens this concept to include economic, social, and cultural rights. Collective, or solidarity, rights has come into prominence since the end of World War II, the collapse of old colonial empires, and the emergence of many new nation-states. These particular forms of rights are best described by the Universal Declaration of Human Rights.

**Individual rights.** These rights were best described by the 17th- and 18th-century political theorists—such men as John Locke in England, Montesquieu in France, and Jefferson and others in the United States. They are the rights to life, liberty, privacy, the security of the individual, freedom of speech and press, freedom of worship, the right to own property, freedom from slavery, freedom from torture and unusual punishment, and similar rights as spelled out in the first ten amendments to the United States Constitution. Basic to individual rights is the concept of government as a shield against encroachment upon the person. Little is demanded from government but the right to be left alone. Government is not asked for anything except vigilance in safeguarding the rights of its citizens.

**Social rights.** This concept of rights grew out of the socialist and Communist criticisms of capitalism and its perceived economic injustices: low wages, long working hours, unsafe working conditions, and child labor, among others. Social rights make demands on government for such things as quality education, jobs, adequate medical care, social-insurance programs, housing, and other benefits. Basically they call for a standard of living adequate for the health and well-being of the individual and the family.

**Collective rights.** The General Assembly of the United Nations adopted the Universal Declaration of Human Rights on Dec. 10, 1948. It urged the right to political, economic, social, and cultural self-determination; the right to peace; the right to live in a healthful and balanced environment; and the right to share in the Earth's resources. It also pledged the rights of life, liberty, and security of person—the basic human rights. (For text of the Universal Declaration of Human Rights, *see* Fact-Index.)

*Alexander von Humboldt works with flowers in this detail of an 1806 painting by Friedrich Weitsch.*

**HUMBOLDT, Alexander von** (1769–1859). Along with Napoleon, Alexander von Humboldt was one of the most famous men of Europe during the first half of the 19th century. He was a German scholar and explorer whose interests encompassed virtually all of the natural and physical sciences. He laid the foundations for modern physical geography, geophysics, and biogeography and helped to popularize science. His interest in the Earth's geomagnetic fields led directly to the establishment of permanent observatories in British possessions around the world, one of the first instances of international scientific cooperation. Humboldt's meteorological data contributed to comparative climatology. The Humboldt Current off the west coast of South America (now called the Peru Current) is named after him.

Friedrich Wilhelm Karl Heinrich Alexander von Humboldt was born in Berlin, Germany (then Prussia), on Sept. 14, 1769. He and his brother Wilhelm were educated at home during their early years. (Wilhelm eventually became one of Europe's most noted language scholars and educational reformers.) Alexander was at first a poor student and for some years could not decide on a career. Finally botany stirred his interest, then geology and mineralogy. He studied at the University of Göttingen and at the School of Mines in Saxony. In 1792 he obtained a position with the Prussian government's Mining Department. He worked prodigiously to improve mine safety, invented a safety lamp, and started a technical school for young miners. All the while, he was becoming convinced that his goal in life was scientific exploration.

The remainder of Humboldt's life can be divided into three segments: his expedition to South America

(1799–1804); his professional life in Paris, where he organized and published the data accumulated on the expedition (1804–27); and his last years, which were spent mostly in Berlin. The Spanish government permitted him to visit Central and South America. This little-known region offered great possibilities for scientific exploration. Accompanied by the French botanist Aimé Bonpland, Humboldt covered more than 6,000 miles (9,650 kilometers) on foot, horseback, or by canoe. After the trip Humboldt went to the United States and was received by President Thomas Jefferson.

Humboldt and Bonpland returned to Europe with an immense amount of information about plants, longitude and latitude, the Earth's geomagnetism, and climate. After brief visits to Berlin and a trip to Italy to inspect Mount Vesuvius, he settled in Paris readying the 30 volumes containing the results of the South American expedition.

Humboldt returned to Berlin at the insistence of the king of Prussia. He lectured on physical geography to large audiences and organized international scientific conferences. In 1829 he traveled through Russia into Siberia, as far as the Chinese frontier. The last 25 years were occupied chiefly with writing his 'Kosmos', one of the most ambitious scientific works ever published. In it Humboldt presented his cosmic view of the universe as a whole. He was writing the fifth volume of this work when he died in Berlin on May 6, 1859.

**HUME, David** (1711–76). A Scottish philosopher and historian, David Hume was a founder of the skeptical, or agnostic, school of philosophy. He had a profound influence on European intellectual life.

David Hume was born in Edinburgh, Scotland, on April 26 (Old Style), 1711. His father, Joseph Hume (or Home), and his mother, Katherine Falconer, had grown up together as stepbrother and stepsister on the family estate of Ninewells in Berwickshire. Under the system of primogeniture Hume's older brother was heir to the estate.

David Hume was expected by his family to follow a traditional career in law. By the age of 18, however, after attending the University of Edinburgh from 1724 to 1726 and finding law distasteful, he enthusiastically plunged into the study of literature and philosophy. Hume later observed that his studies were "the ruling passion of my life, and the great source of my enjoyments."

From 1734 to 1737 Hume lived in France. There he wrote his first work, 'A Treatise of Human Nature'. He was disappointed by its hostile reception and later dismissed it as an immature work that did not accurately reflect his views. In spite of this, the part on understanding continues to be widely read. Hume's more immediately successful 'Essays, Moral and Political' was published in 1741–42 after he had returned to Ninewells.

For a while Hume worked as a tutor. In the late 1740s he served as secretary to General James St. Clair on military missions in Brittany, Vienna, and Turin. With the publication of 'Political Discourses' in 1752, he began his rise to international fame.

In 1751 Hume had been appointed keeper of the library of the Faculty of Advocates in Edinburgh. Using its historical collection for his research, he wrote his spectacularly successful 'A History of England', published in four volumes between 1754 and 1761. For decades this history, or a shortened version of it, was used as a standard text in English schools.

Hume served for some years as secretary and then as chargé d'affaires in the British embassy in Paris. He returned to London in 1766 and worked for a while as undersecretary of state. In 1769 Hume retired to live with his sister. In 1775 he was stricken by an incurable intestinal cancer. Upon learning of his illness Hume wrote, "I now reckon upon a speedy dissolution." He coolly added, ". . . a man of sixty-five, by dying, cuts off only a few years of infirmities." Hume died in Edinburgh on Aug. 25, 1776.

Hume's philosophical writings cast doubt on the truth of church-supported dogmas. Charges of religious heresy permanently barred him from appointment as a professor in Scottish universities. Not only did he deny miracles and other religious dogmas, but his theory of knowledge seemed to undercut the reality of the world itself. He maintained that knowledge came from observation and experience. These, however, were purely individual. A person's perceptions of objects were just that—perceptions. No underlying reality could ever be proved, because every individual's perceptions are his alone—even if they agree with someone else's. The "someone else" is also only a perception of the senses.

In his political writings Hume held that government organization, though basically evil, is necessary to guarantee human happiness. In economic theory Hume argued that goods rather than money are the basis of wealth. He believed that each part of the world has special products or services to offer and was an early advocate of increased trade among the nations of the world. Despite the intellectual controversy he aroused, Hume was admired and loved by his many friends, which included members of the clergy. He never married but contented himself with assuring the education of his brother's children.

**HUMMINGBIRD.** The Portuguese call it *beija-flôr*, meaning "kiss-flower." The Aztecs adorned Montezuma's ceremonial cloaks with its feathers. The dazzling hummingbird still captures people's fancy.

Because of special flight muscles that control wing beats of 38 to 78 times per second, a hummingbird can hover in the air and is the only bird that can fly backward. The smallest hummingbirds can attain wing-beat frequencies of 200 per second during courtship flights when the males show off their brilliant plumage. The female builds a cup-shaped nest from moss, seed down, and spider webs. She alone incubates the tiny eggs, of which there are usually only two, and rears the young.

© Tom Vezo—Peter Arnold, Inc.

*A female Anna's hummingbird* (Calypte anna) *native to western North America, feeds her young.*

Hummingbirds drink nectar at the rate of about 13 licks per second. They also eat insects. The specialized tongue bones of the hyoid apparatus allow the tongue, which is divided into two equal lobes at its front half, to extend beyond the tip of the long narrow bill. This enables the hummingbird to reach nectar deep within the flower.

Most of the 338 species in the hummingbird family, Trochilidae, live along the equator across the countries of South America, but they range from Alaska to Tierra del Fuego. The giant hummingbird, 8 inches (20 centimeters) long, lives at altitudes of 15,000 feet (4,600 meters) in the Andes Mountains. The Cuban bee hummingbird is the smallest bird in the world, measuring 2 ¼ inches (6 centimeters). (*See also* Birds.)   Barbara Katz

**HUMOR.** The Roman writer Seneca once commented: "All things are cause either for laughter or weeping." The 18th-century French dramatist Pierre-Augustin Beaumarchais echoed Seneca's words by stating: "I hasten to laugh at everything, for fear of being obliged to weep." Both Seneca and Beaumarchais understood that laughing and crying are closely related emotional responses to some kind of outside stimulation. They knew that in life as in drama comedy and tragedy are never far apart. Both laughing and crying serve to relax tension.

Laughter, like weeping, is a reflex action rooted in the central nervous system and its related hormones. It is expressed in the contraction of certain facial muscles and in altered breathing patterns. The stimulation that brings forth laughter is called humor. To define laughter and humor in this way, however, is to leave unanswered two questions. Why do people laugh, and what is funny, or humorous? The questions are difficult to answer because emotions and the reasons for them are not easily analyzed.

Something humorous does not necessarily amuse everyone. Sometimes the reason is cultural. Each society has its own notion of what is comic. An American viewing a British comedy on stage or television may find little to laugh at because the origin of the humor is not understood. The foreigner does not know what the rest of the audience finds funny. Even within one culture there are different responses to humor. Young children, teenagers, and adults do not laugh at the same things.

Values and morals also affect one's views of humor. Prior to the civil rights movement, ethnic humor of all types was popular in the United States. Jokes about ethnic groups were commonly told on radio, television, and the stage. The resurgence of ethnic pride in the early 1960s virtually ended the widespread use of such humor. Telling ethnic stories through the public media became very risky unless the teller was a member of the group about which the stories were told. Thus Myron Cohen could continue regaling audiences with his brilliant Jewish humor, but Bill Dana could no longer perform his José Jiménez routine on television because he is not Mexican. The barrier against ethnic humor was partially broken by the television series All in the Family, in which the lead character, Archie Bunker, freely insulted everyone who was different from himself.

Humor appeals primarily to two senses—hearing and seeing. Before television, professional comics on radio had to rely on words and sounds alone to convey humor. When an audience can see a performer on stage, in movies, or on television, both verbal and visual humor are possible.

**Verbal humor.** Humor in the form of words may be either written or spoken. As such it usually requires some amount of understanding by the hearer or reader for which visual humor may not call. One of the most common kinds of verbal humor is the play on words. This type includes puns, riddles, and some limericks. Puns especially involve the use of soundalike words that have different meanings (*see* Word Games). A parody is a comic piece of writing that gets its humor by imitating a serious piece. 'Don Quixote' by Miguel Cervantes is probably the best parody ever written. Satires are usually long, written attempts at humor. They are designed to make fun of human folly and weakness. The ancient Greek dramatist Aristophanes used satire masterfully to lampoon the persons and institutions of Athens.

Of all types of verbal humor, the joke, or witticism, is probably the most popular. The joke may be as short as a one-liner, or it may be a long and complex story with a surprise ending. Many jokes depend for their success on the unexpected, or bringing together two ways of thinking about the same thing that would not normally occur to someone. Others depend on exaggeration, insult, or absurdity.

**Visual humor.** Almost everything that can be seen may be perceived as humorous by someone, no matter how serious the intent. A grisly horror film may cause an audience to laugh because its dramatic effects are exaggerated or seemingly ridiculous. Visual humor frequently relies on transforming the normal or serious into the unexpected, ludicrous, or absurd. A car chase in a television police drama has little humor, but when used in the movie comedy 'It's a Mad, Mad, Mad, Mad World' it proves hilarious.

The creation of absurd or intentionally ridiculous situations can be quite comedic. In the movie 'Tootsie' Dustin Hoffman played the part of a woman in order to get acting roles that otherwise eluded him. And in 'Victor, Victoria' Julie Andrews carried this type of joke further by pretending to be a man acting as a woman to get stage roles. The man-as-woman ruse was carried to amazing extremes by Milton Berle in the early years of television.

Slapstick is the coarsest and most obvious type of humor. It gets its name from the paddles that clowns use to hit each other. To be effective, slapstick must be sudden, unexpected, and exaggerated.

**HUNAN.** A province in the southeastern part of China, Hunan extends along the middle course of the Yangtze River. It covers an area of 81,300 square miles (210,500 square kilometers) and is bounded by the provinces of Hubei to the north, Jiangxi to the east, Guangdong and Guangxi Zhuangzu (autonomous region) to the south, and Guizhou and Sichuan to the west. Changsha, its capital and leading city, is located in the northeast.

The subtropical monsoonal climate provides long and humid summers. Summer cyclones bring heavy rains, resulting in extensive flooding. Irrigated rice is Hunan's major crop. It exports a large surplus of rice to nearby provinces. Other crops are sweet potatoes, corn, wheat, millet, cotton, ramie, jute, peanuts, and tea. Forestry, fishing, and livestock raising are also major activities. Hunan's mineral wealth is considerable with deposits of coal, iron ore, manganese, antimony, tungsten, lead, and zinc.

Industries include iron and steel, electrical machinery, textiles, paper and pulp milling, and food processing. Traditional handicrafts include embroidered clothing, duck-down quilts, leather goods, and pottery. Waterways are major means of transportation for both goods and people. Nearly 80 percent of Hunan's goods are moved over waterways.

Mostly rural, Hunan's population is largely concentrated in the Dongting Lake basin and river valleys. Village life has changed markedly since the 1949 revolution. Mao Zedong, the revolutionary leader, was born in Hunan. Most villages have civic centers and libraries. Changsha, Xiangtan, and Zhuzhou are major cities that form a single vast urban region. Population (2000 estimate), 64,400,000.

**HUNDRED YEARS' WAR** (1337–1453). The struggle between France and England called the Hundred Years' War was the longest war in recorded history. It lasted, with some interruptions, through the reigns of five English kings (Edward III to Henry V) and five French kings (Philip VI to Charles VII).

The underlying cause of the war lay in the feudal system. Since the time of Henry II the English king had been duke of the great duchy of Guienne in southwest France. For this fief he did homage to the king of France (*see* Feudalism). Philip VI, the French king, was bent on destroying the power of his feudal vassals. England would not meekly submit to the loss of Guienne.

Indeed, Edward III claimed that he himself was rightfully the king of France because his mother was a sister of the late French king, while Philip VI was only a cousin. The French declared that it was a law in France that no woman could inherit the throne, nor could the crown be inherited through a woman.

The immediate cause of the war was economic. English sheep growers sold their long fine wool to weavers in Flanders, across the English Channel. Flemish weavers as well as English sheep growers depended on this trade for their livelihood. In 1336 Philip VI arrested all English merchants in Flanders and took away the privileges of the Flemish towns and the craft guilds. The Flemings revolted against French control and made an alliance with England.

### Crécy—A Great English Victory

In July 1346 Edward III landed in Normandy with an army of about 10,000 men. The French pursued him to Crécy, where the English occupied the side of a little hill. On the plain below, outnumbering the English four to one, Philip VI commanded a disorderly host of mounted French men-at-arms and hired Genoese crossbowmen on foot. Edward had all his men dismount because they were armed with the new longbow.

Suddenly the Genoese advanced to the attack. But they were tired after a long day's march, and their crossbow strings were loosened by the wetting received in a terrific thundershower. Although they "shot fiercely with their crossbows," they were no match for the more rapid shooting of the English longbowmen, whose shafts "fell so thick that it seemed snow." When the Genoese saw the arrows falling thick among them they threw down their bows and ran. At this King Philip flew into a rage and cried out, "Slay these rascals, for they will trouble us without reason!" Whereupon his men-at-arms dashed in among the Genoese and slew a great number of them.

"And ever still," says the chronicler Froissart, "the Englishmen shot where they saw the thickest press.

The Granger Collection

*England defeated the French fleet in the battle of Sluys on June 24, 1340, making it possible for the English to move troops and supplies into France.*

The sharp arrows pierced the knights and their horses, and many fell, both horse and man. And when they were down they could not rise again, the press was so thick that one overthrew another."

In one place the French managed to reach a band of dismounted English knights under the command of the Black Prince, the 16-year-old son of Edward III. In haste the knights dispatched a messenger to the king asking aid. The king was watching the battle from the tower of a windmill. When their request was made known to him, he inquired: "Is my son dead, or hurt, or felled to earth?"

"No, sire," said the messenger, "but he is overmatched and has need of aid."

"Then," replied the king, "return to them that sent you, and say to them that they send no more to me, so long as my son is alive; and also say to them that they suffer him this day to win his spurs, for I will that this day's work be his, and the honor thereof."

As darkness fell the remnants of the French army were fleeing in confusion. The English lines remained firm in their position on the hill.

Thus the English won the first great land battle of the long war. Before this battle they had already won command of the English Channel by a spectacular naval victory at Sluys, and after Crécy, the town of Calais, the door into France, surrendered to them on Sept. 28, 1347, after a year's siege.

For almost ten years after that the fighting lagged. This was caused in part by a great pestilence called the Black Death, which swept over Europe and killed more than a third of the population (*see* Bubonic Plague).

Not until 1355 was the struggle between the two countries renewed. The English now carried the conflict into southern France instead of confining it to the northern section as before. At Poitiers (1356) the Black Prince with a small army of Englishmen was confronted by an overwhelming French force. In vain the prince offered to surrender his spoils and his prisoners and to promise not to fight for seven years if he might be allowed a safe retreat. This offer was rejected, so certain did the French feel of victory.

**Poitiers and Agincourt**

The Black Prince arranged his troops on a plateau where they were protected at the flanks by a hedge and by rough and marshy ground. The brave but inefficient French King John lost his advantage of superior numbers by ordering his knights, weighted down with their armor, to dismount and advance on foot against the hail of English arrows. One after another the three divisions of the French army were thrown into confusion. King John and his youngest son, refusing to flee, were taken captive by the English forces. Once again the victory was the result of the new English weapon—the longbow.

The horrors of a peasants' revolt and civil strife were now added to the miseries of France. A treaty with England was finally concluded at Bretigny in 1360, by which King John was to pay a large money ransom and Edward III was to have Guienne, Crécy, and Calais in full sovereignty. In return Edward renounced all claim to the French crown.

But in 1369 the new king of France, Charles V, physically weak but intellectually strong, found an excuse for breaking the treaty and renewing the war. Aided by the able Breton general Bertrand du Guesclin, he organized an army of professional soldiers instead of knights and by cautious maneuvering brought one place after another into his hands. Only Calais in the north and Bordeaux in the south remained to the English at the time of Charles's death in 1380.

For nearly a generation the war then languished because of factional strife for power in both England and France. In France the situation was aggravated by the fact that Charles VI, who was now king, suffered frequent periods of insanity. Soon after the accession in 1413 of Henry V, the hero king of England, the struggle began again.

The next engagement took place at Agincourt near Crécy, where in 1415 a small English force was once more confronted by a large French army. The French, it seemed, had learned nothing from the disasters of Crécy and Poitiers or from the exploits of Charles V and Du Guesclin. As in the two former great battles, their forces consisted of dismounted knights weighted down with heavy armor. Again they were packed close together in a narrow newly plowed field between two woods. They sank almost to their knees in the soft soil. A third great English victory, equal to those of Crécy and Poitiers, was the result.

By the Treaty of Troyes (1420) the defeated and disunited French agreed that Henry V should marry Catherine of Valois, the daughter of Charles VI of France. It was further agreed that during Charles's lifetime Henry should act as regent and that after Charles's death Henry should reign as king of France as well as of England. Henry did not live to wear the French crown, for he died in 1422. Seven weeks later Charles also died, and the death of these two monarchs left the claim to both thrones to Henry VI, the 9-month-old son of Henry V and Queen Catherine.

The English claims in France, however, were disputed by the disinherited dauphin of France, later Charles VII, who refused to accept the Treaty of Troyes. For a time he was too weak to be feared, and at the end of seven years it seemed that Orléans, his last considerable stronghold, would surely fall.

### Maid of Orléans

Just at this darkest moment in the fortunes of France, a new force appeared in the person of Joan of Arc, the Maid of Orléans (*see* Joan of Arc). Inspired by her patriotism, the French forced the English to raise the siege of Orléans. Victory followed victory in rapid succession, until finally Joan led the dauphin through a hostile country to be crowned at Reims as King Charles VII. Even after Joan's capture and execution by the English and Burgundians, her spirit seemed to inspire the French and to wake in them a new national sentiment. Little by little they drove the English back. Finally the war ended in 1453 with only Calais remaining in English hands.

Instead of winning the French throne for the English king, the Hundred Years' War had lost for him the last of those continental possessions that had once been held by Henry II. The French king, who no longer numbered a powerful rival monarch among his vassals, soon established an almost absolute power in his kingdom. He enjoyed a permanent revenue and could count on the advice of able counselors. He was also supported by a standing army equipped with modern artillery—for cannon had come into use either at the battle of Crécy or shortly thereafter.

One lasting result of the hundred years' conflict was that the struggle to expel the foreigner from their soil had planted in the French the seed of the intense patriotism that came to characterize France. But nationalistic sentiment had been bought at a heavy price. More than 100 years of intermittent warfare had

taken place on French soil. Any advantages that France gained were countered by the fearful losses inflicted on its land and people, the check to population, and the brutalization that accompanied the long-continued conflict. (*See also* Henry, Kings of England, "Henry V.")

**HUNGARY.** In the spring of 1989 the Hungarian government symbolically opened its frontier by removing stretches of the barbed wire that formed the Iron Curtain. After more than 40 years of one-party Communist rule and Soviet domination, in October 1989, during a period of broad political and economic liberalization in the Soviet Union and Eastern Europe, the Hungarian parliament amended its constitution to pave the way for multiparty elections. The country changed its name to the Republic of Hungary and proclaimed itself to be a free democratic republic.

### Land and Climate

The area of Hungary is 35,919 square miles (93,030 square kilometers). It is bounded on the north by Slovakia; on the northeast by Ukraine; on the east by Romania; on the south by Slovenia, Croatia, and Serbia and Montenegro; and on the west by Austria. It is 328 miles (528 kilometers) from east to west and 167 miles (269 kilometers) from north to south.

Much of Hungary consists of the Great Alföld, which is part of the Mid-Danube, or Pannonian, Plain. In the northwest a range of low hills separates the Great Alföld from the Little Alföld. In the southwest are the Transdanubian Mountains, and the western edge contains a small part of the Alps. A chain of hills extends along the northern borders. The highest summit is Kékes Peak in the Mátra Hills, which reaches 3,330 feet (1,015 meters) in height.

The major river is the Danube, which flows for 255 miles (410 kilometers) in Hungarian territory. The Tisza flows from the northeastern corner to the south for 360 miles (580 kilometers). The largest lake is Lake Balaton, about 45 miles (70 kilometers) long and very shallow.

*The Fisherman's Bastion, left, overlooks Budapest and the Danube River. It was built between 1901 and 1903 and owes its name to the fact that it was constructed over the site of a former fishermen's village.*

Chad Ehlers—Tony Stone Worldwide

The soils of Hungary show considerable variety. The plains contain areas of fertile black-earth and alluvial soils, though some less fertile sandy soils occur in places. The hill country has brown forest soils of medium fertility.

The climate is relatively uniform as a result of the flatness of most of the country. It is continental in type, having cold winters and hot summers. In January the whole country has average temperatures below freezing, while in July the plains have average temperatures of over 68° F (20° C). Budapest, in the center of Hungary, has an average January temperature of 31° F (–0.6° C) and an average July temperature of 72° F (22.2° C), with a yearly average of 25 inches (63.5 centimeters) of precipitation.

Hungary's resources for industry are modest. Coal is the major energy resource. Black coal is found in the southwest but is not sufficient for domestic requirements. Scattered deposits of brown coal and lignite are located on the flanks of the northern hills. In the west and south small deposits of petroleum and natural gas are found. There is also a natural gas field in the east. Bauxite is the most abundant metallic ore and is exported.

### Plants and Animals

The natural vegetation of Hungary can be divided into three groups. The Great Alföld was once a grassland with scattered trees, but now most of the trees have vanished. In some areas acacias, oaks, and beeches are found along with brushwood. The main vegetation

. . . . . . . . . . . . . . . . . . . . . . . . . . . . . . . . . . . . . . . . . . . . .

*This article was contributed by Ian M. Matley, Professor of Geography, Michigan State University.*

consists of varieties of grass. In the Transdanubian Mountains beech forests occur. The most densely forested region is the northern ranges of hills, where beeches, oaks, hornbeams, and maples grow.

The animals of Hungary include deer, foxes, hares, and squirrels. Wild boars, wolves, jackals, lynxes, and beavers are also found. Lake Balaton supports a variety of birds, while storks are common. Carp, pike, perch, and other fish are found in rivers and lakes.

### People

The population of the country is some 10 million, of whom about 85 percent are ethnic Hungarians. There are small numbers of Roma (Gypsies), Ruthenians, Germans, Romanians, Slovaks, and Jews.

The Hungarians are descended from the ancient Magyars, who came from an area near the Ural Mountains more than a thousand years ago. The Hungarian language belongs to the Finno-Ugric group and is distantly related to Finnish.

About 60 percent of the people are Roman Catholics and about 20 percent are Protestants, mainly Calvinists. The Protestants live mainly in eastern Hungary. Most of the rest of the people do not actively practice any particular religion.

About 62 percent of the population live in cities, of which the largest is Budapest, the capital. Its more than 1.75 million people make up nearly 20 percent of the country's total population. Smaller cities include Debrecen, Miskolc, Szeged, and Pécs.

### Culture

Among the major contributions of the Hungarians to European culture are literature, science, music, and painting. It was not until the 19th century that

*From vineyards on the terraced hillsides of the Tokaj-Hegyalja region come Hungary's world-famous Tokay wines.*

Hungarian literature flowered. During the early part of the century, the best-known poets were Dániel Berzsenyi and Mihály Csokonai Vitéz, while András Dugonics wrote the most successful novel of the period. They were followed by the novelists Miklós Jósika, József Eötvös, and Mihály Vörösmarty, who also wrote poems. Károly Kisfaludy edited a literary magazine and wrote plays. The greatest lyric poets of the century were Sándor Petfi and János Arany. Mór Jókai was one of Hungary's most popular novelists, while Imre Madách's dramatic poem 'The Tragedy of Man' was translated into many languages and is still performed.

The greatest Hungarian novelists of the early 20th century were Zsigmond Móricz, Menyhért Lengyel, Dezsö Szabó, and Margit Kaffka, the country's first significant woman novelist. Ferenc Molnár wrote popular plays. The major 20th century poets were Attila József, Gyula Illyés, and Endre Ady. Later writers include László Németh, Tibor Déry, Peter Veres, and Ferenc Juhász. In 2002 Imre Kertész became the first Hungarian to win the Nobel prize for literature.

Hungarian-born scientists have won several Nobel prizes. Among these are Georg von Békésy, Albert Szent-Györgyi, Edward Teller, and Eugene Wigner.

Hungary has a rich heritage of folk music. This music is interpreted by the Roma (Gypsies), who make up the traditional folk orchestras. The Hungarian composers Béla Bartók and Zoltán Kodály incorporated this folk music into Western classical forms, though both are also known for their piano and chamber music, concerti, operas, songs, and choral works. The great 19th-century composer Franz Liszt,

though born in Hungary and inspired by Hungarian folk music, lived most of his life abroad. In the 20th century a number of Hungarian orchestra conductors had notable careers abroad, including Fritz Reiner, Antal Dorati, Georg Solti, and István Kertész.

Hungarian painting is less renowned than its literature and music. The best Hungarian artist of the 19th century was Mihály Munkácsi. French influence on Hungarian art is seen in the paintings of such artists as Pal Szinyei Merse, István Szönyi, and István Csók. Hungarian folk culture is also rich in art, costumes, dances, and cookery.

## Economy

After 1949 farmland was collectivized and divided between cooperative and state farms. Although originally based on the Soviet model, the Hungarian authorities introduced reforms after 1965, permitting considerable family participation in the operation of cooperative farms. Less than 10 percent of the labor force is employed in farming and forestry.

About 70 percent of the total area of Hungary is used for farming. More than 75 percent of this area is in field crops. Major crops are corn and wheat, with some barley, rye, and oats. Fodder crops, sugar beets, and vegetables are also grown. Onions and paprika are exported. Fruit and wine production are significant. Apples, pears, apricots, plums, cherries, figs, and almonds are grown, and many of these are exported to Western Europe. Vineyards produce a number of good wines. Livestock production equals field agriculture, and cattle, pigs, and sheep are kept throughout the country. In general, Hungarian agriculture is successful because of good climate and soils and relatively good organization. The country does not need to import much food and provides surpluses for export.

Industry has become a significant part of the Hungarian economy. The iron and steel industry is concentrated mainly at Dunaújváros on the Danube, using mostly imported raw materials. An aluminum industry, based on domestic bauxite deposits, is located in a number of production centers. Most industry is located in the Budapest area. Major products are machine tools, transport equipment (especially buses), chemicals, pharmaceuticals, and textiles. In 1989, final agreements on commercial and economic cooperation were signed between the European Union members and Hungary, marking a new stage in the evolution of the country toward a more market-based economic system.

### Transportation, Communication, Education

An extensive network of long-distance bus lines, railways, and roads are used to transport both passengers and freight throughout Hungary. The main internal waterway route is the Danube, with Budapest as the major port. The national airline is Malév, which is based in Budapest.

Radio and television broadcasting were controlled by the state until 1990. Postal, telephone, and telegraph services were also state owned. Several Hungarian

*Students arrive for class at the Technical University of Budapest, founded in 1782 by the Austrian Emperor Joseph II.*
Interfoto MTI—Eastfoto

newspapers were purchased in 1990 by groups of private investors outside Hungary.

Education is compulsory between the ages of 6 and 16. Students can attend secondary, vocational, or technical schools from age 10 to 18. There are universities at Budapest, Pécs, Szeged, and Debrecen in addition to a number of technical universities and other institutes of higher education.

**Government and History**

The Hungarian People's Republic was established in 1949. The supreme organ of government is the National Assembly, or parliament. Until 1989 members of the Hungarian Socialist Workers', or Communist, party held all political power, which was exercised

through the Politburo of the Central Committee. On Oct. 7, 1989, the party renounced Communism and renamed itself the Hungarian Socialist party. Later that month the country's parliament ended the party's monopoly on power. Parliament also put into law an accord agreed to by the regime and opposition groups that Hungary would become a democratic republic with a legislature elected by universal suffrage, a relatively weak president to be chosen by parliament, and a constitutional court. The name of the country was changed to the Hungarian Republic.

The settlement of the Magyar tribesmen under their leader Árpád on the Mid-Danube Plain in the 10th century marked the beginning of the Hungarian state. In 1000 Stephen was crowned as the first Christian

*The horseshoe-shaped Esterházy Palace at Fertöd, Hungary, was built between 1760 and 1770 by Prince Miklós József Esterházy, a member of Hungary's most prominent family. With its 126 rooms, it is now one of the country's chief tourist attractions.*
© Berlitz—CLICK/Chicago

king of Hungary. For the next 300 years the house of Árpád ruled Hungary, but in 1308 the crown passed to Charles Robert of Anjou as Charles I. His son Louis I conquered much of the surrounding territories, but most of these were lost by Sigismund of Luxembourg, who was king of Hungary from 1387 until 1437. He was followed by the Hunyadi family. János Hunyadi defended Hungary against attacks by the Turks, and his son Matthias Corvinus annexed Bohemia and Austria to the Hungarian state. Matthias was one of Hungary's greatest kings and improved the administration and economy of the country. He did little, however, against the increasing threat of the Turks, who in 1526 defeated the Hungarians at Mohács.

The Turks occupied the central area of Hungary, including Budapest. Much of the population left the region. Western Hungary came under the control of the Austrians, while the province of Transylvania in the east became a princedom, largely independent of the Turks. The failure of the Turks to take Vienna in 1683 led to their retreat from Hungarian territory. In 1699 the Hapsburg ruler of Austria, Leopold, also became king of Hungary. Under the Austrian empress Maria Theresa (1740–80), conditions for the Hungarians improved.

A long period of relative peace enabled Hungarian culture to flourish. Count István Széchenyi not only encouraged the development of the Hungarian language around 1830 but urged political reforms. He believed in maintaining a strong link with the Hapsburgs. Non-Hungarian peoples, such as the Croats and the Romanians, resisted Hungarian rule, however, and local revolts took place.

In 1848 the Hungarian patriot Lajos Kossuth took advantage of the general unrest in the Austrian territories to declare an independent Hungarian state. In 1849 a Russian army, sent to aid the Austrian emperor Franz Joseph, defeated the Hungarians and reestablished Austrian control. In 1867, realizing that the Hapsburg empire could not exist without Hungarian support, the Austrians arrived at a compromise (Ausgleich) whereby Hungary was given control of its internal affairs and the emperor was crowned as king of Hungary. This dual monarchy of Austria-Hungary lasted until 1918. (*See also* Austria-Hungary.)

## Hungary Fact Summary

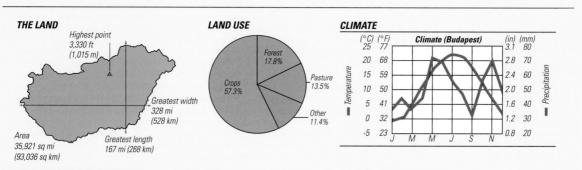

**THE LAND**
Highest point 3,330 ft (1,015 m)
Greatest width 328 mi (528 km)
Area 35,921 sq mi (93,036 sq km)
Greatest length 167 mi (268 km)

**LAND USE**
Forest 17.8%
Pasture 13.5%
Crops 57.3%
Other 11.4%

**CLIMATE**
Climate (Budapest)

**Official Name.** Republic of Hungary.
**Capital.** Budapest.

**NATURAL FEATURES**
**Prominent Feature.** Great Alföld.
**Highest Peak.** Kékes, 3,330 feet (1,015 meters).
**Major Rivers.** Danube, Tisza.
**Mountain Range.** Alps.
**Largest Lake.** Balaton.

**PEOPLE**
**Population** (2002 estimate). 10,162,000; 282.9 persons per square mile (109.2 persons per square kilometer); 63.6 percent urban, 36.4 percent rural (2000 estimate).
**Major Cities** (2001 census). Budapest (1,775,203), Debrecen (211,038), Miskolc (184,129), Szeged (168,276), Pécs (162,502).
**Major Religions.** Roman Catholicism, Protestantism.
**Major Language.** Hungarian (official).
**Literacy.** 99.4 percent.
**Leading Universities and Colleges.** Attila József University (Szeged), Budapest University of Economic Sciences and Public Administration (Budapest), Lajos Kossuth University (Debrecen), Loránd Eötvös University (Budapest), Semmelweis University of Medicine (Budapest).

**GOVERNMENT**
**Form of Government.** Republic.
**Chief of State.** President.
**Head of Government.** Prime Minister.
**Legislature.** National Assembly, or Parliament.
**Voting Qualification.** Mandatory at age 18.
**Political Divisions.** 19 counties.
**Flag.** Three horizontal stripes of red, white, and green (*see* Flags of the World).

**ECONOMY**
**Chief Agricultural Products.** *Crops*—corn (maize), wheat, sugar beets, barley, sunflower seeds, grapes, apples. *Livestock*—pigs, cattle.
**Chief Mined Product.** Bauxite.
**Chief Manufactured Products.** Food and beverages, chemicals and chemical products, motor vehicles, refined petroleum products, base metals, computers.
**Chief Exports.** Food, office machines and computers, power generating machinery, clothing, road vehicles and parts.
**Chief Imports.** Nonelectrical machinery and apparatus, electrical machinery and apparatus, mineral fuels, road vehicles.
**Monetary Unit.** 1 forint = 100 filler.

In 1918 most members of minority groups became citizens of such new states as Yugoslavia and Czechoslovakia. The province of Transylvania was given to Romania. By the Treaty of Trianon in 1920, Hungary lost more than 10 million of its population and about two thirds of its territory.

In the next two decades there was considerable political and economic instability. At the outbreak of World War II, Hungary hoped to remain neutral, but in 1941 Hungarian troops were sent to join the Germans on the Soviet front. Attempts to break away from German control were unsuccessful, and Germany occupied Hungary in 1944. By April 1945, however, Hungary was in the hands of Soviet troops.

A provisional government set up by the Soviets was replaced by a Communist-dominated government in 1947. The leader of the Communist party, Mátyás Rákosi, tried to make Hungary a model state in the Soviet sphere of influence. With the death of Soviet Premier Joseph Stalin in 1953, Imre Nagy, a more moderate Communist, became the leader. But in 1955 Rákosi regained power. In October 1956 a full-scale uprising against the Communists took place, and Nagy again became national leader. Soviet troops put down the revolt after several days of bitter fighting, mainly in Budapest. Nagy was executed two years later. Many thousands died, and 200,000 people fled the country.

After the revolt János Kádár became first secretary of the Hungarian Socialist Workers' party. He introduced liberal reforms and declared a general amnesty for political prisoners in 1962. In May 1988 Kádár was ousted for failing to keep pace with the party's desire for more economic and political changes. By the spring of 1989 a large number of political parties had come into being. They formed the Opposition Round Table to negotiate with Communist party leadership for an orderly transition from Communism to democracy. In December the parliament voted to dissolve itself on March 16, 1990, and scheduled elections for March 25. In the first free elections in 45 years, Hungarian voters split their vote between two newly formed anti-Communist parties. Jószef Antall, president of the Hungarian Democratic Forum, became prime minister. Árpád Göncz, a founder of the Free Democrats party, was chosen as president by the parliament.

In June 1990 the parliament voted to leave the Warsaw Pact and establish diplomatic ties with the North Atlantic Treaty Organization. Later that year Hungary became the first former Soviet-bloc country to join the Council of Europe. Voters weary of the transition to a free-market economy gave a parliamentary majority to the Hungarian Socialist party, composed of former Communists, in 1994 elections. In March 1999, Hungary along with Poland and the Czech Republic, officially joined the NATO alliance. The move marked the first eastward expansion of NATO into lands once dominated by the Soviet-led Warsaw pact. In 2003 Hungary signed an accession treaty to join the European Union.

**FURTHER RESOURCES FOR HUNGARY**

**Complete Guide to Hungary,** 3rd rev. ed. (Hippocrene, 1990).
**Lye, Keith.** Take a Trip to Hungary (Watts, 1986).
**Nemeth, Sy.** Hungary: A Comprehensive Guide (Hippocrene, 1986).
**St. John, Jetty.** A Family in Hungary (Lerner, 1988).

**HUNGER AND FAMINE.** In its simplest sense, hunger is merely a desire. The teenager arrives home from school and heads straight to the refrigerator looking for something to eat. He has already had breakfast and lunch, and dinner will soon be ready, so he is not in great need of food. For millions of people on Earth, however, hunger represents a genuine need—a large-scale lack of food. This lack may be partial: there is some food, but never enough. The lack of food may also be total. A total lack of food for a whole population is called a famine—obviously related to the word famished. The Latin word *fames* from which it comes means "hunger." The result of famine is mass starvation, something that has often happened in world history (*see* table in Fact-Index under Famine).

A famine is defined as an extreme and long-term shortage of food. A famine can affect a whole country, as it did Somalia in the early 1990s. Or it may be regional, as in Ethiopia during the 1980s. In Germany, just after World War II, there was regional famine because the country had been so devastated by the war, but some areas were hit harder than others. Warfare has been the most common historical cause of famines; it destroys not only food supplies but distribution systems as well.

There are two main causes of famine: natural and human. Natural causes include disasters such as drought, insect plagues, excessive rainfall and flooding, and unseasonably cold weather. In a large nation such as the United States these factors may operate to cause shortages and high prices. But they have never caused a famine, because food can be imported or carried from one part of the country to another. In a smaller, less diverse society a natural disaster can cause extreme hardship. In Ireland, during the 1840s, the failure of the potato crop led to the deaths of at least 1 million people and the emigration of thousands. In ancient societies, a flood or drought could easily cause famine because there were no outside sources of food relief.

Overpopulation, a kind of natural cause, has led to severe famines in China and India since 1700. Between 9 and 13 million persons died of starvation in China in the years 1876–79, for example. Significant 20th-century improvements in agriculture—the Green Revolution—have eased this problem considerably.

In the 20th century, human causes of famine were at least as prevalent as natural causes, especially in Asia and Africa. Apart from warfare, misguided economic reform programs carried out in the name of Communism and socialism led to the deaths of millions in the Soviet Union (notably Ukraine in the 1930s), China after 1949, and Ethiopia and Mozambique in the 1980s. Farm families were driven from villages or tribal lands by force and herded into collective farms. Individual initiative was abolished, and agricultural production suffered badly. Agriculture was run by government bureaucracies, with little freedom of choice for producers or consumers. Russia and China were recovering from these mistakes by the 1990s, but famine persisted in Africa.

**HUNS.** During the 3rd century BC some of the earlier segments of the Great Wall of China were connected to keep out a fierce nomadic people from Mongolia to the north. These tribes were called the Hsiung-nu. In the West they became known as the Huns. They were a nonagricultural people—animal herders who became expert horsemen. Gradually they worked their way westward across the grasslands of Central Asia until, in about AD 370, they appeared in Southeastern Europe in the last days of the Roman Empire. There, and also in Central Europe, they built a large empire of their own. In spite of the similarity in name, they are not connected with the modern Eastern European population of Hungary.

The Huns first overcame the Alani, another nomadic group, who lived on the plains between the Volga and Don rivers. They then moved on to overthrow the Ostrogothic kingdom between the Don and Dnestr rivers. By 376 they attacked the Visigoths in the area of what is now Romania, on the western shores of the Black Sea. (*See also* Goths.) For 50 years after their conquest of the Visigoths, the Huns remained a chronic irritant to both the Western and Eastern Roman Empires. They had established themselves in Europe and raided the Roman provinces along the Danube River. Early in the 5th century they apparently extended their authority over Germanic peoples to the west. Some Huns became soldiers for the Byzantine, or Eastern Roman, Empire (*see* Byzantine Empire).

The Huns were outstanding warriors. Their feats as mounted archers astonished the Romans to the extent that they inspired great fear throughout Europe. For most of their history the Huns were governed by chieftains. Even on their military campaigns they seem to have had no single general. This situation changed in the 5th century.

By 432 the leadership of the Huns had become centralized under a strong ruler or king, like Rome and some of the Germanic tribes. King Rugila, or Rua, died in 434 and was succeeded by his two sons, Bleda and Attila. The two shared power until 445, when Attila killed his brother. Military and political leadership fell to him, and he proved to be a strong and autocratic ruler. Attila administered his vast empire through a group of emissaries. They went on diplomatic missions, served as commanders of military campaigns, and collected tribute from subject peoples.

It was the subject populations who eventually brought the downfall of the Huns' empire. Attila suffered a military defeat in Gaul (now France) in 451 and was driven from Italy by a plague and famine in 452. He died the next year and was succeeded by his many sons. They soon began fighting among themselves, and the subject peoples took the opportunity to launch a series of rebellions.

The Huns were decisively defeated in 455. The Byzantine Empire closed its frontiers and broke off trade relations with them. Sporadic raids by some of Attila's sons continued for a few years, but by the end of the century the Huns had disintegrated as a separate people. (*See also* Attila.)

**HUNTING.** Game hunting began as a means of supplying food. Dogs were probably trained to hunt as early as Neolithic times and came to be bred for their specialized skills. Native peoples obtained much of their food by killing buffalo, bear, deer, and waterfowl. Settlers also depended largely upon wild animals and birds for meat.

Later, as farming and stock raising spread and many societies became more industrialized, hunting ceased to be a significant means of livelihood. By now it has come to be primarily a sport. It involves the seeking, pursuing, and killing of wild animals and birds, called game and game birds, and is done primarily with firearms today.

Critics of game hunting refer to it as a blood sport that causes needless suffering and death to harmless animals in order to satisfy primitive desires in those who do not need to hunt to live. They also point out that the tons of lead from shotgun cartridges and bullets deposited in the environment each year have

*A hunter dressed in camouflage and his dog, wait patiently during pheasant season.*
© Hanson Carroll—Peter Arnold, Inc.

*A hunter out in an open field takes aim with his shotgun at a pheasant that has been flushed from the weeds. About 20 million pheasants are taken each year in the United States.*

caused a steady rise in toxic lead poisoning in animals, including endangered species, who ingest it.

Proponents of game hunting point out that killing animals quickly is often more humane than letting them starve slowly in regions where the animal population may be too large to be supported by the limited food available in the habitat.

Through the years the steady increase in the number of licensed hunters threatened to wipe out the game supply. Since the late 1930s, however, sound conservation practices have been keeping the population of many species of game at a high level despite increased hunting pressures. To protect the present game supply hunters should follow the principle that guided the Indians: Kill only the game you want for food; never waste it.

The four major types of hunting in the United States are upland-game, waterfowl, big-game, and pest. Upland game includes rabbits, squirrels, quail, pheasants, grouse, and woodcock. Geese and ducks are the favorite waterfowl targets. Big-game hunters stalk deer, bear, elk, antelope, and moose. Pest hunting may be coyotes in the West, crows on the farm, or woodchucks (groundhogs) almost everywhere.

### Rules of Safe Gun Handling

The chief firearms used by hunters are .22-caliber rifles, large-caliber rifles, and shotguns (*see* Firearms). All these are deadly weapons and should not be handled unless certain rules of gun safety are followed. Nine basic rules are:

1. Treat every gun as if it were loaded.

2. When entering an automobile, home, or camp, carry a gun with the action open or taken apart.

3. Be sure the gun barrel is free of obstructions.

4. Carry a gun so that the direction of the muzzle can be controlled, even in falling.

5. Be sure of the target before pulling the trigger.

6. Never point a gun at anything except in shooting.

7. Never leave a gun unattended without first unloading it.

8. Never climb a tree or fence with a loaded gun.

9. Never shoot at hard, flat surfaces or at water.

### Hunting with a Rifle

The first firearm that most hunters learn to use is the .22-caliber rifle. This gun serves best for shooting rabbits and squirrels. It is also used on crows, woodchucks, and other animals that are hunted for sport or as pests and not primarily to eat. These rifles are most commonly made in four styles: single shot, pump, bolt action, and automatic. All can be used in the field or on a target range.

For larger game, the most popular rifles are the .270, .30, and .375 calibers. The basic styles are pump, bolt action, and automatic. These rifles are used chiefly for hunting bear, deer, elk, and other big game found in forested or mountainous country. Heavier caliber rifles are sometimes used for shooting elephants, rhinoceroses, and other big game hunted in Africa and elsewhere.

### Other Types of Hunting

Upland game and waterfowl are hunted with a shotgun. There are six types of such guns: single barrel, single shot; side-by-side double barrel; over-and-under double barrel; bolt action; pump; and automatic. There is also a choice of shotgun gauges ranging from the small .410-inch bore through the heavy 10-gauge guns. For most hunters, the 20-, 16-, or 12-gauge guns are best.

Selecting the proper choke and the correct barrel length is important. The choke means that certain barrels are constricted (tapered) at the front end, with the amount of this constriction designated as choke. It varies from a true cylinder (which has no choke) to modified and full choke. The cylinder barrel tends to spread the shot pattern of the pellets. The more a barrel is choked, the smaller the shot pattern becomes. A full choke barrel makes the smallest pattern, holding the pellets closer together at any given distance. Mechanical choking devices permit the hunter to use a variety of chokes on a single barrel.

For quail and rabbits, where shooting is at close range and in brushy country, the cylinder choke is best. Usually, a barrel length of 26 inches serves well with this choke. For shooting pheasants, waterfowl, grouse, and other game at long ranges, the full choke barrel works more successfully, and barrel lengths of 28 or 30 inches are recommended. Actually, a longer barrel does not give a hunter much additional killing range, but it does make sighting easier.

A shotgun should feel comfortable to the shooter if accurate gunning is to result. The stock may be adjusted to fit the shooter's shoulder. Another important point is the weight of the gun. A hunter must be able to throw the gun quickly to his shoulder and swing it with the target fast and accurately.

Some hunters find greater sport in killing game with a bow and arrow rather than with a firearm. If properly used, this weapon is as deadly as a rifle.

Much of the fun of hunting comes from being outdoors enjoying nature. Many hunters add to their pleasure by using a trained hunting dog, which can find game that would escape a hunter's eye.

### Laws and Rules Governing Hunting

The federal government and all state governments have passed laws to conserve the supply, or correct an oversupply, of game birds and animals. In general, migratory game birds are protected by federal laws; other forms of game, by state laws. These regulations prohibit the killing of game except during open seasons. The exact dates of these hunting seasons vary from state to state and sometimes by zones within states. In some cases a state may specify different dates for hunting the same animal, if different types of weapons are used—bow and arrow versus guns for deer, for instance. Other regulations govern the method of taking game, the amount of game that can be killed in one day, and the amount of game that hunters may have in their possession.

In addition to government regulations, modern hunters face a new challenge—animal rights activists who are determined to stop all hunting. Some activists have directly confronted hunters to attempt to prevent the killing of animals. Others have promoted their goals through lobbying state legislators. (*See also* Animal Rights.)

Jim Mitchell

**HUNTINGTON BEACH, Calif.** A haven for surfing enthusiasts, Huntington Beach is in Orange County on the Pacific coast 35 miles (56 kilometers) southeast of Los Angeles and boasts a beach 8½ miles (14 kilometers) long. Huntington Harbor has Orange County's first marina city, and the Bolsa Chica Ecological Reserve draws many visitors to its protected wetland. Golden West College is located in the city. September brings an annual surfing competition.

Much of Huntington Beach's industry is petroleum-related. Tremendous industrial development followed early discoveries of oil both on- and offshore. The city also has a space center, but it is promoted most often as a seaside resort.

Originally part of Rancho Las Bolsas and La Bolsa Chica, Huntington Beach was first called Shell Beach. After subdivision in 1901 it became known as Pacific City. The city was renamed for Henry E. Huntington, who was the owner of the Pacific Electric Railway. It was incorporated in 1909. Petroleum was discovered in 1919, and offshore oil was found in 1930. Huntington Beach has a council-manager form of government. Population (2000 census), 189,594.

**HURON, LAKE.** The second largest of the Great Lakes, Lake Huron has an area of 23,000 square miles (59,570 square kilometers), including Georgian Bay. It is bounded on the south and west by Michigan and on the north and east by Ontario. The United States–Canada border passes through the lake. The lake is irregularly shaped, with Saginaw Bay indenting the coast of Michigan. The northeastern part of the lake is dotted with islands, especially in Georgian Bay. Its level and depth are about the same as those of Lake Michigan, with which it connects through the Straits of Mackinac. Its greatest depth is 750 feet (230 meters). The lake carries extensive ship traffic despite the mountainous waves that northeasters drive upon its western shore.

Lumbering and fishing are part of the economy around Lake Huron. The area also draws many tourists. Some consider Georgian Bay, in Ontario east of the main body of the lake, to have the most beautiful scenery in all the Great Lakes. It is separated from the lake by a peninsula and the island of Manitoulin. The picturesque area between Manitoulin and the rocky bluffs of the Ontario mainland is best seen from the waters of North Channel. Georgian Bay is one of the most popular vacation spots on the continent.

Trent Canal, near the eastern end of Lake Ontario, was designed to provide a shorter water route for shippers between the St. Lawrence River and the Lake Superior–Lake Michigan region (*see* Canal). Started in 1833, the canal once served a flourishing lumber trade; it is significant now as a source of hydroelectric power. Through the St. Clair River, Lake St. Clair, and the Detroit River, the waters of Lake Huron flow into Lake Erie. The passage between the lakes is continually dredged, keeping open a channel of fixed depth.

Lake Huron was the first of the Great Lakes to be explored by Europeans. Samuel de Champlain and Étienne Brûlé reached Georgian Bay in 1615. Louis Jolliet canoed down Lake Huron in 1669. In the 18th century the British captured Fort Detroit. The lake was named by the French after the Huron Indians. (*See also* Great Lakes.)

**HUS, Jan** (1369?–1415). A forerunner of the Reformation, Jan Hus of Bohemia was burned at the stake as a heretic rather than recant his religious views and his criticisms of the clergy. Hus founded the Moravian church.

Jan Hus was born in the Bohemian village of Husinec in about 1369. He studied for the priesthood at the University of Prague. After graduation he lectured there on philosophy and for a time served as rector of the university. Hus and his fellow scholars wrote in Latin as did all learned men throughout Europe, but Hus also wrote in his native Bohemian, or Czech, helping to establish Bohemian as a literary language.

He also preached in Bohemian, winning the trust of the people and a devoted following.

As a young priest Hus was drawn to the writings of the English priest and reformer John Wycliffe, who denounced evil practices that had grown up among the clergy. Hus carried on Wycliffe's protests, and as a result he gained many enemies. Hus disagreed with some of Wycliffe's beliefs. He did not reject the church's doctrine of transubstantiation, for example. When he opposed the burning of Wycliffe's books, however, he was charged with heresy and was forbidden to preach or to teach. (*See also* Wycliffe.)

This was the time of the Great Schism in the church (1378–1417), caused by rival claims to the papacy. One of the antipopes, John XXIII, proclaimed a crusade and promised indulgences to volunteers. Hus attacked this procedure. His followers burned the pope's decree. The church excommunicated Hus, laying an interdict on any place that sheltered him. Friends defied the interdict and hid Hus in the countryside.

In 1415 the Council of Constance met to heal the Great Schism and to discuss reform. Called by the council, Hus was given safe-conduct by the German king Sigismund. While Hus was at Constance, however, Sigismund repudiated his pledge. Arrested and thrown into prison, Hus was called before the council and accused of beliefs that he had never held. He refused to take back things he had not said and was put to death on July 6, 1415. He is the national hero and saint of Bohemia.

**HU SHIH** (1891–1962). The writing of Chinese was revolutionized in the 20th century by the diplomat and scholar Hu Shih. Through his efforts, spoken Chinese was given a literary dignity it had never before achieved. He was also a guiding force in building the Chinese Nationalist revolution through mass education.

Hu Shih was born in Shanghai on Dec. 17, 1891. While being educated in the traditional Chinese classics, he discovered that the rigidities of language hampered the development and expression of new ideas—so remote was the written from the spoken language. From 1910 until 1917 he studied in the United States at Cornell and Columbia universities. At the latter he was strongly influenced by the philosophy of John Dewey. Hu Shih joined the faculty of Peking University in 1917, the same year he published his essay "Tentative Proposal for Literary Reform."

The literary revolution he started was but one aspect of a broad campaign directed against traditional values. Under Dewey's influence he attacked all simplistic ideologies that were competing for attention in China. In so doing he became a foe of the new Communist party. Hu served as ambassador to the United States from 1938 to 1945 and as chancellor of Peking National University (1945–49). After the Communist revolution he lived in New York City as Taiwan's ambassador to the United Nations. He moved to Taiwan in 1958 and died there on Feb. 24, 1962.

**HUSSEIN** (1935–1999). On May 2, 1953, when he was only 17 years old, Hussein ibn Talal was enthroned as king of Jordan. He succeeded his father, King Talal, who had been deposed in 1952 because of mental illness. After becoming king, Hussein played a crucial role in the incendiary politics of the Middle East. In contrast to more radical Arab leaders, he maintained close relations with the United States and worked to mediate the Arab-Israeli conflicts that troubled the region.

Hussein was born on Nov. 14, 1935, in Amman, Jordan, the oldest of four children born to Talal and Princess Zain. Hussein attended the Muslim College of Amman and Victoria College in Alexandria, Egypt. After being proclaimed crown prince in 1952, he pursued advanced academics and military studies in England.

As king of Jordan Hussein fostered a slow but steady economic growth, but in doing so he relied on financial aid from the West, especially the United States. Because so many of the Jordanian population felt no strong attachment to his rule, he was forced to increase the military establishment. In the face of internal unrest in 1957, he imposed martial law.

Israel's victory in the 1967 Arab-Israeli War cost his country land on the West Bank of the Jordan River, including portions of Jerusalem. This defeat also brought many Palestinians into Jordan, which they used as a base from which to attack Israel and undermine Hussein's rule. In 1970 full-scale warfare broke out between the Palestinians and the Jordanian army. Eventually the Palestinians were expelled. Despite pressure from Syria, Iraq, and Iran, Hussein maintained control in Jordan. As a result of Egypt's peace agreement with Israel in the Camp David accords of 1978, Jordan severed ties with Egypt, but relations were again established in 1984.

During the Persian Gulf crisis of 1990–91, Hussein tried to remain neutral but found himself drawn to give at least public support for Iraq's Saddam Hussein. His own citizens, and thousands of resident Palestinians, overwhelmingly supported Iraq. After the war good relations were once again established with the United States. (*See also* Jordan.)

**HUSSEIN, Saddam** (born 1937). After Saddam Hussein became president of Iraq in 1979, he proved to be one of the most brutal and warlike of late–20th-century political figures. In 1980 he launched his country into an eight-year war with neighboring Iran that neither nation could win. In 1990 his armies invaded and annexed tiny Kuwait. In response, a massive United Nations coalition attacked Saddam's forces in January 1991 and defeated them decisively in six weeks. Saddam also used his armed might against his own people, especially the minority Kurds in the north.

Saddam Hussein was born to a peasant family in the village of Tikrit on April 28, 1937. Orphaned early in life, he was raised for a time by an uncle. In his youth he became an ardent nationalist, determined to rid Iraq of foreign influences. Soon after moving to Baghdad in

1957 he joined the Ba'th Socialist party. In 1958 he took part in the coup that overthrew the monarchy and made Abdul Karim Kassem prime minister. After trying to kill Kassem, Saddam fled Iraq for Syria, then to Egypt. There he studied law and came under the powerful influence of Gamel Abdel Nasser (*see* Nasser). When Kassem was overthrown in 1963 Saddam returned to Baghdad and joined the Ba'th party's new government. The regime was short-lived, however, and Saddam was imprisoned. By 1966 he was free and a party leader.

In 1968 Saddam helped bring the Ba'th party back into power. Iraq's new president was Ahmed Hassan al-Bakr, but Saddam quickly became the most powerful individual in government. He became chairman of the Revolutionary Command Council and worked relentlessly to get rid of opponents and put his friends and family in positions of authority. His first goal was revitalizing the economy in order to build up his military power. He had gained enough control by 1979 to push Bakr aside and become president.

A United Nations (UN) cease-fire agreement that followed the 1991 Persian Gulf War prohibited Iraq from possessing biological, chemical, or nuclear weapons. Over the next decade, Saddam's refusal to cooperate with UN weapons inspectors brought worldwide economic sanctions and periodic air strikes by the United States and the United Kingdom. In early 2003 those countries warned Saddam that they would take swift military action if Iraq did not complete its disarmament promptly. In March 2003, United States President George W. Bush ordered Saddam to leave the country or face removal by force. Saddam refused to leave, and on March 20, 2003, an American- and British-led coalition invaded Iraq. Saddam, along with his family and closest advisers, went into hiding. In July 2003, two of Saddam's sons were killed during a raid of their hideout by United States troops. Saddam eluded capture until Dec. 13, 2003, when United States troops discovered him in an underground hideout near Tikrit. Although armed, Saddam surrendered without a struggle and was taken into custody.

**HUTCHINS, Robert M.** (1899–1977). Some of the 20th century's boldest and most influential educational reforms were undertaken by Robert M. Hutchins during his tenure as president of the University of Chicago. He reorganized the undergraduate and graduate departments of the university. His Chicago Plan for undergraduates encouraged a liberal education at an earlier age, and it measured accomplishment by comprehensive examination rather than by time spent in classrooms.

His chief criticisms of modern education were aimed at overspecialization and the extraordinary emphasis on careers while in school. His aim was to introduce students to the intellectual traditions of Western civilization before they turned their attention to learning skills for making a living.

Robert Maynard Hutchins was born in Brooklyn, N.Y., on Jan. 17, 1899. His father was a Presbyterian clergyman who later became president of Berea College in Kentucky. Hutchins attended Oberlin College in Ohio before going overseas to serve in military ambulance services during World War I. After the war he attended Yale University. He graduated in 1921 and received a law degree there in 1925. He stayed at Yale Law School as a teacher until 1929 (as dean from 1927 to 1929), when he was elected president of the University of Chicago. He remained at the university until 1951, the last six years as chancellor.

Hutchins was an excellent administrator, but the extraordinary changes he made were considered so sweeping by the faculty that they aroused furious opposition. With the help of his longtime associate Mortimer J. Adler, he introduced the Great Books program at the university.

The Chicago Plan, a four-year program in the humanities, called for students to start college after the sophomore year in high school. Students were required to take courses in mathematics and the sciences as well as in the traditional liberal arts. Hutchins denounced early specialization, and he also deplored the undue emphasis on nonacademic pursuits. The university abandoned intercollegiate football in 1939 despite the great football tradition that had been established there by Amos Alonzo Stagg over several decades (*see* Football). Hutchins published his educational ideas in 'The Higher Learning in America' (1936), still one of the classic works on the subject.

When Hutchins left the university in 1951, it was to become a director of the Ford Foundation. In 1954 he became president of the foundation's Fund for the Republic. The fund founded the Center for the Study of Democratic Institutions in Pasadena, Calif., and he became its president and moved the organization to Santa Barbara. He also served as chairman of the board of editors of Encyclopædia Britannica from 1943 until his death, and he was editor in chief of the 'Great Books of the Western World' (1952). Among his later books were 'The Conflict in Education' and 'The University of Utopia', both published in 1953, and 'The Learning Society' (1968). He died in Santa Barbara on May 14, 1977.

**HUTCHINSON, Anne** (1591–1643). One of the first New England colonists to challenge the authority of the Puritan leaders in religious matters, Anne Hutchinson preferred following her conscience over blind obedience. Her protest helped to establish the principle of freedom of religion.

Anne Marbury was born in Alford, England, and she was baptized on July 20, 1591. Her father was an English clergyman. Twice he was imprisoned for preaching against the established Church of England. Although Marbury had no formal education, she learned much by listening to her father and his friends discuss religion and government.

When Marbury was 14 her father was appointed to St. Martin's Church in London. At 21 she married

*Firm in her faith, Anne Hutchinson hears the sentence of the General Court banishing her from Massachusetts Bay Colony.*

William Hutchinson, her childhood sweetheart, and they returned to Alford to live. They had 14 children. Despite her busy household affairs, Hutchinson was active in religious affairs. She often made the 24-mile (39-kilometer) journey to Boston, England, to hear John Cotton preach. In 1633 Cotton was forced to leave England because of his Puritan sympathies. With Hutchinson's eldest son, Edward, he fled to New England. The Hutchinsons with their other children followed the next year and settled in Boston, Mass.

Soon she held weekly prayer meetings for the women of the colony. At these meetings she often criticized the preaching of the clergy. Hutchinson believed that the Lord dwelt within each individual, and she felt that faith alone would win salvation. This was in opposition to the teachings of the Puritan fathers. By 1636 she had made many converts, including her brother-in-law, the Rev. John Wheelwright, and the young governor, Henry Vane. John Cotton supported her at first, but later he publicly renounced her teachings.

With Governor Vane a convert, the other leaders feared civil disobedience and tried to regain control. When Vane returned to England in 1636, they obtained the governorship for John Winthrop. At once he banished Wheelwright to New Hampshire and brought Hutchinson to trial. She was banished in November 1637, but because of ill health she was permitted to spend the winter in nearby Roxbury.

During the winter Cotton and other clergymen tried to get Hutchinson to deny her beliefs. When she refused, she was excommunicated from the church. She and her family and friends moved to Aquidneck, R.I.,

in 1638 and founded a new colony. After her husband's death in 1642, Hutchinson moved with her younger children to Pelham Bay in New York. In 1643 she and most of her family were killed by Indians.

**HUTTON, James** (1726–97). The Scottish scientist James Hutton originated one of the fundamental principles of geology: uniformitarianism. This principle assumes an enormously long span of time during which the different kinds of rocks composing the Earth had been formed by diverse natural processes. Although vigorously attacked at the time, this theory became the cornerstone of modern geologic studies.

Hutton was born in Edinburgh, Scotland, on June 3, 1726. He tried his hand at chemistry, law, medicine, and farming before taking up geology. With James Davie he developed a cheap process for making sal ammoniac (ammonium chloride) from coal soot, for use in industry.

With the money he made from the process he bought a farm and worked it for several years. While farming he began studying rocks and the effects of natural processes, such as rain, running water, tides, and volcanoes, on the development of the Earth. His theories received little notice until 1785 when he presented two papers on his uniformitarian principle to the Royal Society of Edinburgh. They were published in 1788, and two volumes of his 'Theory of the Earth' came out in 1795. He was working on a third volume at the time of his death on March 26, 1797, in Edinburgh.

**HUXLEY, Thomas Henry** (1825–95). The foremost British champion of Charles Darwin's theory of evolution was the teacher and biologist Thomas Henry Huxley. He popularized the findings of science by lecturing and writing in language that all could understand. Today his essays and speeches are still read for their clarity.

Thomas Henry Huxley was born in Ealing, Middlesex, England, on May 4, 1825. During his youth, Huxley attended school only from the ages of 8 to 10. He studied much on his own, however.

Huxley taught himself the German language, and at the age of 12 he was reading advanced works on geology and logic. During early adolescence he began conducting his own scientific experiments. At 15 Huxley was apprenticed to a London physician but soon won a scholarship to Charing Cross Hospital Medical School in London.

In his 21st year, Huxley's scholarship came to an end, and, though still unqualified, he secured a post as assistant surgeon in the British navy aboard the HMS *Rattlesnake*. The studies he conducted of sea creatures during the next four years gained him the respect of the leading biologists of the day.

Darwin once declared that Huxley was one of the three men in England whom he needed to convince of the theory of evolution in order to satisfy himself. (*See also* Darwin, Charles.) So thorough and earnest a convert did Huxley become that his popular lectures and writings in defense of Darwin's theory have somewhat obscured his own original work in biology and zoology.

From 1854 to 1885 Huxley was professor of natural history at the Royal School of Mines, London. He was the first great teacher of biology to use the laboratory method, and he began the first courses of effective practical training for science teachers. Toward the end of his life Huxley devoted much time to educational reform and was the dominant member of the first London School Board.

Among Huxley's best-known writings are 'Evidences as to Man's Place in Nature' (1863); 'An Introduction to the Classification of Animals' (1869); 'Lay Sermons, Addresses and Reviews' (1870); and 'Scientific Memoirs' (5 vols., 1898–1903).

**HUYGENS, Christiaan** (1629–95). The shape of the rings of Saturn was discovered by Christiaan Huygens, a Dutch astronomer, mathematician, and physicist. Huygens also developed the wave theory of light and made significant contributions to the science of dynamics and the use of the pendulum in clocks. His reputation in mathematics as well as his wealth and parentage enabled him to correspond with some of the leading scientists of his time, including René Descartes, Blaise Pascal, and Gottfried Wilhelm Leibniz. Late in life he met Isaac Newton, with whose theory of gravitation he disagreed.

Huygens was born in The Hague on April 14, 1629. He was trained by his father in languages and drawing, and at 13 he began the study of mechanics. In 1645 he entered the University of Leiden to study mathematics and law. Two years later he transferred to the College of Breda.

At 21 he published his first treatise on mathematics and followed this with work on probability theory. At the same time, he and his older brother discovered a new method of grinding and polishing lenses for use by astronomers. In 1655 he discovered a Saturn satellite. He identified the components of the Orion nebula in 1656 and three years later published his discoveries of the shape of Saturn's rings. His construction of a pendulum clock with an escapement aided in his observation of planetary motion. Huygens lived in Paris from 1666 until 1681, when he returned to Holland. Written much earlier, 'Discourse on the Cause of Gravity' and 'Treatise on Light' were published in 1690. He died on July 8, 1695, in The Hague.

**HYDERABAD, India.** One of India's largest cities, Hyderabad is the capital of Hyderabad District and Andhra Pradesh State. It is situated on the banks of the Musi River on the Deccan Plateau in southern India. The city has a warm climate with mean annual temperatures of 80° F (27° C). Monsoon rainfall, occurring between June and September, averages 30 inches (75 centimeters).

There are several palaces and royal tombs in and around Hyderabad. The 400-year-old Golconda Fort is nearby. The Charminar, built in 1591, with four ornate minarets, forms the center around which the original city was planned. The Mecca Masjid is a richly ornamented granite mosque. The Salar Jung Museum is well known.

Hindus and Muslims form the majority of the population. Telugu, Urdu, and English are widely spoken. Its educational institutions include Osmania University (founded in 1918), one of the finest in India. Other noteworthy institutions are the American Studies Research Centre and the German Institute of Oriental Research.

A major center of trade and transportation, Hyderabad is well served by roads and rail and air services. Cotton, millet, wheat, and oilseeds are grown in the surrounding areas. One of the major industrial centers of southern India, it manufactures cigarettes, cotton and silk textiles, weapons, railway rolling stock, glass, paper, machine tools, pharmaceutical goods, motor vehicles, and tiles. The city is connected by a 1-mile- (1.6-kilometer-) long embankment on Husain Sagar Lake to the nearby town of Secunderabad. The embankment serves as a promenade.

Founded in 1591 as the capital of the Golconda kingdom, Hyderabad was conquered in 1685 by Mughals. In 1724 it broke away from the Mughal Empire and was ruled by Muslim governors as an independent kingdom until 1948, when it became part of India. Population (2001 census), 3,449,878.

**HYDRA.** One of the most hideous creatures of Greek mythology is the nine-headed hydra. For each head that was cut off, the monster grew two new ones. The hydra known to zoologists is a small aquatic animal only about 1.2 inches (3 centimeters) long. Like its namesake, however, it can regrow parts of its body.

The hydra lives in quiet, freshwater ponds or streams. At the top of its thin, stalklike body is a mouth opening, used both to ingest food and eject waste, surrounded by four to 25 tentacles bearing stinging cells. The hydra uses these cells to paralyze small marine creatures that it eats.

Of this tiny animal's many unusual characteristics, the most remarkable is its ability to regenerate parts of its body. All living things can regrow some new tissue to replace damaged parts. The hydra, however, re-creates whole new bodies from sliced tissue.

The hydra is one of the oldest of the many-celled animals. Although simple, its body structure contains many of the tissues common to more complex forms of life. The body wall is composed of two layers of cells separated by a thin, structureless layer of connective tissue and a cavity containing digestive organs. Individuals are usually hermaphroditic—they possess functional reproductive organs of both sexes. They may reproduce in two ways. The hydra may

© Arthur M. Siegelman

*The hydra constantly regenerates itself. Photomicrographs capture the progression of an intact, adult hydra with a bud (top) and after mouths and tentacles were sliced off (second from top). The hydra regenerated a new body tube and mouth (second from bottom) and tentacles (bottom) within 15 days.*

release gametes, and fertilization may take place in the water; or the hydra may reproduce by budding, in which small outpouchings of its wall nip off at the base to form separate new individuals.

The hydra moves either by creeping on its base or by looping, or flipping end over end. The genus *Hydra* belongs to the class Hydrozoa and includes 20 to 30 species.

**HYDRAULICS.** The study of the forces and motions encountered in liquids, such as water or oils, is known as hydraulics. It is part of the larger field of fluid mechanics, which includes gas flows and aerodynamics (*see* Airplane, "Aerodynamics"). Hydraulics is used to design piping systems, pumps,

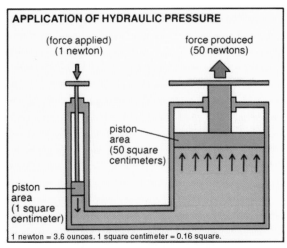

**APPLICATION OF HYDRAULIC PRESSURE**

1 newton = 3.6 ounces. 1 square centimeter = 0.16 square.

*An incompressible liquid can be used to transmit an increase in pressure. Similarly, a small force, acting on a small surface area and through a large distance, can produce a large force that acts on a larger surface and through a smaller distance.*

propellers, water turbines, hydraulic presses, and flow-measuring devices. It is subdivided into hydrostatics, the study of forces encountered in liquids at rest, and hydrodynamics, the study of liquids in motion. Hydraulics is applicable to essentially incompressible fluids, fluids that do not contract under pressure, and low-speed air flow.

**Hydrostatics**

The French mathematician Blaise Pascal stated that the pressure at any point at the same elevation in a confined liquid is the same. Since pressure is force per unit area, the total force exerted on a body containing a fluid is proportional to the surface area exposed to the fluid. This forms the principle of the hydraulic press. Leakproof pistons are fitted in two arms of a U-shaped vessel with different cross sections, and the pressure on both pistons remains the same. If the area of the large piston is 50 times that of the small piston, the total force on the large piston is 50 times that on the small one. The work done (force × distance), however, remains the same in the absence of friction. Thus the small piston must be pushed down 50 times farther than the large piston rises. This force amplification is used in hydraulic jacks to lift automobiles and building slabs and in hydraulic presses for forging and to form car-body components and airplane sections.

Archimedes discovered in the 3rd century BC that a body immersed in liquid experiences an upward buoyant force equal to the weight of the fluid displaced, and a floating body displaces its own weight in the liquid (*see* Archimedes). Accordingly, a ship weighing 10,000 tons will float at a depth where it displaces the same weight in water. Pressure increases with depth due to the weight of the liquid. The increase in pressure is proportional to the density of the fluid times the height of the liquid column. This

## CONTINUITY PRINCIPLE FOR LIQUID FLOW

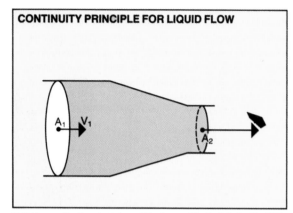

## BERNOULLI'S PRINCIPLE FOR LIQUID FLOW

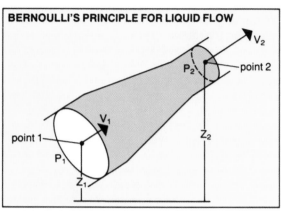

*Both the continuity principle and the Bernoulli principle for liquid flow account for the increased velocity of a volume of liquid as it flows through a contracting pipe.*

principle is applied in manometers, which are used to measure the pressure of water flowing in a pipe at above atmospheric pressure. One leg of a U-tube, filled with mercury at the bottom, is connected to the pipe. The other leg is open to the atmosphere. The water pushes the mercury up the open leg, and the water pressure in the pipe is related to the difference in the height of the mercury in the U-tube.

### Hydrodynamics

The principle of continuity in hydrodynamics is based on the assumption that liquid flowing steadily through a contracting pipe has a constant volume flow rate at any cross section (*see* top of next page). The volume flow rate at each interval is equal to the velocity of the liquid times the cross-sectional area. Since the cross-sectional area decreases as the pipe narrows, the velocity must increase.

For an incompressible ideal, or frictionless, liquid, the total mechanical energy in the flow of liquid through any contracting pipe is preserved according to Daniel Bernoulli's principle, proposed in 1738. According to this principle, illustrated on the following page, the total mechanical energy at any cross section through the pipe is the same. Bernoulli's principle is represented by the following equation:

$$\frac{P_1}{Q} + \frac{V_1^2}{2} + gZ_1 = \frac{P_2}{Q} + \frac{V_2^2}{2} + gZ_2$$

| flow energy | + | kinetic energy | + | potential energy | = | flow energy | + | kinetic energy | + | potential energy |

| total mechanical energy at point 1 | = | total mechanical energy at point 2 |

Here Q = density, P = pressure, V = velocity, g = acceleration due to gravity, and Z = elevation above an arbitrary horizontal line.

The Torricelli theorem, proposed by Italian mathematician Evangelista Torricelli in 1644, is based on Bernoulli's principle. It enables the prediction of the flow velocity through a small nozzle at the bottom of a large open tank. Since the pressure is atmospheric at both the tank top and at the nozzle, the difference in potential energy from the top of the liquid to the nozzle is converted to kinetic energy. Assuming that the velocity at the top is essentially zero, Bernoulli's equation can be used to estimate the velocity of the fluid leaving the tank with Torricelli's equation:

$$V = \sqrt{2gH}$$

In this equation V is the velocity of the liquid flowing out the nozzle, g is the acceleration due to gravity, and H is the distance between the liquid surface and the center of the nozzle.

Both the Bernoulli equation and the Torricelli equation apply only to the steady flow of frictionless, incompressible fluids. They must be adjusted for high-speed gas flows, unsteady flows, and for friction, which is encountered in all real applications.

Although the need to modify these equations was known by the late 18th century, no solutions were available. Different corrections seemed applicable for slow-flowing oils and water flowing at normal velocities. The explanation was found by Osborne Reynolds in 1883. He showed that if dye was carefully injected into a low-speed flow of liquid in a pipe, it did not disperse but stayed in layers. This is called laminar flow. As the flow velocity in the pipe was increased, however, the dye stream broke up into eddies. Reynolds found that this turbulent flow was related to the fluid's viscosity, a liquid property proportional to the force required to shear it. Turbulent flow occurs when the ratio of the velocity, diameter, and density to the viscosity, now called the Reynolds number, exceeds about 2,500. The flow always remains laminar below a Reynolds number of 2,100.

Reynold's experiment led to an understanding of the different behaviors of laminar and turbulent flows over surfaces such as wings and ship hulls and in channels. It also laid the groundwork for modern hydraulics and fluid dynamics. Another major advance was made by Ludwig Prandtl, who in 1904 suggested that the viscous (friction) effects on a streamlined body are limited to a thin boundary layer

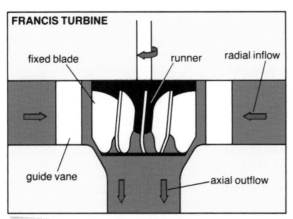

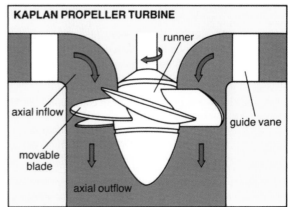

*Turbines are used to convert the energy in a stream of fluid into mechanical energy in a runner. The runner blades on the Francis turbine are fixed, and those on the Kaplan turbine are adjustable.*

along the body surface. This discovery led to developments in aerodynamics and forms the basis for many advances in fluid machinery.

### Piping Systems, Dams, and Canals

Hydraulics enters in the design and construction of municipal water systems. Water is taken from a lake or river and pumped, after treatment, through a distribution system to the users. The system is laid out to ensure that customers far away are not deprived of water if there is heavy use closer to the pumping station.

The construction of dams for flood control and power generation is also a task for the hydraulic engineer. Since water pressure increases with the depth of the water, the dam must be thicker at the bottom than at the top. Other hydraulic applications involve the design of sewer and irrigation systems and of ship canals and locks.

### Hydraulic Machinery

Pumps, propellers, and turbines are examples of hydraulic machinery. In a centrifugal pump an impeller imparts tangential velocity to the fluid through vanes that are driven by an external power source (*see* Pump and Compressor). The vanes increase the kinetic energy, and sometimes the pressure, of the flow. The high-speed flow leaving the impeller is then slowed through a set of diffusing passages where the kinetic energy is converted to flow energy and the outflow pressure increases. In ship propellers the difference in pressure between the forward and backward side of the blades creates thrust, which propels the vessel.

Waterwheels date from Roman times when water flowing past a rotating paddle wheel was used to produce power for milling. These waterwheels, however, extracted only a small portion of the energy in a stream. Modern hydraulic power-producing machines, known as turbines, work on different principles (*see* Turbine). Their design depends on the height between the reservoir and the turbine outflow.

For a large height difference, or head, and low flow rates, the Pelton wheel or turbine is used. Here the water flowing down a pipe, or penstock, accelerates through a nozzle at the bottom. The high-speed water is then directed onto a wheel. Pelton turbines are typically used if the head is greater than about 500 feet (150 meters). For smaller heads the Francis turbine is commonly used. It is the counterpart of a centrifugal pump. Water flows into the turbine in a radial direction and is discharged at lower pressure nearly axially downward. For low heads and high flow rates, vertically installed propeller or Kaplan turbines are used. Whereas in ship propellers the turning propeller moves the water, propeller turbines use flowing water to turn the propeller. Another hydraulic machine, the torque converter of an automobile, permits smooth transmission of power from the engine to the drive shaft (*see* Automobile).

Fluid forces transmitted in a pipe have many applications. The hydraulic brake in a car depends on the pressure exerted on a fluid reservoir by the brake pedal. This force is then transmitted through oil lines to move the brake shoes. Power steering uses a hydraulic system to magnify the torque applied to the steering wheel to turn the car. Hydraulic power is also used in airplanes to move control surfaces, such as the tail and rudder. (*See also* Airplane.)          Fred Landis

**HYDROCHLORIC ACID.** Without a constant supply of hydrochloric acid, many of the nation's businesses would shut down. Hydrochloric acid is a solution of hydrogen chloride gas (HCl) in water. About 1,000 cubic feet of this gas can be dissolved in one cubic foot of water. For commercial use hydrochloric acid is usually marketed as a solution containing 28 to 35 percent hydrogen chloride by weight.

Some of the main industrial uses of hydrochloric acid are the cleaning, or pickling, of metals, the production of glucose and corn sugar from starch, and the refining of cane sugar. It is also used in making glue and gelatin and is essential in the manufacture of synthetic rubber and plastics.

There are three principal commercial methods of manufacturing hydrochloric acid. First, hydrogen chloride is obtained as a by-product in the chlorination of hydrocarbons. This is how much of the hydrochloric acid is produced in the United States. In the second process, sulfuric acid and salt are roasted to form hydrogen chloride. In the third method, hydrogen chloride is produced by the combustion of hydrogen in chlorine.

Gaseous hydrogen chloride is colorless and has a pungent, irritating odor. The water solution is yellow in color because of impurities, usually dissolved iron. Hydrogen chloride gas is soluble in some organic solvents. Hydrochloric acid reacts with many metals to form salts known as chlorides. Hydrochloric acid is secreted in gastric juices by glands in the walls of the stomach, where the acid aids in the digestion of foods. Small quantities of hydrochloric acid occur in nature in the gases given off by active volcanoes and in waters from volcanic mountain sources.

In the 18th century scientists called hydrochloric acid muriatic acid, from the Latin word meaning "pickled." During the early 19th century, hydrogen chloride was a waste product of various industrial processes, such as the production of soda ash. Until its many industrial uses were realized, it was dissolved in liquids and dumped at sea.

**HYDROGEN.** The lightest and most abundant element in the universe, pure hydrogen is a gas without taste, color, or odor. It is believed to have formed, with helium, all of the heavier elements and is estimated to compose three quarters of the mass of the universe. On Earth, hydrogen occurs chiefly in combination with oxygen in water (its name comes from the Greek for "water-forming"). It is also present in organic matter such as living plants, petroleum, and coal, and sparingly as a free element in the atmosphere. It combines with other elements, sometimes explosively, to form hundreds of thousands of compounds. It reacts with other hydrogen atoms to form hydrogen molecules ($H_2$).

Hydrogen can be produced by passing steam over heated carbon (coke or coal). When heated, natural gas decomposes into hydrogen and carbon black. Hydrogen is also produced by the electrolysis of water, by displacement from acids, and by the action of certain hydroxides on aluminum.

### Varieties of Hydrogen Atoms

Hydrogen is the lightest element because it is composed of only two particles—the smallest number that can form a neutral atom. Its nucleus consists of a single proton bearing a positive electrical charge. Associated with this nucleus is an electron bearing a negative electrical charge.

This simple atom of two particles is the most common type, or isotope, of hydrogen. Chemists call it protium. Two other isotopes have been found. Double-weight hydrogen, with a mass number of 2, has one neutron as well as a proton in its nucleus. It is

| Properties of Hydrogen | |
|---|---|
| Symbol . . . . . . . . . . . . . . . . H | Density at 32° F (20° C) |
| Atomic Number . . . . . . . . . . 1 | . . . . . 0.08988 grams per liter |
| Atomic Weight | Boiling Point |
| . . . . . . . . . . . . . . . . . 1.0079 | . . . . –423.17° F (–252.87° C) |
| Group in Periodic Table | Melting Point |
| . . . . . . . . . . . . . . . . . . . . Ia | . . . –434.45 ° F (–259.14° C) |

called deuterium. "Heavy water," which is denser than ordinary water, can be prepared by burning deuterium. Triple-weight hydrogen, or tritium, has two neutrons and one proton in its nucleus. It is radioactive and is produced naturally in the Earth's upper atmosphere. It can be prepared artificially by bombarding lithium with neutrons in an atomic reactor. Both deuterium and tritium are used in the manufacture of hydrogen bombs (see Nuclear Weapons).

In 1929 it was demonstrated that, apart from isotopes, hydrogen gas under ordinary conditions is a mixture of two kinds of molecules, known as ortho- and para-hydrogen. These forms of hydrogen differ from one another by the spins of their electrons and nuclei, and thus their physical properties differ as well. (For more information on particle spin, see Nuclear Physics.) Normal hydrogen at room temperature contains 25 percent of the para form and 75 percent of the ortho form.

### Hydrogen in the Sun and on Earth

Hydrogen is found in most stars, including the sun. This great furnace converts hydrogen into helium by means of the same chemical reaction exploited in hydrogen bombs (see Nuclear Energy). The energy produced by this chemical reaction is sent to Earth in the form of heat, light, and other forms of radiation (see Radiation; Sun). Without hydrogen, the sun could not generate the energy necessary to sustain life on Earth.

On Earth, hydrogen is used commercially in the synthesis of ammonia and methanol, in processes for desulfurizing petroleum fuels, and for producing stable, volatile products from certain refinery by-products. It is also used in hydrogenation of organic compounds to make solvents, industrial chemicals, and food products such as margarine and shortenings. Hydrogen has been used to inflate lighter-than-air craft such as balloons and dirigibles. Because it is highly flammable, however, it has been largely replaced by helium, which does not burn. (See also Balloon and Airship; Helium.)

**HYDROMETER.** A floating body sinks deeper in a light liquid than in a heavy one. This principle is applied in the hydrometer (from Greek words meaning "water measurer"). The hydrometer is a device used for determining such characteristics of a liquid as its density, or weight per unit volume. Hydrometers are also used to determine a liquid's specific gravity, or the weight of the liquid as compared to an equal volume of water.

The hydrometer is usually a sealed glass tube, weighted at one end to keep it upright and marked with a scale. When it is immersed in the liquid being measured, the depth of the flotation depends on the liquid's density. The scale on the neck of the tube is calibrated to read density, specific gravity, or some other related characteristic.

A typical instrument is the storage battery hydrometer, which is used to measure the specific gravity of battery liquid and to determine the condition of the battery. Another instrument is the radiator hydrometer, in which the scale is calibrated in terms of the freezing point of the radiator solution. The Baumé hydrometer, named for the French chemist Antoine Baumé, is calibrated to measure specific gravity on evenly spaced scales. One scale is for liquids heavier than water and the other is for liquids lighter than water. Hydrometers may also be used to determine the richness of milk, the "proof" of liquors, the percentage of sugar in sugar solutions, and the strength of saline solutions. (*See also* Water, "The Density and Weight of Water.")

**HYDROPONICS.** The science of growing plants in water or some substance other than soil is called hydroponics, from the Greek *hydro,* meaning "water," and *ponos,* meaning "labor." In hydroponics, also called soilless culture, the stems and roots of the plants are supported. The necessary nutrients for plant growth are provided in the solution surrounding the roots.

All plants need the oxygen, hydrogen, and carbon available from either air or water. They are also dependent on 13 essential elements, the nutrients that are normally acquired from the soil. Some elements, called macronutrients, are taken by plants in large amounts. In other situations only trace amounts of elements, micronutrients, are necessary. The macronutrients are nitrogen, phosphorus, magnesium, sulfur, potassium, and calcium. The micronutrients are iron, chlorine, boron, manganese, zinc, copper, and molybdenum. In hydroponic culture these chemical elements are supplied to the plants by adding salts that contain them to the solution surrounding the roots.

Laboratory experiments designed to determine the factors controlling plant growth were conducted as early as the 17th century. During the subsequent centuries scientists discovered that plants could be grown in inert substrates or in water alone, provided the proper nutrients were available. The significance of hydroponics was revealed in the 1930s by W.F. Gericke at the University of California at Berkeley. By controlling the nutrient levels provided for crop plants grown in water baths, Gericke's laboratory experiments resulted in tomato plants more than 20 feet (6 meters) high. His findings led to the worldwide use of hydroponics in agriculture.

To begin a hydroponic culture medium, a nutrient solution is prepared in a storage tank by dissolving salt mixtures containing the necessary elements for

*Styrene boards are used as a substrate to grow beans and lettuce in a nutrient solution in concrete raceways.*

proper plant growth. Since the plants remove nutrients from the water, the solution is periodically revitalized with the addition of salt mixtures. The acidity level is adjusted to a pH of 6.0–6.5 for most types of plants. Because of the enormous water uptake by the plants, there is an increase in the sodium-chloride concentration in the water. This is remedied by frequently replenishing the solution in the storage tank.

Although plants may be grown with the roots suspended in a water solution, a variety of other substrates are available. Natural substrates such as gravel, sand, and peat provide support for roots but do not have the nutrients typical of soil. They are used in hydroponic culture with the addition of nutrient-rich solutions. Other substrates include mixtures containing sawdust, pumice, vermiculite, and even peanut shells. A recent development is the use of certain plastics as an inert substrate surrounded by water. Regardless of the substrate used, the plant roots must be supplied with enough oxygen. The approach of suspending roots in a humid enclosure and spraying them periodically with a nutrient solution is also highly effective in promoting plant growth.

Hydroponics has many advantages over standard soil agricultural practices. Weeds and soil diseases, for example, are not a problem. The area required for a particular crop is considerably reduced because of the greater efficiency of plants at obtaining nutrients directly from the water solution. In addition, crops can be grown in regions where poor soil conditions prevail. The practical application of hydroponics was initiated during World War II by the United States on many remote islands where fertile soil was absent. Gravel was used as the primary substrate.

Experimental sites for hydroponic farming exist in regions where poor soils and harsh climates make traditional farming practices inadequate to meet the food requirements of the inhabitants. Major prospects for the use of hydroponics in agriculture are in arid parts of northern Africa and the Middle East.

J. Whitfield Gibbons

© S.J. Krasemann—Peter Armold, Inc.
*Spotted, or laughing, hyena* (Crocuta crocuta)

**HYENA.** Widely mistaken as a pure scavenger, the hyena is actually a brave nocturnal hunter in its own right. The animals' famous laughing sounds are uttered as they seize prey and fight among themselves for food. The cry often draws lions and other large carnivores, which may then try to steal the food.

Hyenas generally travel in packs of up to 100 members and have firmly established territories. The adult hyena is about the size of a large dog, with four toes on each foot and long forelegs, and is easily distinguished by its peculiar hunched profile.

The three species of hyenas belong to the family Hyaenidae. The animals are native to Africa and Asia. Two of the species—the striped and brown hyenas—are endangered.

**HYGROMETER.** A standard weather report usually includes information about humidity, which is the weight of water vapor in a certain weight of air in the atmosphere. Constant measurements of the temperature and of the humidity help the weather forecaster to predict rain or snow with greater accuracy. The instruments used to measure the humidity are called hygrometers. Relative humidity is given in percentages to reflect the amount of moisture in the air compared to that of dry air.

The simplest mechanical hygrometer uses a single hair to determine the humidity. The hair is attached to a spring and dial. When the relative humidity increases, the hair contracts, or shortens, pulling the spring and dial hand. At a lower relative humidity it lengthens, releasing the tension on the spring, which allows the dial hand to move in the opposite direction.

A more accurate measurement is achieved with an electronic hygrometer. It measures the change in electrical resistance of a thin layer of lithium chloride, or of a semiconductor device, as the relative humidity changes. Other hygrometers sense changes in weight, volume, or transparency of various substances that respond to relative humidity.

The dew-point hygrometer is a polished metal mirror that is cooled until moisture just begins to condense onto it. This occurs when the surrounding air reaches its dew point. The temperature of the metal is then the same as the dew point temperature. Knowing the atmospheric temperature and the dew-point temperature, the relative humidity can be determined by means of a table.

Another type of hygrometer, called a psychrometer, consists of a wet-bulb thermometer and a dry-bulb thermometer placed side by side and read simultaneously. The wet-bulb thermometer has a thin, wet cloth covering the bulb. The dry-bulb thermometer has a bulb exposed to the atmosphere. Both bulbs are exposed to the air, and the wet wick cools by evaporation depending on the air's humidity. A decrease in the humidity of the air brings an increase in the difference between the dry- and wet-bulb temperatures, called the wet-bulb depression because evaporation cools the wet bulb. From these temperatures it is possible to determine, usually from a table, the relative humidity and dew-point temperature of the air.

**HYPNOSIS.** Such an extraordinary phenomenon is hypnosis that no completely satisfactory definition has ever been developed. In fact, debates still rage over its exact nature. The British Medical Association and the American Medical Association have tentatively defined it in part as "a temporary condition of altered attention in the subject that may be induced by another person," but there is still much about hypnosis to be understood. Although the condition resembles normal sleep, scientists have found that the brain wave patterns of hypnotized subjects are much closer to the patterns of deep relaxation. Thus, rather than a psychic or mystical phenomenon, hypnosis is now generally viewed as a form of attentive, receptive, highly focused concentration in which external or peripheral events are omitted or disregarded.

### Trance Phenomena

The remarkable and characteristic feature of the hypnotic trance is that hypnotized persons become

*Franz Mesmer, an 18th-century Austrian physician, used hypnotism to heal patients in his Vienna salon.*
Mary Evans Picture Library

highly suggestible, or easily influenced by the suggestions or instructions of others—generally the hypnotist. They retain their powers to act and are able to walk, talk, speak, and respond to questions. Their perceptions, however, can be radically altered or distorted by external suggestions. At the command of the hypnotist, subjects may lose all feeling in a limb, and a pin prick will cause them no pain. The heartbeat can be made slower or faster, and a rise in temperature and perspiration can be induced. They can be made to experience visual or auditory hallucinations or to regress in mental age and live the past as if it were the present. Subjects may forget part or all of the hypnotic experience or be made to recall things that they had otherwise forgotten.

The hypnotist may also make certain "posthypnotic suggestions"—instructions to the hypnotized subject to respond to a specified signal at a later time, after awakening. For instance, the hypnotist might suggest that, at some time after the hypnotic session, the subject will resume the hypnotic state on signal. Such suggestions are sometimes used by certain medical specialists to repress or suggest away such symptoms in a patient as anxiety, itching, or headaches.

**Trance Induction and Termination**

The state of hypnosis is produced essentially by inducing deep relaxation and focused concentration. Subjects become quite unresponsive to ordinary forms of stimulation, and though they are told to sleep, they are also told to listen and be ready to respond to commands or suggestions made by the hypnotist.

The suggestion that they are asleep and the fact that they have previously agreed to cooperate with the hypnotist make the subjects less critical than they would be if normally awake. In this state they will accept commands and suggestions, even if the suggestions are illogical. In general, however, subjects cannot be made to follow instructions that conflict violently with their moral sense. For instance, subjects would not be likely to commit murder or robbery if directly instructed to do so.

The classical methods used to produce hypnosis are usually simple and frequently employ direct commands or monotonous suggestions repeated continuously. Subjects are requested to concentrate on the hypnotist's voice, or they may be asked to fix their eyes on some object or to concentrate on some repetitive sound. The hypnotist tells the subject over and over again to feel drowsy or relaxed, to let his or her eyelids grow heavy and close, to breathe deeply and comfortably, and to go into a deep sleep. The degree of hypnosis is tested by challenging subjects to perform some simple task while suggesting that they will find it impossible. For instance, the hypnotist may say, "You will be unable to open your eyes no matter how hard you try, and the more you try, the more tightly they will close." The entire process of induction may take a few minutes or a few seconds, depending on the subject. Usually, if suggestions are made during hypnosis that it will be easy to induce hypnosis again, the subject will subsequently enter a trance almost instantly upon an agreed signal from the hypnotist.

In conjunction with these classical induction methods, drugs such as sodium pentothal, alcohol, and certain barbiturates may be used to make the procedure easier, but these are rarely necessary. Aside from classical methods, there are a number of specialized techniques used by some psychiatrists to hypnotize their patients. There are a number of other techniques as well—for example, a blow to the side of the neck (a method used by some stage magicians)—that are not approved by the medical profession and that can be highly dangerous.

Subjects are usually wakened at the command of the hypnotist, who generally orders them to return to their normal state and suggests that they will feel alert and well afterward. Some subjects may nevertheless feel disoriented and drowsy for a period following a hypnotic trance.

In order to produce hypnosis, the hypnotist should have a certain amount of authority in the eyes of the subject. Many experts believe that the more firmly the subject believes in the power of the hypnotist, the more readily he or she will give way to hypnotic suggestion. Many factors seem to contribute to hypnotic susceptibility, however, though it is still unclear what these factors are. There is evidence to indicate that a good subject tends not to be anxious, to be interested in new experiences, imaginative, and intelligent; some research also suggests that hypnotic susceptibility is in part genetically determined. Many investigators report that about 10 percent of adults cannot be hypnotized at all and that between 20 and 30 percent can be deeply hypnotized. Some researchers believe that only 5 or 10 percent of the population can be hypnotized deeply enough to experience visual hallucinations.

Estimates of susceptibility vary greatly because of the continued disagreement concerning the exact nature of hypnosis. Some authorities claim that anyone is potentially hypnotizable and that failure to induce a hypnotic trance is due to either poor technique on the part of the hypnotist or resistance on the part of the subject. In contrast, there are researchers who assert that hypnotism, as it is generally understood, does not exist at all, and thus the question of susceptibility is irrelevant. They believe that hypnosis is not a result of some alteration in the subject's capacities or mental state but is a consequence of "role playing" based upon the subject's preconceptions of how hypnotized persons behave, their expectations, and their willingness to volunteer and eagerness to experience something unusual.

### History

When hypnosis first claimed the attention of scientists, it was called animal magnetism or mesmerism, after Franz Mesmer of Vienna. In the late 18th century, Mesmer claimed to use it to heal certain nervous ailments. He thought some sort of magnetism was transferred from him to his patients, and that it redistributed their body fluids. For many years mesmerism was denounced by medical practitioners and generally associated with stage performances, fraud, and superstition.

In the 19th century, before the discovery of anesthetics, physicians began to use mesmerism in surgery. They found that a deeply hypnotized patient would lie perfectly still and appear unaffected by pain, even during operations as serious as an amputation. Around 1840 a doctor named James Braid coined the term hypnosis, which means a "nervous sleep." The new name was more acceptable than mesmerism, with its implications of fraud, and it soon supplanted the older term. In the mid- to late 19th century several physicians, including Jean-Martin Charcot and Sigmund Freud, became interested in the use of hypnosis in the practice of medicine.

Today hypnosis is widely and successfully used by such medical practitioners as surgeons, dentists, and psychotherapists. Physicians may use it to relieve anxiety or as an anesthetic. Psychotherapists use it to relax the patient, to reduce resistance to therapy, to facilitate memory, and even to treat some conditions. Hypnosis is also used in specialized therapies such as those that help a person to stop smoking, eat less, or fight specific fears, such as fear of flying. It is unclear, however, if such procedures have any positive long-term effects. Hypnosis has also been used during police interviews to enhance the memory of witnesses.

Regardless of the application, hypnosis should be left to those who are properly trained. When used by untrained persons it may have undesirable and even dangerous effects.